SON OF
PROPHECY

SON OF
PROPHECY

THE RISE OF HENRY TUDOR

NATHEN AMIN

AMBERLEY

First published 2024

Amberley Publishing
The Hill, Stroud
Gloucestershire, GL5 4EP

www.amberley-books.com

British Library Cataloguing in Publication Data.
A catalogue record for this book is available from the British Library.

ISBN 978 1 3981 1047 2 (hardback)
ISBN 978 1 3981 1048 9 (ebook)

1 2 3 4 5 6 7 8 9 10

Typeset in 10.5pt on 13pt Sabon.
Typesetting by SJmagic DESIGN SERVICES, India.
Printed in the UK.

Contents

To Lucy & Vera

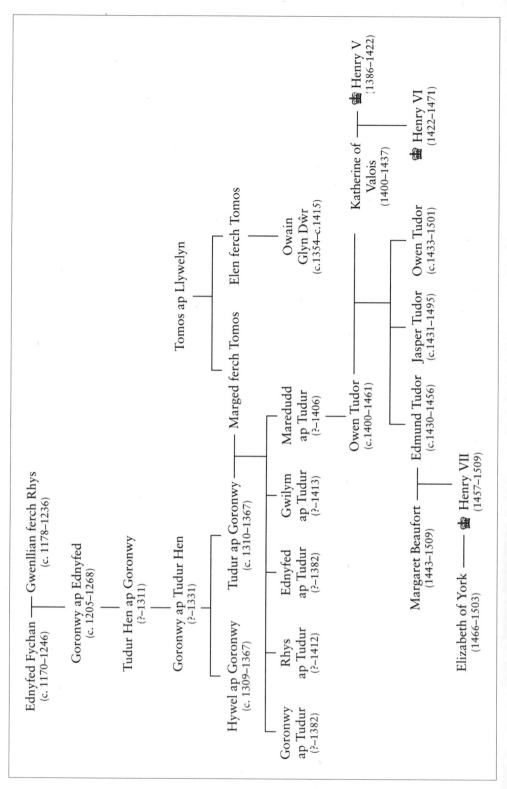

The descendants of Edynfed Fychan.

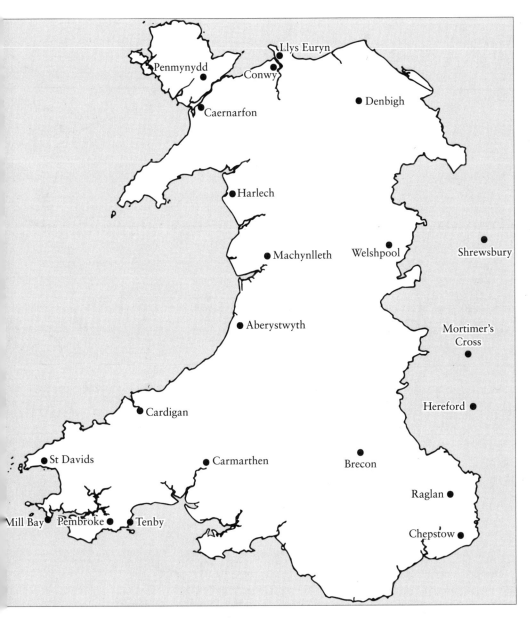

Wales in the time of Henry Tudor.

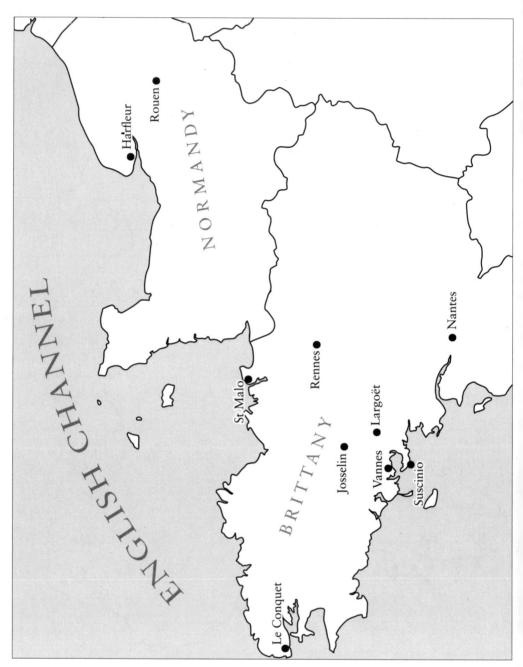

Brittany and surrounds in the time of Henry Tudor.

Introduction

'They [the Welsh] may now ... be said to have recovered their former independence, for the most wise and fortunate Henry the 7th is a Welshman.'[1]

The words of a Venetian visitor to England in 1496 leave no room for ambiguity. It was being reported by foreign dignitaries that after centuries under the heel of the English occupier, the Welsh nation had been liberated by one of its own. The Tudors are the most celebrated dynasty to occupy the English throne, three generations that presided over monumental political and religious change that gave birth to the modern British state. Yet, as our Venetian friend noted, the founder of the dynasty, Henry VII, was born and bred a Welshman. How did it come to pass that the boy born in Pembroke, West Wales, once a penniless teenage exile in Brittany, rose to be a king of England?

The Tudors' relationship with their native Wales has sadly not always generated the level of mainstream discussion that the subject deserves. Every aspect of the 118-year Tudor reign has been intensely examined in a wide range of books, articles and, increasingly, new media formats like podcasts and social media. Yet their Welsh background has oddly escaped a focused analysis, save for a few crucial publications by a handful of esteemed Welsh historians who have shone their lamps in this neglected corner. It is hoped that this work builds on the fine scholarly research conducted by luminaries like Ralph A. Griffiths, Glanmor Williams, H. T. Evans, Roger S. Thomas, and more.

When the Tudors' Welsh background has been explored, it has typically been given short shrift. Outside Welsh academia, there has long been the tendency to downplay Henry VII's Welshness. If the subject is mentioned at all, it is often in dismissive terms, the reader habitually reminded that, biologically, Henry was but a quarter Welsh, equally French and half-English. His upbringing in Wales, and indeed his lived experience until he became king at twenty-eight, is usually pushed to the side. The most prominent biographer of Henry during the twentieth century, the much-admired S. B. Chrimes, even opened his exceptional and hugely influential 1972 account of the king's life with the line, 'The Welshness of Henry Tudor can easily be, and often is, exaggerated.' Suffice to say, this seems a somewhat unsatisfactory assessment when there is an abundance of evidence to the contrary.

This book, it is hoped, will build on the work of Griffiths, Williams, Thomas *et al.* to fully explore the paternal lineage of Henry VII, the first Tudor king, and examine in detail the life and times of his Welsh ancestors. Delving back eight generations through the family tree, close attention will be paid to the accomplishments and misdeeds of the figures who paved the way for Henry's eventual triumph, to the wider struggles of the Welsh, and in particular their clamouring for a national deliverer to surface after many false dawns. The Tudor accession in England came not in spite of their Welshness, as we're often led to believe, but in many ways *because* of this Welsh inheritance.

Spanning 1170 to 1485, this is the enthralling story of one remarkably resilient family, a close-knit and redoubtable force that thrived during lean years of political chaos, national instability and inter-generational bloodshed. We will learn how Ednyfed Fychan carefully laid the foundations for his sons and grandsons to cling onto their influence after the English completed their piecemeal conquest of Wales, and how they levied their standing among their countrymen to even go to war with the king of England. We will follow as an entire generation of brothers lead their people in the last Welsh War of Independence against the might of the English crown, only to disastrously fall short, and join one member, Owen Tudor, as he seeks fresh opportunity outside his native land.

How did Jasper Tudor evade the chopping block throughout the Wars of Roses? Why was his nephew Henry so roundly supported in his native Wales as the Son of Prophecy, a national deliverer who would rescue his people from the miserable servitude in which they had long dwelled? Did he prove the champion it was claimed he would be? All will be revealed.

Nathen Amin
Spring 2024
London

1

The Terror of England

The grunts, groans and anguished screams of gasping men filled the morning air as metal relentlessly crashed into metal. A mass of exhausted bodies swayed against one other as momentum ebbed and flowed. Blood stained the grass and mud beneath their feet as confusion and terror took hold of those who still had breath in their burning lungs. Around them lay their slaughtered peers, their lives extinguished in an instant through a slight misstep or lapse in concentration. The stench of death lingered in the air, irritating the nostrils of those who lived to see another dusk.

When the fighting had ceased, one weary commander jostled his way through the ranks of his exhausted soldiers, his bloodied spear now at a well-earned rest. In his hands he clutched a gruesome memento of his role in this skirmish: the heads of three of his Anglo-Norman enemies, their eyes lifeless, jaws clenched and skin discoloured. These, he had determined, would prove a welcome gift for his master.

This formidable warrior's name was Ednyfed Fychan, and the man he served was Llywelyn ab Iorwerth, Prince of Gwynedd and the principal native Welsh ruler of his day. When Ednyfed returned from the field of battle and presented his lord the three heads, Llywelyn was delighted. The prince commended Ednyfed for routing the English army, and according to a later sixteenth-century account ordered his victorious commander to henceforth adopt a new coat of arms, replacing the Saracen's head he previously wore on his shield. Ednyfed's new arms featured three helms on a red background with a white chevron, proudly recalling for posterity the heads he had so boldly taken.[1]

This violent episode brought Ednyfed Fychan to the fore of the early thirteenth-century Welsh political scene, rewarded for his valour and reviled by his enemies for his ferocity. But this was just the start of an accomplished career, the legacy of which would be assumed by his descendants with extraordinary, even incomprehensible, consequences that spread far beyond the borders of his native Gwynedd. Llywelyn ap Iorwerth may have received the epithet 'Great' after his death, but in many ways it was through Ednyfed's line that lasting greatness would be achieved.

Ednyfed Fychan – or, more properly following the Welsh patronymic style of the day, Ednyfed ap Cynwrig ap Iorwerth, or Ednyfed son of Cynwrig son of Iorwerth – was born in the early 1170s in Gwynedd, the dominant North Welsh kingdom. The epithet Fychan usually translates to 'small' or 'little', and was often ascribed to the younger party in cases where an elder figure with the same name survived. As there is no obvious person in the known historical record around Ednyfed bearing the same name, Fychan in this situation may even be an indication of his physical stature, or lack thereof.

Though not royal himself, because of a later commission by his descendant Henry VII, Ednyfed Fychan's lineage is nevertheless traceable – to an extent.[2] The commission found that Ednyfed's father was Cynwrig, who in turn was the son of Iorwerth. His great-grandfather was Gwrgan, son of Maredudd. The line continued through the generations to Coel Godebog, better known as Coel Hen, a fourth-century Briton living under Roman rule. From Coel, the lineage grows more fanciful, taking in legendary figures like Beli Mawr and Brutus of Troy, and should be treated with caution by the modern historian or genealogist. There is no reason to doubt the several generations before Ednyfed, however, which are plausible. Ednyfed's mother, meanwhile, is named by the commission as Angharad, a daughter of Hwfa, whose lineage was supposedly traced to the fifth-century warrior Vortigern. Even without the more fictitious elements of the family tree, it is reasonable to assert that Ednyfed possessed a solid North Welsh pedigree, one he would have worn with honour and could recite at will.[3]

The geopolitical scene of early medieval Wales was markedly different to the unified entity we would later know. After the Romans withdrew from Britain in the early fifth century, a series of autonomous petty kingdoms formed to fill the void, some of which proved more dominant than others. Vulnerable to invasion, in subsequent centuries sub-Roman Britain was repeatedly overrun from the seas, with Irish settlers arriving from the west and hordes of Angles, Saxons, Jutes, Frisians and Danes from the east, altering the political and ethnic make-up of the island below Hadrian's Wall. This encroachment gradually consigned the majority of native British rule to the area roughly known today as Wales, the division once demarcated by an earthwork known as Offa's Dyke.

Unlike in England, where by 927 several Saxon kingdoms had amalgamated into one under a single ruler, a united and enduring Welsh polity failed to develop, and indeed never would. The Welsh were a broadly homogenous people with a shared legal system, a common language and a thriving culture, and recognised one another as the *Cymry*, or fellow countrymen. They also considered themselves the *Brythoniad*, or Britons, refusing to recognise the term Welsh, a Saxon term understood to mean foreigner.[4] Despite acknowledging they were a distinct people, however, a natural national affiliation there was not. Any sense of a shared identity was chiefly driven by a common foe, first the Saxon and then the Norman, but Welsh loyalties and personal ties first and foremost remained with the local leader rather than any national figure.

By the eve of the Norman Conquest of neighbouring Anglo-Saxon England in 1066, the three principal Welsh kingdoms were Gwynedd in the north, Powys in the east, and Deheubarth in the south, though boundaries were routinely changeable. Once the Normans created a foothold in England, lesser Welsh kingdoms like Morgannwg, Brycheiniog and Gwent were quickly overrun by opportunistic invaders, with inroads made westwards through the fertile lowland plains of Deheubarth. To subdue the Welsh he could not overrun, William I, the famed Conqueror, incorporated the captured territory into a series of new semi-autonomous lordships running from the Dee Estuary in the north to the Severn in the south and occupying much of the territory westwards from the Wye to the Irish Sea. This area became known as the March, from the Norman-French *marche*, or boundary, a fluid buffer zone that served as the first line of defence against Welsh raids. William I installed three of his leading knights, hardy soldiers with vast experience of warfare and colonisation, to govern much of the March, creating them the earls of Chester, Shrewsbury and Hereford, and initiating a complex and often violent aspect to Anglo-Welsh relations that would prove troublesome to unravel for centuries to come.[5]

Though these barons owed their allegiance to the English king, as their possessions had been obtained by force they were free to govern their conquered lands as they saw fit, typically replacing native Welsh law with their own standalone feudal system. Former Welsh-ruled areas such as Radnor, Brecknock, Glamorgan and Gwent soon developed a markedly mixed Norman-Welsh culture, strategically centred around new towns such as Monmouth, Chepstow and Ludlow, and bolstered by scores of motte-and-bailey castles which littered the countryside. It was a firm foothold among the Welsh, a formidable physical presence patrolled by ambitious Norman lords, and once established it would not be reversed. Though there were no efforts to complete a programme of total conquest of the Welsh as was achieved in England, that the Normans proved to be politically, economically and militarily superior to their new neighbours proved a significant hindrance to the establishment of an enduring and united Welsh polity.

The world a youthful Ednyfed Fychan would have known in the late twelfth century was a turbulent one in which many perished in a never-ending cycle of ethnic violence. The broad division between a *Pura Wallia* in the north and west, where the Welsh were ruled over by native princes and chieftains, and the *Marchia Wallie*, the Norman-controlled lordships in the south and east, was more pronounced than it had ever been, and often prone to conflict. Much of what is known about Welsh society at this time comes from the work of Giraldus Cambrensis, or Gerald of Wales, an energetic Norman-Welsh cleric who travelled throughout the land recording his observations for posterity.

Gerald experienced the same land and culture that Ednyfed knew, and both men may even have briefly crossed paths during the former's sojourn into Gwynedd. Gerald reported that daily life at this time was an overwhelmingly rural affair, with communities rarely settling in one location for an extended period. The usual practice was to temporarily erect modest wattle-and-daub huts on the edge of forested areas and relocate during the seasons from the hills into the valleys, taking with them their livestock of sheep, swine and cattle.

Except for the fertile Anglesey, the rugged, vertiginous terrain that dominated large parts of Gwynedd proved unsuited to crop cultivation, with sustenance typically coming from livestock in the form of milk, butter, cheese and meat. Meals were simple, and often taken seated on the floor in threes. Beds were communal, stuffed with rushes and covered with a stiff sheet known as a *brychan*, while entertainment was often provided by young girls in the household playing the harp. Both men and women wore their hair short, with the males only wearing moustaches rather than the full beard. Exercise centred on the practice of arms, with which the Welsh were noticeably obsessed. In Gwynedd, the spear was the weapon of choice. It was a taxing and tribal lifestyle that produced a robust and resilient people; someone like Ednyfed Fychan likely grew into a tough and resourceful man, a born wanderer who, judging from his later actions, clearly possessed laudable physical and mental attributes that held him in good stead.[6]

Ednyfed's early adulthood coincided with the rise to prominence of one of the most successful Welsh rulers, Llywelyn ap Iorwerth, later known to Welsh history as the 'Great'. After emerging successfully from a bitter dynastic feud between various heirs of Gwynedd, by the turn of the thirteenth century Llywelyn presided over a principality comprising the towering heartlands west of the River Conwy that included the cantrefs, or hundreds, of Arllechwedd, Arfon, Llŷn, Ardudwy and Meirionnydd, the mostly flat and fertile island of Anglesey, and another four highly disputed cantrefs to the east of the Conwy known as the Perfeddwlad, regularly the arena of violence between Welsh and English. It was a domain that stretched from the River Dee in the east to the Dyfi in the south-west and encompassed everything in-between, including the forbidding mountains of Eryri,[7] an enduring redoubt for the Welsh in times of woe.

It is unclear when Ednyfed entered the direct royal service of the man one Welsh bard styled 'the bold darling of fortune', but considering the lengthy service the former provided the prince of Gwynedd across the next forty years, an early connection between the two men is likely.[8] The skirmish in which he claimed a trio of English heads is likely to have occurred in early 1211, when, after a decade of peace, Prince Llywelyn came under attack from his father-in-law, King John of England, for overseeing a series of 'cruel attacks on the English'. An operation led by Ranulf de Blondeville, 6th Earl of Chester, was repelled that year by the men of Gwynedd, during which Ednyfed may have excelled himself in the field, but it drew a heavy response from John, who considered Llywelyn a wayward vassal.

In May that year, the king entered Gwynedd with a vast army intent on 'utterly destroying' Llywelyn and letting 'not one living soul remain alive throughout the whole country'. When Llywelyn and his men, including Ednyfed, retreated deep into the rugged mountains, out of the king's reach, John razed the town of Bangor to the ground. With Llywelyn 'unable to bear the cruelty' much longer, the prince capitulated and was forced to surrender the Perfeddwlad as well as 20,000 cattle and 40 horses.[9]

Though momentarily humbled, Llywelyn ap Iorwerth was not to be underestimated, and quickly recovered his position. John proved heavy-handed in trying to tighten his grip in Wales, and soon lost the support of the other Welsh rulers who had supported his campaign against Llywelyn. When war resumed in the summer of 1212, Llywelyn entered an alliance with those rulers who had stood against him a year earlier, men like Gwenwynwyn ab Owain of Powys Wenwynwyn and Rhys Gryg and Maelgwn ap Rhys of Deheubarth, the latter two brothers-in-law of Ednyfed Fychan, to resist John's expansionist ambitions. In a three-pronged campaign, Llywelyn recaptured the Perfeddwlad, Gwenwynwyn besieged the king's commander Robert de Vieuxpont in his new castle at Mathrafal, and in the south Rhys Gryg torched Swansea.

When John was informed of this uprising that had briefly united the Welsh princes against him, preparations were made for another invasion, with an army numbering 8,000 men ordered to muster at Chester. As the final arrangements were made, in the middle of August 1212 John arrived at Nottingham where he refused to eat or drink until twenty-eight young Welsh hostages were hanged for the 'transgressions of their countrymen'. Before he could press ahead with his plan to punish the Welsh princes, however, Llywelyn's wife Joan, King John's daughter, made a timely intervention. She warned her father that his barons were planning to betray him if he ventured out on campaign again, and, perhaps aware of the depth of his unpopularity, two days later the king postponed his invasion to deal with more pressing issues in England.[10]

That John had trouble with his barons is an understatement. As the king's reign progressed, his reputation had steadily declined among his subjects, who chafed under his oppressive, suspicious and often malicious rule. As the king entered the second decade of his reign, crippling taxation, a relentless pursuit of feudal debts, extortion of the clergy, a bitter dispute with the Papacy that led to an interdict placed on England, and the humiliating loss of Normandy to the French made John a deeply unpopular figure presiding over a reign that had descended into suffocating tyranny.

Though the king attempted to mitigate the grievances of his nobility, by May 1215 many rebellious barons took the extraordinary step of formally renouncing their fealty to John, publicly rejecting him as their king. The rebels marched into London and took control of the greatest city in the realm, including the royal treasury. John in turn based himself at nearby Windsor, and a tense stand-off between the two sides ensued. As support grew for the reformers, among those who now rounded on the king was Prince Llywelyn, who offered his backing to the rebels' cause by capturing Shrewsbury.[11]

By 10 June 1215, with the king at Windsor and the rebels just a handful of miles away at Staines and refusing to back down, John had little option but to meet his adversaries face to face and negotiate his way out. On the riverbank at Runnymede, roughly halfway between their respective bases, the barons formally presented John with their grievances, a devastating critique of his kingship thus far. The expectation was that a widespread programme of reform to limit royal abuse in future would be implemented. The king agreed to the terms presented, though the chronicler Roger of Wendover maintained he only 'deceitfully pretended' to accept peace as he knew he was outnumbered. Nevertheless, five days later, John put his seal to a document containing sixty-three clauses that became known as *Magna Carta*, or Great Charter.[12]

Three of those clauses related specifically to the Welsh; one stipulated that any lands and liberties deprived from Welshmen without lawful judgement were to be returned immediately, as were those stolen from the English by the Welsh, though another added this didn't extend to property seized under the two previous monarchs, Richard I and Henry II, in the event John went on crusade. The third clause ordered that Llywelyn's son Gruffudd ap Llywelyn, a hostage of John's, should be restored to his father, as well as all other Welsh hostages that had yet to be hanged by the English king.

Peace between the king and the baronial party was short-lived, as suspicion on both sides endured. Magna Carta had been an ambitious project, but it immediately failed, and England descended into civil war before the year was out. Between September 1215 and March 1216, the king journeyed with vengeful purpose throughout the heart of England, furiously laying waste to the estates of his enemies. It was, said Roger of Wendover, 'a miserable spectacle to all who beheld it'. The rebels' response was dramatic; they extended an invite to Louis, the son and heir of Phillip II of France, to invade England in May 1216 and seize the crown, an offer that was eagerly accepted by the French prince.[13]

Before there could be a decisive encounter between John and the rebels, the English king contracted dysentery. Unable to shake the malady, he died in Newark on the evening of 18 October 1216.[14] By any measure, it had been a failed reign; John presided over the collapse of the Angevin Empire, cruelly exploited his people beyond what was customary and suffered excommunication from the church for several years on account of his disobedience. That he also engaged in warfare with his own barons, falling victim to sickness before he could be deposed in favour of a foreign prince, was perhaps the greatest indictment of all. With John's death, most of the English barons determined that his innocent nine-year-old heir should not be punished for the sins of his father. On 28 October 1216, in Gloucester, the young boy was crowned Henry III.

While England had been warring with itself, Prince Llywelyn exploited the turmoil not only to consolidate his position in Gwynedd, but to extend his sway over the other Welsh principalities. A relentless campaign into Deheubarth in December 1215 included the sacking of Carmarthen and the capture of Llansteffan, Laugharne, Cardigan, Emlyn and Cilgerran castles, firmly establishing Llywelyn's status as the principal native ruler of his day and leaving him 'happy and joyful'.[15]

To aid matters of governance and guide future ambitions, in 1215 Llywelyn appointed a new figure to serve as his seneschal. This was in effect the senior diplomat and counsellor in the principality, tasked with the most important missions both domestic and foreign, and Llywelyn chose Ednyfed Fychan. An office known to the Welsh as *distain*, the duties of the seneschal were originally constrained to the prince's domestic household, with responsibility for overseeing supplies, waiting on guests, managing the servants and any matters relating to lodging. By the time Ednyfed filled the role, it had evolved into an office of considerable prestige that required a well-rounded individual to provide administrative, judicial and military guidance to his prince. With a hand in shaping policy and recognition as the prince's most trusted confidant, to be named seneschal was to wield considerable influence over one's peers, occupying a highly visible role next to the throne. Holding this office until his death thirty years later, the gifted Ednyfed Fychan was plainly uncommon among the common.[16]

Ednyfed's first assignment was to oversee a council that assembled in Aberdyfi the following year, a summit at which all the Welsh princes and native nobility were present. During the proceedings, and possibly due to Ednyfed's guidance, Prince Llywelyn exercised his new authority to partition Deheubarth between four feuding heirs, dealing a fatal blow to any pretentions it could rival Gwynedd as it had in the past. By the close of 1216, he had also annexed Powys Wenwynwyn by forcing his adversary Gwenwynwyn ab Owain into permanent exile, was overlord of Powys Fadog, and had extended his patronage across Gwent and Glamorgan. In short, Llywelyn's authority across the Welsh was absolute.[17]

As he neared fifty years old, Ednyfed's next contribution to Welsh history was of greater significance. After King John's death, the cause of the rebellious barons gradually dissipated as many sought reconciliation with the representatives of the new child king of England, Henry III. This baronial climbdown left Prince Llywelyn and Ednyfed alienated, and when two princes of Deheubarth, Rhys and Owain ap Gruffudd, revolted against English rule in the summer of 1217, a host from Gwynedd swept south to raid English-held lordships including Brecon and Swansea.[18]

In the spring of 1218, Llywelyn was invited to a peace summit in Worcester and, with Ednyfed Fychan and seven others at his side, left the safety of Gwynedd to complete the 140-mile hike through Powys and across the River Severn. As the king was just eleven years old, the Welsh delegation was confronted by the figurehead of the regency council, William Marshal, 1st Earl of Pembroke, a wise and aged veteran charged with restoring royal authority. Between 12 and 18 March, the seneschal of Gwynedd played an integral role in securing advantageous terms for his prince – an indication not only of the comparative weakness of English rule as they wrestled with the fallout of Magna Carta and the recent civil war, but also of the strength of Llywelyn's position in 1218.

While Llywelyn agreed to do homage and fealty to the young king and accept his vassal status, he was formally recognised as overlord of his fellow Welsh princes. To ensure he fully honoured the terms of the treaty, four men, one of them Ednyfed, were released from their homage to Llywelyn and tasked by the English crown with holding their prince to account. Once the terms were finalised and sealed, the Welsh party could be satisfied with their achievements. As they returned home, they did so in the knowledge they had secured from the English government recognition of Llywelyn's supremacy in Wales; just seven years after being humbled by King John, the treaty marked the apex of both Llywelyn's reign and Ednyfed's career.[19]

The arena of medieval Welsh politics was complex and unstable, a treacherous cycle of violence and betrayal with successful episodes few and far between. Despite recent military and diplomatic triumphs, few people would have known this more than Ednyfed Fychan. He had been entrusted with guiding the fortunes of Prince Llywelyn, and likely spent much time in private ruminating on each decision with his prince. Although Gwynedd's supremacy was never domestically threatened again after the Treaty of Worcester, matters relating to the English crown and the Marcher lords would compete for his attention in the coming decades.

In 1222, Ednyfed, alongside his teenage son Goronwy ab Ednyfed, was one of fourteen witnesses to a pact between Llywelyn and the earl of Chester, sealed with the marriage of the former's daughter Elen and the latter's nephew John of Scotland, Earl of Huntingdon.[20] The following year, meanwhile, Ednyfed was one of six representatives tasked by the minority government of Henry III with conducting a review concerning all lands in South Wales, presumably for the English crown to update their records as to who held what estates. The commission was given on 4 November 1222, with the assignment expected to be completed by the Feast of St Nicholas on 6 December.[21] His reputation as a figure of authority who could be entrusted with fulfilling crucial administrative duties clearly extended beyond the Welsh border, and he continued to witness various charters in his role as seneschal across the remainder of the reign.[22]

The cordial relationship with the earl of Chester notwithstanding, the remainder of the decade was dominated by Gwynedd's various conflicts with Marcher lords. A series of back-and-forth campaigns between Llywelyn and William Marshal the Younger, 2nd Earl of Pembroke, caused widespread carnage between 1220 and 1223, and when Hubert de Burgh, Henry III's chief justiciar, started constructing a new stone castle at Montgomery in 1228, the Welsh prince led a 'vigorous resistance' to what he viewed as a provocative development on the periphery of his principality. This resistance drew the attention of the king, who supported his justiciar with an army regarded as 'the strength of England', but Llywelyn's men used their home advantage and made 'vast slaughter of them' in the woods before gleefully pulling down de Burgh's half-built castle. By May 1231, an emboldened Llywelyn had even started styling himself 'Prince of Aberffraw and Lord of Snowdon', setting himself apart from the other Welsh princes.[23]

The destructive conflict with de Burgh continued into the early 1230s, a period during which the Welsh repeatedly 'burst forth from their hiding places like rats from their holes, and spread fire and devastation' before fading back into the woods. When during one skirmish the customary Welsh retreat was blocked, an exasperated de Burgh ordered any captives to be summarily beheaded, 'and their heads to be sent to the king'. When Llywelyn learned of these executions, 'in great indignation at this deed' he furiously swept south and harried the March, committing 'severe depredations on the lands and possessions' of the English lords that included burning several churches 'together with some noble women and girls who had fled there for safety'.[24]

Llywelyn scored another notable victory in the summer of 1231 over an English garrison at Hay. Waiting with his men in some marshes near the River Wye, the prince sent a monk from the abbey of Cwmhir to the castle to inform the garrison there was a Welsh force loitering nearby. The English soldiers queried whether they could cross the river but were informed Llywelyn had broken the bridge, though the waters were shallow enough to be navigated on horseback. When this was relayed to Walter de Godarville, the local governor, he ordered his men to advance in Llywelyn's direction.

When Llywelyn spotted the garrison approaching, he and his men retreated into a nearby wood, leading the English to believe they had fled in fear. The garrison were so intent on catching their Welsh prey they rode straight into the marshes, sinking into the swamp up to the bellies of their horses. With the trap set, the Welsh re-emerged from the woods armed with lances and 'caused a cruel slaughter' as the English desperately 'rolled about in the mud'. Though reinforcements from the garrison arrived, 'after much slaughter on both sides', the English chronicler Wendover conceded 'the Welsh were victorious'. Henry III's response was to plunder Cwmhir Abbey and order a new stone castle erected at Paincastle, just a few miles outside Hay.[25]

Ednyfed Fychan's age may have precluded him from taking part in much, if any, of the latest wars, but he was intimately involved in brokering the one-year truce that was negotiated on 30 November 1231.[26] In the first week of December 1232, meanwhile, the venerable seneschal was handed a safe conduct by Henry III to travel to Shrewsbury to meet with Richard Marshal, 3rd Earl of Pembroke, chief justiciar Stephen de Segrave and the bishop of Chester to negotiate another truce, followed by a further safe conduct in June 1233 to discuss a lasting peace, this time in person with the king in Worcester.[27] A full treaty was finally ratified by both sides in 1234 at Myddle in Shropshire, one which would be renewed each year until Prince Llywelyn's death six years later.

Having played an integral role in bringing a decade of war to a close, Ednyfed started to consider opportunities outside Gwynedd for the first time. In late 1234, Pope Gregory IX announced the intention for a fresh Crusade to the Holy Land to revive waning Christian interest in the Eastern Mediterranean and to free the territories which remained, in his words, 'under the yoke of impious tyranny'. Though Jerusalem and Bethlehem were still under Christian rule, the truce which had been arranged between the Holy Roman Emperor, Frederick II, and the Ayyubid Sultan of Egypt, Al-Kamil, was vulnerable, prompting Pope Gregory to implore Christians throughout Europe not to be 'backward in undertaking the pilgrimage to the succour of that land'.[28]

One person who responded enthusiastically to news of a fresh crusade was Ednyfed, who during 1235 took the cross and vowed to travel to the Holy Land. There were many reasons why an ageing man would pledge to undertake the arduous trip across land and sea to the Middle East, a journey fraught with dangers such as drowning, theft, disease and malnourishment. Genuine faith and a desire to answer the pope's call to arms were naturally a significant pull, though for some there was the additional promise of gaining monetary reward in the form of plunder, particularly for younger sons who did not stand to inherit any great patrimony. For others, it may have been an opportunity to travel far beyond their homeland, to sample new cultures and visit renowned cities they could scarcely imagine.

For someone like Ednyfed, however, who already held considerable property of his own, the motivation is likely to have been penance, perhaps for the men he had killed in warfare across his career or even his part, if indeed he played any, in Llywelyn's torching of churches during the 1231 outbreak of violence. Participation in a crusade brought forgiveness of all sins from the pope, and owing to his advanced age, it would not be unusual if Ednyfed's thoughts were turning increasingly to the afterlife.

In any event, Ednyfed does not appear to have ventured further than London, though his time in the English capital during the summer of 1235 was not uneventful. When Henry III discovered the seneschal of Gwynedd was lodging in the city, he granted Ednyfed and those travelling with him the promise of safe conduct to continue through his realm, as well as during their anticipated return.[29] The king furthermore ordered his treasurer, Hugh de Pateshull, to find out where Ednyfed was staying and bring him a silver cup worth five marks as a gift from the Crown. That Henry III honoured his guest in this manner suggests whatever the turbulent relations between the Welsh and English in recent times, Ednyfed was worthy of respect even from the king.[30]

It is unclear when Ednyfed returned to Wales, but in 1236 his wife, Gwenllian ferch Rhys, passed away, and if the death was not sudden one would expect her husband to have been present for her final days, especially in light of his failure to embark on crusade.[31] Ednyfed married Gwenllian around the turn of the thirteenth century, a prestigious match that suggests that even before his rise to prominence his character and ability were sufficient for a royal match. Gwenllian, herself later described as 'a lady of great beauty and accomplishments',[32] was the daughter of Rhys ap Gruffudd, the revered prince of Deheubarth who ruled his principality with distinction for four decades between 1155 and 1197.

Known to history as *Yr Argwlydd Rhys*, or the Lord Rhys, the lineage of Ednyfed's father-in-law was distinguished and could be traced back to Rhodri Mawr, the highly capable and ambitious ninth-century warrior-king of Gwynedd who, like his near-contemporaries Alfred and

Charlemagne, was later bestowed the epithet Great. Hywel Dda, whose committed expansionist programme gradually extended his influence across the Welsh so that by 942 he ruled the kingdoms of Gwynedd, Powys, Brycheiniog and Deheubarth, was another admirable ancestor, remembered by the Welsh as 'chief and glory of all Britons' and 'ruler of all Wales'.[33]

Hywel's enduring legacy, however, which led to later generations bestowing upon him the epithet Dda, or Good, was a series of sensible and progressive laws ascribed to him that would become the cornerstone of the medieval Welsh legal system. Known as *Cyfraith Hywel*, or the Laws of Hywel, in the prologue to the later written manuscripts it was recounted that he had summoned learned figures from every part of Wales to his hunting lodge on the River Taf near modern-day Whitland to revise and codify a consistent written system for the Welsh to live by. Based on the ancient customs which had been verbally passed from generation to generation, many of these laws would remain in place until Wales was fully annexed into the English system in the mid-sixteenth century under Henry VIII – who was, incidentally, Hywel's direct descendant. Separate to English or canon law, Welsh law depicted a hierarchical society in which each person was assigned a value relating to their position in the community. There was no capital punishment for murder, though the perpetrator's family was compelled to make financial restitution, known as *galanas*, to the victim's relations, with the death penalty confined only to certain cases of theft.

Welsh law was noticeably fair to women in some respects compared to other legal systems of the day, apportioning the queen one-third of her king's income for personal use, for example, and assigning her a status above that of any other court official or person in the kingdom. Should a woman require a divorce, she could request one, even reclaiming property brought to the marriage, while all children were considered equal, whether born in or out of wedlock. The laws were practical for everyday life and designed to reconcile kinship groups and communities through common sense; even as Marcher and English law had made their incursion into Welsh life by the thirteenth century, it was these laws that men like Ednyfed Fychan still lived by, a potent symbol of native identity and unity. Though Hywel may not have been personally responsible for codification of the laws, with the earliest extant manuscripts only dated to the twelfth century, his reputation as a just ruler and benevolent legislator was nevertheless well established in the Welsh public consciousness by Ednyfed's day, who would have recognised him as 'the Good'.[34]

Another notable ancestor of Ednyfed Fychan's wife Gwenllian was her great-grandfather Rhys ap Tewdwr, who as king of Deheubarth was the principal power amongst the South Welsh just a decade after the Normans arrived in England. Though Rhys ap Tewdwr fostered a cordial relationship with the Conqueror, even paying financial tribute to the English king, he was unable to halt the Norman expansion west after William's death and was slain at Brecon in 1093, a killing some chroniclers considered the end of kingship in Wales.[35] The temptation is to suggest a link between the name Tewdwr and the Tudor borne by his later royal descendants, but the latter derives from the given name Tudur, a name of separate origin with a dissimilar pronunciation that entered the family line only through the offspring of Ednyfed and Gwenllian ferch Rhys.

The Lord Rhys, Ednyfed's father-in-law, meanwhile, had restored the reputation of Deheubarth during his four-decade tenure as prince, reassembling the fragmented principality and leading a spirited revival against Norman incursions. It was through a personal if pragmatic accord with Henry II, however, that Rhys attained lasting security, using his friendship with the English king to become the dominant Welsh prince from 1170 until his death in 1197. For much of this period, Rhys was the king's justiciar in South Wales, and surviving documents reveal he used the titles *princeps Wallie* (prince of Wales) and *Walliarum princeps* (prince of the Welsh) to demonstrate his supremacy.[36]

Though Rhys's remarkable reign ended in somewhat strained fashion, facing aggressive overtures from his own sons and contending with the emergence of Llywelyn ap Iorwerth who started to reassert Gwynedd's supremacy over Deheubarth, when he died aged sixty-five on 28 April 1197 his legacy as one of the most successful of Welsh princes was assured.[37] He had embarked on an ambitious programme of castle-building, for example at Dinefwr, Cardigan and Carreg Cennen, and also established two religious houses, the Premonstratensian abbey in Talley and the Cistercian nunnery at Llanllyr. The 'grand festival' of poetry and song he hosted over Christmas 1176, meanwhile, proved an innovative pursuit widely regarded as the forerunner of the modern Eisteddfod, which exists as a celebration of Welsh culture. It is perhaps with good reason Rhys was lauded in the *Brut y Tywysogion* as a 'lion of furious heart' who for much of his reign was 'the head and shield and strength of the South and of all Wales', in whose capable hands had been 'the hope and defence of all the tribes of the Britons'.[38] To his distant cousin Gerald of Wales, who knew Rhys well, he was particularly worthy of praise on account of his 'liberality and independent spirit'.[39]

These princes, figures of vision like Rhodri Mawr, Hywel Dda and the Lord Rhys, ranked among the most esteemed men to have ruled over the *Cymry*. Their names were uttered with reverence by later generations, who whispered their myriad achievements with admiration. There is certainly no basis for any accusation that the later Tudors, descended from this 'noblest line of kings', were of base stock.[40] By any measure of the day Ednyfed married well, and Gerald of Wales's comment that the

Welsh 'would rather marry into a noble family than a rich one' indicates the match would have been well received.[41] Gwenllian is sadly absent from the historical record, but despite theirs being a clear political match designed to strengthen relations between Gwynedd and Deheubarth, that the couple shared several children suggests they bonded personally. Multiple offspring of both sexes are attributed to Ednyfed by later writers, but the six that can be solidly accounted for are Goronwy, Gruffudd, Tudur, Cynwrig, Rhys and Hywel ab Ednyfed.[42]

Though Ednyfed and his sons grieved the passing of their wife and mother, the seneschal had one more role to perform for his ailing prince, and that was to oversee the succession. On 8 July 1238, along with three others, he swore upon some relics on behalf of Llywelyn to observe a one-year extension to the peace with the English, while in October that year all the Welsh princes and magnates were summoned to a council at Strata Florida Abbey, where Llywelyn demanded their fealty to his younger son, Dafydd.[43] This summit marked the prince's final public engagement, for on 11 April 1240, in the abbey of Aberconwy, 'to the great grief and dissatisfaction of all the Welsh', the defiant titan who had revived a fractured principality and proven 'a plague to the English' for nearly five decades succumbed to his illness.[44] Though Llywelyn had imposed his authority over the leading Welsh rulers of the day and even united them against the king of England, like many of his ancestors he nevertheless failed in his objective to establish a lasting political and military Welsh hegemony.

Llywelyn's death was devastating for his longstanding companion, Ednyfed Fychan. Few had known the prince as intimately as he, who mourned not only his leader but his friend. As Llywelyn's seneschal, he had played an integral role in shaping Gwynedd throughout the reign, and the prince's successes, by extension, belonged to both men. Thoughts now, however, had to turn to his own mortality, and setting in motion plans for his sons' future. Through his rise to the summit of Welsh politics, Ednyfed accumulated a collection of estates and titles which reflected his exalted position, 'divers goodly houses' that were 'royally adorned with turrets and garrets'.[45]

Though there are no known surviving documents or grants to give a full picture of his property portfolio during his lifetime, analysing contemporary chancery rolls and later royal surveys provides some insight into the extent of Ednyfed's holdings across Wales, some of which were tribal and some acquired. Based on studies of his kindred, the wider family unit appears to have settled in the Perfeddwlad around the ninth century, specifically near Abergele. In the royal survey of this region in 1334, this kindred, including Ednyfed's direct descendants, is shown to still have an interest in a cluster of ancestral vills including Brynffanigl, Abergele, Llwydcoed, Cefnllaethfaen, Trofarth, Dynorban Fychan, Twynan and Llysaled.[46]

Ednyfed, however, soon acquired, either by purchase, royal gift or a combination of both, a collection of further holdings that extended his sway far beyond his ancestral lands in the Perfeddwlad. Further west in the commote of Arfon, he owned Dinorwig, Cwmllanerch and Gloddaeth, while on the Isle of Anglesey he had a presence in Tregarnedd, Trecastell, Erddreiniog, Gwredog and Penmynydd, a tight collection of vills that provided the family with a significant and stable foothold from which to operate. Perhaps pointedly, the Anglesey lands were close to the principal Gwynedd royal court at Aberffraw, giving Ednyfed quick access to his prince whenever his duties as seneschal were required. A record in the English Chancery Rolls further confirms that he also held land outside his native Gwynedd for in 1229 he was given letters of protection from Henry II to visit holdings in Llanrhystud, Cellan and Llansadwrn. These lands likely came into his possession through his marriage to Gwenllian ferch Rhys, daughter and sister of the local princes.[47]

It was on the Creuddyn Peninsula, however, close to the sea and at the foot of a limestone hill known as Bryn Euryn, that Ednyfed established his chief residence.[48] Known as Llys Euryn, the location may have been chosen as it had links with the seat of the fifth- and sixth-century kings of Rhos, to whom Ednyfed may have wanted to establish a connection to raise his own prestige. It is likely the origins of Llys Euryn are linked to the patent granted to Ednyfed by Llywelyn the Great on 1 May 1230, one sealed in green wax bearing the prince's equestrian emblem. Styled 'Idneved Vachan' in the document, an eighteenth-century transcription reveals a formal notification that the seneschal had 'bought with Llywelyn's consent the land of Rhosfynaich', a moor on the Creuddyn Peninsula that forms part of modern-day Rhos-on-Sea.

The terms stipulated that Ednyfed would hold the land free of all secular service, perhaps an indication of the high regard in which the prince held him, though he and his heirs would be compelled to offer two shillings each year to the local church for their Easter lighting. Ednyfed would also retain ownership of a local channel of water known as Aberdowith, including all buildings, mills and fisheries built along the banks so that nobody else could fish in the waters.[49] As Llys Euryn lay within the boundaries of the land bought by Ednyfed, his palace was likely constructed shortly thereafter. The ruin which now adorns the site is a later fifteenth-century manor house, described in the Elizabethan period as 'decayed for want of reparations', with no trace of Ednyfed's earlier erection visible to offer clues as to its splendour.[50] When all his holdings are considered, many of which were held free of dues or services to the Crown, save for providing military service during time of war, Ednyfed's influence extended across the whole of Wales, and there appears little doubt the eminent seneschal ranked among the most prosperous Welshmen of his day.

A seasoned and respected veteran of Welsh politics armed with invaluable experience of diplomacy and protocols, despite entering his seventh decade Ednyfed's service to the crown of Gwynedd did not end with the death of Llywelyn the Great. Retained as seneschal and possibly mentor to the new prince, Dafydd ap Llywelyn, one of Ednyfed's first acts was to witness an agreement made between Henry III and Dafydd at Gloucester on 15 May 1240 in which the king accepted his nephew's claim to be the rightful ruler of Gwynedd. Wearing a coronet to reflect his status as prince, Dafydd was knighted before he and his men did homage, submitting to Henry's overlordship.

Though Dafydd was permitted to inherit Gwynedd, the agreement stipulated that the rest of his father's disputed conquests, in particular Cardigan, Builth and Powys Wenwynwyn, were to be submitted to a body of arbitrators, partly English and partly Welsh and including Ednyfed Fychan, to determine their future. Though Dafydd swore to observe this proposal, and Ednyfed to uphold the outcome, over the next year the prince repeatedly ignored summonses to appear before the arbitrators until in August 1241, an infuriated Henry III denounced his recalcitrant nephew as 'a traitor and rebel in every respect'.[51]

The king invaded Gwynedd that month to force Dafydd's subjugation. Aware he could not withstand the martial superiority of his uncle, the prince wisely submitted before his principality was overrun. The terms of a fresh pact between the pair, again negotiated on Dafydd's behalf by Ednyfed, forced the prince to reimburse the king's expenses and hand over both the disputed territories and his elder half-brother Gruffudd ap Llywelyn.

As intended, this latter condition severely curtailed Dafydd's behaviour; should he step out of line in future, the prince risked the English king equipping Gruffudd, a man 'beloved by the Welsh',[52] with an army to launch a bid for a throne many felt had been unfairly denied him as his father's eldest son. Henry III further requested that Dafydd deliver several hostages as surety, with the records showing that that 'Rees son of Edenaveth, the son of Thuder Abidenavet, the son of Griffin son of Edenaveth, the son of Wronob son of Edenavet' among others were turned over. These appear to be Ednyfed Fychan's son Rhys plus three grandchildren drawn from each of his three other sons, Tudur, Gruffudd and Goronwy, perhaps as punishment for failing to enforce the May 1240 agreement. Pledging to uphold the terms of the treaty, Prince Dafydd swore upon a holy cross, before ordering Ednyfed to do the same. Neither man had much choice.[53]

The fragile peace that existed between Gwynedd and England was shattered by none other than Gruffudd himself. Having grown to resent his captivity, on the night of 1 March 1244, St David's Day, he lowered himself out of his Tower of London chamber using a makeshift rope fashioned from torn bedsheets and wall hangings. Described by Matthew Paris as 'very corpulent', Gruffudd's weight caused the rope to give way and he plummeted to his death, his 'pitiable corpse' discovered in the morning with a broken neck.[54]

Freed from the fear of his brother fronting an English-backed invasion, in June 1244 Prince Dafydd launched a blistering campaign to regain the territories he had ceded to Henry III three years earlier. The king responded in kind, marching into Gwynedd at the head of 'an abundant army' featuring 'a great band of soldiers' that despoiled the fields and towns they passed through.[55]

In one notable exchange, recounted in a letter written from the king's camp by one of Henry III's weary soldiers, an Irish ship bringing a cargo of wine to the English ran aground on a sandbank on the western side of the Conwy estuary, an area under Dafydd's control. When the men of Gwynedd noticed the stranded vessel, they hurried from their mountain hideouts to assault the exposed ship, though before much damage could be caused they were repelled by a 300-strong detachment of English soldiers, urgently charged with rescuing the shipment.

Before completing their mission, however, the rash Englishmen, 'like greedy and needy men', looted Aberconwy Abbey, the resting place of Llywelyn the Great, plundering the countryside and burning the library 'amongst other profane proceedings'. When the Welsh were informed, they furiously regrouped and set upon the English soldiers, 'wounding and slaying many' and capturing more. When Dafydd's men discovered that Henry had executed Welsh captives, parading their heads around camp, they in turn butchered the English in their possession, 'decapitating and mangling them dreadfully' before leaving their mutilated corpses along the river. One of those Welsh prisoners slain had allegedly been a young son of Ednyfed's, likely Rhys ab Ednyfed, who had been handed over as per the terms of the peace four years earlier.[56] It was a particularly brutal episode in a violent age.

Frustrated to be making 'but little progress', at the start of October Henry III issued a safe conduct for Ednyfed to lead a Welsh delegation into the king's temporary camp at Deganwy to discuss a winter truce.[57] One must wonder whether the seneschal of Gwynedd was able to hide any anguish at his son's death, an act ordered by the very man with whom he now had to negotiate peace. The resultant treaty may have been necessary, but it hardly represented a victory for either side, both having suffered considerable loss of life, supplies and trade.

Before hostilities could resume the following spring, Dafydd ap Llywelyn, 'worn out by various troubles' and 'after enduring innumerable sorrows of mind' owing to the slaughter of his men and destruction of his lands, died at Abergwyngregyn. He was laid to rest next to his father in Aberconwy, the Cistercian abbey so recently torched by the English.[58]

Ednyfed Fychan, a persuasive influence on the Welsh political landscape for nearly half a century, did not long outlive Dafydd.

Before 1246 was over, the Chronicle of St Werburg's Abbey in Chester reported that Ednyfed, this imposing counsellor and tenacious champion of Gwnyedd's interests, had also passed away. No specific date was given for his demise. He was buried in the chapel he had himself constructed near his home at Llys Euryn, having earlier gained a licence from the Vatican for Masses to be sung for his and his family's souls after death.[59] Heavily rebuilt in the fifteenth and seventeenth centuries and later adopted as the parish church of the Rhos-on-Sea, there are minor traces of Ednyfed's thirteenth-century chapel in the north aisle, with two pointed arches and a closed doorway still visible. It was believed his tombstone lay near the altar before it was removed to the entrance porch as this monument bore the name 'Ednyfed'. Though it seems likely he would have been buried in a prominent position within his own chapel, this particular headstone, which also carried the wording '*quondam vicarius*' (or 'sometime vicar'), belonged to Ednyfed ap Bleddyn, who was the local priest in the first decade of the fifteenth century.[60]

Ednyfed Fychan had presided over an impressive career. A hardened soldier and assiduous diplomat, he had used his extensive talents to dominate Welsh politics, dining and negotiating with princes and kings alike. Few outside royalty had wielded the levels of influence Ednyfed had exercised during his many decades in service to the princes of Gwynedd, often employed to serve as a conduit between the native Welsh and the ascendant English regime. It was his bureaucratic efficiency that had proven integral to the endurance of Gwynedd and native Welsh rule while the other principalities gradually fell by the wayside. It was for good reason the poet Elidir Sais mourned the seneschal's passing:

> Above the new grave of Ednyfed I stood,
> The tears flowed to my bosom –
> The terror of England; of the subduing throng,
> Complete in liberality, valiant in action[61]

Ednyfed's death left a colossal void, both on a personal and a political level. As expected from one so thorough in every task he conducted, the mighty seneschal of Gwynedd had prepared his sons well for the heavy burden they would now shoulder as their father's heir. To confront the coming tribulations that all Welshmen in the late thirteenth century faced, the sons of Ednyfed needed to heed every lesson their indomitable father had taught them.

2

War and Bloodshed

The deaths of Ednyfed Fychan and Prince Dafydd ap Llywelyn in 1246, coming just six years after the demise of Llywelyn the Great, in many ways represented a generational shift. The old guard of thirteenth-century North Welsh politics gave way to their respective heirs, an ambitious set determined to advance on their forefathers' progress. If the names and faces had changed at the head of the Gwynedd royal court, however, old troubles endured.

Dafydd left no legitimate male heir, prompting two of his nephews, Llywelyn ap Gruffudd and Owain Goch ap Gruffudd, sons of the unfortunate Gruffudd ap Llywelyn who had plunged to his death from the walls of the Tower of London, to jointly claim the throne of Gwynedd that had eluded their father. The siblings also inherited Dafydd's war with Henry III, though they quickly sought peace as they focused on rebuilding their harassed principality. Gwynedd was reported to be 'in a most straitened condition' so that 'the inhabitants began to waste away through want'; the continuation of war was not in their interest.[1] On 30 April 1247, the Treaty of Woodstock recognised the brothers as co-rulers of a reduced and partitioned Gwynedd, resigning the much-contested plains of the Perfeddwlad to the English once more.[2]

Ednyfed Fychan's death, meanwhile, transferred the burden of maintaining the family's hard-earned position at the summit of Welsh politics to the sons he left behind. Though the historical record is vague when tracing how many children Ednyfed fathered, five, probably six, sons can be identified. Goronwy, Gruffudd and Tudur achieved a considerable degree of political success following in their father's footsteps, with a fourth brother, Cynwrig, assuming a lower profile in their shadow. Another sibling, Rhys, was handed over to the English as a hostage in his youth and may have been the 'handsome and brave youth' executed during the war of 1245 that triggered such violent reprisals from the Welsh. A sixth figure, Hywel ab Ednyfed, who in 1242 was consecrated as bishop of St Asaph, was also likely one of his sons.[3]

Much of Ednyfed Fychan's estates were divided between his sons, as per Welsh law. Gruffudd ab Ednyfed inherited Tregarnedd on Anglesey and Dinorwig in the cantref of Arfon, and from his mother Gwenllian four townships near modern-day Llandeilo in South-West Wales, namely Llansadwrn, Tyllwyd, Taliaris and Cwmliog. In contrast to his faithful father, Gruffudd's devotion to the princes of Gwynedd appears to have been less than steadfast. Even during Ednyfed's lifetime, Gruffudd fell foul of Llywelyn the Great for slandering the reputation of the prince's adulterous wife, Joan. With his life at risk, Gruffudd fled to Ireland where he remained until Llywelyn's death in 1240.[4] This rebellious streak was inherited by Gruffudd's sons Rhys and Hywel ap Gruffudd, who would later side with the English crown against many of their cousins during the final conquest of Wales between 1277 and 1282, to their personal gain.

Tudur ab Ednyfed, meanwhile, also received land on Anglesey, notably the vill of Twrcelyn.[5] Though little is known of his earlier life, in November 1245 Tudur was captured by English forces and imprisoned in the Tower of London. He was not released from prison until 4 September 1246, earning his freedom by swearing to serve the king faithfully and doing homage.[6] On 27 January 1247 at Windsor, Henry III formally recognised Tudur's inheritance 'of that portion of the lands of his father in Wales which falls to him by hereditary right', providing he remain 'in the king's fealty and service'. Leaving two sons behind as surety, Tudur left England four months later and would remain loyal to Henry for much of the next decade, receiving lands and payment as reward for his continuing service. Tudur was even employed as one of the king's representatives in peace negotiations with the Welsh delegation as late as May 1260, fifteen years after his capture. It was a situation that must have caused some friction within the family, though the fact that one of his sons, Heilyn ap Tudur, was only released from the Tower in February 1263 may have explained in part Tudur's reluctance to return to the fold.[7]

It was Goronwy ab Ednyfed, however, who initially stepped into the vacuum left by Ednyfed Fychan's death, succeeding his father as seneschal and devotedly fulfilling the role of chief counsellor to the new co-prince of Gwynedd, Llywelyn ap Gruffudd. Judging by the success of his career thereafter, it is likely Goronwy was heavily prepared for the role by his father; as early as 1222 he was at Ednyfed's side as a young man witnessing a pact between Llywelyn the Great and the earl of Chester.[8]

It is reasonable to assume there was something in Goronwy's character, perhaps a natural aptitude for diplomacy, that distinguished him from his peers, including his brothers. To support his lifestyle, he inherited his father's Anglesey lands in Trecastell, Erddreiniog, Penmynydd and Gwredog, a tight cluster of properties that provided a strong base from which to operate. It is unclear which son of Ednyfed, if any, inherited his principal residence at Llys Euryn, though Goronwy did also inherit some property on the Creuddyn Peninsula which may have been his father's palace.[9] It was Goronwy, the new seneschal of Gwynedd, who would be the progenitor of the line that ultimately included not just Henry VII, but every English and thereafter British monarch to the present day.

Of course, as had been evident throughout the history of Gwynedd and the other Welsh principalities, lasting peace between siblings was a rarity when it involved power and land. When another brother of the co-princes, Dafydd ap Gruffudd, reached adulthood, Henry III announced his intention to further partition the already-truncated Gwynedd. When Llywelyn ap Gruffudd resisted further division of the principality, his brothers Dafydd and Owain Goch entered an alliance to seize their brother's lands by force. In the short but 'unnatural civil war' that followed, it was Llywelyn who emerged victorious, defeating his brothers within an hour at the Battle of Bryn Derwin and assuming full control of Gwynedd west of the Conwy.[10]

The lives of Ednyfed Fychan's four surviving sons – Gruffudd, Tudur, Goronwy and Cynwrig – were no less peaceable thereafter, however. In 1254, Henry III invested his already-imposing fifteen-year-old heir, Edward, with the earldom of Chester and handed him control of all the Crown possessions in Wales, including the Perfeddwlad, the lordships of Cardigan, Carmarthen, Montgomery and Builth, and, in Upper Gwent, the three castles Skenfrith, Grosmont and White Castle.[11]

Prince Edward's direct rule over the Perfeddwlad proved tough, and within two years the native people were raising complaints to their former lord, Llywelyn ap Gruffudd, about the harsh governance of the English officers. In their eyes, they 'would rather be killed in war for their liberty, than suffer themselves to be trodden down by strangers in bondage'.[12] Moved to tears by their plight, Llywelyn broke the Woodstock treaty and crossed the River Conwy to avenge these 'most cruel' atrocities. By the close of 1256, the Perfeddwlad was back under his control, soon followed by Powys Wenwynwyn. His allies in the south then defeated an English army near Llandeilo and quickly captured the castles of Laugharne, Llansteffan and Narbeth, granting him extensive authority over a large section of the Welsh people.[13] Matthew Paris could only note with dismay that 'the hatred between the English and Welsh daily gained ground' as a consequence of these unexpected and widespread Welsh successes.[14]

At Llywelyn's side throughout this period was Goronwy ab Ednyfed, 'one of the chief lords of the prince's council' and his leading advisor.[15] On 18 March 1258, Goronwy was one of twenty-seven Welshmen who established a 'mutual alliance and friendship' between Llywelyn and a collection of Scottish nobles, headed by Walter Comyn, Earl of Menteith, and the earls of Buchan, Mar and Ross, who were in charge of the Scottish kingdom during the minority of Alexander III. One of the fundamental principles of the pact was that neither party could enter an agreement with the king or magnates of England, nor provide assistance in any form that would undermine Scots–Welsh relations. It was hoped that by securing a trade deal with Scotland, the faltering Welsh economy could be stimulated through new trading routes, lessening the downturn in Anglo-Welsh commerce because of war.[16]

This alliance also represented the earliest surviving document in which Llywelyn ap Gruffudd laid claim to the title Prince of Wales, betraying his ambitions not only to govern his subjects in Gwynedd, but to press forward with a lasting political unification of all the individual principalities and lordships now under his sway. It was a resurrection of his grandfather's ultimately failed policy, but the younger Llywelyn was determined to succeed – at a meeting later that same year, his growing authority received a further boost when he welcomed the homage of all the leading Welsh lords of his day, save for his long-term rival Gruffudd ap Gwenwynwyn, the exiled prince of Powys Wenwynwyn. This moment, perhaps above all previously aborted attempts, marks the moment Welsh nationhood was truly born.

Despite the Scottish agreement, the Welsh adopted a pragmatic policy when it came to England, and on 25 June 1259 at Montgomery, Goronwy, recorded by Llywelyn as 'our seneschal', helped negotiate a one-year truce with the English king's representatives.[17]

The longstanding conflict between Henry III and his English barons, meanwhile, principally his brother-in-law Simon de Montfort, 6th Earl of Leicester, was exploited by Llywelyn. In late 1262, the prince sought to expand his dominions into the March, capturing Brecon and ravaging as far east as Herefordshire. In February 1263, Goronwy ab Ednyfed launched a destructive raid of his own deep into Gwent, leading 'a very great host' considered 'the pride of Wales'. He was able to penetrate as far as Abergavenny before his soldiers dismounted their horses and retreated to the nearby Blorenge mountain, intending to dupe the English into an ambush.

The king's man in the region, Peter de Montfort – no relation to the rebellious baron – did not fall for the trap, however, and instead targeted the Welsh plunderers who remained active in the area, later claiming in his report that he killed or captured around 300. He did, however, urgently request the king send monetary aid as this was the fifth time he had been forced to fend off an attack, and if Goronwy was not stopped they would 'destroy all the land of our lord the king' as they 'ask nothing but to have the land of Went'.[18] Before the year was out, Llywelyn was even extending the hand of friendship to his rival Gruffudd ap Gwenwynwyn, agreeing to restore the exiled prince to his lands in Powys if he paid homage. With three 'sons of Ednyfed' – Goronwy, Tudur and Cynwrig – assuming a central role in the lengthy negotiations, Gruffudd ap Gwenwynwyn agreed to the stipulation and for a short period Gwynedd and Powys stood united against English rule.[19]

After Henry III and his two sons were captured in May 1264 by Simon de Montfort, now established as the de facto ruler of England, Llywelyn sought to gain recognition of his status over the Welsh from the new ruling power. By now heavily experienced in diplomatic matters, Goronwy ab Ednyfed was one of the crucial figures involved in securing an agreement from de Montfort the following summer that recognised Llywelyn as the rightful prince of all Wales. Before any further progress could be made, however, a month later de Montfort was slain in battle at Evesham. With royal authority restored, any agreement that established Llywelyn ap Gruffudd as Prince of Wales was declared void.[20]

Llywelyn's supremacy across the Welsh remained firm, however, and a fresh treaty was urgently sought with a recovering English crown. The prince knew that if his hegemony was to endure after his death, he required royal recognition of his status. On 29 September 1267, at a ford just a few miles north-west of Montgomery, Llywelyn finally secured what he and his predecessors had long desired. After much negotiation on both sides, the papal legate to England, Cardinal Ottobuono de' Fieschi, announced that 'seeing that the English and the Welsh had long been divided and afflicted by conflicts and wars', Llywelyn of Gwynedd and Henry III of England had finalised what was hoped to be a lasting peace. The terms negotiated were certainly generous; in return for Llywelyn's homage and the hefty payment of 25,000 marks in instalments, the king agreed the prince could retain disputed territories in the March like Brecon, Gwerthrynion and Builth, while also receiving Cedewain and Ceri and the Perfeddwlad.

Most important, however, was King Henry's solemn acknowledgement that, to 'magnify the person of Llywelyn and honour his successors', he granted to him 'the principality of Wales, so that Llywelyn and his heirs shall be called and shall be princes of Wales'. This recognition constitutionally enshrined the principality of Wales as a political and administrative entity for the first time, under the aegis of the king of England but crucially distinct from the kingdom of England. To ensure they upheld the terms agreed, the prince and five of his leading counsellors, led by Goronwy ab Ednyfed, 'the prince's steward', and his brother Tudur ab Ednyfed, all swore on the Gospels 'not [to] break this peace and settlement but observe it in all the aforesaid articles for ever'.[21]

If the Treaty of Montgomery marked the high point of Llywelyn's reign, the first and last time a Welsh ruler received official recognition as prince of Wales from an English king, it also represented one of the final accomplishments in the storied life of his dependable right-hand man, Goronwy ab Ednyfed. Though his services were retained as late as the end of September 1268, when he was appointed to a four-person delegation alongside his brother Tudur to settle a land dispute with Gilbert de Clare, Earl of Gloucester,[22] on 17 October 1268 the distinguished and highly regarded seneschal passed away at the height of a productive career.

Having become involved in royal service with his father Ednyfed Fychan from an early age, in later life Goronwy had assumed an essential role in not just establishing Llywelyn ap Gruffudd on his throne, but leading his countrymen to heights scarcely before achieved. In the final decade of his life, Goronwy had helped secure a novel Scottish alliance, arranged peace between the longstanding rivals Gwynedd and Powys Wenwynwyn, and negotiated a deal with the brief de facto ruler of England, Simon de Montfort, before his principal achievement at Montgomery, which established for the first time the principality of Wales. Not merely a statesman, Goronwy had also led armies into the field, most notably during the 1263 raid on Gwent.

Like his father before him, Goronwy was mourned by his contemporaries, an indication of the respect in which he was held. To the author of *Brut y Tywysogion*, who presumably reflected the attitudes of many around him, the seneschal had been 'a man illustrious in arms, and generous in gifts, wise in council, and upright in deed, and humorous in words'.[23] To the bard Dafydd Benfras, Goronwy's 'word was completely wise', while another court poet, Bleddyn Fardd, regarded him reverentially as 'the buttress of Gwynedd' and observed that 'hard it is to learn to be without him'.[24] In short, Goronwy was undoubtedly the ideal figure a prince needed in his corner, and not a disciple easily replicated. One must speculate whether the marked decline in relations between England and Gwynedd thereafter, and the difficulties Llywelyn had in maintaining his hard-won Welsh principality, was linked to the absence of Goronwy's proficiency for policymaking and diplomacy. His death was a loss to all Welshmen.

Succeeding Goronwy ab Ednyfed as Prince Llywelyn's leading councillor was his brother Tudur, soon regarded by English and Welsh alike as the 'steward of Wales', a status neither his sibling nor his father attained. Despite his flirtation with the English crown between 1247 and 1260, Tudur had been an established part of the Welsh court for the previous decade and the transition into his brother's role was one of minimal disruption. As the seneschal of a fledgling principality of Wales, he certainly had enough to keep him occupied, including witnessing an agreement between Llywelyn and his brother Rhodri ap Gruffudd in April 1272 whereby the latter resigned his hereditary lands in Wales for 1,000 marks.[25]

If securing English recognition of his supremacy in Wales had proven a remarkable success for not just Llywelyn ap Gruffudd but tireless servants like Goronwy and Tudur ab Ednyfed, a golden age for the Welsh would prove elusive. Llywelyn's financial obligations to the

English crown and the cost of his many military campaigns forced him to heavily tax his frustrated subjects, and in building and then extending his principality he had made many enemies in the March, including his cousin Roger Mortimer, 1st Baron Mortimer, Humphrey de Bohun, 3rd Earl of Hereford, and Gilbert de Clare, 7th Earl of Gloucester. The tense situation was exacerbated after Henry III's death in the winter of 1272, bringing to a close more than half a century on the throne. As the new king, Edward I, was away on crusade at the time of his accession and in no rush to return to England, Gloucester and Mortimer were just two of the barons who wielded royal authority in his absence.

Llywelyn's woes were increased in February 1274 when an assassination plot against him was exposed and its would-be architects were unmasked as his brother Dafydd ap Gruffudd and Gruffudd ap Gwenwynwyn of Powys. At a summit on 17 April at Dolforwyn, Llywelyn's leading counsellors investigated and convicted the Powysian prince, led by the prince's justiciar Tudur ab Ednyfed, and his sole surviving brother Cynwrig. Dafydd, however, fled to England, and was given refuge by the calculating English king.[26]

When Edward I arrived back in England during the height of that summer, the Welsh prince did not find a willing arbitrator but a ferocious enemy who stood over six feet tall. What followed was a stubborn stand-off between two formidable figures who refused to back down. Llywelyn seethed that Edward not only continued to harbour his 'felonious barons' but refused to deliver some of the Marcher lordships as stipulated in the Treaty of Montgomery. Edward, meanwhile, was infuriated to discover the Welsh prince had repeatedly withheld his homage, had refused to attend the coronation, and was struggling to maintain his financial obligations to the crown. When Llywelyn, in his early fifties and still childless, then pursued a marriage with Eleanor Montfort, daughter of the rebel earl and through her mother a granddaughter of King John, a return to war seemed unavoidable. The king travelled to Chester in September 1275 to personally command Llywelyn to do homage, but the prince turned and retreated into the mountains of his heartlands to await the inevitable onslaught.[27]

Edward's incendiary response later that winter was to have sailors from Bristol intercept Lady Eleanor, a woman Llywelyn 'extremely loved',[28] during her voyage from France to assume her position as princess of Wales. Eleanor was imprisoned in Windsor Castle, beyond the reach of her waiting husband, who could only seethe in resentment when informed of her capture. Despite this setback, the prince remained unwilling to compromise on his demands for the Marcher lords to have their power curbed, the Treaty of Montgomery to be honoured in full, and his brother Dafydd to be handed over, so in November 1276 Edward I declared Llywelyn ap Gruffudd a rebel.

Assembling a vast army more than 15,000 strong to punish the Welsh prince, by the summer of 1277 Edward had subdued Powys, Deheubarth, Ceredigion and the Perfeddwlad. Orders were given for new castles to be constructed at Flint, Rhuddlan, Hawarden, Hope and Ruthin, while the harvest on Anglesey, on which much of Gwynedd and beyond depended for sustenance during the winter months, was seized. Sensing defeat, many Welsh lords started to defect, including Ednyfed Fychan's grandchildren Rhys and Hywel ap Gruffudd. Prince Llywelyn evaded capture but was nevertheless trapped in the mountains of Eryri, surrounded by a daunting English force that included a growing contingent of Welshmen who no longer believed in his ability to lead them. Hungry, tired and dispirited, Llywelyn had little option but to surrender.[29]

The outcome of the war of 1277 was a complete repudiation of the Treaty of Montgomery, which was replaced by a new agreement that was sealed at Aberconwy on 9 November. Though one of the negotiators was Tudur ab Ednyfed, who put his seal to the document, this latest 'severe and merciful' treaty was weighted heavily in favour of the English crown.[30] The prince was forced to pay £50,000 for what was termed 'disobedience, damages and injuries', and also had to relinquish the Perfeddwlad and his lands in South and Mid Wales, shattering the single Welsh principality he had worked so hard to establish.

Llywelyn was no longer permitted to receive homage from his compatriots and was ordered to partition what little remained of his truncated principality with his brothers. He was also to be restricted to the mountainous terrain west of the Conwy, with the Llŷn Peninsula bestowed upon Owain Goch, released from captivity after two decades. Dafydd, meanwhile, was handed two of the four cantrefs of the Perfeddwlad by Edward I, which allowed him a modest foothold on the eastern side of the Conwy. Finally, ten hostages were to be delivered to the English king to guarantee Llywelyn abided by the terms, with Tudur swearing on behalf of the prince he would hand them over by a date to be fixed by the king.[31]

Though Llywelyn was permitted to retain the style prince of Wales, now an empty title lacking substance, thirty years of progress had been reversed in an instant. He had overreached himself and unwisely antagonised a formidable foe; unable to hold together a united Welsh front, he was back to where he started. After belatedly paying his homage during Christmas 1277, Llywelyn was permitted to formally marry Eleanor Montfort. The ceremony was conducted at Worcester Cathedral in October 1278, in the presence of the English king and queen who bore the cost of the festivities. There was a message being sent – Llywelyn was now dependent on the English king's goodwill.[32]

Just as Goronwy ab Ednyfed had passed away following the Treaty of Montgomery in 1267, his brother and successor Tudur ab Ednyfed likewise passed away soon after he had sealed the Aberconwy agreement. Perhaps owing to the low ebb of Gwynedd at the time, his death did not herald much attention from the bards, but just like his brother and father, Tudur nonetheless played a faithful role in advancing the cause of his homeland in less than prosperous circumstances and was justly recognised as the first-ever seneschal of Wales.[33] His final role had been to help negotiate an uneasy peace between the Welsh and English, but it was a truce that lasted just four years.

Though Llywelyn ap Gruffudd generally resolved to live within the harsh terms of the 1277 Aberconwy treaty, the prince nevertheless failed to quell rising discontent among his subjects, who grew frustrated at strict taxation and the creeping encroachment of English law across Welsh territory, often enforced by stern royal officials who had little time for complaints. Llywelyn himself was just one victim whose native rights were being eroded in a manner that hardened Welsh hearts – in a lengthy legal dispute with Gruffudd ap Gwenwynwyn of Powys over the lordship of Arwystli in Mid Wales, he demanded it was judged according to Welsh law, which would likely have resulted in a favourable outcome, though after a protracted period of deliberation Edward I ultimately favoured English law.

One of those who furiously resisted this development was Dafydd ap Gruffudd, who, in his own words, had 'laboured greatly' on behalf of the English king in the past, often to the detriment of his own brother, Llywelyn. By early 1282, however, Dafydd felt that not only was the king failing to observe the terms of Aberconwy, but he was making war on the Welsh 'out of inveterate hatred and avarice'. As he felt 'unable to obtain any justice, amends or grace', therefore, Dafydd 'began to defend himself and his people as well as he could'.[34]

On 22 March 1282, Dafydd took decisive action that would have catastrophic repercussions for his compatriots. On his orders, English garrisons at Hawarden, Rhuddlan and Flint were attacked, and in just a few days the revolt spread with a remarkable alacrity that took Llywelyn by surprise. In the south, the castles at Llandovery, Aberystwyth and Carreg Cennen were captured in what rapidly developed into a fervent national insurrection against English rule.[35]

Having been humbled already by Edward I, Llywelyn was hesitant to support the revolt. Public clamour against English governance grew by the day, however, and the prince had to choose between leading his people or being overthrown by them. His decision to cast his lot with the uprising was also likely influenced by the death of his wife, Eleanor Montfort, during childbirth in June. As the child was a daughter, any hope of establishing a lasting dynastic future was lost with Eleanor's demise. Llywelyn may have had more to lose than to gain by joining his brother's campaign but, stricken by grief and lacking the measured counsel of pragmatic and wise seneschals like Goronwy and Tudur ab Ednyfed, perhaps reasoned it no longer made a difference.

This Welsh insurgency captured Edward I's full attention, and at once he became fixed on completing what his predecessors had started more than two centuries earlier – the complete conquest of Gwynedd, and with it the Welsh at large. The king assembled his nobility and mustered a vast army, one fully prepared for a winter campaign in the forbidding wilds of Eryri if required. Following the strategy that had proven successful five years earlier, he easily subdued the Perfeddwlad before capturing Anglesey, hampering Llywelyn's movements and starving his men.

Such was the scope of the uprising that while Edward himself headed the northern invasion, Roger Mortimer was responsible for tackling Mid Wales, with the earls of Gloucester and Pembroke covering the south. Despite facing a superior military force, the Welsh did secure two notable victories that boosted morale. On 17 June 1282, Gloucester's men were ambushed near Dinefwr Castle and overrun, while at the start of November an English force attempting to cross to the mainland from Anglesey was destroyed on the banks of the Menai Strait.[36]

In a final attempt to quell a war that had rapidly spiralled out of control, John Pecham, Archbishop of Canterbury, wrote to Llywelyn hoping the prince would 'submit to a peace with the English'. Pecham was hardly tactful in his approach, however; he criticised the 'excessive cruelty of the Welsh', which he believed was 'even beyond that of the Saracens and other infidels', and disparaged their culture, society and manners. The peace proposal, in fact, was little more than a veiled threat. Llywelyn retorted it was the English 'that delight themselves with war and bloodshed' and his people were 'glad to live quietly upon their own' but were prevented from doing so by their neighbours 'who coming to the country, utterly destroy whatever comes in their way, without regard either to sex, age, or religious places'.[37]

Pecham presented Llywelyn's grievances to Edward, who granted the archbishop authority to offer the prince an English earldom in exchange for peacefully surrendering Gwynedd, supplemented with a generous annuity of £1,000. Llywelyn's newborn daughter would be provided for after her father's death as befitting her status, while Dafydd was promised a safe conduct to live out his days on crusade. If Llywelyn found such drastic terms disagreeable, Pecham promised gravely that Edward's army would not only 'oppress them, but in all probability totally eradicate the nation'.[38]

Llywelyn's response to this ultimatum, upon deliberation with his council, was resolute. He could 'in no wise agree' to a deal that sought the destruction of his people, and he could not in good conscience 'resign his paternal inheritance, which has for many ages been enjoyed by his predecessors', as far back as the time of Brutus.[39] The prince, in fact, was almost incredulous he should be asked to abandon his homeland, which he possessed by 'unquestionable right', for merely defending it against 'tyrannical government'. Unlike in previous generations of Welsh princes and English kings, a peaceful compromise was not within sight. This was to be a decisive confrontation, with neither side willing to give any quarter.

Forced to navigate this deadly situation was Tudur Hen ap Goronwy, who had assumed leadership of his family and was thus charged with the unenviable task of following in the accomplished footsteps of his father Goronwy ab Ednyfed, uncle Tudur ab Ednyfed and grandfather Ednyfed Fychan. There is some evidence he was groomed to step into the role of seneschal, having witnessed several documents between 1274 and 1278 and presumably provided some degree of counsel to Llywelyn. However, he also had connections to the English king; in September 1278, Edward I had restored to Tudur Hen and his brothers Goronwy ap Goronwy and Hywel ap Goronwy a cluster of lands in the Perfeddwlad that had been previously seized by the crown, a conflict of interest that placed the trio in a compromised position when war between Gwynedd and England became an inevitability.[40]

Each man was forced to weigh up the cost of patriotism versus pragmatism, of upholding Welsh traditions and rights against moderate prosperity and influence within the expansionist English system. Further division among the Welsh was sown by King Edward's promise that any person who submitted to his authority would retain full possession of their lands and privileges, an appealing concession when weighted against Llywelyn's increasing financial burdens on his people to help fund his ambitions for an extensive Welsh principality, which some may have considered an unachievable project.[41]

If Tudur Hen was the 'son of Wronob son of Edenavet' handed over to Henry III as a hostage in 1241, then this suggests he was at least middle-aged by the summer of 1282. He had responsibilities as a husband, father, landowner, counsellor and Welshman, some of which may have been pulling him in different directions. It was a fraught and fluid period in which men like Tudur spent considerable time contemplating their position and how they could survive the fallout of what was proving a particularly fierce episode in the history of Anglo-Welsh relations. It is unclear precisely what position Tudur Hen adopted, but ultimately any decision to betray Llywelyn in pursuit of personal prosperity was taken out of his hands by a fateful journey the prince took at the beginning of December.

Though much of the circumstances surrounding Llywelyn ap Gruffudd's demise are lost to the mists of time, it is known the prince emerged from his refuge in the heart of Eryri a few days into December to launch an attack on the lordship of Builth. On 11 December 1282 at a ford near Cilmeri, just a few miles west of Builth, Llywelyn's army encountered an English force under the command of Edmund Mortimer, the new Baron Mortimer and a distant cousin of the Welsh prince. During the skirmish that followed, Llywelyn became separated from his main host and was set upon by an English detachment. He may have been scouting his opponents or lured away by treachery. While riding without armour and away from his bodyguard, a knight by the name of Frankton chanced upon the prince and fatally pierced him with a lance. It was only when his helm was removed that his identity was revealed.[42]

The elated Frankton promptly severed Llywelyn's head and sent it on to Edward I at Conwy, a gruesome if well-received memento. This brief but bloody incident marked a dramatic turning point in the story of Wales, with repercussions that in many ways still endure. Though Welsh resistance to foreign rule would survive Llywelyn, destined to be remembered as Llywelyn the Last, no Welshman would again bear the title prince of Wales as recognised by the English crown.[43]

Llywelyn's death did not stop his brother Dafydd laying claim to the title, which he had long sought, but in doing so he accepted the most poisoned of chalices. Dafydd was unable to reverse the destruction wrought on the weary and famished Welsh, and by June 1283 was a prisoner of the English king. On 3 October in Shrewsbury marketplace, Dafydd was executed in the most brutal and agonising manner; according to the Annals of St Werburgh 'he was first torn in pieces by being dragged by horses to the gallows, then after being hanged and his head cut off, he was divided into four quarters'. It was a most 'miserable death'. Dafydd's head was sent to London where it very visibly adorned London Bridge next to his brother's – two princes of Wales, their lifeless eyes staring across the Thames in the heart of England's capital city.[44] There could be no prophecy calling for either man's return.

The short-lived independent principality of Wales had been brought to a violent and bloody conclusion. Llywelyn died without an acknowledged male heir, his only child, a daughter named Gwenllian, taken into English custody to spend the rest of her days shut away from the outside world in a Lincolnshire priory. Dafydd's sons would also remain in English captivity until their respective deaths, locked in an iron cage deep within Bristol Castle to prevent escape. Of their other brothers, Owain Goch was already dead and Rhodri ap Gruffudd had freely resigned his ties to Gwynedd to live out his days in relative obscurity in south-east England.[45]

Where possible, therefore, Edward I had taken decisive action to thwart a Gwynedd resurgence, even removing all regalia to London, where it was triumphantly paraded through the street. Other Welsh dynasties were likewise disinherited or imprisoned. With native rule ended, after 1283 the English crown's status as the greatest landowner in Wales was indisputable. For Welshmen who survived the tumult of the early 1280s, like Tudur Hen ap Goronwy, it was a new and uncertain world. Would they prosper under English rule, or be eradicated completely? One thing was clear – the war and bloodshed had not ended.

3

Hardship

The successive military campaigns of 1277 and 1282–83 had proven a conclusive triumph for Edward I, reducing and then finally overrunning Gwynedd, completing the Anglo-Norman conquest of the Welsh that had begun more than 200 years previously. Bringing the Welsh to heel, however, had not been a straightforward process for one of the most formidable men to sit on the throne of England. Edward had been forced to mobilise a vast number of troops, including Gascon knights and Savoyard builders to supplement English levies and Welsh dissenters, all funded through unpopular taxation and burdensome loans. The conquest had been hard won and costly, and the king sought at once to permanently secure his position in Wales, militarily, administratively and constitutionally.

After repairing a string of Welsh castles which had come under his control, Edward turned his attentions towards an expensive and extensive castle-building programme of his own across the newly conquered principality. From March 1283, huge state-of-the-art fortresses were erected at Caernarfon, Harlech and Conwy, formidable if sophisticated symbols of English royal power designed not only to become the seat of government in Gwynedd, but to intimidate the local population into submission by visibly asserting crown authority. Though often perceived to be provocative symbols of colonial subjugation, these castles may also be viewed in some respects as a testament to the dogged resolve of the Welsh to resist English rule, demonstrating the extraordinary steps the king had to take to ensure royal supremacy could be insurmountably enforced.

The building progress was protracted, noisy and hugely disruptive, with woodlands felled, deep ditches excavated, and stone quarried and dragged to the construction sites by a cosmopolitan gathering of labourers, carpenters, masons and diggers numbering several thousand.

Craftsmen from across England and the continent were recruited for the work, overseen by the masterful leadership of the Savoyard James of St George, who incorporated features he had encountered from his travels across Europe and the Middle East.

On 19 March 1284, meanwhile, the governance of the lands Edward had 'annexed and united' to his crown were constitutionally reformed by the Statute of Rhuddlan, or the Statutes of Wales, a royal charter addressed by the king to 'all his Subjects of his Land of Snowdon, and of other his Lands in Wales'. Pointedly, there was no mention of prince or principality in the entire document, just repeated references to the 'land of Wales'.[1]

The statute's purpose was to extend the English legal and financial system to the Welsh lands now under direct English royal control, with the Welsh henceforth subject to English criminal law and courts conducted in the Norman French language, though in some instances native customs were permitted to remain. The former principality of Gwynedd, meanwhile, was carved into three new English-style shires – Caernarfonshire, Merionethshire and Anglesey – with other crown holdings becoming the shires of Cardigan, Carmarthen and Flint. These were to be administered by two justiciars, one in the north and one in south, who were effectively royal governor, supreme judge and chief military commander combined. A new chamberlain accountable to central government was responsible for collecting all revenues due to the crown, which were sent on to the royal exchequer in London. Below these two offices were scores of sheriffs, coroners and bailiffs working to maintain the royal authority in the region, none of whom were to be Welsh. These changes were all considered 'expedient for the security of us and our land of Wales'.

Though Edward I spared little expense to subjugate the Welsh, there would naturally remain some stout resistance to what was viewed as the removal of traditional rights and disregard for ancient customs and laws. Overzealous royal officials and forced territorial resettlements were an additional source of consternation, creating a febrile atmosphere. In 1286, for example, Tudur Hen ap Goronwy appears to have fallen foul of the new regime when he was forced to make a modest payment to the chamberlain for committing 'a certain offence', though the nature of this transgression is not clarified.[2]

Of greater consequence, in late September 1294 Tudur joined a local rebellion fronted by a minor lord named Madog ap Llywelyn ap Maredudd, who claimed descent from the twelfth-century prince Owain Gwynedd. This quickly erupted into a well-coordinated, cross-country rampage that drew wide support. After a dozen years of direct English rule, there was growing resentment in North and West Wales towards the severe nature of unscrupulous and arrogant royal officials, particularly regarding the rigorous collection of a tax on movable property and enforced conscription for Edward I's French war. Wounded national pride in the years since the conquest of Gwynedd also played a role in triggering this latest outbreak of violence. According to a later account written by the knight Sir Thomas Grey, based heavily on his father's experiences during this period, that the English settlers 'led a jolly life, and took much delight in hounds and hawks, and in horse racing and leaping, and especially in killing deer' hardly enamoured them to the deflated locals.[3]

It was Madog ap Llywelyn who exploited this discontent among his compatriots, resorting to arms and declaring himself the rightful bearer of the title of prince of Wales. The Conwy, Clwyd and Dee valleys were quickly overrun by insurgents, with the king's unfinished project at Caernarfon looted and burned. Several other castles in the north were targeted, including Harlech, Conwy, Flint, Ruthin, Mold, Hawarden and Denbigh, before the movement shifted south, with rebel activity occurring in Pembroke, Glamorgan and Brecon. Edward I's loathed officials also came under fire – the hated sheriff of Anglesey, Roger Puleston, was even dragged through the streets of Caernarfon and hanged in front of a baying mob.[4]

On 19 December 1294 at Penmachno, Madog's leading supporters met to witness the 'prince of Wales and Lord of Snowdon' grant lands to someone named Bleddyn Fychan. Among those listed as present were 'Tuder ab Gronw, our steward' and 'Gronw vychan, his brother', proving that the sons of Goronwy ab Ednyfed had yet to fully abandon a restoration of Welsh independence, even if this required following a minor figure like Madog. There was undoubtedly a sense of hereditary continuity at play, with Tudur Hen designated steward, or seneschal, the position his father, uncle and grandfather had held. It was a mark of respect for the family's standing in North Wales, a pedigree that was widely known.[5]

Edward I was in Portsmouth preparing to embark on campaign to France when he was informed of the latest Welsh uprising and decisively turned his army around. By Christmas 1294, the energetic king, intending to 'quell the pride and stubbornness of the Welsh', had marched his army across the border to set up camp at Conwy, just 20 miles north of Penmachno. Though Edward was briefly besieged in his new castle over the winter, and ambushed in early January during one foray deep into Eryri, Madog's cause did not seriously undermine the English hold in Wales. After suffering heavy losses in March 1295 during a surprise attack near Montgomery in Powys, the leader was apprehended with little incident and conveyed to London where he was condemned to 'perpetual imprisonment' for the remainder of his life.[6]

This latest episode of Welsh defiance compelled Edward I to tighten the restrictions he had already imposed on the Welsh before embarking on the construction of yet another castle, Beaumaris, on Anglesey. The ease with which the English king suppressed Madog's uprising, as well as the lack of viable candidates to front any future insurgency, is likely to have persuaded Tudur Hen to fully reconcile with English domination to safeguard his ample inheritance. Perhaps hoping to conceal the level of his involvement in the rebellion, on 3 December 1296 Tudur formed a delegation of four who approached the king at Waldingfield in Suffolk on behalf of the 'good men and commonalty of Snowdon and Anglesey' protesting rumours 'which disturbed and grieved them' that the king 'held them in suspicion'. Tudur and his companions begged Edward not to doubt their loyalty, prompting the king to reply that 'by reason of their late good service' he held them 'for his faithful and devoted subjects'. Whether this was the truth or not is debatable, but both sides appeared content to move forward together, sharing a mutual desire for peace.[7]

King Edward needed men like Tudur Hen working within the system rather than undermining it from outside, exploiting their considerable influence and expertise to bolster his standing with a restless native populace. Tudur, for his part, understood that although he was professionally restricted by the presence of the king's new chamberlain and justiciar, the path to stability, and perhaps even prosperity, lay in serving the English king as diligently as he and his ancestors had served the princes of Gwynedd in the past.

After the king's namesake heir, a tall, handsome, youth born in Caernarfon Castle, was created the new Prince of Wales on 7 February 1301, the most prominent Welshmen were summoned to swear fealty to their new feudal lord, the first English bearer of this ancient title. On 22 April in Flint Castle, Tudur Hen ap Goronwy pledged to faithfully serve the seventeen-year-old prince in whatever capacity he was required, to uphold his authority and to never act again against the royal interest. Among those listed swearing fealty alongside him were Goronwy ap Tudur and Hywel ab Goronwy, Griffin ab Goronwy and Goronwy Fychan, which may indicate that in total three generations of the same family swore fealty to the prince across several days. This wasn't intended to be merely symbolic, but rather a concerted effort by Edward I to bond the Welsh to his heir; the prince was granted possession of all the royal territories in Wales, including but not limited to Anglesey, the Perfeddwlad and the heartland of Gwynedd in the north, and the lordships of Builth, Montgomery, Carmarthen, Cardigan and Haverford in the mid and south. It was an expansive endowment that offered the Welsh an opportunity to secure patronage in return for pledging their loyalty to a feudal lord who wasn't the conquering king of England.[8]

Tudur Hen took advantage of the English heir's involvement in Welsh affairs; in 1305 he complained to Prince Edward that the justiciar had deprived him the office of *rhaglaw* of Dindaethwy, an office similar to the English bailiff charged with ensuring efficient and peaceful local government, as well as unfairly demanding rent for land he claimed had been freely gifted to him by Llywelyn the Last. Tudur further requested the prince permit him to hold his own courts within his territories for all pleas except those of a serious nature, which was granted.[9]

During this latter petition, Tudur Hen described himself as an old man. With thoughts turning to the next life, he would soon begin dedicating his final years to the restoration of the Dominican friary in Bangor. It had been heavily damaged by fire during the 1282 war, and though the English crown provided some compensation to the prior for its repair, as well as timber, local benefactors like Tudur assumed much of the responsibility. Tudur's role, in fact, was prominent enough that he has been erroneously believed to be the friary's founder, though this honour can likely be bestowed upon Llywelyn the Last several decades earlier. One must wonder, considering Tudur's enthusiasm in overseeing its rebuilding and the friary's speculated date of foundation a few years after his grandfather's death, whether this was the final resting place of Ednyfed Fychan.[10] When Tudur passed away on 11 October 1311, it was within the south wall of the friary chapel that he was buried, though unfortunately any trace of his work was lost when the friary was dissolved in 1538, ironically at the behest of his descendant, Henry VIII.[11]

Before his death, Tudur Hen had been able to exploit the useful English property laws which now applied in the principality of Wales to allow for just one son inheriting the bulk of his estates, as opposed to dividing his possessions equally as stipulated under the Welsh system. This was an advantage which, perhaps above all other reasons, attracted Tudur to the new regime, allowing him to bestow his patrimony upon his eldest son alone in the expectation that with each generation it could expand, as occurred across the border. He made the system work for him. His heir with Angharad ferch Ithel Fychan,[12] Goronwy ap Tudur Hen, therefore had a distinct advantage over previous generations of Welshmen forced to partition their inheritance, and would subsequently prosper as one of the leading native landowners in fourteenth-century North Wales. His brothers Hywel and Madog would sink into obscurity.

Goronwy ap Tudur Hen, honoured with the name of his grandfather, followed his father's example in pledging his loyalty to the English crown. One imagines Tudur Hen had counselled Goronwy that the path to prosperity and influence was to bind oneself to the English king, to provide tireless service in advancing royal power in Wales and to rise within the system rather than risk destruction operating outside of it. It worked for Tudur, so there was no reason it could not work for Goronwy. Not that there was much alternative, in any case.

Goronwy, therefore, pledged his full support towards the tall and athletic new king, Caernarfon-born Edward II, upon his accession in the summer of 1307. When the English king mustered a vast army in 1314 to invade Scotland and overthrow the defiant King of Scots, Robert the Bruce, he made committed use of his Welsh subjects. One of those summoned to serve Edward was Goronwy, personally tasked with raising twenty men for the campaign. It is unclear if Goronwy made it as far as Bannockburn, where the English army was famously routed across two brutal days by Bruce's troops on 23 and 24 June 1314, but he was certainly paid by the chamberlain of North Wales on Edward's command for travelling as far as Newcastle upon Tyne that tense summer.[13] Much had changed since the days when Goronwy's namesake grandfather was busy not just fighting the English but forming anti-English alliances with the Scottish nobility.

The younger Goronwy clearly made a positive impression on Edward II during the Bannockburn campaign, as he was retained in royal service thereafter; he was created a King's Yeoman, to attend upon the king when he visited his lands in North Wales, and for fourteen months between 18 May 1318 and 16 July 1319 served as forester of Snowdon. The position of forester is not clearly defined, but Goronwy was likely charged with maintaining law and order in the woodland areas that fell within North-West Wales in general, overseeing the detainment of fugitives or the apprehension of would-be poachers hunting any protected game. He would also have been expected to ensure the livestock numbers were kept suitably high and to supervise the production and sale of timber where needed. It could be a profitable role, but it was certainly a demanding one and may have brought Goronwy into conflict with local ruffians whom he was responsible for policing.[14]

Edward II's two-decade reign proved to be one of 'great tribulation and adversity', with the king's inflammatory and often haughty behaviour provoking substantial discontent among his nobility, chiefly the Marcher Lords. Though he could be 'wise, gentle, and amiable in conversation', Edward was 'not industrious, neither was he beloved by the great men of his realm'.[15] His repeated refusal to renounce his intimate relationship with Piers Gaveston early in his reign provoked a furious backlash which ultimately led to the latter's execution in 1312 by a group of barons, to the king's great fury.

Edward's reputation plummeted further with frequent military failures in Scotland, an escalating financial crisis, and a devastating multi-year famine that caused the price of food to rise to exorbitant levels. The king's inability to control or placate his noble critics, plus his dependence on a divisive and ambitious new favourite, Hugh Despenser the Younger, led to the outbreak of civil war in early 1321. Though Edward managed to emerge from this conflict victorious, his merciless vengeance only served to harden the resolve of his enemies, principally led by Roger Mortimer, 3rd Baron Mortimer. In August 1323, Mortimer escaped from captivity in the Tower of London and fled across the Channel to France, where he was soon joined by Isabella, Edward II's queen, who likewise simmered in resentment at Despenser's hold over her malleable husband.

Forming a political and romantic alliance, Mortimer and Isabella assembled an army on the continent and in September 1326 invaded England, landing on the Suffolk coast before sweeping west and overwhelming the king's party. Before the year was up, Despenser and his father were both executed for usurping royal authority while Edward, who had fled into South Wales, was humiliatingly taken prisoner by his queen and her lover.[16]

In early January 1327, it was agreed that the king should abdicate in favour of his fourteen-year-old namesake heir, who would be raised to the throne as Edward III. Oaths were sworn to the new king as well as his mother Isabella, appointed her son's regent until he reached majority. It was Mortimer, however, who assumed de facto control of the kingdom, exploiting his authority to further establish his hold over Wales – he assumed the role of justiciar and as 1st earl of March extended his possessions from Wigmore as far north as Denbigh, taking in the lordships of Clun, Montgomery and Oswestry. The ousted king, meanwhile, was reduced in rank to just Edward of Caernarfon, and would shortly suffer 'a horrible death' in Berkeley Castle on the apparent orders of Mortimer.[17]

Despite Edward II's political difficulties and patent unsuitability to wear the crown, he had generally retained the loyalty of his Welsh subjects, including Goronwy ap Tudur Hen. This Welsh contingent was led by Sir Gruffudd Llwyd and included a young Rhys ap Gruffudd, the former a great-grandson and the latter a great-great-grandson of Ednyfed Fychan respectively and therefore distant cousins of Goronwy. Gruffudd Llwyd's father had fought for the English during the war of 1282 and this enabled his son to advance in royal service earlier than his cousins, who stood with Llywelyn the Last. Gruffudd is mentioned as early as 1284 succeeding to lands in Rhos, and again in 1297 to the estate of Tregarnedd on Anglesey, both which had been connected with Ednyfed. He had remained loyal to the English crown during the 1295 uprising, and certainly by 1298 was the principal royal agent in North Wales, trusted with levying Welsh troops for the English king's campaigns in Flanders and Scotland and serving in turn as sheriff of Anglesey, Caernarfonshire and Merionethshire. Regarded as a 'stout and a valiant gentleman', he was a yeoman of the king's household and by 1301 was listed as a knight, one of the earliest Welshmen afforded the honour under English rule. By the end of his years Gruffudd had been one of the most conspicuous Welshmen in public life, rewarded handsomely for his service to the English crown. Bonded by kinship, Goronwy now resolved to follow the example set by Gruffudd Llwyd, a 'loyal Welshman of Snowdon', to achieve modest success for himself and his family.[18] Men like these, the '*Wyrion Eden*', or descendants of Ednyfed Fychan, now emerged to take the place of the princes as the heads of Welsh society.

Despite this loyalty to Edward II, however, there was no hesitancy in extending that same courtesy to his successor, Edward III. In 1330 the young monarch launched a dramatic counter-coup against the unpopular, cruel and grasping Roger Mortimer, who after three tumultuous years revelling in his role as the most powerful figure in the kingdom was arrested on a litany of charges, not least the murder of Edward II. Mortimer was hanged, drawn and quartered at Tyburn on 29 November 1330, an execution that heralded a new era in Welsh and English history under a bold, vigorous teenage king who would develop into one of the most celebrated monarchs to wear the crown of England.[19]

Goronwy ap Tudur Hen would not long survive this stormy episode, passing away on 11 December 1331. He died an established and prominent royal servant with a lengthy and laudable track record of service to three consecutive bearers of the English crown named Edward. Likely per his final wishes, Goronwy was buried near his father, Tudur Hen, in the friary at Bangor. Just under a year later, on 10 November 1332, Edward III formally recognised Goronwy's three sons, Hywel, Tudur Fychan and Gruffudd, as their father's rightful heirs, in return for which they swore fealty to the English king.

As they were of full age, all being twenty-one or older, the king ordered Gilbert Talbot, the new justiciar of South Wales, to deliver the three men their share of Goronwy's lands in Cardiganshire, as per Welsh law. An inquisition taken earlier that summer revealed these lands included a third of the township of Cellan in Mabwynion, a third of Rhydonnen in Perfedd, and a third of Llechweddlwyfan in Creuddyn.[20] Though Goronwy's North Welsh estates are not mentioned, a similar settlement was likely reached with the estates he held in Dindaethwy on Anglesey, particularly the vills of Penmynydd, Trecastell and Erddreiniog. Much of the other estates once held by Ednyfed Fychan, particularly those on the mainland in the area once known as the Perfeddwlad, had passed down the family into other lines of descent, but though this particular generation was chiefly restricted to Anglesey, the three men nevertheless grew to wield significant influence that extended beyond the island.

This inquisition notwithstanding, information about Gruffudd ap Goronwy is non-existent, suggesting he may have died soon after, while

Hywel ap Goronwy entered the priesthood, serving initially as a canon at Bangor Cathedral. Responsibility for the family's secular position rested on the shoulders of Tudur ap Goronwy, the second of his family to bear that name after his grandfather. To avoid confusion, he was known by the epithet Fychan, or 'younger', and may even have been born before his grandfather's demise in 1311, which makes it possible to suggest a minimum age of at least twenty-one at the moment of his inheritance in 1332. Based principally at Trecastell, Tudur Fychan served as a royal officer on the island, notably fulfilling the role of *rhaglaw* of Dindaethwy in 1343, a position his namesake grandfather had held nearly forty years earlier.[21]

Despite the political upheaval in England during the first quarter of the fourteenth century that had culminated in the deposition of Edward II in January 1327, the same period had proven generally stable for the Welsh, a few minor episodes apart. As English settlers and native Welsh learned to coexist, even intermarrying in some cases, many towns experienced prosperous growth in the generations following the Edwardian conquest of 1282, becoming centres of international commerce that raised the general standard of living. In rural communities where the population was wholly Welsh, local leaders who established cordial relations with their English lords were able to flourish, and though the highest offices continued to elude their ambitions, several Welshmen nevertheless thrived in public service, becoming burgesses, foresters and sheriffs.

These men, typically members of the gentry who could boast some degree of Welsh royal descent, served as the traditional leaders of their communities and were able to amass considerable wealth and privileges by adopting some of the English ways, even as they retained Welsh cultural and literary traditions. Prominent figures such as Tudur Hen ap Goronwy and his son Goronwy ap Tudur became integral cogs in the English machinery of local governance in Wales, for which they were well rewarded, even if a racial ceiling limited the scope of their advancement.

The outbreak of war with France in 1337, however, fuelled by Edward III's coveting of the French crown, upset the equilibrium. Frequent taxation to support the king's military demands across the Channel exposed fresh discontent among his Welsh subjects, exacerbated by intensifying corruption and patent misgovernment by scores of royal officials who manipulated both Welsh and English law for their own personal enrichment. Unlike his father, Edward III had never served as prince of Wales, and, lacking personal attachment to the Welsh, indifferently harvested the country for money and men without consideration for the hardship he generated.

Moderately peaceful Anglo-Welsh relations, judiciously cultivated across a delicate half-century by Edward I and Edward II, were consistently undermined during the reign of the third Edward. The racial hatred the Welsh harboured for English rule, under which they were regarded in law and in reality as an inferior people in their own country, was revived with renewed vigour. Rumours of revolt abounded in 1338 and 1339, with the investiture of the king's heir, Edward of Woodstock, as the new prince of Wales in May 1343 failing to quell the growing unrest. In 1344, the English community of Rhuddlan complained to the new prince's council that they had been viciously accosted by the Welsh when attending the fair of St Asaph, with similar letters dispatched from the town and burgesses of Conwy, Denbigh and Caernarfon bemoaning the 'great damages and destructions' and 'divers extortions and hardships' they experienced when attempting to go about their trade. The prince was warned to remedy the toxic situation at once, for 'the Welsh have become so proud and cruel and malicious towards the English' that they 'dare not go anywhere for fear of death'. It was clear, they stressed, that the native population had 'never since the conquest been so disposed as they are now to rise against their liege lord to conquer the land from him', and if a solution was not sought, the English officials would 'desert his towns and castles and leave the country'.[22]

Matters came to a head with a particularly violent incident that occurred near Bangor on St Valentine's Day in 1345. At the centre of this episode, the ringleaders even, were Hywel and Tudur ap Goronwy. On the evening in question, one of the prince of Wales's attorneys, Henry de Shaldeford, was travelling towards the town on horseback when near Hywel's house in Bangor his party of six were ambushed by Tudur ap Goronwy 'with a great number of Welshmen'. In the confusion that followed, Shaldeford was butchered, 'feloniously and against the peace', with goods to the value of £100 stolen by the assailants before they fled the scene.

It was a murder that appalled the terrified English administration in North Wales, provoking a wide-ranging investigation in the days that followed, led by the prince's clerk John de Pirye, his steward Richard de Stafford and the burgesses of Caernarfon, Conwy and Rhuddlan. Though Tudur was accused of leading the attack, 'one of the greatest mischiefs that has ever happened in North Wales', it was claimed he did so 'by the compassing of his brother Hywel ap Goronwy', the mastermind behind the plot. It was Stafford's grave verdict that if Shaldeford's murderers were not immediately rounded up then the Welsh 'will be such that it will be impossible for any Englishman or English official to dwell in these parts – and all this through the maintenance of Hywel ap Goronwy'. It was already a concern of the burgesses that Tudur and Hywel ap Goronwy had grown 'so powerful that no Welshman dare to indict them' of Shaldeford's murder, nor 'other trespasses which they commit daily against the peace' – only royal intervention could suppress the destruction the brothers were causing in North Wales.[23]

Briefed by the prince's council about the incident and the wider unrest, on 25 February Edward III announced that those who had 'feloniously killed' Shaldeford had been identified as Robert Dilby, Griffin Tue, David ap Jerman Rees and Griffin Castel Meryon, with 'Howel ap Gronough, clerk, a Welshman' having given 'his counsel and assent to the felony'. As the accused had fled the region, the king was determined that 'the felony may be duly punished', and appointed his serjeant-at-arms to apprehend Hywel 'wherever found within the realm of England and deliver him to the nearest gaol'.[24]

Hywel was captured in Cheshire around a year after the murder of Shaldeford, with a record for June 1346 ordering the Constable of Beeston Castle to be paid to convey Hywel 240 miles to Launceston Castle in Cornwall. Hywel was not moved from Beeston, however, until mid-December when another payment was made to Sir Nicholas Pynnok to complete the arduous journey. The constable of Launceston, meanwhile, John de Moveroun, was ordered to receive Hywel and keep him in close confinement, limiting visitors to only those he trusted unreservedly.[25]

Hywel remained in custody until August 1347 when, at the request of Richard FitzAlan, 3rd Earl of Arundel and justiciar of North Wales, he was released into the care of four sureties who were tasked with presenting him before the justices one month later. While Hywel had been languishing in prison for at least a year, it was not until 13 June 1347 that the prince of Wales appointed three men to 'take and arrest' Tudur Fychan and deliver him to Chester Castle, with orders to imprison any of his followers who proved 'contrariant or rebellious' when confronted.[26]

What happened next to the brothers is not clear, perhaps owing to the devastating outbreak of the Black Death, which did little to ease the economic pressure the Welsh were under. Originating in Asia, this virulent plague spread west into Europe along trading routes, with the first known case reaching the south coast of England in the summer of 1348. The disease, which caused fierce headaches and swelling in the armpit or groin invariably followed by a painful death, rapidly infested the kingdom. The following year it reached Wales, where it ravaged entire tight-knit communities, particularly in the north, claiming around a third of the population before its progress slowed in the winter months. In the spring of 1349, the poet Ieuan Gethin captured how contemporary Welshmen viewed the plague, lamenting 'the death coming into our midst like a black smoke'.[27]

For those who survived the plague's worst, there was considerable societal upheaval in the disruptive years that lay ahead, exacerbated by insufficient food production, rural depopulation and a crippling shortage of agricultural labour that wasn't always reflected in the wages paid by unscrupulous landowners. Rents, taxes and fees continued to be collected without respite despite the deep economic slump, exacerbating the intense resentment many of the Welsh felt for their English lords. Life was hard, with few signs of recovery to assuage the anxiety of a population desperately seeking solace from the poverty in which they found themselves.

There do not appear to have been any permanent ramifications for Hywel and Tudur Fychan for the attack on Shaldeford, however, nor any lasting trauma or financial ruin arising from the pandemic. The 1352 royal survey of Anglesey confirms they remained in full ownership of Trecastell while sharing Penmynydd and Erddreiniog with a second cousin, Rhys ap Dafydd. A similar survey of Caernarfonshire further confirmed they had also retained ownership of the part of Bangor known as Gafael Goronwy, which may have been near where the Shaldeford incident took place.[28] The pair were also permitted to hold court on Anglesey and regulate the price and measure of ale while claiming exemption from certain fees and duties payable to the crown, a privileged exemption they owed to their descent from Ednyfed Fychan. This was in addition to their holdings in Cardiganshire, namely the townships of Cellan, Rhydonnen and Llechweddlwyfan.[29] Despite committing a grave crime against royal authority that seemed destined to lead them to the executioner's block, Hywel and Tudur's standing in their ancestral heartland remained high.

That Hywel ap Goronwy was always listed before Tudur Fychan in the chancery rolls suggests he was the elder of the brothers. A prominent cleric, Hywel certainly enjoyed a higher profile during their lifetimes and, as he spearheaded the Shaldeford episode, appears to have exerted a degree of authority over Tudur that was likely age-based. This may account for a curious legend that first appeared about Tudur Fychan in the late seventeenth-century work of William Wynne, *History of Wales*.

Wynne alleges that Tudur, 'either of ambition or fancy', had assumed the rank of knighthood without royal authority, 'requiring all people to call him and style him Sir Tudor ap Grono'. When Edward III was informed of 'such unparalleled presumption', he summoned the Welshman to his presence. When commanded to justify 'with what confidence he durst invade his prerogative by assuming the degree of knighthood', Tudur haughtily responded he did so 'by the laws and constitution of King Arthur' as he possessed the three necessary qualifications: 'First, he was a gentleman. Second, he had a sufficient estate, and thirdly, he was valiant and adventurous.' He then theatrically declared to those present, 'If my valour and hardiness be doubted of, lo, here I throw down my glove, and for due proof of my courage, I am ready to fight with any man, whatever he be.' The king was much amused by this display of defiance, and choosing to reward rather than punish his guest, was 'easily persuaded' to confirm Tudur Fychan in the rank he had brazenly assumed.[30]

It is likely this well-known tale of Tudur Fychan's boldness was shaped, if not invented, by Welsh antiquarians like Wynne writing long after the Tudor ascendancy in England. It was a colourful invention to exalt the otherwise modest character of a man who through Henry VII was the ancestor of every English, and later Scottish, monarch. Wynne was accurate, however, when he described Tudur Fychan as 'one of the chiefest in North Wales', and when Tudur died on 19 September 1367, his passing was marked with a touching elegy composed by the renowned bard Iolo Goch. To Iolo, who made his living performing in the homes of Welsh nobles, the wise Tudur Fychan was a 'fine patriarch' who was 'the most beloved man of all'. Regarded as the 'stag of Trecastell', Tudur's military prowess was also recognised by references to him as a 'good knight of the tournament field'.[31]

Tudur Fychan was buried near his celebrated father and grandfather in Bangor Friary, joining his brother Hywel, who died the previous year.[32] He married twice, though as a later record reveals he died without legitimate heirs; his five known sons – Goronwy, Rhys, Ednyfed, Gwilym and Maredudd – were a product of his second union with Marged ferch Thomas ap Llywelyn of Cardiganshire.[33] In the Welsh patronymic style, the quintet adopted their father's name as a surname (ap Tudur) and, based principally out of one of their ancestral holdings on Anglesey, are known to history as the anglicised, if geographically erroneous, Tudors of Penmynydd. It is a convenient term that connects this distant Welsh clan to the royal dynasty that were later ascribed the name in England.

Though the five brothers would emulate their recent ancestors in serving the English crown, this support would later be rescinded in devastating fashion. After more than a century of subservience, a brutal and divisive war of national struggle returned to the undulating hills and deep valleys of Wales; at the forefront of this internecine conflict were the bold great-great-great-grandsons of Ednyfed Fychan, a close-knit band of committed royal servants who abandoned their influential and prosperous offices to assume the mantle of patriots seeking to unshackle themselves and their countrymen from oppressive colonial rule. It was an act that would transform the family's destiny in a manner no one could have foreseen.

4

The Great Rebellion

Since Ednyfed Fychan's death in 1246, his descendants, the '*Wyrion Eden*' (literally Ednyfed's grandsons or descendants), had resiliently maintained the tribe's ubiquitous presence at the apex of North Welsh politics. Following Ednyfed's admirable career as seneschal to two princes of Gwynedd came his sons Goronwy and Tudur ab Ednyfed, who both served as seneschal to Llywelyn the Last. Thereafter, Tudur Hen ap Goronwy, his son Goronwy ap Tudur Hen and the brothers Hywel and Tudur Fychan ap Goronwy represented another three generations of dynastic stability under direct English rule, which even two rebellious episodes in 1294 and 1345 did not undermine. While their influence, and perhaps affluence, had diminished since the Edwardian conquest of Wales, the family's stature nonetheless remained high among the native Welsh and recognised by the English crown.

As the fourteenth century drew to a close, the burden of upholding the family's considerable legacy on the island of Anglesey fell upon the five sons of Tudur Fychan, the revered 'stag of Trecastell' – Goronwy, Rhys, Ednyfed, Gwilym and Maredudd ap Tudur. As had been customary in earlier generations, as the sons approached adulthood they were steadily introduced to royal service by their father and groomed to dominate the island's political scene after his death in 1367. While preparing a visit to Anglesey at some point before 1382, Iolo Goch penned a fawning elegy to Tudur's sons, 'a golden litter' he reverently regarded as the 'chief jousters' of the island. His work also revealed how the quintet had partitioned their father's extensive inheritance.[1]

To Goronwy ap Tudur went Penmynydd, 'a fine fair place' where he kept a 'pleasant court'. Rhys ap Tudur held Erddreiniog, 'which ennobled the island', while Ednyfed ap Tudur, 'a gift-bestowing lord' named for his esteemed ancestor, possessed Trecastell, a 'chamber of gifts' on 'heavenly land'. Gwilym ap Tudur, meanwhile, 'a keen spear', was based at Clorach, a 'brilliant building' that was 'a mansion full of herbs' and held interests in the townships of Trysglwyn and Crymlyn and a burgage at Newborough.[2] All were 'fine magnanimous princes' who served 'without fear', 'bulls of battle' who were 'relentless in conflict'. There is no mention, however, of the youngest son, Maredudd ap Tudur, which suggests he either held no land of note or was absent from the area and thus merited no mention. Though often collectively regarded by later generations as the Tudors of Penmynydd, a convenient label, that designation can only be accurately attributed to Goronwy ap Tudur.

Regarded as 'lords of the island' by Iolo Goch, Rhys and Goronwy alternated the role of *rhaglaw*, or bailiff, of Dindaethwy, following in the footsteps of their father and great-grandfather in overseeing local law and order. Both would also attain offices that had hitherto been reserved solely for Englishmen across the previous century. Rhys served as sheriff of Anglesey for a year in 1374 and again for three years between 1381 and 1384, though he would still fall foul of the law himself.[3] During an unspecified dispute in June 1389, Rhys was bound over to keep the peace, and ordered to 'do no hurt or harm to' several significant members of the English administration in North Wales, including Sir Henry Conway, constable of Rhuddlan, John Wodehouse, chamberlain of North Wales, William de Frodsham, a future chamberlain of North Wales, and Richard de Pykemere and William de Hunton, former sheriffs of Anglesey and Caernarfonshire respectively, who were likewise directed not to injure Rhys. Whatever the quarrel between the parties, clearly there was fear it would turn violent – a foreshadowing, perhaps, of what Rhys was capable of.[4]

On 18 March 1382, meanwhile, Goronwy, described as the king's esquire, forester of Snowdon and steward of Anglesey, was appointed constable of Beaumaris Castle, one of the principal English fortresses in North Wales, constructed by Edward I nearly a century earlier during his efforts to subjugate the Welsh. Regarded as a 'wild boar in battle', Goronwy had likely excelled himself in a military capacity earlier in his life, possibly in France under the command of Edward of Woodstock, Prince of Wales, qualifying him to be given charge of the largest garrison on the island. Only the second Welshman to be honoured with this responsibility, Goronwy was to be paid £40 a year for the office but was expected to provide a chaplain, a deputy constable, a porter and a watchman at his own expense.[5]

Goronwy would never assume the role in person – within six days of his appointment, he was described in the chancery rolls as 'deceased', having drowned alongside his brother Ednyfed while disembarking a ship in a Kentish port.[6] One poet referred to Goronwy as a 'wine-loving leader' and speculated his death occurred due to 'excess of mead', and there certainly doesn't appear to be any report of foul play. Perhaps Ednyfed perished attempting to save his drunken brother? According to a sombre Iolo Goch, the 'grievous accident' shattered the men of Anglesey, all of whom took to wearing mourning black. The brothers' bodies were recovered from the water, with Goronwy interred in Llanfaes friary, the monastic house founded by Llywelyn the Great nearly 150 years earlier.[7]

The richly carved and elaborate alabaster tomb which was placed over Goronwy's grave was later removed from Llanfaes, either following the destructive Welsh uprising two decades after his death or when the friary was dissolved and dismantled in 1538. It would find a new home in St Gredifael's Church, close to Goronwy's principal estate at Penmynydd, where it remains to the present day. Placed in a little chapel on the north side of the nave, it is topped by the recumbent figures of Goronwy, depicted as an armoured knight in a surcoat, and his wife Myfanwy, their heads resting on a pillow supported by two small angels. Though heavily weathered, around the base are numerous shields that once bore Goronwy's coat of arms, as well as those of his brother Maredudd's descendants – what later became the Tudor dynasty. It was a costly monument, a vivid reminder of the family's standing in a region they had politically and socially dominated for multiple generations. It may also have betrayed the despair felt at Goronwy's untimely demise, which curtailed a promising career. He left a young son, unimaginatively named Tudur, from whose line a branch of the family, later known as the Theodors, would live at Penmynydd throughout the entire reign of their distant English royal cousins.[8]

Though it is unclear where the youngest brother, Maredudd, called home, he nevertheless followed in similar manner to his brothers, serving as a burgess of Newborough, *rhaglaw* of Malltraeth and escheator of Anglesey. The latter position was vital in protecting the king's feudal rights, and often profitable, for the escheator was responsible for overseeing and managing all lands that reverted to the crown in cases where someone had died without a legal heir.[9]

From the offices they held, it is clear the Tudur brothers of Anglesey enjoyed an ample degree of royal favour, with two of them even directly retained by the king of England himself. Richard II had succeeded his grandfather Edward III in 1377 at just ten years old, and even before he reached his majority he was proving a headstrong ruler, inclined to rely on a small band of unpopular favourites. As an adult, the king nonetheless enjoyed widespread support in Cheshire and North Wales, and showed particular trust in Rhys and Gwilym ap Tudur to uphold royal authority on his behalf, at home and beyond their native land.

Amid rumours the French were preparing an invasion in 1386, Rhys and Gwilym were charged with raising a contingent of 120 archers from Caernarfonshire, while in July 1398 the pair were 'retained to stay for life with the king', a mutually beneficial and exclusive service for which they were paid £10 a year. This retaining of the Tudurs may have been linked to Richard's wider attempts to bolster his affinity and strengthen his power at a time when he was facing significant opposition to his rule from his nobility. When the king crossed to Ireland the following year 'with many great lords', it is possible the Tudur brothers accompanied him through Wales, and perhaps even completed the sea journey with him.[10]

Though the Tudurs enjoyed prominent roles as part of the English administration of the Principality, many of their countrymen proved restless as the fourteenth century progressed. The social disruption triggered by the Black Death and the escalating costs of the protracted war with France merely exacerbated persistent Welsh dismay with English governance, and the influential bards, following a well-established, continent-wide literary tradition, stoked the flames by employing the art of political vaticination to stir the hearts and hopes of their audiences.

The reign of Edward III between 1327 and 1377 had seen a significant upturn in the development of an English national identity, and this likely helped foster unity among the once-fragmented Welsh, who increasingly identified as a distinct people with a common history, culture and language, no matter from which part of Wales they hailed. It was within the talents of any perceptive poet to exploit this burgeoning sense of nationhood to nurture resentment of perceived political and cultural subjection, particularly in times of economic or social instability.

Many of the Welsh bards were well versed in *canu darogan*, or prophetic poetry, the central element of which was often *Y Mab Darogan*, or the Son of Prophecy, a messianic figure who would return to deliver the Welsh from servitude. With roots as far back as Nennius' legendary *Historia Brittonum* in the early ninth century, prophetic poetry was typically preoccupied with a struggle for independence, and this promise of a redeemer was constructed around a national myth that the island of Britain was once united under a common people, the Britons, who had been scattered by the Saxon heathen. Though they had lost considerable lands to a series of foreign invaders, it was promised that a British hero descended from the ancient line of kings would emerge to drive the foreigners into the sea and recover the crown for the Britons for the first time since Cadwaladr ap Cadwallon flourished in the late sixth century. This was a potent tradition transmitted from generation to generation, from parent to child, across hundreds of years. When all seemed lost, the Welsh were at least able to cling to this hope of salvation.[11]

Much of the prophecy's origins were traced to an early tenth-century poem, *Y Armes Prydein Fawr*, or *The Great Prophecy of Britain*, which was written to express dissatisfaction with Saxon meddling in Welsh affairs during the reign of Athelstan, the first king of the English. In the poem, which features the first known reference to the *Kymry*, or the Welsh, the druids made a passionate appeal for the Brittonic-speaking people of what later became Wales, Cornwall and Strathclyde to ally with the Vikings of Dublin and violently expel the Saxons from the British mainland for good.

The appeal to the Welsh apparently went unheeded, for in 937 Athelstan roundly defeated an allied army of Scots, Strathclyde Britons and Norsemen from Ireland at the battle of Brunanburh, asserting his dominance over the island and preserving the unity of the newly established England.[12]

The prophecy that reached the fourteenth-century Welshman was further shaped by the inventive quill of Geoffrey of Monmouth, who in the 1130s embellished established bardic traditions for his own work, *Historia Regum Britanniae*. This purported history of the kings of Britain tells of the founding of the British royal line by Brutus of Troy before the island was divided among his descendants and thereafter conquered by the invading Saxons, concluding with the death of Cadwaladr in 688. Geoffrey's writings also prominently featured the legendary Arthur, whose exploits were amplified to make him the archetypal hero against whom all prospective redeemers would be measured in future, and Merlin, a sorcerer responsible for prophesying the eventual British victory over the heathen Saxons.

Though most of the content which formed Geoffrey's highly influential work was fictitious, it nevertheless informed the medieval Welsh of their supposed glorious history while introducing the concept of an impending British insurrection to a wider audience. Arthur, notably, did not merit a mention in the earlier *Armes Prydein*, perhaps revealing his relative insignificance before the twelfth century. In the three centuries since, however, the feats of Arthur and the prognostications of Merlin had been regarded highly by the Welsh, with scores of bards employing the Son of Prophecy narrative to great effect.[13]

It is important to note that, to its medieval audience, such prophecies were taken seriously, and certainly not dismissed as the mere fantastical ramblings of the bardic circles. For a conquered people these works, both oral and literary, harkened back to past glories while providing much-needed hope for the future – they helped shape the political and cultural outlook of both the Welsh gentry and the common folk. More than mere poetry, they were pieces of powerful political propaganda. A name commonly employed by fourteenth-century bards for the prophesied hero was Owain, and when a 'valiant knight' of clear princely lineage bearing that name lay claim to the title prince of Wales in 1372, people took notice, particularly a nervous English administration.[14] Owain Lawgoch, or Owain of the Red Hand, was the grandson of Rhodri ap Gruffudd, the younger brother of Llywelyn the Last who renounced his claim to the principality of Wales in the late thirteenth century and retired to south-eastern England. Though born and raised in Surrey, an English subject, Owain Lawgoch crossed the Channel in his youth and, taking the name Yvain de Galles, or Owen of Wales, fronted a free company of mostly Welsh mercenaries supporting the French king Charles V in war against the English.[15]

For such overt treachery, Owain's lands in Surrey, Cheshire and Gloucestershire were confiscated by Edward III, which merely hastened his decision in 1372 to openly lay claim to the dormant crown of Wales. Though he intended to launch an invasion of his ancestors' homeland, Owain's obligations to the French crown thwarted any campaign reaching fruition, and he spent much of the next five years fighting for Charles V across southern France and Castile. When fresh rumours reached the English court in 1377 that Owain was finally available to press his claim to Wales with French support, the minority council ruling on behalf of the new boy-king Richard II took decisive action to eliminate the threat before any national uprising could be provoked.

A spy named John Lambe was sent to Owain's camp near Poitou, charged with infiltrating the self-styled prince of Wales's innermost circle. One method Lambe employed to gain Owain's confidence was to encourage the Welshman's ambitions, advising that he knew from personal experience that the 'whole principality was desirous of having him for their lord'. Owain appointed Lambe his chamberlain, allowing him intimate access to his private quarters each morning. On one particular morning in July 1378, Lambe entered Owain's room with a concealed dagger and stabbed the unsuspecting and half-dressed Welshman before fleeing the scene. Though Lambe collected his reward of £20, what he did would be remembered as a 'wicked and treasonable act' of 'base wickedness'. As Owain slumped to the floor, his ambitions never amounting to little more than a misty-eyed vision, the direct male line of Llywelyn the Great, and that of the House of Gwynedd, died with him.[16]

It remains unknown what impact Owain Lawgoch would have had on the Welsh people had he successfully landed in Wales. It is certainly true loyalties were divided during this period, with Welshmen active in both the French and English armies, but whether Owain could have persuaded enough of his compatriots to unite behind his cause is open to debate. Notably, one member of the gentry accused of financially supporting Owain's endeavours was Rhys ap Robert, a direct descendant of Ednyfed Fychan and another distant cousin of the Tudur brothers.[17] The Tudurs' involvement in any conspiracy at this stage is unknowable, but considering their burgeoning careers under English rule it seems unlikely.

The assassination of Owain Lawgoch unintentionally cleared the path for a younger Owain to be regarded as not only the senior Welsh magnate of his generation, but also the latest incarnation of the Son of Prophecy. Owain ap Gruffudd ap Gruffudd, Lord of Glyndyfrdwy and better remembered as Owain Glyn Dŵr, was born between 1354 and 1359 and boasted an impeccable pedigree that predictably drew the attention of the bards soon after Lawgoch's demise.

Through his father, Gruffudd Fychan, Glyn Dŵr was descended in the male line from the princes of Powys, while through his mother, Elen ferch Tomos ap Llywelyn, he also claimed descent from the princely houses of Gwynedd and Deheubarth, connected to many of the most celebrated Welsh princes of any age. After Lawgoch's murder, it was an ancestry widely lauded as the finest among his contemporaries, and one that appealed to Welshmen no matter which corner of Wales they called home.[18] To the bard Iolo Goch, for example, this 'boy of princely stock' possessed nothing less than the 'highest lineage' in his veins, a fact of which he would have been aware from his earliest years.[19]

For surviving Tudurs Rhys, Gwilym and Maredudd, however, it was Glyn Dŵr's more immediate family connections that proved crucial in shaping their destiny at the dawn of the fifteenth century. The Tudurs' mother, Marged, and Glyn Dŵr's mother, Elen, were sisters, their sons developing a close rapport to form an influential and tight-knit faction in the North Welsh political arena.

Like his Tudur cousins, earlier in his career Glyn Dŵr understood the necessity of fostering positive relations with the English crown; he profited, for example, from the patronage of the FitzAlan family, who as well as holding the wealthy English earldom of Arundel were also lords of Chirk, Oswestry and Welsh Maelor, which bordered Glyn Dŵr's estates. His father and grandfather had likewise served previous FitzAlan magnates. Through the agency of another English patron, Glyn Dŵr's guardian and future father-in-law Sir David Hanmer, a chief justice of the King's Bench, he studied law as an apprentice at the Inns of Court in London – a privileged education for a member of the English gentry, much less the Welsh.[20]

Returning to his native Flintshire during the early 1380s to establish his position as the new lord of Sycharth and Glyndyfrdwy, Glyn Dŵr embarked on a varied military career defending the crown of Richard II. In March 1384, he was part of the Berwick garrison that fended off a furious Scottish attack, excelling as a soldier and winning 'great renown' for his feats. The following year he accompanied the king on another campaign into Scotland, while in 1387 he enlisted in the retinue of his neighbour Richard FitzAlan, 4th Earl of Arundel, to lead a small force in fending off a French invasion along the coast of Kent.[21] Glyn Dŵr's military apprenticeship proved a formative experience, offering valuable insight into the intricacies of border warfare which would serve him well in years to come.

The Welshman's standing in English social circles was recognised in September 1386 when he was summoned to give evidence in Chester relating to a bitter heraldic dispute between the Scrope and Grosvenor families. His privileged upbringing near the border, his warm relations with widely connected and influential figures like Hanmer and Arundel, and a flourishing military career on behalf of the crown meant that by his early thirties he was as comfortable operating in English society as he was in Welsh. He moved with ease between the two worlds and profited handsomely, personally and professionally. He was part of the system, a Welshman conformed to English rule and unburdened by much of the hardship experienced by his compatriots.

The 1390s proved a quieter decade for Glyn Dŵr, however, his opportunities were limited as he grew older. There is no suggestion, though, that at this stage in his career Glyn Dŵr, or the Tudurs for that matter, were plotting a revolution against English rule. They were, after all, approaching middle age and living more than comfortably. As David Powel asserted when discussing the era two centuries later, they all remained 'in very great favour and credit' with the king, Richard II,[22] Glyn Dŵr in particular fathering a 'fine nestful of chieftains'. Risking all at this juncture made little sense.[23]

This is not to suggest there was not growing unease, even outright resentment, towards English rule among well-educated members of the Welsh gentry as the fourteenth century drew to a close. Claims of misgovernment, extortion and corruption remained at the forefront of Welsh complaints, with English officials and acquisitive landowners often manipulating the two extant legal systems to jealously preserve their privileges. There was little to no equality when offices, whether ecclesiastical or secular, were dispensed – between 1372 and 1400, for example, of sixteen bishops appointed in Wales, only one, John Trefor of St Asaph, was Welsh.

Pockets of violence continued to undermine Anglo-Welsh relations, such as the murder in 1385 of John Lawrence, deputy justiciar of South Wales. Each passing year brought fresh grievances, exacerbated by a general upsurge in bardic activity, once more desperately attempting to summon a saviour of princely extraction. Welsh hostility fed English fears, while English suppression galvanised Welsh spirits, creating an increasingly toxic climate of mutual suspicion which threatened to explode into open revolt given the right spark. That spark proved to be the alienation from royal favour of Owain Glyn Dŵr.

It is unknowable, even acknowledging the myriad grievances they had with the unpopular English administration, if Owain Glyn Dŵr and his Tudur cousins would have revolted had Richard II not been deposed in September 1399. Richard had proven a deeply unpopular king in England, his arrogant dependence on a small circle of favourites provoking conflict with a collection of influential nobles known as the Lords Appellant. His actions had also led to an extensive redrawing of political power in North Wales that paved the way for Welsh national ambitions to emerge after a century of acquiescence.

Though Richard II found his power limited between 1387 and 1389, the unrepentant king rebuilt his authority over the next decade before exacting revenge on the leading Appellants, triggering a fresh period of tyranny that would usher in his downfall. In September 1397, Thomas of Woodstock, 1st Duke of Gloucester and Richard II's uncle, was murdered in captivity, with Glyn Dŵr's neighbour Richard FitzAlan, 4th Earl of Arundel, also beheaded. Thomas Beauchamp, 12th Earl of Warwick, was exiled to the Isle of Man, with Henry Bolingbroke, 3rd Earl of Derby and 1st Duke of Hereford, also banished from the kingdom. The removal of four commanding Marcher barons in Gloucester, Arundel, Warwick and Roger Mortimer, 4th Earl of March, who had died on campaign in 1398, only served to exacerbate the instability of many Welsh lordships that had been under their sway. The death of Arundel certainly weakened Glyn Dŵr's opportunities for further advancement, for the earl had proven a generous patron under whom the Welshman had flourished.[24]

When Bolingbroke's father, the supremely wealthy John of Gaunt, 1st Duke of Lancaster, died in February 1399, Richard cruelly intervened to block his cousin's sizable inheritance, declaring all lands, titles and possessions forfeited to the crown. In the blink of an eye, Richard had seized the greatest inheritance in England before callously extending Bolingbroke's exile to life. Rather than meekly accepting his fate, however, Bolingbroke chose to act, and his response altered the political landscape of England, and indeed Wales, forever. Amassing a modest force of around 300 men, on 4 July 1399, while Richard was in Ireland on a campaign on which Rhys and Gwilym ap Tudur may have been present, Bolingbroke landed on the East Yorkshire coast and started marching south.[25]

Richard's absence gave Bolingbroke a golden opportunity to advance through what was effectively an unguarded kingdom, steadily recruiting supporters to his cause until he had assembled 'an innumerable army'.[26] Forced to confront this challenge, the king returned from Ireland 'in the full glory of war' and landed at Milford Haven on the west coast of South Wales. Richard, however, soon deserted his army, desperately riding north to where he still enjoyed great support. The beleaguered king reached Conwy Castle on 11 August, possibly in the presence of the still loyal Tudors, only to discover Bolingbroke had anticipated his movements and was at Chester with his army. Within five days, a humiliated Richard was in Bolingbroke's custody, his captor 'having gloriously, within fifty days, conquered both king and kingdom' without the need for battle or bloodshed.[27]

What followed next is disputed, with conflicting accounts appearing in the contemporary chronicles, but whatever transpired would have significant implications for the lives and careers of the Tudors. On 29 September 1399, the day before parliament was due to convene, Adam of Usk alleged that the lords and clergy abruptly renounced their allegiance to the king, 'and holding him henceforth not for a king, but for a private person, Sir Richard of Bordeaux, a simple knight', he was deposed. The *Brut* corroborated this to some extent, adding that once the king was locked up in the Tower he was deposed by 'all his lords counsel, and by the common assent of all the realm'. Thomas Walsingham believed Richard willingly conceded his crown, provided he 'was given a livelihood suitable to his position'. The *Crowland Chronicle* meanwhile notes the king appointed others 'in his name to resign the crown of his kingdom', as did the *Chronicles of London*.[28]

When parliament reconvened, the throne was conspicuously empty until Bolingbroke rose from his seat and boldly declared he, as a grandson of Edward III, would gladly accept the crown. One by one, the assembled lords voiced their approval. To justify this deposition – the second of the fourteenth century after Edward II seven decades earlier – thirty-two articles were read out, outlining each instance in which Richard had violated his oath. For good measure, the deposed king was accused by Walsingham of being 'deeply inadequate and lacking the intelligence for ruling and governing his kingdoms'.[29] He was transferred from London to Pontefract in Yorkshire, where, after a failed uprising to free him in January 1400, it was revealed he had died by starvation.[30] Richard had been a spiteful and temperamental prince, often paranoid, ruthless and vain, and it is a telling fact that once Henry Bolingbroke invaded, large parts of England deserted his side.

Despite it being an English royal conflict, the demise of Richard and the ascendancy of Bolingbroke as Henry IV had far-reaching consequences in Wales. The political map of Wales, in the north in particular, had been extensively redrawn during this tumultuous period. Richard had crushed the Arundel powerbase in the north-east to create a new royal demesne for himself, while great Welsh landowners such as Mortimer, Gloucester, Warwick, Mowbray and Despenser had either died of natural causes or been executed. Because of his own inheritance, and as a by-product of Richard's tyranny, Henry IV meanwhile acceded to the throne with a territorial supremacy in Wales unlike any previous king of England – as well as the Principality lands in the north-west and south that he now claimed as monarch, he also held a significant stretch of land in the south-east, including the lordships of Monmouth, Brecon and Hay.[31]

This severing of traditional feudal ties left many Welshmen disoriented and increasingly unsure of their place in society. Men like the Tudurs, who had been closely associated with Richard II, found themselves leaderless and facing an anxious future devoid of opportunity after their patron's sudden fall. Likewise, the execution of Arundel in 1397 proved a vexing source of consternation to Glyn Dŵr, who already felt spurned by his lack of appointment to public office. It was, however, an acrimonious land dispute with a neighbour that sealed Glyn Dŵr's transformation from demoralised if loyal subject to celebrated figurehead of the first national uprising in more than a century – and he found a restless native population ready to follow his lead.

Part of Glyn Dŵr's estates shared a boundary with Reginald Grey, 3rd Baron Grey of Ruthin and one of the principal landowners in north-eastern Wales. In 1399, Glyn Dŵr alleged that Grey had unlawfully seized some common land which lay between their respective estates, anticipating his grievances would be addressed by parliament. Grey, however, was a close ally of the new monarch, Henry IV, having participated in the latter's coronation, and held a coveted place on the king's council. Glyn Dŵr's appeal was, unsurprisingly, indifferently dismissed.

Matters were hardly helped by a series of heated letters exchanged between the feuding landowners in June 1400 in which the pair traded threats. Glyn Dŵr, irked that a promise he would be made master forester and warden of Chirkland had not been kept and warned that Grey was planning to burn his lands, boasted he had stolen some of the baron's horses. Grey in return not only pledged to have Glyn Dŵr hanged for theft, but withheld a royal summons requesting military service for a forthcoming Scottish campaign.[32] When the oblivious Welshman failed to present himself, his behaviour was viewed by Henry IV as treasonous and his lands were threatened with forfeiture. Though John Trefor, Bishop of St Asaph, anxiously warned the English lords not to unduly provoke Glyn Dŵr or the Welsh, he was haughtily informed that parliament 'cared naught for bare-footed buffoons'.[33]

Bishop Trefor was right to be concerned; Glyn Dŵr's response was explosive. Surrounded by an intimate collection of kinsmen, in-laws, neighbours and friends, on 16 September 1400 at his ancestral home of Glyndyfrdwy he boldly proclaimed himself Prince of Wales, drawing on his well-known lineage as justification for his claim in what also served as a clear repudiation of English rule.[34] There is little doubt he was the ideal figurehead to lead his countrymen; regarded by the poet Iolo Goch to be a 'bold wolf' who was 'savage in the thick of battle', Glyn Dŵr was cultured, well connected and boasted extensive military experience that would hold him in good stead for the war he had just instigated. His cause was further emboldened by the passionate prognostications of his seer, who declared Glyn Dŵr, now regarded as 'the sole head of the Welsh', to be *Y Mab Darogan*, the long-promised Son of Prophecy who, after a few false starts, had finally surfaced to put the English to the sword.[35]

Two days after proclaiming himself prince, Glyn Dŵr and his spirited band of followers raided the nearby town and castle of Ruthin, one of Reginald Grey's principal strongholds. From Ruthin, they destructively swept north through Denbigh and Rhuddlan before advancing with unbridled fury on Flint, Holt, Oswestry and Welshpool, all English-held towns perceived to be centres of oppression. As well as punishing Grey, the objective was to severely diminish English authority in the region.[36]

At the same time, in Anglesey, Rhys and Gwilym ap Tudur commenced their own uprising, exploiting the family's long-established influence on the island to muster widespread support. The spark of Glyn Dŵr's feud with Grey had become a roaring blaze, suggesting the events of September 1400 were not a spontaneous revolt, but rather a well-coordinated, cross-country movement fuelled by decades of festering resentment. Though on the surface it may have appeared surprising that after a lifetime of commendable royal service the Tudurs had chosen to move against the English crown, risking the forfeiture of their estates and offices, their motive to rebel was clear. Like most of their compatriots, the Tudurs were deeply aware of their lineage, conscious of both the role their ancestors had played in stoutly resisting English subjugation and their own close ties with Glyn Dŵr, whom they now recognised as their prince. Though not acting solely out of nationalistic concern, the sheer weight of history played its part in turning their heads.

Of more pressing consideration to the Tudur brothers, however, was the deposition of Richard II, who had been a generous patron in recent decades. As retainers of Richard, Rhys and Gwilym were left out of pocket by Henry IV's usurpation and were undeniably driven by personal revenge as much as patriotic fervour. It is reasonable to speculate that a series of discussions took place between the Tudurs and Glyn Dŵr in the months before the cousins took up arms, combining their separate grievances against a common foe and deliberating upon a mutual course of action for the maximum effect. From the moment both parties rose in revolt, their interests were entwined, their successes and failures shared.

News that the Welsh had broken out into revolt drew a robust response from Henry IV, who had already faced one rebellion in England against his authority. With 'a strong power of men-at-arms and of archers', at the end of September the king ordered his men to advance from Shrewsbury into Wales, progressing steadily along the northern coast. It was the first military campaign personally led into Wales by an English sovereign in over a century. By 7 October the king and his men had reached Bangor, and two days later they established a temporary base within the towering walls of Caernarfon Castle. What is noticeable about Henry's route is that it patently ignored Glyn Dŵr and instead made a beeline for the Tudurs, suggesting it was they, not the figurehead of the Welsh uprising, that the crown feared first and foremost in military terms.[37]

Crossing the Menai Strait, the royal army laid waste to Anglesey before setting fire to Llanfaes Priory, the resting place of Goronwy ap Tudur, and killing some of the friars. Rhys ap Tudur, Goronwy's grandson, was not inactive during this violent rampage through his ancestral heartland. Carefully monitoring Henry's expedition from afar, Rhys gathered some of his men and ambushed the king when he passed by Rhos Fawr, a highland moor on the eastern side of island. Taken by surprise, Henry signalled for his army to retreat behind the walls of Beaumaris Castle, desperately seeking refuge from Rhys's sudden attack.[38]

Though the uprising had opened with a ferocious inferno in the final weeks of September 1400, the formidable presence of a royal army parading around Anglesey and Caernarfonshire dampened Welsh spirits as winter approached, and the revolt quickly lost momentum without spreading further afield. Seeking to punish Glyn Dŵr for having the gall to declare himself Prince of Wales, Henry IV stripped the Welshman of all his manors and lands, in both North and South Wales, 'forfeited to the king by reason of his treason'.

Intending to curb Glyn Dŵr's territorial influence, on 8 November the estates were granted to the king's half-brother John Beaufort, 1st Earl of Somerset, whose bloodline would ironically mix with Tudor blood just half a century later.[39] Garrisons at Caernarfon, Criccieth, Harlech, Conwy, Denbigh and Beaumaris, meanwhile, were strengthened with additional men-at-arms and archers, notably in the north-west of the country where the Tudurs had been particularly active.

When parliament met at Westminster in January 1401, Henry IV employed a range of legal mechanisms to bring a swift resolution to what he anticipated was merely a brief episode of civil unrest already in its death throes. A series of punitive ordinances were passed by the king, each designed to blunt the influence of the Welsh gentry and strengthen the English administration in Wales. While Glyn Dŵr and the Tudurs remained at large, both Crown and parliament were keen to take preventative measures against a revival of what had been termed a 'great rebellion', particularly when a petition was presented by the Commons nervously warning that Welsh scholars at Oxford and Cambridge as well as Welsh labourers on English farms were hurrying home armed with 'weapons of war' in preparation for a new rising.

Before parliament dissolved, it had been ordained that henceforth no full-blooded Englishman could be convicted in Wales on the word of a mere Welshman, while those same Welshmen were prohibited from purchasing land not just in certain border towns such as Chester, Shrewsbury and Worcester, but also in English borough towns throughout Wales. Intermarriage was also outlawed, while public offices such as bailiff, chamberlain and constable could no longer be held by Welshmen, who could no longer openly bear arms of any kind. All garrisons in Wales, meanwhile, were to be reinforced at the expense of the Welsh, and all public gatherings were banned. Lastly, in recognition of the widespread influence of the peripatetic bards, men such as Iolo Goch, all poets and minstrels were henceforth restricted in movement to limit the power of their words.[40] Henry IV gave his assent to the ordinances on 18 March 1401, and four days later the documents were sealed with the Great Seal, becoming the law of the land.[41] These measures were, in short, racist laws designed to punish all the Welsh solely on account of their nationality rather than target individual transgressors.

Despite the severity of these laws, on 10 March 1401, the final day of parliament, at the supplication of the king's heir, the teenage Prince of Wales, Henry IV issued a general pardon to all Welsh rebels 'for all treasons and insurrections' committed between January 1400 and January 1401. Conscious that the rebellion had ground to a halt, many gladly accepted the opportunity of mercy, including Glyn Dŵr's own brother. There were, however, three notable exceptions to whom the hand of friendship was not extended – Owain Glyn Dŵr, Rhys ap Tudur and Gwilym ap Tudur, singled out as the ringleaders of the revolt.[42]

As the uprising collapsed around them, the Tudurs found themselves in a precarious position. Less than two years earlier, the two eldest surviving brothers, Rhys and Gwilym, were widely respected and competent leaders of Welsh society who had thrived within the English framework for two decades. They were highly regarded by their countrymen, lauded by the poets and personally recruited by the king, Richard II, to be part of his affinity. By spring 1401, however, their circumstances had altered dramatically. Richard II was dead, Wales was once more awash with English soldiers, and the Tudur brothers were outlaws, all their possessions, lands and offices stripped from them by an edgy Lancastrian regime disinclined to ignore challenges to its authority. Out of separate loyalties to Richard II and Owain Glyn Dŵr, the Tudurs had gambled, and come up short.

Designed to guard English interests and protect English residents in Wales, the so-called Penal Laws imposed upon the Welsh did not have the intended result for the government. Quite the contrary, in fact. When the terms of the laws became widely known in the days following parliament's dissolution in early March, far from meekly accepting their lot, Welsh hearts grew inflamed at what they perceived to be excessive punishment. Many of those infuriated by the laws had not necessarily been sympathetic to Glyn Dŵr's grievances and had remained aloof from the revolt. Now, however, a large cross-section of Welsh society felt unfairly harassed by an English crown that had crossed the line.

Sensing the atmosphere to be febrile, Rhys and Gwilym ap Tudur exploited the discontent to emerge from their redoubt in the mountains with devastating effect. Unlike most of their compatriots who partook in the September 1400 uprising, the Tudurs had no royal pardon to fall back on. If captured by English forces, they faced imprisonment, and possibly even execution. They needed leverage, a strategy to bring Henry IV back to the negotiating table. As the Easter period of 1401 approached, the brothers put their heads together and devised a cunning ruse intended to capture the king's attention. It would take an abundance of courage, a degree of trickery and plenty of luck to succeed. The alternative was certain death.

5

Men of Fame

Conwy Castle, compactly constructed upon a rocky outcrop with eight immense round towers, two barbicans and an unscalable curtain wall, was designed to be impenetrable. The brainchild of James of St George and built on the orders of his master Edward I, work started on the castle in 1283, less than a year after the Conquest of Wales was complete. It took four years to finish and was one of the most formidable fortresses ever erected on the British Isles, strategically placed to cow the native Welsh into an enduring submission. It very much served as a palpable symbol of English supremacy.

As imposing as the whitewashed exterior of Conwy was, the interior was designed to offer comfort to its guests, who were occasionally royal. The Inner Ward, for example, contained a great hall and luxurious private apartments which hosted Edward I and his queen in 1283, and in more recent times accommodated Richard II and Henry IV. In short, Conwy Castle was highly prized by the English crown, and controlling it was integral in upholding law and order across North Wales.

On the evening of 1 April 1401, Good Friday, a tight-knit band of just over forty Welshmen stealthily approached the castle and made their way up the steep ramp and over the drawbridge until they stood before the west barbican. At the head of this throng was Gwilym ap Tudur, who had been condemned as a traitor when he was excluded from the general pardon granted by Henry IV just a few weeks earlier. The timing of his abrupt appearance outside Conwy's towering castle walls wasn't a coincidence – most of the garrison were away from their posts attending a service in the town's parish church, which crucially stood just outside the castle's protection. Only two guards remained on duty on what was the holiest of days in the Christian calendar, one usually dedicated to peace and mourning – and certainly not one for acts of war.[1]

According to Adam of Usk, a 'certain carpenter' approached the gateway, putting the guards at ease that he was merely returning to complete some unfinished work. Certainly, in the years leading to 1401 there were at least three Welsh carpenters employed in Conwy, and any one of these may have assisted in the ruse. However they achieved the diversion, the Welsh rebels stormed into the barbican and swiftly overpowered the stunned guards with ease, slaying both in the brief scuffle which followed. Before the rest of the garrison in the church were alerted to what was happening, a significant part of the town around the Mill Gate area, including the offices of the local exchequer, was torched, possibly by Rhys ap Tudur's separate band, which was not part of the main assault. All records of debts and other financial obligations were destroyed, and it is probably no coincidence that Rhys was in arrears to the crown of £60; as recently as 1398 he had been reprimanded for his debts.[2]

That one of the most formidable English castles had fallen to a gang of wily Welshmen with modest equipment proved a momentous coup for the Tudur brothers. It was also a bitter humiliation for the English crown. News of the audacious raid quickly swept through the homes and taverns of North Wales, swelling the hearts of dejected Welshmen and indicating that despite their patent limitations against a superior foe, victories were there to be stolen. It was this episode which truly rekindled a stuttering revolt that would take the best part of a decade to suppress.

Once the castle was secured, the drawbridge lifted and the portcullis lowered, Gwilym ap Tudur and his companions assessed their position, satisfied to discover the fortress was 'well stored with arms and victuals', including copious amounts of meat and boar. Rhys ap Tudur, meanwhile, retreated into the nearby mountains to observe matters from a distance, ready to pounce with his followers if Gwilym required backup.[3] The intention of the Tudurs was clear – to surrender the castle, they demanded the king grant the pardon earlier denied to them. As far as bargaining chips go, the brothers held one of the largest.

The man tasked with recovering Conwy Castle was Sir Henry Percy, son and heir to the 1st Earl of Northumberland and highly regarded by Adam of Usk as the 'flower and glory of the chivalry of Christendom'.[4] Nicknamed 'Hotspur' by the Scots for his eagerness to join battle, Percy had been rewarded well by Henry IV for supporting the latter's usurpation and his prize included a huge concentration of royal power in North Wales – in late 1399, he was named justiciar of North Wales and Cheshire, and given a lifetime grant of Anglesey plus the castles of Conwy, Chester, Flint, Caernarfon and Beaumaris.[5] As the principal royal official in the region, therefore, on Percy's shoulders now fell the responsibility of recapturing the castle from the Tudurs.

On 18 April 1401, just over a fortnight since the castle had been taken, Percy was handed a commission by the king 'to treat with William ap Tudur and other rebels of North Wales who have taken and hold the castle of Conewey and Rees ap Tudur his brother and others who have risen in insurrection in North Wales'. These negotiations, led by Percy and Sir Arnold Savage on the one side and Gwilym and Rhys on the other, provided the Tudurs with an opportunity to publicise their demands. First and foremost, the brothers demanded a comprehensive pardon for all activities since the start of the revolt, along with recovery of all lands and possessions which had been confiscated, with a fine of 100 marks payable. It was further expected that no charges would be brought for six months for burning the town of Conwy, nor for despoiling the homes of the burgesses and destroying official documents.[6]

Percy was content to accept these terms to recover Conwy, noting that the rest of North Wales remained obedient to the king. In a letter to his son, however, Henry IV made it clear he was not prepared to grant the rebels such favourable conditions which, it was feared, would set a 'most evil precedent'. Prince Henry had 120 men-at-arms and 300 archers at his disposal, 'a good arrangement' that the king believed would be sufficient to recover a castle only lost 'through the negligence of your Constable', namely Percy. The king was willing to fund the soldiers throughout the summer and into the autumn so 'the rebels might be punished according to their deserts, or that we should have at least some other treaty which should be agreeable to us'.[7]

Further talks followed between Percy and the Tudurs, with a deal only finally concluded on 24 June 1401, twelve weeks to the day since the castle had been so spectacularly captured. It seems likely by this stage Percy was growing impatient, while the occupiers' enthusiasm started to wane as their supplies dwindled by the day. On 5 July, the terms were formally agreed by the king's council, and three days later at Westminster a pardon was granted to thirty-five men for 'all offences committed', first among them 'Gwyllym ap Tydur'.[8] He had, in effect, received a pardon for committing treason by committing another act of treason. His brother Rhys ap Tudur, however, who wasn't present in the castle at all during the siege, was not exonerated.

Adam of Usk reported that the Tudurs' surrender of Conwy was not without bloodshed, however. 'Cowardly for themselves and treacherously for their comrades', according to Adam, Gwilym and some of his accomplices 'bound nine of their number' by 'stealth as they slept after the night watches', handing them over to the English 'on condition of saving their own and the others' lives'. The unlucky nine were immediately hanged, drawn and quartered, while the rest of their collaborators walked out of the castle free men with their lands and possessions returned.[9] The official records hold no information about this incident, but that is not to say it did not occur. The king was sure to have asked that some form of penalty be exacted on at least a handful of rebels.

The capture of Conwy Castle, a detested symbol of English domination, was a remarkable feat led by a small but determined band of Welshmen that proved deeply embarrassing for three Henrys – the king, the prince of Wales and the Percy justiciar of North Wales. It was cunning in its implementation, bold in its ambition and unquestionably successful in its immediate objective of gaining pardon.

Furthermore, the Tudurs' daring scheme had political consequences that extended far beyond Conwy's town walls. That a towering stone structure with a reputation of impregnability had fallen, however briefly, into Welsh hands offered encouragement to scores of indignant Welshmen who were bristling at the recently passed Penal Laws. It is perhaps the Tudurs, the sons of Tudur ap Goronwy who had rebelled against English oppression in 1345, and not their much-extolled yet conformist cousin Owain Glyn Dŵr, who should be credited with initiating the last Welsh War of Independence, an uprising that only truly took hold after the extraordinary capture of Conwy Castle.

After a quiet winter and uneventful spring hidden in his mountainous redoubt, Glyn Dŵr reemerged in June 1401, and 'harassed with no light hand the parts of West and North Wales'.[10] Evading attempts to ensnare him, he even succeeded in defeating an English force on the western slopes of Pumlumon, another morale-boosting triumph. He continued to press south as the summer progressed, the uprising spreading through the country and drawing new followers throughout the Tywi Valley as well as parts of Cardigan and Powys.

Rather than delegating responsibility for suppressing the resurgent Welsh threat to one of his barons, Henry IV assumed direct responsibility and in October 1401 returned to Wales for a two-week campaign at the forefront of a 'strong power'. This time he chose to advance through the heart of Powys, ravaging the area with 'fire, famine, and sword'. With Glyn Dŵr nowhere to be found, the king pressed south to Llandovery, where even the public mutilation of Llywelyn ap Gruffudd Fychan in the marketplace failed to draw out the elusive Welsh leader.[11] Despite gaining his hard-won pardon just three months earlier, Gwilym ap Tudur was suspected of partaking in the latest outbreak of violence, for on 7 October he was once more stripped of his lands in Anglesey, which were duly transferred to Prince Henry.[12] With the weather turning, Henry IV had little option than to strengthen his garrisons in places like Cardigan and Aberystwyth before returning across the border as winter set in.[13]

The peripatetic Glyn Dŵr, meanwhile, surfaced once more in the north, capturing Prince Henry's baggage train before he 'sorely harried with fire and sword' the town of Welshpool, slaying many Englishmen in the process. By early November, he attacked another English force near Caernarfon, although not without sacrificing around 300 of his men. It was in the aftermath of this encounter that Glyn Dŵr confidently raised a golden dragon banner, a symbol popularly associated with ancient Brythonic legend, intended to strengthen his claim to be regarded as the longed-for Son of Prophecy. Glyn Dŵr further invoked ancient mythology by scribing ambitious letters to his 'well-beloved cousins' Robert III of Scotland and the various lords of Ireland appealing for aid to defeat their mutual oppressor, 'the Saxons'.[14] Many of Glyn Dŵr's recent decisions, in fact, appear to have been grounded in the sincere belief he was truly the fulfiller of these ancient prophecies.

After another low-profile winter, reduced to sporadic raids for much-needed sustenance, Glyn Dŵr resurfaced in dramatic style during April 1402 when he ambushed his hated rival, Reginald Grey, carrying the humiliated baron off into the mountains. On 22 June, meanwhile, he showed himself to be more than a mere bandit when, in open battle, he inflicted 'woeful slaughter' on an English force at Bryn Glas near Pilleth in Powys. During the latter stages of the battle, Glyn Dŵr's men even took possession of his opposite number, an influential and wealthy Marcher nobleman named Edmund Mortimer.[15]

These two very different victories in early 1402, alongside the capture of Conwy by the Tudurs the previous year, proved a precious psychological boost to the Welsh forces. Despite the obvious disadvantages of their general situation, such as inferior numbers, substandard military technology and a consistent dearth of provisions, they had shown they were nevertheless able to inflict bruising defeats on their English foe. Glyn Dŵr, in particular, had proven his martial credentials by overcoming a considerable English levy deep in the central March and close to the Herefordshire border. After his victory at Pilleth, support freely flowed towards him in subsequent weeks and months, encouraging him to press further south into Gwent and Glamorgan.

The lax English response to Edmund Mortimer's capture further strengthened Glyn Dŵr's hand. While Henry IV had approved the enormous sum of 10,000 marks to ransom Reginald Grey, he proved unwilling to entertain any notion of funding Mortimer's freedom. When Henry had usurped the throne in 1399, many believed Mortimer, and certainly his young namesake nephew, the 5th Earl of March, possessed a superior claim to the throne. The Mortimers were descended from the third surviving son of Edward III, albeit through a female line, while Henry could only boast descent from his fourth son, John of Gaunt. Though the Mortimers did not press their claim at the time, Henry IV now questioned Edmund Mortimer's loyalty, suspecting he had allowed himself to be captured as part of a conspiracy to force another change of dynasty upon the English throne.[16]

Whether Mortimer was plotting against Henry IV at this juncture has never been determined, but the king's conduct only served to drive the captive Marcher lord into Glyn Dŵr's embrace. A formal bond between Glyn Dŵr and Mortimer was struck when the latter married the former's daughter, and both men together pledged to overthrow Henry IV. Two separate anti-Lancastrian causes, in effect, became united against a common foe.[17]

Glyn Dŵr's alliance with Edmund Mortimer also opened the channels of communication with Mortimer's famous brother-in-law, Henry 'Hotspur' Percy, a connection that bolstered the Welsh cause by further exploiting English political instability. Percy, alongside his father and uncle, the earls of Northumberland and Worcester respectively, were aggrieved that, after their integral role in Henry IV's rise to the throne, the cash-strapped king was not honouring his financial obligations for the family's military service in Wales and Scotland. During the spring and summer of 1401, Percy wrote to the king on at least five occasions pleading for more funds to repress the reinvigorated Welsh revolt. The first request came just nine days after the Tudurs had taken control of Conwy Castle, the loss of which the king blamed on Percy.[18]

The relationship between the king and the Percys deteriorated further in April 1403 when Henry IV reorganised the military command in Wales to fall under the authority of his son, Prince Henry. Percy and his uncle Worcester, justiciar of North Wales and lieutenant of South Wales respectively, were affronted by this lack of confidence in their abilities. It was the king's persistent refusal to consider ransoming Edmund Mortimer, however, that particularly rankled the Percy camp, giving way to 'a deadly quarrel'.[19] In early July 1403, the Percys broke rank and raised the banner of rebellion, openly accusing Henry IV of callously murdering the rightful sovereign, Richard II, to provoke popular outrage.[20]

Having spent three years attempting to suppress Glyn Dŵr in Wales, Henry Percy also now aligned himself with the Welsh rebels, an alliance that may have been facilitated by the Tudurs. During the negotiations over Conwy two summers previously, it is possible that Percy and the Tudurs developed a rapport, a mutual respect now exploited to good effect. Three years into his revolt, it was clear Glyn Dŵr was proving adept at exploiting English political fissures to transform his own prospects, content to extend the hand of friendship to erstwhile enemies once their relationship with the king had irrevocably broken down. English monarchs had long taken advantage of Welsh divisions to maintain their grip on power; by cultivating close friendships with Mortimer and the Percys, Glyn Dŵr and his cohort now turned the tables.

With confidence growing, 1403 was the year Owain Glyn Dŵr's flourishing campaign developed from a series of loosely connected violent incidents into a truly national revolt that covered the breadth of

Wales. After an eventful winter of raiding, the summer brought frenzied activity as Glyn Dŵr's men once more turned their attentions to the south with such vigour and violence it made Adam of Usk's heart tremble to reminisce.[21] Widespread defections in the south-west brought new support to Glyn Dŵr's cause, and together they captured the castles of Dryslwyn, Newcastle Emlyn and Carmarthen. Elsewhere, attacks were recorded at Kidwelly, Brecon, Abergavenny and Cardiff, prompting the receiver of Brecon to warn Henry IV that 'the whole of the Welsh nation' have 'treacherously raised against you'.[22]

It was while Glyn Dŵr was occupied in South Wales that Henry Percy revolted in Chester. The plan was to combine both forces into one formidable unit to take on the king of England, but Percy's rebellion lasted just ten days. Having recruited an army in Cheshire, an area heavily associated with Richard II and hostile to the Lancastrian regime, Percy engaged with a royal army at Shrewsbury on 21 July 1403, and in this 'most fearful battle' he was killed before Welsh reinforcements could arrive. The engagement was notable as the first to involve the future Henry V, then a precocious sixteen-year-old prince, who was severely wounded on the cheek by an arrow which left a dreadful scar.[23] Percy's body was impaled on a spear in Shrewsbury marketplace before his corpse was quartered, a gruesome warning to Glyn Dŵr and the Welsh rebels. The earl of Worcester was executed two days later, while Percy's father Northumberland fled into exile before he could be captured. The sprawling Percy power across vast swathes of northern England had been broken in one afternoon.

Glyn Dŵr was not deterred by this setback, nor by the torching of his ancestral homes at Glyndyfrdwy and Sycharth by Prince Henry, and by the end of summer 1403 no part of Wales was exempt from rebel activity. Glyn Dŵr's status as a national leader of the Welsh was assured. If he had initially intended to merely use the title of prince of Wales as a bargaining chip to seek redress in his quarrel with Reginald Grey, Glyn Dŵr's military successes and political alliances soon made clear to him that this revolt was no short-term affair with limited scope. It is from this year that Glyn Dŵr truly stepped into his role as prince – his clerks started dating documents in the year of his reign, while a seal was created that depicted him enthroned with a legend that read 'Owain by the grace of God prince of Wales'.[24]

The uprising reached its zenith in April 1404 when, with mighty fortresses like Aberystwyth and Harlech falling under his control, Glyn Dŵr hosted his first parliament at Machynlleth. This was a novel experience for the Welsh – since the conquest in 1282, they had been granted no parliamentary representation within the English system. Recent defectors to Glyn Dŵr's side, such as John Trefor and Lewis Byford, bishops of St Asaph and Bangor respectively, brought the

Welsh significant bureaucratic and diplomatic experience including knowledge of parliamentary procedure. All those who recognised Glyn Dŵr's authority were summoned, and one may assume there was an enthusiastic uptake not just from his supporters, but from those curious to learn more.[25]

Though there is no extant evidence to indicate who was present, it would seem highly likely that the three surviving Tudur brothers, Rhys, Gwilym and Maredudd, Glyn Dŵr's cousins and his closest supporters, were at the gathering. Glyn Dŵr outlined his grand vision for an independent Wales, one that would feature a separate Welsh church, two national universities, and a return to the laws of Hywel Dda. In the presence of envoys from France, Scotland and Castile, who took news of this development back to their homelands, he was even formally crowned prince of Wales, the first native ruler to bear the title since 1282.[26] Welshmen from the ancient kingdoms of Gwynedd and Deheubarth, from Gwent and Morgannwg, united to pledge their support to this princely son of Powys. Glyn Dŵr's achievement, bringing so many together under his banner to stand against the English king, was an exceptional one that marked him out from his predecessors. As Welsh morale soared, England's grip on Wales was flagging.

Glyn Dŵr followed up his parliament by sending a letter to Charles VI, King of France, requesting arms, money and soldiers, even invoking the memory of Owain Lawgoch to bolster his case. The appeal was favourably received, particularly as Wales offered the French an additional front in their own war with England. On 14 July 1404, a Franco-Welsh treaty was concluded, establishing a formal friendship between the parties and raising Glyn Dŵr from a lowly rebel squire to a credible prince who negotiated with kings of major European powers.[27]

In February 1405, meanwhile, an extraordinary plan was drawn up in anticipation of the Percy–Glyn Dŵr–Mortimer alliance proving victorious. Known as the Tripartite Indenture, this agreement arranged for the kingdom of England to be carved into three independent territories. Mortimer was to receive southern England, the Percy Earl of Northumberland central and northern England, and Glyn Dŵr an enlarged Wales that included large swathes of land on the English side of the border, including most of Cheshire, Shropshire and Herefordshire.[28]

That the proposal coincided with an extraordinary plot in England that same month to spring Mortimer's two nephews from custody indicates the three signatories were genuine in their ambition to crush the House of Lancaster. The boys, who possessed a potent claim to the English throne, were successfully removed from their chamber at Windsor by Constance of York, who maintained her own grudge against Henry IV for executing her husband, Thomas Despenser, 1st Earl of Gloucester, five years earlier. With the Mortimer boys in her control, Constance rode hard for Wales, though her party was intercepted by pursuing troops before she could cross the Severn. If the Mortimer boys had reached their uncle and Glyn Dŵr in the Welsh mountains, the indenture's potency would have increased tenfold and triggered civil war in England.[29]

Though May 1405 proved a difficult month for Glyn Dŵr, his brother killed during an attack on Usk Castle and his son Gruffudd taken prisoner, he nevertheless managed to host a second parliament that summer in Harlech, which had become established as his royal court and military headquarters. August, meanwhile, witnessed the remarkable spectacle of a few thousand French soldiers landing at Milford Haven, a gift to the Welsh prince from Charles VI who, in keeping with kings of France both before and after, sought to further unsettle the beleaguered English crown. The French were under the command of the highly competent Jean II de Rieux, Marshal of France and Brittany, and joined their numbers with Glyn Dŵr's to create, in the judgment of the well-informed French chronicler Jean de Wavrin, a single 'great force'. Together, the army progressed steadily inland through the heart of South Wales, attacking the towns of Tenby, Haverfordwest and Carmarthen until at the end of the month it was stationed near Worcester, just a mile from an English army which blocked their path. For reasons undetermined, battle was not joined, and after eight days the Franco-Welsh army retreated without so much as an arrow loosed in anger. From the moment the French soldiers departed for their homeland in the autumn of 1405, Glyn Dŵr's fortunes fell into rapid decline as his influence waned and desertions increased.[30]

Many of those who took the opportunity to defect from Glyn Dŵr's side in 1406 were based on Anglesey, which was being heavily pressed by Prince Henry's troops. The widespread submission prompted the collapse of Tudur authority on the island as their affinity, which could be traced to the early thirteenth-century heyday of their revered ancestor Ednyfed Fychan. It crumbled under intense pressure. Rhys, Gwilym and Maredudd ap Tudur were among the few who refused to submit, and were included in a list of men convicted of outlawry in their absence, a clear indication that despite their pardon in 1401 for the capture of Conwy they had never abandoned the uprising. For such patriotism, their lands across North-West Wales were declared forfeit to the crown, the family hegemony irrevocably ruined.[31]

As the first decade of the fourteenth century neared its close, the back of the Welsh uprising had been broken, particularly as Henry IV's grip on the English throne grew stronger with each passing year. The king's economic situation started to improve, external threats from Scotland and France had diminished, and in February 1408 the rebellious earl of Northumberland was slaughtered by royal forces at Bramham Moor in Yorkshire. For the first time since the war had erupted, Henry was able to give the situation in Wales his undivided attention. The financial toll of the rebellion, not to mention the physical and mental demands on a war-weary population, was also having a detrimental effect on Welsh morale. In 1406 and 1407, significant parts of the Welsh populace put down their weapons and submitted to a revitalised English authority, including at Anglesey, Flint, Denbigh, Dyffryn Clwyd, Usk, Caerleon, Abergavenny, Monmouth and Glamorgan.[32] Support for Glyn Dŵr was dissolving as rapidly as it had materialised.

With the revolt pushed back into its north-western heartland, namely the recalcitrant counties of Caernarfonshire, Merionethshire and Cardiganshire, the recapture of Aberystwyth and Harlech castles was prioritised, the king furnishing his commanders with several hundred men-at-arms and archers to force their capitulation. English control of Wales depended, ultimately, on holding strategic castles such as these two, together with other vital fortresses like Caernarfon and Conwy. The Welsh garrisons did not make their English besiegers' mission a straightforward one, but by early 1409 both castles were forced into surrender, unable to withstand the fierce and determined onslaught. During the fall of Harlech, another of Glyn Dŵr's English allies, his son-in-law Edmund Mortimer, was slain, with the Welsh leader's unprotected wife, daughters and granddaughters taken prisoner and sent to London.[33] Deprived of his principal redoubt at Harlech, an increasingly isolated Glyn Dŵr had little option but to gather the small band of supporters which remained by his side and withdraw into the same Eryri caves that had offered protection at the outset of his revolt. With the demoralised prince were Rhys and Gwilym ap Tudur, their younger brother Maredudd having apparently perished in recent years.[34]

As the rebels tirelessly hiked through an array of deep valleys and clambered over endless jagged rocks to escape capture, there was plenty of time for the surviving Tudurs to reflect on their present predicament. The previous decade had presented exhilarating highs like the bold capture of Conwy in April 1401 and Glyn Dŵr's progressive parliament of 1404, which outlined a new path for the Welsh people to follow. By 1410, all was lost. They were impoverished, dispossessed and without hope of redemption. Food and shelter were scarce, and they lived in constant fear of betrayal by a friendly face. Adam of Usk, who had briefly joined the rebels, mentioned how during his time in Wales he had been 'sorely tormented with many and great perils of death and capture and false brethren, and of hunger and thirst, passing many nights without sleep for fear of the attacks of foes'.[35] His experience is likely one that was shared by men like Rhys and Gwilym ap Tudur, who endured a restless and miserable existence on the run. This hopeless outlook may account for some of the sporadic raids associated with the Tudurs and Glyn Dŵr in the final days of the uprising, desperate excursions from which they perhaps didn't expect to return alive.

In 1411, a small band of the rebels emerged from their hiding spots and led a ferocious raid deep into the Shropshire countryside, during which some of the English who resisted them were killed. At least three Welsh 'men of fame' were captured near Welshpool, however – Rhys Ddu, Glyn Dŵr's captain of Aberystwyth Castle; Phillip Scudamore, the former royal captain of Carreg Cennen who had defected early in the revolt; and Rhys ap Tudur. The three were tried, but their sentence was never in question. All were to die. In Chester, Rhys ap Tudur was drawn to the gallows where he was hanged before a cheering crowd. Though unstated, it is likely his head was cut from his body and spiked upon a local bridge as a macabre trophy.[36]

There is little doubt Rhys ap Tudur had been a figure of significant importance in Anglo-Welsh politics during the late fourteenth and early fifteenth centuries. For several years he had proven a dependable royal servant, serving as sheriff of Anglesey on two occasions and raising a contingent for military service before being retained by the king, Richard II.[37] When the Welsh broke into revolt, Rhys was integral in leading the men of Anglesey against Henry IV, harassing the king's forces before fronting the audacious band that captured Conwy Castle on Good Friday 1401. He is almost certain to have retained a principal role in the rebellion thereafter, for which he paid the ultimate price at the hands of a Chester executioner. Rhys's death was lamented in verse by Gruffudd Gryg, a native of Anglesey who likely knew his subject well. To Gryg, Rhys had been a man of wisdom, a figure merry, modest and brave.[38]

Rhys's brother Gwilym ap Tudur, meanwhile, does not appear to have suffered the same horrific fate. After Henry V came to the throne in March 1413, there was a conscious programme of reconciliation as the crown extended pardons even to the most hardened of rebels. The new king endeavoured to draw a line under the revolt as his attention turned towards an invasion of France, and one of the men who benefited was Gwilym. On 6 May 1413, a pardon was granted to 'William ap Tudur' that absolved him of 'all treasons, insurrections, rebellions and felonies' except for murder and rape. However, stripped of his estates, his affinity and his influence, he soon faded into obscurity. It is likely Gwilym ap Tudur did not long outlive his pardon.[39]

As for the third Tudur brother who participated in the revolt, Maredudd ap Tudur, even less is known about his end. Though he played no discernible part in the capture of Conwy in 1401, Maredudd was included in the list of rebels outlawed in 1406, so appears at least to have been alive by this crucial juncture in the revolt. It has been suggested he was employed as an esquire to the bishop of Bangor, Lewis Byford, and as the cleric had been a notable defector to the Welsh this connection is certainly plausible. Later claims he was merely a butler or brewer do not align with his well-established record of public service, having served as burgess and an escheator before the rebellion. There is no known mention of Maredudd in the revolt's later stages, and none after 1406, which raises the likelihood he had either died of natural causes or had been killed during one of the many skirmishes between the Welsh and the English royal forces soon thereafter. He simply disappears from the historical record, though not before fathering at least one son, Owain ap Maredudd ap Tudur, in the years between 1400 and 1406.[40]

Though Glyn Dŵr had one last success in early 1412, capturing the leading Welsh opponent to his uprising, Dafydd Gam, the revolt was effectively over. In a war of attrition, the financial might, superior manpower and military resources of the English crown proved insurmountable. After a dozen years in the field, the Welsh were exhausted from evading repeated royal expeditions, frustrated as most English castles repelled their assaults with little difficulty and starved by a dearth of provisions. Psychologically, much less militarily, the Welsh were done.

After 1412, the defiant squire of Sycharth who had dared to call himself a prince of Wales retreated into the mountains for the last time, his whereabouts lost to history, his fate unknown. Despite large rewards offered for his capture, Glyn Dŵr was never betrayed, a measure of the respect he retained even at his lowest ebb. On 10 March 1414, English royal administrators led by Thomas FitzAlan, 5th Earl of Arundel, and Edward Charlton, 5th Baron Charlton of Powys, held sessions in Bala where 600 local Welshmen pledged their loyalty to the English crown. Bala lay just 10 miles from Glyndyfrdwy, Glyn Dŵr's ancestral home and where, fourteen years earlier, he raised the banner of rebellion. By compelling Glyn Dŵr's own affinity to submit to the authority of the new king, Henry V, the English sent a palpable message to the wider Welsh population that there was no cause left to fight for. The Lancastrian reconquest of Wales was complete.[41] By 1415, the year Adam of Usk gives for Glyn Dŵr's death, Welshmen drawn from both sides of the revolt were fighting side by side in Henry V's armies in France, including at the famed Battle of Agincourt. The following year, the king was even able to make an uneventful pilgrimage on foot to the shrine of St Winefride in North-East Wales. There was no one left to oppose him.[42]

This subdued end to a tumultuous period in Welsh history shouldn't detract from Glyn Dŵr's extraordinary accomplishment in stirring a loyalty in his compatriots greater than any of his predecessors, particularly since the odds had been stacked against a favourable outcome from the outset. Hundreds, possibly thousands, of Welshmen, including at least one of his Tudur cousins, Rhys, were willing to sacrifice their lives in pursuit of his grand vision for an autonomous Welsh state.

Though an astute political operator in the present, Glyn Dŵr had also shrewdly drawn on the blessings of ancestry and native bardic tradition to integrate his cause with ancient prophecies that promised a messiah would free the Welsh from tyranny. He employed a seer who was present when he proclaimed himself prince of Wales in 1400, consulted another renowned expert on divination three years later, and alluded to the tradition in diplomatic communications with the French, the Scots and his English allies. It is telling that Henry IV banned the gathering of bards as part of his Penal Laws, hoping to suppress their intoxicating message. Though his cause ultimately floundered, Glyn Dŵr would not be the final Welshman to adopt such a persuasive strategy to draw his countrymen to his banner.

A later Tudor tradition first recorded in the 1540s work of Elis Gruffudd recounts how Glyn Dŵr was walking one morning near Valle Crucis Abbey when he remarked with surprise that the abbot had risen early. The abbot scolded Glyn Dŵr in response, pointedly replying that it had been Glyn Dŵr, in fact, who had risen early – by 100 years.[43] Though an apocryphal account written with the benefit of hindsight, as the fifteenth century progressed and the glowing embers from a failed revolt burned out, it became clear neither Owain Glyn Dŵr, nor indeed Owain Lawgoch, Llywelyn the Last or any other previous candidate, had been the Son of Prophecy the legends foretold. Glyn Dŵr's uprising, the only mass revolt against English rule that truly encompassed all of Wales, had been comprehensively crushed, his final whereabouts unknown. Within half a century, however, would be born one more aspirant who would capture the attention of the bards, a figure rooted in the noble stock of Wales on both sides of his bloodline, and in whose veins ran the bellicose blood of Ednyfed Fychan and the Tudurs. His story would begin with another Owain.

6

A Gentleman of Wales

The years following the collapse of Owain Glyn Dŵr's 'great rebellion' were challenging for the Welsh, a fraught period in which they suffered considerable judicial, economic and social hardship. The racially motivated and repressive series of laws passed by parliament in response to the revolt had cowed the populace into compliance, stripping many individuals of crucial opportunities to flourish. A decade of soldiers rampaging across the undulating hills and through the bustling townships of Wales had devastated much of the landscape, with monasteries, farms and mills – the sources of entire livelihoods – left in smouldering ruins.

Communal fines levied to replenish a stretched royal treasury crippled entire communities for many years, with a lack of crops and trade starving an already impoverished people. Whether an individual had revolted was irrelevant; all were punished solely on account of their nationality. Many families simply never recovered their positions, with the Penal Laws reissued four more times across the first half of the fifteenth century.[1] Wales's first truly national revolt, one which encompassed all of the country, proved its last, and for good reason; no parish had escaped unscathed by the war. Far from freeing the Welsh from the servitude in which they languished, Glyn Dŵr's actions instead provoked more draconian measures than before and fuelled anti-Welsh sentiment in the English government.

Welsh history had been littered with phases of desperate adversity, but prospects for almost any Welshman of ambition were dire after the English crown reestablished its royal authority. Continuing with the terms of the Penal Laws set in 1401, they were barred from attaining public offices such as bailiff, mayor, sheriff or constable, and could not bear arms, buy land in towns or even gather in public lest they be regarded as a menace to the king's peace. The modest opportunities afforded to their ancestors across the previous century had been withdrawn, with little prospect of a reversal in government policy. The Welsh, so the king's council and parliament believed, could not be trusted.

When an emboldened Henry V invaded France in the summer of 1415, resuming a war which had lain dormant for a quarter-century, scores of young Welshmen flocked across the Channel in search of an opening denied them at home. The king was more than content to welcome them; as prince of Wales throughout the peak of the rebellion, Henry had discovered first-hand the extensive military capabilities of the Welsh, which he now put to good use against the French. That Wales was drained of a vigorous generation of young men, many also finding domestic positions in the vast households of English magnates, also had the benefit of purging an aggrieved corner of the king's dominions of hundreds of potential agitators.

One of those who sought pastures new during this troubled period was Owain ap Maredudd ap Tudur, the son of the youngest of the Tudur brothers of Anglesey. An unfinished account from 1723 contends that Maredudd fled his native land after committing murder and fathered Owain in exile, but there is no solid contemporary evidence to support such a claim. The likelihood is the child was born in Wales after 1400 but before 1406, when Maredudd disappears from the historical record after being outlawed for his role in the Welsh rebellion. It is certain, however, that Owain never knew his father well.[2]

Whether a newborn, infant or toddler, Owain was young when his home of Anglesey was overrun by the royal troops of Prince Henry, the future Henry V, in 1406. The bountiful island that had enriched generations of his family was greedily plundered of its resources and the Tudur affinity scattered by force. Though Owain's uncles Rhys and Gwilym ap Tudur persisted with the revolt for another six years, the family never recovered their position and forfeited their prized inheritance to the crown, to be subsequently regranted to those who had sided with the king. Though some Welsh families of princely stock were able to recover their erstwhile positions in subsequent years, often paying exorbitant fines for the privilege, from 1406 onwards the Tudurs as a dynasty of influence were extinguished.

One Welshman who deftly navigated the fallout of the revolt, and contributed to the Tudurs' downfall, was their distant cousin Gwilym ap Gruffudd, a descendant of Ednyfed Fychan who had married a daughter of Goronwy ap Tudur, Owain's uncle. Gwilym initially supported his Tudur kin when the uprising exploded in 1400 but later, sensing the way the wind was blowing, sought reconciliation with Henry IV. Once the revolt was suppressed, Gwilym was able to acquire the forfeited estates of the Tudurs, including Penmynydd, and establish his family as the leading North Welsh power of their day; his son Gwilym Fychan would serve as deputy chamberlain of North Wales under Edward IV, and his grandson William

Griffith as chamberlain under Richard III and, ironically, his distant cousin Henry VII.[3] Gwilym did, however, fail to obtain the lands of Maredudd ap Tudur, which on 8 December 1408 were granted to an Englishman named Richard del Wode and his heirs as reward for his 'good service'.[4]

Through events not of his making, therefore, a young Owain ap Maredudd was denied inheritance or opportunity, regardless of any political, administrative or military promise he demonstrated as he moved into adolescence. There was little to keep him in Anglesey, or even North Wales. It is unknown when, or even how, Owain migrated to England, but on 13 May 1421 protection was given to an Owen Mereddith to join the France-bound retinue of a rising English magnate named Walter Hungerford.[5] Considering his later progression in English society, exploiting connections he developed early in his career, and consistent references to him under this name, it is fair to assume the young man that crossed the Channel with Hungerford in 1421 was Owain ap Maredudd. If accurate, this represents the earliest known record of Owain; there are certainly no grounds to substantiate later claims he was present at Agincourt six years earlier, which appear to be dubious attempts to associate the ancestor of the later Tudor dynasty with Henry V's famed victory over the flower of French chivalry.

Once Owain started to establish his position in England, his name caused ample bewilderment among his non-Welsh peers, with a clear inconsistency in how he is documented by parochial English clerks grappling with Welsh patronymics. Following the tradition of his native land, Owain was born Owain ap Maredudd ap Tudur, or Owen son of Meredith son of Tudor, his name proudly displaying his recent ancestry. During a later appeal for denizenship in 1432, he provided the name Oweyn fitz Meredyth, which follows a similar form, while two years later he appears in the Recognizance Rolls of Chester as Oweyn ap Meredith, and again in 1437 as Owen ap Mereduth.[6]

This is also the year in which Owain's name is first contracted as Oweyn Tidr, perhaps the result of a clerk misunderstanding Welsh patronymics and adopting the latter name of the three, that belonging to Owain's grandfather, as an English-style surname. The following year there are references to Owini ap Tuder, Owen ap Tedir, Owin ap Tuder and Owen ap Meredith ap Tidur, before two further mentions in 1439 of Owen Meredeth and Owen Meridith.[7] Owain likely always regarded himself as Owain ap Maredudd, and would have found Owen Meredeth or Meridith acceptable anglicised versions of his name. Towards the end of his life, however, and certainly by the accession of his grandson to the English throne in 1485, he was firmly known as Owen Tudor.[8] It is the name by which he is remembered in history – England was just a stroke of a quill away from having a royal dynasty known by the name of Meredith rather than Tudor.

Hungerford was not an inconsequential figure for Owen Tudor to attach himself to; born into a moderately prosperous West Country family, Hungerford's father had been a steward in the household of the prodigious John of Gaunt, and when Gaunt's son usurped the throne in 1399, opportunities were aplenty for Walter. He was knighted in the first year of Henry IV's reign and served as a Member of Parliament, sheriff and Speaker of the Commons between 1400 and 1414. When Henry V invaded France in 1415, Hungerford acquitted himself well during a campaign in which lasting military reputations were formed, not least his own. By the time Owen entered Hungerford's sphere, his master was an established presence in the highest echelons of government, a distinguished diplomat, soldier and administrator who served as admiral of the fleet, steward of the king's household and constable of Windsor Castle, among other positions.[9]

Hungerford's principal residence was at Farleigh Hungerford Castle on the Somerset–Wiltshire border, and this may be the place a young Owen Tudor first called home in England. Farleigh Hungerford was an old Norman manor rebuilt by Walter Hungerford's father, Thomas, in the 1370s. It was a modest quadrangular compound with four circular towers, the southern pair of which flanked a twin-towered gatehouse and drawbridge controlling access to the inner court. In the centre of the courtyard was the tapestry-lined great hall, where guests of the Hungerfords were entertained with food and drink from the adjacent kitchen and bakehouse, and the residential ranges overlooking a steep but scenic bank falling towards the River Frome. Though it could not compete with the grander castles of the period, the Hungerford seat at Farleigh was nonetheless a robust base from which the family could drive its ambitions, and an idyllic location in the West Country for Owen Tudor to find his feet in English society.

This connection with the Hungerfords is likely to have been the conduit through which Owen first reached the fringes of the royal household, for if he remained in Walter Hungerford's service after 1421 there would have been regular opportunity to accompany his lord to the court on state business. In 1422, Hungerford was named one of the executors of Henry V's will, and the following year was appointed to the regency council assembled to govern the kingdom on behalf of the child king, Henry VI. By 1426, Hungerford had established himself as an integral part of the royal machinery, rising to become lord treasurer and serving another stint as steward of the king's household. Incidentally, though Owen likely served Hungerford throughout this period, sixty years later the roles were reversed for their descendants when Walter's namesake great-grandson fought under the Tudor banner at Bosworth Field.

Whether it was through service to Hungerford or by other means, Owen first became acquainted with Katherine of Valois, Henry V's widow and mother of Henry VI, around 1428. He has traditionally been considered to have progressed from Hungerford's service into Katherine's, rising quickly to become keeper of either the queen's household or her wardrobe, though there is no evidence to support such claims. Considering his subsequent access to Katherine, some middling post in her service seems likely, perhaps more modest than keeper itself.[10] In contemporary records Owen is consistently regarded as a squire, which though below a knight in social status suggests he had some knowledge of the code of chivalry and the rules of heraldry and was proficient in the basics of horsemanship and swordsmanship. In short, he had abilities appropriate for a modest post in a noble household, but no more.[11]

Katherine was the youngest daughter of Charles VI, King of France, and his Bavarian wife Isabeau, born in the Hôtel Saint-Pol in Paris on 27 October 1401. A Valois princess, as early as 1409 there were discussions of a potential match with Henry, Prince of Wales, though this was quickly dropped as both England and France grappled with internal issues that demanded the undivided attention of the respective monarchies. When the prince acceded to the English throne in 1413 as Henry V, however, one of his strategies to unite his kingdom behind him was to advance a popular policy of war, reviving Edward III's claim to the French throne and invading France in the summer of 1415. Within four years, Henry's single-mindedness had brought a large swath of France to its knees, including all of Normandy. Paris was in sight, raising the prospect of an enduring peace between the warring Houses of Valois and Lancaster that would be sealed in marriage.

Katherine's father Charles VI was a weak and ineffectual monarch prone to bouts of incapacitating mental illness, his unstable kingdom bitterly divided between rival factions. The French could not withstand the English onslaught, and in the negotiations that followed, it was not only agreed that the thirty-three-year-old Henry V would marry the eighteen-year-old Katherine but that upon her father's death the crown of France would pass to her English husband and then to any children they would have.

Henry and Katherine were married in Troyes on 2 June 1420 before returning to England together, where the new queen was crowned in Westminster Abbey on 23 February 1421. While Henry wasted little time in returning across the Channel to defend his gains, his pregnant bride stayed behind, giving birth on 6 December 1421 to a baby boy who stood to one day inherit the dual crowns of England and France. Henry V would never lay eyes upon his son, however, for on 31 August 1422 England's warrior king died of dysentery near Paris, just two months before his father-in-law Charles VI. At the tender age of twenty, and after just twenty-six months of marriage, Katherine was not only a widow in an alien land hostile to those of French blood, but mother of an infant who was king of England and of France. It was a heavy burden for one so young to bear.[12]

As per the conditions laid out in her husband's will, Katherine remained in the household of her infant son for much of the next decade, personally supervising his upbringing and contributing to the costs from her substantial dower.[13] The child king was chiefly based at Windsor and Eltham, also spending considerable time at Katherine's residences of Hertford, Waltham and Wallingford, and this ever-present access allowed the king's mother to become an influential force in his early development. Her role was only significantly reduced in the spring of 1428 when Henry reached the age of seven, at which point responsibility for his education and upbringing was passed to a male governor, Richard Beauchamp, 13th Earl of Warwick, and an all-male entourage comprising four knights and four esquires.[14]

Warwick was a suitable choice to raise a disciplined and virtuous king; an experienced soldier and prudent diplomat, the very embodiment of the chivalric ideal, the earl was charged with not just guarding the king's person but educating him in 'good manners, letters, languages, nurture and wit'.[15] Katherine would, however, retain a highly visible ceremonial presence next to her son during feast days and other public appearances, including Henry's coronation as king of England on 6 November 1429 in Westminster Abbey, where she was seated to his right throughout the rituals.[16]

During the early years of Henry VI's reign, however, England was a politically troubled realm, with the corridors of power rife with suspicion as competing ambitions relentlessly clashed. The regency government created in 1422 to govern the kingdom during the king's minority involved the most influential and highest-ranking members of the nobility, comprising a council of eighteen figures including four dukes, four earls, one archbishop and four bishops. Though in France there had been precedents for female regents governing for kings, like Blanche of Castile for her underage son between 1226 and 1234, Joan of Burgundy for her absent husband in the 1340s and even Katherine of Valois's mother Isabeau during the various illnesses of Charles VI, the custom of a woman ruling England was not known or considered. With her brother fronting a vigorous campaign to expel the English from France, the potential conflict of interest was sufficient for Katherine to be deemed unsuitable to hold the reins of her adopted kingdom, though there is no evidence she pressed the matter in any case.[17]

With Henry V's eldest surviving brother, John, 1st Duke of Bedford, heavily preoccupied with defending the English position in France, the regency council in England came to be dominated by two figures with divergent ideas on how they should govern in both domestic matters and the French war. Bedford's younger brother Humphrey, 1st Duke of Gloucester, had anticipated being appointed regent and entrusted with the overall governance of the realm but did not account for the vociferous opposition of parliament and his seasoned half-uncle, Bishop Henry Beaufort, who argued a lord protector accountable to the council was a more appropriate role.[18] This political quarrel and the disputes that followed marked the start of a deeply personal feud between uncle and nephew that would last for the next two decades, drawing in their respective factions and sparking considerable unease around the royal court. In October 1425, amid accusations from Gloucester that Beaufort intended to kidnap the young king and seize the throne for himself, the rivalry intensified further until the armed retinues of both sides faced each other across London Bridge, a calamitous skirmish on the Thames averted only by the desperate intervention of the archbishop of Canterbury and the visiting Prince Pedro of Portugal.[19]

The queen dowager was not safe from the fallout of Gloucester's feud with Henry Beaufort. By 1427, Katherine had been widowed for five years and yet was still just twenty-six years old. It is unclear what the council's collective attitude was towards the widowed queen taking another partner, but history had shown the romantic endeavours of French mothers to young English kings could be politically challenging. When Henry III became king at nine years old in 1216, his mother Isabella of Angoulême was just twenty-eight, and four years later took a French magnate, Hugh X of Lusignan, as her second husband. As Isabella failed to seek the consent of the king's council, her dower lands were confiscated and her pension was withdrawn.

A century later, Isabella of France famously embarked on a highly divisive affair with Roger Mortimer, toppling her husband, Edward II, from the throne and ruling in her son Edward III's name for four years between 1326 and 1330. During that period, the acquisitive Mortimer exploited his unprecedented access to the crown to accumulate an extraordinary array of lands and titles, including the earldom of March, and even oversaw the murder of the deposed king and the judicial killing of his brother. Mortimer's deeply unpopular and corrupt reign was only curtailed when the teenage king was able to launch a dramatic counter-coup to reclaim control of his crown. In more recent memory, the English mother of Richard II, Joan of Kent, was fifty when her ten-year-old son acceded to the throne, and never remarried. No queen dowager of England, in fact, had married one of her husband's subjects since Adeliza of Louvain in the mid-twelfth century, and even then she was Henry I's second wife and had no royal children to complicate matters.

When rumours surfaced around 1426, therefore, that Katherine of Valois was growing noticeably close to Edmund Beaufort, the twenty-year-old nephew and protégé of Bishop Henry Beaufort, the churchman's bitter foe Humphrey of Gloucester grew alarmed. Though there is no evidence the Beaufort faction had any agenda to secure Katherine's hand in marriage, the protector nevertheless feared such a development would make their position at court insuperable – a Beaufort stepfather with unfettered access to the crown could exert unchecked influence on a susceptible child king, which would prove particularly propitious as Henry grew into adulthood. The bishop had form for securing advantageous royal matches for his family, after all – just two years earlier he had overseen his niece Joan's marriage to King James I of Scotland, even hosting the wedding celebrations at his palace in Southwark.

Matters were exacerbated during the tense parliament that sat in Leicester between February and June 1426, a gathering in which all weapons were forbidden, such was the fear of violence between the Gloucester and Beaufort factions, though many retainers nevertheless armed themselves with clubs and bats. During the proceedings, a petition was presented by the Commons which sought to permit queens dowager to remarry if they desired, and though it was deferred for further consideration this appeal spurred Gloucester into action. When parliament next met between October 1427 and March 1428, the protector and the regency council proposed a remarkable act that would make it a financially ruinous offence to marry any queen dowager without the explicit permission of the king.

The draft statute, which was designed to protect the supremacy of the council and deny any ambitious subject the opportunity to accrue undue influence beyond the traditional channels, read:

> It is ordained and established by the authority of the present parliament for the salvation of the most noble estate of queens of England for the time being that no man of whatsoever estate or condition he may be shall make contract of espousals or matrimony nor shall be married to any queen of England without the special licence and assent of the king himself having attained the years of discretion, and he who shall do the contrary and shall be duly convicted thereof shall forfeit to the king for the term of his life and all his lands and tenements.[20]

The statute readily received the assent of the temporal lords, though the spiritual peers only did so conditionally, conflicted because of the church's doctrine that anyone was free to marry. The Commons, meanwhile, were not petitioned at all. This lack of universal approval may account for the draft's failure to be formally enacted when the statute rolls were drawn up, thus raising doubt whether Gloucester and the council succeeded in making it illegal to marry Katherine. It could, of course, have simply been made redundant by consequent events, for shortly after leaving the king's household the defiant Katherine pursued her own desires in a manner that boldly rejected any legal mechanism designed to police her personal life. However, the object of her desires was not a Beaufort.

Historians, poets and novelists throughout the centuries have speculated over how a modest Welsh squire like Owen Tudor and a

French-born queen dowager of England met, though contemporary accounts reveal frustratingly little. The two most well-known accounts originate from the work of a pair of Welshmen, Elis Gruffydd and Robin Ddu. According to Gruffydd, a soldier and chronicler who completed his work in 1552, one summer Owen was swimming in a river near Katherine's court when he was pointed out to the queen dowager by one of her handmaidens. This maid disclosed to the queen that Owen claimed to be in love with her, and would approach her whenever she left Katherine's side. The queen noted the fairness of Owen's body, her eyes following him as he frolicked in the water with his colleagues. Turning to her maid, Katherine ordered her to schedule another tryst with Owen, though this time she would attend in the maid's place.

Dressed as the maid, Katherine met an unwitting Owen in a darkened gallery as had been arranged, her face obscured. The couple gently conversed before Owen took the disguised queen by the neck and tried to kiss her on the mouth, though she calmly turned her face to present her cheek. A flickering shadow in the light under the door unsettled Owen, who worried the queen might interrupt, oblivious to the fact she was already in the room. As he rose to leave, Owen attempted another kiss on the mouth, but when he was rejected for a second time started to suspect the lady before him was not the handmaiden of previous meetings and that he was the subject of a prank. Determined to uncover the mysterious maid's identity, Owen nibbled her on the cheek, causing a small mark that would reveal her to him the following day, before fleeing the gallery.

The following morning, Katherine instructed her chamberlain to order Owen to attend to her table during dinner. As he placed the food before the queen dowager, she crossly pointed at her bandaged cheek, shaming Owen for his conduct the previous evening. Terrified he was in grave danger for assaulting the king's mother, Owen hurried to the stables, intending to flee to Wales. Katherine, however, hampered his escape by commanding the gates closed and sending a messenger to bring Owen into her presence. It was from this second meeting that an unlikely romantic relationship between the pair developed, though Gruffydd is vague on the details.[21]

The story of Owen sexually assaulting and then injuring a disguised Katherine before she fell in love with him seems far-fetched, and surely less likely than the account of Robin Ddu. Also hailing from Anglesey, Robin Ddu knew Owen personally, and if his information did not originate with Owen himself then it is likely to have been obtained from someone within his inner circle. In an elegy composed shortly after Owen's death, Robin claimed that he had 'clapped his ardent humble affection on the daughter of the King of the land of wine' during a feast celebrating a holy day. This is the earliest known account of how Owen and Katherine met and was a version favoured by later Tudor writers and poets like John Stow, Michael Drayton, and Hugh Holland, who added that he even fell into the queen dowager's lap.[22]

There may have been another scenario through which Katherine and Owen became acquainted. After Henry V's death, Katherine was granted several lands in Wales, including Hawarden, Montgomery, Builth, Menai, Flint, Mostyn and Caldicot, the revenues from which she used to contribute to her place in the king's household. She was also granted property at Beaumaris, Newburgh, Cemaes and Aberffraw on Anglesey, an island Owen was intimately connected with.[23] If indeed he was around the royal household at this time, it raises the possibility his local knowledge was exploited by the queen's officials, perhaps with Owen even personally assisting in the collection of her revenues. As two young adults living in a country in which they were strangers, a strictly formal interaction could soon have developed into a close bond as they explored shared experiences, a connection that over time evolved into a romance. Owing to the difference in their stations, however, the impetus surely came from the queen.

The relationship between Katherine and Owen progressed quickly once they became involved, and soon the pair were married. As could be expected from a clandestine union that defied the council's wishes, there is no extant record of how, where or indeed when the marriage took place. A reasonable assumption can be made that the nuptials occurred between November 1427 and November 1429 due to the testimony of Sir John Steward, who, according to a manuscript compiled by his descendants, was questioned by the council shortly thereafter about his knowledge of Katherine and Owen's affair.

Steward was the son of a Scottish knight raised in the English court, and in adulthood became closely affiliated with the household of Katherine. In February 1421, Steward was knighted at Katherine's coronation as queen of England, after which he was given a gold goblet for serving as cupbearer during the feast. Shortly thereafter, he was appointed keeper of the queen's horses, fulfilling the role for the next five years, working from the royal stables and responsible for overseeing her travel arrangements. Steward was with the queen when she learned of Henry V's death, and part of the household that escorted her back to England. He also later served as master of the king's horses when accompanying Henry VI to his French coronation in 1431. There is little doubt Steward knew Katherine well, and in his later years with her household may have become acquainted with Owen.[24]

During Steward's interrogation, which took place during Katherine's lifetime and confirms the council were aware of the queen's remarriage before her death, the Scotsman proved discreet, declaring he could in no good conscience reveal his lady's secrets. To do so, he affirmed, would be 'to the perpetual shame of his name and estate'. Steward did however deny any involvement in Katherine and Owen's plans to marry, noting he was serving in France at the time, the dates of his service falling between November 1427 and November 1429.[25]

That no contemporary ever cast doubt on the wedding in subsequent years, nor the legitimacy of their offspring, strongly indicates a ceremony took place, and if Steward's testimony is truthful, it happened before the end of 1429. Even Richard III, when later attempting to denigrate Henry Tudor's background in the months before their confrontation at Bosworth, never remarked upon the validity of Katherine's Welsh marriage. All that can be surmised from the crumbs of material available is that once Katherine had extricated herself from prying eyes and inquisitive minds around the king's household, she was almost certainly joined in holy matrimony with Owen, requiring just a single priest to conduct the rituals and their own consent. Considering their background, the vows were likely expressed in English, the one language they had in common. The union was unquestionably consummated, as proven by their later children.

History has not judged Katherine, a French princess by birth and an English queen by marriage, kindly for entering a union with a man who, though of gentle birth and descended from Welsh royalty, was patently beneath her social status. One of the earliest contemporary accounts which covered Katherine's second marriage was the *Incerti Scriptoris Chronicon Angliae*, compiled around 1460, which chastised the queen for her apparent inability 'to control her fleshly passions', a condemnation rooted in misogynistic attitudes towards female behaviour prevalent throughout written history.[26]

This approach proved influential, and similar judgements were repeated throughout the sixteenth century and beyond. In 1534, Polydore Vergil contended that 'being but young in years' Katherine was 'of less discretion to judge what was decent for her estate',[27] while in 1548 Edward Hall condemned her behaviour as that of a woman who was 'young and lusty' and regarded 'more her private affection than her open honour'.[28] These accounts were repeated in 1577 by Raphael Holinshed, who in turn inspired playwrights like Marlowe and Shakespeare and later generations of historians.[29] Owen, meanwhile, was predictably excused from responsibility and rather praised on account of his appearance and character – to Vergil, he was a 'gentleman of Wales, adorned with wonderful gifts of body and mind', confirmed by Hall who added he was 'a beautiful person', both of 'nature and grace'.[30]

Putting aside dated misogyny, just what drove Katherine, a queen dowager, to become involved with Owen, a mere squire? She may have grown frustrated with stern counsellors, only concerned with politics and safeguarding their own positions, meddling in her personal life and elected to take matters into her own hands, undermining the statute by choosing an unmarried man from her household who was without title or land. In matters of her remarriage, Katherine has typically been viewed as a willing participant in the possible pursuit of her hand by Edmund Beaufort, but it must also be considered the queen dowager perhaps resented her status as a pawn in the ambitions of others, and took the pragmatic if bold step to remove herself from the marital market by marrying a man of little consequence.[31] Young and independently wealthy, Katherine certainly did not need a nobleman of means to sustain her lifestyle, and if she chose this course to escape unwelcome attention, she need not be scolded as lusty or dishonourable for preserving control of her own situation.

Of course, the matter may be no more complex than Katherine and Owen sharing a mutual attraction after encountering one another around court – later accounts praise the Welshman on account of his natural charm and attractiveness, while the queen dowager was described by the French chronicler Enguerrand de Monstrelet as 'very beautiful, of high birth and of decorous comportment'.[32] After nearly a decade bereaved, and with her daily involvement in her son's upbringing diminishing after 1428, Katherine was not unreasonable in pursuing simple companionship with someone who appealed to her for who he was in private, rather than what he represented in public.

Much of the Tudor–Valois relationship was conducted at Katherine's principal country residences of Hertford and Waltham, outside the regency council's immediate reach and around those whose loyalties were first and foremost to the queen dowager. Situated on flat lowland on the south bank of the River Lea, Hertford was granted to Katherine by her first husband in 1418 and was certainly a comfortable royal abode for her to enjoy with her new partner. Whether they were hosting guests in the lively great hall, sharing sumptuous feasts in the opulent king's chamber or taking morning strolls through the elaborate gardens and the peaceful grounds, Hertford was a pleasure palace contained within flint rubble walls, an idyllic stage on which love could blossom.[33]

Waltham, meanwhile, offered a change of scenery. A manor house close to the Augustinian priory of Waltham Holy Cross on the periphery of a vast royal forest, it was here on 30 November 1431 that Katherine met with Walter Hungerford, now serving as treasurer of England. Though superficially this appears to have been a matter of state business, it is tempting to suggest Hungerford also met with Owen Tudor, his former retainer, though what conversation, if any, passed between the men remains speculative.[34] It may be through this meeting that the regency council on which Hungerford served first became aware of Katherine's remarriage.

Katherine and Owen's union proved nothing if not fruitful in the seven or eight years they shared together, with three sons and a short-lived girl born to the couple during that period.[35] Known as Edmund of Hadham in later Chancery Rolls, the eldest child came into the world around 1430 at Much Hadham Palace, an ecclesiastical property belonging to the bishops of London.[36]

That the boy's name was shared with Edmund Beaufort, once the rumoured object of Katherine's affections, has raised a degree of modern conjecture that it was Beaufort, rather than Owen Tudor, who was the true father. This is highly speculative; there is no credible evidence Beaufort and Katherine engaged in a physical affair other than court gossip, and there could be various explanations to account for the boy's name. Beaufort may have stood godfather to the boy, who then took his name as was traditional, or perhaps the name was inspired by St Edmund the Martyr, particularly if the birth occurred on the saint's feast day of 20 November. Much Hadham was less than 50 miles from St Edmundsbury, which housed the shrine of St Edmund, and this may have proved influential when deliberating upon names.

The typically English name is a curious choice for a child of Welsh and French pedigree, but this should not necessarily cast doubt on his parentage. When knowledge of the children became widely known, their paternity was never challenged, and when Richard III later questioned the legitimacy of Henry Tudor's ancestry in 1485 on both sides of his family tree, his failure to query the validity of Katherine's marriage with Owen suggests a tacit acceptance it was matrimonially sound. Edmund of Hadham was explicitly described by Richard III as 'son of Owen Tydder'.[37]

The second son was given the more unusual name Jasper, which does not feature in English or Welsh royal history. A name of Persian origin but known in France, it may suggest that the boy possessed a fiery shock of red hair, similar to the opaque brownish-red mineral from which the name is ultimately derived. In an early sixteenth-century genealogical chronicle, it may be noted that the depiction of Jasper suggests he had the red hair famously associated with his later kin, Henry VIII and Elizabeth I.[38]

Like his brother, Jasper was also born at an ecclesiastical residence, the bishop of Ely's manor of Hatfield.[39] It may be significant that the incumbent bishop, Philip Morgan, was a Welshman, a compatriot of Owen's who shared a common cultural and linguistic background. He was also an experienced diplomat in French affairs and had previously served as chancellor of Normandy, which made him well-known to Katherine. Much Hadham was around 9 miles east of Hertford, while Hatfield was 7 miles west, suggesting Katherine sought out the protection and privacy of the church to give birth. It is difficult to believe either bishop would have offered their homes if they weren't content the children were born lawfully.

The birth of another son, named Owen for his father, occurred in Westminster. Judging from the more urban location compared to his siblings' births, Owen's delivery may have been premature, taking his mother by surprise while she was away from her usual abodes. Information about Owen is non-existent other than that he was entrusted to the care of the Benedictine monastery, perhaps a pragmatic step by Katherine to spare her secret being revealed to the wider world. Here, he was raised and educated by the monks, taking his own vows once he reached adulthood. His head was shaved save for a band of hair just above the ears, and he was provided with a woollen tunic tied at the waist by a simple leather belt, over which sat a black scapular and a deep-hooded cowl. He owned very little, except perhaps for a pen, a comb and a small sewing kit, and slept on a straw or feather mattress beneath a woollen blanket. He dedicated most of his daily life to communal and private prayer, religious reading and manual labour, spending what little remained of his personal time relaxing around the cloister or taking meals in the refectory. As the rest of the English nobility tore itself apart during the civil wars that plagued the second half of the fifteenth century, deeply affecting his own family, Owen enjoyed a peaceful existence, rarely having reason to leave the confines of the abbey.

The names for the three children – Edmund, Jasper and Owen – were noticeably English, French and Welsh in origin, reflecting the diverse background of the family unit. Little is known of the fourth child, a daughter who likely died soon after her birth.[40] Though the children were descended from Welsh royalty on their father's side and the mighty House of Valois on their mother's, they had no English royal connections other than being half-siblings to the present king. At no moment in time could Katherine have entertained thoughts it would be through her eldest son with Owen, a boy with no English royal blood in his veins, rather than her only son with Henry V, that her descendants would see out the century on the throne of England.

In fact, on account of his Welsh birth, until May 1432 Owen had none of the rights of an Englishman, forbidden from any public office and prohibited from owning even the smallest strip of land. In the parliament which assembled that month in Westminster, Owen petitioned the Commons for exemption from the restrictive Penal Laws which placed him at an economic and professional disadvantage to his English colleagues, particularly now he had sons of his own who were likewise constrained. In return for swearing an oath to the crown and pledging to be the king's liegeman, on the opening day of parliament, 12 May, Owen was solemnly granted letters of denizenship. Henceforth, he was permitted to purchase property and land, though still barred from becoming a burgess, officer or minister in any city, borough or market town. This concession may indicate the marriage had become widely known among the regency council, and attempts were being made to minimise any legal difficulties further down the line. Welshmen had also been barred from marrying Englishwomen, and though the queen dowager was not of English birth herself, as the king's mother she was most certainly regarded as an English subject.[41]

Owen's new rights did allow Katherine to grant her Welsh husband custody of the Flintshire lands of the late John Conway two years later on 11 May 1434, to be held during the minority of the Conway heir and providing a modest source of income.[42] It is, however, otherwise difficult to glean any noteworthy insight into Katherine and Owen's personal life. We can only speculate whether relations between the pair were typically passionate or quarrelsome, or how they preferred to whittle away the hours. The number of children does at least hint that lack of intimacy was not an issue. Regarding childcare, noble mothers during the fifteenth century were not expected to handle the physical care of their children, which was entrusted to a select group of nurses and servants. Without the political demands and strict court formality that often interfered with her involvement in the upbringing of her eldest son, Henry VI, however, Katherine did at least have more flexibility when it came to raising her Tudor offspring.[43]

The remarkable union between a queen dowager of England and the audacious, perhaps even insolent, son of a Welsh rebel was not destined to survive into old age. In late 1436, during a debilitating winter in which a 'great, hard, biting frost' hit London, 'good Queen Katherine' left her husband and children behind and entered the Benedictine monastery of Bermondsey, despairingly seeking spiritual and medicinal respite from a lingering illness she lamented as a 'long, grievous malady, in the which I have been long, and yet am, troubled and vexed'.[44] A widespread shortage of wood and coal may have influenced her decision, the dearth of fuel for heat causing many deaths throughout December and beyond.

While at Bermondsey, on the south bank of the Thames opposite the Tower of London, Katherine received a new year's gift from her royal son of a 13-ounce tablet of gold on which stood a bejewelled crucifix of pearl and sapphire, sourced from a local Bermondsey goldsmith named John Pattesby.[45] Although the gift may have briefly raised her spirits, Katherine's illness was sufficiently troubling that she finalised her will the same day. Addressed to her 'full entirely beloved son', the king, in whom 'stands all my trust', much of her last testament was conventional for the period, concerned with ensuring all creditors were paid outstanding debts, that loyal servants were rewarded and that prayers were obtained for her soul. No explicit mention, however, was made of Katherine's second husband, Owen, nor the children they shared, except perhaps for the vague line directed at the young king which mentioned her hope he would oversee the 'tender and favourable fulfilling of mine intent'.

Appealing to Henry's 'full, high, wise, and noble discretion' to act in her favour, had Katherine made her son privately aware of an additional, unwritten, provision for his Tudor stepfather and half-brother?[46] It cannot be dismissed. Just two days later, on 3 January 1437, Katherine died at the age of just thirty-five.

After her interment in Westminster Abbey's Lady Chapel, Henry VI ordered an alabaster tomb erected to honour his mother's memory, on which was engraved a Latin epitaph celebrating Katherine, 'a perfect flower of modesty' who had been the 'joy of this land'. Like her will, the inscription made no reference to her family with Owen Tudor, regarding her as simply a 'maid and widow' of Henry V.[47] It would be surprising if her son, also named Owen and a monk within Westminster Abbey, did not pay regular private visits to the tomb of his mother in subsequent years.

After her grandson Henry VII came to the throne, Katherine's memorial was updated to reflect current affairs. A series of Latin verses were composed on a tablet which hung near where she was interred, and unlike the epitaph on her tomb these did make overt reference to Owen Tudor in the later passages:

> Of Owen Tudor after this
> The next Son Edmund was,
> Of Catharine, a renowned Prince,
> That did in Glory pass;
> Henry the Seventh, a Britain Pearl,
> A Gem of England's Joy,
> A Peerless Prince was Edmund's Son,
> A good and gracious Boy;
> Therefore a happy Wife this was,
> A happy Mother pure,
> Thrice happy Child, but Grandam she,
> More than thrice happy sure.[48]

Katherine's body was sadly not left to rest. In 1502, Henry VII ordered the old Lady Chapel pulled down and a far more ornate replacement constructed in its place, one that would not only serve as a royal sepulchre for himself and his descendants but also house the shrine of his uncle, and Katherine's son, Henry VI, who he hoped would be canonised in the near future. Katherine's coffin, which had lain undisturbed for sixty-five years, was removed during this process, with Henry VII leaving orders in his will that 'the body of our grand dame of right noble memory' should also be placed in a prominent spot within his new chapel. When the grand new Lady Chapel was completed early in the reign of Henry VIII, however, for reasons that are unclear, Katherine's dilapidated coffin was not reinterred as intended and remained in situ on the floor near the tomb of her first husband, Henry V, throughout the sixteenth-century reigns of her various Tudor descendants.[49]

In his 1598 *Survey of London*, a detailed topographical and historical tour of the city and its many buildings, the antiquarian John Stow remarked in an entry on Westminster that though Katherine's rotten coffin had been raised nearly a century earlier, she was 'never since buried, but remained above ground in a coffin of boards behind the east end of presbytery'.[50] Few people would have cast their eyes upon the partly visible remains before the dawn of the seventeenth century, but with renewed interest in the life of Henry V and his French queen as a result of Shakespeare's play *The Life of Henry the Fifth*, there was an upsurge in tourism to the abbey after 1600. On 23 February 1669, Samuel Pepys took his wife and daughters to the abbey for a private tour of the royal tombs, noting:

> Here we did see, by particular favour, the body of Queen Katherine of Valois; and I had the upper part of her body in my hands, and I did kiss her mouth, reflecting upon it that I did kiss a Queen, and that this was my birthday, thirty-six years old, that I did first kiss a Queen.[51]

This macabre event may not have been a solitary occurrence, with many other prominent society figures perhaps having direct access to Katherine's corpse through the years for the furtive exchange of a modest fee. Passing mentions of Katherine's visibility continued throughout the following century, though James Ralph was moved to write of the wooden chest of bones in 1734, 'I think nothing can be a greater violation of decency, or more injurious to the memory of such illustrious personages, than to expose their relics in so licentious a manner, and make a shew of what once commanded respect and adoration.'[52]

It was not until 1787, after Katherine's partially exposed remains had been above ground for 276 years and become a well-known curiosity for eighteenth-century antiquarians, that the former queen of England was belatedly reinterred into the Percy family vault beneath the Chapel of St Nicholas. Regrettably, in recent years her corpse had been subject to ghoulish vandalism by indecent scholars of the abbey school, who 'amused themselves with tearing it to pieces'.[53]

After Sir Gilbert Scott was appointed to oversee the maintenance and preservation of Westminster Abbey in 1849, it was his recommendation to the dean and chapter that Katherine was moved once more, this time to beneath the altar in the Chantry Chapel of her first husband, Henry V. Under the guidance of the dean, Arthur Stanley, the sympathetic movement of the wooden chest carrying what remained of the queen's bones was conducted in 1878. A new epitaph was erected, illustrating

Katherine's status as daughter of a French king and wife, and mother and grandmother of English kings, though again with no reference to her Welsh spouse.[54] She remains there to the present day, finally at rest.

Back in January 1437, Owen's emotional reaction to the death of his wife is unknowable, though with no suggestion the marriage was under any noticeable strain, it may be assumed he was grief-stricken by the early demise of a woman he had taken an extraordinary risk to marry. Now lacking her protection, he certainly seems to have developed a justified wariness regarding his welfare. According to the minutes of a privy council meeting held on 15 July 1437 in the chapel chamber at Kennington Palace, a royal residence south of the Thames in Surrey, not long after the death of Katherine the king requested Owen, 'the which dwelled with the said queen', to come to his presence. Owen, who had already decamped to Daventry in the Midlands en route to his native North Wales, refused to entertain such a notion unless the king could guarantee he was able to 'freely come and freely go'.[55]

When informed his request had been snubbed, Henry VI commanded his uncle the Duke of Gloucester to convey the king's guarantee Owen would be given a safe conduct, a message handled by the duke's retainer Miles Sculle. Owen heard out Sculle but, without the promise in writing, again refused the offer. Although he did head back towards London, rather than hastening to the king's presence as requested, he entered sanctuary at Westminster Abbey where he dwelled for 'many days'. Providing the dates of his sanctuary took place after 18 February, Owen may even have paid a poignant trip to the site of Katherine's recent interment, a belated goodbye that had been denied them when she retired in great pain to Bermondsey Abbey. He was surely granted an audience with his youngest son, who had been entrusted to the care of the monastery as a newborn a few years previously.

Owen was persuaded by 'diverse persons', out of 'friendship and fellowship', to leave sanctuary for a tavern, and though he brushed off such questionable offers, he did shortly thereafter finally come to the king's presence. Stood before his sovereign and stepson, Owen declared the reason for attendance, which is not revealed in the council minutes, adding he 'understood that the king was evilly informed of him'. Owen defiantly 'declared his innocence and his truth' to the king, affirming to all present that he had done nothing that should have caused Henry offence or displeasure. On the contrary, he professed himself the king's true liegeman before taking his leave as per the conditions of his safe conduct. Having appealed directly to the impressionable sixteen-year-old, Owen no doubt trusted that the matter was closed.

Shortly after this summit, however, Owen was arrested on the council's command and all his possessions seized. Valued at £137 10*s* 4*d*, these were not insignificant. Among the 'certain jewels and goods' turned over to the exchequer were a dozen gold cups, six silver salt cellars, a golden chalice, a silver jug, six silver cups made in Paris, four silver flagons, a pair of silver candlesticks, another handheld candlestick, two spice plates, four basins, two of which were decorated with roses and heraldic arms, and a silver pax bearing an image of St Christopher. It is unclear if Owen stood accused of theft, unlawfully seizing items which belonged to either Katherine's estate or the church, but they were later known to settle a crown debt to William Eastfield of London, one of the king's creditors and a recent Lord Mayor of London.[56] With his Welsh background and fears his presence in Wales could stimulate rebellion partly motivating his capture, Owen was thrown into Newgate jail, the oldest and most notorious prison in the capital.

It was Owen's imprisonment that provided the reason for the council's gathering on 15 July at Kennington, during which they sought to portray his seizure as lawful and not contrary to the safe conduct the king had extended to his stepfather earlier in the year. Among those present were Humphrey of Gloucester, the senior counsellor in rank; the bishop of Bath and Wells, then chancellor; the archbishop of York; the bishop of Lincoln; the earls of Stafford, Northumberland and Suffolk; the lords Hungerford, Tiptoft and Cromwell; plus William Lyndwood, Keeper of the Privy Seal, and William Phillip. In short, some of the most influential figures in the kingdom deliberated over Owen Tudor's fate, including his former master Walter Hungerford, who may have ventured some light defence of his erstwhile squire. The king himself was not present.

The council's judgement was that Owen's conduct in demanding surety from the king had been odious for one who claimed to be his liegeman, and as a safe conduct could not be used more than once, his imprisonment was therefore defensible to any who questioned its legality. Most importantly, the king's honour could not be challenged. At no stage during the council minutes, however, is the reason for Owen's original summons to appear before the king and council revealed, and though it is often assumed to have been connected to his relationship with Katherine it may have involved some other private matter unconnected to the queen dowager. Whatever the reasoning behind his sudden predicament, it is clear Owen had incurred the displeasure of some influential members of the council and, deprived of Katherine's protection, was vulnerable to their malice.

Confused, nervous and quite possibly aggrieved, myriad thoughts would have swirled through Owen's mind as he struggled to acclimatise to his daunting new surroundings. Life within the walls of Newgate was tough, cold and violent, with prisoners restricted to the same filthy clothes in which they entered for the duration of their stay, which could last more than a year before they were tried. The water was contaminated, the air rancid, the keepers cruel and corrupt, and starvation and disease were rife among the overcrowded inmates. Conditions were so terrible that many Londoners left bequests for the prison's repair, including three-times mayor and later folk hero Richard Whittington, and following decades of public outcry demanding its overhaul, Newgate was pulled down and rebuilt between 1423 and 1431. Little had changed, however, and the prison that received Owen in 1437 remained one of the most forbidding places in which to languish.[57]

Owen's faith in justice when brought back before the regency council was non-existent. Aided by a priest who was later found to have the significant sum of £89 on his person,[58] in early 1438 Owen successfully broke out of Newgate, grievously wounding his keeper in the process.[59] A prisoner of utmost importance to the council, the search for Owen was energetic and by 24 March it was reported he was in the custody of John Beaumont, 6th Baron Beaumont, a figure of rising influence in the king's household, who was rewarded twenty marks. Though they had failed to prevent the escape, royal pardons were issued to a pair of sheriffs, William Hales and William Chapman, for Owen's flight; it was accepted it had been accomplished 'deceitfully and subtly'.[60]

Owen's dramatic escape and the commotion regarding his recapture likely drew the attention of Henry VI, perhaps inquisitive about his stepfather's fortunes, or lack thereof. Around this juncture, Owen was transferred out of Newgate and into the custody of William de la Pole, 4th Earl of Suffolk, at Wallingford Castle in Berkshire. Owen may have known Wallingford intimately, for this royal fortress had most recently been part of Katherine of Valois's dower – if he had visited here once as her partner, he did so now as a prisoner. Shortly thereafter, Owen was on the move again, this time handed over to Walter Hungerford, the constable of Windsor, who was ordered on 14 July 1438 to receive his former squire and 'keep him in custody' until further instructed.[61] Windsor was another location with deep connections to Katherine – it was here, seventeen years earlier, she had given birth to the king.[62]

Owen's tenure at Windsor had lasted almost exactly a year when, on 15 July 1439, incidentally two years to the day since the council met to discuss his arrest, an order was passed down to Sir Thomas Stanley to allow Owen to 'go at large'. The cost of freedom was not insignificant; a mainprise of £2,000 was paid into the exchequer, with an added provision that Owen would appear before the king and council on 12 November to answer anything 'what shall be laid before him'. In the meantime, Owen was commanded to maintain 'good behaviour' and not to enter any part of his native Wales, the March, or even border counties like Shropshire, Herefordshire, Gloucestershire and Cheshire. Once again, the royal administration felt compelled to account for Owen's family background and was nervous about the prospect of fresh Welsh insurrection.[63] Just three years earlier, an English poet implored his countrymen to 'beware of Wales, Christ Jesus must us keep, that it make not our child's child to weep'.[64] The spectre of Glyn Dŵr haunted the House of Lancaster.

Owen adhered rigidly to the conditions of his release, for on 13 November 1439 at Kempton Manor in Surrey he was granted a 'general pardon' of all offences, and the mainprise itself was cancelled on 1 January 1440.[65] It had been a gruelling three years since Katherine's death, but from the outset of 1440, Owen Tudor was judicially regarded a free man. The deciding factor in his release was almost certainly Henry VI voicing his preference to have his mother's husband acquitted of any wrongdoing; once he did so, no figure on the regency council, even his uncle Gloucester, could continue to pursue Owen without incurring the royal wrath once the king attained his majority.

As Owen neared his fifth decade, he walked wearily away from the strains of the previous years, which had been chiefly spent courting, then concealing, a relationship with a queen dowager whose untimely demise left their children motherless and placed him at the mercy of hostile enemies at court. The years 1437 and 1439 had been particularly demanding, with a series of desperate imprisonments taking their toll on Owen's mental and physical wellbeing. As Robin Ddu later lamented, Owen had been 'neither a thief nor a robber, neither debtor nor traitor', but rather merely 'the victim of unrighteous wrath' in that 'his only fault was to have won the affections of a princess of France'.[66]

His freedom hard-won and his spirit subdued, Owen retreated into the shadows, maintaining a low profile to grieve for his wife in private. For the two boys removed from his care, however, a new life beckoned, one far removed from that experienced by their father. At the start of the fifteenth century, the family had fought to their near-demise a bitter war with the House of Lancaster, Owen's father Maredudd and uncles Rhys and Gwilym ap Tudur forfeiting their inheritance and forcing his migration to England as a youth. Through a potent mixture of personal charisma, self-confidence and an ability to seize opportunities, Owen had shed the stain of rebellion that ran through his veins to share the bed of the king of England's mother. In the dramatic annals of English and Welsh history, his story stands apart.

That story had not reached its terminus. Scarcely two decades since the end of the brutal war which had been waged across Wales, Owen's sons, half-Welsh and half-French by blood, were not only raised as members of the English nobility but embraced into the beating heart of the Lancastrian royal family by their half-brother Henry VI, King of England. The wheel of fortune had turned rapidly for Edmund and Jasper Tudor, and its unpredictable revolutions had yet to cease.

7

The King's Uterine Brothers

For any two boys in mid-fifteenth-century England whose mother had died and whose father was in prison, the outlook would have been bleak. Worse still if that mother was a recent immigrant with no other family of her own in the land, and the father descended from a tribe of rebels and forced to flee his homeland as a youth. Fortunately for young Edmund of Hadham and Jasper of Hatfield, the stranded sons of Katherine of Valois and Owen Tudor in need of a saviour, there was one crucial factor in their favour – their half-brother, their only close relation in England and sole kin of note, happened to be the king.

Though Owen Tudor was not in favour with the council in the summer of 1437, languishing in his cell in Newgate and awaiting his fate with trepidation, his offspring were destined for a different path. Rather than being abandoned, Edmund and Jasper, still no more than seven years of age, were taken into the care of Katherine de la Pole, the abbess of Barking, almost certainly at the insistence of the compassionate sixteen-year-old king. Orphaned with no brothers and sisters save for the Tudor offspring of his mother's second marriage, Henry VI is likely to have requested his half-siblings were taken care of, and as one of the king's rising confidants and a member of the royal council closely acquainted with the sensitive matter, William de la Pole, 4th Earl of Suffolk, arranged for his sister to receive and raise the boys at Barking. When Owen was later moved into Suffolk's custody at Wallingford, he may have been privy to regular updates on his sons' welfare, heartening snippets which helped lessen the burden of his predicament. The youngest of the Tudor children, meanwhile, named after his father, remained under the care of the monks at Westminster.

Barking in the fifteenth century was a rural outpost around a day's travel from the bustling city of London, in the centre of which was the well-endowed, richly furnished and royally founded Benedictine abbey.

To the north and east were extensive woodland, to the west the River Roding, and to the south flat floodplains that stretched out towards the mighty Thames as it surged towards its estuary and out into the sea. Founded in the seventh century for St Ethelburga, and accommodating an array of widowed noblewomen and daughters from aristocratic or upper gentry backgrounds who had chosen to dedicate their lives to charity and prayer, the abbey had grown into the most significant female monastic house of the age. Four abbesses of note had been royal ladies named Matilda or Maud, namely the queens of Henry I and Stephen and the daughters of Henry II and John. Barking, by any measure, was politically, religiously and royally important. That the Tudors had been sent there was a statement.[1]

As abbess of Barking, Katherine de la Pole held precedence over all others in England. Of good reputation and high social status, she was regarded an appropriate guardian for two boys closely connected to, if not descended from, the ruling house of England. Katherine oversaw more than 1,000 acres of land with manors under her jurisdiction spread across England; she was one of just four abbesses endowed with a landed and financial responsibility on par with an English baron.[2]

When the boys entered the vibrant abbey courtyard on 27 July 1437, the Welsh aspects of their name were butchered by confused English clerks, just as their father's had been in recent years. Edmund was registered as Edmond ap Meredith ap Tydier and his brother as Jasper ap Meredyth ap Tydier, rather than the correct Edmund and Jasper ap Owen ap Meredith, their father's name having been omitted.[3] Like Owen, however, they would be regarded by history, if not their contemporaries, simply as Edmund and Jasper Tudor.

Life at Barking was certainly not dire for the Tudor boys, despite the strict religious aspect of growing up in a Benedictine abbey. Though aged around seven and six respectively when they entered Abbess Katherine's care, Edmund and Jasper benefited from the abbey's well-stocked library, with religious and secular texts distributed for the education and enjoyment of residents, likely read to them by the nuns. The diet was varied and rich, with beef enjoyed three times a week except during advent and lent, and pork, mutton, chicken, geese, fish and eels regularly available. Bread, ale, oatmeal, butter, milk, eggs and spiced pies were also frequently on the menu.[4]

The surrounding gardens and outbuildings provided ample opportunity for youthful exploration, and the constant stream of pilgrims and visitors brought an exciting array of people. The year 1437 had been traumatic for Edmund and Jasper, their mother leaving while sick and not returning and their father being cast into prison. Barking Abbey had a long tradition of caring for the children of noble patrons, and under the guidance of the abbess the Tudor boys were provided a stable and protective environment to flourish, sheltered from the malicious gossip and cruel judgement of court.

Half-brothers of the king, the Tudors' care proved a strain on the abbey finances, though the abbess never wavered in her duty. It was expected the abbey would cover, to a noble standard, the education, entertainment, clothing and lodging of Edmund, Jasper and their attendants, which cost a not inconsiderable 13s 4d a week. On 16 July 1440,[5] Katherine was granted a payment of £50, but had to regularly write to the king and his council for further reimbursement; on 5 November that year, her petitions were finally heard when a warrant was made to grant the abbess an overdue payment of £53 12s for the Tudors' upkeep, though the money would not materialise until July 1443, three years later.[6] This was not a slight on the king's feelings towards his siblings, but rather symptomatic of a cash-strapped crown.

Henry VI was a well-educated and pious youth who prized the literary arts and religious learning, and there is little doubt he intended for his brothers to follow suit. According to the work of John Blacman, a spiritual advisor of the 'chaste and pure' king, during the Tudors' youth they were provided 'most strict and safe guardianship', overseen by 'virtuous and worthy priests, both for teaching and for right living and conversation, lest the untamed practices of youth should grow rank if they lacked any to prune them'. It was hoped by Henry such stern tutoring would encourage Edmund and Jasper to 'eschew vice and talk of the vicious and dissolute', but rather follow the king's example and 'lay hold on virtue'.[7] At Barking, the Tudors observed, if not partook in, all religious rituals during their five years at the abbey, including the many plays and festivals which punctuated the liturgical calendar. There may even have been plans the brothers would, in time, join the monastery themselves. They almost certainly were raised to understand the basics of Latin and French as well as their native English, perhaps in addition to the smattering of Welsh they may have picked up from their father.

In February 1443, another warrant of £55 13s 4d was sent to the exchequer, covering the Tudors' expenses for sixteen months up to 6 March 1442.[8] As this is the final payment for their upkeep, it is likely that, after five years in Barking, in the spring of 1442 the boys left the abbey, though the circumstances behind their removal are unknown. Aged around twelve and eleven, there are no known references to Edmund and Jasper around this period, and in fact for the next decade their whereabouts are untraceable in the chancery rolls and chronicles. They likely disappeared into the swollen ranks of the royal household, continuing their education away from notice, though it is also possible they were reunited with their father Owen, now pardoned and free to take care of his sons. In fact, Owen was steadily rehabilitating his reputation. On 19 May 1441, he witnessed a charter made between Robert Banastre and Humphrey, Duke of Gloucester, and on 25 August 1442 was one of five men granted a share in some land in the parish of St Mary Newington, Lambeth.[9] On 20 October 1442, meanwhile, King Henry granted his stepfather £40 in cash, with three more instalments of £40 paid to his 'well-beloved squire' on 12 February, 20 July and 18 September 1444.[10]

In November 1444, a party crossed to France tasked with escorting King Henry's new French bride, Margaret of Anjou, back to England, and among those listed were an 'Owen ap Maredudd'. As Owen Tudor was later reimbursed £18 4s by the chancellor for expenses incurred during his service to the new queen, this is almost certainly indicative of his presence in France.[11]

The king's wedding proved controversial even as it was negotiated, and in later years it would become a significant contributing factor in the bitter division which tore England apart for a generation. By the mid-1440s, the extraordinary political and military achievements of Henry V in France a generation earlier were a distant memory. Financially unable to withstand a dogged French resurgence under Henry VI's maternal uncle, now widely recognised among his countrymen as Charles VII, the prevailing mood around the English court was despair. Buoyed by the emergence of Joan of Arc, Charles had united the once-divided French nobility behind his cause and was able to recapture Reims in 1429 and Paris in 1436, before turning his attentions towards the steady recapture of Normandy and the ultimate expulsion of the English invader from France once and for all. Though the principal players may not have appreciated it at the time, the Hundred Years War, as this series of Anglo-French wars became known, had turned a decisive corner.

The pursuit of peace with Charles VII was the English government's favoured policy, Henry VI's military aptitude paling in comparison with that of his forebears, though his steadfast insistence on retaining his French title had proven a stumbling block in negotiations. A marriage between the English king and a French princess was proposed as a compromise, and the bride put forward was Margaret, the fourteen-year-old daughter of René, Duke of Anjou and titular king of Sicily, Naples, Hungary and Jerusalem. It was an impressive array of titles, but in truth, René held little land and had limited funds; the principal appeal of Margaret stemmed from her status as a niece by marriage of Charles VII and the hope this would increase chances of a truce between the warring kingdoms. To her new husband, Margaret represented peace and, it was anticipated, a fruitful future for the House of Lancaster in more ways than merely financial.

Margaret was formally betrothed to Henry by proxy in May 1444, and on 13 November that year a considerable embassy departed England to accompany the future queen of England to her new home. Leading the expedition was chief negotiator William de la Pole, recently raised to the rank of Marquess of Suffolk, along with seventy ships carrying five barons, seventeen knights, sixty-five esquires – likely including Owen Tudor – and 215 yeomen. Suffolk's embassy spent the winter in France finalising the treaty until, in early spring, Margaret was handed over to the 300-strong English entourage at Pontoise on the road between Paris and Rouen, where she was met by Richard, 3rd Duke of York. Margaret was taken to Harfleur and boarded the *Cock John*, sailing for Portchester on the English south coast. Incidentally, this was the same port from which Owen's grandson would set forth exactly fifty years later in his own quest to claim a crown.

How much of Margaret's journey to England was attended by Owen is unknown. He may even have been present for her marriage to Henry at Titchfield Abbey on 23 April 1445, or part of the entourage that escorted her into a teeming London at the end of May for her coronation, his sons Edmund and Jasper perhaps among the excitable crowds hoping to catch a glimpse of their new queen. The brothers were around the same age as the nervous fifteen-year-old Margaret, and again may also have been inside Westminster Abbey on 30 May to watch her coronation from the wings.[12] Jasper, in particular, could not have appreciated just how closely he would come to be aligned with the slight teenager holding the city's attention that mild spring day. The boys might have been regaled with tales from their elders of the last time a Frenchwoman was crowned queen of England – their mother, Katherine, a quarter-century previously.

With further references to an Owen Meredith forming part of the royal household between 1444 and 1453, it is reasonable to suggest the king's stepfather was employed around the court during this period, Henry perhaps honouring his mother's final wishes to safeguard her second husband's professional and personal wellbeing.[13] On 1 March 1459, Owen was one of four men, including his son Jasper, commissioned to bring before the king or council seven political dissenters. On 19 December that year he was granted a lifetime annuity of £100 from the confiscated Kent, Sussex and Warwickshire estates of John Clinton, 5th Baron Clinton. On 5 February 1460, meanwhile, Owen was granted for life the office of parker of some of the royal parks in Denbighshire, to hold either by himself or through his deputies, close to the ancestral heartlands of Ednyfed Fychan.[14] Henry VI was a compassionate young man minded to be merciful to those who had transgressed, and it isn't difficult to imagine that once he became personally acquainted with Owen he extended a warmth towards the man who had shown his mother love in the last years of her life.

As King Henry's half-brothers, however, Edmund and Jasper Tudor were destined for greater heights than an obscure role around the royal household and the occasional modest grant. Considering their upbringing at Barking Abbey and the king's deep piety, it is unclear if Henry had originally intended his half-brothers enter the church once their education had been completed, but by the early 1450s the king's political, economic, military and dynastic woes merited their summoning to his side to assume a far more visible and secular role. Closest in blood to the king, the Tudor boys' unlikely, and ill-prepared, catapulting to the forefront of the royal family came at a critical juncture for the House of Lancaster.

The king's marriage to Margaret of Anjou had thus far failed on two fronts – after several years together, no heir had been born, and the war with France had resumed to England's heavy financial and territorial cost. The capitulation of Normandy between 1449 and 1450 was a particularly damning indictment of Henry's inept government, and the alarming decline in English fortunes in France showed no sign of abating in the coming years, provoking vicious recriminations against the king's collection of royal favourites, widely chastised for providing deplorable counsel.

Foremost among those held responsible were William de la Pole, 1st Duke of Suffolk, and Edmund Beaufort, Count of Mortain and Earl of Dorset before he was raised to the dukedom of Somerset in 1448. Both men owed their prosperity and political pre-eminence to the king's generosity, and, acquisitive of titles, lands and offices in a period of military and economic turmoil, they developed many enemies among lords and commons alike. Queen Margaret was also the subject of growing hostility, suspected of unduly influencing her husband in matters relating to the French war prejudicial to English interests. For example, it was through the terms of her marriage, arranged by Suffolk, that England ceded Maine to Margaret's father, a deeply unpopular move.

The loss of Normandy had proven deadly for Suffolk, the king's foremost advisor and Owen Tudor's onetime jailor. When parliament convened in November 1449, there was widespread clamour for the duke's destruction, and during the Christmas break tensions manifested themselves violently when his adherent Adam Moleyns, Bishop of Chichester and until recently Lord Privy Seal, was murdered in Portsmouth by disgruntled sailors. Suffolk was unable to fend off accusations of 'heinous and horrible treasons', which included a charge he intended to claim the throne through the pedigree of Margaret Beaufort, the young heiress and great-granddaughter of Edward III he had betrothed to his young son, John. Suffolk was condemned to death but the king intervened to reduce the sentence to a five-year banishment, a deep dissatisfaction to the duke's enemies.[15] When Suffolk departed England, his ship was intercepted by another vessel and he was subjected to a mock trial. On 3 May 1450, the disgraced duke's head was stuck from his body using a rusty sword. It is unknown who perpetrated the bloody deed, but the outcome appeased many in England, including some among the nobility.[16]

It was Edmund Beaufort, 2nd Duke of Somerset, meanwhile, who stepped into the void Suffolk left, becoming both the most powerful magnate in the kingdom and the new focus of discontent for the government's critics across the social ranks. In May 1450, a rebellion rose in Kent under the shadowy figure of Jack Cade, his numbers swelled by disgruntled soldiers returning from Normandy and growing further as they marched on London. The revolt spread through southern England, and among those slaughtered were William Ayscough, Bishop of Salisbury and the royal confessor who had married the king to Margaret of Anjou, and James Fiennes, Baron Saye and Sele and Lord Treasurer. Cade held many grievances, but they were chiefly centred around the 'insatiable, covetous, malicious' persons surrounding the king, who had been stripped of his dignity and his wealth. They intended to replace the king's 'false progeny and affinity' with other figures, most notably Richard, 3rd Duke of York.[17]

Though Cade's revolt was ultimately suppressed, the leader cornered and stabbed while resisting capture, the rebels' message retained its potency in the following years. The principal consequence of this episode was the return to frontline politics of Richard of York, untarnished by recent losses in France. York was the greatest landowner in the kingdom, and since Humphrey of Gloucester's death in 1447 arguably next in line to the throne, boasting descent from two of Edward III's sons. It hadn't escaped anyone's attention that Jack Cade employed the alias Mortimer, a pointed allusion to York's maternal ancestors whose claim had been swept aside during the Lancastrian usurpation in 1399. York positioned himself as a populist reformer who could re-establish good governance, restore law and order, and return financial probity to the crown while eradicating corruption and incompetence from the king's court. This placed him in direct opposition to Somerset, who 'ever prevaileth and ruleth about the King's person', and a deeply personal feud developed between the two royal dukes that divided the court into two camps.[18]

Confident that there were grounds to forcibly remove Somerset from power, and frustrated his calls for reform had so far been snubbed, in March 1452 York assembled his supporters and marched on London. He was intercepted at Dartford by a royal army, and a skirmish was only avoided when Henry VI extended a promise he would consider York's articles for reform. The offer was not made in good faith, and Somerset remained at the king's side throughout the remainder of the year, continuing to wield 'great rule' over him.[19]

It was in this tense environment, with accusations of royal misgovernment gathering pace and positions hardening on both sides of the political divide, that the Tudor brothers made their debut at court.

The recent challenges to the Lancastrian leadership, together with the depleted state of the royal family, necessitated Henry's summoning of his half-siblings to his side, starting with their ennoblement in the autumn of 1452. On 23 November in Reading, just nine months since the standoff with Richard of York at Dartford, the king inducted Edmund Tudor into the peerage, issuing letters patent he had created his half-brother the earl of Richmond, having likely recently reached twenty-one years of age. The king further declared that Edmund would hold precedence over all other magnates and laymen of the realm save for those holding dukedoms, which at the time were five: York, Norfolk, Exeter, Buckingham and Somerset. Though he is not mentioned on the Charter Roll, Jasper was also likely created the earl of Pembroke at the same time.[20]

The titles themselves were significant; the earldom of Richmond was created in 1071 by William the Conqueror to reward his Breton ally and cousin Alan Rufus, responsible for erecting in the centre of his new lands an imposing fortress designed to cow the local populace. The earldom was typically held by members of the Breton nobility across the next few centuries, though it had recently become associated with the House of Lancaster; Henry VI's great-grandfather John of Gaunt, 1st Duke of Lancaster, and uncle John, 1st Duke of Bedford, both held the title during their lifetimes. The earldom of Pembroke, meanwhile, was first created in 1138 by King Stephen for Gilbert de Clare, passing through the distinguished Marshal, de Valence and Hastings families until it was granted to Henry VI's other uncle, Humphrey, 1st Duke of Gloucester, between 1414 and his death in 1447. The gift of these prestigious earldoms was a clear indication of the Tudors' new status as celebrated members of the Lancastrian royal family. Notably, this also made them the first Welshmen, albeit English-born, to be inducted into the peerage of England.

The solemn investiture ceremony was scheduled to take place during the height of the Epiphany celebrations that marked an end to the year's Christmas festivities, providing maximum exposure for the Tudors' ennoblement before the entire court. Both were provided new wardrobes, packed with a variety of velvets, furs, and cloth of gold, as well as other trappings including a selection of equestrian equipment including spurs and a harness. They no doubt received quiet instruction as to what the ritual involved, and the expected role they would assume at the heart of the royal household.

On 5 January 1453, Twelfth Night, Edmund and Jasper were brought to the Tower of London where that evening they kneeled before the king and were dubbed on each shoulder with the flat side of a sword, a ceremonial rite of passage that conferred upon them the rank of knight.[21] Typically, the process of becoming a knight started in childhood, when children began learning the basics of chivalry as a page, before becoming a squire around fourteen, serving a thorough military apprenticeship under a knight. If considered a worthy candidate, from the age of twenty-one squires could be dubbed knights, binding themselves to a lord and providing military service and support where necessary. The Tudors, through their connection to the king, appear to have bypassed much of this process. Kneeling beside them for the same honour was William Herbert of Raglan, a Welshman of growing repute who would become a pugnacious foe of the Tudors across the next two decades.[22]

The following day was the Feast of the Epiphany, an elaborate celebration of the Three Wise Men's visit to the Baby Christ, and one of the most important days in the liturgical calendar. Once all religious observances had been completed, Edmund and Jasper were summoned to the king's presence once more. King Henry was handed a pair of sword belts and carefully fastened them around his half-brothers' waists. It was a personal moment between the siblings, and a degree of hushed conversation surely broke some of the solemnity. Having symbolically invested the Tudors with the dignity of earls, the act of their creation was also read aloud before the assembled lords, reiterating once again, and publicly before their peers, the titles and honours they now held.[23]

The final stage in the brothers' ennoblement was their maiden appearance in parliament, which occurred on 6 March in Reading Abbey. During the proceedings, the Commons presented a petition imploring the king to formally recognise Edmund and Jasper as his legitimate siblings born of the same mother, or the king's 'uterine brothers'. The petition pointedly noted the Tudors were the product of lawful matrimony, an acceptance that any marriage between Owen Tudor and Katherine of Valois was regarded in the corridors of power as above reproach. The petition further requested the king release his half-brothers from any statutory impediments that remained on account of their ancestors on both sides not being English, though no specific reference is made to Owen himself.

Henry gladly granted his assent to the request, openly accepting Edmund and Jasper as his legitimate brothers and confirming their titles. The king added this was of his own free will and not at the insistence of others, perhaps an acknowledgement of criticism he was in thrall to certain advisors. Henry took full responsibility for the Tudors' rise.[24]

To mark their induction into the peerage, the brothers were granted new coats of arms reflecting their kinship to Henry VI and emphasising their membership of the royal family. Both Edmund and Jasper were granted use of the quartered royal arms of England and France as borne by the Lancastrian kings, but enclosed within a solid blue border. Edmund's was distinguished from his brother's by employing alternating golden martlets and fleurs-de-lis in the border, while Jasper's arms bore martlets alone.[25]

The fleurs-de-lis on Edmund's arms were a clear tribute to his French mother, Katherine of Valois, but the reason behind the martlets that appeared on both brothers' arms is more difficult to ascertain. A mythical bird without feet said to never roost, the martlet represented relentless perseverance, and could have alluded to Owen Tudor's journey from son of a Welsh rebel to husband of a queen and then father of earls. Martlets had also been borne on the arms of the de Valence and Hastings earls of Pembroke in the thirteenth and fourteenth centuries, though this doesn't explain Edmund's usage of them on his arms as earl of Richmond. His son would, however, go on to be referred to as *cyw'r wennol*, or young of the swallow, in later prophetic poetry, a swallow being another name for the martlet.[26]

The granting of the royal arms to the king's half-brothers does seem unusual, but there was precedent for this; Richard II granted his elder half-siblings John and Thomas Holland use of the royal arms in the late fourteenth century, though, like the Tudors, differentiated with a border. From 1452 onwards, the Tudors may not have been of English royal blood themselves but, as their new arms broadcast to the world, they occupied a conspicuous role at the forefront of the royal family. Their father Owen, meanwhile, presumably retained the arms of Ednyfed Fychan with pride.

With the titles of Richmond and Pembroke came a generous landed endowment that instantly turned Edmund and Jasper into prosperous young men. Between 24 November 1452 and 24 July 1453, a series of grants transformed the brothers' fortunes and allowed them to sustain the high estate now expected of them, the gifts coming to a halt only when their royal benefactor fell into a catatonic stupor in August 1453.

With the earldom of Richmond, Edmund also received two-thirds of the separate honour of Richmond, one of the most important and extensive feudal baronies in England, with a reversion of the final third after the death of the dowager duchess of Bedford. The honour comprised many prosperous holdings spanning the breadth of northern and eastern England; though heavily concentrated in northern Yorkshire and around the stronghold of Richmond itself, it included the rugged lordships of Kendal in Westmorland and Wyresdale in Lancashire, the fertile Lincolnshire manors of Frampton and Wykes along with seventy-five tenements in the bountiful staple town of Boston, the manors of Bassingbourne and the bailiwick of Babraham in Cambridgeshire, and the manor and lordship of Swaffham in Norfolk.[27]

Aside from the honour of Richmond, on 30 March 1453, Edmund was granted Baynard's Castle in the centre of London, a grand townhouse near Paul's Wharf that overlooked the Thames and which had most recently been extensively rebuilt and enjoyed by Humphrey of Gloucester. Despite its imposing curtain walls, the house was one of the finest noble residences in the city; boasting several courtyards, a striking great hall and a series of lush gardens, it was more a palace than a castle. That same day, Edmund also received the lordship and castle of Hadleigh in Essex, a favoured residence of Edward III, and the office of master of the royal hunting forest of Bradon in Wiltshire. A week later, he also assumed possession of the lordship and manors of Atherstone in Warwickshire and Ludgershall in Wiltshire, followed by Frodsham in Cheshire.[28]

Jasper, meanwhile, was the beneficiary of a more geographically homogenous series of estates, chiefly based in West Wales. His new seat was in the heart of Pembroke itself, a formidable Marcher fortress erected upon a rocky promontory dominated by an early thirteenth-century cylindrical stone keep, five stories high, that had once been integral in safeguarding the Anglo-Norman position in Wales. The lands associated with the earldom spread out in every direction from Pembroke, encompassing the lordships of Castlemartin, St Florence, Tenby, Rhos and Milford, added to which were the castle and lordship of Cilgerran plus the settlements of Ystlwyf, Trane Clinton and St Clears.[29]

Beyond Pembrokeshire, Jasper was granted the lordship of Llansteffan in Carmarthenshire, the manors of Cloigyn and Pibwr across the Tywi estuary in Kidwelly, and the lordship of Aber in Caernarfonshire. One notable, even touching, grant made to Jasper from his royal half-brother was the castle and lordship of Caldicot, which between 1422 and her death in 1437 had formed part of their mother Katherine's dowry.[30] While many of his paternal forebears had actively mobilised against Anglo-Norman Marcher lords during the thirteenth and fourteenth centuries, Jasper was himself now one of the principal Marcher lords in Wales, charged with upholding royal authority in the south-west. In England, meanwhile, he was given all the manors, lordships and castles which had been stripped from William Oldhall, Speaker of the Commons, who had been attainted for treason, plus the manors of Whitley and Worplesdon in Surrey, the manor of Kingsthorpe in Northamptonshire and Pollestedhall in Norfolk.[31]

The brothers were also granted further lands and manors to be held jointly, further swelling their already respectable revenues. On 1 May 1453, they were together granted the manor and lordship of Hyde in Hertfordshire, an estate that comprised 100 acres of land, 2 acres of meadow and 20 acres of wood, as well as the lordship of Bonby in northern Lincolnshire. On 1 July, they received the manors of Solihull and Sheldon in Warwickshire, and three days later were handed control of the castles and lordships of Horston and Bolsover in Derbyshire and the manors of Mansfield, Linby and Clipstone in Nottinghamshire. On 24 July, they added Magor in South-East Wales to their extensive, kingdom-wide portfolio.[32]

All taken together, Edmund and Jasper could expect an annual income each of at least £925 from their assorted lands, which was half what the dukes of York and Buckingham could command but still placed the earls high in any ranking of the richest men in the kingdom. Considering the crown's financial woes, it represented a remarkable concession from the king, and reveals some of the depth of feeling Henry had for his younger half-siblings.[33] With no claim to the throne themselves, or independent power outside the crown, such royal favour also brought utter loyalty, which was no doubt a consideration.

One of the most noteworthy grants the Tudor brothers received from the king, however, and one with extraordinary long-term consequences, was the joint custody of the wealthy heiress Margaret Beaufort. The Beaufort family owed their origins to an extramarital affair conducted throughout the 1370s between Edward III's son John of Gaunt, Duke of Lancaster, and his mistress Katherine Swynford. The four children born out of wedlock to Gaunt and Swynford were retrospectively legitimised in 1396, and thereafter they rose high in court circles, particularly once their elder half-brother usurped the throne three years later as Henry IV.

After the stain of illegitimacy was formally removed by parliament, the first generation of Beauforts proved remarkably competent members of the nobility during the first half of the fifteenth century, producing an earl, a cardinal, a duke and a countess who offered vital military, political and financial support to the fledgling House of Lancaster. The second generation initially flourished under the reign of their cousin Henry VI, though a series of deeply humiliating military and administrative failures in France tarnished the family reputation during the 1440s. Margaret's father, John Beaufort, 1st Duke of Somerset, was haunted by his disappointments and died in disgrace in 1444, leaving behind his one-year-old daughter as the sole heir to his estates. The ducal title passed to John's brother Edmund Beaufort, who as a young man had been rumoured to be romantically involved with Katherine of Valois and later occupied a highly contentious role in the king's highly unpopular government. Though the Beauforts had to rely on royal patronage to prosper, like the Tudors, they nevertheless remained close to the throne in both blood and favour and were an influential force to be reckoned with in fifteenth-century English politics.

Even at ten years old, the wardship of Margaret Beaufort was a highly sought-after prize. She was, after all, not just wealthy in inheritance – her lands were estimated to be worth around £1,000 a year, greater than either of the Tudors – but a legitimised great-granddaughter of Edward III.[34] During the Beauforts' process of legitimisation, an Act of Parliament was passed which stipulated the family were not only 'begotten of royal blood' but entitled to acquire any estate, attain any office or inherit any title as though they had been born in 'lawful matrimony'.[35] Despite later confusion over whether they were barred from the throne itself, this particular act was never repealed by parliament and remained enshrined in the law of the land fifty years later, which only served to enhance Margaret's status.

In fact, her potential claim to the throne had already caused controversy. Just four days after her father's death in June 1444, Margaret's wardship, along with all her lands and possessions, had been granted to Henry VI's leading advisor, William de la Pole, then earl of Suffolk.[36] On 7 February 1450, Suffolk married the seven-year-old Margaret to his son and heir, John, later provoking accusations he had intended to steer his blood towards the throne by 'presuming and pretending her to be next inheritable to the crown'.[37] Despite Suffolk's murder just three months later following impeachment for his adjudged political and military failures, Margaret's marriage to John de la Pole went ahead. It was only annulled in February 1453 by the king, who had developed other plans for his Beaufort kinswoman.

On 24 March 1453, a month after hosting an audience with Margaret's mother, Margaret Beauchamp, in which he likely outlined his desire, Henry VI transferred the child's lucrative wardship to the Tudors, his 'uterine brothers'.[38] Aside from being named the beneficiaries of her vast landed inheritance, spread across twelve counties but largely centred in the English south-west, where they had no current interests of their own, like Suffolk before them Edmund and Jasper also received the rights to her hand in marriage.[39] Despite the age difference between Margaret and the brothers, fully grown men in their early twenties, there seems little prospect she was lined up to marry anyone other than either Edmund or Jasper in the near future.

Thirty-one years old and lacking an heir, and with all three of his uncles having died without issue, Henry VI's thoughts naturally turned towards matters of succession should he fail to father a son. There was no shortage of potential claimants; many of the nobility were able to boast some degree of descent from Edward III, including Margaret's uncle Edmund Beaufort, 2nd Duke of Somerset, Humphrey Stafford, 1st Duke of Buckingham, and Henry Holland, 3rd Duke of Exeter. Of greater concern to the king may have been the very plausible claim possessed by Richard, 3rd Duke of York, one of the government's most vocal opponents and so recently politically alienated.

The transfer of Margaret Beaufort's wardship to his brothers, then, may be seen as a tentative step by Henry VI towards creating an alternate line of succession, imbuing any Tudor offspring she had with legitimate English royal blood. However, as Queen Margaret was found to be pregnant in the same month, any long-term aspirations for a prospective Tudor–Beaufort succession were shelved.

By the spring of 1453, the Tudors were embarrassingly rich in titles, land and income, and assumed their lofty positions as the premier earls of the realm. Closest in blood to the king, at least until the heir was born, despite their inexperience they were being groomed by the Lancastrian leadership to play a pivotal role in the future governance of England, and to support and defend their royal half-brother's personal and political interests. For two descendants of Ednyfed Fychan, the 'Terror of England', it was a remarkable situation.

In April 1453, at least one of the Tudor brothers, and perhaps even both, accompanied Margaret of Anjou on her extensive progress of Norfolk, their service to the king also extending to the queen, their sister-in-law. In a letter to her husband John Paston, a prominent Norfolk landowner, Margaret Paston reported that the queen entered Norwich on 17 April in the company of 'the king's brother', with the pair staying in the city for two days. They were accompanied by Blake, the bailiff of Swaffham, which suggests that Edmund, recently created lord of Swaffham, was likely present and perhaps conducting a personal survey of his new holdings. The Norwich city records do provide evidence that both brothers were given a gift of £5 each by the city elders, so Margaret Paston may simply have not noticed both Tudors when they passed her by. The fact that neither Edmund nor Jasper were named in either record exposes their relative obscurity to the wider English public this early in their career – they had, for all intents and purposes, appeared from nowhere.[40]

As the summer of 1453 approached, there was cause for great optimism around the Lancastrian court, not least for the thriving Tudors. After a difficult few years that had witnessed the devastating loss of Normandy, the duke of Suffolk's disturbing execution, an alarming revolt under Jack Cade that brought bloodshed to the streets of London, and Richard of York's emergence as the popular and principal advocate of widespread governmental reform, the tide finally appeared to be turning for the beleaguered court party. Though the situation in France remained dire, the previous autumn the elderly John Talbot, 1st Earl of Shrewsbury, had retaken the city of Bordeaux and with it control of western Gascony, a chastened York was in retreat, stripped of his offices and with his political capital in ruins, and after eight years of marriage Margaret of Anjou was pregnant with, it was hoped, a long-awaited male heir. The crown was in the strongest position it had been for several years. As the king's closest adult relations, welcomed deep into his favour, Edmund and Jasper Tudor were on the cusp of promising careers at the heart of the royal family. But then, disaster struck the House of Lancaster.

On 17 July 1453, Castillon-sur-Dordogne, one of the last remaining English-held towns in Gascony, fell to Charles's army after Shrewsbury was lured into a trap. As the triumphant French swarmed through the Gascon countryside, the loss of Castillon left Bordeaux an isolated English outpost facing imminent capture. This devastating reverse stunned the English court, and the effect on the distraught king, resting at a hunting lodge near Clarendon Palace, was immense. The unwelcome news triggered a complete mental collapse in Henry, who according to one chronicler was 'indisposed suddenly', unresponsive to any attempt to rouse him from his catatonic state. It was, it appeared to onlookers, as though the inert king had been 'smitten with a frenzy', his 'wit and reason withdrawn'. He neither moved nor spoke, had no control of his limbs, and had to be waited upon day and night. No amount of remedies, including ointments, laxatives, head-purges, baths and bleedings, had an effect.[41]

King from the cradle, Henry VI had never been the most proactive of monarchs, preferring to empower a small group of favourites to administer the realm on his behalf. A medieval kingdom, however, required a functioning king to nominally oversee day-to-day governance, even one who was weak, pliant and patently unsuited to the role. Henry's collapse took the council by surprise, as well as the queen and his Tudur half-brothers. Aware of the constitutional uproar that would ensue once knowledge of the king's illness became widespread, Somerset, Margaret and the aged chancellor, Cardinal John Kemp, strove to conceal the truth, issuing commands in the witless Henry's name and giving the impression it was business as usual.

The repeated mental illnesses of Henry's French grandfather Charles VI had allowed conflict between rival court factions to spiral into a deeply destructive civil war, destabilising France to such an extent the English were able to exploit the resultant chaos. When Queen Margaret was safely delivered of a healthy prince on 13 October 1453, even news of his long-awaited heir failed to shake Henry out of his stupor.[42]

On 19 October, less than a week after the prince's birth, Bordeaux surrendered and brought to an ignominious end 300 years of English control over Gascony. Just thirty years on from the glorious Treaty of Troyes, the Lancastrian dynasty had been humiliatingly expelled from France, save for a thin strip of land around Calais. In a state of crippling national crisis, and against the will of Somerset and Queen Margaret, the frantic council took just five days to recall Richard of York to London. At a tense meeting held in the Star Chamber of Westminster Palace on 21 November 1453, twenty-five lords met to discuss the path forward, including the archbishops of Canterbury and York, the bishops of London, Winchester, Ely, Norwich, St David's, Chester, Lincoln and Carlisle, the dukes of Buckingham and York, and the earls of Salisbury, Warwick, Wiltshire, Shrewsbury and Worcester. As earl of Pembroke, Jasper Tudor was also listed as present, though his brother Edmund was not. York, as the 'king's true liegeman', declared he had returned upon receiving his summons, and intended to see to the 'welfare of the king and of his subjects'.[43]

Shortly thereafter, John Mowbray, 3rd Duke of Norfolk, an avowed ally of York and firm critic of the government in previous years, launched a remarkable attack against the duke of Somerset, demanding an investigation into his role in the loss of the noble duchies of Normandy and Gascony and accusing his target of offering bribes so that some turned their hearts from truth and justice. Without the king's protection, Somerset was vulnerable to his enemies' hostility and within days was sent to the Tower of London, ostensibly for his own protection. He would remain there for the next fourteen months, completely removed from power and nervously awaiting his fate.[44]

Jasper observed this tense, often uncomfortable, series of meetings with interest, and though there is no record of him taking any particular role in the febrile proceedings, it served as a thorough education in the perils of power during the mid-fifteenth century. Just months earlier, Somerset's position at the king's right hand appeared unassailable, his adversaries' complaints about his competence nonchalantly dismissed. Now, before the year was out, Somerset was in the Tower, his critics primed to seize control of the council and with it governance of England. Aged roughly twenty-two, the inexperienced and youthful Jasper listened from the wings, and he learned a lesson about the capricious nature of court politics that would hold him in good stead in coming years.

On 6 December 1453, another, more intimate, council meeting of ten people took place to discuss the parlous state of the king's finances, for which Jasper was again present. The meeting was chaired by Richard of York and was filled with the duke's supporters, including the earls of Warwick and Worcester, and the viscount Bourchier. That Jasper was present indicates that York was keen to extend the hand of friendship across the divide and had determined that the support of the king's younger half-brother would be vital in lending credibility to his calls for reform of the royal household.[45]

After the Christmas break, Jasper continued to be associated with York, indicating his political, and perhaps even personal, sympathy indeed lay with the duke. Edmund's outlook at this critical juncture is harder to determine, his presence around court business less discernible than his younger brother's, but by the end of January 1454 both siblings were reported as part of York's 'goodly fellowship' when the duke arrived in London for the forthcoming parliamentary session. The Tudors' apparent friendliness towards York risked their falling foul of Queen Margaret, who was far more distrustful of the duke's ambitions than her brothers-in-law. After failing to rouse the king by showing him their child, Margaret launched a desperate bid that month to retake control of the government. She presented the council five articles she expected them to pass, 'whereof the first is that she desires to have the whole rule of this land'.[46] Her confidence was misplaced, and unsurprisingly she was politely, if firmly, rebuffed. Unlike Margaret's native France, fifteenth-century England was not ready for a female ruler, even if only in a temporary capacity.

During the heated parliamentary session which sat between February and April 1454, there was much crucial business to discuss, not least the king's continued incapacity. On 13 February, York, with the council's assent, was given limited rights to reopen and preside over parliament in the king's name, but many elected to stay away from Westminster to avoid being drawn into a sensitive constitutional matter.[47] The duke introduced heavy fines for those who failed to attend, and despite Jasper's presence one of those penalised 100 marks was Edmund Tudor. In total, only 45 peers out of 105 answered their summons.[48]

For those who did attend, the king's condition naturally took precedence over all other issues, and on 15 March Jasper was part of another council meeting tasked with deliberating the wisest court of action. The council comprised the leading nobles of the realm, including the dukes of York and Buckingham, and the earls of Warwick, Devon, Oxford, Salisbury, Shrewsbury and Wiltshire, and their conclusion was to commission three physicians and two surgeons to attend to the king at once.[49] Their report was not promising; the king continued to be utterly unresponsive. The death of the chancellor, Cardinal Kemp, on 22 March deepened the administrative crisis the council faced. The king was keeper of the Great Seal, a device used to denote the sovereign's approval of any documents of state. In the monarch's absence, this privilege could only be assumed by a regent or protector, so a new custodian could not be appointed. The government was paralysed.

In a final desperate attempt to rouse Henry from the madness that had gripped him for more than half a year, a delegation of twelve lords led by the bishop of Chester rode to Windsor on 25 March to try and encourage the king to nominate a new chancellor. They were greeted by a languid figure who had to be supported by two attendants, his demeanour indifferent to visitors he should have recognised. In their debrief to the council the delegation advised that, to their 'great sorrow and discomfort', in three separate attempts they could obtain 'no answer, word, nor sign' of the king's will, and were forced to leave his presence 'with sorrowful hearts'.[50]

No longer could Henry's absence from state business be concealed, and on 27 March, 'by advice and assent of the Lords Spiritual and Temporal and of the Commonalty of England', and 'in consideration of the king's infirmity', Richard of York was formally nominated Protector and Defender of England.[51] His role was, as the name suggested, to protect England from its enemies domestic and foreign, and to serve as chief of the council. The role would cease when the young prince, Edward of Westminster, was old enough to take upon himself the title of protector. The king, it seemed, was not expected to recover anytime soon.

Having long established himself as a reformer who would remove from government the scourge of corruption, York proved an impartial protector, earnestly adopting a non-partisan stance to the many disputes that pervaded the noble ranks. Though employing a firm hand after years of weak rule, the duke nevertheless extended friendship to those associated with the previous regime, the duke of Somerset apart, ensuring the council was balanced between those drawn from both the Lancastrian and Yorkist factions. Notably, he continued to foster good relations with Edmund and Jasper Tudor.

Empowered to pursue his reformist programme, York set about reducing expenditure and easing the financial burden on the king's subjects out of 'very necessity', in particular targeting the swollen royal household. The duke found ready support from the Tudors, even though any limitations on spending directly impacted their own positions. In the ordinances which York pushed through, it was decreed that the brothers themselves were to be forthwith restricted to just one chaplain, two esquires, two yeomen and two chamberlains each, though this allowance was matched only by the king's confessor in what was a clear concession to their now-acknowledged royal kinship.[52] Being relatively new to the nobility and having had no opportunity of their own to build up a large affinity, this was likely no particular hardship to Edmund and Jasper, who gave their assent.

York and the Tudors were not natural allies; the brothers represented the kind of privileged parvenu that a proud landed magnate of royal pedigree like the duke typically resented, their position at the top table of English politics owing to the king's generosity rather than the blessings of ancestry. In Jasper's case, the previous year the new earl of Pembroke had even benefited from the forfeited Norfolk estates of York's chamberlain and ally, Sir William Oldhall.[53] York, however, needed friends of all political shades to advance his programme of reform, and the Tudors, new to the court and unblemished by the faults of the previous regime, were ideal collaborators. As long as York restricted his ambitions to the removal of Somerset, the restructuring of royal finances and the restoration of law and order, Edmund and Jasper were sympathetic to the duke's objectives. Anything which benefitted the dignity, wellbeing and estate of the king, after all, was in the Tudors' own long-term interest. Henry VI's chosen manner of governance in recent memory, placing his faith in a select group of favoured counsellors, had proven deeply unpopular with both lords and commons alike, which wouldn't have escaped Edmund or Jasper's notice. This was an opportunity to carve a new path, for the benefit of the many, not just the few.

The new administration was not to everyone's liking. Queen Margaret had resisted York's recall, and Somerset was still incarcerated in the Tower. In the north, York's own haughty son-in-law, Henry Holland, Duke of Exeter, attempted to rouse the populace against the Protector, believing he had been unfairly overlooked for the role. He found a willing audience for his frustrations in the Percy family, who likewise felt sidelined in favour of the Nevilles, York's close allies and their bitter dynastic adversaries in the north of England.

With the nobility increasingly polarised as 1454 progressed, there was a decidedly explosive and resentful atmosphere around the royal court, a febrile mood the Tudors could not have failed to notice. When on Christmas Day 1454 Henry VI regained his senses as quickly as he had lost them, Edmund and Jasper may have hoped their half-brother's guiding hand could ease some of the bad blood that had festered in his absence.[54] Henry's recovery, however, merely deepened the 'unhappy plague of division' that spread through the kingdom, setting England, and the Tudors, on the path to civil war.[55]

8

War in Wales

Though no one dared lament the king's sudden Christmas Day recovery, Henry VI's re-emergence into the world after fifteen months spelt trouble for England. A cognisant king could not be denied his right to rule, so his recovery heralded the termination of Richard of York's flourishing protectorate. The duke faced removal from power, the reversal of his reforms and the restoration of his sworn nemesis, Edmund Beaufort, Duke of Somerset.

Events moved fast once the king was caught up with the seemingly overwhelming turn of events: Cardinal Kemp's death, the imprisonment of the dukes of Somerset and Exeter, York's political supremacy. There was good news, however – Henry was introduced to his son, Edward, the long-awaited Lancastrian heir who represented the future hopes of the dynasty. As soon as the king was able, he took back the reins of power and ordered Somerset and Exeter, his most senior supporters, released from captivity. By early February 1455, York's protectorate had been terminated and he was stripped of his other offices, including the lucrative captaincy of Calais, which was restored to Somerset. By March, York and his allies, the Neville earls of Salisbury and Warwick, had abandoned court, the former having resigned as chancellor.[1]

This was the second time that York had been forced into retreat, but this time he did not begrudgingly accept political exile. During his protectorate, the duke's reforms had been well received by the wider nobility, vindicating his repeated calls for reform. Emboldened by his success and the passionate advocacy of Salisbury and Warwick, York plotted his next move.

In the meantime, his rival Somerset not only set about re-establishing his position at the king's side but swore vengeance on York, bitterly complaining before the council that he had been held for over a year 'without any reasonable ground or lawful process'. Henry, for his part, assured everyone that Somerset was 'his true and faithful liegeman and cousin'. Clearly, there was no future in which both York and Somerset could be accommodated by the king, even if Henry was the only person unable to grasp that fact.[2]

Edmund and Jasper Tudor were placed in a delicate position by their half-brother's recovery. On a personal level, there can be no doubt they were pleased Henry had returned to his senses after so long withdrawn from the world. The king had shown the Tudors compassion and generosity after their mother's death, and to him alone they owed every opportunity they had been given, including the right to call themselves earls. The Tudors' ennoblement had been arranged with full expectation they would prop up the Lancastrian court party, offering visible support to Somerset and the king's closest advisors.

The brothers, however, and Jasper in particular, appeared to warm towards York during the king's illness, developing good relations with the protector and contributing to his council. York had, after all, proven efficient and effective in his role, returning much-needed stability to a troubled realm. With the king's welfare their principal concern in every matter, it had served the Tudors' interests to adopt a pragmatic stance when it came to York and his protectorate. Now, they had to look on in dismay as a vengeful Somerset sought retaliation.

When plans were announced for the assembly of a great council in Leicester on 21 May 1455, York hesitated. The Midlands was a region heavily dominated by Lancastrian estates, centred around formidable powerbases like Coventry, Kenilworth, Tutbury and Leicester itself, and the duke feared, probably with justification, that if he attended he would fall into to a trap. When York's mentor, Humphrey, Duke of Gloucester, attended a similarly hostile council meeting in 1447, he had been seized and arrested on trumped-up charges of treason.

York was not willing to let history to repeat itself. Instead, the duke reached out to his disaffected Neville in-laws, Salisbury and Warwick, and together they combined their respective resources and marched south, bypassing Leicester before setting up camp near the Old North Road in Ware, Hertfordshire. When the king learned of their mobilisation, he demanded York stand down and disband his force, a request that was politely rebuffed.[3] Careful to avoid any language that could be construed as treasonous, York replied that he and his companions had no intention of overthrowing the king, but rather merely sought the permanent removal of Somerset. They remained, the duke cautioned, Henry's 'true and humble liege men'.[4]

The royal convoy that departed Westminster for Leicester comprised a fine array of nobles, an impressive retinue numbering around 2,000 men fronted by a refreshed king showing no sign of the debilitating illness which had sidelined him for more than a year. Accompanying Henry on the journey north were the dukes of Somerset and Buckingham, and their respective sons the earls of Dorset and Stafford, plus the earls of Northumberland, Devon and Wiltshire, the lords Clifford, Dudley, Sudeley, Berners, Roos and Fauconberg, and many other lesser knights, household retainers and servants. Also present in his capacity as the premier earl in the realm, and likely riding close to the king's side throughout, was Jasper Tudor.[5] Despite the king's political shortcomings and personal flaws, he unquestionably retained the support and sympathy of most of his nobility.

When the court party reached St Albans, it was clear they could not progress further without confronting York's force, which blocked the route into the Midlands. The 'fire, rancour and envy' that had been permitted to fester between York and Somerset for much of the previous decade now threatened to erupt into 'great and hot flames of open war and wrath'.[6] Henry sent Humphrey Stafford, 1st Duke of Buckingham, to negotiate with the Yorkist camp, trusting he would make headway with York and Salisbury, his brothers-in-law. Buckingham reminded his audience of their oaths to the king, but his pleas for their submission went unheeded. York, in fact, grew more agitated, declaring boldly that he would not rest until those 'which have deserved death' either met their end, or he his.[7]

Steps were taken by the royal camp to barricade the town, and in the shadow of St Peter's Church the king's banner was raised near his tent. Though it was widely recognised as treasonous behaviour to attack the royal banner, the Yorkists were not deterred. Frustrated at Buckingham's refusal to be drawn on whether the king would turn over Somerset, around eleven o'clock in the morning the Yorkists started hacking away at the makeshift blockades, which groaned under the attack. Although the barricades were robust and able to withstand York and Salisbury's assaults, other sections of the eastern approach were left unmanned, allowing Warwick to take advantage of the stretched Lancastrian resources by creeping through back gardens with a small but hardy force of his finest soldiers. Crucially, they evaded detection until they reached the centre of the town.[8]

As the Lancastrian army ambled about, many only partially armoured, Warwick and his men pounced from the shadows upon their prey with a great cry, 'slaying alle those that withstood them'. The local abbot, John Whethamstead, would later claim he witnessed a man fall 'with his brains dashed out, there another with a broken arm, a third with a throat cut, and a fourth with a pierced chest', adding that 'the whole street was full of dead corpses'. It was a bloodbath.[9]

There is no record detailing Jasper's role during what is regarded the first battle of the Wars of the Roses, and though he is known to have been present with the royal convoy leaving London, he is not listed among the combatants or the injured in one contemporary report.[10] With this his first real experience of warfare, Jasper may have been paralysed by the carnage around him, emerging unscathed from the violent disorder by luck as much as choice.

While some members of the Lancastrian leadership were actively sought out and eliminated, ruthlessly hunted down by their enemies in the confusion, Jasper's warm relations with York may have held him in good stead. Perhaps orders had been dispatched down the ranks to leave the earl of Pembroke be. The king, however, suffered a wound in the neck, likely from an errant arrow that had been loosed toward his bodyguard. If Jasper busied himself tending to his stricken half-brother, his shaking hands stemming the flow of blood, this may also explain his absence from the fighting.[11]

When the bloodshed ceased, it was clear the Yorkists had inflicted significant harm on their foes. The frightened and wounded king was sheltering in the nearby abbey and was alarmed when the duke of York thundered into his presence. Somewhat incongruously, considering the blood that stained the streets directly outside the abbey walls, York fell to one knee and declared himself the king's true liegeman. Taking the king tenderly by the arm, he led Henry outside. In every direction lay mutilated corpses, some only identifiable by their armour or badges. Among the casualties were York's detested adversary Edmund Beaufort, Duke of Somerset, and two northern rivals of the Nevilles, Henry Percy, 2nd Earl of Northumberland, and Thomas Clifford, 8th Baron Clifford.[12] In one fell swoop, the Yorkist leadership had annihilated their principal foes, taking minutes to accomplish what they had desired for years. In death, there would be no reprieve for Somerset.

The blood spilt on 22 May 1455 stunned the English nobility. Although York and his associates must take blame for how events unfolded at St Albans, their actions were the product of a weak king ruling without direction or conviction for years on end, allowing a small cabal to assume the mantle of governance and wield it to their personal benefit. Henry VI may have been a kind, decent and pious man who had proven generous to his closest companions, including Edmund and Jasper Tudor, but he lacked the authoritative fist required in a time of political, economic and military turmoil. His want of foresight in navigating the many disputes which fragmented his nobility at a time of national crisis had ended in calamity. As he dabbed away the blood that still trickled from his neck and reflected upon the aftermath of St Albans, Henry must have seen that a lot of trouble could have been prevented if he had simply taken greater personal accountability for his kingdom.

Turning the distressed royal convoy around, the Yorkists led the pliant nobles back towards London. Warwick entered the capital first, carrying the sword of state, while Salisbury and York flanked the king behind. Henry may have worn a crown, but it was clear he was directed by new advisors who had wrested the reins of power from the dying Somerset's hands. In a letter forwarded to the duke of Milan from one of his emissaries, though Somerset had 'ruled as usual' prior to St Albans, now 'York has the government, and the people are very pleased at this'.[13]

On 9 July, parliament opened in the Painted Chamber in Westminster, with Jasper in attendance. Though there was some resistance, the proceedings were heavily controlled by the Yorkists. Responsibility for the recent violence was placed firmly on Somerset, who was posthumously charged with intending the 'hurt and destruction' of York. The Yorkists were, predictably, pardoned of any offence and accepted as the king's true liegemen.[14] It was a deliberate rewriting of history, an attempt to erase from the public consciousness the recent skirmish, one it was hoped would never be spoken of again. Concluding the coup, York was appointed constable of England, Warwick was made captain of Calais, and Viscount Bourchier was handed the office of treasurer.[15]

York took a firm grip of government thereafter and resumed his interrupted reformist agenda, addressing urgent matters of defence and seeking to reverse financial mismanagement around the king's household. A fresh Act of Resumption was put to parliament, demanding severe regulation of royal expenditure and the cancellation of all grants made since the start of the reign. The bill was supported by the Commons, who further requested that Queen Margaret's dower be restricted along with funding of the Tudors. The bill encountered robust opposition from the Lords, who deeply resented the notion of relinquishing grants they had received over the last thirty years, and no progress was made before parliament prorogued for the summer. Before the lords took their leave, on 24 July in the great council chamber at Westminster, to show the 'truth, faith and love' they bore towards their king, a fresh oath of allegiance was sworn by each of the lords, including Jasper.[16]

When parliament reassembled on 12 November for its second session, it did so without the presence of the king, possibly suffering a recurrence of his illness. Sixty-five peers were also absent from the month-long assembly, including Edmund and Jasper Tudor. Edmund had not participated in many recent council meetings, but Jasper's non-attendance was more striking. It is tempting to suggest that, having had time to reflect, he started to develop misgivings about the direction of York's government and elected to stay away. As a result, the brothers did not personally witness, or have any involvement in, York's appointment to the office of protector for a second time.[17]

Edmund's absence is explained by the need for his presence elsewhere, both personally and politically. While the English nobility had been distracted by its own internal disputes, a crippling breakdown of law and order in Wales had been left unchecked, with violence and corruption endemic in the royal counties of the south and west. When the general disorder became such that it desperately needed remedying, the man the council turned to was the Welsh-blooded Tudor earl of Richmond.

After the collapse of the Glyn Dŵr uprising at the start of the fifteenth century, an uneasy calm existed in Wales. In a period of weak government, absentee lords and indifferent officials often handed over the administration of their Welsh interests to local tenants, paying little attention to suspect practices so long as the collection of rents and fees was maintained. A group of emboldened Welshmen soon amassed considerable influence in this vacuum, abusing their positions to subjugate their compatriots. In Pembrokeshire, the Wogans of Wiston and Perrots of Haroldston came to hold sway, while in Brecon there were the Vaughans of Tretower and in Monmouthshire the Herberts of Raglan.[18]

By the mid-fifteenth century, the most prominent figure who had risen to the fore among the South Welsh was Gruffydd ap Nicholas, an experienced, intelligent and ruthless Carmarthenshire landowner. Though 'very wise', Gruffydd was described in a later family account as 'a man of a hot, fiery, and choleric spirit', and this seems to be an accurate characterisation. Though an indispensable agent of the crown, he had repeatedly shown himself to be utterly contemptuous of toeing the line, exploiting the disintegration of royal power to suppress his rivals and enrich himself and his family. He arrogantly dismissed repeated summonses from the council, and on one occasion even had a pair of royal commissioners flayed for daring to darken his door.[19]

Hampered by their own systemic weakness, the impotent council could do little other than look the other way. Gruffydd ap Nicholas continued in crown service across the next decade, establishing near supreme control in matters of royal governance in West Wales and known by the poet Lewys Glyn Cothi as 'the eagle of Carmarthen'. An example of Gruffydd's unscrupulous and unchecked rule occurred in Carmarthen on New Year's Day 1448. When Owain ap Ieuan ap Philip accused Ieuan ap Gruffydd Gogh of a felony, as deputy justiciar, Gruffydd ap Nicholas took a personal interest in the case. He ordered the men to face one another in a judicial duel, producing white leather jackets and decorating the chosen location that would play host to this macabre spectacle. The bewildered pair fought as commanded, with Owain slaying Ieuan and justifying by the law of the day the charges he had levied against his fallen foe. In an act of great cruelty, Owain was seized by Gruffydd's men and promptly beheaded. His head was sold to his friends for the sum of £40, the entire proceedings amounting to little more than one man's morbid entertainment.

Gruffydd ap Nicholas's power reached its zenith in the early 1450s, his position safeguarded by a limp Lancastrian rule that was incapable of restraining wayward subjects. It was only through Henry VI's descent into illness that Gruffydd's supremacy in West Wales was threatened. When Richard of York became protector for the first time in March 1454, the duke's intention to restore order, reduce lawlessness and revive royal authority, the latter extending to the Principality lands in Wales. Gruffydd was compelled to surrender custody of the lordships of Cilgerran, Emlyn Is Cuch and Dyffryn Bryan to Jasper Tudor, the new earl of Pembroke, and on 25 May 1454 the York-dominated council wrote to Gruffydd and his two sons outlining its deep displeasure at complaints of extortion and a general dereliction of duty in matters of justice. No longer would Gruffydd's gross misconduct be tolerated.

The Lancastrian defeat at St Albans in May 1455 removed from power one of Gruffydd ap Nicholas's long-standing sponsors in the duke of Somerset. York assumed many of Somerset's offices after the latter's death, including the constableship of three principal royal castles in West Wales – Carmarthen, Cardigan and Aberystwyth – while his nephew Edward Bourchier was granted responsibility for Kidwelly and Carreg Cennen. York's requests that Gruffydd relinquish his hold on these castles came to naught, and by the November 1455 session of parliament, the indifferent Welshman was directly accused of presiding over a reign of terror that included robbery, destruction of the king's subjects and murder. He was charged with a £1,000 recognisance, or bond, for his future good behaviour and ordered to appear before the king within three weeks or he would forfeit another £2,000; these were huge sums Gruffydd ap Nicholas couldn't afford.[20]

If royal authority was to be recovered in West Wales, it was imperative the area was brought under the control of someone who valued the interest of the crown above that of the self. When casting his eyes around the English nobility for such a figure, York's gaze came to rest on Edmund Tudor. As the king's half-brother, his devotion to Henry VI was beyond reproach. With a well-known and deeply respected Welsh pedigree which would appeal to the local populace, Edmund was the ideal candidate to bring Gruffydd ap Nicholas back into line.

It is uncertain why Edmund was preferred to his brother Jasper, whose lands were centred around West Wales rather than in Yorkshire and the East of England, but seniority may have played a part in the decision. Jasper may have expressed a preference to stay close to the court and the king, or Edmund may simply have been the more military-minded of the pair for a mission in which some competency in warfare would be required. The persuasiveness of ancestry, meanwhile, so valued among the Welsh, unquestionably played its role in a Tudor appointment. Before Edmund departed for Wales, however, he had some personal business to attend to.

At some point during the summer of 1455, Edmund Tudor married Lady Margaret Beaufort, the young ward he shared with his brother. She was just twelve years old at the time, the groom around double her age. The wedding likely took place at the home of the bride's mother, Margaret Beauchamp, Baroness Welles, in Bletsoe, Bedfordshire and, in consideration of her royal ancestry, must not have been arranged without the approval of the king. Edmund's father Owen and brother Jasper may have been present, though there are no records to confirm.

Edmund's motivation in marrying Margaret despite her tender age appears to be simple greed. Though there is no evidence that the recently ennobled Edmund was in any financial difficulty, Margaret stood to bring to her marriage a considerable landed inheritance that ranked among the wealthiest in the kingdom. Edmund now moved to exploit his legal privilege at the earliest possible opportunity. It does need to be considered whether orders to do so originated from Edmund's half-brother, Henry VI. Though it is highly unlikely Richard of York had any designs on the throne at this juncture, the development of an alternative line of succession may have been considered prudent by a suspicious crown, a quasi-Lancastrian Beaufort-Tudor line, should anything untoward happen to Henry VI or his young heir, Prince Edward.

Margaret, for her part, later claimed it was she who was responsible for choosing her groom. According to her confessor, Bishop John Fisher, Margaret recounted late in life that she had been presented a choice between two suitors: John de la Pole, the son of the duke of Suffolk, or Edmund Tudor. 'Doubtful in her mind what she were best to do', Margaret asked an old gentlewoman 'whom she much loved and trusted' for advice. The elderly lady advised her young companion 'to commend herself to St Nicholas', the patron and helper of all true maidens, for guidance. The night before she was due to give her answer, a figure appeared to Margaret as she prayed, 'arrayed like a Bishop', and bade her take Edmund as her spouse. Just a child at the time, it seems unlikely Margaret was, in fact, given any agency in whom she would marry; the decision to transfer her wardship to the Tudors, and with it her hand in marriage, rested with the king alone.[21]

Shortly after the wedding celebrations concluded, Edmund and his household began the long journey from Bletsoe into Wales, a strenuous expedition of over 200 miles which would have taken several difficult weeks to complete. By 30 November 1455, the earl's convoy had reached as far west as Lamphey, a secluded hamlet just 2 miles from Jasper's imposing seat at Pembroke. The palace that dominated Lamphey was a spacious and regal residence owned by the absentee bishop of St David's, John de la Bere, Henry VI's chaplain and almoner of the king's household. It was likely through this connection that Edmund and his young bride came to stay at Lamphey, a more opulent, and private, base than his brother's huge Norman fortress just up the road.[22]

A rich estate which provided great comfort to guests, Lamphey was a serene and pleasant abode for the pair during their time in West Wales, even during the bleak winter months when husband and wife got to know one another, both personally and physically. It was in these otherwise tranquil surroundings in April 1456 that Margaret conceived what would prove her only child. The bedding of a mere twelve-year-old by Edmund was a distasteful and ruthless act, even by the standards of the day. Though the church accepted that twelve was not below the minimum age of consummation, it was rare for this to be the case while the female body was still in its early stages of development. Edmund's motivations were clear, then and now; an heir would entitle the earl to a lifetime interest in the extensive Beaufort inheritance, to be enjoyed as he saw fit until his death. If Edmund had any concerns over the physical or mental wellbeing of his young countess, they were callously set aside in favour of his own self-interest.

Comfortably settled in at Lamphey and buoyed by the prospect of an heir, by the end of spring Edmund Tudor had turned his full attention towards the problem of Gruffydd ap Nicholas. The presence of the earl of Richmond in West Wales, not a local lord but a man to whom he owed no feudal commitment, incited the aged Gruffydd. Rankled an outsider had been tasked with constraining his authority, he was unlikely to surrender a position he had spent years carving out for himself, and extended Edmund little respect based solely on the earl's Welsh background.

By early 1456, Gruffydd ap Nicholas and his sons were in possession of the royal castles of Aberystwyth, Carmarthen and Carreg Cennen, an embarrassment to the crown and in particular Richard of York, appointed constable of the three the previous summer. Any attempt by Edmund to persuade Gruffydd to yield up the castles voluntarily and abide by the king's law proved futile, for by 7 June 1456 the pair were described as 'at war greatly in Wales'. By August, Edmund had recaptured Carmarthen, the centre of royal government in Wales and its richest and most populated town. It was a triumph which elevated the earl's military credibility and provided a suitable launchpad to retake control of the wider region.[23]

The situation back at court was rapidly evolving, however, and would greatly impact Edmund Tudor's position, and indeed his life. York had continued to try and push the severe Act of Resumption through parliament, even conceding a range of exemptions for the queen and the Tudors to try and garner support. The Lords, however, proved an insurmountable barrier for the protector, who despite his high office failed to persuade most of his apathetic peers in his argument. When York and Warwick reached London on 9 February 1456 for the final session of the parliament, they arrived with 300 men in jackets of mail and brigandines, anticipating the potential outbreak of violence. Though their principal adversaries had been killed at St Albans nine months earlier, the Yorkist lords now had to contend with the emergence of another opponent who loathed their presence around government, a strong-willed, tenacious and aggressive rival with unfettered access to the king – Margaret of Anjou.

Now in her twenty-fifth year, Queen Margaret was no longer the timid young girl who had arrived in England a decade earlier, but a 'great and strong-laboured woman' who would 'spare no pain' to turn things to her intent.[24] As her husband had weakened over the years, physically, mentally and politically, it was through necessity that Margaret emerged as the real driving force behind the Lancastrian dynasty. It is likely through her that complaints about York's Act of Resumption reached Henry's ear, and on 25 February the king's return to front-line politics compelled the vexed duke to resign the protectorate. Not for the first time, York withdrew from court.[25]

During the summer of 1456, as Edmund Tudor was engaged in war with Gruffydd ap Nicholas, relations between York and Queen Margaret continued to deteriorate. From their respective bases, they viewed one another from afar with a deep suspicion that could not be overcome. Margaret had left her husband in London to tour Lancastrian estates in the Midlands and Cheshire, assessing the strength of the royal forces at her disposal and strengthening in person her relationships with the nobility and gentry. The queen was also laying the groundwork for a full royal retreat from London, the Lancastrian headquarters to be split in future between Coventry, Kenilworth and Tutbury, fulfilling what had been intended the previous summer.[26]

York's response to what he interpreted as aggressive overtures was to strengthen his own, already robust, position in Wales. As a consequence of its turbulent past, Wales in the 1450s was a complex patchwork of Marcher lordships and royal counties where competing loyalties and tangled webs of kinship had produced a febrile atmosphere exploited by powerful absentee magnates. The Lancastrian presence in Wales was considerable; in the south-west, Cardiganshire and Carmarthenshire were royal counties, buttressed to the north by the principality of Caernarfonshire, Merionethshire and Anglesey. The profitable lordship of Kidwelly, meanwhile, was held by Henry VI as part of the duchy of Lancaster, also maintaining control of Monmouth in the east. To the west, the earldom of Pembroke was held by the king's half-brother Jasper Tudor, and in Mid Wales the king's cousin Buckingham was lord of Brecon, Hay and Newport.

Owing to his Mortimer inheritance, however, Richard of York also held sway over a vast concentration of lordships stretching from Caerleon in the south to Denbigh in the north, a striking hegemony he administered from his imposing fortresses of Wigmore and Ludlow. His nephew and ally the earl of Warwick also retained a significant presence in South Wales as the lord of Glamorgan and Morgannwg, which included the formidable castles of Caerphilly and Cardiff. Warwick's brother Edward Neville, another Yorkist adherent, was Baron Bergavenny.[27]

Already in firm control of a sweeping arc of lordships along the Welsh March, the wary York decided to pursue his claim as constable of Carmarthen and Aberystwyth castles, personal control of which would establish a strong Yorkist foothold in the heart of Lancastrian West Wales. That this would severely weaken his adversaries in the process was unquestionably a driving factor. It was an approach that brought York into conflict with the man currently occupying Carmarthen on behalf of the crown. The focus of Edmund Tudor's war in Wales had unexpectedly shifted.

With York staying on his Yorkshire estates, the men he employed to wrest control of Carmarthen from the Tudor earl were two of his most trusted tenants in the March, Sir Walter Devereux of Weobley and Devereux's son-in-law Sir Walter Herbert of Raglan. Devereux had been a long-time adherent of York's, serving with the duke in France and Ireland during the 1440s and later filling the office of constable of Wigmore.[28] Herbert, meanwhile, was a figure of considerable influence in Gwent, and known to Edmund Tudor – they had been knighted together in the Tower of London in January 1453, and in October that year Herbert was granted an annuity of £10 by Edmund from the lordship of Bassingbourn in Cambridgeshire.[29] Herbert was also retained as a member of Jasper Tudor's administrative council, helping manage the earl's extensive portfolio in South Wales, and may have regularly encountered Edmund in this capacity.[30]

The Herbert and the Tudor family shared an acrimonious history, however, of which both men likely had some degree of knowledge. Herbert's maternal grandfather was Dafydd Gam, a Welsh soldier of great renown who lost his life fighting for Henry V at Agincourt. According to a later family legend, Gam's demise came while rescuing the stranded king from certain death. His reputation within Wales, however, had been shaped by his prominent resistance to the ambitions of Owain Glyn Dŵr at the turn of the fifteenth century. Gam led much of the opposition to Glyn Dŵr in South Wales on behalf of the English crown, for which his lands were repeatedly razed and, on one notable occasion towards the end of the uprising, he was briefly taken hostage. In this role, Gam was the greatest Welsh adversary of not only Glyn Dŵr but also Edmund Tudor's grandfather Maredudd ap Tudur and the Tudurs of Anglesey.[31]

Herbert's vigorous father William ap Thomas, meanwhile, firmly established his reputation as a figure of local importance through his marriage to Dafydd Gam's daughter Gwladys. Developing close relations with Richard of York when he was appointed the duke's chief steward of his Welsh estates, William was succeeded with great competence in this role by his son. By 1454, Herbert was even described in a letter to York as 'no man's man but only yours'.[32]

Through his mother's first marriage, Herbert, who had adopted an English-style surname to consciously disassociate himself from lingering anti-Welsh bias, was also the younger half-brother of the Vaughan family of Tretower, these grandsons of Dafydd Gam forming a tight affinity to spread their influence deep into the administration of their corner of Wales. As the Tudurs of Penmynydd had demonstrated a generation earlier, brothers working in concert could yield considerable rewards.[33]

Herbert adeptly stepped into the role of Richard of York's leading tenant in Gwent after his father's death in 1445, establishing his commercial reputation in the international wine trade and demonstrating military competency as a soldier in France.[34] When York required someone loyal and reliable to move against the king's Tudor half-brother in the summer of 1456, it was to Herbert and Devereux he turned. In fact, the pair had already made a nuisance of themselves earlier that year. In a heavy response to the murder of a kinsman, across the Easter period Devereux and Herbert intimidated the king's justices in Hereford, before imprisoning the mayor and hanging those they judged to be guilty. On 12 April, meanwhile, Herbert robbed a servant of the earl of Wiltshire in Cowbridge, Glamorgan, and rumour spread in June that his brother, Richard Herbert, had gathered men in Ross-on-Wye intending to kill the king.[35]

At the start of August 1456, Devereux and Herbert once more assembled their respective forces, a considerable host that numbered around 2,000 well-armed men, and left Gwent behind. A hardy military unit that included several esquires and gentlemen, they marched westward, passing through Brecon, into Llandovery and Llandeilo, and across the fertile plains of the Tywi Valley. They only came to a rest once they reached the high stone walls encircling the town of Carmarthen. Though Edmund had brought some men with him to West Wales, there had been no expectation he would need enough to fend off the small, well-provisioned army which now stood menacingly in the distance.[36]

Carmarthen Castle was not just one of the largest Welsh fortresses of its day but the seat of royal government and law enforcement in South Wales, a crucial administrative centre from which English royal authority was exercised in every direction. A fort had existed here since the Roman period 1,000 years earlier, and the present stone castle, built atop a steep rocky crag overlooking the meandering River Tywi, dominated not just the medieval town but the surrounding landscape for many miles. It was strategically placed, near a crossing point in the river, controlling the lines of communication and trade into, and out of, South-West Wales.

It is unclear how much violence occurred at Carmarthen in the late summer and early autumn of 1456, or whether the forces of Herbert and Devereux engaged with Edmund's garrison at all. What is known, however, is that the Yorkists quickly entered possession of Carmarthen, placing Edmund under their custody before advancing on Aberystwyth to reduce another royal fortress.[37] Having seized the seal of the chamberlain of South Wales in the process, Herbert and Devereux audaciously appointed themselves as a royal commission to hold the judicial sessions, claiming to act on behalf of York, the legitimate constable of the royal castles.[38]

There is no contemporary source to provide insight into Edmund's time as prisoner in a castle he had briefly possessed, but it is possible he was detained in the Southwest Tower, once known as the Prison Tower. Originally standing four stories high, the cylindrical tower had been constructed against a steep slope which led down to the river, and contained a series of rectangular, stone-vaulted chambers, reached by a spiral stairway. It is not known for how long Edmund was kept locked up, but by early November 1456, aged only twenty-six, the earl of Richmond was dead. The date of death given on his tomb is 1 November, though a payment in the privy purse of Elizabeth of York in 1502 for the observance of his obituary is recorded on 3 November.[39]

Edmund's death has commonly been attributed to an outbreak of the plague, but there is no contemporary indication this was the case. It must be considered that the earl perished because of injuries sustained during the siege, having perhaps stoutly resisted Yorkist attempts to seize the castle. Less likely, but impossible to rule out, is the suspicion Edmund was murdered on the orders of Richard of York. As events at St Albans the previous year had shown, the duke and his allies were not averse to draconian acts to safeguard their position. With news spreading that Margaret Beaufort was pregnant with a child of English royal blood, was there a suspicion in Yorkist circles that Edmund Tudor had designs on greater power, ambitions which did not sit easily with York, repeatedly denied political prominence?

Tensions at court were certainly heightened a few weeks before Edmund's death when the queen oversaw the dismissal of York's allies Viscount Bourchier and Archbishop Bourchier as treasurer and chancellor respectively, replaced by Lancastrian loyalists John Talbot, Earl of Shrewsbury, and Bishop William Waynflete. Margaret may have, with some degree of justification, interpreted the taking of Carmarthen and Aberystwyth castles to be an act of war by York, and moved to punish him by stripping his supporters of their offices. In absence of any credible source, all possibilities must be considered in the context of a marked escalation of hostility between the duke and the queen.

In any event, Herbert and Devereux were eventually exonerated of any wrongdoing in the death of Edmund Tudor, though only after being pursued for several months by a suspicious crown. On account of the widespread 'mischief and grievance' the pair had presided over across South Wales, they stood accused of robbing, beating, maiming and killing the king's subjects, for which they were thrown into prison, Herbert at the Tower of London and Devereux at Windsor.[40] Herbert was bailed in March 1457 but within days had fled back to Wales, 'to pursue his evil course'. The council ordered the sheriffs of London, Gloucestershire, Herefordshire, Worcestershire, Shropshire, Bristol and Coventry to be alert to his whereabouts, warning that 'no man of whatsoever estate, degree or condition shall receive, comfort, aid or favour' the errant knight but to consider him 'a rebel put out of the king's grace'. His capture would be rewarded with 500 marks.[41]

At an inquisition held in Hereford on 5 April 1457 to examine events at Carmarthen the previous autumn, Herbert was one of at least fifty-seven people investigated. Among those who travelled to Hereford to hear the indictments were the king and queen, the duke of Buckingham, the earl of Shrewsbury, and very likely Jasper Tudor, who would have paid close attention to the details surrounding his brother's capture and death. In an effort to prise Herbert's loyalty from York, and further bolster the royal position in Wales, the queen extended a pardon to the knight, promising his life would be spared if he appeared before the king on 7 June in Leicester. Herbert duly appeared, swore his fealty to the king and was formally pardoned of wrongdoing. Seven tuns of Gascon wine that had been earlier seized from him were even returned. Twenty-one other men, drawn from throughout the Yorkist lordships of Usk, Abergavenny and Herefordshire, were also exonerated, though not Walter Devereux, who remained in prison until February 1458. The cause of Edmund Tudor's death, therefore, remained an unanswered question no longer pursued by the crown.[42]

However he met his end, the earl of Richmond's body was claimed by the austere Franciscan monks of the nearby Greyfriars and buried within the walls of their monastery church. This was intended to be only a temporary measure; in a will dated 2 June 1472, Edmund's widow, Margaret Beaufort, made provision for his remains to be translated out of Wales to Bourne Abbey in Lincolnshire, where she planned for a tomb to be erected and a chantry founded.[43] As Margaret saw her station transformed in later life, ultimately becoming mother and grandmother of kings, her modest first will was cancelled and Edmund remained in his original crypt.

A new Purbeck tomb was, however, commissioned by Edmund's son in November 1496, forty years after his death. Rhys ap Thomas, the most prominent Welshman of his day, and incidentally a grandson of Gruffydd ap Nicholas, was assigned £43 10s by Henry VII for 'the making of a new tomb for our most dear father', which has survived to the present day, albeit not in its original position.[44]

When Greyfriars was dissolved in 1538, the tomb was saved from the widespread desecration that ensued and removed to a new location, though not in Lincolnshire as Margaret had originally intended. Likely overseen by a collection of enterprising local officials acting independently of the distant Tudor court, Edmund's tomb and possibly his remains were transferred 50 miles west to St David's Cathedral, the holiest site in Wales.

To this day, the tomb stands in a site of prominence before the altar, capturing the attention of many a pilgrim across the previous five centuries. Around the base of the tomb chest are twelve restored shields bearing the arms of Edmund's immediate and extended family, including those of Owen Tudor and Katherine of Valois, Margaret Beaufort and the previous three generations of her family, plus those borne after Edmund's death by his son and grandsons, two kings of England and one prince of Wales.

In all but two of the twelve shields, the quartered royal arms of England and France appear, a conscious reminder to visitors of Edmund's many royal connections in life and in death. Indeed, at the moment of his demise, his half-brother Henry VI occupied the English throne and his uncle Charles VII was seated on the French. In just another generation, his sole offspring would come to occupy the former. Edmund's past, present and future can be gleaned by a simple circuit of his tomb.[45]

There are no surviving accounts of Edmund's appearance, and no record reveals his character. The monumental brass that adorns his tomb, a later addition and not contemporary, depicts a grave armoured figure with shoulder-length hair and hands in prayer, a rather generic representation of a fifteenth-century nobleman. Above Edmund's left shoulder rests a dragon, and at his feet is the Richmond greyhound. An epitaph around the tomb chest, added after 1485, reads proudly:

> Under this marble stone here enclosed resteth the bones of the noble Lord, Edmund Earl of Richmond, father and brother to kings; the which departed out of this world in the year of our Lord God, 1456 the first day of the month of November; on whose soul Almighty Jesu have mercy. Amen.

Away from his family, Edmund's death drew the attention of the Welsh bards, who deeply lamented his passing. A sorrowful Dafydd Nanmor composed a moving elegy, expressing his sadness at the pleasure of Edmund's enemies but also his certainty that Jasper would offer protection to his brother's unborn child. Edmund may be gone, but mercifully the lineage survived in this young deer that would surely grow into a proud stag.[46]

The Carmarthenshire poet Lewys Glyn Cothi shared Nanmor's sense of loss and despair; while Owen Tudor pined for his son, a 'fine stag' who was a lover of peace, Glyn Cothi anxiously feared for Welsh hopes, comparing a Wales without Edmund to a hearth without smoke, a house without a bed, a town without palaces, a beach without water, and even a church without a priest. Wales was empty without its Tudor earl, and for that, the sorrowful poet adds, 'we are distressed'.[47]

Edmund Tudor died in Wales before he could realise his potential as a great magnate of England. Thrown deep into the political mix through his royal half-brother's generosity, his career was just beginning when he perished during his first significant commission, for which he was arguably ill prepared. The earl of Richmond's legacy, however, would prove enduring, far outstripping anything he was able to accomplish in his brief life. From Edmund would spring a line of kings and queens no one could have foreseen, a dynasty that would shape Welsh, English and, in time, British history.

9

Roots of Rancour

While Edmund Tudor had travelled into West Wales, tasked with curbing the wayward behaviour of the recalcitrant Gruffydd ap Nicholas, Jasper Tudor had not been wholly inactive himself. In the spring of 1456, a series of spontaneous anti-Italian riots erupted in London, xenophobic English traders enviously targeting merchants drawn to England from cities like Venice, Florence, Lucca and Genoa. The violence was such that, on 30 April 1456, Henry VI handed a commission to twenty-four men to investigate the disturbances in his capital, led by the dukes of Exeter and Buckingham, the earls of Salisbury, Northumberland and Worcester, and, in his capacity as earl of Pembroke, his half-brother Jasper. On 6 June, Jasper formed part of another commission granted authority to examine similar disorders further afield in Kent and Sussex.[1]

At Sheen Palace on 7 June 1456, meanwhile, it was reported that Jasper was the only lord in the king's presence. Sheen had been a favoured riverside retreat of Edward III, Richard II and Henry V, a peaceful haven upriver from the bustle of London where successive monarchs sought respite from the daily pressures of kingship. Henry VI's mental burdens were widely known by this period, and it may be that while his queen Margaret of Anjou was on progress around Cheshire and the Midlands he took the opportunity to savour the sunshine and rest his weary mind. That it was Jasper who was the king's sole companion is an indication of the close familiarity between the half-brothers, with the earl of Pembroke able to offer quiet support, sibling to sibling rather than subject to king.[2]

As the summer days of 1456 shortened, updates concerning Edmund's difficult campaign in Wales reached Jasper in London, including the disturbing news of his imprisonment at the hands of the Yorkist tenants William Herbert and Walter Devereux. At the end of September, Jasper gathered his council and held a meeting at the King's Head in Cheapside, a tavern erected a century earlier during the reign of Edward III and which stood in the shadow of St Paul's soaring spire. Every magnate had their own council, men selected for their local knowledge and administrative capabilities to handle every facet of their lord's financial and political interests. Council meetings typically followed a routine agenda, focused on approving repairs to manors, the lord's domestic requirements, the collection of revenues and the payment of wages. At this particular council meeting, however, it was Edmund Tudor's predicament which surely dominated much of the discussion, although, strangely, among those listed present 'considering various matters' was a William Herbert. If this William Herbert was the same man who had imprisoned Edmund – the scribe doesn't identify the attendees by their social rank – the summit likely involved tense negotiations regarding Edmund's release from captivity, with accusations flying back and forth across the tavern floor.[3]

If such negotiations were indeed fruitful and Edmund was released, the earl of Richmond's days were nevertheless numbered. On 15 November, just two weeks after his brother's death, Jasper was granted a share in Thomas Vaughan's house, 'Le Garlek', located on Brook Street in Stepney. Vaughan was a kinsman of Herbert, and also one of the councillors present at the King's Head meeting in September, so the surrendering of half his countryside residence to Jasper may have been punishment for his family's role in Edmund's demise.[4]

When Jasper received news of Edmund's death, he embraced his brotherly duty at once, springing into action to safeguard his young sister-in-law, Margaret Beaufort. Carrying Edmund's child in her womb, under Jasper's direction she was brought from Lamphey to his imposing baronial seat of Pembroke, an uncomfortable but mercifully short journey of just a couple of miles. She was likely incapable of travelling further.

On 28 January 1457, just under three months since Edmund's death, Margaret gave birth to their son in a darkened chamber specially prepared for the purpose. It had not been an easy delivery, and Margaret's underdeveloped body, still just thirteen years old, struggled with the strain of childbirth so that for some time her life was thought to be in danger. In a sermon delivered forty years later, Bishop Fisher recounted that, though the child was 'wonderfully born', it 'seemed a miracle that at that age, and of so little a personage, anyone should be born at all'.[5] It is probable the traumatic effects of labour so young caused Margaret lasting harm; despite two later marriages, she would never conceive a child again. It is particularly telling, poignant even, that many years later Margaret protested plans to marry her namesake granddaughter to the king of Scotland when just nine years old, compassionately drawing on her own harrowing experience to protect the young princess's wellbeing.[6]

According to the poet and antiquarian John Leland, writing between 1536 and 1539, Margaret's child was born in a thirteenth-century guard's chamber that formed part of the outer bailey's defensive wall. Leland claimed to have been shown a chimney that bore the arms and badges of the first Tudor king during the visit, but, though he may very well have been reporting a local tradition, the claim seems to be dubious.[7] Despite her tender age, Margaret was a noblewoman of a great and royal lineage, her baby a close relative of the king on both sides of his family tree. In consideration of her ancestry, station and most of all her physical condition, Margaret likely gave birth in the more comfortable domestic quarters reserved for the use of the lord, her brother-in-law Jasper, or other honoured guests. Recent excavations have revealed the stone foundations of such a building in the outer bailey of the castle, away from the bustling environs of the inner ward, where the great hall, chapel, chancery and dungeon were in heavy daily use. A private dwelling of high status fitted with the latest amenities, such a noble suite was a far more appropriate environment for Margaret's labour than a guard's chamber near the gatehouse.

Another sixteenth-century tradition, recounted by Elis Gruffudd, who claimed to have heard the story from his elders, suggests the boy was originally named Owain. This, however, was likely influenced by knowledge of the Tudor accession to the English throne and the assertions then current among Welsh bards that the ancient prophecies foretelling of a national deliverer of Wales had been fulfilled.[8] In the absence of a father, the reality is that Margaret had almost certainly named her son as intended, bestowing upon him the name Henry in honour of her cousin Henry VI. It will also be noted the king was the boy's half-uncle on his Tudor side, making it an appropriate and respectful name in every sense, however romantic the claim of Elis Gruffudd.

The enduring bond between mother and child, a connection that would prove unshakable across the course of their turbulent lives, was forged in their first few moments together inside the whitewashed stone walls of Pembroke, where Margaret 'wisely attended' to her son's care.[9] She was, in truth, still a child herself – a mother and a widow at just thirteen years old – and after a terrible ordeal may have only been able to summon the strength to look into her baby's small blue eyes and feel relief. She, like the son she now held, had never known her father. In letters exchanged between the pair in later life, Margaret calls Henry 'all my worldly joy' and 'only beloved son'. In turn, he would respond noting his appreciation for 'the great and singular motherly love and affection' his 'most loving mother' had always shown him.[10]

From his very first breath, young Henry joined the noble ranks, inheriting his father's title as earl of Richmond. History would remember this boy as Henry Tudor, though by the practice of the day in which he lived he was properly known from birth as Henry of Richmond. The course of an internecine war played out on battlefields across England and Wales would, in time, cost Henry his earldom and his freedom, forcing him to navigate unsteadily through a frightening adolescence of hardship and danger while exiled for more than a decade, separated from his mother's embrace and his homeland. He would, against all odds, emerge as the unlikeliest candidate ever proposed for the English throne.

Back in January 1457, however, a helpless babe in the arms of a mother not much older than him, the birth of this remarkable survivor who would one day don a crown passed with little comment from contemporaries. Just another noble mouth to feed in a nation distracted by inward conflict, nobody outside his immediate family and their household paid any attention to the arrival of Henry Tudor.

After surviving the harrowing experience of childbirth, Margaret Beaufort continued to convalesce at Pembroke, supported by a compassionate and experienced local network of midwives, wet nurses and mothers. One of those nurses was a Welshwoman named Joan, wife of Philip ap Howell, later rewarded by Henry when king with an annuity of 20 marks for her services.[11] Together, this collection of aides tended to Margaret's physical needs while assuaging any concerns she had about her son's welfare. Once her strength had recovered sufficiently to be reintroduced to society, she was delicately escorted to the porch of a nearby church, probably the nearby thirteenth-century St Mary's, to experience an important ceremonial ritual known as churching. This was a religious practice intended to restore purity after the birthing process.

Bearing a lighted candle, Margaret was sprinkled with holy water in the form of a cross by a local priest, who recited a psalm and offered blessings for mother and child. Permitted to enter the church, she then knelt before the altar to be blessed once again, with thanks given to the Virgin Mary for her protection. Once ritually shed of the uncleanliness associated with childbirth, Margaret celebrated the safe delivery of her child, and of course her own survival of such a traumatic episode, with a lively purification feast. Held within the grandly decorated walls of Pembroke's great hall, ale and wine were consumed in immense quantities and entertainment was provided by an assortment of dancers, musicians and minstrels.

The festivities were possibly presided over by the earl of Pembroke himself. In the absence of the father, Jasper was expected to step into the central male role after the birth of a child, celebrating the newborn's paternity and, most importantly, their shared lineage. A social and political event, the feast also provided an opportunity for the earl to strengthen his ties with the local community, further establishing relations that would hold him and his nephew in good stead in years to come.

Young Henry's christening, meanwhile, had taken place a few days after his birth, as was customary. Local tradition maintains the ceremony took place in St Mary's Church, and this is possible, with Henry's presentation to the wider public serving as a statement of his survival. A modern stained-glass window commemorates the joyous event, and a font pre-dating the fifteenth century is still in use. The temptation is to suggest this unassuming stone structure was once used to baptise a future king.[12]

Though Jasper had provided commendable care and protection to his sister-in-law in her time of utmost need, her long-term situation needed to be addressed. With wider political and regional concerns at the forefront of his mind, in March 1457 the earl travelled to Greenfield in the lordship of Ebbw near Newport for a summit with Humphrey Stafford, 1st Duke of Buckingham. Travelling with him was the nearly fourteen-year-old Margaret, who had only recently completed her churching.[13]

Buckingham was a magnate of the highest esteem, an experienced commander of the Hundred Years War, a long-time councillor of Henry VI and himself a great-grandson of Edward III. One of the most powerful and wealthy nobles in the kingdom, with vast estates scattered across central England, Buckingham was also lord of Brecon and Newport in South Wales. With Jasper in possession of the lordship of Caldicot, the pair were technically neighbours, but more importantly in the current climate they shared a political outlook that now brought them into closer association.

Both men had recently sought to heal much of the division in England and had been cautiously supportive of Richard of York's protectorates, perhaps even sympathising with some of his reforms. Buckingham had assumed a principal role in the negotiations with York, his brother-in-law, before the violence at St Albans, and his Bourchier half-brothers were closely aligned with York's party, keeping the lines of communication open. Buckingham was also brother-in-law to another of the leading Yorkist lords, the earl of Salisbury, which certainly placed him in a delicate position as the troublesome decade of the 1450s wore on. The duke's loyalty to the court party, however, like Jasper's, could not be broken by his personal connections. When his Welsh estates were threatened by the same ambitious Yorkist retainers who had waged war on Edmund Tudor, Buckingham was minded to foster closer relations with the earl of Pembroke. This Tudor–Stafford alliance was to be sealed with a Beaufort marriage.

Topics of discussion at the Greenfield meeting likely included York's continued exclusion from power, the escalation in ill-feeling among the nobility, and perhaps even the recent investigation into Edmund's death and the arrests of William Herbert and Walter Devereux. The true purpose of Jasper's journey to Buckingham's manor, however, was to arrange a union between the two parties. It was proposed that Margaret Beaufort would marry Buckingham's second son, Henry Stafford, providing the prospective groom with a more than respectable income through his new wife's estates and the bride a husband of noble blood with extensive connections. Indeed, through his mother, Lady Anne Neville, Henry Stafford, like Margaret, was a great-grandchild of John of Gaunt and closely related in blood to the House of Lancaster. This detail would not have gone unnoticed by either side. That he was twice her age was not considered relevant.

After a dispensation for the proximity of kinship was granted, the pair were wed on 3 January 1458, less than a year since Margaret had given birth to her Tudor son. With her remarriage, she now departed Jasper's care to assume her new life as Lady Stafford. After Edmund's death, the income from Margaret's extensive estates had transferred into the hands of her brother-in-law as sole custodian of her wardship. She may have been a widow and a mother, but Margaret was still a minor in the eyes of the law. Now, upon her remarriage, Jasper relinquished those sizable proceeds from the Beaufort inheritance to the Staffords, who probably took up residence in one of Margaret's manors, Bourne in Lincolnshire.[14] For Jasper, the political alliance with Buckingham was worth more than the money.

When Margaret departed Pembroke, in a turn that must have caused considerable distress, her son did not accompany her. On 8 January 1458, five days after Margaret's wedding, Jasper was granted joint custody of his nephew's estates in England, Wales and the Marches, to be shared with John Talbot, 2nd Earl of Shrewsbury. Between them, the earls of Pembroke and Shrewsbury would hold all young Henry's lordships, castles, manors and lands until he turned twenty-one, receiving any rents, revenues and fees but charged with preserving the inheritance.[15] In the meantime, guardianship of the one-year-old earl of Richmond remained in his uncle's hands, and he continued to be reared within his birthplace of Pembroke.

Jasper, however, had bigger concerns than the day-to-day upbringing of his nephew, entrusted to a governess and an array of household staff. The earl of Pembroke's five-year career had been chiefly spent around court, offering close political and personal support to a king weighed down by the burden of rule. The death of his brother, however, triggered a change in priorities for Jasper, who now assumed a hands-on role in the administration of royal lands in Wales, consolidating the crown position and hindering Yorkist ambitions. His presence in the land of his father would herald the start of a lengthy association with Wales and the Welsh that would endure to his death, and laid much of the groundwork that would facilitate his nephew's rise in future.

Already earl of Pembroke and in control of vast swathes of land in the most south-westerly corner of Wales, to aggrandise his authority on 21 April 1457 Jasper was granted the constableships of the royal castles of Carmarthen, Aberystwyth and Carreg Cennen. These had most recently been held by Richard of York, though his reluctant appointment as Lieutenant of Ireland had drawn him away from West Wales. York was compensated for yielding the castles, though the strategic cost was far greater than the sum offered.[16]

Jasper was not ignorant of the task that faced him. It is likely he had already journeyed into West Wales before these appointments, having paid his tributes at the graveside of his brother. Since his ennoblement five years earlier, Jasper had always been minded towards seeking a peaceful resolution to the political division at court, freely associating with York and attending several Yorkist-dominated council meetings, even after the slaughter of the royal leadership at St Albans. The escalation in Yorkist hostility, however, which possibly included the murder of his brother, forced Jasper's hand. At the minimum, York's tenants Herbert and Devereux had committed an act of war against the Tudor position in Wales, and increasing suspicion of York's intentions was enough for Jasper to wholeheartedly set himself against any attempt to inflict further bloodshed on his kin. The line had been crossed.

Jasper was able to study his brother's approach in Wales the previous year and adapt his strategy to avoid falling into the same trap. One of his first objectives was to immediately court the friendship of Gruffydd ap Nicholas and his tenacious sons, all of whom remained men of substance in Carmarthenshire and beyond. Despite his predilection for disobedience, Gruffydd had been recently pardoned by Queen Margaret for his past misdemeanours, clemency he rewarded by supporting the court party in its quarrel with York.[17] Jasper's friendship with Buckingham, meanwhile, strengthened through the marriage of Margaret Beaufort to the duke's son Henry Stafford, ensured considerable military and political reinforcement if needed from a like-minded individual of great national influence.

Jasper was shrewd to take such a precaution, and it suggests he was more keenly aware of the depth of disunity in the kingdom than his naïve half-brother, Henry VI. The Yorkists' intentions at St Albans on 22 May 1455 had been to eliminate their enemies and, in the bloody aftermath, seize the reins of government. In the short-term, their plan worked, though the Yorkist ascendancy was to prove brief. Within a year, the court party had rallied, the queen in particular proving spirited in the revival of Lancastrian fortunes. One of those at the forefront of the fightback against the Yorkists had been Henry Beaufort, 3rd Duke of Somerset, who at just nineteen years old had witnessed his father slaughtered in the tightly packed streets of St Albans.

Somerset maintained a ferocious hatred for the Yorkists in the years following his father's death, and relentlessly pursued his foes at every opportunity, encouraged at every step by the queen. When a great council was summoned in Coventry in October 1456, Somerset arrived heavily armed, intending to confront the duke of York and the earls of Salisbury and Warwick, provoking a 'great affray' in the town that left a handful of watchmen dead. At the meeting itself, Somerset had to be restrained from physically attacking York, while the following December in London he tried to maim Warwick's younger brother John Neville. In November 1457, Somerset even stood accused of attempting to kidnap Warwick, possibly an impulsive reaction to news of Edmund Tudor's suspicious demise in Wales.[18]

Somerset was not alone, for there existed a group of implacable magnates who craved the shedding of Yorkist blood as retribution for St Albans. Men like the duke of Exeter and the earl of Shrewsbury colluded with Somerset, supported by other bereaved sons like the earl of Northumberland, and the barons Egremont and Clifford. All had lost their fathers in violence at St Albans. Lancastrian vengeance was the mood of the moment, and could not be contained.

It was in this context that Jasper turned his mind to establishing a defensive base for himself that would provide protection and a means of escape if – or, to his mind, when – violence between the warring factions resumed. Despite Pembroke Castle having a long-established and well-earned reputation as one of the most impregnable fortresses in Wales, the seat of successive earls which had withstood Welsh sieges across the centuries, Jasper identified the coastal port of Tenby as crucial to his purpose.

Tenby lay around 10 miles east of Pembroke, facing eastwards out into Carmarthen Bay, with vital trading routes with England, Scotland, Ireland and continental Europe. With a natural deep-water harbour sheltered from the rough winds of the Atlantic Ocean, Tenby had long been identified as an ideal settlement point. When the Normans first invaded the region in the early twelfth century, Tenby was one of their principal targets, a strategic seaside base from which to establish a thriving trading port. A stone tower garrisoned with Norman troops was erected on a rocky promontory which projected out to sea, though this did not discourage attacks from native Welsh armies. The town was sacked multiple times, including by the Tudors' ancestor Rhys ap Gruffudd in 1153. In the late thirteenth century, further attacks from Welsh leaders prompted the erection of an extensive curtain wall around the parts of the town not guarded by the cliffs, this defensive structure buttressed with towers, gateways and an external barbican. These improvements in the town's defensive infrastructure were robust enough to repel another assault in 1403 by Owain Glyn Dŵr.

Tenby gradually declined in political, if not economic, importance, and by the time Jasper inherited the town as part of his earldom of

Pembroke the fortifications were in a dire state. On 1 December 1457, letters patent from Jasper to the mayor of Tenby, Thomas White, and the burgesses approved an extensive programme of repairs designed to fortify the town's modest defences. As per Jasper's instructions, the town officials were instructed to thicken the town walls to 6 feet, from cliff to cliff, raising the height and installing a continuous parapet walk. The moat was to be cleaned and widened to 30 feet across. To ensure the work was completed with great urgency, Jasper ordered the mayor to recruit carpenters, masons and other tradesmen from throughout Pembrokeshire, paying statutory rates for their time. The cost would be shared between the earl and the townspeople, lessening the financial burden on each party but holding both responsible for its completion.[19]

Once this programme of repairs and improvements was finished, Tenby's Welsh name, Dinbych-y-Pysgod, or 'little fortress of the fish', was more than apt. The town now presented a formidable challenge to any would-be assailant, and a place of refuge in time of need. It is clear to any modern visitor why Jasper chose Tenby as his new political and military headquarters. The town enjoys a beautiful natural setting with a favourable microclimate, boasting a range of rich, sandy beaches and extensive sea views in more than one direction. Profitable trade routes brought an array of cuisines and languages to fifteenth-century Tenby, and a wealthy, multicultural mercantile class likely appealed to Jasper's sensibilities, most of his adulthood having been spent around London's elite. The deep harbour, meanwhile, provided abundant opportunity for the lucrative importation and exportation of goods, and would later play a significant role in saving Jasper's life. The work Jasper had directed was of such a good standard that considerable remnants of this defensive infrastructure can still be glimpsed 600 years later, particularly the noticeably stout western wall and its two square towers that adorn the southern section.

In a reign woefully short of royal leadership, at the end of 1457 Henry VI uncharacteristically issued a sharp summons to his nobles, demanding their attendance for a great council in Westminster to commence on 27 January 1458. The king's intention was to, once and for all, 'eradicate the roots of rancour' that plagued his kingdom and find a compromise that would ensure a lasting peace.[20] His plan involved a bizarre ceremony known as a Loveday, a peacefully mediated arbitration employed to bring to an end a bitter feud. True to form, the king had completely misjudged the mood.

A steady stream of dukes, earls and barons travelled to London for the council as directed, including Jasper Tudor, accompanied by thousands of armed troops that swamped the city's streets. The nervous citizens were understandably alarmed and feared an outbreak of violence outside the doors of their homes. The duke of York brought with him 400 men, and Salisbury 500. Exeter and Somerset brought 800, and the combined Percy contingent from the north numbered around 1,500. Warwick was the last of the great magnates to arrive, bringing with him about 600 professional retainers from the Calais garrison.[21]

The concerned mayor, Geoffrey Boleyn, great-great-grandfather of a future Tudor queen in Elizabeth I, was moved to ban the carrying of weapons in his city and mobilised troops of his own to patrol the streets overnight, alert for anything untoward. While Richard of York and his allies were lodged just inside the walls, at Baynard Castle and the Greyfriars, the more provocative Lancastrian elements were billeted outside. Though London appeared on the brink of violence, such measures were successful in temporarily enforcing a very uneasy peace.[22]

An intense period of arbitration followed, conducted between intermediaries representing each faction. Recriminations were levelled across the chamber during heated summits. But with tempers fraying and no breakthrough on the horizon, the king delightedly announced on 24 March a truce had been agreed. To placate Lancastrian malcontents like Somerset and Northumberland, the Yorkist lords accepted responsibility for the blood shed at St Albans, providing it was recognised, somewhat incongruously, they had always been the king's true liegemen. The Yorkists further agreed to compensate the widows and sons of those they had killed, and to pay for masses to be said for the souls of the dead.

The following morning, the Feast of the Annunciation and known in England as Lady Day, the joyful monarch led a celebratory procession from Westminster to the doors of St Paul's. Walking before him, their hands awkwardly joined in a contrived gesture of friendship, were the duke of Somerset and earl of Salisbury. Following Henry, looking equally uncomfortable holding hands, were Queen Margaret and Richard of York, with the duke of Exeter and earl of Warwick bringing up the rear.

Upon reaching St Paul's, a service of thanksgiving was heard which praised God for delivering peace to England, brokered by his representative, the king. Despite the optimism of Henry VI, it would take far more than holding hands in public to overcome three years of acrimony; indeed, the sixteenth-century chronicler Edward Hall would later note with some accuracy that while 'their mouths lovingly smiled', for those who took part in the procession, their 'courages were inflamed with malice'.[23]

The hollow Loveday charade changed nothing. Though there was a brief thawing in hostility, Somerset and his companions remained fixated on vengeance, the queen suspicious, and York excluded from the power he so desperately sought. A lasting peace eluded the witless king, who had failed once more to address the underlying grievances and understand he could not accommodate both sides. Contending political factions were a recurring symptom of Henry's weak rule, and his partisan promotion of favourites throughout his reign had fomented a deep-seated bitterness and rancour that could not be overcome with one gesture. In November 1458, just eight months later, the earl of Warwick was attacked by royal cooks armed with spits after attending a council meeting in Westminster, and forced to flee via the Thames.[24] York retired to his estates in the Welsh March, and Salisbury returned north. Despite the public spectacle of the Loveday, the English nobility was anything but united.

Jasper's role in the Loveday is not clear, though, as one of the lords who had thus far favoured reconciliation, he may simply have played the part of a hopeful observer. He likely returned to Wales shortly thereafter to conduct his responsibilities as earl and royal constable and observe the redevelopment of Tenby in person. He had also authorised rebuilding work on Kidwelly and Carreg Cennen castles, strengthening their garrisons and reinforcing the Lancastrian position throughout West Wales.[25]

As the leading authority figure in West Wales, on 1 March 1459 Jasper was handed a commission to arrest seven malefactors in Carmarthenshire. This included a servant of the Kidwelly landowner John Dwnn, a great-grandson of Owain Glyn Dŵr and long-term associate of Richard of York. Despite their distant kinship, Jasper and Dwnn would become bitter rivals in years to come. The men handed the commission alongside Jasper, and who presumably carried out much of the investigative work, were his father, Owen Tudor, and the sons of Gruffudd ap Nicholas, Thomas and Owain ap Gruffudd. That Gruffudd ap Nicholas himself is not named suggests he had either died by this point in time, or perhaps was not physically up to the task any longer. Any lingering hostility between the families from Gruffudd's war with Edmund Tudor three years earlier had been resolved and they now tenaciously worked together as a unit to reduce York's influence in West Wales.[26]

Jasper's general standing was further enhanced in 1459 when he was inducted into the Order of the Garter, the most prestigious order of chivalry in England, which had been founded by Edward III in 1348.[27] Though the order offered no material benefit, it was intended to honour the 'bravest and noblest in England' and demanded from its members loyalty, courage and proficiency in arms.[28] Restricted to only twenty-four living members at any one time, the death of Alfonso V, King of Aragon, Sicily and Naples, provided a vacancy, and once elected Jasper was permitted to hang his sword, helm and banner in St George's Chapel at Windsor alongside those of his companions in the brotherhood. Other current members included the dukes of York, Buckingham and Norfolk, the earls of Salisbury, Shrewsbury and Wiltshire, and even Afonso V, King of Portugal, and Frederik III, Holy Roman Emperor. On 23 April 1459, as a knight of the Garter, Jasper took part for the first time in the traditional St George's Day procession at Windsor.

In a further demonstration of the high regard in which Jasper was held by his half-brother, on 2 May the king granted him lifetime use of a tower 'in the lower end of the great hall' in the Palace of Westminster, 'for the safeguard and keeping of the earl's evidences and for the communication and easement of the earl and his council' when in the city. The tower at the other end of the hall was occupied by the queen. Keeping Jasper close for personal reasons was also a factor in Henry's grant, and it certainly provided a more convenient base for the former than his other holding out in Stepney.[29] Around twenty-seven years old, a clear favourite of the king and increasingly prominent in a political capacity, Jasper's star continued to rise. But war was headed Jasper's way, and this time he could not stay on the sidelines.

Regardless of Loveday, animosity between the buoyant Lancastrian court party and the disenfranchised Yorkists continued to escalate throughout 1459. In May, the court decamped once more to Coventry, a continuation of Queen Margaret's transparent strategy of establishing a provincial Lancastrian capital in the Midlands dominated by courtiers and officials loyal to her and her son. Many of the most significant Midlands landowners, men like the duke of Buckingham and the earls of Wiltshire and Shrewsbury, were openly allied with the queen, and even Jasper Tudor was in possession of the manors of Sheldon and Solihull. Owing to his Lancastrian inheritance, which included the earldoms of Derby and Leicester, the king's sway in the region was also widespread. Together, the Lancastrian lords were able to pool their extensive resources and influence through their retainers and officials, forging a hugely formidable royal bloc that stood united against the House of York.

Queen Margaret now sought to take advantage of the Lancastrians' strong position in the Midlands by recruiting men from the surrounding counties into her service, broadening her affinity while stockpiling weapons at Kenilworth, the greatest royal fortress in the region. She even distributed small livery badges depicting a swan with a crown around its neck, a well-known Lancastrian emblem now appropriated on behalf of her six-year-old son, Prince Edward. Such was her campaigning, rumours abounded that Margaret's intention was for the king to soon abdicate in favour of his son, for whom she would govern during his minority.[30] When another great council was scheduled for June, this time to be held in Coventry, York suspected treachery and declined to attend, as did his closest allies Salisbury and Warwick. Their refusal to heed the royal summons exposed them to fresh accusations of sedition from the queen.[31]

York was in a vulnerable position. The queen was intent on his destruction, which was likely to be accomplished in the upcoming council through an Act of Attainder that would strip him of his lands, titles and offices. The duke busied himself in preparation, once more calling on his affinity in the Welsh March and sending urgent messages to the earls of Salisbury and Warwick to muster their men and come to his side at once. It was the third time York had raised a force within a decade. Margaret was alert to the danger a combined Yorkist army could pose, recalling the slaughter at St Albans four years earlier, and sought to frustrate their ambitions.

On 21 September 1459, Warwick's army encountered the young duke of Somerset's force in Warwickshire, though after a tense stand-off they failed to engage and withdrew.[32] Two days later, Warwick's father Salisbury was heading from Yorkshire on his own journey to Ludlow when, on barren sloping heathland near Blore Heath in Staffordshire, his path was blocked by a Lancastrian force under the command of the elderly James Tuchet, 5th Baron Audley. Salisbury feigned a retreat and the elderly Audley fell for the ruse, his mounted cavalry racing into the brook that stood between the two armies. In a brutal skirmish that lasted all afternoon, the Yorkists overturned their numerical disadvantage and routed the stranded Lancastrians.[33]

Salisbury and Warwick reached the duke of York in Worcester without further incident, their resolve strengthened by their respective experiences on the way. In the town's cathedral, oaths were sworn to one another, and the embattled lords finalised plans to confront the king and refute accusations of disloyalty. Notified by their scouts that a vast royal army blocked their path towards London, they retreated west to York's stronghold of Ludlow, protesting one final time by letter they were the king's faithful subjects, their ambition merely stretching to the removal of his incompetent counsellors.[34] The king responded that he would offer a pardon to York and Warwick should they surrender within six days but that, having spilled noble blood at Blore Heath, Salisbury was to be condemned a traitor. There was no prospect of such terms being acceptable to Salisbury's son Warwick, or his brother-in-law York.

On 9 October 1459, the Yorkists assembled their combined forces in the fields near Ludford Bridge, just across the River Teme from Ludlow, and waited. The only other lords with them were York's teenage sons, the earls of March and Rutland, and John Clinton, 5th Baron Clinton. Three tense days passed before the royal army they had been expecting appeared on the horizon. Present on the Lancastrian side was the queen, with the armed retinues of the dukes of Somerset, Exeter and Buckingham, and the earls of Northumberland, Arundel, Devon, Shrewsbury and Wiltshire. Foremost among their number, however, was the fully harnessed king himself, his royal standard fluttering in the Shropshire breeze. Morale among the Yorkist rank and file plummeted when word of Henry's presence spread, and their despair was infectious.

When the duke of Buckingham offered a royal pardon to any Yorkist soldier who defected, York's position weakened considerably as his men's heads were turned. Under the cover of darkness, Warwick's Calais garrison, the only professional standing English army of its day, submitted to the king, claiming they had been deceived as to the Yorkists' true intentions. Already outnumbered and facing certain defeat when morning came, York, Salisbury and Warwick retreated beyond the walls of Ludlow under the pretence of finalising their strategy. In truth, they had dishonourably abandoned their soldiers, who woke in the morning confused, leaderless and frightened.

The Yorkist lords split into two parties following their flight, with York and his second son Rutland fleeing to Ireland. York's eldest son, Edward of March, and the earls of Salisbury and Warwick headed for the Devon coast before making for Calais. In their absence, York's principal seat of Ludlow was sacked, Lancastrian soldiers robbing taverns of their stock and shamefully defiling women in the streets. Among those the royal leadership encountered were York's deserted duchess Cecily Neville, his younger sons George and Richard, and his daughter Margaret.[35]

Having orchestrated the hounding of her enemies out of the kingdom, it was said by one chronicler that 'every lord in England at this time dares not disobey the Queen',[36] and it is certainly true she was emboldened by her success. Writs were quickly issued summoning those lords to a parliament in Coventry on 20 November, where the partisan proceedings were singularly focused on irrevocably crushing York's influence.

There is no evidence Jasper had been present at Ludford Bridge, but he is noted as present for the parliament, albeit arriving late in its proceedings. According to one observer, the earl of Pembroke only appeared in Coventry on 6 December, entering the city at the head of 'a good fellowship'.[37] His tardiness may have been connected with York's flight to Ireland through North Wales, with Jasper having perhaps been tasked with leading an ultimately unsuccessful pursuit through terrain he knew well. If Jasper had been advancing on Ludlow from the south-west with his affinity, part of a Lancastrian pincer movement, it certainly explains York's decision to flee, breaking the bridges behind him.

Later dubbed the Parliament of Devils, the purpose of this session was the destruction of the Yorkist lords who had raised arms against their sovereign for the third time in four years. Richard of York, cast as an ungrateful and persistent traitor, was formally attainted, which amounted to legal death; his titles, lands and possessions were declared forfeit and returned to the crown in a rich windfall for the king. Salisbury and Warwick received the same punishment for their malicious intent. Their treason was cried openly in every town, city and burgh throughout the kingdom, leaving no subject in doubt that the Yorkist faction were outlaws. Fresh oaths were sworn to the king, queen and heir by all present, including Jasper, a collective reaffirmation of their allegiance to the House of Lancaster, present and future.[38]

The forfeiture of Yorkist lands and the dismissal of all their officials allowed the king to reward his faithful servants across the following months, including his Tudor kin. On 19 December, the penultimate day of parliament, Owen was handed a pension of £100 a year to be funded from six forfeited manors belonging to Lord Clinton, attainted for his association with the Yorkists at Blore Heath. This was followed in May by a lease for seven years on some of Clinton's estates, including the manors of Folkestone, Benstead, Huntingdon and Millbroke in Kent, and Blakeham and Hamsey in Surrey.[39] The extra income would have been a useful boost for Owen, for in 1459 in Pembroke he had fathered another child with an unknown woman. This son, who took the name David Owen, was likely raised in Pembroke alongside his nephew Henry, two years his senior. David would later serve the crown under the reigns of his Tudor nephew and great-nephew, who openly acknowledged his paternity.[40]

On 12 February 1460, meanwhile, Jasper was granted for life full rights to Le Garlek, the Stepney townhouse he shared with Thomas Vaughan, also recently attainted for his connection to York.[41] On 5 May, York's lordship of Newbury in Berkshire was likewise transferred to Jasper.[42] The most politically significant grant to Jasper at this time, however, came on 5 January 1460 when he was gifted Denbigh Castle, York's strategically crucial fortress in the heart of one of the wealthiest baronies in North Wales. Jasper was now created constable of Denbigh for life, as well as steward and master forester of the lordship, with his father Owen appointed parker and woodward a month later.[43] It may not have gone unnoticed by both men that their paternal lineage, through Ednyfed Fychan, had its roots in the Denbigh area.

Before his downfall, York had heavily garrisoned Denbigh, and part of the conditions of Jasper's new grant was an expectation that he would suppress this pocket of Yorkist resistance in North Wales. As he had done on many occasions before, the earl of Pembroke set about his latest mission with utmost urgency, although he first issued a series of demands of the king and council, conveyed through his esquire Thomas Wyriot. First, he requested a commission to raise a besieging force in West Wales, intending to delegate responsibility for raising troops and tradesmen to fifteen subordinates he trusted, experienced military and administrative officials bound to him by ties of service, personal loyalty and a shared political attitude. Also sought was permission to pardon any rebels prepared to submit to his authority, or to execute them at his discretion. Jasper further petitioned the king to be granted all moveable goods seized from the Yorkist garrison so he could reward his supporters.[44]

The king immediately acquiesced to all his half-brother's requests, and on 16 February wrote to his chancellor, William Waynflete, ordering their swift execution. There was a request, however, that any English or Irish outlaws captured were to be detained at the king's will, to be tried at a later date.[45] The measures did their job; by 13 March 1460, Jasper was reimbursed the sum of 1,000 marks to cover his expenses in 'crushing the rebels' of Denbigh, as well as suppressing other Welsh castles in the hands of Yorkist rebels. Pointedly, the money would be funded from the revenues of York's own forfeited lordships.[46]

Jasper was also part of two other extensive and powerful commissions designed to seek out and crush Yorkist sedition in Wales in the spring of 1460. Under the nominal authority of his nephew Edward, the young Prince of Wales, leading Lancastrian magnates like Jasper, the duke of Buckingham, the earl of Shrewsbury and Viscount Beaumont were tasked with investigating the Welsh lordships of York, Salisbury and Warwick, collecting evidence of treason and exposing any conspiracies, insurrections, robberies, plunders, rapes or murders. To help ease Jasper's financial burden in rooting out and eradicating lingering Yorkist support, he was also declared exempt from any outstanding or future fines for charters, letters patent and other writs.[47]

By 25 May 1460, Jasper was back at his baronial seat of Pembroke dealing with another pressing matter of defence. A Yorkist ship had entered Milford Haven waterway, the deep and wide natural channel around which several inlets and coves offered several locations to make landfall for a hostile force. The waterway also provided seaborne access to Pembroke, a fact which concerned the Tudor earl. From his apartments in the castle, Jasper wrote to John Hall, the mayor of Tenby, giving notice he had ordered a ship called *Le Mary* to be handed over to his esquire Thomas Wogan, who was charged with attacking the enemy vessel. The mayor was also tasked with providing sailors for the mission, men of local standing to be urged to defend their homeland at all costs. It is unknown if Wogan engaged with the Yorkists at sea, but no attempted landing on the coast of West Wales was recorded at this time, suggesting he fulfilled his duty.[48]

Perhaps owing to Jasper's cautious diligence in marshalling the Welsh coast, the Yorkists focused their attentions elsewhere. In January 1460, Warwick led a lightning raid on Sandwich in Kent, demolishing part of a royal fleet, and in March boldly sailed through the Channel to Ireland to liaise with York in person, discussing strategy for their return to England. It may have been he who appeared in Milford Haven waterway that spring, assessing the feasibility of an invasion through Wales. When Warwick returned to Calais, he assembled another strong fleet and, together with his father Salisbury and his strapping seventeen-year-old cousin Edward of March, sailed for Kent once again. This time, they intended to fully invade England. The Yorkists landed at Sandwich on 26 June without much difficulty, and marched onwards to London with ease, advertising a manifesto which repeated their well-worn grievances about misgovernment and corrupt counsellors. It was familiar rhetoric, an apparent desire to bring misrule to an end, but one that had resonated with the commons of the south-east for generations.[49]

While Salisbury laid siege to the Tower of London, Warwick and March hurried into the Midlands, their army swelling with followers along the way, including the lords Fauconberg, Saye and Sele, Clinton, Abergavenny, Scrope of Bolton and Audley, plus papal legate Francesco Coppini, the archbishop of Canterbury and the bishops of Salisbury, Exeter, Ely and Rochester.[50] Audley was the son of the baron killed just nine months earlier by Warwick's father at Blore Heath, but in a rare example of a son not seeking revenge during this period, he had elected to defect. Coppini had been sent to England by Pope Pius II to heal the division and promote a crusade against the Turks but, having found Queen Margaret unwelcoming, had instead become a committed Yorkist mouthpiece.

When the Lancastrian leadership learned of Warwick's advance, a royal force under Buckingham's command was hastily assembled, assuming a defensive position just south of the flooded Nene near Delapré Abbey in Northampton. They did not have to wait long for the Yorkists to appear. On the wet morning of 10 July 1460, Warwick sent some of the bishops to the royal tent to ask the king to grant the earl an audience. It was a request rejected by Buckingham, who upbraided the churchmen as mere 'men of arms' before warning that if Warwick entered the king's presence 'he shall die'. Resigned to battle to get his way, at two o'clock in the afternoon, Warwick's army launched into the right flank of the royal army, commanded by Edmund Grey, 4th Baron Grey de Ruthin.[51]

Rather than standing their ground, Grey's men downed their weapons in the bog and helped pull Warwick's men over the barricades, moving aside to allow them to charge at the ill-prepared main body of the Lancastrian host. Confused and panic-stricken by the sudden onslaught, the Lancastrians' resistance was feeble, and victory was Warwick's within half an hour. Ordering the common soldiers to be spared, Warwick's soldiers pursued the nobles, a tactic reminiscent of the battle of St Albans five years earlier. Those hunted down and slain beside the king's tent included Buckingham and Shrewsbury, as well as the lords Egremont and Beaumont. Of greater significance, however, was the capture of Henry VI, found alone in his tent and oblivious to the slaughter around him.[52]

With the king once more under their control, the Yorkist takeover of government was swift. By the end of July, supporters of York filled the great offices of state: Bishop George Neville, Warwick's brother, was appointed chancellor, while Viscount Bourchier, York's brother-in-law, was made treasurer.[53] The council, meanwhile, was dominated by Warwick, Salisbury and Archbishop Bourchier, the viscount's brother. When news of Warwick's victory reached York in Dublin, the duke readied himself for his return to England after nearly a year in exile. He landed in Lancashire on 9 September 1460, notably evading Wales, where Jasper's men were patrolling the coast, and marched casually towards London. Once he was reunited with his duchess in Oxfordshire, York was forthwith accompanied by trumpets and clarions, with his sword drawn before him in the manner of a king. His banner also bore the royal arms of England, rather than those of the House of York. Already subject to an attainder and unlikely ever to be reconciled with the Lancastrian regime, York had nothing to lose, and was raising the stakes.[54]

The duke entered London on 10 October, timing his arrival to coincide with the first week of parliament. Strutting into the Painted Chamber of the Palace of Westminster, his sword still borne before him, York confidently walked past his fellow lords and headed straight to the dais. Standing before the empty throne, he reached out and rested his palm on the royal cushion. His gesture needed no interpretation: York now coveted the throne. Rather than enthusiastic applause, however, the duke was greeted with an awkward silence.[55] Even York's closest supporters, the earls of Salisbury and Warwick, were outwardly unsettled by his behaviour.

York's dissatisfaction with Lancastrian rule had been a central theme of politics stretching back a decade, his criticisms of crooked officials and scandalous misgovernment a well-trodden subject. But the duke had never expressed any desire to provoke a change on the throne, nor had he sought to have his lineage broadcast as superior to that of the Lancastrian dynasty. Previously deposed kings like Edward II and Richard II had displayed tyrannical behaviour that cost them the support of much of the nobility, but despite his flaws as ruler no one could call Henry VI a despot. He was not hated, and certainly not feared. If anything, Henry's chief crime had been that he was merely a poor judge of character, and easily led. There was very minimal clamour, if any, to unseat the king from a throne he had occupied for nearly forty years. York had severely misjudged the mood of the nobility, even among his closest allies.

Encouraged by the prudent archbishop of Canterbury to submit his claim to the throne in writing, York withdrew, although not before presumptuously laying claim to the royal apartments. On 16 October, his claim of dynastic precedence was duly presented to parliament, illuminated with a genealogical roll which documented his descent from the separate royal lines of Mortimer and York. The duke argued that through the York side he was descended in the male line from Edmund of Langley, 1st Duke of York and the fourth son of Edward III to survive to adulthood. Through the Mortimer side, York showed that he was descended, albeit in a female line, from Lionel of Antwerp, 1st Duke of Clarence, the second son of Edward III to survive to adulthood. The House of Lancaster, on the other hand, were descended from John of Gaunt, the third surviving son of Edward III. York, then, had a superior claim according to cognatic primogeniture, in which female claims are considered, but not through agnatic primogeniture, which considers the male line only. To emphasise the point, York now assumed the surname

Plantagenet in honour of his dual royal descent, the first recorded use of this name to describe all royal descendants of Henry II.[56]

York's claim was considered by the foremost minds in the realm, many of them reluctant to be drawn on its legality for fear of offending either of the affected parties, York and Henry VI. Any objections to his argument were easily countered by the duke. After two weeks, a remarkable compromise known as the Act of Accord was suggested. Henry VI was to retain his throne for the remainder of his natural life, but upon his death the crown was to pass into the Yorkist line. In the meantime, York was created prince of Wales, duke of Cornwall and earl of Chester – titles traditionally reserved for the heir apparent – and appointed protector for the third time. To avoid the shedding of more Christian blood, King Henry meekly gave his consent.[57] On 31 October, the assembled lords spiritual and temporal swore an oath recognising York as the 'rightful heir' to the kingdom.[58] It was a middle path that appeased no one, and merely postponed the pressing matter of who should rule England.

A consequence of the Act of Accord was the total disinheritance of Henry VI's son, Edward of Westminster, the prince of Wales. The worst fears of Queen Margaret had been realised, but unlike her pliant husband she was not prepared to accept the situation. Her gender may have precluded Margaret from personally assuming rule in England, but her force of character and decisive nature galvanised a core of Lancastrian nobles willing to resist the Yorkist ascendancy. These included the dukes of Somerset and Exeter, themselves both in the Lancastrian line of succession, and of course the staunchly loyal earl of Pembroke, Jasper Tudor.

While York had been in Westminster demolishing her son's future and snatching away his birthright, Margaret had wisely fled England, taking with her Prince Edward. The man to whom she turned for protection was her brother-in-law, Jasper. After Warwick's victory at Northampton, the Yorkist party had seized the reins of government once more and set about recovering some of their lost power, particularly in Wales. On 9 August, Jasper was tersely ordered by the new Yorkist-controlled council to surrender Denbigh Castle to York's nephew, Edward Bourchier. Similar orders were sent to the Lancastrian constables in charge of Beaumaris, Conwy, Flint, Ruthin, Montgomery, Holt and Hawarden castles, each a strategic North Welsh fortress in its own right. Not recognising their authority, Jasper refused. On 17 August, therefore, the Tudors' old foes, Walter Devereux, William Herbert and Roger Vaughan, were granted 'full authority and power' in 'all possible haste' to take Denbigh by force, triggering a protracted siege which Jasper's kinsman and deputy constable Roger Puleston bravely repelled for several months.[59] How the tables had turned at Denbigh in just five months.

Throughout the autumn of 1460, however, Jasper still retained great authority in Wales and was able to shelter Queen Margaret and his nephew Prince Edward in Harlech Castle.[60] Erected by Edward I at the end of the thirteenth century, Harlech was an imposing fortress perched high on a rocky crag that overlooked the Irish Sea to the west, while in every other direction it was enclosed by the rugged snow-capped peaks of Eryri. In recent memory, the castle had briefly served as the military, political and family headquarters of Owain Glyn Dŵr during his war of independence, and held a worthy reputation as one of the most impenetrable strongholds found anywhere in the kingdom. Harlech was not a palace, but a gloomy stone compound singularly designed for soldiers and conflict. Having been assaulted and robbed by one of her servants during her flight, Harlech and its sturdy defences were the perfect redoubt for a queen desperately seeking protection for herself and her young son.[61] In a world where loyalties were changeable, Margaret knew she could depend upon Jasper.

At Harlech, safe for the moment and able to reflect on recent events, Margaret's anguish over her son's disinheritance poured out. If Jasper was able to offer any comforting words, they likely did little to soothe the queen's anger. When a series of letters purporting to be from the king reached her hand, begging the queen to bring her son south, Margaret suspected something was amiss. Before she had left Henry's side, the king had kissed his wife and instructed her he would only communicate using a secret token, or code, known only to the pair. This code was not present on the letters, revealing them to be counterfeits designed to draw her into a trap.[62] With Jasper's assistance, in late November 1460, Margaret and Prince Edward boarded a ship and sailed for Scotland.

The Act of Accord was also a devastating development for Jasper. He owed everything to the generous patronage of his half-brother, and though Henry VI would be permitted to reign until his natural death, there was no guarantee Jasper or his heirs would enjoy any particular favour under Yorkist rule. Jasper's only recourse was to throw in his lot with the queen's party and seek York's destruction.

Between 1457 and 1460, the earl of Pembroke's challenging assignment to secure Wales for the crown had proven productive; he had succeeded in quelling lawlessness in Carmarthenshire and Cardiganshire, had established a strong political friendship with his neighbouring magnate Buckingham in Gwent, strengthened his own position in Pembrokeshire and particularly Tenby, and subjugated York's treasured lordship of Denbigh. Jasper had established his reputation as one of the most tenacious defenders of Lancaster, demonstrating with every success a deeply unselfish devotion to the flagging cause of his half-brother, Henry VI. He had little choice. The future of the Tudors depended on him, for the Wars of the Roses had truly ignited.

10

Interminable Treachery

The act which settled the crown on the line of Richard, Duke of York, after the death of Henry VI solved nothing. York was forced to wait for the natural end of the king, ten years his junior, while Queen Margaret and her faithful band of followers were galvanised by the distressing prospect of Lancastrian disinheritance. The king may have meekly accepted the act, but his proud queen was disinclined to stand idly as her son's future crown was snatched from his grasp.

Unfairly painted by later commentators as a belligerent warmonger who stepped outside the traditional role expected from a queen consort, there is little evidence that Margaret imposed herself on political matters before her husband's sickness. If he would not, or even could not, fight to safeguard his son's inheritance then, through necessity rather than choice, Margaret was willing to step up.

The queen was not alone in opposing the act, of course. Among those on whose support she could count were the Lancastrian-descended dukes of Somerset and Exeter, cousins of Henry VI and high in the current line of succession. Other magnates content with the current order were the earls of Northumberland, Wiltshire, Devon, and Westmorland, the lords Clifford, Roos and Dacre, and of course Margaret's brother-in-law, Jasper Tudor, Earl of Pembroke. After sheltering with Jasper's assistance at Harlech Castle on the north-west coast of Wales, Margaret and her son Henry sailed out into the Irish Sea and headed north to Scotland, where she found a sympathetic audience in Mary of Guelders, the French widow of King James II and regent to her nine-year-old son, James III.

From her Scottish base, Margaret now coordinated an ambitious two-pronged invasion of England, hoping to capitalise on Northumberland's northern insurgency. Messengers were sent to the hot-headed Somerset and his ally Devon, demanding they gather their troops in the south-west of England and journey through the heart of England for a general

Lancastrian muster in Hull.[1] Despite the bleak winter months and the poor condition of the tracks north, the pair doggedly set about their mission.

From his position in Wales, Jasper Tudor learned with dismay how, on 30 December 1460, Richard of York had been duped into leaving the safe confines of his castle at Sandal in Yorkshire and was quickly set upon from every direction by his enemies. The duke was caught 'like a fish in a net' and slaughtered, as was his young son, Edmund of Rutland, cruelly butchered attempting to flee the assault. York's brother-in-law, Salisbury, was captured alive and taken to Pontefract, where he would shortly meet his end on the chopping block.[2] For the sons of those slain at St Albans five years earlier, men like Somerset, Northumberland and Clifford, it was sweet revenge to bring death to the Yorkists' door but could only yield yet more bloodshed in return.

A full descent into civil war was now inevitable, and Jasper hurriedly raised his affinity, calling on his indentured retainers to provide men, weapons and supplies for the inevitable campaigns to come. He must have known that York's eldest son, Edward of March, had spent the Christmas period touring the family's estates in the Welsh March, and would be eager for vengeance. That Edward of March also blocked Jasper's path north to combine his Welsh army with Queen Margaret's force would have concerned the earl of Pembroke.

Among the many knights, esquires and tenants whose service Jasper now called upon were Owain and Thomas Gruffydd, the hardy sons of Gruffydd ap Nicholas who had proven steadfastly loyal to the Tudor earl in recent years. Others mobilising for him included Thomas Perrot of Haverfordwest, Lewis ap Rhys and Hopkin Davy of Carmarthen, Philip Mansel and Hopkin ap Rhys of Gower, Rheinallt Gwynedd of Harlech, Lewis Powys of Powysland and Thomas FitzHenry, a Herefordshire lawyer and acting chamberlain of South Wales at the time. Sir John Skydmore of Ewyas Lacy, Jasper's constable of Pembroke and a brother-in-law of Owain and Thomas ap Gruffydd, was able to raise thirty men by himself, including his sons James and Harry, and his brother William.[3]

Apart from FitzHenry and Skydmore's Herefordshire contingent, Jasper's men were chiefly drawn from the counties of Pembrokeshire and Carmarthenshire, and his army was noticeably referred to by one chronicler as 'the Welshmen'.[4] Also present among Jasper's force was his father, Owen Tudor. For much of the previous decade, Owen had maintained a lower profile than in his younger days, quietly tending to his modest estates in Surrey and even fathering another son, David. Despite his advanced age, in his eldest surviving son's time of need Owen now emerged once more from the shadows. In a treacherous period rife with danger and betrayal, his father's companionship and commitment probably eased Jasper's anxieties on the march to war.

Jasper's Welsh contingent was also joined by the Irish levies of James Butler, the handsome if fainthearted earl of Wiltshire, plus a unit of French and Breton mercenaries that swelled the numbers.[5] Together, this disparate, multinational, multilingual force journeyed through the Tywi Valley, passing through Carmarthen, Llandovery and Brecon before fording the Wye near Glasbury. Once north of the river, they followed the path of the Wye through hamlets like Kinnersley, Sarnesfield and Weobley, making for the great Yorkist political base of Wigmore. Conscious they were deep in enemy territory, the Lancastrians travelled cautiously.

It was only when they were around 4 miles south of Wigmore, steadily heading north on the old Roman road between Hereford and Shrewsbury, that Jasper's foreriders reported the presence of a well-arrayed Yorkist army blocking their path.[6] As expected, Edward of March had known of Jasper's advance for several days, his own scout network bringing him regular dispatches of the Lancastrians' progress and the quality of their host. March was deliberately based close to his ancestral seats of Wigmore and Ludlow, his well-rested force largely drawn from the local Herefordshire gentry, who had little concern over provisions running low. Also responding to March's call were Sir William Herbert and his brother Richard, their half-brother Roger Vaughan of Tretower and Sir Walter Devereux, the same tight collective that had invaded South Wales in 1456 and clashed with Edmund Tudor. Yorkist retainers from across South and East Wales, including Glamorgan, Brecon, Monmouth, Radnor and Montgomery, were also present, thousands of men prepared to die in the cause of Edward of March and the House of York.[7] Jasper's fatigued men, on the other hand, although no less devoted to their lord, had travelled more than 100 miles in around ten days in the middle of a miserable Welsh winter.

The path in front of him blocked, Jasper had little choice but to array his forces for battle. The Yorkists had assumed an aggressive position on a southwards-facing plain, their left flank protected by the meandering River Lugg and their right by dense, rising woodland. The stage was set for a hugely significant military confrontation deep in the Welsh March between two armies heavily recruited from different quarters of Wales. The outcome would help determine who would wear the English crown.

As principal commander, Jasper conferred with his most trusted advisors and ordered their men to set up camp. With battle likely to be joined in the morning, that evening the camp was a hive of anxious activity as the troops steadied themselves to face what could be their last day on Earth. Some focused on prayer while others congregated around firepits, discussing any and all topics other than the obvious. After several days in the field together – weeks in the case of the Irish and French recruits – a natural camaraderie had been fostered, with howls of laughter intermittently shattering the heavy tension in the air. All, no doubt, inspected their weapons and armour before bedding down for the night on the cold, unforgiving ground.

Jasper's tent, located near the centre of camp and likely the largest, doubled as a strategic command centre. Maintaining morale was crucial to prevent desertions under the cover of darkness, and the earl may even have wandered through the camp, checking in with the lower ranks and offering measured words of reassurance. Regardless of who emerged from the battle victorious, many of the calloused hands Jasper shook belonged to men who would not survive to see another sunset. His fate was likewise uncertain.

When the Lancastrians woke on the bitterly cold morning of 3 February 1461,[8] their attention was quickly drawn to the sky where a strange sight greeted thousands of bleary-eyed men. As they adjusted to the sunlight, it soon became apparent they were gazing upon three suns rising on the horizon, which gradually combined to form one. This is an atmospheric phenomenon known as a sun dog, caused by the refracting of sunlight from ice crystals in the cold atmosphere. To the observer, the two sun dogs, or parhelia, appear to the right and left of the Sun, particularly when the Sun is near the horizon, giving the appearance there are three in the sky rather than one.[9]

In a superstitious age, this was a terrifying portent, one which particularly troubled the soldiers on the Yorkist side. When Edward of March grasped the despair that was brewing among his men, he addressed them with a confidence and maturity far beyond his eighteen years. This, Edward charismatically explained, was a providential omen – the three suns represented the Holy Trinity, and they should be of 'good comfort', for they were fated to prevail against their enemy. Almost to a man, their grave countenances were transformed.[10]

Warfare in the fifteenth century was typically guided by the principles laid out by the Roman writer Flavius Renatus Vegetius in his fifth-century handbook *De re militari*, which also formed much of the basis for Christine de Pizan's influential 1410 military treatise *The Book of Deeds of Arms and Chivalry*. Kings and commanders across Europe had access to their teachings on martial organisation, and Jasper, like his contemporaries, probably drew his basic strategy from Vegetius and de Pizan. He had followed their advice on selecting fit men capable of wielding an array of weaponry, on setting up a fortified camp and on managing his troops to prevent mutiny or desertion, at least as far as circumstance allowed.

As per Vegetius, English armies were typically organised into three divisions, or battles. In the front, or occasionally on the right, was the vanguard, with the mainguard in the middle and the rearguard following behind or on the left. Each division was allocated to someone the commander respected and trusted, a subordinate who would follow the agreed strategy. In his first military engagement as commander, Jasper assumed leadership for the main body of troops, assigning one battle to the earl of Wiltshire and the other to his father, Owen, and Sir John Throckmorton.

As a wealthy earl, a half-brother of the king even, Jasper was enclosed from head to toe in full-plate armour crafted from the finest well-tempered steel, the whole suit being known a harness. Though it was heavy, he retained his ability to move with comparative ease. Beneath the armour, he wore a thick arming doublet fashioned from fustian lined with velvet, with gussets of mail protecting vulnerable areas like the neck, armpits and hips. On his head, Jasper donned a steel sallet with a visor pulled down across his face, only a narrow slit providing sight of the chaos unfolding before him. To lift the visor in the heat of battle was a risk that could prove deadly, as Henry V nearly discovered as a teenager at the Battle of Shrewsbury in 1403 when an arrow lodged in his cheek. The ordinary troops under Jasper's command were not so fortunate. Most were protected only by their padded doublets, perhaps aided by the odd breastplate or brigandine they had pilfered from a dead opponent during a previous engagement.

Though the extent of Jasper's childhood military education is unclear, being raised chiefly at Barking Abbey and not in a noble household, in keeping with all his contemporaries he was probably competent at swordplay. En route to battle, he certainly carried a sword of some type, either a double-edged arming sword or the two-handed longsword, and on his person had fastened a dagger, typically used to deliver a mercy blow to a dying adversary or to thrust through plate armour in close-combat scenarios. Other weapons brought to the battlefield included a variety of polearms, such as halberds, bills, glaives and poleaxes, and other instruments including hammers, axes, spears and maces, each designed to inflict dreadful injury on its target.

The backbone of any respectable Welsh and English army of the day, however, was the archer, who bore a huge yew longbow capable of loosing between twelve and fifteen arrows a minute. Often wearing just a simple skullcap for protection and sometimes barefooted to gain better traction with the ground, the archers would loose their arrows in a high arc so they rained down on their opponents, inflicting considerable injury and even death before the armies engaged on foot.

As with most fifteenth-century battles, the fighting that took place on the morning of 3 February 1461 started with those archers. Having been able to inspect the terrain long before the arrival of his foe, Edward had shrewdly concealed a unit of archers in the woods to the west of the battlefield. At his command, they unleashed a relentless arrow storm that quickly caused considerable distress to the Lancastrian left flank. As the soldiers attempted to move away from the unremitting aerial assault that was finding its target with deadly accuracy, they started to compress on the Lancastrian centre, a distraction that impacted negatively on their overall positional discipline. As Jasper's army was being driven towards the river by the volley of arrows, he had little option but to order his men to advance before the core of his force plunged into the icy Lugg.

Once both sides released the bulk of their forces, the fighting was fierce, chaotic, loud and extremely bloody. It is unknown if Jasper took part in any combat personally, or rather directed matters from afar, but his counterpart, the fearless Edward of March, was immediately in the centre of the action. Still only eighteen years old, Edward towered above his contemporaries and slashed through his enemy with the consummate experience of a veteran twice his age. In many respects, he was a throwback to great Plantagenet warrior kings like Henry V and Edward III. As the fighting wore on and gaps developed where once had stood men, it became clear the Yorkists' numerical advantage was having an effect. Jasper could only look on in dismay as his men were slaughtered in the thousands, with Wiltshire's ill-equipped Irishmen particularly bearing the brunt.[11] Even if his tactics had been beyond reproach, Jasper's army was outnumbered and outmuscled by a better-prepared, higher-quality adversary.

With the day plainly lost, the Lancastrian troops started to abandon the battlefield, and hot on their heels were their weary commanders. The rout that followed was frantic and brutal, as the Yorkists mercilessly hunted down their prey, stopping only to strip the dead of their armour and valuables. The Yorkist archers now demonstrated their lethality in close combat, now picking off individual targets instead of loosing towards the mass. Prospero di Camulio, the Milanese ambassador to France, reported that as many as 8,000 men were killed, and much of the bloodshed is likely to have taken place near Kingsland, where a 1799 stone pedestal in the Tuscan style still commemorates the battle.[12] The nearby hamlet was soon named Mortimer's Cross, likely inspired by the victory of Edward of March, the inheritor of the great Mortimer legacy. Other local features, such as the Battle Oak and Battle Acre Cottage, hint at the area's bloody legacy.

Though the common soldier was slaughtered where he stood, the principal targets were the nobility and gentry. When it became clear they had lost control of their men, Jasper and Wiltshire abandoned their positions and bolted from the battlefield, 'put to flight' in the words of one scornful chronicler. They only stopped to shed their armour and don disguises, hoping to be mistaken for commoners. Jasper wisely headed west as quickly as he could ride, intending to work his way through Wales to his coastal fortress at Tenby. In the haste of his flight, he lost contact with his father, Owen, who had also desperately tried to make his escape. He didn't make it far.[13]

Not even a knight, Owen's capture should hardly have warranted much attention, but these were chaotic times where the normal rules no longer applied. His captor was Roger Vaughan of Tretower, who was no friend of the Tudors, and word was likely sent to Edward of March regarding his apprehension. With Edward still grieving for the killing of his father, brother and uncle just five weeks earlier, Owen Tudor represented his first opportunity for retribution.

Dragged through the streets of Hereford with his hands bound,[14] his face bloodied and muddy from the battle, Owen cut a tragic figure. He was an old man, in his early sixties, though murmurs among the crowds recalled how in his younger days the prisoner before them had wedded the dowager queen in secret. He was led into the Market Square, where he caught sight of a makeshift stage upon which stood a wooden chopping block and an axe. Even at this late stage, Owen expected a pardon, with a tough period of imprisonment or perhaps ransom back to his son. It was not customary in England, after all, to conduct summary executions in this manner. But times were changing. When the collar of his red velvet doublet was torn away from his neck, Owen at last grasped the severity of his situation.

His life about to be brought to an end, Owen's final words recalled happier times with the queen he had been so audacious to court thirty years earlier. With the eyes of the crowd upon him, standing between his captors and facing the executioner preparing to take his life, Owen said, 'That head shall lie on the stock that was wont to lie on Queen Katherine's lap.' Fully accepting of his fate, Owen dropped to his knees and placed his bare neck onto the coarse block. Putting 'his heart and mind holy unto God', this bold Welsh squire who dared to rise high above his station 'full meekly took his death'. With a mighty swing of the axe, Owen Tudor's extraordinary life was extinguished.

Owen's bloodied head was raised before the baying crowd and thereafter set upon the highest point of the market cross, a grisly symbol of the Yorkists' recent victory. Edward of March's role in the execution of Owen Tudor is unclear, but, whether matters were directed by him or simply conducted on his behalf by an underling like Roger Vaughan, the killing of Henry VI's stepfather was retribution for the death of Edward's father, Richard of York. The unfortunate Owen was in the wrong place at the wrong time.

In the following days, a lady was observed approaching Owen's decapitated head and combing his hair, even gently washing some of the blood away as though she was lovingly bathing a family member. Around his head she had painstakingly placed dozens of burning candles, perhaps more than 100. Her identity is unknown, and she was regarded by one chronicler as little more than a local madwoman. It must be considered that this was a grieving mistress of Owen's, perhaps even the mother of his two-year-old son, David. This may have been a final act of love towards a man whose romantic exploits caused significant commotion in life, and perhaps even in death.

Owen's body was buried in a chapel of the local Greyfriars priory, possibly later followed by his head, though since the priory's dissolution no trace exists. As to be expected, considering his lineage, his demise drew comment from the sorrowful Welsh bards. Robin Ddu, an associate of the Tudors, raged at the 'interminable treachery' that led to Owen's death, a 'bitter loss for Anglesey'. A 'beloved lord' and 'eminent kinsman to Arthur', Owen Tudor had been a 'gallant and blameless man'.[15] His death rankled with the Welsh for many years to come.

Events moved quickly after Mortimer's Cross. On 17 February 1461, just three weeks later, a second battle was fought at St Albans. On this occasion, a Lancastrian army under the command of Somerset and Northumberland tactically outwitted an ill-prepared Yorkist force led by Warwick. Though the latter managed to flee the field before capture, in his flight he left behind King Henry, found by the Lancastrians singing under a tree and unconcerned by the slaughter around him.[16] Any hopes of the Lancastrians re-establishing authority in London, however, were hindered by word of their army's widespread plundering of St Albans and general looting of the English countryside, which prompted officials in the capital to close the gates at the behest of their frightened citizens. With provisions running low, Queen Margaret commanded her men to return north, unable for the moment to reverse the political settlement of the previous year that had disinherited her son.[17]

For the Londoners, Edward of March was a different proposition. Reuniting with Warwick in Oxfordshire, at the end of February the cousins were welcomed into the capital 'with unbounded joy'.[18] Here, there was a marked shift in their strategy. On 1 March, Warwick's brother George Neville, Bishop of Exeter and Chancellor of England, preached a sermon in which he encouraged the crowd to accept Edward of March as king, followed the next day by bills being dispersed through the city documenting the Yorkist claim to the throne. On 4 March, Edward rode in procession from St Paul's to the Palace of Westminster, where the handsome, confident and vigorous eighteen-year-old took his place on the throne while holding the sceptre. There, before the enthusiastic London crowds, he was proclaimed king.[19]

Losing possession of Henry VI to the Lancastrians damaged any credibility the Yorkists had in claiming to be governing on his behalf. Since the Act of Accord had been broken by the killing of his father, Edward now asserted he no longer had to wait for Henry's death to inherit the crown – it was already his through the treason committed at Wakefield.

Edward stopped short of being crowned, however, and after a brief rest gathered his troops and travelled north for a decisive showdown with the Lancastrians. Just four months earlier, his father had pursued a similar path, only to meet a brutal end. Still elated from his crushing victory at Mortimer's Cross, Edward, described by one contemporary as 'valiant in arms' and 'well fitted to endure the conflict of battle', was unfazed by the prospect of heading into the enemy territory.[20] This was the kind of decisive leadership absent from England since the death of Henry V four decades earlier.

With the crown of England at stake, the two forces met in terrible conditions on 29 March 1461, Palm Sunday, near the village of Towton in Yorkshire. Since December 1460, the Lancastrians had secured victory at Wakefield, St Albans and Northampton, and the Yorkists at Mortimer's Cross. With both sides accusing the other of treasonous insurgency, something had to give.

Once the forces engaged, hampered by the swirling winds, blinding snowfall and icy ground, no quarter was given by either side. Thousands, perhaps even tens of thousands, met their end at the hands of their compatriots. It was a 'great and cruel' slaughter, mused the Milanese ambassador, 'as happens when men fight for kingdom and life'.[21] Towton would prove the bloodiest battle ever fought on English soil, an afternoon of relentless bloodshed that turned the snow claret and filled nearby waterways with the mutilated bodies of those who perished as they fled the slaughter. It was also a resounding victory for Edward and the Yorkists.

Among those who died on the Lancastrian side, or were executed in the aftermath, were the earls of Northumberland, Wiltshire and Devon, just three of the countless men who lost their lives. The dukes of Exeter and Somerset made a successful flight. King Henry, Queen Margaret and their prince, Edward of Westminster, had been placed 10 miles away in York where they anxiously awaited tidings from the battlefield. When the dreadful news of their army's annihilation arrived from a panting messenger, they wasted no time in fleeing north, retreating across the Scottish border 'full of sorrow and heaviness'.[22]

After taking down his father's spiked head in York, Edward of March returned south to London a conquering hero. On 28 June 1461, he was crowned Edward IV in Westminster Abbey, the first monarch of the now royal House of York.[23] Described by one contemporary chronicler as 'tall of stature, elegant in person' and 'of unblemished character',[24] the contrast couldn't have been more marked between this mentally sharp teenage warrior king and the inert character who had passively occupied the throne for the previous four decades. Despite his youth,

Edward already enjoyed great favour with the commons and much of the aristocracy, who were drawn to him with 'wonderful affection'.[25] In short, he commanded respect from his subordinates and love from his subjects.

The reversal at Mortimer's Cross had been a deeply traumatic experience for Jasper, responsible for leading hundreds of men to their deaths, and compounded by the devastating news of his father's execution a few days later. Overwhelmed with rage and grappling with his grief, Jasper retreated beyond the robust walls of Tenby. From his coastal fortress, the grieving earl busied himself dictating a series of wrathful letters to his followers, attempting to raise flagging spirits and demanding vengeance.

One letter, dated 25 February 1461 and addressed to Roger Puleston and John Eyton, has survived. Puleston, who shared a great-grandfather with Jasper in Tudur ap Goronwy, and Eyton had been tasked with holding Denbigh Castle against an anticipated Yorkist siege. They were now reminded of the 'great dishonour' done to them by the 'traitors' Edward IV, William Herbert and John Dwnn in 'putting my father your kinsman to the death'. Jasper expected it was a betrayal that they would collectively 'within short time ... avenge'. Though some degree of retribution would take a decade and more, Denbigh, at least, held out for several months. On 23 July, Jasper was again in contact with Puleston, praising his distant cousin's 'faithful diligence' for the castle's safeguarding and promising extra money would soon be provided by the receiver of the lordship, Gruffydd Fychan.[26] Similar letters were likely dispatched to other Lancastrian strongholds like Carreg Cennen, Kidwelly and Conwy.

The suppression of Lancastrian Wales, and in particular the neutralising of Jasper's extensive influence, was one of Edward IV's principal objectives in the summer of 1461. Rumours in June that 20,000 Frenchmen were preparing to land somewhere on the South Welsh coast only served to hasten Edward's movements.[27] To accomplish his goal, and oversee the administration of Wales going forward, the new Yorkist king turned to men he knew and could trust, those who had much to gain from the destruction of their Tudor rival.

Chief among the Welsh Yorkists now rewarded was Sir William Herbert, who had fought against Jasper at Mortimer's Cross and who was referred to in one contemporary account as the new king's 'chosen and faithful' follower.[28] On 8 May 1461, Herbert was appointed chief justice and chamberlain of South Wales, as well as steward and chief forester of Carmarthenshire and Cardiganshire. The following day, he was handed a commission with his brothers Thomas and John Herbert to enter Jasper's lordship of Pembroke and take it 'into the king's hands', along with any other possessions the Tudor earl held in England and Wales.[29]

After Edward's coronation at the end of June, Herbert was further rewarded for his unyielding service to the House of York with induction into the peerage, becoming 1st Baron Herbert of Raglan, as well as lord of Chepstow and Gower.[30] In September, meanwhile, he was granted custody of the wealthy Stafford estates in Brecon, Newport and Gwent, to be held for the duration of the duke of Buckingham's minority, being just six years old at the time.[31] His authority over Wales, particularly for a member of the gentry, of full Welsh blood and no familial relationship to the crown, was unequalled. Herbert was reliable, energetic and, above all, loyal.

The suppression of Jasper Tudor was William Herbert's principal mission, and so on 8 July, 'for defence against the king's enemies', the new lord of Raglan, his brother Thomas Herbert and his brother-in-law Walter Devereux, newly created Baron Ferrers of Chartley, were commanded to array all able-bodied men in the counties of Hereford, Gloucester and Shropshire. Throughout the summer they were further empowered to inquire into all treasons, insurrections and rebellions in South Wales, and to pardon all men who submitted to the Yorkist king except for four – Jasper Tudor and his adherents John Skydmore, Thomas Cornwall and Thomas FitzHenry. To assist them in this matter, their ally John Dwnn, one of the king's ushers and explicitly blamed by Jasper for his loss at Mortimer's Cross, was appointed constable of Aberystwyth and Carmarthen castles. In the Welsh north, meanwhile, prominent Yorkist lords William Hastings, Baron Hastings, and John Tiptoft, Earl of Worcester, were granted the positions of chamberlain and justiciar of North Wales respectively, while Richard Grey, Lord Powis, became steward of the strategic lordships of Montgomery plus Ceri and Cedewain.[32]

With his Yorkist administration of Wales in place, by September the king was ready to turn his Welsh might on the Tudor earl, now regarded as little more than 'a rebel'.[33] Edward had spent much of the late summer in or near the Welsh March, visiting places such as Bristol, Gloucester, Hereford, Ross and Ludlow, which allowed him to maintain regular contact with Herbert and pay close attention to Jasper's movements.[34] Now, Herbert and Devereux were ordered to finish gathering their troops, head into West Wales to shore up Yorkist support and 'cleanse the country' of Lancastrian resistance.[35]

The Yorkists marched along the South Welsh coast, shadowed from the sea by the king's naval fleet, and encountered no opposition of note until they reached Jasper's seat of Pembroke. The constable there was John Skydmore, a Lancastrian combatant at Mortimer's Cross, but despite his close association with Jasper he surrendered Pembroke at the end of September without much incident.[36] Skydmore's decision was swayed by the promise his lands would not be confiscated, a guarantee not upheld when he was nevertheless forced to forfeit his possessions two months later for supporting Jasper.[37] Pembroke secured with minimal fuss, Herbert and Devereux moved on to Tenby, which, despite the expense of its bolstered fortifications, also succumbed without evidence of a struggle.[38] There was little to be gained from holding out and defying the will of an energetic new king determined to crush any lingering Lancastrian sedition.

Once the Yorkists took control of Pembroke and Tenby, it became quickly clear that their principal target, Jasper Tudor, was not in the vicinity. He may have been confident his two principal baronial bases would hold out in his absence, leaving them behind to open up another Lancastrian front in North Wales. His exact whereabouts during the summer and early autumn of 1461 are unclear, but Jasper journeyed north sometime after the end of July when he had written to Roger Puleston from Tenby. It is probable he spent some time on the north-west coast at Harlech Castle, another Lancastrian redoubt, perhaps even intending to reach Denbigh before he received word that it, too, had fallen, surrendered to the Yorkists by the start of October.

Like many of his Welsh ancestors before him, as the net closed in around Jasper, he withdrew into the wilds of Eryri to regroup and gather his thoughts, pursued by 'divers lords' and 'men of worship'. Just when escape seemed impossible, word reached the anxious and trapped earl that the duke of Exeter had arrived by sea with a small force. Despite being a brother-in-law of Edward IV, married to the king's sister Anne, Exeter had fought for the Lancastrians at Wakefield, the second battle of St Albans and Towton. Like Jasper, he was also on the run, having refused to reconcile to Yorkist rule despite his kinship by marriage to the new king.[39]

On 16 October 1461, Jasper, Exeter and Thomas FitzHenry made a last stand at Twt Hill, to the north of Caernarfon's town walls. The Lancastrians were again bested in this poorly documented skirmish, but they were able to succeed in retreating to Exeter's boat, eluding capture and sailing wearily for Scotland to join the rest of the Lancastrian exiles.[40] Aside from Harlech Castle, famously associated with Owain Glyn Dŵr and which would stubbornly hold out for another seven years, and Carreg Cennen Castle, under the defiant command of Owain and Thomas ap Gruffydd, sons of Gruffydd ap Nicholas, every other fortress across the breadth of Wales had surrendered into the king's hands.[41] The country had been cleansed as directed.

On 4 November, the first parliament of the reign opened in Westminster, where it laid out that the Lancastrians had usurped the throne in 1399 against the laws of God, man and nature. As the direct descendant of Edward III's second son, Lionel of Antwerp, it was reasoned that Edward of March, now Edward IV, was the rightful heir to the throne. The

Lancastrian attacks on the House of York throughout the winter of 1460 and 1461 were contrary to the Act of Accord, particularly the 'piteous and sorrowful' killing of Richard of York, the 'true and rightful heir'. For this treason, and presiding over a reign in which extortion, murder, rape, riots and the shedding of innocent blood had been commonplace, the Lancastrians were subject to a wholescale attainder, with their collective estates, titles and offices declared forfeit. For returning to the Lancastrian fold after the battle of St Albans, Henry VI, now regarded in the parliamentary rolls by terms such as 'usurper' and 'late king', had 'against good faith, truth, conscience and his honour' broken the act, and therefore 'forfeited his crown and ought to be deposed'.[42] It was a damning judgement of a king as ill-suited to reign as any who had ever sat on the English throne.

Standing accused of 'false and cruel violence' against Edward in Wales, as well as urging foreign enemies to invade England, Jasper was one of the principal figures stripped of everything he owned.[43] In the judgment laid out against him, and on account of his 'traitorous offences and transgressions', he and his heirs were forever barred from having, holding or enjoying any dignity, estate or pre-eminence within England, Ireland, Wales or Calais.

Nine years to the month since he had been summoned to the Tower of London to be raised to the peerage, Jasper Tudor no longer had the right to call himself earl of Pembroke. He was lord of nowhere, owned no castles or manors, could receive no fees or rents, and held not a single office. He was even stripped of the right to call himself a knight of the Garter, his place in the prestigious order taken by Edward's younger brother, George, Duke of Clarence.[44] As long as the Yorkists ruled, Jasper was legally dead.

Perhaps most galling of all, Jasper could only observe helplessly from afar as his enemies were rewarded at his expense. In February 1462, for his 'good service' William Herbert was granted a range of Jasper's former possessions, including the castles, towns and lordships of Pembroke, Tenby, Cilgerran, Llansteffan and Caldicot, and the lordships of Castlemartin, St Florence, Emlyn and Penrhyn.[45] In April, Herbert was also inducted into the Order of the Garter.[46] Herbert's brother Richard was granted the confiscated lands of Jasper's loyal supporters FitzHenry and Skydmore, while John Dwnn received Laugharne as reward for 'his good service to the king's father Richard, late duke of York' in his struggles against Henry VI and Jasper Tudor.[47]

After a decade of sustained advancement in English royal circles, the Yorkist accession represented an impregnable barrier to continued Tudor progression. Not for the first time in the family's history, they were a victim of dynastic upheaval outside their control with devastating consequences. The deposition of his royal half-brother deeply troubled

Jasper, who owed his livelihood, wealth and earldom to Henry VI. From the moment of his ennoblement in 1452, he had tried valiantly to ease tensions at court between Lancastrian and Yorkist factions. As the horrifying bloodshed of early 1461 had demonstrated, the depth of ill feeling on all sides had proven insurmountable.

Jasper's losses had been significant; in the space of just six years, his brother and father had died, at least one in the most brutal of circumstances, and he had been unable to prevent his ailing half-brother being toppled from a throne he had occupied for forty years. He had witnessed the shocking bloodshed at St Albans, and was haunted by his responsibility for leading thousands of men to their deaths at Mortimer's Cross. At an age when marriage and the fathering of an heir should have been his foremost preoccupation, the thirty-year-old Jasper had been forced to abandon his estates and his homeland, scurrying through the mountains to the coast, before sailing out into the unknown. Apart from a brief return and a few lightning raids, he would remain in exile for nearly a quarter-century.

To Jasper's mind, Edward IV was not the rightful king, but merely a usurper, the son of a disgraced duke who had overreached himself by deposing an anointed monarch. His government was illegitimate, his council a nest of traitors who deserved death for raising the House of York to the throne. He certainly did not entertain any notion that he was a rebel. Even so, the reality was that Jasper had lost everything, and no amount of outrage could alter that fact. Where others favoured submission to the new order, Jasper vowed never to abandon the cause of his half-brother, Henry VI. He would become the House of Lancaster's most tenacious defender, never losing his spirit even in moments of overwhelming odds. In the confusion and anxiety of his flight, however, one thing rankled with Jasper above all others.

When William Herbert was preparing his attack on Pembroke Castle in September 1461, Jasper fled north. Whether through design, anticipating the castle could withstand a siege, or for practical reasons, he had left behind his four-year-old nephew Henry, the young earl of Richmond. When Herbert entered the castle he stumbled across this boy, not the Tudor he was pursuing but a richer prize in many ways. The child was likely removed to Herbert's seat of Raglan in Monmouthshire at this time, and 'by reason of his minority', on 12 February 1462, Edward IV formally granted his loyal lord custody of Henry of Richmond. This significant grant included Henry's future marital rights, an appealing prospect for Herbert considering the boy's English, French and Welsh royal lineage on both sides of his family tree. The wardship cost Herbert 'a thousand pounds in hand paid', an extraordinary sum funded by the estates he had received in recent months, many of them forfeited by Jasper Tudor.[48]

Just as the tumult of 1282 and 1399 had transformed the political scene of Wales, so too did the dynastic revolution of 1461 and the Yorkist ascendancy. As king of England, Edward IV not only commanded the vast Mortimer estates along the Welsh March that had been wielded to great effect by his father, Richard of York, but also controlled the principality of Wales and the duchy of Lancaster. Jasper Tudor's earldom of Pembroke was declared forfeit and returned to the crown, and two other leading Marcher lords, the dukes of Buckingham and Norfolk, were minors. The lordship of Glamorgan, meanwhile, was in the hands of Edward's cousin and ally, the earl of Warwick. The English crown, now Yorkist, was stronger in Wales than it had been at any time since the advent of the Normans. The Yorkists, it could be confidently said, had 'the whole possession of all the whole realm', England as well as Wales.[49] As the bishop of Elphin reported in a letter to Francesco Coppini, the Apostolic legate to England, 'everything is turning out successfully for King Edward and all in England rejoice greatly at this time, and reverence him as sole lord and king in the land'.[50] Master Antonio, Coppini's physician, went one step further and noted in his own letter to an Italian merchant that, while the Lancastrian faction had been 'practically destroyed', Edward was adored and loved by the commons of England 'as if he were their God'.

Conversely, Jasper Tudor's authority in Wales and over the Welsh, even his own family's destiny, was at its lowest ebb. Deprived of his possessions, his title and even his nephew, there was no reason for Jasper to expect fortune's wheel to revolve in his favour any time soon. He had, however, shown courage and tenacity in recent months, with a streak of resourcefulness that would hold him in good stead in the difficult years ahead. He may have taken some solace from the sanguine words of the Welsh bards, if their work reached his tired mind. Robin Ddu, though deeply mourning Jasper's defeat at Mortimer's Cross, predicted ultimate victory for the Tudors and Wales, writing that 'the dishonourable white dragon has triumphed, but the red dragon will yet win the field'.[51] Another noted that, though Owen Tudor had been slain, 'hope remains for our people', for Jasper still lived.[52] Time would tell if Jasper could somehow repay their faith. The outlook did not favour his chances.

11

The Masterlock

The deafening thunder of horses, growing louder as they advanced upon Pembroke Castle's towering Great Gatehouse, served as a warning to those inside to prepare for visitors. A cursory glance from the battlements would reveal if it was friend or foe, often determined by identifying the banners and livery of the riders. As they came nearer, the echoing din giving way to a repetitive clip-clop as the horses slowed to a gentle trot, the guards on duty could make out the deep-red and sky-blue livery, the banners bearing a proud rampant white lion. The alarm was raised that Lord Herbert, the Yorkist king's man in Wales, was approaching, with orders sent down the ranks to lower the drawbridge.

Inside the castle, household officials hurried through the crowded corridors. They busied themselves arranging food and drink for Herbert and his companions, likely exhausted after their long journey across South Wales. The great hall was also prepared for the evening ahead, with tables and chairs laid out and the fireplaces lit. Somewhere within Pembroke's labyrinth was a curious five-year-old boy, alert to the sudden change in pace. When called upon, young Henry Tudor was led into the great hall and introduced to the imposing figure others were deferentially calling lord. It was explained that Lord Herbert had been granted Henry's wardship and he was soon to leave Pembroke, his home and birthplace, the only place he had known. As with most children who experience a significant change in routine for the first time, Henry was probably scared, highly anxious and resistant to what was happening, but he had no choice in the matter.

The Yorkist triumph of 1461 and the accession of Edward IV naturally affected the lives of those close to the deposed Lancastrian regime. Their options were stark: they could fall in line, or they could be attainted as rebels and condemned to death or exile. As half-brother to the fallen king Henry VI, Jasper Tudor was never going to be reconciled to the House of York, who in his eyes had unjustly usurped the crown contrary to the laws of man and God. Having been chased from the realm on account of his resistance to the Yorkist ascendancy, Jasper anticipated this to be a brief interruption of the Lancastrian reign and had therefore made no provision for his Tudor nephew in Pembroke.

The boy's mother, Margaret Beaufort, meanwhile, had remarried three years earlier and was steadily establishing her position elsewhere as Lady Stafford. Her husband, Sir Henry Stafford, was a younger son of the duke of Buckingham killed at the Battle of Northampton in July 1460, and like his father had been closely aligned with the Lancastrian cause, fighting for Henry VI at the Battle of Towton. Stafford, however, did not follow the more senior Lancastrian nobles into exile and instead submitted to Edward IV soon after Towton, gratefully accepting a pardon from the new king in June 1461.[1] Stafford likely made good use of his kinship to the Yorkists; he was a first cousin of Edward, their Neville mothers being sisters, as well as Richard Neville, the commanding earl of Warwick. Stafford would remain a committed Yorkist until the end of his life, despite his and his wife's Lancastrian pedigree. Margaret, still just eighteen years old, quickly adapted to the new order. Like her son, she had limited options.

Despite the Staffords' submission, which protected Margaret's ancestral inheritance, she was unable to defend her son's interests. In August 1461, Edward IV stripped Henry Tudor of the castle, county, honour and lordship of Richmond, which he granted to his youngest brother, Richard, the new duke of Gloucester. One month later, the lucrative honour and lordship were transferred to the king's other brother, George, recently created duke of Clarence, and his heirs. The earldom itself was declared forfeit to the crown. Margaret had also been unable to obtain the permanent wardship of her son, which was granted to Lord Herbert on 12 February 1462, in exchange for £1,000.[2]

With the Welsh lord a committed enemy of Jasper Tudor and implicated in the deaths of her previous husband Edmund Tudor and father-in-law Owen Tudor, Margaret must have had deep concerns about Herbert's suitability to raise her son. Her fears would prove unfounded. Despite his acrimonious relationship with the Tudors, Herbert was widely regarded as 'a hardy knight and expert captain' and proved a worthy guardian of young Henry.[3] He embraced the boy into his family and provided a stable environment in which he could flourish.

The only account of Henry's upbringing dates from later in his life, written during his reign by a French poet named Bernard André. An Augustinian friar who suffered from vision issues, perhaps even blindness, André first came to Henry's attention during his years in France and was brought to England once Henry became king. The Frenchman was highly regarded by Henry, who rewarded him with an annual pension, the title of poet laureate and a covetable job as a royal tutor. Around 1500, André was commissioned to write a biography of his master, a panegyric which flattered its subject and accentuated his legitimacy as king. The unfinished result, *The Life of Henry VII*, was undeniably biased towards André's patron, but nevertheless there may be a seam of truth running through much of its composition, particularly as Henry is likely to have been his principal source.

According to André's account, Henry was an 'often sickly' child, and his place of education varied according to the weather to 'protect his health'.[4] No further detail is given on where exactly he was taken other than that it was in Wales, but upon reaching 'the age of understanding', Henry was put under the supervision of 'men upright and wise' to be 'tenderly educated', presumably at Raglan.

As he grew, Henry was taught the 'first principles of literature', how to read and write, and introduced to some basic mathematics, algebra and Latin. One of his tutors was Edward Haseley, later rewarded by Henry as an 'instructor of the king in grammar in his tender age'.[5] When introduced to literature, André declares that Henry 'surpassed his peers with the same quick intellect he had displayed as a boy', adding that he had personally spoken to one of his teachers, Andrew Scott, a master of theology at Oxford, who recalled a student 'with such great mental quickness and capacity for learning'.

Theology does appear to be where Henry shone, for according to André the young Tudor was 'endowed with such sharp mental powers and such natural vigour and comprehension' that he learned 'everything pertaining to religious instruction rapidly and thoroughly, with little effort from his teachers'. In fact, reports André, Henry was so 'attentive in reading and listening to the divine office that all who watched him saw signs of his future goodness and success'. During these formative years, Henry also encountered Sir Hugh ap John, a veteran of the wars in France who had aligned with the House of York during the conflict in England. On 15 October 1485, less than two months into his reign, Henry, 'in consideration of the good service' the knight 'did unto us in our tender age', rewarded ap John a payment of £10. Those services, frustratingly, are not mentioned but are likely to have been martial in nature.[6]

One discipline that Henry likely developed at Raglan, if he hadn't already started learning at Pembroke, was the Welsh language. Wales remained a deeply monoglot nation until the early nineteenth century, and four centuries earlier the language was spoken widely and frequently among the Welsh, from north to south and even extending beyond the Severn in the east. William Herbert boasted an ancient Welsh pedigree and was certainly a Welsh speaker himself, a proud champion of Welsh arts and literature who established a thriving cultural centre at Raglan. Here, native bards and musicians passed through with great regularity, performing their work to an audience who shared their tongue. There is no tangible evidence Henry was able to recall any Welsh in later life, but as a skilled linguist known to freely converse in French, English and Latin, there is no reason to doubt that in his youth he could hold at least a basic conversation in the language of his ancestors.

It was also at Raglan that Henry would have first been exposed to Welsh mythology, learning about the exploits of King Arthur and perhaps even the political prophecies that would help shape his outlook in later life. Matters of genealogy, heraldry and the history of the Welsh people would also have become subjects of interest to Henry as a youth. He certainly had a deep understanding of such matters by the time he was king.

It is tempting to dismiss André's writings as state-sponsored propaganda designed to flatter a paying master, but there is ample evidence of what Polydore Vergil called Henry's 'pertinacious memory' as an adult, his quick wit and his renowned perspicacity. It is reasonable that such a mentally sharp man had been no ordinary child.[7] That Henry was a precocious youth who demonstrated a deep intelligence from his earliest years may partly explain Herbert's ambition to someday make his Tudor ward a son-in-law. In the will he hastily completed shortly before his death, Herbert left clear instructions to his wife, Lady Anne, that his daughter Maud 'be wedded to the Lord Henry of Richmond'.[8] This prospective match would have bonded the feuding Herbert and Tudor families together before God, creating an insuperable Welsh affinity operating at the apex of English politics.

There was no shortage of companions for Henry at Raglan, either. Lord Herbert had a large family, having fathered several children in the dozen years before Henry's arrival. The eldest Herbert child, named William after his father, was around ten or twelve in 1462, a year older than his brother Walter. There were also George and Philip, joining their sisters Cecily, Maud, Katherine, Anne, Isabel and Margaret. Lord Herbert also had at least one illegitimate son, Richard Herbert of Ewyas, whose presence around Raglan was not unknown.

In 1467, the Herbert family were joined by another ward, the nineteen-year-old Henry Percy, disinherited heir to the earldom of Northumberland. Percy's father had died fighting for the Lancastrians at Towton, and, like Henry Tudor, he was placed with a Yorkist guardian in the expectation he would be reconciled to the new order. In the fullness of time, and after being married into his family, Herbert likely envisioned that he would be able to encourage Edward IV to return his two wards their hereditary titles of Richmond and Northumberland.[9] Some of these childhood connections would hold Henry Tudor in good stead during his march to Bosworth Field two decades later, when he looked to old companions to help forge a new path together.

Despite their separation, Margaret Beaufort nevertheless maintained an interest in her son's religious wellbeing, securing for him a place in the confraternity of the Order of the Holy Trinity at Knaresborough.[10] In September 1467, meanwhile, she was able to pay her son a rare visit as part of a south-western progress of her husband's lands. It is unclear how often Margaret had been able to see Henry since her remarriage nine years earlier, but any absence from the boy she would later regard her 'worldly joy' must have been tough to endure.[11] A record in Henry Stafford's accounts shows a payment for a ferry to take him and Margaret across the Severn to Chepstow, continuing their journey to Raglan by land. The Staffords were warmly welcomed by the Herberts and stayed for a week, precious time during which Margaret caught up with her son, now ten years old and likely approaching her in height, if not already surpassing her.[12]

A building site for most of Henry's time there, Raglan was nonetheless a fine place for any child to be reared. Already affluent for a Welshman under Lancastrian rule, Herbert's rise was accelerated under Yorkist patronage. After his induction into the peerage in 1461, Herbert set about upgrading his baronial seat, an extensive and ambitious project that transformed an otherwise unremarkable Marcher fortress into one of the grandest homes to be found anywhere in the kingdom.

A castle of some manner had existed at Raglan since the advent of the Normans, though its most recent sandstone iteration was begun by Herbert's father, William ap Thomas, soon after he acquired it in the summer of 1432.[13] He was responsible for erecting the imposing Great Tower, a hexagonal five-story structure known locally as the Yellow Tower of Gwent, and the South Gate, both retained by his son three decades later.

Chief among Herbert's upgrades was the extraordinary three-story gatehouse, its two towers inspired by the *châteaux* of southern France he had encountered while serving in the English army in his younger days. Extensive machicolations ran along the top of the towers, arched openings through which missiles could be dropped onto attackers, and entry into the heart of the castle was regulated by a pair of portcullises and a drawbridge. Inside, a library was constructed to house the greatest collection of Welsh literature, a lauded cultural centre which may have been where Henry Tudor first became acquainted with the King Arthur legend and prophecies foretelling a national deliverer.

The great hall, meanwhile, was updated, as were the private quarters of Herbert and his family. Located in the inner court, where Henry likely spent much of his time, the two-story private suites included large fireplaces, wood-panelled walls, private latrines and intricately decorated bay windows fitted with large stone seats to relax on, away from the bustle of the outer court. The suites were reached through the Great

Stair, and Henry likely shared his space with some of the Herbert boys, developing petty rivalries and firm friendships as they grew older. The view from the apartments was extensive, offering a scenic panorama of the soaring Brecon Beacons in the distance as well as the deer park and gardens which extended from the castle wall. It is easy to imagine Henry staring wistfully from his window, wondering what had become of his uncle Jasper. He would be careful, of course, not to voice such thoughts around Herbert circles.

There can be little doubt that the Herberts lived in splendour at Raglan. Under Yorkist rule, Lord Herbert had spent his newfound riches well, strengthening his reputation as not just the mightiest Welshman of his day, a position usurped from Jasper Tudor, but one of Edward IV's most trusted lieutenants. Despite his Lancastrian background, Henry was the beneficiary of Herbert's success and exposed to a rounded social, religious, military and cultural education in which he wanted for little.

A disinherited Lancastrian earl handed over to a rival Yorkist family to be raised, Henry always maintained in later years that he had not been at liberty during his youth, his fate controlled by others. According to the Burgundian diplomat Philippe de Commines, he was told personally by Henry 'that from the time he was five years old he had been always a fugitive or a prisoner'.[14] Nevertheless, there are hints that Henry recalled his time at Raglan with some warmth, regardless of the wider political and dynastic considerations that forced him into the Herberts' control in the first place. Polydore Vergil, who, like Commines, probably obtained much of his information directly from Henry, wrote that though 'kept as a prisoner' in childhood, Henry conceded that he had nevertheless been 'honourably brought up with the wife of William Herbert', Anne Devereux.[15] Six months into his reign, Henry even granted 'special protection and safeguard' to his 'dear cousin' Lady Anne to come to London, though it is unknown if this emotional reunion did occur.[16]

Outside Raglan's grand gatehouse, however, the brutal dynastic wars entered their next phase. Since Henry VI's deposition in March 1461, a group of Lancastrian exiles had been working tirelessly to reverse the Yorkist triumph, not least Jasper Tudor. Initial attempts to rouse northern England from Scotland floundered, and Margaret of Anjou cast her glances further afield for assistance. Though she anticipated support from the French king, Charles VII, maternal uncle of her husband Henry VI and Jasper, his death in July 1461 apparently put paid to such hopes. Charles's successor, Louis XI, favoured peace with Yorkist England and shunned talks of aid to the Lancastrians.

Nevertheless, in early 1462 rumours swept through the Yorkist court that a vast invasion was being prepared, a 'great conspiracy' that involved Jasper and the duke of Exeter landing at Beaumaris in North Wales. At the same time, another force led by Henry Beaufort, 3rd Duke of Somerset,

Margaret of Anjou's brother John, Duke of Calabria and Lorraine, Walter Hungerford and John Morton was believed to be heading for East Anglia with a supplementary French army targeting Kent. This initial onslaught was to be followed by a secondary assault funded by the kings of Aragon, Portugal, France and Denmark, a collective force numbering more than 200,000 with the sole objective of restoring the House of Lancaster to the English throne.[17] Supposedly overseeing this extraordinary conspiracy within England was the previously neutral John de Vere, 12th Earl of Oxford, who for good measure would also assassinate Edward IV. The plot, unlikely to have been anywhere as extensive or organised as the rumours claimed, collapsed when one of Oxford's messengers revealed the intrigue to Edward, prompting the earl's arrest on 12 February 1462 and execution two weeks later.[18]

According to an Italian envoy of the duke of Milan, Francesco Sforza, Jasper was in Brittany around the middle of March 1462, though soon returned to Edinburgh to check on his half-brother Henry VI.[19] By June, he was on the move once more, sailing across the Channel with John Fortescue, chancellor to the Lancastrian king. By 13 June, the pair had reached Rouen in Normandy when they were dismayed to discover that Louis XI had rescinded freedom of movement within France for the Lancastrians. Stranded, they appealed to Charles of Charolais, heir to the duchy of Burgundy, and through his intervention were able to secure a safe conduct to continue their journey. By 24 June, Jasper reached the scenic French royal retreat of Chinon, deep in the Loire Valley, where he was warmly greeted by Margaret of Anjou. The Lancastrian queen had arrived in France two months earlier to personally appeal to King Louis for his support, and Jasper arrived in time for the conclusion of those negotiations. He was able to present Louis with letters of credence from Henry VI, bolstering their argument.[20]

The petitions of Henry VI, Margaret of Anjou and Jasper Tudor, all first cousins of Louis XI, proved persuasive, and a deal was struck with the calculating French king. Louis was prepared to provide a loan of 20,000 *livres tournois* and a small body of soldiers, but the cost was high should the Lancastrians be returned to the throne. As well as a 100-year truce and a promise not to aid each other's enemies, Louis secured a promise that either Jasper or the Gascon knight Jean de Foix, Earl of Kendal, would be appointed captain of Calais and expected to deliver the town to the French within a year. If this clause was not adhered to, the loan would need to be repaid in full. Each side content with the terms, the treaty was publicly signed in Tours on 28 June, with Jasper one of the principal signatories on the Lancastrian side.[21] The promise of surrendering Calais was a desperate step by the Lancastrians, one that would prove deeply unpopular in England when discovered, but they were negotiating from a point of considerable weakness.

Finally armed with the financial, military and diplomatic backing of France, in late October 1462 Queen Margaret and Jasper sailed for northern England to support the duke of Somerset's struggling Northumberland campaign. Together, the Lancastrians made 'open war' on the Yorkists and were able to capture the strategically significant castles of Bamburgh and Alnwick, but their presence failed to rouse any wider groundswell of support and the decision was taken by Margaret to return to France. Somerset was installed as constable of Bamburgh and ably supported by Jasper with a garrison of around 300 men.[22]

Life in Bamburgh was tough for Jasper and his companions. The restoration of Yorkist authority in Northumberland was a priority for Edward IV, who couldn't afford to allow the Lancastrians too much opportunity to foment rebellion. Using a loan from the citizens of London, he assembled a huge army, gathering support from two dukes, seven earls and thirty-one barons. Unable to travel further north than Durham due to illness, he handed command of the formidable host to the earl of Warwick, and the castles of Bamburgh, Alnwick and Dunstanburgh were subjected to punishing sieges. Warwick's objective was clear: destroy the Lancastrians' spirit and then starve them out.

Heavily outnumbered and with food supplies running low, the disheartened Lancastrian rank and file were forced to survive on horse meat. Their leaders' resolve weakened with each passing day, and heated discussions likely took place between Somerset and Jasper about their options. Since his father's assassination seven years earlier, Somerset had been the most implacable enemy of the House of York, but his hatred diminished when faced with the stark choice of starvation or surrender. On Christmas Eve of 1462, Somerset not only ordered Bamburgh to be handed over to the Yorkists but switched sides, in one fell swoop depriving the Lancastrians of their most vital stronghold and their most competent military commander. Jasper, on the other hand, stoutly refused to submit, and accepted a safe conduct to withdraw to Scotland.[23] The Yorkists would, in time, rue that small act of mercy.

Fortunately for Margaret of Anjou, all was not lost. In March 1463, Sir Ralph Percy and Ralph Grey, who had switched sides with Somerset, defected once again, returning to the Lancastrian fold. As Edward IV had allowed Percy and Grey to continue holding Bamburgh, Alnwick and Dunstanburgh castles, those mighty fortresses also reverted to the cause of Henry VI.[24] Satisfied that the Lancastrians at least had a foothold in the north-east of England, Margaret belatedly set sail for France that summer with her son Edward, the disinherited prince of Wales. Having paid his half-brother a visit in Edinburgh, Jasper also crossed the Channel that summer, in the company of the duke of Exeter, Lord Ros, John Fortescue and John Morton among others.[25]

Despite the earlier promise of aid from King Louis, on 8 October 1463 Lancastrian ambitions were rocked by the news that the French monarch had negotiated a one-year truce with Edward IV. One of the principal terms the English king had secured from his French counterpart was a promise he would offer no support to the Lancastrians. As a consequence, before the year was out, Jasper was forced to leave France, heading initially to Scotland and later onwards to Brittany, then an independent duchy outside the French king's direct control. Queen Margaret and some of the other Lancastrians sought refuge with her father, René, Duke of Anjou and titular king of Sicily, Naples, Hungary and Jerusalem. Despite this impressive array of titles René held little land, but he was able to accommodate the exiles at his castle of Koeur.[26]

In November 1463, tidings reached the downbeat Lancastrian exiles that Somerset had turned his coat once again, abandoning the Yorkists and fleeing to Northumberland to be reunited with his former troops.[27] The loss of the duke the previous year had been devastating for Lancastrian morale, but his return to the fold provided a much-needed boost to a flagging cause. By March 1464, a reinvigorated Somerset had captured several castles in the Tyne Valley, as well as Norham on the Scottish border and Skipton in Yorkshire. It was the most promising position the Lancastrians had been in since they had lost the throne three years earlier.[28]

In the meantime, Jasper was busy trying to put together an invasion force concerned with replenishing the Bamburgh garrison, which now hosted Henry VI. A Breton envoy named Guillaume de Cousinot had personally visited Henry and Somerset over Christmas 1463, reporting back that though their situation was grave, general sympathy for the Lancastrian cause in the north of England persisted. The deposed king had handed Cousinot letters requesting King Louis and René of Anjou furnish Jasper with weapons and men so that he could return to Wales to raise support. As Jasper remained in Brittany, Louis commanded the Breton duke to provide whatever assistance he could, which would include a fleet of ships under the control of his vice-admiral Alain de la Motte. Before they could embark, however, disturbing tidings from Northumberland negated the need to set sail.[29]

Somerset's betrayal and subsequent success had only served to provoke Edward IV into a heavy response to rid himself of this lingering Lancastrian insurgency in the furthest reaches of his otherwise peaceful realm. The Yorkist king dispatched into the north his cousin John Neville, 1st Baron Montagu and younger brother of the earl of Warwick, a man valued for 'his hardiness and sage conduct in martial affairs'. On 25 April 1464, Montagu encountered a Lancastrian army near Hedgeley Moor, their weapons drawn and arrayed for battle. Montagu made light work of Somerset's troops, who broke and fled after an exchange of arrows.[30]

Somerset was not discouraged by this setback, quickly regrouping his forces and deciding to challenge Montagu once more. On 15 May, the two forces met for the second time in less than a month 2 miles south of Hexham, and this time there would be no escape for Somerset. Montagu's superior royal army destroyed the Lancastrian force, which suffered heavy casualties. Somerset was captured alive and brought before Montagu. Unwilling to give Edward the opportunity to pardon Somerset a second time, Montagu ordered his unrepentant rival to be beheaded in Hexham marketplace.[31]

In the following days, Somerset's half-brother Lord Ros and four others were executed in Newcastle, with seven more put to death in Middleham. Fourteen others were sentenced to death a week later in York. Together with the hundreds, if not thousands, lost during the battles of Hedgeley Moor and Hexham, the late spring of 1464 was catastrophic for the Lancastrian cause. By the end of June 1464, Alnwick, Dunstanburgh and Bamburgh castles surrendered for the final time. The Lancastrian insurgency in the north of England was over.[32]

Meanwhile, Henry VI had been left isolated after the death of Somerset and the flight of Jasper Tudor. He evaded capture for over a year until he was finally apprehended in July 1465, bedraggled and deeply confused. The fallen king was brought to London where he was paraded through the streets by a delighted Edward IV. Now regarded as mere Henry of Windsor in Yorkist circles, this sad figure, more monk than monarch, was sent to the Tower of London where he would remain under close observation for the next five years.[33] From this nadir, Lancastrian fortunes would ultimately be revived from the unlikeliest of sources.

In the middle of September 1464, barely four months after the resounding Yorkist victory at Hexham, Edward IV announced to his startled lords that he had secretly taken a wife, one Elizabeth Woodville, widow of a Lancastrian knight named John Grey. It was a match most unsuitable for a king of England, 'prompted by the ardour of youth' according to one commentator, and which 'greatly offended the people' in the judgement of another. The person it affronted the most, however, was the earl of Warwick.[34]

For supporting the House of York in the struggle for the throne, Warwick had been rewarded well. Upon the accession of Edward IV, he received offices and lands on an extensive scale, including the chamberlainship and admiralship of England and wardenship of the Cinque Ports and Dover Castle. In the north of England, he was created warden of the east and west marches and steward of the duchy of Lancaster, all the while retaining his influential post as captain of Calais, host of the largest standing army of its day. There was no one wealthier, or more powerful, than Warwick other than the king. His family likewise rose higher under Yorkist rule; his brother John was created Baron Montagu and then earl of Northumberland, and their uncle William Neville, Lord Fauconberg, was created earl of Kent. Another brother, George, had been appointed chancellor and translated to the archbishopric of York. It was for good reason that in 1464 an official from Calais reported that England had two rulers, 'Monsieur de Warwick, and another, whose name I have forgotten'.[35]

In his capacity as the king's mightiest subject, the proud earl had spent considerable time and effort in arranging a French marriage for Edward, a strategy that would remove the king of France's support for the Lancastrians and help secure the Yorkist crown. It was politically embarrassing for Warwick that Edward had taken another wife, one who offered no financial or diplomatic gain, and personally troubling that his cousin had hidden it from him for months. Though he begrudgingly came to terms with the marriage, Warwick's prominence at court lessened as the decade progressed, the king favouring the counsel and company of his extensive Woodville kin at the earl's expense. Edward went to great lengths to provide for his in-laws, 'enriching them with boundless presents and always promoting them to the most dignified offices about his person'. At the same time, the king banished from his presence his 'kinsmen sprung from the royal blood'.[36]

Where Warwick had once been the sole hand guiding his younger cousin, his ascendancy now waned, replaced by others who grew in influence around the maturing king. One of those was William Herbert, who through Edward's friendship had grown hugely wealthy and politically powerful in a short space of time. As early as 1462, the year he was elected a knight of the Garter, Herbert was being referred to as a member of the 'King's house', an indication of the growing closeness between the pair.[37] The following summer, Herbert was appointed constable for life of Harlech and chamberlain and chief justice of Merionethshire, extending his influence into the north of Wales. At the same time, he was confirmed as steward of Carmarthenshire and Cardiganshire, soon adding Crickhowell and Tretower to his portfolio and the honour, castle and manor of Dunster in Somerset.[38]

On 9 March 1465, meanwhile, 'for his good service' against Henry VI and Jasper Tudor, the king created for Herbert the lordship of Raglan, formed from parts of his own hereditary lordships of Monmouth and Usk to fashion 'one united royal lordship'. It was an impressive reward for his trusted lieutenant and was, in fact, the first Welsh lordship created since the conquest of Wales in 1282. On 26 September 1466, Herbert was granted a collection of other lands, including the manor of Haverfordwest, and confirmed in the office of chamberlain and chief justice of South Wales. Finally, on 28 August 1467, the 'king's knight' was created constable of Denbigh, chief justice of North Wales and steward of the lordships of Denbigh, Montgomery, and Ceri and Cedewain.[39] Save for Warwick's lordship of Glamorgan, no corner of Wales was untouched by Herbert's influence. His authority over the Welsh, outside the king, was nearly supreme.

Warwick's resentment of Herbert was four-fold. First, as lord of Glamorgan, Warwick was hostile to Herbert's growing influence in South Wales, particularly when Herbert also received control of the extensive Stafford lands during the minority of the duke of Buckingham.[40] Second, Herbert was closely aligned with the Woodville faction, arranging the marriage of his son and heir, William, to Queen Elizabeth's sister Mary in September 1466. Third, when Warwick's brother George Neville, Archbishop of York, was stripped of the chancellorship in June 1467, it was Herbert who accompanied Edward IV to retrieve the Great Seal. Fourth, Herbert had long-term ambitions to restore his two wards, Henry Tudor and Henry Percy, to their hereditary earldoms of Richmond and Northumberland, which would have proven prejudicial to the Neville family in the English north, an arena they had dominated for much of the fifteenth century. Warwick was simply jealous of the king's increasing reliance upon Herbert, an upstart Welshman of modest origins who now had Edward's ear.[41] When Edward IV dismissed Warwick's tireless efforts to secure a French alliance by consenting to the marriage of his sister Margaret of York to Charles the Bold, the new duke of Burgundy, Warwick's disgust pushed him towards rebellion. In a case of recent history repeating itself, he intended to reassert his political supremacy over the king by force.

In the meantime, the Lancastrian court-in-exile was in dire straits as the decade neared its end, an impoverished collection of malcontents clinging to a crown that had long been wrested from their grasp. At Koeur in France, Margaret of Anjou continued to plot with men like the earls of Devon and Wiltshire, while Edmund and John Beaufort, brothers of the deceased duke of Somerset, were based at the Burgundian court awaiting further opportunity to prove themselves. Some of the Lancastrian exiles, it was said, 'were reduced to such extremity of want and poverty' that it was observed 'no common beggar could have been poorer'. The duke of Exeter was even allegedly found barefoot and barelegged, begging door to door for bread.[42]

If the marriage of Charles the Bold to Margaret of York in July 1468 pushed Warwick towards mutiny, for very different reasons it also spurred Louis XI of France into action, dismayed by the burgeoning friendship between two of his adversaries, England and Burgundy. Louis's response was to undermine the Anglo-Burgundian agreement by distracting Edward IV's attention. The French king's weapon of choice was his cousin Jasper Tudor, who was now brought in from the cold and prepared for another Lancastrian invasion of Wales.

Since the Yorkist victory in 1461, the Lancastrian garrison of Harlech Castle had doggedly resisted all overtures to submit, holding out in the name of their lord, Jasper Tudor. A man of great resilience and patience, Jasper had not been disheartened by the events of the previous few years, and was able to count on the support of a core group of Welsh followers to retain a foothold in Wales. Some of those supporters – Phillip Mansel of Gower, Hopkin ap Rhys of Llangyfelach and Lewis ap Rhydderch of Strata Florida – attempted an uprising near Dryslwyn in the Tywi Valley in Carmarthenshire in 1464, only to be suppressed by John Dwnn and Roger Vaughan, long-time foes of the Tudors.[43]

During this period, Jasper moved 'from country to country, not always at his heart's ease, nor in security of life', and directed such insurgency from afar. Careful measures were taken to ensure he remained outside the grasp of the Yorkists.[44] According to the poet Tudur Penllyn, Jasper typically sailed into Barmouth, 10 miles south of Harlech, and passed on intelligence and orders to the garrison before retreating to the sea from whence he had quietly arrived.[45] To curtail Jasper's sedition, on 26 October 1464 a commission was handed to William Herbert, his brother Richard and brother-in-law Walter Devereux granting them powers to pardon any Harlech rebel below the rank of baron, though it did not encourage any defections.[46] The parliament that sat this year further demanded the garrison surrender, charging Dafydd ap Ieuan ap Eynon and Rheinallt ap Griffith ap Bleddyn with harbouring known Lancastrian malcontents and 'with great might' seeking to destroy the 'most royal person' of Edward IV. The king even ordered the mayor of Chester to have a proclamation read in his city three days in a row that threatened the garrison with death unless they submitted before 21 January 1465.[47] Again, such threats had no impact.

By the summer of 1468, the remote Harlech was still holding out for Lancaster, more than seven years since Edward IV had wrested the crown away from Henry VI. No other fortress in England or Wales still had a Lancastrian element dwelling inside. On 1 June, Louis XI of France signed an order authorising his treasurer of war, Antoine Rougier, to provide Jasper a modest sum of money, around fifty men and three ships to sail to Wales. Jasper assembled his small force and headed out from Honfleur and through the English Channel, sailing around the south-west coast of Pembrokeshire and into the Irish Sea. On 24 June, he landed at his usual spot near Barmouth, though this time the extent of his ambitions would not be restricted to merely touching base with the Harlech garrison.[48]

Though he only had limited supplies, and certainly not enough to sustain any prolonged military campaign, Jasper sought to use the opportunity afforded him to launch a direct assault on Yorkist authority in North Wales. Once his men were refreshed after their voyage, Jasper roused the garrison at Harlech before they collectively headed north-east, a punishing upland trek through the heart of Eryri until they reached the gentler plains of the Conwy Valley. During this march through the Principality counties of Merionethshire and Caernarfonshire – areas strongly Lancastrian in sentiment – many flocked to Jasper's standard, his highly regarded Tudor lineage a potent recruiting tool in a region where his ancestors had once held sway.

By 24 June, Jasper had reached his destination. Arriving at the wealthy Yorkist lordship of Denbigh, his men wasted little time in setting the town ablaze. The houses were plundered, the taverns burned and the citizens generally terrorised by hundreds of soldiers, many of them strange French mercenaries who showed little restraint. Though the castle itself was able to fend off the assault, Jasper held sessions in the town in the name of Henry VI, a bold move that mocked the authority of the Yorkist king, Edward IV.[49] So great was the raid that just one week later it was remarked upon by the Milanese ambassador at the French court, though estimates that Jasper had put 4,000 Englishmen to death were wildly inaccurate.[50]

The assault on Denbigh, a lordship that formed an integral component of his Yorkist inheritance, hardened Edward's resolve to crush all lingering Lancastrian resistance in North Wales. Jasper Tudor had played his final hand when it came to fomenting anti-Yorkist sedition through Harlech. On 3 July 1468, the king handed a fresh commission to William Herbert to array the counties of Gloucestershire, Herefordshire and Shropshire, his mission to raise an army with the sole purpose of capturing the Lancastrian coastal stronghold.[51] According to the estimates of contemporary poets and chroniclers, he was able to gather a force numbering between 7,000 and 10,000 soldiers. One detachment was entrusted to the command of his brother Richard Herbert, who captured and put to death twenty of Jasper's men in the Conwy Valley.[52]

Lord Herbert, meanwhile, advanced on Harlech from the south with the main Yorkist host, following the winding route of Sarn Helen, the ancient Roman road. The pincer movement worked; on 14 August, the Harlech garrison surrendered, bringing to a close seven stout years of Lancastrian defiance on the Welsh coast. Fifty members of the garrison were sent to the Tower of London, where two were promptly beheaded by earl Rivers, the constable of England. The castle's leader, Dafydd ap Ieuan, however, the man responsible for rejecting all previous calls to surrender, evaded severe punishment, and would even regain the favour of the Yorkist king later in his reign. Other followers of Jasper, underlings like his kinsman Roger Puleston, who had for so long risked their lives keeping his cause afloat, now grudgingly accepted pardons.[53]

Frustratingly for the Yorkist crown, Jasper was nowhere to be seen in the weeks and months after the fall of Harlech. A later sixteenth-century Welsh tradition recalled that he had managed to evade capture by donning the disguise of a peasant, hauling a bale of straw on his back as he navigated through hostile country around Denbigh to the Flintshire coast. Whatever the means of his escape, by October 1469 Jasper was back at the French court of Louis XI. In a tacit acknowledgement that his campaigns in Wales had likely reached their end, he formally entered the service of his French cousin, for which he was compensated with a generous pension of £100 *tournois* a month.[54]

William Herbert's prize for bringing all of Wales to heel for the Yorkist king was significant, and politically loaded. On 8 September 1468, the 'king's kinsman' was raised to the earldom of Pembroke, the same title that had been stripped from Jasper seven years earlier.[55] He also acquired Chepstow Castle from the duke of Norfolk and was made master forester of Snowdon, constable and captain of Conwy, and chamberlain of North Wales.[56] Already chamberlain of South Wales, Herbert's pre-eminence over the Welsh was indisputable; he was by far the most powerful full-blooded Welshman since the Edwardian conquest nearly 200 years earlier. He naturally did not escape the attention of the bards, with Lewys Glyn Cothi noticeably regarding Herbert as 'King Edward's master-lock'.[57]

As he prepared to defect from the king's side, Warwick cultivated a closer relationship with Edward's ambitious twenty-year-old brother George, Duke of Clarence. When a series of shadowy northern rebellions broke out in spring 1469, suspicion fell upon Warwick's vast affinity. When the king rode north to personally face down the threat, he wrote to Warwick and Clarence demanding their submission. Instead, the wayward pair fled to Calais where a month later Clarence was married to Warwick's daughter. Firmly committed to one another, father and son-in-law now openly broadcast their support for the northern rebels and issued a damning manifesto outlining their issues with Edward's 'mischievous rule'. They shared their unhappiness at being excluded from power in favour of 'seditious persons' who only desired 'their own promotion and enriching', and promised to remedy such evil government.[58]

One of those criticised for rising above their natural station was William Herbert, the new earl of Pembroke. Clarence, in particular, feared Herbert's sponsorship of Henry Tudor and the boy's right to the honour of Richmond posed a threat to his influence in the English north. It was recalled in the rebel manifesto that previous kings who had excluded princes of the blood to make room for small cliques of grasping favourites had been removed, most recently Henry VI. Warwick had been instrumental in propelling Edward to the throne, and trusted he could do it again with the naïve Clarence.[59]

When Warwick and Clarence duly invaded England in early July, Edward's response was to turn to William Herbert to lead the military resistance.[60] As he had done for Mortimer's Cross eight years earlier, Herbert raised his affinity in the south-east of Wales, recruiting heavily among his and the king's Welsh lordships to assemble a force expected to crush whatever manpower the rebels could muster. Most of his men were drawn from his native Gwent, with some recruited from Brecon, Gower, Pembrokeshire and Kidwelly. It was a thoroughly Welsh force in every way. Together, Herbert's army progressed out of Wales to Gloucester, following the old Roman roads towards Northampton, eventually encountering the rebels near Edgcote.[61]

The evening before the battle, Herbert was forced to deal with the belligerent behaviour of his fellow commander, Humphrey Stafford, the newly created earl of Devon, who voiced his displeasure at the billeting arrangements of his troops. On the morning of battle, 24 July 1469,[62] a sulking Devon refused to combine his men with Herbert's, forcing the earl of Pembroke to engage alone from a position of tactical disadvantage. Herbert's army was formed chiefly of men-at-arms and had little answer to the arrow storm from the rebels, with Devon's archers nowhere to be seen. Herbert had little choice but to abandon his strong position on a hill and commit his men to hand-to-hand fighting. For some time, victory appeared in his grasp; Herbert's brother Richard acquitted himself particularly well, armed with a poleaxe and passing through the enemy lines twice without injury. When a small number of rebel reinforcements joined the field bearing Warwick's standard, however, Herbert's Welsh troops panicked, believing it to be the bulk of the mighty earl's entire host. They abandoned their positions and fled, only to be cut down in 'a most dreadful slaughter'. Devon's belated arrival was too late to change the course of the day.[63]

Herbert, 'the one whom men honoured' in the words of the Welsh poet Hywel Swrdwal, was captured alive and taken to Northampton to be tried before the earl of Warwick. It is likely Warwick cherished this opportunity to lambast Herbert, mocking his low birth and chastising him for daring to rise so high. When Herbert begged for the life of his brother Richard, who had performed with great vigour on the field of battle, Warwick coldly dismissed his pleas and ordered the younger man executed.[64] Warwick conceded one small act of mercy to his foe, however, permitting Herbert to pen a final letter to his wife Anne. Among the brief instructions Herbert gave his 'heart and soul' was a clear request his countess should arrange the marriage of their daughter Maud to Henry Tudor. With that, Herbert followed his brother to the chopping block.[65]

The Battle of Edgcote is not a fifteenth-century engagement particularly well recorded, perhaps as it was fought between rebel northerners and Welshmen, the details falling outside the interest of chroniclers based in

London and the south-east. Its political significance was only noted from afar.[66] One group did pay close attention to Edgcote, however: the Welsh poets and bards, who viewed Herbert's defeat as a national catastrophe. In the opinion of Guto'r Glyn, Edgcote was a 'day of disgrace' in which cruel 'vengeance was exacted, upon fair Wales'. Hywel Swrdwal, a champion of Herbert, roundly called for the ruin of the English.[67] For many generations, the battle would be remembered in Wales as a dark day, with an intense grudge against northern Englishmen remarked upon deep into the sixteenth century.[68]

The core of his royal forces destroyed, a stunned Edward IV could not evade Warwick's grasp and was arrested alone at Olney Manor. As well as Herbert's death, the king was distressed to discover that in the weeks following Edgcote his father-in-law Earl Rivers and brother-in-law John Woodville had also been executed. Under Warwick's custody, Edward was briefly imprisoned in Warwick Castle before being transferred to Middleham, one of the earl's ancestral seats in the north. With Henry VI still locked in the Tower of London, Warwick effectively had two kings of England under his control, one Yorkist and one Lancastrian.[69]

Warwick's ascendancy, however, clearly couldn't last, for he had no mandate to govern the realm in the place of Edward IV. Unlike Henry VI fifteen years earlier, Edward was not sick or otherwise incapacitated, and retained much of the goodwill of his subjects and nobility. Warwick's authority was undermined by the continuation of widespread disorder and private feuding, with both lords and commons alike reluctant to bend to his will. By early October Edward was released from Warwick's captivity and resumed direct control of his kingdom, even offering pardons and renewed friendship to his cousin and his brother, Clarence. In a shrewd attempt to placate Warwick's disquiet and appease his ambitions, the king announced he would betroth his eldest daughter, Elizabeth of York, to the earl's male heir, his nephew George Neville, now raised to the dukedom of Bedford, trusting this would bring the earl back in line.[70] It didn't work.

Excluded from any serious influence, Warwick's ambition could not rest. He soon returned to thoughts of replacing Edward on the throne with the king's brother Clarence, intending to use his impressionable son-in-law as a puppet. When yet another rebellion surfaced in Lincolnshire in March 1470, Edward rode north once more and made light work of the uprising near Empingham. Documents found on the battlefield, however, implicated Warwick and Clarence in a fresh conspiracy and opened them to accusations of insurrection. Rather than defend themselves when summoned by the furious king, now alert to their treachery, the pair fled the kingdom.[71] Their next move surprised everyone, and would impact greatly on the fortunes of the Tudors.

12

The Bloody Sword

Warwick's despair was palpable. So recently England's greatest magnate and the hand that guided the crown, the proud earl now contemplated his options as he sat aboard a ship stranded in the English Channel. He had planned to sail into the impregnable Calais, of which he had been captain for the previous decade, raising the garrison and returning to England to depose Edward IV. In the king's place he would have put his son-in-law and Edward's younger brother, George, Duke of Clarence.

When approaching the heavily militarised port, however, Warwick was shocked to come under fire from his own deputy captain, John Wenlock, Baron Wenlock, and repeated attempts to dock were thwarted. While they were anchored just out of range, the earl's daughter Isabel gave birth to a child that didn't survive, a traumatic experience for everyone on board. With Calais blocked and all avenues of reconciliation with Edward exhausted, a demoralised and grief-stricken Warwick and Clarence were forced to seek refuge in France. Worse still, Warwick was forced to reach out to the person who detested him above all others: Margaret of Anjou.[1]

A cousin to Henry VI, Margaret of Anjou and Jasper Tudor, Louis XI of France was sympathetic to the Lancastrians' plight but unwilling to act in anyone's interest other than his own. When Warwick surfaced in his kingdom at the start of May 1470, however, Louis quickly identified an opportunity to nullify the burgeoning friendship between Yorkist England and his chief foe, Charles the Bold, Duke of Burgundy. If the prudent French king was to divert Edward IV from an Anglo-Burgundian alliance, he needed Warwick and Margaret to join forces.

When the deposed Lancastrian queen arrived at Amboise on 25 June 1470 to negotiate with Louis, the pair quickly agreed a thirty-year alliance between England and France in the event Henry VI was returned to his throne. When the French king broached a rapprochement with Warwick, however, she proved 'hard and difficult'; despite many assurances, she mistrusted him. As Warwick had been instrumental in her present predicament, Margaret's hesitancy was understandable.[2]

It would take another month of persuasion for Margaret to agree to meet Warwick face-to-face, their first encounter since the earl had toppled her husband from his throne nine years earlier. Warwick arrived in Angers on 22 July and endured a humbling afternoon in Margaret's presence. In the tense confines of the castle's great hall, the proud earl was forced to his knees soon after his arrival, begging the Lancastrian queen's forgiveness for 'injuries and wrongs done to her in the past'. His humiliation complete, Margaret eventually entertained his proposal. It was put forward that the queen's only son, Prince Edward, would marry Warwick's youngest daughter, Anne, uniting their causes into one anti-Yorkist movement.[3] When the kingdom was recovered, with his father demonstrably unfit to rule, the prince would serve as regent but would be guided by his father-in-law. In return, Warwick would remain loyal to Henry, Margaret and their prince, 'unto death'.

Warwick would thereafter set to work recovering the crown for the House of Lancaster, a crown he had been integral in wresting away from Henry VI in the first instance. As well as Margaret of Anjou, he also had to win around Lancastrian stalwarts like Jasper Tudor and John de Vere, 13th Earl of Oxford, who had lost their fathers to the Yorkists. Though any encounter between the three earls at Angers is not recorded, Warwick presumably pointed to his own father's execution and sought to find some common ground, urging them all to consider the future rather than the past. It could not be denied by Jasper, Oxford or indeed Margaret that, from a most unlikely source, the Lancastrian cause was suddenly imbued with a glimmer of hope. That Warwick had ruthlessly set aside Clarence, the duke's ambitions for the crown quashed, would prove problematic not too far down the line.

On 9 September 1470, the Lancastrian army sailed from Saint-Vaast-la-Hougue on the Cotentin Peninsula in Normandy, cautiously optimistic after several years of bruising military setbacks. Despite the expectation that Wales would be their destination, owing to Jasper's deep associations there, they instead landed at Dartmouth in southern Devon four days later and disembarked after nightfall.[4] Once refreshed, proclamations were dispersed in Henry VI's name, urging all men 'to prepare themselves to fight against Edward duke of York, which contrary to all right, justice and law, had untruly usurped the crown'. They quickly attracted widespread support, with the area traditionally Lancastrian in sentiment.[5] While Warwick set off towards London, Jasper headed towards Wales to raise whatever remained of his affinity.[6]

Edward IV was in the Midlands when he discovered the Lancastrians had landed in Devon, and was alarmed to learn that Warwick's brother

Right: The tomb of
Goronwy ap Tudur
in St Gredifael's
Church, Penmynydd.

Below: Beaumaris
Castle, associated
with the Tudurs of
Anglesey.

Above: Conwy Castle, which the Tudurs of Anglesey captured in 1401.

Left: Farleigh Hungerford Castle, where Owen Tudor may have been based as a youth.

Above: Barking Abbey Curfew Tower, through which Edmund and Jasper Tudor arrived as children.

Right: Katherine of Valois and Owen Tudor, with their three sons Edmund, Jasper and Owen. (The British Library, BL King's 395 f.33)

The Tower of London, where Edmund and Jasper Tudor were created earls in 1452.

The tomb of Edmund Tudor in St David's Cathedral.

Statue of Henry Tudor outside his birthplace of Pembroke Castle.

Above: Harlech Castle, Jasper Tudor's redoubt during the Wars of the Roses.

Left: Denbigh Castle, which Jasper Tudor attacked in 1468.

Above: Raglan Castle, where Henry Tudor was brought up between 1461 and 1470.

Right: William Herbert and Anne Devereux, Henry's guardians at Raglan Castle, kneeling before Edward IV. (The British Library, BL Royal MS 18 DII f.6)

Above: Tenby Harbour, from where Jasper and Henry Tudor fled in 1471. (*Tenby Harbour* by Dylan Moore, Wikimedia Commons)

Below: The tomb effigy of Francis II of Brittany, who provided refuge to the Tudors. (Jibi44, Wikimedia Commons)

Above: Chateau de Suscinio, where Jasper and Henry Tudor were based between 1472 and 1474.

Below: The main residential block and moat at Suscinio.

Above: Chateau de Josselin, where Jasper Tudor was based between 1474 and 1476.

Left: The keep at Josselin which housed Jasper Tudor.

Above left: Chateau de Largoët, home of Henry Tudor between 1474 and 1476.

Above right: The 144-foot Tour d'Elven, which housed Henry for two years.

Below: St Vincent Cathedral, St Malo, where Henry sought sanctuary in 1476.

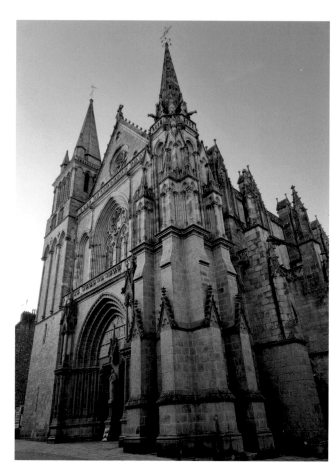

Left: St Peter's Cathedral, Vannes, where Henry made several offerings between 1476 and 1483.

Below: Rouen, where Henry Tudor was shown to the public as the king of England in April 1484.

A document signed by 'Henry of Richemonte' acknowledging the loan of 10,000 crowns from Duke Francis II. (The British Library, BL Add MS 19398 f.33r)

Above: Mill Bay, where Henry Tudor's army landed on 7 August 1485.

Right: Margaret Beaufort's recording of the day her son landed at Mill Bay in her Book of Hours. (The British Library, BL Royal MS 2 A XVIII f.31v)

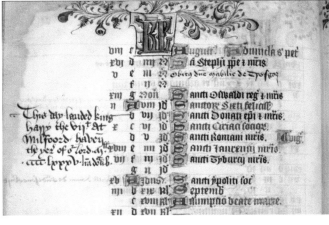

The house on Wyle Cop, Shrewsbury, where Henry Tudor traditionally rested on his way to battle.

The remains of Merevale Abbey, where part of the Tudor force traditionally stayed before Bosworth. (By kind permission of Jenny Deadman, Abbey Farm B&B, Merevale)

Above: Bosworth Battlefield, where Henry Tudor won the crown on 22 August 1485.

Below: The effigy of David Owen in St Mary's Church, Easebourne.

The Welsh Dragon visible on Canterbury's Christ Church Gate.

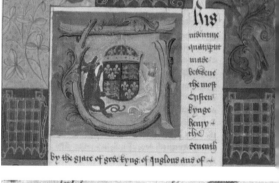

Henry VII's coat of arms, featuring a Welsh Dragon on a green and white background. (The British Library, Harley MS 28 f.1r)

Henry VII and Elizabeth of York. (The British Library, BL King's 395 f.33)

John Neville, recently stripped of the coveted earldom of Northumberland despite no evidence of prior disloyalty, was heading south from Yorkshire having chosen to side with his sibling. Trapped in a pincer movement, Edward chose to flee, heading eastwards towards the coast and sailing across the North Sea to Burgundy without giving battle or collecting his pregnant wife. With him was just a small collection of his closest advisors, led by his youngest brother Richard, Duke of Gloucester, and brother-in-law Anthony Woodville, Earl Rivers.[7]

With the kingdom abandoned, on 6 October 1470 another of Warwick's brothers, George Neville, the archbishop of York who had been humiliatingly stripped of the chancellorship, entered London and went directly to the Tower. Once there, he entered the chamber housing Henry VI, dishevelled and confused after five years of captivity. Henry was informed of what had occurred – it is unclear if he understood – and was escorted out of his prison. Just one week later, the bishop of Novara was reporting that Warwick had 'practically the whole of the island in his power', a coup completed 'without the least slaughter or bloodshed'.[8] For this, he would be remembered in history as the Kingmaker.

The return of Henry VI to his throne after a decade in the wilderness was termed the Readeption, though to one foreign observer it seemed more like 'a miracle or a dream' had occurred.[9] Nothing had changed in the interim, however, regarding Henry's ability to personally govern his realm. In fact, the forty-eight-year-old king was less capable than before he had been deposed, half a decade in captivity taking its toll on his already fragile mental state. As Margaret of Anjou had elected to stay behind in France with her son for the time being, it was Warwick who would rule England as de facto protector in the interim.

The restoration of Lancaster heralded a return to prominence for Jasper Tudor, that indefatigable champion of his half-brother's cause. Throughout the 1460s he had been busy, operating relentlessly between Northumberland, Scotland, Ireland, Flanders, Brittany and France, stubbornly rebuffing any notion of reconciliation with the Yorkists. Now, it was time for Jasper to return home and revive his position and that of his family. One of his first acts was to seek out his Tudor nephew in rural Herefordshire.

At the battle of Edgcote on 24 July 1469, the twelve-year-old Henry Tudor had watched helplessly from the sidelines as the army of his guardian, William Herbert, was routed by rebel northerners. Herbert's motivation for bringing Henry to the battlefield was to advance his military education, a rite of passage that would provide the boy with an invaluable opportunity for hands-on experience among hardened soldiers within a working camp. Considering Henry's age, he likely performed some minor duties, passing messages between various commanders, helping in the cleaning and handling of weapons, and perhaps even dressing or arming Lord Herbert before battle. This was vital for an earl of royal pedigree like Henry, laying the foundations for future advancement to knighthood and preparing him to command armies of his own in adulthood.

Herbert's misjudgement in having Henry accompany him on this expedition had threatened the life of his Tudor ward, but the boy was spirited to safety by Richard Corbet of Moreton. The nineteen-year-old son of a Shropshire knight, and Lord Herbert's nephew by marriage, Corbet later recounted to Henry that he had been responsible for rescuing him 'out of the danger of your enemies', taking him from the battlefield back to Hereford. It is likely Corbet more specifically took Henry to Weobley, 12 miles north-east of Hereford and the seat of the Devereux family, to which Herbert's grieving wife belonged.[10] Here in the gentle Herefordshire countryside, Anne Herbert, now dowager countess of Pembroke, continued to raise her children, including her Tudor ward.

Henry's feelings towards his guardian are unknown, for no record has survived documenting their personal relationship. In his eight years under Herbert's protection, however, an impressionable youth is likely to have acquired some of his master's traits. Herbert was a diligent administrator, meticulously scrutinising his landed interests, commercial affairs and finances with a vigour his erstwhile ward would later emulate. He was courageous in his endeavours and ambitious in his building projects, possessed a sage political mind and was a noted family man, again characteristics evident in an adult Henry Tudor.[11] It must be considered that, in many respects, William Herbert was the first father-figure Henry had, and the young man may have sincerely mourned his death.

When news of Herbert's demise reached Margaret Beaufort, she immediately recognised the opportunity to be permanently reunited with her Tudor son. Since Henry's guardian was no longer around, it made sense that the boy could return to his mother to continue his upbringing. Edward IV, however, was unmoved and had no pressing desire to terminate the Tudor–Herbert project. The new Herbert earl, named William like his father, was still a minor but control of his lands and estates had been granted to his mother until he was old enough to fully succeed to his inheritance.

The king did, however, also need to satisfy the ambitions of the Stafford family, whose influence rivalled the Herbert affinity in South-East Wales. The present duke of Buckingham was also a minor, just fourteen years old, with the family interests overseen by his uncle Sir Henry Stafford. This Stafford happened to be married to Margaret Beaufort, and furthermore was brother of John Stafford, Earl of Wiltshire, and nephew of the Bourchier brothers, one of whom was archbishop of Canterbury and another earl of Essex. Stafford, therefore, was well placed in Yorkist royal circles to raise a quarrel on his wife's behalf. Edward IV had to manage the matter delicately to avoid alienating either the Herbert–Devereux faction or the Beaufort–Stafford party.

By the autumn of 1469, Margaret was avidly pursuing every legal avenue to retake possession of her son. She enlisted her receiver-general, an up-and-coming administrator named Reginald Bray, to liaise with parliamentary clerk Thomas Bayan to search through exchequer and chancery records, trying to find a loophole that would invalidate the Herberts' wardship of Henry. To aid their research, Bray purchased a copy of the original patent, scrutinising the contents for any ambiguities which could be exploited. He even travelled to Weobley to discuss the matter with Lady Herbert, taking with him messages and money for young Henry, as well as a bow and some arrows for his enjoyment. It was the start of a lengthy association between Bray and Henry Tudor, one that would prove astoundingly beneficial for both men in later years.[12]

Bray appears to have made some headway, for on 31 October 1469 in the Bell Inn on London's Fleet Street, Margaret Beaufort and Henry Stafford entertained Anne Herbert and her brother, Walter Devereux, Lord Ferrers of Chartley. With Bray covering all expenses, the summit was a matter of business, with legal counsel present in the form of Master Humphrey Starkey, recorder of London, and the lawyer Richard Eton. The dispute remained unresolved when Edward IV lost his crown a year later and another interested party entered the scene.[13]

Shortly after the Lancastrians regained control of the kingdom in October 1470, Jasper Tudor presented himself before Lady Herbert at Weobley and let it be known he was to resume care for his now teenage nephew.[14] Any previous discussions about his legal status were dismissed, and the dowager countess had little choice but to acquiesce to Jasper's will. According to the later testimony of Richard Corbet, it was he who was responsible for conveying Henry into his uncle's hands. Certainly by the middle of the month uncle and nephew were reunited, for the pair were in London together by 27 October. The nearly 150-mile journey was an ideal opportunity for Henry to reacquaint himself with Jasper, and for Jasper to get to know the young man whom his greatest adversary, William Herbert, had raised. Uncle and nephew would grow noticeably close in the coming years, but in these early moments together they were forced to develop a relationship almost from scratch. Once in London, they dined with Margaret, her husband Henry Stafford, and the king's chamberlain Sir Richard Tunstall. Although mother and son likely spent much of their time relishing each other's company after so much time apart, Henry's long-term situation most certainly dominated the discussions.[15]

It was while Henry was visiting the capital – probably his first ever visit to London – that he was granted an audience with the royal uncle he had likely never met but after whom he was named. The two principal accounts written of this meeting between a nearly fifty-year-old Henry VI and a teenage Henry Tudor were only crafted after the latter had acceded to the English throne, and must be interpreted with considerable caution, such is the hindsight with which they were penned.

According to Bernard André, the Lancastrian king hosted a splendid feast for his nobles and summoned his young Tudor nephew into his presence as he was washing his hands. In front of everyone, the king 'prophesised that some day the boy would undertake the governance of the kingdom and would have all things under his own power'. Bishop Fisher, speaking before Henry VII and his mother Margaret in 1506, also mentioned Henry VI's foretelling of the Tudor accession.[16] This was later embellished by Polydore Vergil, who claimed it was Jasper who brought the boy to Westminster to meet with his uncle. When the king beheld his nephew, Vergil reports he turned to the nobles present and uttered, 'This truly, this is he unto whom both we and our adversaries must yield and give over the dominion.' Thus, adds Vergil, 'the holy man showed it would come to pass that Henry should in time enjoy the kingdom'.[17]

It is plausible that Henry Tudor met his uncle in London during the autumn of 1470. His uncle Jasper was the king's half-brother, and his mother Margaret was the king's adoring cousin; both had good reason to introduce the boy to Henry VI during their own emotional reunions with the king. It is highly doubtful, however, that the king predicted his Tudor kinsman would one day wear the crown. At the time in question, the Lancastrian succession was vested in the king's own son, Prince Edward, and there was no consideration that anyone other than he would follow his father on the throne, providing they could fend off the Yorkist challenge. Even if Henry VI's line failed, there were others in England with more striking Lancastrian lineages than Henry Tudor – Henry Holland, Duke of Exeter, and Edmund and John Beaufort to name but three. As part of the settlement between Warwick and Margaret of Anjou, even George, Duke of Clarence, was ahead of young Henry in any hypothetical line of succession. In October 1470, no one could have foreseen all of those would be dead within a decade.

Upon leaving the king's presence, Henry stayed with his mother for the next fortnight. He was thirteen years old, and his mother still a youthful twenty-seven. Accompanied by Margaret's husband, Henry Stafford, they left the bustling city behind and briefly decamped to the more serene environs of her riverside manor at Woking. From here, they moved on to Guildford, Maidenhead and finally Henley-on-Thames in Oxfordshire. On 11 November 1470, probably at Henley, Henry was returned to Jasper's care, and together uncle and nephew travelled westwards into South Wales. Unbeknown to both at the time of their parting, Henry would not see his mother again for nearly fifteen years.[18]

The resurgent Lancastrians, meanwhile, held their first parliament in a decade, though Jasper doesn't appear to have been present. The parliament assembled at Westminster on 26 November, and though no records have survived to provide in-depth details, it was chiefly concerned with confirming the change of king, restoring attainted Lancastrian lords to their former positions and reversing nine years of Yorkist governance. Jasper was restored to the earldom of Pembroke and most of the offices and estates he had held before 1461, though he had of course never accepted they had been surrendered in the first place. Edward IV, notably, was proclaimed throughout London during this period to have been a 'usurper of the crown'.[19]

It is unclear what role the duke of Clarence played in the proceedings, but his status was noticeably lower than he had been promised two years earlier by Warwick. With Henry VI returned to the throne, it was established that the heir presumptive was once again his only son, Prince Edward. Only if Henry's line failed would the crown pass to Clarence, and even this was contentious to the Holland and Beaufort families, both members of the wider Lancastrian bloodline with claims of their own.

Despite the efforts of Margaret Beaufort and her husband Henry Stafford, Clarence was also permitted to retain the earldom, lordship and honour of Richmond for life, to the exclusion of Henry Tudor. Stafford, who pointedly referred to the Tudor boy as the 'Earl of Richmond' in his will,[20] visited Clarence six times between 6 October 1470 and 16 December 1470, with Margaret also attempting to reach a settlement with the duke in person at Baynard's Castle on 27 November. It was agreed that Henry would succeed to the honour on Clarence's death, but as the latter was only eight years the former's senior it wouldn't have been seen as much of a concession.[21] This fragile balance between restoring attainted Lancastrian loyalists and placating turncoats like Warwick, his brother Montagu and son-in-law Clarence hinted that the Readeption regime faced some difficult days ahead, particularly in the absence of a commanding king who could enforce his will. An uneasy impasse persisted.

After a decade of Yorkist rule, however, the Lancastrians urgently needed to secure the realm rather than quibble over hereditary rights, especially if Edward IV was preparing his return as anticipated. One of the main areas of concern was South-East Wales and the neighbouring border counties, a region where support for the House of York was deep-rooted and long-standing. Despite his absence for much of the past decade, Jasper Tudor still commanded widespread influence in South-West and North Wales. Steps were quickly taken to enhance his power where it was found wanting.

On 14 November 1470, with his old adherent Thomas FitzHenry standing as a guarantor, Jasper was granted the revenues from the extensive estates of the late William Herbert, to hold for seven years. As one of the Yorkist king's closest confidants, Herbert's holdings at the end of his life had been widespread, and Jasper was now to draw considerable income from the castle and lordship of Raglan, the lordship of Dunster in Somerset, the Herefordshire lordships of Goodrich and Archenfield, plus rents from Haverfordwest, Gower, Loughor, Kilvey, Swansea, Crickhowell, Tretower and Chepstow. A few weeks later, with Henry in tow, Jasper was based in Monmouth, able to inspect some of his new holdings personally. On 20 December, while he was still in the region, he was appointed a justice of the peace for Herefordshire and Gloucester.[22]

The appointments and grants didn't end there. On 23 January 1471, 'for defence against Edward the usurper', Jasper was commissioned to array all able-bodied men in South Wales and the Marches, and to further aggrandise his authority in the region he was appointed constable of Gloucester Castle on the feast day of St Valentine. The same day, he further benefitted from the fact two significant Marcher lords were minors; he was granted control of all lands belonging to the Lord Powis, including the castle of Welshpool, and with Warwick was given a share of the duke of Buckingham's lordships of Brecon, Hay and Huntingdon.[23]

Jasper's remit was clear. He was to uncover then suppress the lingering Yorkist threat and prevent Yorkist-aligned families like the Herberts, Vaughans and Devereuxs from ever recovering their dominance. By the early spring of 1471, with his authority over the Welsh covering the breadth of Wales south of Welshpool and extending into England, his territorial authority was at its pinnacle.

While Jasper and the Lancastrian party steadily rebuilt their authority, holding together a fragile alliance that placed the earl of Warwick at the centre of its operations, Edward IV had been plotting his return to England. After his humiliating flight in September 1470, the deposed Yorkist king had made his way to Flanders where he sought protection from his brother-in-law Charles the Bold, Duke of Burgundy. Despite his recent marital connection to the House of York, the ambitious duke was a great-grandson of John of Gaunt and close in blood to the Lancastrians. Charles had even sheltered exiled Lancastrians in the past, which included providing Jasper safe conducts on a handful of occasions to pass through his lands.[24]

Warwick's aggressive foreign policy, however, in which he fully supported France in its conflict with Burgundy, pushed Duke Charles towards modestly sponsoring a Yorkist invasion of England. Edward gathered around him the small number of supporters who had joined him in exile, perhaps a few hundred men, and with the duke's blessing was able to secure further financing from wealthy Flemish merchants. In early spring 1471, he sailed for England, landing at Ravenspur in Yorkshire on 14 March 1471.

Though the Yorkists failed to find much support in the north of England, an area in which the principal landowners were presently aligned with the Lancastrians, Edward drew more interest as he moved south into the East Midlands, dropping his initial pretence that he only returned to claim the duchy of York. At Coventry, he attempted numerous times to lure his cousin Warwick out from behind the town walls before pressing on. It is also at this juncture that Edward was reconciled with his brother Clarence, who now abandoned the Lancastrians to return to the family fold. All three brothers of York, united once again, purposefully pushed towards London. On 11 April, they entered the city and encountered no resistance, the duke of Somerset and earl of Devon having fled south-west. The Yorkists found Henry VI abandoned and alone in the bishop of London's palace in Lambeth, and returned him to the Tower. London secured, Edward turned his attentions to inflicting a fatal blow to his adversaries, stopping only to reunite with his queen, Elizabeth Woodville, who had given birth to an heir while in sanctuary at Westminster Abbey.[25]

With London pitifully surrendered without any resistance, Warwick belatedly emerged from Coventry and headed south, linking up with the duke of Exeter and earl of Oxford. Edward IV was more than prepared to meet them in battle, and the two forces clashed in a 'dreadful engagement' just north of Barnet on the misty morning of 14 April 1471. Though Oxford was able to make quick work of Lord Hastings on the Yorkist left flank, even chasing them from the field back towards London, when he led his men back into battle they were attacked by Warwick's brother Lord Montagu. With fog making it hard to see, Montagu had mistaken Oxford's badge of stars with rays for the Yorkist sun in splendour, and the latter's men, not unreasonably, cried, 'Treason! treason!' Believing they had been betrayed by Warwick, Oxford's men abandoned the field, prompting the remainder of the panicked Lancastrian force to collapse shortly thereafter. In the Yorkist rout that followed, both Montagu and Warwick were killed.[26] The notorious Kingmaker, a man of 'stout stomach' and 'invincible courage' who dared to meddle with the throne, was no more.[27]

As battle raged at Barnet, 140 miles away Margaret of Anjou finally landed back on English soil, disembarking at Weymouth with her son, Prince Edward. As per her understanding with Warwick the previous autumn, Margaret had only been willing to bring her son back to England once the earl had returned her husband to the throne. From a position of great optimism for the future, it was with considerable terror that she now learned that not only was Warwick dead, but her husband was back in the Tower. The Yorkists were on the verge of reclaiming the kingdom.[28] The queen's timing could not have been more unfortunate.

Ordering Somerset and Devon to raise an army from the surrounding counties, Margaret placed her seventeen-year-old son, Prince Edward, front and centre of the force to invoke further support. Her intention was to head towards the Welsh March where she could combine her army with Jasper Tudor's Welsh recruits before advancing into Cheshire and Lancashire, areas known to be 'well affected to the Lancastrian line'.[29]

Edward IV, however, had been made aware of Margaret's plan, and quickly assembled a fresh force to head west and decisively crush her host before it could reach either Wales or the north-west of England. Issuing a proclamation reiterating his right to be king, Edward condemned the Lancastrians, including Jasper, as rebels he intended to destroy.[30] He made efficient use of his scouts to track the Lancastrians' movements and, pushing his troops at a punishing speed, was soon on their tail. Exhausted after three weeks trekking through 'foul country' without 'any good refreshing', the Lancastrians eventually halted their march in Tewkesbury and started preparing for battle. They had not been able to cross the Severn and reach Wales, and could only hope that Jasper would make it to Tewkesbury quicker than the Yorkists.[31]

Jasper had probably been in or near Wales since collecting his nephew from Margaret Beaufort in November 1470, concentrating on re-establishing his authority in the Marches throughout winter. His exact whereabouts during the seismic events of March to May 1471 are unknown, and he may have been in any one of a number of properties he held across South Wales. It may be assumed that a messenger from Margaret of Anjou had alerted Jasper to raise his troops and prepare to meet the main host, which he set about with his customary zeal. However, for whatever reason – difficulties mustering his forces at such short notice, hesitancy among the men of South Wales to move against the Yorkists, or simple shock at the swiftness of Edward IV's advance – Jasper never made it to Tewkesbury.

While based at Chepstow, a long-established frontier town first settled by the Romans, word was brought to Jasper of events at Tewkesbury on the morning of 4 May. He learned that, unable to shake off the Yorkists, the Beaufort duke of Somerset had taken command of the Lancastrian army, aided by the earl of Devon, Baron Wenlock and, in his first military engagement, the young Prince Edward. Despite their strong position and greater numbers, they were harried by a shower of arrows and gunshot, provoking Somerset into engaging early in the battle, a move considered 'more courageous than circumspect' in the official Yorkist account. The Lancastrians crashed into the main Yorkist host, and though they held their own for some time, they were eventually overawed and slaughtered 'with great violence'.[32]

To his horror, Jasper was then informed that his nephew Prince Edward, on whose young shoulders rested the hopes of the Lancastrian dynasty, had been killed in the fighting, 'slain in the field' according to the pro-Yorkist account. Another near-contemporary account reported that just before his death the prince cried out to his brother-in-law Clarence for help, only for his pleas to be coldheartedly rejected. Others killed in the fighting included John Beaufort and the earl of Devon, while the Lancastrians' principal commander, Somerset, was dragged out of sanctuary in Tewkesbury Abbey and summarily executed in the marketplace. It had been an annihilation for Lancaster, and a 'glorious victory' for York.[33]

There was no time for Jasper Tudor to lament his failure to reach Tewkesbury. Edward IV was anxious to mop up any lingering Lancastrian complications and, 'not being out of fear' of Jasper's ability to rouse the Welsh, sought to strike first. The man he tasked with trapping the Tudors was Jasper's old foe Roger Vaughan of Tretower, a 'very valiant man' who was dispatched immediately after Tewkesbury to track them down. While deliberating upon the shrewdest course of action, Jasper was tipped off by 'certain friends' about Vaughan's mission, and set a trap of his own. When Vaughan reached Chepstow, it was he who was taken by surprise, ambushed by his prey.[34]

Jasper relished having Vaughan in his possession, taking the opportunity to upbraid his prisoner for his role in the execution of Owen Tudor a decade earlier. Much heated conversation passed between the two men, which according to an account later given to the antiquarian John Leland ended with the desperate Vaughan begging Jasper 'to be good to him'. The response was cold and decisive – Jasper snapped that Vaughan 'should have such favour as he showed to Owen his father', and had his head 'smitten off'.[35]

The bloody deed done, Jasper and Henry wasted little time in heading west, recognising that 'matters were past all hope of recovery' for the Lancastrians in England.[36] They followed some of the old Roman routes that took them through Cowbridge, Neath and Carmarthen, a gruelling, anxious trek completed in under a fortnight. Vaughan may have been dispatched, but other Yorkists would soon be in pursuit. The Tudors reached Henry's birthplace of Pembroke and barricaded themselves inside the castle, dropping the portcullis behind them and hoping to buy some time while they figured out their next step. Their options were more than limited; they were sitting ducks.

When a small force surfaced outside the castle walls under the command of Morgan ap Thomas, a grandson of Jasper's old ally Gruffydd ap Nicholas, the trapped earl may have been led to believe they were riding to his rescue. The family of Gruffydd had, after all, been defiant Lancastrians during the early phases of the Wars of the Roses, including Morgan's father, Thomas ap Gruffydd, who had once been entrusted with holding Carreg Cennen Castle for Jasper. Morgan, however, was not at Pembroke to assist Jasper. As son-in-law of the recently executed Vaughan, he intended to exact his own brand of vengeance and do what his father-in-law had been unable to do.

According to the account of Polydore Vergil, crafted later from first-hand recollections, Morgan besieged the Tudors at Pembroke for eight full days, digging a series of trenches that encircled the castle to prevent their escape. The situation appeared precarious for Jasper and Henry when Morgan's brother Dafydd ap Thomas arrived with a small force of his own. Unlike his sibling, Dafydd remained a 'faithful friend' of Jasper's, and turned his hastily assembled mob, armed with hooks, prongs and glaives from their fields, on his brother. During this fraternal skirmish outside Pembroke's towering walls, Jasper and Henry were able to slip away, perhaps through the large prehistoric cavern that lay beneath the castle.[37]

From Pembroke the Tudors hurried to Jasper's coastal fort at Tenby, which he now hoped would justify his considerable investment some fourteen years earlier. A later tradition states the Tudors were assisted by 'Mr White', then mayor of Tenby.[38] This was likely to have been Thomas White, a wealthy merchant who served as mayor five times between 1457 and 1472 although not, it should be noted, in 1471 when the office was filled by a Walter Eynon.[39] If it was indeed White who aided the Tudors, he would never live to see Henry ascend the throne, dying during the reign of Edward IV on 8 May 1482. In St Mary's Church in Tenby's centre one can still see the fine tomb of this man who possibly helped save a future king of England when he was but a frightened teenage boy.

It is likely that snippets of information continued to arrive from England, helping Jasper plot his next move. Still reeling from the death of his nephew Prince Edward, Jasper now learned that his half-brother Henry VI, a 'good, simple and innocent man' who had shown him great compassion as a child and generosity as an adult, had also been 'put to death'. The official Yorkist source reported the Lancastrian king had expired through 'pure displeasure, and melancholy' upon hearing of his son's death, but the truth was betrayed by his body bleeding over the floor of St Paul's Cathedral the following day.[40] With no son and therefore no cause left to fight for, the once redoubtable Margaret of Anjou, meanwhile, had meekly surrendered to Edward IV.

Jasper could spare little time to mourn. He may have been unable to reach Tewkesbury in time to save one nephew, but with him at Tenby was his other nephew, the fourteen-year-old Henry Tudor. Even in his shock, Jasper grasped the severity of the situation. With the Yorkist king having 'chosen to crush the seed' of Lancaster, slaying Prince Edward and wiping out the Beauforts in the male line, young Henry's lineage became of greater interest to the Yorkists.[41]

On his father's side, the Tudor teenager was a widely acknowledged nephew of Henry VI, though this close kinship to the fallen Lancastrian king provided no claim to the English throne. On his mother's side, however, there was a decent argument to be made that Henry Tudor now represented the slight Beaufort claim borne by his deceased relations. Any objection that a claim through the female line disqualified Henry had been somewhat nullified by the Yorkists acceding to the throne using their Mortimer descent from Philippa of Clarence. Regardless of how weak Henry's Lancastrian claim to the English throne may have been, however, the Yorkist regime could allow no more dynastic complications going forward. The Tudor boy was a target, a fact Jasper was immediately able to appreciate.

The Tudors sheltered behind Tenby's 6-foot-thick walls throughout the uneasy summer of 1471. On 16 July, the Milanese ambassador at the French court, Sforza de Bettini, reported to the duke of Milan that Jasper maintained 'a good number of places in Wales', a 'strong country' noted for its 'constant opposition' to the Yorkist king. Despite the gravity of his situation, Jasper was still attempting to stir up trouble. On 6 August, Bettini wrote again that Jasper was keeping matters 'unsettled' in the region, 'with some other lords and the help of the Scots'.[42] It is likely in response to this that, on 27 August, Edward IV commissioned the namesake heir of William Herbert to array the men of South Wales, Worcestershire, Gloucestershire, Herefordshire and Shropshire 'to resist Jasper Owen, calling himself earl of Pembroke'. The use of Jasper's father's name as his English-style surname, correct in the manner of Welsh patronymics, rather than the modern usage of Tudor, is notable. The junior Herbert, regarded as the new earl of Pembroke by the Yorkists, was further empowered to accept into the king's allegiance any remaining Lancastrian rebels in South Wales, save for five: Jasper, his old ally the duke of Exeter, and his loyal supporters John Owen, Hugh Mulle and Thomas FitzHarry.[43]

Not for lack of trying, Jasper was unable to make any headway in organising fresh conspiracies to unseat Edward IV. The Lancastrian cause was dead, and everyone knew it. Bernard André reported that Margaret Beaufort, conscious it was only a matter of time before Yorkist troops flooded the narrow streets of Tenby, implored her brother-in-law and son to flee the country, saying 'the great distance of the sea will help us avoid all perils'. At the forefront of Margaret's mind was the knowledge that Edward IV was ruthlessly purging potential Lancastrian claimants, not least two of her Beaufort cousins at Tewkesbury. They had shared the same royal lineage as her son, descended from a grandson of Edward III named John Beaufort. For Margaret, her son needed to escape 'the bloody sword' of the Yorkist king.[44]

Whether or not Margaret directed orders from afar, the Tudors did indeed conclude that to stay within reach of the Yorkists was unwise. Local tradition states Jasper and Henry made their escape through an extensive network of tunnels that led from the town down to Tenby's harbour. They possibly entered this underground passage through one of the large merchant houses near St Mary's Church, perhaps from a basement belonging to Thomas White. Evidence of a vaulted tunnel still exists beneath the modern-day High Street, including a small chamber that once contained a vented fireplace, an ideal subterranean place of refuge. Though now blocked, a tunnel once continued down towards the harbour, passing beneath Crackwell Street and through the cliff, terminating near the slipway. It is more than plausible these dark tunnels once sheltered the Tudors. As they crept through the dark, careful not to trip over the uneven, rocky surface, the only sounds they would have heard were their footsteps and the thumping of their hearts.[45] As they worked towards a sliver of moonlight that eventually gave way to the harbour and the gentle ebb and flow of the sea, thoughts of cruel betrayal at this late hour surely played on their minds.

Whether it was Mayor White who assisted them or another unidentified conspirator, the Tudors did not fall victim to treachery. In the harbour they boarded a small barque, probably with a modest, close-knit crew they could trust, and sailed out past St Catherine's Rock and around Caldey Island. They headed out into the Celtic Sea, bound for France, where Jasper trusted they could claim asylum at the court of his cousin Louis XI.[46] As they left Wales behind, both uncle and nephew could breathe a sigh of relief. They were safe, for now.

13

The Only Imp

The destination was France, but during their blustery passage through the English Channel the Tudors were blown off course and forced to seek shelter in Brittany.[1] The spot where uncle and nephew came ashore was near Le Conquet, a small fishing port on the westerly tip of the Breton mainland. It is possible they caught sight of a lonely monastery from the water – the clifftop Abbey of Saint-Mathieu de Fine-Terre – and, worn out from their difficult voyage, desperately sought aid from the small community of Benedictine monks. News reached London of the Tudors' flight and their reappearance in Brittany around the start of September 1471.[2]

Jasper had intended to seek refuge at the court of his French cousin Louis XI, with whom he already had a personal relationship. During a previous flight from his homeland, Jasper spent time in the French court and even drew a royal pension from his Valois kinsman. The expectation was that Jasper would once more be warmly welcomed by Louis, and in time perhaps transform the Tudors from Anglo-Welsh aristocracy into a family who would serve the French crown exclusively. A fruitful future in Yorkist England or Wales, after all, appeared improbable with the fall of the House of Lancaster.

Once it became apparent that they had in fact disembarked in Brittany, not France, the Tudors' only recourse was to appeal to the Breton court for a safe conduct to continue their journey by land. Brittany in the 1470s was an independent duchy, a sovereign state that had existed since the early tenth century when the Bretons expelled the Vikings from their midst. The duchy's commanding position on the western reaches of the English Channel, protruding out into the Atlantic Ocean, ensured Brittany was a vital player in Anglo-French relations across the centuries, with successive dukes pawns in the wider struggle for regional supremacy. In particular, the Breton War of Succession between 1341 and 1365 drew

French and English attention to the duchy, with the warring kingdoms sponsoring rival claimants to succeed John III as duke of Brittany. John of Montfort's triumph, secured with English support, served to strengthen Brittany's determination to resist annexation by France, a situation that continued deep into the fifteenth century under a succession of Montfort rulers.

The incumbent duke of Brittany in the autumn of 1471 was Francis II, a 'kind and good prince' who had inherited his ducal crown thirteen years earlier.[3] Like Louis XI, Jasper also knew Francis well, having once sought refuge in Brittany in 1462. The two men were a similar age, around thirty-eight years old, and also second cousins, sharing a great-grandfather in Charles V of France. There was no need for the Tudors to fear Francis, but whether he would be cooperative at this juncture was not certain.

Once recovered from their challenging voyage, the Tudors and the modest band of followers that had accompanied them, possibly in single figures, started trekking inland from the windswept coast. They quickly came upon the town of Brest before continuing, possibly under guard thereafter, to either the formidable ducal capital at Nantes or perhaps the Château de l'Hermine in Vannes, roughly 60 miles north-west of Nantes. Upon their arrival, the Tudors were granted an audience with the inquisitive duke, during which Jasper formally submitted himself to the protection of Francis. The duke received his weary guests graciously, and with 'honour, curtesy, and favor entertained them as though they had been his brothers'.[4] Still aged just fourteen, the journey may have been significantly taxing for young Henry, and he likely welcomed the opportunity to recuperate.

Francis, however, was in a delicate situation. Although independent, Brittany faced persistent hostility from the acquisitive king of France, Louis XI, and subsisted under a state of significant economic, military and diplomatic pressure. The French king intended to enlarge his royal demesne by annexing the duchies around his kingdom, such as Burgundy, Berry, Normandy and Orléans, and centralise all power. Brittany, however, was Louis's principal target. This existential threat led to the foundation of the League of Public Weal in 1465, a military alliance between the defiant dukes that sought to restore their feudal prerogatives and thwarted Louis's ambitions for the time being. Maintaining his autonomy was proving an expensive endeavour for Francis, however, forcing him to rely on the political and military support of successive English kings to withstand French expansion.

When it became known in London that the Tudors had survived their voyage and arrived safely in Brittany, Edward IV immediately sought to manipulate Duke Francis's domestic concerns to coerce him into their handover. After all, the two parties were allies, having agreed a thirty-year pact just three earlier in which they agreed not to support one another's adversaries.[5] In April 1472, when France threatened once more to invade the vulnerable duchy, Edward sent his two brothers-in-law, Anthony Woodville, Earl Rivers, and Edward Woodville, across the Channel armed with 1,000 archers placed at the Bretons' disposal. A probing French advance was duly repelled that summer, followed by an amicable exchange of envoys that took place between the English and Breton courts. A treaty was ultimately negotiated in September, but attempts by Edward's representatives to persuade Francis to surrender his Tudor guests proved fruitless.[6]

The duke's rationale for frustrating his ally was sound; if Francis handed over the Tudors to the English, he'd have no bargaining chip during future negotiations when seeking military or financial assistance to withstand the French. By retaining Jasper and Henry, a diplomatic gift yielded by the sea, Francis could gently blackmail the Yorkist king to remain generously disposed to Breton concerns, lest the duke deliver the Tudors to Louis XI. The French king, meanwhile, had to be wary of his dealings with the duchy as long as they were backed by the English. Because of this complex if fragile Anglo-Franco-Breton stand-off, the Tudors found themselves reduced to little more than pawns in a cautious game. Like ships ensnared in a tempest, their fates lay outside their control.

Despite such political complexities, Francis did prove a generous host to his Tudor kinsmen, prompting the Frenchman Philippe de Commines to observe they were treated 'very handsomely for prisoners'.[7] Wardrobe accounts dated to June 1472, for example, show that the still growing 'monsieur de Richemont' was gifted a long robe of fine black velvet and a stuffed doublet of black Damask, clothing appropriate to Henry's noble rank, rather than reduced to the rags of a captive.[8] Though greatly in demand, Francis promised 'upon his honour' to safeguard the Tudors from harm, and apart from some brief episodes during bouts of sickness he proved true to his word.[9] Aside from the matter of honour, this approach was likely driven by the personal relationship that quickly developed between the duke and his two guests, Henry in particular – the poet Bernard André would later remark that, owing to the younger Tudor's 'goodly form' and 'natural talents, the longer Francis spent in his company the more he was inclined to 'love him'.[10]

Despite Francis's goodwill towards the Tudors, as a consequence of his discussions with the English envoys in September 1472, the duke was obliged to ensure Henry and Jasper were securely lodged and closely observed going forward. There was concern in English circles that through an act of duplicity they could be snared by French infiltrators at any time. Around this period, therefore, uncle and nephew were removed from the lively ducal court and transferred to the picturesque Château de Suscinio.[11]

Situated on the Rhuys Peninsula near the quiet coastal town of Sarzeau, Suscinio was an idyllic countryside fortress that had long been a treasured hunting retreat of the dukes of Brittany. Originally a modest manor house erected in the heart of a dense forest, Suscinio was first fortified in 1229 by Duke John I and gradually developed across the centuries. The grand ducal palace that now greeted the Tudors certainly impressed, and was far removed from its humble beginnings.

As they cautiously made their way along the muddy path that snaked through the forest, beyond the branches and greenery uncle and nephew caught teasing glimpses of stone towers, seven in total. Particularly noticeable was the largest of the seven, La Tour Neuve, which dominated the north-western corner. The final approach revealed the full glory of the gatehouse, comprising three imposing cylindrical towers reached by a wooden drawbridge that controlled access across a deep moat. As Henry passed through the gatehouse for the first time, he may have noted the extensive range of machicolations that crowned the top of each tower, triggering memories of his youth at Raglan Castle. Just three years distant, his childhood with the Herberts may have felt like a different lifetime.

Once into the main courtyard, Henry was transferred into the care of another guardian who took his responsibility seriously. Jean de Quélennec, Viscount du Faou, was the highly regarded admiral of Brittany and strongly supported the duke's determination to protect the Tudors from injury. At Suscinio, the Tudors were permitted to live freely around the castle estate, and were likely based in the duke's own residential block, a comfortable and modern four-story construction littered with wide fireplaces and large mullioned windows that provided views of the not-too-distant ocean. Jasper and Henry likely enjoyed the many pleasurable opportunities Suscinio afforded to them, including hunting in the bountiful parkland, exploring the marshland and beaches, or simply resting in the landscaped gardens. Perhaps Henry enjoyed visiting the dovecote and spending time with the birds it housed. After their recent travails, the relative calm of this coastal château was surely very agreeable to the pair.

Suscinio played host to the Tudors for the next two years until Duke Francis once more came under pressure to turn them over. This time, the petition was from Louis XI. The wily French king, known as the Universal Spider on account of the webs of intrigue he was fond of spinning, sent Guillaume Compaing, dean of Saint Pierre-en-Pont in Orléans, to the Breton court to convey his fury that Francis persisted in harbouring Jasper. Compaing contended on behalf of his royal master that since Jasper was Louis's close kinsman, had briefly formed part of the king's household and intended to sail to France when he left Wales, it was only just he was transferred at once to French safekeeping. The duke rebuffed Compaing's passionate argument, responding that since the Tudors had failed to obtain a safe conduct to travel through his lands they had rightly been detained as prisoners. With little recourse, like the English envoys two years previously, Compaing departed empty-handed to face an irritated master.[12]

Francis, however, was mindful of his guests' unique value to different parties, and knew their presence in Suscinio was no longer tenable. Situated within sight of the open sea, the castle provided ample opportunity for the Tudors to escape but also, and more likely, to be kidnapped by the French during a lightning raid. In addition there remained, of course, the risk of assassination by English cutthroats; as another Welshman with royal pretensions, Owain Lawgoch, learned a century earlier, it wasn't beyond kings of England to have their threats neutralised, even if they were overseas. Before the end of 1474, therefore, Henry and Jasper were not only moved inland but, for the first time since their flight from Wales, separated. Their few English-speaking servants were also dismissed, replaced by Breton guards tasked with applying greater standards of security.[13]

Jasper's new home was Josselin, a bustling town in the very heart of Brittany that rested on the northern bank of the Oust.[14] The château that loomed high above the river was first built in 1008, though much of the work that greeted Jasper upon his arrival dated from the tenure of Olivier de Clisson during the 1370s. A wealthy if feared Breton lord, Clisson had loyally served Jasper's great-grandfather Charles V of France, and earned the deep enmity of the English during the height of the Hundred Years War for his savage practice of mutilating prisoners of war. For this, he had earned the nickname 'the Butcher'.[15]

Having initiated an extensive rebuilding programme at Josselin, which involved the expensive construction of nine cylindrical defensive towers enclosing a broad keep, Clisson married his daughter into the powerful Rohan family, who inherited the castle upon his death. It was one of Clisson's descendants, John II, Viscount de Rohan, who was now entrusted with the care of Jasper Tudor. The fallen earl of Pembroke was likely to have been stationed in one of Clisson's towers, his movement restricted along with his communication with the outside world. Jasper may have received regular updates on Henry's status, but otherwise he appears to have been cut off from his nephew.

Henry's destination was the Château de Largoët, an altogether more imposing moated compound concealed deep within a vast expanse of dense woodland.[16] Located just a couple of miles outside the village of Elven, and only 10 miles from the mighty port of Vannes, Largoët's crowning glory was the seven-story Tour d'Elven. Only constructed a decade earlier, at 144 feet tall it was reputed to be the highest tower in France, and an arresting sight to the first-time visitor.

Though day-to-day life at Largoët, a near impenetrable and self-contained military headquarters defended by deep ditches, would prove considerably more constrained than at Suscinio, Henry's tenure here would not be without its comforts. The man entrusted to oversee Henry's captivity was Jean de Rieux, Marshal of Brittany and one of the wealthiest figures in the duchy, and he did not intend to treat his charge meanly. Henry was given a room on either the sixth or seventh floor of the soaring, state-of-the-art octagonal keep, living close to the Rieux family who occupied each level of the tower below him; on the first level was the chamber of Rieux's wife Françoise, with the marshal on the second level. The third, fourth and fifth levels, meanwhile, were inhabited by the Rieux children, whom Henry may have got to know well.[17]

Henry's small room, reached by a spiral staircase, afforded him a degree of privacy high up in the keep. It had a window seat, a fireplace, its own garderobe and even a restful view over the forest below, allowing him to watch the seasons change. Even so, he was still just seventeen years old at the time, and the forced separation from the one person whom he could trust must have affected his spirit. Henry was likely scared, and uncertain of what the future held for him. Assured that no harm would come to him under the care of the marshal, however, he could lean on the Rieuxs for some support, perfecting his French, studying Breton culture and its myriad connections with his native Wales, and competing in various physical pursuits around the castle grounds.[18]

It is during his time in Brittany that Henry first became familiar with the story of St Armel, a South Welsh monk known as Arthfael in his native tongue who emigrated to Brittany in the early sixth century. Armel was highly regarded for his gentle and compassionate nature, and came to be recognised for his work with the lame and sick. On one occasion, he was even credited with curing a woman covered in blood by simply allowing her to touch his cloak. As word spread of his many virtues, Armel was summoned by King Childebert to the Frankish royal court, where he remained in service for several years, performing a series of miracles which only served to enhance his stature.

When he returned to Brittany, however, Armel was disturbed to learn a fearsome dragon was inflicting great havoc on the terrified local populace. One morning, having completed his prayers, Armel laid down his religious vestments and hiked to the dragon's forbidding lair. Standing bravely at the mouth of a dark cave, Armel commanded the beast show itself, placing his trust in God that he would come to no harm. When the snarling dragon duly appeared, Armel quickly bound it using his stole before dragging the thrashing animal to the peak of a nearby mountain. High above the land it had terrorised for so long, Armel condemned the unholy creature to death and cast it down into the fast-flowing river below.

The courageous Armel was credited with liberating the people from evil, and they venerated his name for centuries to come. An abbey was founded at Plourarzel bearing his name, as were other churches throughout Brittany, including in Ploërmel, Ergué Armel, Plouharnel and Saint-Armel. Like St George, to the present day Armel is routinely depicted dominating the monster he subdued, though it wasn't until the advent of the Tudors that the heroic saint's cult surfaced in his native Wales and neighbouring England.[19]

Plourarzel was only around 6 miles north of Le Conquet, and it can be speculated that after a difficult crossing in 1471, during which he feared for his life, the teenage Henry Tudor adopted such a prominently venerated local saint as his personal saviour. In depictions, Armel has sometimes been portrayed beside a ship, and the locals who tended to the Tudors soon after their arrival may have suggested to Henry that it was the saint he should thank for his salvation. He would have been intrigued to discover that Armel had followed a similar path to his own, crossing from Wales to Brittany, and when shown images of the saint would have noted the armour he wore beneath his vestments and the gauntlets which covered his fists. Though Henry was untested on the field of battle during his years in exile, as a magnate of illustrious bearing, he would have identified deeply with both the martial and the religious aspects of Armel's character, particularly in later years when he, too, yearned to deliver his people from the spectre of tyranny. However Henry came to worship Saint Armel, he maintained a lifetime devotion, one that he would bring back across the Channel.[20]

Elsewhere in his private life, Henry may even have become familiar with a local lady during those early years in Brittany. Upon his return home in 1485 to fight for the English crown, Henry brought with him a young Breton boy named Roland de Vielleville, or Velville. Not yet of military age nor old enough to be a companion to Henry, it has been speculated, even taken as fact by successive generations of antiquarians, that Vielleville was in fact the illegitimate son of the Tudor king.[21] This speculation has been fuelled by Vielleville's comparative prominence under the Tudors, a standing that appears unearned and demands explanation.

The earliest reference to this elusive Breton was as 'Roland de Vielle' during the Michaelmas term of 1488, when he was granted 10 marks 'by way of reward'.[22] He appears to have stayed close to the Tudor court thereafter, though without any official position or office for the duration of Henry VII's reign. He served as part of a military expedition back to his native Brittany in 1489 and was present as an esquire for Henry's invasion of France in 1492, for which the king had to lend him money for equipment.[23]

In recognition of his 'faithful services' as the 'king's servant', on 28 May 1496 Vielleville was granted a lifetime annuity worth 40 marks to be paid from the issues of the county of Wiltshire, although a year later the local sheriff was tersely ordered to settle all arrears as it was shown that no payments had yet materialised.[24] In June 1497, Vielleville took part defending the crown against Cornish rebels at the battle of Blackheath, after which he was one of thirty men knighted on the battlefield. In June 1500, Vielleville was one of thirty-four knights summoned to wait on the king during his reception of Duke Philip of Burgundy in Calais.[25] All are clear signs of royal favour, but nothing out of the ordinary.

Vielleville was also closely involved with the royal falcons and likely spent considerable time in Henry's company when the king was hunting and hawking.[26] There are myriad hawking-related payments to 'Sir Rowland' in the king's account books, such as the £10 he received in December 1496 and September 1497, and £4 in December 1497 and January 1498. In January 1506, Vielleville was given money to purchase new tunics for the king's falconers, and two years later was even gifted an expensive horse worth £136 8*d*, likely intended to be used accompanying the king on hunts.[27]

Vielleville also earned a tough reputation as a competent, even obsessive jouster, participating in many tournaments throughout Henry's reign.[28] In November 1494, he played a leading role in a tournament held to celebrate the creation of the king's son Prince Henry as duke of York, a privilege typically restricted to either noblemen or gentlemen. A mere esquire, Vielleville required royal authorisation to compete among men drawn from higher ranks like the earls of Suffolk, Essex and Shrewsbury, and knights like Sir Robert Curzon, Sir Edward Darrell and Sir John Cheyne. This is not to suggest he was singled out for special treatment, however – alongside him in the lists for this tournament were a handful of entrants from a similar social status granted permission to partake, including some of the king's other favourite courtiers like John Peche, Thomas Brandon, Matthew Baker and Guillame de la Riviere. Vielleville ran six courses in total and acquitted himself well against the queen's cousin, Essex.[29]

Vielleville appeared in two further competitions in 1501, including one held to welcome Katherine of Aragon to England, and others held in 1502, 1506 and 1507 as the reign drew to a close. There was even an incident where the bold Vielleville issued a challenge at Kennington to compete single-handedly against anyone who dared to answer his challenge, regardless of rank or status.[30]

Henry VII's death in May 1509 would mark a significant change in Vielleville's story. On 3 July, the new king Henry VIII bestowed upon Vielleville his first office of note, the constableship of Beaumaris Castle on Anglesey. That he was given an office far from London and the royal court, indeed on a distant Welsh island with deep connections, has not gone unnoticed by historians. An earlier constable of Beaumaris was Henry VII's great-granduncle Goronwy ap Tudur, and the wider island had served as the family's base of influence throughout the fourteenth century.[31] The suspicion is Henry VIII was removing from his capital an elder half-brother who could prove a complication to the Tudor succession. That Arthur Plantagenet, an acknowledged bastard son of Edward IV, and Charles Somerset, a direct if illegitimate male-line descendant of the Beauforts, remained around the Tudor court without proving a problem has been ignored.

The Breton-born Vielleville was granted letters of denizenship on 23 March 1512, giving him the rights of an Englishman and allowing him to acquire land and property. A hardened military man prone to violence, he proved a troublesome constable in North Wales, falling foul of the influential Bulkeley family and suffering imprisonment on a few occasions for his misconduct. At some point in the 1520s, Vielleville, by then deep into middle age, took for his wife a widow named Agnes Griffith, a descendant of Ednyfed Fychan and a very distant cousin of the Tudors. He also took ownership of some land in Penmynydd, estates once associated with the Tudors' Welsh forebears, which only serves to add weight to the idea Vielleville had deeper connections with the family than merely being part of the Bosworth campaign.[32]

Vielleville died in early June 1535, nearly fifty years after the battle that had brought him to the British mainland, and was buried in St Mary's Church in Beaumaris. It has been considered of consequence that his will was proven in the Prerogative Court of Canterbury under the jurisdiction of Archbishop Thomas Cranmer, but this was likely due to the value of his lands being above a set value.[33] He ranked, after all, among the richest men in North Wales at the time of his demise.

Complicating matters regarding Vielleville's paternity has been his treatment by the Welsh bards, informal custodians of genealogical matters, and the prominence of his granddaughter Catrin o Ferain, or Kateryn of Berain. Kateryn's mother was Jane Vielleville, and her father a Welshman named Tudur ap Robert Fychan of Berain in Denbighshire. Though known contemporaneously as Kateryn of Berain, or in turn by the surname of her four husbands, she has also been remembered in English history as Katherine Tudor. Following Welsh naming customs, this makes some degree of sense as her name in her native tongue would be Catrin ferch Tudur, or Katherine daughter of Tudur. It has, however, only served to confuse the discussion regarding her potential royal Tudor descent, as does the period she spent as a lady-in-waiting to Elizabeth I, both matters strengthening the argument they were related.[34]

In a poem by Robert Ifans that praises Vielleville's great-grandson Sir John Salisbury of Lleweni, Kateryn of Berain's son and a Welsh knight who rose to prominence towards the end of the sixteenth century, vague mention is made of a 'lineage of kings', adding that the aspirational Salisbury was descended from the ancient and pure blood of Britain (*dyna lin y Brenhinoedd, Bur at hen waed Brytain oedd*). This may simply refer to Salisbury's Breton ancestry, Britain and Brittany being words with a shared etymology, but it can be interpreted as none-too-subtle allusion to his supposed Tudor pedigree.[35]

Another poem written around 1586 by William Cynwal also refers to Vielleville's lineage as that from 'the blood of kings', more specifically 'of the race of the earls of all England' (*Dy lin of waed Brenhinoedd, Ac o ryw Ieill holl Loygr oedd*). Henry Tudor and his father Edmund Tudor were earls of Richmond, and the former at least had blood connections through his mother Margaret Beaufort to other English earls like those of Somerset, Kent, Arundel and Lancaster. Lewys Dwnn in 1602, meanwhile, praises Salisbury's offspring, noting they were 'of a line near the crown and its blood' (*ach bron y goron a'i gwaed*).[36]

Perhaps most pertinent of all was a contemporary mention in the elegy composed upon his death by Dafydd Alaw that Vielleville was of 'a kingly line' (*a gŵr o lin brenhinoedd*).[37] This suggests, at the very least, that Vielleville's rumoured Tudor ancestry was perhaps current in Anglesey as early as 1535. It was certainly hinted at in 1636, a century after his death, as shown in private correspondence between two of his descendants. From such vague beginnings, a fact which may not be true has taken hold.[38]

The circumstantial evidence that supports Vielleville being a son of Henry VII appears persuasive but falls short of convincing. There is little doubt that the first two Tudor kings were drawn to Roland de Vielleville, a somewhat unremarkable and undistinguished character, though this doesn't necessarily indicate kinship. There is no evidence that Henry ever acknowledged he had an illegitimate son, as kings before and after would do, and the favour shown Vielleville was, in the grand scheme, modest at best. It is admittedly fair to suggest that Henry could not recognise any bastard son, such was the perilous situation around the brittle York–Lancaster settlement at the end of a ruinous civil war. Vielleville, however, while retained around court long after his arrival in England, was hardly elevated to unmerited heights that require close scrutiny or even justification. Even Elizabeth I, if she had been aware of her supposed blood relationship to Vielleville's granddaughter Kateryn of Berain, did not hesitate in executing her lady-in-waiting's son Thomas Salisbury for treason in 1586.

In light of any evidence regarding Vielleville's age, it is not even possible to confirm he was born after 1471, the year the fourteen-year-old Henry Tudor first surfaced in Brittany. If Vielleville was seventeen or eighteen years old by 1489, the year he joined an English military expedition to his Breton homeland, then it is plausible Henry could have fathered a child early in his exile, though how this occurred under such close supervision remains to be explained. Vielleville, however, is likely to have been at least a couple of years older for such a punishing campaign, placing his date of birth before Henry ever reached Breton shores. Though information regarding Henry's exile is unquestionably scarce, there is currently no known reference at any time to a Breton lover, or provision for a bastard child.

There is a good argument, on the other hand, that while Vielleville's lineage was indeed noble, it was rooted in Brittany rather than Britain. According to a record compiled by John Writhe, Garter King of Arms during the reign of Henry VII, Vielleville supposedly used the arms of a rampant red lion on a silver background, charged with a singular golden coin.[39] Writhe was in post until his death in 1504 and would not only have encountered Vielleville around court but observed him closely in action at various tournaments. There is little doubt, therefore, about the accuracy of his work. Vielleville also seems to have been associated with arms that were quartered, suggesting he knew his lineage on both sides of his family tree. None of the heraldry featured implied kinship with the Tudors, contrary to other bastard sons of the period who bore the altered arms of their father, including Henry Tudor's cousin David Owen, and his Beaufort ancestors before their legitimisation.

Vielleville's name may also provide some hints of his parentage. In his native Breton, Vielleville was traditionally styled Cosquer, or Coskaër, *cos* or *coz* meaning old and *quer*, *kaër*, or *ker* meaning village. It is possible therefore that Vielleville descended from this prominent Breton clan, who had their seat at Rosanbo in northern Brittany.[40] The most pertinent connection concerning Vielleville's kinship to the Cosquers is that one of the quartered arms he bore, a black boar on a gold background, was shared by the Cosquer family.

Ultimately, how and why Vielleville left behind his native Brittany to become part of Henry Tudor's invasion, and succeeded in carving out a niche for himself in the early Tudor court, is unknowable. Part of it may be to do with the fact that, like other courtiers to whom Henry grew close, Vielleville was unmarried and therefore untroubled by splitting his time between family and court. He shared many of the king's passions like hawking, hunting and jousting, and both men developed a deep bond and trust in the years before the Tudor accession. It may be that Vielleville was a child of someone close to Henry during his exile in Brittany, and he always intended to provide opportunities for the Breton youth in England if he proved successful in his quest for the throne. With no contemporary recognition by either party, the case that Vielleville was a son of the first Tudor king remains, therefore, far from proven.

Back in England in the 1470s, the Tudors were not forgotten. Quite the contrary, in fact. In July 1475, Edward IV invaded France at the head of a vast army numbering nearly 20,000, part of an anti-French coalition in league with the dukes of Burgundy and Brittany. Resurrecting the grand ambitions of his predecessors, Edward declared himself king of France and duke of Normandy and Gascony, broadcasting his intention to press his claims in person. Conscious that he could not withstand a three-pronged attack, Louis XI sought to appease the English king with a generous peace settlement that effectively amounted to bribery. While the tired English troops were treated, at Louis's expense, to four days with 300 cartloads of wine and two tables loaded with the richest selection of meats and pastries, negotiations for lasting amity were thrashed out.[41]

By 29 August 1465, a treaty was finalised, and the two kings came face to face near the village of Picquigny on a hastily constructed wooden bridge over the River Somme. The terms they swore to uphold were very generous to the English. Louis agreed to pay Edward 75,000 gold crowns to withdraw his army while settling upon the Yorkist king a handsome annual pension of 50,000 gold crowns. In return, Edward would promise not to pursue his claim to the French throne, a seven-year truce would be adhered to and his daughter Elizabeth of York would be contracted to marry the Dauphin of France, Charles, when she came of age. If either party was attacked by their enemies, the other would provide military backing and pledge not to enter any league without the other's agreement.[42]

One article of the peace which particularly affected the Tudors was Louis's promise he wouldn't wage war with Brittany during the specified period of peace. When the French king tentatively quizzed his English counterpart about his intentions towards Francis II, Edward responded he would not attempt to move against the duke, for 'he had never found so true and faithful a friend'. This lack of English appetite to support France in attacking Brittany paved the way for the subsequent Franco-Breton Treaty of Senlis, concluded in October 1475.[43]

By protecting Breton interests, Edward expected that Francis would be grateful for his intervention, and more amenable to his demands in future. In January 1476, Edward's principal secretary, Oliver King, was sent across the Channel tasked with renewing the Anglo-Breton treaty, with Jacques de la Villéon heading in the opposite direction in the summer. Edward was keen to discuss the matter of Henry Tudor with Villéon, sending him home armed with a letter outlining the English king's request to hand over the young man. It was thought that Francis would prove agreeable, but he hesitated. To press the matter, Edward sent another party of envoys across to Brittany to try and force through a resolution, this time travelling on ships laden with gold.[44]

To strengthen his case, Edward claimed he was keen to obtain custody of Henry as he wished to marry the now nineteen-year-old to one of his daughters, pulling up the roots of rancour and completing the Tudors' reconciliation to the Yorks. Assured Henry would be treated honourably in England, and pressured by his own courtiers, who had been swayed by the promise of English gold, Francis's resolve weakened. He ordered the earl turned over to the ambassadors, unaware he had effectively 'committed the sheep to the wolf'.[45] There is no recorded indication of Henry's thoughts at this time, but he likely viewed the English ambassadors with trepidation when placed under their control. The years spent in exile with his uncle had almost certainly influenced Henry against the Yorkist regime, memories of their desperate flight still fresh in his mind. As had been the case since he was first removed from Pembroke Castle as a boy, Henry's fate, however, was not in his own hands.

With 'great joy', the delighted envoys took their leave of the Bretons and, with Henry part of their convoy, headed for their ships in the fortified harbour of Saint-Malo.[46] Situated at the mouth of the Rance estuary on the duchy's rocky north-eastern coast, Saint-Malo was a thriving port that had long controlled access in and out of the English Channel. Fully encircled by grey granite walls, Saint-Malo appeared a forbidding prospect to the first-time visitor, a stern coastal guardian designed to intimidate. As Henry was led through the elaborate St Thomas' Gate and into the gloomy bowels of Saint-Malo, he may have allowed himself a disdainful smirk – the town now playing a central role in hastening his probable demise was founded in the sixth century by a Welsh monk named Maloù.

Fortune's wheel, however, was not yet done with Henry Tudor. In the meantime, the highly regarded admiral of Brittany, Jean de Quélennec, had returned to the ducal court to discover that Henry had been surrendered to the English. Quélennec had grown close to the Tudors during their time with him at Suscinio and was ashamed of his duke's capitulation. With 'great sorrow', the admiral remonstrated at length with Francis, tersely reminding his master that he had sworn a solemn oath to protect 'that most innocent imp', Henry, from danger.

Quélennec almost certainly raised the suspicious death of the duke of Exeter the previous summer, pointing out the questionable official explanation of accidental drowning. Although married to Anne of York, the older sister of Edward IV, Exeter had been an unrepentant Lancastrian during the dynastic wars, participating in the battles of Wakefield, St Albans, Towton and Barnet. The duke had once been closely aligned with Jasper Tudor, and after the deaths of Henry VI and his son Prince Edward in 1471 was the senior Lancastrian claimant. When the Yorkist king launched his French expedition in 1475, distrusting Exeter, he did not allow him to remain behind in England. On the return voyage, Exeter mysteriously fell overboard and drowned, with little more said. It did not escape Quélennec's attention that, with Exeter out of the way, Henry Tudor stood apart as 'the only imp' of Henry VI's blood still living. If the Tudor teenager was to set foot upon English soil, he would surely be 'torn in pieces by bloody butchers'.[47]

Though Francis defended his conduct, Quélennec persisted, pressing the point that if Henry was allowed outside the duke's jurisdiction 'all the world shall not after that be able to save his life'. After a period of reflection, Francis was stirred into action, fearing he had broken his oath to protect his young charge. He commanded his treasurer, Pierre Landais, to chase down the English contingent and try to hamper their progress with some false business. The English envoys had reached Saint-Malo and were preparing their flotilla when Henry, knowing that he was being 'carried to his death', fell into a fever just before he was due to board. Whether a ruse to buy him some time or an onset of sickness brought about by stress, the delay was sufficient to enable Landais to reach Saint-Malo and enter into a heated discussion with his English counterparts. With Edward's men furious at these last-minute complications, tempers quickly frayed.[48]

In the confusion, as English and Breton diplomats jostled with one another, Henry slipped away. Fleeing through the narrow streets of Saint-Malo, he cut his way up alleyways, checking nervously behind him every few seconds. Upon reaching one of the town's many churches, possibly St Vincent's Cathedral, he hammered desperately on the large wooden door, yelling that he wished to claim sanctuary. When the door was opened, Henry rushed inside and beseeched the confused monks to shelter him from the Englishmen at the harbour.[49]

When the envoys discovered Henry had bolted, they tried to force their way into the church to retrieve their prey, an act of aggression which only served to antagonise the local populace. Sanctuary may have been breached in Yorkist England – most notably after the battle of Tewkesbury, when Henry's Beaufort cousins were killed – but the Malouins refused to stand idly by and watch their church be desecrated by hostile foreigners. With little choice but to leave Henry be, the Englishmen sailed back to England empty-handed, pondering how to relay their failure to an expectant Edward IV. He had been in their custody for only three days.[50]

This was the second life-or-death flight that the teenage Henry Tudor had been forced to endure. His later reputation for vigilance, a deep-rooted wariness of those around him that has long been perceived as unwarranted paranoia, has its origins in such distressing episodes in his youth. Even at nineteen years old, Henry ruefully acknowledged that, owing to the smattering of royal blood in his veins, the limited world he nervously inhabited involved danger lurking around every shadowy corner. Despite the great success he later achieved, in many respects, Henry never escaped the psychological trauma of being a helpless Lancastrian youth pursued by sword-bearing Yorkists with bad intentions, first through the tunnels of Tenby and later the streets of Saint-Malo. Trust was not a social characteristic that ever came easily to Henry Tudor, and with good reason.

Once Henry was returned to the custody of the duke of Brittany, he was reunited with his uncle Jasper and in October 1476 the pair were moved back to Vannes.[51] They appear to have remained here for the next six years, with little incident. The person initially responsible for Henry's protection was Vincent de la Landelle, an experienced professional soldier, and later Jean Guillemet and Louis de Kermené took up the role. According to payments in the duke's accounts, Guillemet and de Kermené were paid £2,000 *tournois* during 1481 and 1482 to cover Henry's expenses. Jasper, meanwhile, was placed under the supervision of Bertrand du Parc and, reflecting his lesser political importance at this moment in time, incurred expenses of £607 10s 0d.[52]

These years proved quieter for Henry, and he is likely to have spent this period focusing on his own personal development, working on the firm grounding he had been given during his time at Raglan. As testified by the later testimony of Jean Molinet, a Burgundian poet who met Henry during his exile, as he entered his twentieth year he was growing into a personable young man, if understandably guarded.[53] With the political environment in England more stable than it had been for a generation, in June 1482 Henry's mother, Margaret Beaufort, even initiated negotiations with Edward IV to find an arrangement that would allow her son to return home, and not to a chopping block.

Despite Henry's awkward presence abroad and her own proud Lancastrian rearing, Margaret had been able to establish a respected reputation around the Yorkist court, slowly but surely rising in royal favour. Although small in stature, Margaret's resilience was considerable, as was her emotional and political intelligence. She understood when to suppress any opinions that could be deemed pro-Lancastrian, to alter her aspirations so that they aligned with the ruling Yorkist regime, and to accept the limitations of her station under Edward IV.

Shortly after Henry departed Wales in haste, Margaret's husband, Henry Stafford, succumbed to injuries he had suffered at the Battle of Barnet earlier that year. Within a year, she had remarried for the fourth time, taking for her husband an influential northern magnate named Thomas Stanley, 2nd Baron Stanley. While Henry grappled with life in Brittany, the new Lady Stanley became a constant presence around the heart of the Yorkist court, attending upon Edward IV's queen, Elizabeth Woodville, and even afforded the honour of conveying Princess Bridget, the final child of the royal couple, to the font to be christened in November 1480. Margaret's politically savvy husband, meanwhile, was a member of the king's council and steward of the royal household, and brought to the marriage extensive connections of his own which she was now able to exploit to champion Henry's cause.[54]

Together the Stanleys appealed to King Edward to revisit Henry's situation and consider allowing his return to England not as a prisoner or a threat but as a valued member of court. The dynastic wars, after all, had been settled and Edward was secure on the throne with the Yorkist succession assured. Pressed by Margaret, Edward grew receptive to the idea, and on 3 June 1482 an indenture was drawn up in the king's presence outlining 'certain appointments and agreements' should Henry willingly return to England and submit to 'the grace and favour of the king's highness'. Among those agreements was the arrangement that Henry would receive a portion of the estates of his recently deceased grandmother Margaret Beauchamp, dowager duchess of Somerset, to the value of 600 marks. The king's seal was affixed to the contract, the clearest signal yet that Edward was prepared to allow Henry some degree of liberty once under his control.[55]

Separate discussions also took place regarding the possibility of Henry marrying the king's eldest child, Elizabeth, designed to further bind him to the House of York. Among those involved in the discussions were the king, the bishops of Ely and Worcester, and an emissary from the Pope, who would be required to provide a dispensation in the event any union was concluded, as Henry and Elizabeth were related within the prohibited degrees of kinship.[56]

An undated royal pardon, meanwhile, was drafted on the reverse of the patent that created Henry's father Edmund Tudor earl of Richmond thirty years earlier.[57] Regarded for the first time under Edward IV as 'earl of Richmond', Henry would be 'pardoned, remitted and released' in 'all ways' if he submitted, suggesting his mother had secured a pledge from the Yorkist king that her son would be formally restored to an earldom stripped from him as a child. It was convenient, of course, that the earldom and honour of Richmond had stood vacant since Edward's execution of his unruly and traitorous brother George, Duke of Clarence, in 1478.

In the summer of 1482, Henry was twenty-five years old, unmarried, personally impoverished and politically irrelevant. It made sense for him to place his trust in his mother, consider the proposal and return home to start the next phase of his life, one in which he could help shape the next generation of Yorkist rule. It was only natural, however, that he was heavily influenced by his uncle Jasper, who was offered no such hand of friendship from Edward IV, and likely developed his own deep distrust of the Yorkist regime during his decade in exile. Even so, this was Henry's opportunity to salvage some semblance of a normal life. If he chose to remain in Brittany, he was warned he would be entitled to nothing in future.

Before Henry could decide which path to follow, fate intervened once more. On 9 April 1483, 'neither worn out of old age nor yet seized with any known kind of malady', Edward IV died in Westminster.[58] Since recapturing the throne in 1471, Edward had proven a steadying influence as king and had been able to shore up his support, restore law and order to the realm, neutralise what few enemies he had remaining, and generally savour his success. He had much to celebrate. The Yorkist king had brought two decades of bitter civil war to an end, was in receipt of a huge French pension that swelled his coffers, and by early 1483 had two healthy sons who would secure his succession for generations to come. He appeared insuperable. Every explicit threat to his dynasty had been extinguished, minor complications like Henry Tudor notwithstanding.

In his triumph, however, Edward grew complacent about his physical health. The once strapping eighteen-year-old warrior who vanquished his foes in battle had grown corpulent. He overindulged in food, drink and women, and expired at just forty years old after a brief illness.[59] The king's death would prove disastrous for England. The eldest of his sons, Prince Edward, was only twelve years old and unready to assume personal rule. From a position of stability and peace, the kingdom was plunged once more into factional discord and strife. The path was clear for the Tudors to plot their return after a dozen years in exile – not to serve, but to rule.

14

Another King

Edward IV had been the glue that held England together ever since he had recaptured his throne in 1471. Charismatic, popular and authoritative, his men loved him, respected him and followed him. A larger-than-life presence who towered, figuratively and literally, above his contemporaries, when Edward's firm hand fell lifeless, competing rivalries within the House of York quickly thundered out of control. While Edward's younger brother Richard, Duke of Gloucester, had been away from court tending to his duties in Yorkshire and beyond, by the final year of the dead king's reign, the Woodville family had established a deep hold over the governance of the realm.

From the moment Richard Woodville married Jacquetta of Luxembourg, the widowed duchess of Bedford, in 1437, the Woodvilles had attracted scorn in noble circles for aspiring to a position considered above their natural rank. This disdain had only intensified after Edward IV took Sir Richard's daughter, Elizabeth Woodville, for his wife in 1464. Despite her mother's aristocratic background, Elizabeth was but a mere commoner, one who had already been married to a Lancastrian knight who had died fighting against Edward in battle. This morganatic union between the Woodvilles and a Yorkist king was deeply unpopular with the great magnates of the realm, most notably the affronted earl of Warwick.

Nevertheless, the Woodvilles' omnipresence at the very top of the political structure was assured as long as Edward IV, or indeed his Woodville-blooded heir reigned, and by 1483 they collectively held a range of influential positions. When Edward sent his eldest son to Ludlow to begin his kingly education, his care was entrusted to the boy's maternal uncle Anthony Woodville, Earl Rivers, appointed master of the Prince of Wales's household and expected to mentor the boy in the ways of the world. Elsewhere, the Woodvilles also held command of the royal fleet, the deputy governorship of the Tower of London and the bishopric of Salisbury. Not content with political dominance, the family had also married into some of the noblest families in the land, spreading their soft power through the corridors of power.

A 'kind, serious, and just man' according to Dominic Mancini, Rivers was not only renowned throughout Europe for his jousting ability but also a respected diplomat and skilled in military affairs on land and at sea. Deeply pious, often donning a coarse hair-shirt beneath his noble garments, Rivers possessed an intellectual capacity that lifted him above many of his peers, which he demonstrated through poetry and the translation of French texts. Few in England during the fifteenth century embodied the chivalric ideal like Rivers, in many respects the ideal person to raise any young man, let alone a king.[1]

When the child in his charge became king aged only twelve years old, Rivers and his Woodville kin understandably anticipated a lengthy period in which they would wield unmatched power and influence, governing the kingdom through the young sovereign who shared their blood. What Rivers and his sister Elizabeth, now dowager queen, had failed to foresee was the depth of enmity towards them from members of the deceased king's council, most notably William Hastings, 1st Baron Hastings.

In the days following Edward IV's death, the Woodvilles made unwise moves to secure their position. The royal treasure in the Tower of London was jealously guarded, a small fleet was put to sea under Edward Woodville's command, and the coronation date of the new king was fixed for 4 May.[2] Arguments soon arose in the council, meanwhile, as the Woodville faction protested plans to name Edward IV's brother Gloucester protector of the realm. Sensing power was slipping through their hands, the dowager queen commanded her brother Rivers to bring her son to London as soon as possible, accompanied by a force as large as he could muster.

The council, fronted by Hastings, were not cowed by the Woodvilles, and fully intended to honour Edward IV's request that Gloucester assume the office of protector. It was even voiced by some members of the council that the guardianship of Edward V, 'so youthful a person', must be 'utterly forbidden to his uncles and brothers by the mother's side'. As these relations already occupied 'the chief places about the prince', however, they would prove difficult to remove.[3]

Hastings sensed that Gloucester needed to be in London at the earliest possible opportunity if he was to deliver England from a Woodville-dominated regency. The duke hastened south, concerned by Hastings' report that the Woodvilles planned to have Edward V crowned as soon as the first week of May. Any coronation automatically abolished the office of protector, depriving Gloucester of the authority he had not even had the chance to assume. If that was to occur, the Woodville coup would be complete, control of the king and his government assured perhaps for decades to come.[4]

Gloucester reached Northampton on 29 April 1483, where his path crossed with that of Rivers, embarking on his own journey from Ludlow to London to escort Edward V to his coronation. There was no evident ill will between the two men, both uncles of the young king, and they dined together that evening, with Gloucester proving 'cheerful and joyous'.[5] Nothing is known of what conversation passed between the men, or whether it was cordial, heated or a mixture of both. In the morning, after awaiting the arrival of Henry Stafford, Duke of Buckingham, Gloucester, Rivers and their combined retinues pressed on the few miles to Stony Stratford, where Edward V awaited their arrival. Just before they reached the town, at Gloucester's command, Rivers, his nephew Richard Grey and two others named Thomas Vaughan and Richard Haute were seized, caught unawares and unable to resist.[6]

When Gloucester entered his royal nephew's presence, he removed his hat and bent his knee. The confused king was paid every mark of respect appropriate to his rank. According to the report of Dominic Mancini, an Italian visitor in England during these tumultuous months, when quizzed by the king over his actions, Gloucester justified his behaviour as necessary for both his and Edward's protection, arguing that England was too 'great a realm' to be ruled by 'puny men'.[7] Young Edward objected to this treatment of his relatives, but his protests were dismissed with little more than a wave of the hand from the two dukes. He was advised he was to be escorted on to London by Gloucester and Buckingham, while Rivers, Grey and Vaughan were sent north to Pontefract Castle.[8] Despite his regal status, the boy had little control over matters.

When news of events in Northampton and Stony Stratford reached London, Mancini noted that the 'unexpectedness of the event horrified everyone'. He added, however, that it was generally agreed by the citizens 'it was more just and profitable that the youthful sovereign should be with his paternal uncle than with his maternal uncles and uterine brothers'.[9] The dowager queen, on the other hand, was moved to panic and sought sanctuary in Westminster Abbey, collecting her youngest son, Richard, and his five sisters, 'the most sweet and beautiful children', in the process.[10] Even before they had gained control of the kingdom, Woodville ambitions lay in tatters.

Once in London, Gloucester placed the young king Edward in the bishop's palace near St Paul's before reassuring the lords of his sincere intentions by requesting they swear fresh oaths of fealty to their twelve-year-old sovereign. When the council met to discuss the path forward, Buckingham suggested young Edward be moved to the Tower of London, rather than other suggestions like the Palace of Westminster or the Hospital of St John. Despite its fearsome reputation in later years, this would not have alarmed anyone at the time, for the Tower was one of the more comfortable royal residences at the king's disposal. The coronation that the Woodvilles had been planning was postponed, although only until June, and on 27 May Gloucester was formally created lord protector. He had authority to act 'just like another king', however, so his remit was more akin to a regent. Lord Hastings crowed that the governance of the realm had been rescued from the 'queen's blood', accomplished 'without any slaughter, or indeed causing as much blood to be shed as would be produced by a cut finger'. With the coronation date now set for 24 June 1483, one chronicler anticipated a 'season of prosperity for the kingdom'.[11]

Hastings' joy proved premature, for he was soon 'supplanted by sorrow'.[12] Two separate council meetings were scheduled on 13 June by Gloucester, one at Westminster and another at the Tower. The protector oversaw the latter, and proceedings had barely begun when armed guards flooded the chamber with a cry of treason. Hastings was seized and dragged outside to the Tower Green where, by express order of Gloucester, he was summarily executed.[13] In removing one of the strongest supporters of the young king, 'without judgement or justice' according to one critic, and one who was constable of England at that, Gloucester had set in motion events that would change the course of English history forever.[14]

The following day, Gloucester issued a terse appeal to the City of York to raise some troops 'to aid and assist us against the queen, her blood, adherents and affinity, which have intended and daily doth intend to murder and utterly destroy us'.[15] At this juncture, it is unclear who Gloucester feared enough to justify such words; Rivers was in captivity with his nephew Richard Grey, his brother Edward Woodville had fled the kingdom, and dowager queen Elizabeth Woodville was in sanctuary. Hastings had been executed and his other perceived enemies, men like Bishop Morton and Lord Stanley, had been neutralised.

The protector was taking few chances, however. On 16 June, two days after he wrote to the City of York, Gloucester and Buckingham sailed to Westminster by water, taking with them a force 'armed with swords and staves'. Once outside the abbey's precinct, the dukes urged the elderly archbishop of Canterbury to persuade the dowager queen to turn over her youngest son, the nine-year-old Richard of Shrewsbury. It was claimed that Edward V's coronation could not take place without the presence of his brother at his side, who was needed to 'comfort the king his brother'. Sensing she had little choice, since sanctuary had been breached before under the Yorkists and that Gloucester could not be denied, on 21 June 1483 Elizabeth handed over her boy.[16] Remaining behind in sanctuary with her daughters, she would never lay eyes upon either of her boys again.

It has long been speculated why Gloucester moved so swiftly and decisively in those eight weeks in the spring of 1483. Sources are confused and sometimes their motivations suspect, many having only been put to paper once events had fully played out. Hindsight, of course, and the passing of time further obfuscates matters. When one considers Gloucester's first action after learning of his brother's death was to pen a comforting letter to his recently widowed sister-in-law and assure her of his fealty to her son, the new king Edward V, there is no indication that the duke was planning any seizure of the throne.[17] His remit at this juncture was clear: to serve his nephew as his brother intended, and with him to drive forward the House of York.

Two things are likely to have changed Gloucester's mindset as the weeks passed. The first is that Hastings' warning of Woodville ambitions increased Gloucester's own suspicion that he was about to be side-lined by his nephew's maternal relations. A failure to retain a foothold in government had two decades earlier ultimately cost Gloucester's father his head, and he knew from this traumatic experience how dangerous it was to be out in the cold. Even if appointed protector, he could only hope for a few weeks in the role before his nephew was crowned and the office abolished. An arrangement to continue until Edward V came of age might have been reached with the support of the council, but ultimately this only delayed the inevitable Woodville dominance and Gloucester's alienation.

The second, more pressing, matter related to his landed inheritance. After the death of Richard Neville, Earl of Warwick, in 1471, the vast Neville hegemony in the north of England was inherited by his underage nephew George Neville, Duke of Bedford. In recognition of Gloucester's 'great and laudable service' to his brother Edward IV, however, in the 1475 parliament he was granted possession of Bedford's lands for as long as a male Neville heir lived. This included the vast castles and profitable lordships of Middleham and Sheriff Hutton, as well as over forty smaller manors spread across northern England which formed the core of Gloucester's powerbase for the last decade of his life.[18]

On 4 May 1483, less than a week after Gloucester intercepted Earl Rivers and his nephew Edward V, Bedford died childless. Per the terms of Gloucester's parliamentary grant, the Neville estates were only to be retained by the duke until his own death, at which point they would revert to the crown. He had, in effect, initiated an internecine conflict with the Woodvilles at the moment his long-term dynastic prospects had considerably weakened. With little to pass to his son, Edward of Middleham, Gloucester was understandably anxious at the prospect of a Woodville ascendancy.

It can never be known when Gloucester first intended to lay claim to the throne, but by 22 June 1483, nine days since Hastings' execution and six days since taking custody of his youngest nephew, it became clear to all his objective was to be king. He had backed himself into a corner, and his only way out was to establish a permanent pre-eminence over the Woodvilles by taking control of the crown. That day, public sermons in London were given in Gloucester's favour, the most prominent by Dr Ralph Shaa, a cleric 'of great reputation' and brother of the mayor. Speaking outside St Paul's, Shaa even declared Edward IV's children to be illegitimate.[19]

Shaa argued that when King Edward had married Elizabeth Woodville he had already been pre-contracted to one Eleanor Butler, a daughter of John Talbot, Earl of Shrewsbury, and who had died in 1468. This pre-contract had been brought to light by Robert Stillington, Bishop of Bath and Wells, at a most convenient moment, and raised the unconvincing case that Edward's children with Elizabeth had not been born in lawful matrimony. As the deceased duke of Clarence's son Edward, Earl of Warwick, was exempt from the line of succession owing to his father's attainder, it was Shaa's view that 'no certain and uncorrupted lineal blood could be found of Richard, duke of York, except in the person of the said Richard, duke of Gloucester'.[20] Since Edward V was too young to be personally accused of tyranny, this hastily concocted argument of his father's misconduct was the best that could be levied.

Shaa surely did not act without Gloucester's approval, and the duke's northern affinity under the command of Sir Richard Ratcliffe soon began to swell the capital 'in fearful and unheard-of numbers'. A few days later, 'more of will than of justice', Anthony Woodville, Thomas Vaughan and Richard Grey, the dowager queen's son from her first marriage, were executed outside Pontefract Castle. On that very day, 25 June, Buckingham, who had emerged as Gloucester's closest ally, travelled to Guildhall to petition the mayor, alderman and assembled citizens to recognise his fellow duke's claim to the throne.[21] His oration in favour of Gloucester lasted half an hour and was 'well and eloquently uttered', imploring his audience to admit the protector 'for their liege lord and king'.[22] The following day, just four days since Shaa's sermon, the council approached Gloucester and offered him the crown. With some feigned reluctance, the proposition was accepted, and on 6 July 1483 Gloucester was crowned King Richard III in Westminster Hall.[23]

Richard's rise to the throne was swift and unexpected, shocking many contemporaries. As with previous dethronements in the fifteenth century, the new king had to contend with ample opposition from the outset of his reign. His argument for taking the crown was well-rehearsed, clear, and had crucially received the assent of the three estates of the realm: the Commons, the Lords Temporal, and the church. Nevertheless, despite his tender age, young Edward V commanded great loyalty among a significant portion of the nobility that just months earlier had sworn to the boy's esteemed father to serve, honour and defend his son and heir.

Foremost among those who sought to reverse Edward V's dethroning were of course his maternal relations, the Woodville family. Though their influence had been severely hampered by Edward IV's death, his widow Elizabeth's flight into sanctuary and the executions of her brother and son, those who had survived the recent tumult now rallied. Among them were Elizabeth's other son from her first marriage, Thomas Grey, Marquess of Dorset, and her surviving brothers Richard and Edward Woodville.

Support at this time came from an unlikely place. It is not clear what Margaret Beaufort initially thought about Richard III becoming king, though considering she had known the Yorkist princes from the cradle it is reasonable to assume she took a dim view of their disinheritance. Her principal concern, however, as always, was her son's welfare, and crucially whether the pardon Edward IV had been on the verge of ratifying still stood.

The night before Richard's coronation, 5 June 1483, Margaret met with the new king in Westminster, ostensibly to settle a lengthy legal dispute she had with the French. As her father's sole heir, Margaret had inherited the Beaufort family debt owed to them by the House of Orléans, part of a war ransom dating back to earlier in the century. The new king agreed to lend his support to her suit, placing his chief justice, William Hussey, at her disposal, though it is likely conversation soon turned to a more difficult topic: Henry Tudor's fate. Would Richard honour his brother's plan to allow the exiled earl of Richmond to return home after a dozen years in the wilderness? Whatever concessions Margaret was hoping to wrest from Richard on this matter, she departed the meeting unsatisfied. She had been separated from her son for most of his life, and had fought hard for the pardon she had almost secured from Edward IV before the king's premature death. Henry was now twenty-six, and Margaret hoped to spend the next phase of their lives together, content to prosper under Yorkist rule, tending to their ample inheritance. She had reason to be concerned.[24]

On 13 July 1483, just a week after his coronation, King Richard dispatched a canon of Lincoln Cathedral named Thomas Hutton to Brittany to discuss a range of commercial affairs with Duke Francis II. The mission had another purpose, however. Recently, Edward Woodville had crossed to Brittany, possibly with some of the royal treasure,[25] and Hutton, 'a man of pregnant wit', was tasked with trying to 'understand the mind and disposition of the duke' regarding Woodville and his retinue. 'By all means' at his disposal, Hutton was to establish if an assault was being prepared. Though not mentioned in Hutton's assignment, there can be little doubt that King Richard also intended him to probe into the status of Henry Tudor.[26]

By 1483, Francis II had ruled Brittany for a quarter-century and was skilled in securing military and financial concessions from English kings wary of France's expansionist ambitions. In response to Hutton's embassy in July, one month later Francis sent Georges de Mainbier to England, armed with instructions to advise the English king that, though the duke retained love and affection for Richard III, he was concerned that Louis XI had made repeated overtures in recent months requesting 'to deliver to him the lord of Richmond his cousin'. Louis had made the Bretons 'great offers' to obtain his target, and was now openly threatening 'great menaces' if Francis did not respond favourably. Francis wanted Richard to know that, since no river or brook separated his duchy from its much larger and more powerful neighbour, he would not be able to withstand French aggression unless the English sent military aid at once. More specifically, Francis requested 4,000 paid English archers under the command of good captains to serve in the duchy for six months, with the promise of 2,000 or 3,000 more at the duke's own expense if required. If this aid didn't surface, then Francis would be forced to surrender Henry Tudor to the French. These were extortionate demands – diplomatic blackmail in truth – and Richard could scarcely hope to meet them at such short notice.[27]

Though she would not have been privy to these discussions, Margaret Beaufort was proven right to be bothered about her son's prospects with Richard III upon the English throne. Conscious that Richard was unlikely to be swayed any time soon, she now turned to desperate measures to be reunited with her boy. As a mother, Margaret no doubt deeply sympathised with Elizabeth Woodville's predicament, confined within the walls of Westminster Abbey and uncertain of the fate of her two sons in the Tower. Expressing concern for the York boys, and her own son of Lancastrian pedigree, Margaret now extended the hand of friendship to Elizabeth, and both conspired to bring about the downfall of their common foe, Richard III. The restoration of young Edward V, with a promise to continue Henry Tudor's reintegration into Yorkist England, would satisfy both women.

The two women happened to share a Cambridge-educated doctor, a learned Welsh astronomer and mathematician named Lewis Caerleon. A well-rounded intellectual later described by Polydore Vergil as 'a grave man and of no small experience', Caerleon had been a fixture around the various royal courts for decades and had taken to practising medicine in his old age.[28] Well respected at the highest level, he had been consulted by both Margaret Beaufort and Elizabeth Woodville in recent years. He was now, however, recruited for an altogether different purpose.

Margaret summoned Caerleon to her presence and revealed to the physician her hope of establishing an alliance with Elizabeth. She may even have raised the possibility of her son being betrothed to the dowager queen's eldest daughter, Elizabeth of York, bonding the two parties together before God. Caerleon was tasked with taking this information to Westminster Abbey, where the two Elizabeths were sheltering, and sounding them out. As a recognised member of the medical fraternity, authorised to enter and leave the abbey at will, Caerleon was the perfect vessel for this most crucial assignment. Before the king caught wind of what was afoot and had Caerleon thrown into the Tower, the discreet doctor succeeded in bringing Margaret and Elizabeth to a basic agreement regarding their next steps.[29] That Elizabeth was open to such a proposal strongly hints that she believed, rightly or wrongly, that her sons were no longer living.

There is evidence that attempts to actively move against Richard occurred as early as the end of July, when the king was on progress in the West Country. According to a chronicler based out of Crowland Abbey in Lincolnshire, an important and well-informed contemporary observer of events during this tumultuous period, many in the south and west of England 'began to murmur greatly' about the two captive sons of Edward IV, and started to 'form assemblies and confederacies' to free them, some in secret and some 'in face of all the world'.[30] An assault on the Tower may even have taken place. Writing just over a century later and using sources now lost to the historian, the Elizabethan antiquary John Stow suggested that some of the conspirators planned to divert the attention of the Tower guards with a fire. If this took place as Stow reported, it accomplished little more than probably hastening the princes' deaths.[31]

Despite the sons of Edward IV having been declared illegitimate, and therefore lacking any right to the crown of England, it was widely known that what parliament had once passed it could also reverse. If the boys were successfully spirited out of the Tower, they could have, and almost certainly would have, been used to nominally front a military attempt to retake control of the throne, their illegitimacy scrubbed from the records. If Richard III had little to fear from the boys while they remained under his control, an attempt to liberate them proved a game-changer. Illegitimate or otherwise, the princes commanded great reverence within England and patently remained the most potent threat to their uncle's short- and long-term security upon the throne. There would unquestionably be further attempts to restore Edward V to a throne he had barely known.

As the summer progressed, rumours quickly spread throughout England, and indeed across the Channel to the Tudor court in exile, that the two boys had been put to death. The fate of Edward V and his brother Richard of Shrewsbury is no more certain today than it was shortly after they disappeared more than 500 years ago. Accounts were vague and confused, which fuelled the climate of anxiety around their whereabouts. Richard III, meanwhile, maintained a policy of silence which only served to feed the rumours that they had been done away with, and most likely at his instruction.

The *Great Chronicle of London*, an eyewitness account penned by a figure with considerable insight into governmental business, noted that before the change of mayor in early November 1483, the boys had been seen 'shooting and playing in the garden of the Tower'. The commentator was certain that the two sons of Edward IV were 'departed from this world' before the end of Richard's reign.[32] The Crowland chronicler, meanwhile, noted authoritatively that they had remained in the 'custody of certain persons' throughout the summer of 1483, with rumours spreading they 'had died a violent death, but it was uncertain how'.[33]

Robert Ricart, a town clerk of Bristol, also believed the boys had been 'put to silence' in the Tower, perhaps receiving his intelligence from London merchants who brought gossip from the capital.[34] Another contemporary, Edward Brampton, a converted Portuguese Jew and godson of Edward IV, later agreed that the princes' disappearance was 'the worst evil in the world' and that they had, to his knowledge at least, been quietly slain.[35] Their fate was even discussed in a statement made to the States-General of France at Tours in January 1484, when the French chancellor, Guillaume de Rochefort, openly accused Richard III of having murdered his nephews.[36]

One of the more emotive accounts of 1483 is found in the contemporary work of an Italian churchman named Dominic Mancini. As an outsider, even accounting for any deficiency in the English language and the nation's customs, Mancini's observations are critical in understanding the political climate in London around Richard III's rise to the throne, particularly as they were recorded before, and therefore are not prejudiced by, the later Tudor ascendancy. Mancini noted that during the early summer of 1483, the boys had been 'withdrawn into the inner apartments of the Tower proper, and day by day began to be seen more rarely behind the bars and windows'. Finally, 'they ceased to appear together'.

Mancini did note that Edward V's physician, John Argentine, the last person known to attend upon the young king, had even bleakly reported that the boy, 'like a victim prepared for sacrifice', had pitifully sought daily remission for his sins 'because he believed that death was facing him'. Their disappearance from public view did not go unnoticed by the common Londoner, for the Italian further reported that 'many men burst forth into tears and lamentations' when mention was made of Edward V, and that 'there was a suspicion that he had been done away with'. Mancini was careful to add, however, that whether 'he has been done away with, and by what manner of death, so far I have not at all discovered'.[37]

It may never be known what became of the two children who, in the space of a few weeks, grieved for their father before they were forcibly denied their mother's embrace, never laying eyes upon her again. With no evidence of their whereabouts once they were withdrawn deep into the Tower's countless recesses, any impulse to suppose the Yorkist princes were covertly spirited away to eke out a modest existence in obscurity must be tempered by the cruel truth that with each heartbeat they represented death to their noble keepers.

History had shown the fate of deposed kings to be bleak. Edward II, Richard II and Henry VI were three examples of kings quietly dispatched shortly after surrendering their crowns. Even those close to the crown whose lingering presence was deemed problematic were often removed through violent means. Richard III's two predecessors as duke of Gloucester, Thomas of Woodstock and Humphrey of Lancaster, were each disposed of, and Richard himself did not have to think too far back to recall the fate of his troublesome brother, George, Duke of Clarence. Despite his tender years, Edward V similarly posed an excruciating headache that called for the most ruthless of remedies. Despite their disinheritance, it would be foolish of any monarch bearing a crown to doubt that Edward or, in the event of his demise, his younger brother Richard of Shrewsbury could become a troubling focal point for future rebellions.

From the moment Richard III took the throne, his fate was entwined with that of his nephews, the boys he had sworn to defend, honour and serve. The previous three decades had shown no amount of taut parchment bearing the verbose rulings of lawyers and politicians could prevent dormant or forfeited claims to be resurrected under the right circumstances. Richard's own father had been slow to advance his claim and then outmanoeuvred by his enemies at the final hurdle. His reward had been to have his head spiked upon a battlement. It stands to reason that in the febrile summer of 1483 Richard moved with ruthless decisiveness to secure his position, settle the succession on his own son and crush any conspiracies that sought to restore his nephews to their erstwhile status. Polydore Vergil, writing decades later and prejudiced against Richard, was nevertheless astute to note of the king that 'so long as they lived he could never be out of hazard'.[38]

In removing the so-called Princes in the Tower from the scene, however, whether through murder or other means, Richard III merely opened another front from which to be assailed. Rumours that he had killed his nephews had caused the king to lose 'the hearts of the people', who wept until they could weep no more.[39] Having already secured the support of the Woodvilles, Margaret Beaufort's conspiracy against Richard was thus strengthened as rumours of the princes' demise grew louder. Even if hopes of restoring Edward V to his throne faded with each passing week, his maternal family nevertheless demanded revenge. Margaret now recruited another member of her affinity to move the conspiracy forward, an 'honest, approved and serviceable priest' named Christopher Urswick.[40]

The Cambridge-educated son of a Lancashire lay brother, the thirty-three-year-old Urswick was brought to Margaret's attention through her Stanley husband, becoming her chaplain and confessor by 1482. He would later attest that he had known Henry Tudor well for fifteen or sixteen years, suggesting he had been acquainted with the exiled earl when the latter had been a child.[41] Urswick, then, was a suitable and trusted choice to now carry a message across the Channel to Henry in Brittany, informing the otherwise oblivious exile of his mother's Woodville pact. At the last moment, however, Urswick was pulled from the mission. The reason appears to have been Margaret's discovery that, at the same time she was plotting Richard III's demise with Elizabeth Woodville, a similar though unconnected conspiracy against the king was forming in Mid Wales. There was a new deal to be made.

The man who had been, perhaps above all others, instrumental in Richard III's rise to the throne was Henry Stafford, Duke of Buckingham and a magnate 'of the highest nobility'.[42] It had been Buckingham who joined Richard at Stony Stratford to take possession of Edward V, and it had been Buckingham who suggested the young king be placed in the Tower of London. It was also Buckingham who had travelled to the Guildhall to champion Richard's claim to the throne before the mayor and aldermen of London.

After being something of a forgotten figure under Edward IV, the duke had been extravagantly rewarded by Richard for his support, particularly in Wales and the Marches. Buckingham was made chief justice and chamberlain of both North and South Wales, as well as constable of all the royal castles in Wales, including Carmarthen, Pembroke, Tenby, Builth, Usk, Monmouth, Caernarfon, Conwy, Beaumaris and Harlech. He was also appointed steward of the vast Mortimer estates, the Welsh lands belonging to the duchy of Lancaster, and promised all other senior posts in the region as and when they became vacant. Buckingham in the summer of 1483 was as powerful a figure as Wales had experienced under English rule, a virtual viceroy with unprecedented sway. The duke also played a conspicuous role during Richard III's coronation, bearing the king's train in the procession to Westminster Abbey, before he was appointed to the constableship of England. Aside from the king he had helped make, there was no man in England or Wales mightier than Henry Stafford.[43]

When King Richard left London on his western progress, Buckingham accompanied his friend for much of the journey. When they reached Gloucester at the start of August, however, Buckingham took his leave and retired to his chief seat at Brecon. It was here, deep in the heart of Wales, the duke seems to have pondered his position, and was persuaded into rebellion against the king he had helped enthrone just a few months earlier. The figure responsible for Buckingham's dramatic change of heart was John Morton, the aged bishop of Ely and someone 'trained in party intrigue'.[44]

Morton was approaching his sixty-fifth year in 1483, a highly experienced Oxford graduate who first entered royal service in September 1456 as chancellor of Henry VI's son and heir, Edward, Prince of Wales. Morton entered the church the following year, rapidly rising through various clerical offices such as deacon, rector and subdean. In 1459, his legal expertise was used to help draw up the Act of Attainder against the Yorkist leaders after the Battle of Ludford Bridge, and when he was captured after the Battle of Towton two years later, the new king Edward IV had him attainted and placed in the Tower of London.

The resourceful churchman escaped captivity and fled first to Scotland and then to France, aligning himself closely with the deposed Lancastrian queen, Margaret of Anjou, for much of the next decade. He is also likely to have established considerable relations with another exile, Jasper Tudor, during these lean years abroad. Morton dejectedly returned to England with the rest of the Lancastrians in 1470, but after his party's destruction at the Battle of Tewkesbury in the following year finally accepted the unpalatable political reality and in July 1471 pragmatically accepted the pardon extended to him by a triumphant Edward IV.[45] From this moment on, Morton resumed his career in royal service, although this time under a Yorkist king. Regarded as 'a man of note' during Edward's rule, he held posts in the chancery, travelled overseas on diplomatic missions, particularly to the French court, and by early 1479 had been consecrated as bishop of Ely. It is unclear if Morton was able to maintain contact with Jasper Tudor, though his prominence at the heart of the Yorkist court likely meant old friendships had been long forgotten.[46]

After the death of Edward IV, Morton was focused on arrangements for the coronation of Edward V when, at the council meeting on 13 June 1483 in which Lord Hastings was apprehended and executed, the bishop was also accused of treason against the soon-to-be king. Since it wasn't customary to put a churchman to death, Morton was handed over into the custody of Richard's closest ally, the duke of Buckingham, and imprisoned in the latter's castle in Brecon.

When Buckingham took his leave of Richard and retired to his seat, however, Morton, a 'man of great resource and daring', started to work on the impressionable duke, attempting to prise him from the king's grip.[47] Among the bishop's approaches was a reminder that Buckingham possessed a royal lineage as impressive as any in 1483, being directly descended, three times over, from Edward III. Through his father, the duke was a great-great-grandson of Thomas of Woodstock, Duke of Gloucester, Edward III's youngest son, while through both his mother and father he was also a great-grandson of John of Gaunt, Edward III's third son. Considering recent dynastic turmoil, mused Morton, should he not be king?

Proud Buckingham proved more than receptive to the notion of deposing the monarch he had helped install, aware that a king so recently made could surely be unmade just as swiftly. His principal motivation to rebel so soon after reaching his political and financial apex appears to have been greed. In return for supporting his rise to the throne, Richard had rewarded Buckingham plentifully. The only rank the duke could attain that promised more than what he held in his grasp was that of king. It is highly unlikely Buckingham gambled the influence, wealth and power he had accumulated in quick order under Richard III for any position in which the crown itself did not rest upon his head.

It must not be discounted, however, that the fate of Edward IV's sons played a role in Buckingham's abrupt abandonment of Richard III. The duke left Richard's side suddenly, and he would not return. It may be speculated that the king had revealed to Buckingham that the boys had been put to death, and the duke was outraged by such an unthinkable act. Having been with Richard when they took possession of young Edward V, and having advised the boy be placed in the Tower of London, Buckingham may have felt remorse for his role in the child's death, even if he had not been privy to the actual act. On the other hand, it cannot be ruled out that it was in fact Buckingham who had committed or overseen the dastardly act, with or without Richard's knowledge, an unscrupulous deed designed to malign Richard's reputation and clear his own path to the throne. There are many variables during this period which are frustratingly unknowable.

Having learned of Buckingham's temptation to stray from the king's side, perhaps through a timely message from Bishop Morton, Margaret Beaufort at once reached out to the duke. He was a figure she knew well. Margaret had been married for many years to Buckingham's uncle Sir Henry Stafford, and was also the duke's cousin herself; Buckingham's mother was another Margaret Beaufort, a first cousin of his sometime aunt-in-law. The Stafford family had a proud Lancastrian background, Buckingham's father having been killed defending Henry VI at the Battle of Northampton in 1460. Margaret now leaned heavily on these familial connections to turn the duke's head further.

Buckingham was indeed tempted, as were others. One of Margaret's most devoted servants, Reginald Bray, worked tirelessly during these months to expand the growing conspiracy. Born in Worcester in the 1440s, Bray had long been closely associated with Margaret, his parents leasing the manor he grew up in from one of her maternal Beauchamp cousins. In his youth, Bray entered the service of Margaret's Stafford husband, rising to become their receiver-dealer and one of their principal administrators, using his considerable skills to fix any issues that arose. It had been he whom Margaret had sent to Raglan and Weobley castles in the late 1460s to carry money and messages to her son. Bray continued serving Margaret after Stafford's death in 1471, and now in 1483 was able to put his considerable connections to use, including those he had with the Stafford duke of Buckingham.[48]

Bray travelled to Brecon to firm up the Buckingham–Beaufort alliance, while also recruiting to his lady's party a series of notable knights who had served in Edward IV's household, disenfranchised Yorkists like John and Richard Guildford of Kent, John Cheyne of Wiltshire, Thomas Ramney, and Sir Giles Daubeney of Somerset. All were men of significant standing in their respective counties, and brought considerable political and military experience, spreading the roots of rebellion far and wide. Elizabeth Woodville, meanwhile, employed her son from her first marriage, the marquess of Dorset, for a similar purpose. For good reason, Vergil would later regard Bray as the plot's 'chief dealer'.[49]

As the conspiracy gathered pace, Margaret dispatched another household officer she trusted deeply, the North Welshman Hugh Conway, to her son in Brittany armed with a 'good great sum of money'. Conway's role in the conspiracy may be of significant consequence. The Conways were rooted in the north-east of Wales, a region the Stanley family had dominated in recent generations, with their principal seat at Bodrhyddan in Flintshire. Through his father John's second marriage, Hugh Conway was, in fact, related to the Stanleys, and had long enjoyed cordial relations with the family. Through this connection he became known to Lady Stanley, Margaret Beaufort. Conway had prospered during the reign of Edward IV, and by 1483 had been around the Yorkist court for two decades, developing extensive connections that now served him, and his patrons, well.[50] As well as carrying money, Conway's other charge was to advise Henry to start preparing his invasion. Wales was mooted as an ideal destination, his homeland where he would 'find aid in readiness', but the particulars were left up to Henry and his small circle of advisors. As a back-up should anything untoward happen to Conway, Richard Guildford departed from Kent on a similar mission.[51]

Henry received Conway and his updates from England with great delight, 'rejoicing wondrously'.[52] Aside from the money he received from his mother, however, Henry still had no independent funds of his own to assemble, equip and sustain an army in the field for over a month. He therefore turned to Francis II for aid, hoping that after twelve years under the duke's guardianship his cause would be looked upon favourably. Francis's need to court the English crown for protection against the French had not abated, but he pondered the possibility of closer relations with England if his Tudor charge was successful in his enterprise.

Even though Francis continued to negotiate with Richard III during the summer of 1483, he nonetheless listened to Henry's argument, and set the Tudors at liberty. The duke authorised his counsellors and treasurer to release 10,000 crowns of gold to his 'most dear and well-beloved cousin' so that Henry he could start funding his invasion.[53] Francis had honoured his promise to Edward IV not to set the Tudors against the Yorkist crown, but Edward was now dead. Now, the duke concluded a fresh agreement with Henry, one concluded with a service in Vannes Cathedral with the duchess's own chaplain, Arthur Jacques, receiving the earl's solemn oath.[54]

By the start of September 1483, Henry had a small fleet that had been placed at his disposal for one month. To avoid drawing suspicion from across the Channel, it was officially reported that the fleet had been assembled simply to combat the scourge of piracy. In total, the convoy comprised five ships holding 324 men, and included the *Pinasse*, the *Barque* and the *Trésorière* from Saint-Malo, captained by Pierre Guillaume, Jean le Barbu and Louis Berthelot respectively, the *Marguerite* from Brest under the command of Derien le Du, and Jean Pero's *Michelle* from Auray. Each sailor was paid £4 for their month of service, with the captains receiving £10.[55]

On 24 September,[56] Buckingham followed up Margaret's groundwork by penning a letter of his own to Henry, a distant cousin he did not know personally. He instructed his Tudor ally that he would raise his Welsh tenants on 18 October and invade England from the west. Henry should muster whatever forces he could and time his crossing from Brittany so they could group their resources near Newbury and Salisbury. Here, they would also be joined by a host from Devon fronted by the bishop of Exeter, Peter Courtenay, and his brother Edward, the dispossessed Lancastrian earl of Devon. The marquess of Dorset would also join this West Country contingent, supported by Thomas St Leger, a brother-in-law of Edward IV and Richard III, and Robert Willoughby. In Kent and the south-east, another force would be raised under the command of the Guildfords, including knights once connected with Edward IV's household like John Cheyne, Giles Daubeney, George Browne, Edward Poynings, William Noreys and William Berkeley.[57] It was clear that this was a southern-led movement against a king noted for drawing his powerbase from the north, revealing some of the subtler regional dynamics at play.

Together, all would advance on London and overthrow their common foe, Richard III. It was not yet clear who would become king if Richard was defeated, but considering Buckingham's rank and royal lineage, there is every expectation that he would take the crown if the opportunity arose. It could not be expected of him, after all, to yield to a younger cousin of lesser status and a poorer claim, a stranger to England even, in Henry Tudor. Buckingham even had a more impressive Beaufort ancestry, which was Henry's sole connection to the English crown. Hindsight, however, would influence later commentators to position Henry as king-in-waiting from the outset.[58] It may be noteworthy that as late as 30 October 1483 Henry still signed his name as nothing more than 'Henry de Richemont'.[59] Buckingham, for his part, is not known to have acknowledged Henry as his king at any time.

Two distinct conspiracies with a common goal, therefore, had merged into one. It was a disparate blend of loyalties which rallied behind two Henrys, sons of two different Margaret Beauforts united only by their mutual desire to overthrow Richard III. This loose alliance brought together veteran Lancastrians like John Morton, John de Vere and Jasper Tudor with dissident Yorkists distressed at the removal and possible murder of Edward V. Ambition and revenge are what drove the rebellion of 1483, an opportunistic movement which had its seeds in Richard III's taking of the crown.

When the time came for the plot to commence, however, the execution proved farcical. Through his spies, King Richard first developed inklings about a plot against him in early September. He wrote to Buckingham at Brecon, courteously summoning the duke to court. Buckingham, however, sensed the trap and responded that a stomach illness precluded him from accepting Richard's invitation. The king's follow-up was not so polite, but again Buckingham elected to stay away, which only served to confirm Richard's suspicions.[60]

Buckingham did indeed lead his Welsh tenants out of Brecon on 18 October, but any hope of taking the king by surprise was undone by the hastiness of the Kentish contingent. A county noted for its penchant for rebellion during the fifteenth century, the Kent insurgents rashly raised their banners in the Weald early, revealing Buckingham's disloyalty and undermining the balance of the conspiracy.[61] The king, based in the centre of his kingdom at Lincoln, acted urgently. On 12 October, he furiously wrote to his chancellor, John Russell, Bishop of Lincoln, strongly condemning the duke as a 'rebel and traitor' who was surely 'the most untrue creature living'.[62]

Richard also announced a £1,000 bounty on the head of Buckingham, with further rewards for the capture of the marquess of Dorset, his uncle Lionel Woodville, Bishop of Salisbury, and more minor participants.[63] John Howard, recently created duke of Norfolk by Richard, assembled

100 men to barricade the capital from the south-east and stop the Kentishmen in their tracks, while Ralph de Ashton, Buckingham's deputy as constable of England, was granted power to hunt down the rebels.

Buckingham had his own problems, however. Unlike Jasper Tudor or William Herbert, Welsh magnates who at their height had commanded great loyalty and respect in their respective corners of Wales, the duke inspired little love from his tenants, having a reputation as a 'sore and hard dealing' overlord. These Welsh, therefore, were reticent to lay down their lives for their 'unbeloved general', and proved reluctant participants.[64]

Heavy rainfall flooded the plains around the River Severn, prompting many of Buckingham's demotivated tenants to discreetly abandon the venture as the days passed. When the duke reached Weobley, the home of Walter Devereux, Lord Ferrers of Chartley, and which once housed a teenage Henry Tudor, he was forced to seek shelter for ten days as the waters had washed away many of the bridges which crossed the Severn, cutting off his route forward.[65] In his absence, Thomas Vaughan of Tretower seized the duke's seat of Brecon, denying Buckingham the opportunity of withdrawing behind his castle walls. This Vaughan was the son of the Roger Vaughan executed by Jasper Tudor twelve years earlier at Chepstow, so he had ample motivation to hamper the duke's progress and injure any opportunity for the Tudors to return home.[66]

As his army dwindled, Buckingham recognised his enterprise was hopeless and abandoned his position. While the bishops of Ely and Exeter, the earl of Devon, the marquess of Dorset and a host of other rebels managed to evade capture and reach the coast, the duke was not as fortunate.[67] Donning the disguise of a poor man, Buckingham left Weobley and headed north into Shropshire, seeking refuge in the house of Ralph Bannaster, a man he had known since childhood. With a significant reward for his capture, Buckingham was swiftly betrayed and turned over to the county sheriff, John Mytton. He was taken to Salisbury, where Richard III had recently relocated, and 'without speech or sight of the king', was beheaded on 2 November in the marketplace.[68]

It had been a remarkably quick downfall for a duke who just a few months earlier had played a leading role in making a king. In the heat of July, Buckingham was the most powerful man in the kingdom outside the monarch, wielding vast influence and commanding great affluence. By the chill of November, his head was on a spike.

Henry Tudor's modest fleet set sail as planned, departing from Paimpol in northern Brittany at the end of October.[69] Shortly into their voyage, however, part of the convoy was scattered by a strong northern wind, perhaps the same meteorological event that was causing Buckingham such difficulty on land. Though many ships were forced to return shortly after their departure, Henry's vessel succeeded in navigating through the choppy Channel and was able to eventually anchor in calm waters off the coast near Poole in Dorset.[70] Their arrival had been anticipated by the English king, however.

Richard had suspected that Henry would attempt to land along the southern coast to link up with Buckingham and had taken steps to ensure his defences in that part of his kingdom were stout. Soldiers had been sent to all the significant ports, with watches established all along the coast to raise the alarm once the rebel ships were spotted. When Henry was within sight of Poole, he noticed a group of men beckoning him and his companions ashore. He sent a small barque out to probe further, his men reporting back that those on the beach claimed to be loyal to Buckingham. Henry correctly suspected a trap, and instead the order was given to raise anchor and return to Brittany.[71]

Safe from Richard but not yet from the weather, another storm pushed the retreating Tudor fleet eastward through the Channel, and when the rebels finally disembarked after a strenuous few weeks at sea they found themselves near Valognes on the Cotentin Peninsula in Normandy, France. Once they had recovered sufficiently from their voyage, the party sent messengers to the French court seeking permission to continue their journey onward to the Breton court. The old king of France, Louis XI, had died at the end of August and his thirteen-year-old heir, Charles VIII, was in the guardianship of his elder sister, Anne de Beaujeu. The child king's councillors not only granted Henry safe passage – unthinkable under Louis, who had long desired to get his hands on the Tudors – but sent an esquire of the household, Henri Carbonnel, to escort them as far as the Abbey of Saint-Sauveur in Redon, Brittany. The French may even have given Henry some money to sustain his campaign, hoping to further unsettle matters in England.[72] Their lack of urgency in seizing upon this gift may be taken as a grave indictment of Henry's value to the French following the failed invasion, possession of his person no longer of political consequence under the new regime.

Though it may be expected the mood around the Tudor circle back in Brittany was one of dejection, particularly when they learned of Buckingham's execution, there were reasons to be positive.[73] A steady stream of refugees from England had poured into the Breton court, each arrival fixated on working towards the destruction of Richard III.[74] The removal of Buckingham from the scene also refocused loyalties around a single figure, providing a clear figurehead for any conspiracy going forward in Henry, someone any discontented Englishman could turn to as an alternative to the present king.

This period of rebellion has been historically named after its 'chief mover', Buckingham, but this does not adequately document the scope of the movement against Richard III in 1483.[75] Margaret Beaufort, Elizabeth Woodville, Henry Tudor, Bishop Morton and Reginald

Bray all played leading roles in galvanising support in their individual spheres of influence, their efforts merging with Buckingham's to push against a common foe. The attainders later passed by parliament placed Buckingham as the principal ringleader of the rebellion, and while it follows that he fully intended to become king if the revolt proved successful, this merely concealed the humiliating fact that a significant section of the southern gentry had chosen to reject the kingship of Richard III, not just a solitary grasping duke. Any rudimentary study of the participants who rebelled against Richard reveals many former servants of his brother Edward IV, disenfranchised Yorkists who not only feared the loss of their positions to northern rivals but suspected the new king of having put to death their master's two sons.[76]

On 3 November 1483, the very day after Buckingham's execution in Salisbury, a group of the duke's supporters made a last stand on Bodmin Moor in Cornwall before fleeing overseas to Brittany. They included the Courtenay bishop of Exeter, his brother Edward Courtenay, and men like Giles Daubeney, John Cheyne and John Treffry, a former sheriff of Cornwall. All attempted to issue a call to arms before swearing to raise another king and destroy Richard III. Though no name was mentioned, with Buckingham's death the day before the mention of an '*alium regum*' could only refer to Henry Tudor.[77] 'Word sprang quickly', as one chronicler later said, that Henry was busying himself with making 'speedy provision' to come into England and claim the crown, 'considering the death' of Edward IV's children, 'of whom as then men feared not openly to say that they were rid out of this world'.[78]

The French chronicler Philippe de Commines, who met Henry during the later years of his exile, heard from his very mouth that from the time he had been five years old he had considered himself 'a fugitive or a prisoner'. Enough was enough. This grandson of a Welsh squire born Owain ap Maredudd ap Tudur now stepped forward from relative obscurity, ready to take a momentous leap towards destiny. Though he was regarded by Commines as a 'person of no power, and one who had been long prisoner', even widely considered 'not the next heir to the crown', an opportunity had been presented. Henry just had to seize it.[79]

15

Just Quarrel

Dedicated to St Peter, the cathedral that loomed high in the heart of Rennes dominated the medieval landscape of the city, its tower visible for miles around. Originally erected in the fourth century, the church was extensively rebuilt from 1180 in the Gothic manner, though by the 1480s it had fallen into a state of deep disrepair. To the late fifteenth-century worshipper, the west front and tower appeared on the verge of collapse, and indeed would not see out the century. Deep within the creaking bowels of this proud Breton cathedral, which had long represented the religious heart of the duchy, English history would be changed forever.

On Christmas Day 1483, from the steps which led to the altar, Henry Tudor faced his assembled supporters and spoke.[1] Some, Lancastrian stalwarts like his uncle Jasper Tudor, he knew well, and they were undeniably fervent for his cause. They would be there until the bitter end. Others, recent arrivals to Brittany like Thomas Grey, Marquess of Dorset, or the contingent of Edward IV's household knights, were an unknown quantity. All were, at least, united in a common cause against Richard III. Also present was a Breton delegation, including the duchess of Brittany, Marguerite of Foix, and the duchy's leading minister, Pierre Landais. When Henry, the man this disparate collection of English rebels now looked to as their leader, started speaking, everyone listened. He knew that he was about to be scrutinised closely.

His voice reverberating around the cold nave as men warmed themselves by rubbing their hands together and gently swaying back and forth, Henry voiced his gratitude for their support to this point, and solemnly pledged to do all he could to dislodge the tyrant from his ill-gotten throne. As their rightful monarch, Henry claimed he would return England to prosperity and peace, eradicating the scourge of war from the land once and for all. Those present would soon be back on their abandoned estates, returned to their former positions of influence

242

and able to celebrate with their much-missed families. Their present predicament would soon be a legendary tale shared with laughter among friends, an adventure they conquered together.

Before Henry faced his men in such a public setting, there must have been an acknowledgement in private that his claim to the English throne was mediocre at best. It is likely, for example, that even up to a month previously, the figurehead for the anti-Richard campaign had been the duke of Buckingham, descended thrice over from Edward III. Now that Buckingham's head was upon a spike in Salisbury marketplace, the focus of the rebellion shifted to Henry Tudor.

This latest pretender to the English throne did possess the all-important descent from Edward III that had caused such difficulty in the early stages of the Wars of the Roses. Through his mother, Margaret Beaufort, Henry was a great-great-great-grandson of the mighty king, tracing his lineage to Edward's fourth son, John of Gaunt. Though the product of Gaunt's extramarital affair with Katherine Swynford, the Beauforts were retrospectively legitimised by both church and parliament, allowing them to attain any office in the land 'as freely and lawfully as if ye were born in lawful matrimony'.[2]

There have been later accounts which stress the Beauforts had no right to the throne, and that Henry Tudor's quest for the crown was therefore predicated upon false grounds. This accusation has its roots in three words which have been added at an unknown date and by unknown persons to the original 1397 parliamentary act legitimising the Beauforts, which altered the text's meaning. Wedged in awkwardly between the original words, the interlineation '*excepta dignitate regali*' was added after the word 'dignities' and before 'pre-eminences'. This altered the Latin text to read that the Beauforts could be raised to all honours and dignities, *except to the royal dignity* – that is, the throne of England.

It is unclear when these words were added to the parliamentary roll; it may have occurred in February 1407, when Henry's great-grandfather John Beaufort, who in the decade since his legitimisation had risen to become earl of Somerset, requested an exemplification, or copy, of the 1397 act.[3] Whether the interlineation was added at the instigation of the king, Henry IV, by then bedridden with disease and preoccupied with the succession, or a scheming third party keen to curb Beaufort ambitions is unknowable. What is clear is that this curious codicil, whenever added, was legally dubious in any case. The original act had been ratified by parliament and was a legally binding document in every sense. Any alterations to the act could only be made if parliament repealed the previous bill or endorsed those changes. Neither ever occurred, so the act which stipulated the Beauforts could be raised or promoted to all and any office without restriction remained enshrined in the law of the land until the day Henry Tudor staked his claim to the throne.

The Beaufort claim to the throne was never seriously tested across the next century, the family ardently supporting their Lancastrian kin on the throne and defiantly, if unsuccessfully, defending Henry VI's crown from Yorkist ambitions. In truth, many in the mid-fifteenth century could boast more impressive royal pedigrees, with most of the major players in the Wars of the Roses able to include Edward III in their family trees. The Beaufort claim was, however, recognised during the 1450 indictment of William de la Pole, 1st Duke of Suffolk, suggesting any supposed exception to the royal dignity was either disregarded or unknown. One of the most serious accounts against the fallen duke was that he intended to claim the throne through the royal lineage of his then-six-year-old ward Margaret Beaufort, whom he had betrothed to his son John.[4] By 1483, Margaret's claim, as the sole heir in the Beaufort male line, had been transmitted to her only son, Henry Tudor, by his supporters. There doesn't seem to have been any discussion at the time about Margaret laying claim to the throne in her own right – England, it seems, wasn't quite ready for a queen regnant.

Even so, it was accepted at the close of 1483 that this Lancastrian connection alone was not enough to bind dissident Yorkists to Henry's side, whatever the merits of the Beaufort claim. Now, in Rennes' cold and crumbling cathedral, the deal that had been struck behind closed doors was revealed. When Henry seized the English throne, he swore to take as his wife Elizabeth of York, the daughter of Edward IV and Elizabeth Woodville. This pact would unreservedly unite the Yorkist element of his support to Henry, and he to them, and any heirs would embody the union of the two warring houses, York and Lancaster.[5]

Since Henry and Elizabeth shared a mutual ancestor in John of Gaunt, a dispensation for the marriage needed to be sought from the papal penitentiary, the highest administrative body in the church concerned with the absolution of sins. It was one thing for Henry to pledge to marry Elizabeth in Rennes Cathedral, but to follow through he had to ensure there were no canonical impediments to the union which could be politically exploited in future, particularly in light of Richard III having obtained the crown on account of an apparent anomaly in his brother's marriage just a year earlier. The petitioners in Rome, likely headed by John Morton, the rebel bishop of Ely who had fled England after the collapse of Buckingham's rebellion the previous autumn, proved successful in their mission; on 27 March 1484, 'Henricus Richemont', described as a layman of the York diocese despite having never set foot there, was freed to marry 'Elisabet Plantagenta'. Crucially, any offspring would not be tarnished with the stain of illegitimacy. That there is no reference to their prospective royal titles, or indeed any title, suggests secrecy was uppermost in the minds of the petitioners, keen to prevent news of the dispensation reaching Richard III in England.[6]

By early 1484, then, Henry Tudor, a Welsh-born descendant of Welsh rebels forced to flee his homeland as a teenage boy, stood at the head of a conspiracy that lauded him as the rightful king of England. Men swore homage to him 'as though he had already been created king', and toasts were raised in his direction. Deprived of their lands and possessions back home, all now gravely placed their lives at Henry's disposal, unequivocally rejecting the kingship of Richard III.[7] It was some turnaround in fortunes for the Tudors, though there was much work to be done to make such lofty aspirations a reality. For the moment, he remained an impoverished exile, regardless of how many people now honoured him as though he was already king in fact rather than aspiration.

Since the collapse of the October 1483 rebellion, the English contingent in Brittany swelled with rebels who had escaped the indignant wrath of King Richard. Whereas Jasper and Henry Tudor had for more than a dozen years existed alone across the Channel, largely surrounded by Bretons for company, a steady stream of Englishmen now joined them in exile, possibly numbering as many as 500, establishing a tight-knit community that banded together through necessity as much as desire. Though they had been stripped of their wealth and estates at home, these recruits brought experience, political know-how and gossip, every morsel of which Henry eagerly consumed as he started developing his own strategy for ruling England. He became a student of a game he needed to master if he was to be the final player standing.[8]

The exiles were a varied collection drawn from different political and social backgrounds, but to obtain their mutual objective all now swore to loyally serve a solitary master going forward. Based in Vannes, the community lived in close proximity day after day, month after month, getting to know one another and developing a camaraderie they hoped would drive them towards their common goal. It is known they often attended Mass together, with offerings made at the altar of Vannes Cathedral on 8 February, 15 August and 8 September 1484.[9] Even after he became king of England, Henry would not forget his time at Vannes, making regular gifts to the town's cathedral until the end of his reign.[10]

There were those known to Margaret Beaufort and her husband Lord Stanley, trusted figures like Reginald Bray, John Risley and John Welles who transferred their devotions from mother to son without reservation. Others were brought to the conspiracy through the dowager queen Elizabeth Woodville, knights who had served in her husband Edward IV's household like John Cheyne, Giles Daubeney, William Brandon and Edward Poynings, plus her son Dorset and brothers Lionel, Richard and Edward Woodville.[11] These had no prior connection to Henry and in most instances, if not all, only met him for the first time in exile. No doubt they viewed him through curious eyes, sizing him up not only as a man but as a potential king. After many years suppressing the roots of Lancastrianism in England, it must have been galling for men like Daubeney and Poynings to now pay homage to a minor earl of somewhat Lancastrian extraction. Cheyne, at least, was related to Henry, since his mother, Edith Shottesbrooke, was a half-sister of Margaret Beaufort's mother, Margaret Beauchamp.

These Yorkist knights' wariness would have been noted by Henry, who through circumstance had grown to be an astute judge of character. Satisfied by the promise he would marry Elizabeth of York upon becoming king, however, this Woodville–Edwardian Yorkist faction now resolved to try everything in their power to thrust their Tudor leader towards the English throne. Of course, ever present at Henry's side, although increasingly anonymous in accounts going forward, was his principal confidante and mentor, his redoubtable uncle Jasper.

Bonded solely through a determination to overthrow Richard III, it wasn't always a peaceful coexistence, nor could it be. Aside from any political differences they needed to overcome, the community of English rebels proved a financial burden to the Bretons and, despite occasional grants from the duke or the burgesses of Vannes, money, food and other supplies were often in short supply. Some of the English had thrived in comfortable surroundings at home and were now forced into a hand-to-mouth existence. It was a tense situation and tempers inevitably frayed, if not with one another then certainly with the local Vantois populace, alongside whom the English refugees lived uneasily within the town walls. On at least one occasion, Duke Francis was forced to compensate a subject for the actions of one of Henry's men. A widow from Vannes named Georget le Cuff even received payment on account of her husband being murdered by one of the Englishmen.[12] From such unlikely origins did the face of England change forever.

In January 1484, the only parliament of Richard III's reign convened at Westminster, where the principal business was setting out his right to rule and punishing those who had rebelled against him.[13] The almost implausible Act of Settlement outlining his claim to the throne, a statute known as *Titulus Regius*, ratified the earlier suspect judgment of the Lords, Commons and church that Edward IV's 'ungracious feigned marriage' to Elizabeth Woodville had been invalid on account of a prior precontract of marriage to Eleanor Butler. Their children were legally declared 'bastards, and unable to inherit or to claim anything by inheritance'. For good measure, odd accusations of sorcery and witchcraft against Elizabeth and her mother were thrown in.[14] As York's brother George, Duke of Clarence, had been attainted for treason, this nullified any claims his son Edward, Earl of Warwick, may have had. The result was that Richard III, a man of 'great prudence, justice, princely courage and excellent virtue', was judged the true heir to the crown and 'no other person living'. The pre-contract justification appears far too convenient to have been a true representation of the facts, but, whatever the truth, Richard had what he required: legal recognition of parliament's support.[15]

What followed next was a wide-ranging list of attainders which shine some light on the Tudor–Beaufort–Woodville–Buckingham rebellions of 1483. Bills were passed against Henry and Jasper Tudor and the already-executed duke of Buckingham, as expected, but also against another 104 individuals. These included Bishop Morton and the marquess of Dorset, with an entire bill dedicated to Margaret Beaufort alone, 'mother of the king's great rebel and traitor'. Most involved the southern gentry, with the rebels heavily drawn from Wiltshire, Berkshire, Kent, Surrey and Devon. Elizabeth Woodville, referred to as Dame Elizabeth Grey, her name from her first marriage, had all the lands and estates granted to her by Edward IV removed, on account that their marriage was never considered legal.

As per the terms of her attainder, all Margaret's lands and wealth were stripped from her and regranted to her husband Lord Stanley for the duration of his life, after which they would revert to the Yorkist crown. For one who had proudly guarded her inheritance for so long, this was a devastating development, exacerbated by a sentence of perpetual house imprisonment and the stigma of being publicly branded a traitor. She was to have no servants and was forbidden to employ any messengers, who might spread her seditious commands. Despite her evident crimes, however, Margaret's life was to be spared. His reputation damaged by accusations of child murder, Richard could not be seen executing a woman in an age when such an act remained extreme and unpalatable. Perhaps of utmost importance to Richard at this moment in time, though, was to avoid alienating Margaret's powerful husband, who commanded great influence in the English north-west. Lord Stanley may even have pleaded for his wife's life.[16] In fact, for remaining loyal – outwardly at least – Stanley was further rewarded, appointed steward of the royal household and constable of England. Richard's reluctance to crush the Beaufort–Stanley unit represented a dangerous and naive error, one that would cost him his life.

His title confirmed and enemies subdued, Richard now endeavoured to further demolish the flagging Tudor conspiracy. It was clear that much of Henry's legitimacy rested on the support of the Woodville faction, particularly those household retainers who had served Edward IV and intended to obey a Tudor king provided he marry Elizabeth of York. With each passing month in sanctuary, however, without hope of imminent relief from her predicament, Elizabeth Woodville's spirit diminished, and Richard started pressing her to release her daughters so they could rejoin his court. Though the dowager queen may have suspected her brother-in-law of having murdered her two royal sons, and he certainly executed a son from her earlier Grey marriage, as 1484 progressed her options seemed limited. There was no guarantee, of course, that whatever conspiracy was still brewing in Brittany would ever seriously challenge the clear ascendancy Richard now enjoyed.

To further dampen Elizabeth's spirits, in the middle of February, within earshot of her chambers, Richard gathered all the lords of the realm, along with the emboldened knights and esquires who formed his buoyant household. Each man swore a fresh oath to serve and obey Richard's only son, Edward of Middleham, should anything happen to the king.[17] With hope dwindling with each passing day, it is little wonder the dowager queen started to consider her options. The breaching of sanctuary, after all, as she very well knew, was not beyond Richard any more than it had been beyond her husband Edward IV.

On 1 March 1484, in the presence of his magnates, the leading members of the clergy and London's mayor and aldermen, Richard swore a remarkable oath. If released into his care, he pledged that no harm would come to Elizabeth's five daughters, a protestation that notably included a promise they would not be placed in the Tower of London, the last known location of her two sons.[18] Richard would also ensure that as his kinswomen each would be treated honourably, be found suitable husbands of gentle rank and be modestly provided for. That he was even forced to make such solemn assurances is indicative of the suspicion that surrounded him during his own reign, a king who had ascended a throne on the back of his nephews' probable murder. His public penance worked, and the five York princesses – Elizabeth, Cecily, Anne, Katharine and Bridget – were soon released into the king's custody.[19] Their mother may have also emerged at this point, though her presence around the royal court was not reported upon.

It cannot be said, of course, that Elizabeth releasing her daughters is concrete evidence that she no longer suspected her former brother-in-law of having a hand in her sons' disappearance. It was a pragmatic decision taken when there was little other option than to yield to a foe holding every card. Parallels may be drawn with a previous queen of England, Margaret of Anjou, striking a deal with the earl of Warwick in 1470, despite him having been one of the chief causes of her dire predicament at the time. Elizabeth could only recall similar protestations from Richard III less than a year earlier when she handed over her youngest son, Richard of Shrewsbury, whom she never saw again.

If King Richard had been able to consolidate his control of the crown after the military failure of the combined Buckingham–Tudor conspiracy the previous year, there nevertheless remained a considerable movement outside his immediate grasp that sought his downfall. It was a situation that, despite his recent successes, tormented his mind to the point that he supposedly led 'a miserable life'.[20]

Though the rebels in Brittany did not have much to crow about since their failed invasion, renewed optimism spread with the news that Richard's only legitimate heir, Edward of Middleham, had died on 9 April 1484. As it had been in Edward 'whom all the hopes of the royal succession' had been vested, the king's long-term dynastic ambitions lay in ruins. It was reported by one contemporary observer close to the court that Richard was even reduced to a sudden grief 'bordering on madness'.[21] Aged thirty-one, it may have been expected that he would attempt to father another son as soon as possible, but as history would show both before and after Richard's reign, heirs could sometimes be elusive. The rebels now believed that such concern over the succession could prove fertile breeding ground for fresh sedition.

Underground networks of rebels continued to scheme throughout southern England, working together to try and destabilise the kingdom and pave the way for Henry to invade. On 8 July, a Wiltshire esquire named William Collingbourne paid messenger Thomas Yate £8 to carry a message across the Channel urging Henry to attack the south coast of England before October, promising that on this occasion a landing would be successful. Ten days later, the same Collingbourne pinned a defamatory rhyme to the door of St Paul's Cathedral, an incriminating slip of parchment that read, 'The Catte, the Ratte, and Lovell our Dogg, rulyth all England under the Hogge.' The words referred to Richard III's chief supporters, identified by their names and badges; in order, they were a lawyer named William Catesby, the northern knight Richard Ratcliffe, the king's closest friend Francis Lovell, and the hog was the king himself, who employed a white boar as his principal heraldic device.[22]

For his overt treason in encouraging a Tudor invasion, and not just his witty satire, before the year was up Collingbourne was tried in London's Guildhall and executed on Tower Hill in the most dreadful manner. Fastened to a wooden panel and dragged by horse to a specially constructed gallows, he was hanged until his thrashing legs came to a rest. Moments before death took its irreversible hold, Collingbourne was cut down and revived. Strapped to a counter, he was then cruelly emasculated and finally disembowelled before the masses, some of whom may have jeered as though it was entertainment while others pleaded with the officials for mercy. When the butcher reached into his chest, it was reported that Collingbourne cried out, 'O Lord Jesu, yet more trouble' before succumbing to his mutilation. Even in this bleak time it was remembered as a 'most cruel death'.[23]

Richard, no doubt troubled by such periodic outbreaks of insurrection, spotted an opportunity to finally bring this irksome conspiracy against him tumbling down when in the middle of 1484 it was shown that Duke Francis was severely weakened by another onset of illness. Having funded a modest flotilla the previous autumn and provided more than

300 men, Francis remained cautiously committed to Henry Tudor's cause. Despite their acrimonious history, the Breton duke was even encouraged by the French crown, which had much to gain from unsettling matters in England. On 5 April 1484, a French embassy arrived in Nantes and pledged not to undermine Breton independence if they funded another Tudor expedition to England. A fleet comprising six ships and 890 men does appear to have been readied that month, though ultimately it was not deployed.[24]

When Francis fell ill, the reins of Breton government were taken up by his longstanding, if unpopular, grand treasurer, Pierre Landais. Though Landais had once come to Henry Tudor's aid in 1476, riding to Saint-Malo to prevent him being handed over to the English, his motivations had altered over the years. A man of sharp wit, he was disliked by much of the Breton aristocracy, who resented his 'great authority' over the duke, and now sought to shore up his position by manufacturing a personal and mutually beneficial friendship with the grieving king of England.[25] Richard III jumped at the chance to rid himself of this troubling distraction across the water.

Whereas Francis had been content to offer modest support to Henry, turning away from his longstanding Yorkist alliance in the hope of placing his ally on the English throne, Landais elected to pursue a fresh agreement with Richard. In return for 1,000 English archers under the command of John Grey, Baron Grey of Powis, the treasurer pledged to arrange for the capture of Henry and Jasper Tudor and have them sent back to England, bringing their dozen-year Breton exile to a close.[26] Even now, as an avowed claimant to the English throne, recognised as king by several hundred men all willing to lay down their lives for him, Henry remained little more than a pawn in the games of others.

Richard sent his own negotiators across to Brittany, including one of his most trusted allies, William Catesby, the 'cat' from Collingbourne's rhyme, who was recorded as making an offering at the shrine of St Vincent in Vannes in September 1484. He may even have promised to formally restore Duke Francis to the earldom of Richmond, claimed by Henry Tudor but historically associated with successive dukes of Brittany dating back to 1344. Landais was only too happy to accept such terms on behalf of his master, particularly if he was protected by Richard from any retribution on the part of the Breton nobility.[27]

Fortunately for Henry Tudor, the scheme was revealed to John Morton, though how it reached the bishop's ears is unknowable. Clearly, there was a leak among Richard's council, and it may be speculated the source of such intel was none other than Lord Stanley, Henry Tudor's stepfather. Either way, Morton dispatched Christopher Urswick to Brittany in great haste to warn Henry that he was about to be betrayed. It should be noted that Polydore Vergil's chronicle of these years is considered the greatest account of the various conspiracies and plots that sought Richard III's downfall, and one of the likeliest sources for the Italian's work was Urswick. Vergil arrived in England in 1502, nearly two decades after these events in Brittany, but grew friendly with an aged Urswick, who presumably provided much of the oral testimony that formed Vergil's captivating and enduring account.[28]

Henry, who through necessity had grown into a cautious, even suspicious, adult, took Morton's message gravely. He called to his side a few trusted figures and hatched a plan whereby he would flee across the Franco-Breton border and seek asylum at the French court. Urswick was redeployed at once, this time sent from Vannes to the French court to source a safe conduct for their arrival.[29] Henry had already made two improbable flights during his lifetime, first as a fourteen-year-old in Tenby and again as a nineteen-year-old in Saint-Malo. He now looked to complete a third.

As late as 8 September 1484, Henry was still in Vannes, where he was recorded making an offering in the cathedral's shrine. Soon after, however, he put his plan in motion.[30] Under the pretence of visiting a friend, Henry assembled a small group of his most trusted allies and left his court-in-exile behind. Riding two days ahead of him was his uncle Jasper Tudor, who had already accomplished what Henry now set out to do. Just a handful of miles into their journey, Henry suddenly signalled for his men to leave the road and dart into the dense woodland. He leapt off his horse and quickly changed into the clothes of one of his grooms. Suitably disguised, Henry and his companions rode hard for the French border, scarcely looking behind them so as not to lose any speed.

They were right not to stop other than to briefly water their exhausted horses. As soon as Landais discovered Henry had left the court, just days before he planned to have him bound and returned to England, he immediately dispatched his finest soldiers to hunt him down and bring him back. According to Vergil's account, Henry crossed the border with only an hour to spare. As soon as he caught his breath, not for the first time in his life, he was able to let out a well-earned sigh of relief.[31]

Francis soon recovered from his sickness and was distressed to learn of Landais's duplicity. Aside from tarnishing his honour, Henry's escape significantly weakened Brittany's position, depriving them of the support of England and exposing the duchy to French ambitions. A man of great integrity, however, the chivalric duke offered the several hundred remaining English rebels at his court safe conduct to take their leave and join their leader in France. When they had learned of Henry's flight, many feared for their lives, but Francis proved honourable, even covering the cost of their lodgings and travel expenses. The duke summoned Edward Woodville, John Cheyne and Edward Poynings to his presence and advised them they were free to go, expressing his regret for the deceitful actions of his impetuous treasurer. Henry's abandonment of his men had been ruthless, exhibiting a willingness to risk the lives of his supporters to save his own. When he was reunited with them in France, Henry, perhaps out of guilt as much as relief, was 'wonderous glad'. He pledged never to forget the generosity Duke Francis had shown in this moment.[32]

Landais's shady plotting only served to hasten his downfall. Throughout his later career, the ambitious but low-born treasurer had incurred the enmity of the Breton aristocracy, who resented the power he wielded. In the summer of 1485, Landais's enemies encouraged Duke Francis to try him for extortion among other crimes, and he was sentenced to death. The man who once saved Henry Tudor, and yet was also responsible for nearly delivering him up to certain death, was hanged in a meadow outside Nantes on 19 July 1485.

The arrival of Henry Tudor at the French court in September 1484 promised much for those plotting the downfall of Richard III, though ambitions were initially frustrated from the outset by wider political struggles in France. Mirroring what had occurred in England a few months earlier, on 30 August 1483 the authoritative Louis XI died after twenty-two years on the French throne. His successor, Charles VIII, was just thirteen years old. Again, like England, there was instant tension around who should control the government during the king's minority. The principal rivals for power were the young king's elder sister, the formidable Anne of Beaujeu, and the most senior noble of royal blood, the proud Louis II, Duke of Orléans.

A princess in the mould of her shrewd father, Anne was able to point across the Channel at the apparent murder of Edward IV's sons as a cautionary tale of why they must not allow power to slip away to an ambitious if popular royal duke. Richard III would later lash out at these 'false inventions, tidings, and rumours' which besmirched his reputation on the continent, but such scaremongering did the trick in France. By March 1484, Anne had succeeded in securing the support of the States-General to assume the position of regent at the expense of her indignant rival, Orléans. Unwilling to accept this state of affairs, Orléans sought to bolster his faction by securing the support of the Bretons, and fled to Brittany to strike an alliance with Francis II. One of Orléans' proposals was to have his marriage annulled so he could marry Francis's daughter Anne of Brittany, and he also pursued a friendship with Pierre Landais, supporting the scheme to hawk Henry Tudor to the English to secure the long-term favour of Richard III. Any coalition between Brittany, Orléans and England would have placed Henry Tudor in a hopeless situation from which there could be no reprieve. His flight into France, evading the clutches of Landais, could not have been timelier, and it is little surprise he was warmly welcomed by the French government and regent Anne of Beaujeu.[33]

Returning to the French court at the end of 1484 to pursue his goal of seizing the reins of government, Orléans even attempted to snatch the young king of France, though he was ultimately thwarted. The dynamic duke continued to be a thorn in the side of the French government throughout 1485, his actions triggering a three-year conflict known to French history as *la Guerre folle*, or the Mad War. The French were also deeply involved in another succession crisis at this time, with troops engaged on behalf of Flemish interests as they revolted against the attempted guardianship of Maximilian of Austria, who was also counselling Richard III to invade France. Though sponsoring Henry Tudor's claim to the English throne and forcing Richard to abandon his anti-Beaujeu allies was a sound strategy to pursue, it was clear the French regency council was distracted by its own issues, to say the least.

Charles VIII, the regent Anne and the council were in Montargis dealing with such matters when on 11 October 1484 they were informed of Henry's flight and his subsequent arrival in French territory. The man carrying the message was Christopher Urswick, once more trusted by Henry to undertake such a weighty task. Gilbert de Chabannes, lord of Curton, governor of Limousin, and member of a celebrated military dynasty, was urgently sent in the opposite direction, authorised on behalf of Charles to honourably welcome Henry to France and to arrange lodgings and food. The message from the king, or at least his advisors, was that Henry should be brought to the cathedral city of Chartres as soon as possible so the pair could meet.[34]

When Henry was brought into Charles's presence, a twenty-seven-year-old Welsh exile standing before his thirteen-year-old French cousin, the former thanked the latter for his warm hospitality. He wasted little time in pleading his case for further aid, and Charles, likely following his council's lead, encouraged his guest's ambitions 'and bade him be of good cheer'.[35] According to the later testimony of Henry's French poet Bernard André, the king even marvelled at his guest's 'graceful and distinguished countenance, his natural prudence, and his remarkable fluency in French', so much so that he 'could not help but rejoice greatly at his arrival'.[36]

By 4 November, Henry had moved on to Sens, where accommodation was sourced for Henry's supporters, who numbered around 400 now that they had been allowed to leave Brittany. A further commission was issued for the English to be provided with any utensils or other supplies they would need to be a self-sufficient community.[37] This was followed on 17 November with a grant of 3,000 *livres tournois* to clothe them for the coming winter, though it was stressed that this was to be a solitary grant and that the English exiles should not expect bottomless pockets from the French crown.[38]

If the purse strings weren't exactly opened for Henry, the young king of France was nevertheless willing to publicly champion the Tudor claim to the English throne. There was at first, however, a very disingenuous altering of the truth. In a letter sent throughout his kingdom intended to garner wider financial and military for Henry's cause, Charles VIII referred to his cousin as '*fils de feu roy Henry d'Angleterre*'.[39] Henry Tudor was not a son of the late Henry VI of England, as those close to the French crown knew well, merely a half-nephew in the maternal line. That this kinship between Henry VI and Henry Tudor was through a French daughter of the House of Valois, a great-aunt of the current king, just underscored that this was not an innocent ancestral error on the part of Charles, or more correctly, his adult advisors.

This untruthful embellishment almost certainly did not originate from Henry or his own counsel. If such rewriting of family trees was intended to add credibility to his claim, if anything it merely highlighted the weakness of his Beaufort pedigree concerning the English throne. Everyone in England was very clear that Henry VI had only one son, who had perished in battle in 1471, and that the claimant in France was the only son of Edmund of Richmond. To invade under the premise of such nonsense risked widespread alienation from an English nobility who would treat such falsehood with the scorn it deserved.

It is little surprise that this strategy was soon dropped and does not reappear for the remainder of Henry's time in France. He did, however, begin to assume the royal signature HR or H in his missives, adopting the regal bearing of a king biding his time before he could enter his rightful inheritance and 'recover' his realm. Seeking to capitalise on the support of Charles VIII and his regency council, as a self-styled king, Henry sent a range of letters into England and Wales shortly after he arrived in France, one of which has survived. Undated and carrying no specific addressee, the letter spoke to Henry's 'right trust, worshipful, and honourable good friends', and in it he outlined his intentions once upon the English throne:

Being given to understand your good devoir and entreaty to advance me to the furtherance of my rightful claim, due and lineal inheritance of that crown, and for the just depriving of that homicide and unnatural tyrant which now unjustly bears dominion over you, I give you to understand that no Christian heart can be more full of joy and gladness than the heart of me, your poor exiled friend, who will, upon the instant of your sure advertising what power you will make ready and what captains and leaders you get to conduct, be prepared to pass over the sea with such force as my friends here are preparing for me. And if I have such good speed and success as I wish, according to your desire, I shall ever be most forward to remember and wholly to requite this your great and most loving kindness in my just quarrel. Given under our signet. H.[40]

For as long as he could remember, Henry had regarded himself as the earl of Richmond, a title he inherited at birth from his deceased father, Edmund. As late as October 1483, days before the execution of the duke of Buckingham and the collapse of that phase of the conspiracy to depose Richard III, he was still signing his name as 'Henry de Richemont'.[41] Now, however, a year later, Henry of Richmond fell away, replaced by Henry Rex, king of England in right if not yet in fact. This bold change of attitude proved persuasive in raising Henry's stature among his men and the French court, enhancing his reputation far more than any invented royal lineage could. Emboldened with each passing day, Henry now turned to the final chapter of his crusade to be king, securing from the French tangible backing to emerge victorious in what he now regarded as his 'just quarrel'.

16

The King's Great Rebel

Henry Tudor, or Henry Rex as he now regarded himself, remained attached to the French court throughout the early winter of 1484, accompanying King Charles VIII and his household when they decamped to Paris for the Christmas period. For the first time in his adult life Henry had been able to closely observe regal authority in person, studying how a king carried himself in front of his subjects, and how those same deferential subjects followed strict protocols in the royal presence. It was an enchanting lesson in kingship for one who had been raised far from the English court, and helped instil in Henry some notion of what he could expect should he ever gain a crown.

In January 1485, the French king and his household left the capital behind, heading south to Montargis, again with Henry in tow. Both during the journey and once at their destination, Henry pushed for tangible support to 'recover the Kingdom of England', and on 20 January Henry finally secured a solid pledge in King Charles's name. On account of their 'proximity of lineage' and because he was the person 'who has the most apparent right' to the English crown, the French were happy to help Henry in his 'business and deeds'. Still, however, supply of men and money remained lacking as the French grappled with their own military issues in Flanders.[1]

It was probably sometime in this period, between autumn 1484 and the following spring, that Henry became personally acquainted with Jean Molinet, a French historiographer and poet long in the employ of the dukes of Burgundy. Molinet noted that Henry's arrival at the French court was regarded with 'great joy', adding he found the earl to be a pleasant and elegant character who was a handsome adornment around the French court. Unlike Bernard André, Molinet was not employed by Henry and therefore was under no obligation to flatter him. Of Henry's ambitions, the Frenchman remarked that though he was born far from the English throne, he aspired very strongly to the crown, having long been a prisoner of others. Though treated well in France, however, it was Molinet's suspicion this was mostly to do with distracting Richard III and drawing his attention away from grandiose ambitions of leading his own cross-Channel invasion.[2]

In the spring of 1485, Henry remained attached to the French court, accompanying King Charles to Rouen, the capital of Normandy. It was a city central to Anglo-French rivalries ever since William the Bastard, Duke of Normandy, crossed the Channel in 1066 to wrest the English throne from Harold Godwinson. Situated on the banks of the meandering Seine, Rouen owed its prosperity to its advantageous position, the city's merchants able to dominate the river trade by controlling access upstream to Paris. Wine and wheat were shipped out of Rouen and across Europe in great quantities, and as the fifteenth century progressed the city grew increasingly wealthy through the burgeoning textile trade.

Despite the grandeur of Rouen, however, the city had a storied past, one intimately associated with Henry's family. In 1418, the formidable English army of Henry V inflicted a torturous five-month siege on the Rouennais, reducing the surviving citizens to skin and bone. The commander who formally accepted the city's submission was Henry's great-great-uncle Thomas Beaufort, Duke of Exeter, soon created captain of Rouen. During the celebrations the following Christmas, Henry's grandfather John Beaufort was knighted.[3] Another of Henry's great-great-uncles, Cardinal Henry Beaufort, also had a gruesome connection with Rouen, which since its capture had become the administrative centre of English operations in France. On 30 May 1431, the imposing churchman was present to witness the burning of the peasant-turned-warrior Joan of Arc, later ordering her ashes to be collected and scattered in the Seine.[4]

If the Beauforts had been closely associated with the city's capture, they also played a leading role in its surrender. Surrounded by a vast French host, in the autumn of 1450 Edmund Beaufort, now duke of Somerset, opened the gates, a submission considered deeply dishonourable by his political enemies back in England and which contributed to the febrile atmosphere that would soon tear the kingdom apart.[5] The loss of Rouen after thirty years of English occupation was particularly galling to the Yorkist faction – Richard, Duke of York's eldest son Edward IV had been born in the city in 1442 during his father's tenure as Lieutenant of France. Now, Rouen played host to a Beaufort scion who looked to disinherit a son of York.

On 14 April 1485, Henry Tudor entered Rouen as part of the French royal convoy, perhaps conscious of his family's role in the Norman capital's recent history. In procession, they wound through the tight streets, packed on either side with the citizens who had turned up to not only pay tribute to their young king and other princes of the blood royal but to catch a glimpse of this supposed claimant to the English throne. It was said that the English students in the city even cheered him.[6]

Despite the destruction exacted on Rouen by the English nearly seventy years earlier, the city's grandness remained apparent to Henry as he turned his gaze from the faces in the crowd to the timber-framed shops and houses which thwarted the sun's rays from reaching the cobbled streets. He may have noted the intricate Flamboyant east front and lantern tower of Saint-Ouen's Abbey, which in French shared the name of his grandfather Owen, or caught a glimpse of the fascinating Gros-Horloge, a huge astronomical clock that showed the relative positions of the Sun and Moon as well as telling the time. It is likely somebody pointed out to him the early thirteenth-century donjon, looming high above the castle, that not too long ago housed an English garrison under Beaufort's command, perhaps even being gently needled about his kinsman's failure to hold the city.

Finally, the procession wormed its way towards the Cathedral of Notre-Dame, which even in a city filled with impressive spires dominated the Rouen skyline. A church was first established here in the third century, and progressively expanded across the next 1,000 years. Patronised by successive dukes of Normandy, when the newly rebuilt Romanesque church was consecrated in 1063, the rituals were conducted in the presence of William the Bastard, just three years before he sailed to England to conquer new lands. Subsequently reconstructed in the Gothic manner, with the recently completed Tour Saint-Romain reaching towards the heavens and work already underway on another tower, the church which soared high above Henry Tudor in 1485 rivalled any in Europe for its sheer magnificence.

Entering through the extravagantly decorated west front, Henry may have glanced up to briefly take in the stone scenes above him, identifying intricately carved figures like the Virgin Mary, Christ and the Apostles. Slowly, he advanced through the pillared nave. When he reached the brightly lit transept, Henry perhaps even craned his neck in both directions to take in the pair of fine Rose windows depicting Christ waited upon by the Four Evangelists and an array of bishops and kings. When the procession reached the altar, he bided his time until it was his turn to solemnly step forward and make his offerings. These were recorded by the cathedral's canons as having been received from the king of England.

Before departing the church, one wonders if Henry was shown the various royal tombs of his kinsmen who lay in Rouen. Though his immediate paternal ancestry was rooted in Wales, as a prospective king of England, Henry no doubt paid close attention to those who had ruled before him. There was, of course, William I, the great duke of Normandy who conquered England, a feat Henry hoped to soon emulate. Also visible were the tombs of Empress Matilda, who for seven years laid claim to the English throne, and her grandsons Henry the Young King and the famed crusader Richard I, the Lionheart. If they were too far removed in time for Henry to feel a connection, he may have been more interested in the black marble tomb of John, Duke of Bedford, the son, brother and uncle of Lancastrian kings who died in Rouen fifty years earlier. As he stared at the lifeless carved figures before him, most of whom bore crowns, the scale of what he hoped to achieve became clear. Immortality was at stake.

Luckily, Henry's position had been further boosted by a trickle of new recruits to his established band of supporters, adding to the 400 or 500 men who already looked to him as their leader, their king even. In November 1484, a group of gentlemen fled England to join the rebels in Paris, including John Risley, William Coke, William Brandon, Thomas Brandon and William Stonor. English students in the city's university also flocked to Henry's cause, most notably a Lincolnshire native named Richard Fox, a man of an 'excellent wit' who would become one of the leading clerical figures in the early Tudor regime.[7] During his time in Paris, Fox had in fact been appointed vicar of the parish of St Dunstan in the London suburb of Stepney, though King Richard soon intervened. On 22 January 1485, the king ordered Fox to be denied the appointment on the basis that he was known to be fraternising with the 'great rebel, Henry ap Tudder'.[8] A London draper named William Bret was also noted to have brought several suits of English-style armour to Henry. By far the most consequential addition to Henry's court during this period, however, was John de Vere, the mighty earl of Oxford.[9]

Born in 1442, Oxford was the heir of a great East Anglian dynasty, his ancestors having arrived in England alongside William the Conqueror and quickly establishing their position in and around north Essex. Since the earldom was created for his Norman ancestor Aubrey in 1141, the John de Vere that Henry Tudor now warmly embraced was the thirteenth consecutive member of his illustrious family to bear the title, along with the hereditary office of great chamberlain. When the political dispute between Richard of York and Henry VI turned into a struggle for the crown, Oxford's father, the 12th earl, abandoned his neutrality and pledged his colours and men to the House of Lancaster. For his efforts, the patriarch of the de Vere family was soon apprehended by the Yorkists and convicted of high treason against the new Yorkist king Edward IV, condemned for his involvement in a plot that involved Jasper Tudor landing with his men from France. On 26 February 1462, the 12th earl was beheaded on Tower Hill, six days after his eldest son, Aubrey.[10]

In pursuit of wider reconciliation, Edward IV permitted John de Vere to succeed his father as earl of Oxford once he reached twenty-one years of age, and, with little choice but to fall in line, he proved outwardly loyal to the Yorkist king. When his brother-in-law Warwick rebelled in the summer of 1469, however, Oxford joined the insurrection and fought in a losing effort against Edward IV's forces at Losecoat Field on 12 March 1470. Like Jasper Tudor in Wales, Oxford fled overseas, regrouping at the court of Margaret of Anjou before returning with Jasper and Warwick in September 1470 to help restore Henry VI to his throne. In recognition of his efforts in returning the Lancastrians to power, Oxford was given the honour of bearing the Sword of State before the reinstated king in procession to St Paul's as well as being appointed Lord High Constable. He also took the opportunity to exact vengeance on the man who had overseen the execution his father and brother, John Tiptoft, 1st Earl of Worcester.[11]

When the Yorkists returned to England in the spring of 1471, Oxford commanded the right wing of the Lancastrian army at the Battle of Barnet, when his men were mistakenly attacked by their own side due to confusion in the heavy fog. Now unrepentant in his opposition to Edward IV, when the Yorkists wrested back control of the crown Oxford once more joined Jasper Tudor in exile, fleeing to France where he engaged in privateering throughout the Channel. At the end of September 1473, the earl and around eighty of his men even invaded and captured St Michael's Mount, a tidal island situated off the coast of Cornwall. During the relentless siege that followed, Oxford was able to withstand the Yorkist assault until February 1474, when in return for his life he surrendered the island and turned himself over to Edward. Though Oxford escaped the same fate as his father, he was punished with perpetual imprisonment in Hammes Castle, just outside Calais and far from his natural sphere of influence in East Anglia. He was attained in the 1475 parliament, with most of his estates granted to the king's brother, the future Richard III.[12]

Loath to submit to Yorkist rule, three years later Oxford managed to scale the walls of Hammes and leapt into the moat, though he was pitifully retrieved from the mud and thrown back into his cell. It is unclear if this was a suicide attempt or merely an escape gone awry. Oxford had almost become a forgotten figure in subsequent years, until the advent of Henry Tudor in France and the prospect of a French assault on Calais spurred Richard III into action. In October 1484, the English king issued orders arranging for the rebel earl to be transferred back across the Channel, removing any potential for one of the last great Lancastrian veterans to be sprung from a prison in which he had languished for a decade.[13]

The king was right to be concerned, but perhaps did not anticipate the circumstances of Oxford's flight. As the moment of the earl's return to England neared, Sir James Blount, the captain of Hammes and the man responsible for overseeing Oxford's detention, released his charge from prison and together both men fled the short distance into France. They continued on to Paris and the spirited court of Henry Tudor, pledging their support to the pretender's cause.[14] For Oxford, the toppling of Richard was personal; in 1471, all his forfeited lands had been granted to the then duke of Gloucester, who proceeded to break up the de Vere inheritance once he became king, granting away individual manors to those who had supported his rise to the throne.[15] Greater offence was caused when Richard stripped Oxford's mother of her lands. The reinvigorated Lancastrian earl desired nothing more than Richard's destruction, and Henry was to be his chosen implement. In return, Oxford, a man of 'so great nobility and knowledge in the wars', would place his considerable diplomatic and military experience at Henry's disposal. In a rebel court crowded with Yorkist veterans, Henry was 'ravished with joy incredible' at Oxford's arrival, and the earl quickly established his position as one of Tudor's most intimate advisors and chief champions.[16]

Henry's growing status, his conscious transformation – with gentle French encouragement – from rebel leader to king-in-waiting, had not gone unnoticed in England. In fact, the Tudor pretender's series of scheming cross-Channel missives courting potential supporters had been revealed to Richard III, and elicited an incensed response from the man who actually wore the crown. On 6 December 1484, Richard commanded the mayor of Windsor, and likely many other officials throughout the kingdom, to seize and investigate anyone caught carrying or distributing such treasonable material. They were, he complained, 'false inventions' spread by 'seditious persons' and 'our ancient enemies of France', designed to sow discord between the king and his nobles.[17]

The following day, Richard issued a scathing proclamation of his own taking aim directly at Henry and his cohorts, publicly acknowledging the irksome threat across the Channel.[18] A masterful exercise in propaganda, it was designed to nip in the bud any prospective support within England for the growing conspiracy while convincing his people that he was a 'well-willed, diligent, and courageous prince' who would deliver them from the immoral and unpatriotic intentions of the Tudor conspiracy.

Richard lashed out at the principal 'rebels and traitors' who had turned to Henry as their captain, a man of 'ambitious and insatiable covetousness' with 'no manner, interest, right or colour' to the crown, 'as every man well knoweth'. Those named as the chief plotters around Henry were Jasper Tudor; Peter Courtenay, Bishop of Exeter; John de Vere, Earl of Oxford; Thomas Grey, Marquess of Dorset; and Edward Woodville. All, Richard thundered, had not only forsaken their rightful king and natural country, but were murderers, adulterers and extortioners, moral delinquents who would inflict great harm on the English people if successful in their venture.

Bolstered by support of the French, Richard further warned that if Henry became king of England he had already agreed to relinquish any

English claim to the crown of France, abandoning forever the duchies of Normandy, Gascony and Guienne, and the towns of Calais, Guines and Hammes. It was powerful rhetoric, a patriotic appeal to 'good and true Englishmen' he hoped would persuade any wavering subject to remain loyal. The proclamation also served, however, as a tacit acknowledgment of the pressure Richard was starting to feel from Henry's posturing, and merely brought the latter to greater prominence on both sides of the Channel.

One person omitted from the proclamation was John Morton, and four days later Richard took the surprising step of issuing a pardon to the mutinous bishop, hoping to entice him away from a conspiracy he had been prominent in shaping.[19] Morton had once, after all, accepted a Yorkist pardon under Edward IV. In this instance, however, the veteran churchman spurned Richard's hand of friendship and continued to press Henry's case in the Holy See, where he remained in the company of his nephew Robert Morton, formerly Master of the Rolls to Edward IV, and Oliver King, once that king's secretary.

When Henry's presence in Paris became known to the English king, Richard ramped up his defensive measures at home and abroad. Though the Bretons had failed to surrender Henry while he had been in their possession, Richard nevertheless continued pursuing friendship with Brittany. By early March 1485, a fresh Anglo-Breton truce had been struck, to last for seven years during which both sides pledged not to support enemies of the other. Richard also promised again to send 1,000 archers across the Channel.[20]

That same month, Richard's position had become altogether more vulnerable when on 16 March his queen, Anne Neville, followed their only son to the grave. Rumours quickly spread in London that the bereaved king was scandalously intending to replace Anne with one of his nieces, either Elizabeth of York or her younger sister Cecily. These were shocking allegations, almost certainly unsubstantiated, that the king felt obliged to address.[21] On 30 March, before an assembly of the lords, 'in a loud and distinct voice' Richard formally denied the salacious gossip, saying that such an idea had 'never once entered his mind' and instead publicly grieved for his recently deceased wife. That he was forced to take this step highlighted the reputational damage he had incurred since coming to the throne, and the need to prevent any further defections to Henry Tudor.[22]

In June 1485, Richard continued to anticipate an invasion of his kingdom. On 8 June he finalised a nine-month truce with Brittany, and a fortnight later once more ordered his commissioners to begin mustering their men to be available at just one hour's notice. Sheriffs throughout England were put on high alert to weed out any signs of seditious activity, and a range of beacons were established around the southern coast ready to be lit the moment enemy ships were spotted on the horizon.[23] He also introduced mounted couriers posted 20 miles apart, able to convey urgent messages at great speed across the country. At Nottingham on the 21st, meanwhile, the king signed a warrant for another proclamation against Henry and his enterprise, to be issued two days later.[24] Following much of his previous proclamation six months earlier, Richard focused on the bloody upheaval England would suffer under Tudor conquest. Henry would persist with his plan to surrender England's claim to the French crown, and would remove the fleurs-de-lis from the English royal arms. Men would be deprived of their bishoprics, dukedoms, earldoms and baronies, with lands and possessions seized so Henry could reward his false friends.

This time, however, Richard turned his attack on Henry's lineage, disparaging his pedigree and legitimacy on both sides of his family tree. The king was a man noted for his preoccupation with matters of legitimacy, and it galled him that he could be challenged by someone whose background was legally questionable.[25] Attempting to draw attention to his foe's Welsh paternal descent – which was, after all, hardly ideal for a man claiming to be the rightful king of England after all – Richard mocked the rebels for taking as their leader 'one Henry Tidder, son of Edmond Tidder, son of Owen Tidder'. If this alone wasn't a regal line worthy of the name and title of a royal estate, then Richard claimed that Owen Tudor had been 'bastard borne', though his source for this is unclear. Perhaps notably, Richard did not raise any doubts over the legitimacy of Owen's children with Katherine of Valois, which may be taken as an implicit acceptance that the births of Edmund and Jasper Tudor occurred in lawful matrimony.

Turning his attention to Henry's maternal pedigree, Richard noted that the Beaufort line had illegitimate origins, the product of a famed affair between John of Gaunt and Katherine Swynford. Though later retrospectively legitimised, which Richard surely knew as a descendant of the same union himself, this nonetheless formed a convenient and persuasive argument for the king to cast doubt on Henry's suitability to wear a crown. It appeared evident to Richard 'no title can nor may be in' his foe. Indeed, a Tudor conquest would ensure 'the disinheriting and destruction of all the noble and worshipful blood of this realm forever'.

Regarding his personal troubles, and despite his grief, Richard also started to pursue a new marriage. At thirty-two years old, he needed to remarry in the hope of fathering an heir, but also saw a crucial opportunity to reinforce his position upon the throne while weakening his enemy's hand. After consulting with his advisors, the king settled upon a match with a Portuguese princess named Joanna, sister of King John II. At the same time, Richard also suggested the marriage of his niece Elizabeth of York with the Portuguese king's cousin Manuel, Duke of Viseu. It was a shrewd strategy from Richard, one intended to utterly undermine Henry Tudor. Not only did Henry stand to lose Elizabeth as a prospective bride, which risked alienating much of his Yorkist support, but the Portuguese royals were, like him, descendants of the House of Lancaster, tracing their lineage to John of Gaunt through his daughter Philippa, queen consort of Portugal between 1387 and 1415. Once these matches were concluded, it would be Richard, not Henry, who could be said to be uniting York and Lancaster as one party.

Elsewhere, Richard also turned a wary eye towards Lord Stanley, whose loyalty to the Yorkist king thus far had been accepted as sincere. When Stanley voiced his intention to return to his north-west estates, Richard agreed only on the condition that his heir, George, Baron Strange, remained behind with the court. Such a request hardly showed royal confidence in Stanley, or the awkward position he found himself in.[26] The Stanley family had been noted during the Wars of the Roses for maintaining their position regardless of which way the conflict swung, hedging their bets regardless of who held the crown. It may be of consequence that Strange was married to a niece of Elizabeth Woodville, which likely opened alternative lines of communication between the Woodvilles and the Stanleys. Though a mere baron, Stanley now found himself in a situation where England's fate possibly rested in his hands. The moment was approaching when he needed to decide whether he was for the king, Richard III, or the stepson he had never met, Henry Tudor.

If Richard was receiving regular updates about Henry as 1485 progressed, then likewise tidings from England were brought to Henry in France by refugees, messengers and merchants. The rumour of Elizabeth of York's impending marriage, however, either to her uncle Richard or a Portuguese duke, deeply distressed the Tudor court when it reached France, and no one was more troubled than Henry. Much of the support he enjoyed across the previous eighteen months was because of the pledge he made to marry Elizabeth once king, which the Yorkists in his camp expected would return them to political dominance. If Henry was unable to honour this promise as Elizabeth was no longer available, then it was possible these Yorkist dissidents would either find another candidate or seek a rapprochement with Richard. For good reason, these rumours 'pinched Henry by the very stomach'.[27]

Uncertain how this would play out, Henry and his closest advisors desperately scrambled around for a back-up plan, one that would retain at least some Yorkist support, and perhaps even attract fresh backing from quarters yet to betray their loyalties. One suggestion put forward was for Henry to consider a daughter of his former guardian, William Herbert. The Herberts had impeccable Yorkist credentials, William having been Edward IV's 'master-lock' throughout the 1460s before perishing defending the Yorkist crown. The Herberts even had connections with the Woodvilles; the present head of the family, also called William and now holding the earldom of Huntingdon, had been married to Mary Woodville, the dowager queen's sister, between 1467 and her death in 1481. The families all knew each other well.

The glaring issue with pursuing a Herbert match was that Huntingdon had remarried after Mary Woodville's demise, taking as his wife an illegitimate daughter of Richard III named Katherine Plantagenet. The earl had also been appointed justice of South Wales and granted Brecon Castle, in effect replacing the duke of Buckingham as the king's man in the region. But Huntingdon also had a dynamic and ambitious younger brother named Walter Herbert, a man of 'ancient authority among the Welshmen' closer in age to Henry Tudor and perhaps even a childhood companion of his during their years together at Raglan Castle. Though his official positions were restricted to the constableship of the minor villages of Caio and Manordeilo in Carmarthenshire, Walter was military-minded and politically savvy, a figure of great influence on the ground in South Wales. Unlike his inactive elder brother, who may have suffered from bouts of ill health, Water was every inch his father's son, something remarked upon by Welsh bards who praised his bravery and talent. He resented the hindering of the family's power in their native sphere, his brother having been forced to relinquish the lucrative Pembroke earldom for that of Huntingdon some years previously. Walter was sounded out and, probably in return for some concessions in the event of a Tudor victory, proved open to an alliance.[28]

The Herbert daughter once intended by her father to be a Tudor bride, Maud, had married Henry Percy, 4th Earl of Northumberland, nearly a decade earlier. Maud's sisters Jane, Cecily and Katherine Herbert remained unmarried, however, and in the circumstances made reasonable alternatives at short notice. It didn't escape attention that Northumberland had also been based at Raglan as a youth, and was identified as another potential, and vastly powerful, recruit to the Tudor cause, particularly in light of Herbert involvement. Northumberland had been rewarded well by Richard thus far in the reign, being retained in the offices of great chamberlain, warden general of the Marches and captain of Berwick. Nevertheless, there had been tension between Northumberland and Richard during the latter's tenure in the north of England under Edward IV as the two great northern magnates jostled for regional supremacy. Once more the tireless Christopher Urswick was handed an assignment, and dutifully set off back across the Channel and towards the Percy heartlands carrying a message for the earl. It is unclear on this occasion if Urswick was able to complete his arduous mission.[29]

Other letters sent into England and Wales did reach their intended recipients, however. In particular, several prominent Welshmen were targeted in addition to Walter Herbert. Word soon came back to Henry that Trahaearn ap Morgan of Kidwelly, Sir John Savage and Rhys ap Thomas had responded warmly to his overtures. These were not insignificant pledges, and the message was that Henry should set out for his homeland at the earliest opportunity.[30]

John Savage was a native of Cheshire, but as a knighted nephew of Thomas Stanley he wielded some degree of cross-border influence in North-East Wales. He may also be considered a stepcousin of sorts to Henry Tudor, connected through his uncle's marriage to Margaret Beaufort. Savage fought for Edward IV against the Lancastrians at the battles of Barnet and Tewkesbury in 1471, and accompanied the future Richard III on the campaign to Scotland in 1482. Perhaps owing to their connection with the Stanleys, the Savages were regarded with something akin to distrust under Richard III, who was proven right when John Savage started colluding with the rebels in France. Savage implored Henry to invade, though it is unclear if he was acting independently of his Stanley uncle or doing his bidding.[31]

Rhys ap Thomas was similarly unknown to Henry in a personal capacity, but their respective families were closely entwined in fifteenth-century Welsh politics, sometimes rivals and sometimes allies. Rhys was the youngest son of Thomas ap Gruffydd, a Lancastrian soldier once loyal to Jasper Tudor. He was also the grandson of Gruffydd ap Nicholas, the powerful lord who thirty years previously had clashed with Henry's father Edmund before later aligning with Jasper to stand against the Yorkists. This complex relationship spanned the generations; when Jasper and Henry were besieged at Pembroke in 1471, their assailant was Thomas ap Gruffydd's son Morgan ap Thomas, though their liberator after eight days was another of Thomas's sons, Dafydd ap Thomas.[32]

By 1485, the patriarch of this influential Welsh dynasty was the valiant Rhys ap Thomas, the youngest son of Thomas ap Gruffydd and sole inheritor of his father and brothers' patrimony. Not seeing any worth in supporting the duke of Buckingham in the autumn of 1483, Rhys sat out the first major rebellion against Richard III, and 'as the king's servant' was rewarded in February 1484 with a lifetime annuity of 40 marks.[33] Even so, the emergence of Henry Tudor brought moments of contemplation from Rhys, who considered under which king would he be better served.[34] If a later family biographer is to be believed, Rhys's tutor as a young man was a certain Lewis Caerleon, the messenger who went between Margaret Beaufort and Elizabeth Woodville.[35] Perhaps of greater consequence was the fact that, through his mother, Rhys was a direct descendant of Ednyfed Fychan.

Despite attempts to grow his following, Henry was forced to deal with some discontent among his established support, particularly in the Woodville quarters, which were so integral to any hope of success. Made aware that his mother, Elizabeth Woodville, had recently reached an agreement with Richard III to release his half-sisters into the king's custody, and feeling put out by the arrival of the earl of Oxford to Henry's court, the marquess of Dorset's loyalties wavered. Late one night under the cover of darkness, he stole away from the Tudor court in Paris and made for the Flemish border. In a reversal of what had occurred in Brittany, Henry now ordered men to pursue Dorset at once and bring him back. Not only would losing the marquess at such a critical juncture have demoralised the rest of Henry's men, but he carried with him an abundance of military intelligence that would have been of great use to King Richard. Unlike Henry, Dorset failed to complete his escape and was sheepishly brought back to Paris. Dorset would never recover Henry's faith, and for the rest of his life was kept at arm's length – tolerated, but never trusted.[36]

Nevertheless, plans progressed. Henry remained on good terms with the regent, Anne de Beaujeu, and at every opportunity continued to press his hosts to sponsor an invasion of England.[37] If Henry waited too long to make his voyage he might suffer further desertions, progressively diminishing his force until it was too weak to ever swing a sword in anger. It was French concern for Richard III's military alliance with Brittany and Burgundy, however, that proved decisive in finally putting a Tudor fleet to sea.

A core objective of the regency was that Brittany would become annexed to France, but for that to happen the anti-French fellowship between England and the duchy needed to be broken. If Henry invaded Richard's kingdom, the French anticipated the English king would be distracted from his dalliance with the Bretons, restricting him to affairs on his own patch instead of meddling with those across the Channel. It was also a concern of the Beaujeu administration that another hostile adversary, Maximilian of Austria, continued to urge Richard to invade France, triggering a resumption of the Hundred Years War. It was for selfish reasons that the French ultimately supported Henry Tudor's pretensions for the English throne, and it is questionable if they ever truly believed he stood any hope of success.[38] Regardless of their motivations, however, it is patently true that Henry stood no chance of triumph without French backing; their supply of cash and men would prove the difference between any new assault and a repeat of 1483's failed invasion.

At an assembly on 4 May 1485 in Rouen, the fourteen-year-old King Charles again formally requested financial aid for Henry, reasoning that his cousin was the rightful king of England. It was the very public backing of his invasion that Henry had been seeking. The Norman estates were reminded that Henry had sought French aid to recover his realm and that money was required if they were to provide an army. The royal plea was somewhat successful, and Charles was able to approve a modest grant of 40,000 *livres tournois* to Henry, although this was to be paid quarterly with only 10,000 issued up front.[39] To further demonstrate his importance to the French government, during a procession to mark the feast of the Ascension on 12 May, Henry was afforded the rank of prince of England and placed ahead of everyone except for the king and the three princes of the blood royal, the dukes of Orléans, Bourbon, and Lorraine.[40]

Financial and military aid from the French government, however, quickly dwindled in the middle of June when news emerged from Brittany that the pro-English government of Pierre Landais had been overthrown, with its leader facing execution. With a Breton-backed English invasion of France no longer an immediate threat, interest in following through with Henry's own plans faded away.

Henry remained determined to launch his invasion. Noting the sudden apathy from the French, in desperation he turned to the mercantile trade to further fill his war chest. He was in Rouen as late as 29 June when he struck a deal with a Barfleur merchant named Denis Beton, later rewarded for his 'various services and kindnesses'.[41] The following day he was also mentioned, as the king of England, in the Rouen Cathedral accounts for making an offering in the chapel of the Virgin, possibly in thanksgiving for his recent upturn in good fortune.[42] A Scottish source compiled three decades later also reported that while dwelling in Rouen Henry stayed for a period in the house of a Scotsman named Patrick who, moved to compassion for his guest's cause, bestowed upon him a large part of his fortune.[43]

On 13 July, meanwhile, Henry also entered an arrangement with Philippe Lullier, a royal councillor and lord of Saint-Jean-le-Blanc, to borrow 30,000 *livres tournois*. As surety, Henry was to surrender any personal goods he had accumulated during his time in exile, as well as leaving behind the two Yorkist lords in his camp, the marquess of Dorset and John Bourchier, the young Baron FitzWarin. The choice of sureties was hardly a vote of confidence in Henry; in the event that he was unsuccessful and met his end on his enterprise, Dorset and FitzWarin represented Lullier's best chance of recouping his losses through ransom. Leaving behind the untrustworthy Dorset, however, likely did not greatly bother Henry, who preferred to focus on immediately investing the money to begin assembling the force that would either make him a king or die trying.[44]

The fleet was to be prepared at the mouth of the Seine, at either Honfleur on the southern bank or more likely Harfleur on the northern, and while the French king and his court returned to Paris, Henry remained in Normandy to personally oversee the arrangements. Jean Molinet claims that 1,800 men were first assembled at Honfleur, joined by another 1,800 just before departure.[45] This may have included about 1,500 discharged soldiers from the military base in nearby Pont de l'Arche, who according to Philippe de Commines were 'the loosest and most profligate persons' in Normandy.[46] In truth, any soldiers associated with Pont de l'Arche were almost certainly experienced and highly skilled military veterans, disciplined fighting men well prepared for the forthcoming campaign. This isn't to suggest, however, that the wider French contingent did not include considerable bands of ruffians, dangerous characters attracted by the promise of booty, bloodshed and adventure.

The person responsible for bringing together the French soldiers was the elderly but energetic Philippe de Crèvecoeur, lord of Esquerdes and recently appointed marshal of France.[47] Esquerdes first came to prominence in the service of Charles the Bold, Duke of Burgundy, earning recognition throughout the 1460s for his role in the Burgundians' conflict with Louis XI of France. In 1471 he held the Norman town of Abbeville against the French king, but after the death of Duke Charles in 1477 he transferred his services to his former foe Louis. Esquerdes was soon distinguishing himself once more in continental warfare, though this time under a French banner against the might of Maximilian of Austria. By 1485, Esquerdes was still regarded an 'extremely active commander' by Dominic Mancini despite being around seventy years old, and showed no sign of slowing down, particularly when offered the opportunity of fresh war with England.[48]

Esquerdes likely had little interest in Henry's personal aspirations, merely seeing him as a useful vessel through which to launch a raid on England, and perhaps even take back control of Calais. He had already fallen foul of the Yorkist regime in previous years, attacking English vessels in the Channel after his complaints for restitution for earlier wrongs done to him were ignored. When offered another opportunity to take out his frustrations, Esquerdes was grateful for the chance. In his funeral epitaph some years later, he was even credited with having been the 'arbiter' of Henry's fate.[49]

The wages of these French soldiers – archers, longbowmen, crossbowmen, halberdiers and pikemen – were provided by their king.[50] Another detachment fell under the command of Philibert de Chandée, a young nobleman from Savoy who appears to have developed a fast friendship with Henry. De Chandée, a 'wise and valiant soldier' according to Bernard André and one 'distinguished in his knowledge in the art of war', was connected to the maternal Savoyard relations of Charles VIII, and therefore claimed to be a kinsman of Henry.[51] The Tudor king would later reward Chandée well for his role in the invasion, an open acknowledgement of the captain's leadership during these tense and uncertain weeks.

The ships, meanwhile, were also provided by the French crown, with the fleet commanded by a vice-admiral named Guillaume de Casenove. It is likely that Casenove was recruited for the voyage alone, as before the end of the month he and his ships were recorded as leading an attack on Venetian galleys off the coast of south Portugal; whatever Henry encountered once he disembarked in Wales, there would be no retreat.[52] Bolstering the numbers were a contingent of Bretons Henry had accumulated during his lengthy stay in the duchy and a party of Scotsmen, perhaps even as many as 1,000. These were provided by the Franco-Scottish commander Bérault Stuart, lord of Aubigny, but captained in the field by Sir Alexander Bruce of Earlshall and John Coningham, leader of the Scottish archers in France.[53]

With around 500 English exiles forming the heart of the invasion force, in total it seems Henry left France with about 4,000–5,000 men under his overall command, though some put it as low as 2,000.[54] Made up of English exiles drawn from two sides of a bitter conflict, French mercenaries, and Breton and Scottish opportunists, it was hardly a cohesive, well-drilled unit, but it would have to do. Henry could only hope that the promised Welsh support on the other side of the water would materialise, and that at least one major English magnate would defect to his side before the moment of truth. Otherwise, he was to face the well-provisioned and rested army of Richard III at a significant numerical disadvantage.

Finally, on 1 August 1485, everything was ready.[55] Henry stepped onto the vessel that would take him towards either immortality or death. As he looked back towards the harbour, final preparations were being made, some last-minute loading of the ships, perhaps caskets of weapons or tuns of wine being rolled across shaky wooden planks. The frantic footsteps of men making their way onto the boats gradually calmed as the final soldiers boarded, aware that some of them would not be returning but at peace with their decision. The potential upside was too good to turn down.

As he turned his gaze towards the River Seine and the Channel beyond, Henry may have mused about his journey to this moment; his early years at Pembroke, learning about the father he never knew, the ancient Welsh blood in his veins. As a child, he may have been surprised to learn his half-uncle was the king of England and that he was also related to the kings of France. When the wars between the House of Lancaster, to whom both his mother and father were connected, and the Yorkists erupted, Henry may have recalled the devastation of discovering his grandfather Owen had been executed, his uncle Jasper had abandoned him, and he was to be sent to live far from the only home he had known.

From these earliest years, Henry's life had been turbulent, and at times he encountered moments of grave danger. At just fourteen years old, he had been pursued through Wales by sword-wielding enemies because of the modicum of royal blood in his veins, and forced to shelter underground. Henry had wasted fourteen years of his life exiled from his homeland, a prisoner of the Bretons and sought after by the English and French who desired to exploit him for their own ends. On at least three occasions he'd had to fight for his life, slipping from his enemies' grasp to make it to this very moment in time.

As Henry received word that the southern wind was soft and favourable, and the time had come to raise the anchors and leave his exile behind, he surely pondered what lay ahead in the event of success.[56] A reunion with his mother, perhaps, a coronation, even a marriage? Any fanciful notions of the future had to be dismissed at once. Focus needed to remain on the more pressing concern in front of him.

Such ruminating may have inspired a speech Henry is reputed to have given his men shortly before their departure. Though much of Bernard André's account of these moments may have originated from his own imagination and crafted with the benefit of hindsight to honour his master, it cannot be dismissed completely that the poet may have been present, able to later recall Henry's voice above the din of the final preparations. Dropping to his knees, Henry prayed aloud to God, calling for His blessing to grant him the power to defeat his enemy – if, of course, he was deemed deserving of such victory.

Turning to his 'valiant fellow soldiers', Henry remarked that many had lived away from their wives and children for too long, but bade them take heart for they stood on the verge of returning home to take 'what is rightfully ours'. The bloodthirsty 'tyrant' in England, the one who had 'defiled everything with blood', would be punished by their hands, so long as they placed their faith in God so that the 'few may conquer the many'.[57]

Nearly two years had passed since Henry last attempted to invade England, a stormy voyage that left his fleet scattered and his life in jeopardy. Now, Henry looked to the summer sky and said his prayers, hoping for a 'happy and prosperous' voyage.[58] He perhaps even beseeched Saint Armel for aid. At twenty-eight years old, with no hope of a pardon and a bleak future ahead of him, he had nothing left to lose. It was now or never.

17

The Fated Dragon

High above the wooden deck, the fierce and fiery red dragon stitched on a fabric of green and white grappled with the winds. The ships had been at sea for a week, pounded by the waves in every direction, when they finally started to sail towards land once more. Since departing Harfleur, it had been a nervy voyage through the English Channel before the fleet navigated around the tip of Cornwall and caught the winds that drew it towards the hulking mass of cliffs that marked out their destination. The nights were bitter, and the days were still chilly despite the rays that dazzled off the surface of the water. It may have been the height of summer, but out at sea, hardened men shivered in the breeze as they waited impatiently for this part of their adventure to be over.

Henry Tudor may not have found the journey comfortable, though he was mindful to maintain his regal bearing around his men. As had been made clear in recent months, he was not their equal anymore – he was their king, albeit one without a kingdom, which they now collectively sought to address. He remained, however, a mere mortal, and one who had experienced two tough experiences at sea in the past; first, as a fourteen-year-old boy in 1471, Henry had been forced to flee his homeland in the reverse direction to the one he was now undertaking, when a storm carried him to Brittany; and in 1483, just two years previously, he had again nearly lost his life in a tempest. It is highly likely these memories weighed heavily on his mind as he stared out at the waves that stretched before him.

Just before departing France, Henry probably called together his senior advisors to discuss their strategy. There had been at least a few messages from the British mainland for him to consider landing in Wales, the land of his birth and where he would likely enjoy at least some degree of support for his enterprise, both on account of his ancestry and because many communities retained deep Lancastrian sympathies. Men like the earl of Oxford had significant input, as did the French military commanders in the party, Philibert de Chandée and Guillaume de Casenove, and the Scots, Alexander Bruce of Earlshall and John Coningham. Other English members of Henry's contingent may also have been consulted. Above all, however, Henry is likely to have sought the advice of his beloved uncle, Jasper Tudor.

Around fifty-three years old in the summer of 1485, Jasper's famed vigour in his younger days had long deserted him, but as a man of great resource and experience he would have had ample thoughts on the task ahead. If he was indeed solicited, then Jasper surely championed Wales as the only viable gateway for invasion, particularly the south-west where he once held sway as earl of Pembroke. The Tudors had the promise of support there, they knew the terrain, and it was far from the centres of English power, allowing them to establish their position before encountering the expected Ricardian resistance.

And so it was, just before sunset on 7 August 1485, that the fleet approached St Anne's Head, a rugged red sandstone promontory guarding the northern entry into Milford Haven Waterway. As they navigated carefully into the first sheltered inlet, now known as Mill Bay, the larger ships probably anchored some distance off the coast, evading the treacherous rocks. Scanning the beach and the clifftops for signs of enemy action or the lighting of a beacon, the men slowly disembarked, perhaps using some of the smaller boats to ferry them onto the sand.[1] A mill had long stood above the bay, giving it its name, so it is possible that a bewildered miller or a member of his household was the first person on the British mainland aware that Henry Tudor and his army had landed.[2]

When Henry first stepped onto land after seven days at sea, he could not betray the swell of emotion inside him. For fourteen years he had been away from his home, his friends and his mother. He had left a frightened boy on a small barque carrying just a few souls, and returned a man at the head of an army numbering thousands. Taking in the scene around him and breathing deeply, Henry dropped to his knees, bent forward and, with a 'meek countenance and pure devotion', kissed the ground. He then began Psalm 43, uttering, 'Judge me o God, and distinguish my cause', imploring the lord to help him overcome what he and his followers professed to be godless tyranny. Making the sign of the cross and taking a deep breath, Henry opened his eyes and returned to his feet.[3]

The selection of Mill Bay for his momentous landing was an inspired choice. It may have been considered the unusual option when one considers that landing at Angle, on the southern tip of the waterway, would have meant the first town of note encountered by the invaders would be Pembroke, Henry's birthplace and Jasper's former seat. This, however, would have been the Tudors' expected route, and for that reason Richard III had placed one of his men, a gentleman usher named Richard Williams, in Pembroke with a garrison and plenty of supplies to withstand a siege.

Even if the Tudor army had been able to press on in this direction, much of South and South-East Wales was on high alert and packed with men loyal to the Yorkist king. Richard had been unsure of where Henry would choose to land, demonstrated by sending his closest confidante, Francis Lovell, to Hampshire to monitor all the ports on the English south coast. Henry, of course, had attempted to land in this region two years earlier, and Richard was made aware of a prophecy that foretold his enemy would land at a place called Milford. Just 20 miles east of Poole lay Milford-on-Sea. Wales, however, clearly made the most strategic sense for a Tudor landing, and this was where Richard concentrated his defensive efforts.[4]

As well as receiving custody of the lordship of Pembroke, Richard Williams had been handsomely rewarded across the previous year or so, appointed constable and steward of the castles of Haverfordwest, Tenby, Manorbier, Cilgerran, Penally and Llansteffan, giving him extensive power in the immediate vicinity.[5] Beyond, Sir James Tyrell held the lordships of Gower, Glamorgan and Newport, with Thomas Vaughan and his brothers well placed further north, having been granted the forfeited Buckingham estates around Brecon and competently marshalling the Wye and Usk valleys. Rhys ap Thomas was the most powerful figure in the Tywi Valley, controlling the routes through the heart of Carmarthenshire, but his loyalties were presently uncertain.[6] All fell under the command of the justiciar of South Wales, William Herbert, Earl of Huntingdon, the king's new son-in-law. The well-trodden path eastwards from Pembroke into the heart of southern England was prepared for the Tudors, and for good reason: Richard was confident Henry would meet an 'evil end' soon after landing.[7]

However, three promontories sheltered Mill Bay from the nearest settlement of note, Dale, which until the most recent winter had a small garrison keeping watch for potential sedition.[8] It is likely that this simple cove, just one of many around the jagged Pembrokeshire coast, was suggested by intelligence which had reached Henry before he left France. Perhaps word was sent from a messenger of Trahaearn ap Morgan of Kidwelly, or even Rhys ap Thomas, alerting them to stay away from Pembroke. At Mill Bay, Henry and his men were able to unload their equipment without detection, avoiding an awkward skirmish from a position of tactical disadvantage. Going northward may have been the more taxing option, but experience had taught Henry to always take the cautious step first, particularly when two years earlier he had nearly come ashore at Poole and straight into the arms of Richard's henchmen.

Once everything was ready, Henry turned to his men, and perhaps delivered a speech intended to rouse their spirits for the arduous journey they were about to embark upon while tersely commanding them to maintain discipline at every step. Richard had warned in previous months that Henry's army would inflict great terrors on the people of Wales and England, and it was imperative if they were to be welcomed that the soldiers' kept their hands to themselves and their swords sheathed.[9] It is perhaps to Henry's credit as a commander that no word of his army's indiscipline was recorded, with each unit aware of their responsibilities for the weeks ahead.

Henry also took this opportunity to knight eight of his men, trusted soldiers he expected to bear some responsibility in the coming weeks. Among the men honoured were Edward Courtenay, Philibert de Chandée, John Cheyne, Edward Poynings, John Fortescue, James Blount and his mother's half-brother John Welles. Personally significant was the knighting of David Owen, the illegitimate son of Owen Tudor and half-brother to Jasper Tudor. It is unclear if David was waiting for his kinsmen at Mill Bay or if, as is more likely, he had crossed to the exiled court previously, a touching reunion having occurred between the two surviving sons of Owen and his sole grandson. David would go on to bear his father's coat of arms, the shield of three helms once associated with Ednyfed Fychan.[10] Henry's mother, meanwhile, later marked this momentous day in her own Book of Hours, noting that 7 August 1485 was the day her son 'landed at Milford Haven'.[11] Regardless of the political ramifications, this was a moment of huge personal significance for the family.

Following the example of kings of England dating back to his ancestor Edward III, Henry commanded his men to follow him in the name of the Lord and St George.[12] Privately, he may also have sought the guidance of St Armel and, considering the location, St David. Together, Henry and his army began the steep climb from the beach, winding their way up the coast towards the dim light in the distance that signified the village of Dale. Most, nearly all, of Henry's army was not Welsh and had never been to this part of the world. They knew not what awaited them and had to rely on their leader's word that support would materialise once they started their march.

The most informed reporter of what followed across the next fortnight is Polydore Vergil.[13] Vergil started writing his account of English history, including the reign of Richard III, during the time of Henry VII, which has exposed him to accusations of bias towards his Tudor employer. Nevertheless, though crafted two decades after the fact, Vergil was able to draw much of his information from informed friends who were close to the early Tudor regime, men like Christopher Urswick, Reginald Bray and Richard Fox. His account of the march is astonishingly concise, and detailed in terms of places, names and dates. Vergil's general veracity may be doubted by detractors who question whether he merely parroted a

Tudor-sponsored narrative, but nobody provides anywhere near as much insight into these weeks in mid-August 1485 as the man from Urbino.

Dale Castle was found to be abandoned, so on the evening of the landing Henry and his army rested without having to loose an arrow. At daybreak, after wiping the sleep from their eyes, taking a drink and packing up their few belongings, the soldiers started heading inland. They were conscious that their arrival would soon be reported if it hadn't already, and there was little time to waste. After 12 miles, they reached the first potential obstacle in their path, the town of Haverfordwest. Rather than offering any resistance, however, the people of the town welcomed the army 'with great goodwill', though whether through genuine support or fear of being sacked is unknowable. The presence of Jasper, who had been earl of Pembroke between 1452 and 1461 and again between 1470 and 1471, may have helped.[14]

It was while they were at Haverfordwest that they were told Rhys ap Thomas and John Savage, two men who had pledged their support a few weeks earlier, were now hesitating, 'clean contrary' to what they had promised.[15] In an early seventeenth-century family history written by one of Rhys's descendants, it was claimed that he had been present for Henry's landing, though there is no contemporary evidence for this. Nevertheless, Richard III may have had some doubts about his loyalty, for according to the same account the king had requested Rhys send his son Gruffydd ap Rhys to court as a hostage, similar tactics to that he employed with Lord Stanley. Rhys refused to part with his son, citing his young age, but did swear an oath of fidelity to Richard, one which likely troubled his mind when the time came to break it.[16] That his father and uncle had fought for Jasper at Mortimer's Cross, however, strongly indicates that Rhys's instinct was to side with the Tudors. Again, like the Stanleys, timing was clearly of utmost importance – a matter of life and death even.

Savage, meanwhile, had been arrested in Pembroke three months earlier; though he was released, his card was marked. Both, then, were hampered by self-interest from hurrying to Henry's side, a bitter blow to the invaders who had counted on their support from the moment they had first stepped onto Welsh soil.[17] More welcome news, however, was the arrival of Arnold Butler of Coedcanlas. A 'valiant man', Butler brought with him a contingent of soldiers from Pembroke, who now begged forgiveness for past offences done to their earl, Jasper, while pledging their allegiance forthwith to Henry, born in their town.[18] It was a much-needed boost for morale.

The following day, during a refreshment break just 5 miles into their march, Henry's army was spooked when word spread through the ranks that a considerable host under the command of Walter Herbert was approaching, and that an assault seemed imminent. As

positioning himself as the Son of Prophecy. Only he could deliver them from their misery. One wonders how much this posturing was influenced not only by the presence of his uncle Jasper, but the education he had received from William Herbert as a child at Raglan. It may have been politically prudent at this moment to exploit his Welshness, but that doesn't necessarily mean Henry was not also sincere in his desire to aid his countrymen where he could. He implored his target audience, then, to join him for the remainder of his march, raising whatever numbers they could muster from their local communities. If they failed to heed his words, however, and yield to his command, Henry promised they would rue their hesitancy. Neutrality would not be respected. As with most of his recent communication, Henry again adopted the regal style, beginning the letter 'By the king' and ending it with the royal signet. He was behaving as though he was already king, the present occupiers of power within England mere rebels to be crushed.

Pressing onwards, staying close to the coast so that escape was possible, on 11 August Henry reached the Llwyndafydd home of the poet Dafydd ab Ieuan. His stay here was later commemorated by the magnificent crafting of a silver horn, apparently gifted by Henry to Dafydd in appreciation for his hospitality. The exquisite instrument, known as the Hirlas Horn, was supported by Henry's two principal royal beasts, a dragon and a greyhound, with the rim adorned with Beaufort portcullises and a Tudor rose.[23] It was an heirloom cherished for centuries to come by Dafydd's descendants, the Vaughans of Golden Grove in Carmarthenshire, and proudly displayed to visitors, a symbol of the small role one of their number played in the Tudor accession. A faithful reproduction still exists, and remains in the possession of the barons of Penrhyn.[24] Another tradition states Henry also stayed, or at least visited, the home of Einion ap Dafydd Llwyd at Wern Newydd in the Llanarth parish, though what was discussed during such brief meetings can only be guessed at. As he would throughout his march, Henry was courting locally prominent figures to help spread his message throughout their communities, exploiting their deep knowledge and connections to open the path ahead of him.

The following day, 12 August, the army reached another historic town of note, Aberystwyth, and it may be that here they finally met some military resistance to their progress, however token. In his account, Vergil notes that some fortresses needed to be subdued en route, including a castle under royal jurisdiction, which must have been a reference to Aberystwyth.[25] The absentee constable was Walter Devereux, Lord Ferrers of Chartley, who had a lengthy history of conflict with the Tudors. Ferrers's father had been implicated in the death of Edmund Tudor in Carmarthen in 1456, and together with his brother-in-law William Herbert had robustly repressed Jasper Tudor's influence in the years thereafter.[26] Following Herbert's death it was Ferrers who represented his sister, Herbert's widow Anne, in discussions with Margaret Beaufort concerning Henry Tudor's guardianship.[27] Henry had, incidentally, even spent some time at Ferrers's seat of Weobley. Now, all these years later, the acrimonious Tudor–Ferrers dynamic erupted back into life at Aberystwyth. If Henry did encounter some opposition here – and considering Ferrers's strong devotion to the Yorkist cause it is likely his men put up some degree of resistance – it was swiftly overcome, for the march continued unhindered the next day.[28]

If they were to enter England, at some point during their 'rugged and indirect' trek north Henry's army needed to start heading eastwards, and this decision was made once they reached Machynlleth on 13 August.[29] This made some degree of sense. To head further north would mean navigating the extremely tough and complex terrain of Eryri, which even in the heat of summer could be a forbidding environment. By turning east at Machynlleth, there was still a taxing climb to be navigated, but after that the fertile plains of Shropshire would open before them, in the heart of which lay Shrewsbury, where the River Severn could be crossed.

Machynlleth represented the lowest crossing point of the Dyfi, and it was here Henry may have been shown some sights relating to events that occurred eighty years earlier. In 1404, his distant kinsman Owain Glyn Dŵr hosted his first Welsh parliament at Machynlleth, an assembly at which Henry's great-grandfather Maredudd ap Tudur may have been present alongside his brothers Rhys and Gwilym ap Tudur. Though Henry had no intention of pursuing Glyn Dŵr's vision for an independent Wales, one that featured a separate church, university and legal system, it may nonetheless have been of personal interest to him. It hardly hurt his credibility at this moment in time to be associated with Glyn Dŵr, rebel to the English crown he may have been. In 1404, Glyn Dŵr and the Tudur brothers had even leaned heavily on the support of the French, something Henry himself was now emulating. He, of course, sought a more favourable outcome.

Perhaps spurred on by tales of his warrior kinsmen, on 14 August Henry wrote another letter, this time addressed to a Shropshire knight of Welsh extraction named Roger Kynaston. This Kynaston was sounded out as he was safeguarding the estates of his nephew by marriage John Grey, Baron Grey of Powis, whose neutrality in the Marches was necessary if Henry and his army were to pass through his sphere of influence in coming days. The historic lordship of Powys that had succeeded the independent Welsh kingdom had been divided between two branches of the Charlton family after the death of Edward Charlton in 1421. The Powys estates were partitioned between two of Charlton's daughters; the eastern portion through which Henry Tudor now wished to travel was granted to Joan, who married Sir John Grey, while Arwystli and Cyfeiliog in the west were bestowed upon Joyce and her descendants.[30]

The great-grandson of Joan, Lord Powis was a member of Richard III's council, trusted enough by the king to have been given command of the unit of archers sent to Brittany the previous year. In the summer of 1485, however, Powis was absent from his ancestral dominions, so the decision over what to do about the Tudor invasion fell to Kynaston. As constable of Harlech Castle on the north-west coast, the fortress once loyal to Jasper but whose present garrison could yet pose an irritant to the Tudors, Kynaston wasn't without influence in his own right.

Warming to the style of kingship, Henry opened the letter 'By the King' but, in a tacit acknowledgement that his recipient was one of Richard's agents, astutely avoided any mention of his adversary's supposed abuses. In fact, Richard is not even mentioned. Henry instead focused on Lord Powis, referencing an apparent pledge of support that had previously been made between the men. It is not known when or how this occurred, but it could conceivably have happened when Powis was in Brittany between June and September 1484. Henry was in Brittany up until September 1484 when he fled into France. Back in August 1485, Kynaston was now commanded 'in all haste possible' to assemble his nephew's servants to come to Henry's aid and assistance. He was, however, warned sternly that if he failed to raise the Powis affinity he would incur Henry's 'grievest displeasure'. Kynaston's reaction is unknown, but his lack of presence on either side at Bosworth suggests he simply froze and let the matter pass him by.[31] He wasn't the only figure during these weeks to adopt a policy of non-involvement, maintaining a low profile and hoping the victor would not hold them to account.

Henry's journey through Powys could not have been timed better. Lord Powis's absence was clearly an advantage, but he was also unwittingly the beneficiary of another stroke of luck. When the Charlton estates had been divided, the western portion of Powys granted to Joyce was inherited by her son John Tiptoft, the cruel Yorkist lord created earl of Worcester in 1449 and executed in 1470 by the vengeful Lancastrians. Worcester's widow remarried a year after her husband's death, taking as her partner a certain William Stanley. Since the Tiptoft heir, Edward, was still a minor, for more than a decade Stanley had presided over his stepson's inheritance in Powys. When Henry Tudor reached Machynlleth, therefore, he was effectively already marching under Stanley jurisdiction, perhaps even protection. On 12 August, when Henry was at Aberystwyth, Edward Tiptoft died, having never reached his majority. If he had died a few weeks later, there is every likelihood Richard III would have been able to move men loyal to him into the region, blocking Henry's path. As it was, Henry was able to pass through the entirety of Powys, the very heart of Wales, without opposition.[32]

While at Machynlleth, Henry also sent messages to his mother, the Stanleys and Gilbert Talbot, informing them of his intention to head towards Shrewsbury, then onwards towards London if possible.[33] Moving on, Henry spent the night in Mathafarn with another Welshman of local repute, an esteemed seer named Dafydd Llwyd. Here, another later tradition suggests that Henry sought the judgement of the prophet for his cause, but Dafydd was uncertain how to advise him. Deferring to his wife, Dafydd was counselled to prophesise a great victory for Henry, for if he was successful the new king would bestow a reward upon him for his services; if Henry fell in the field, on the other hand, he clearly would not be returning to exact his vengeance on the seer anyway.[34]

From Machynlleth, the punishing push eastwards through the Dyfi, Twymyn and Banwy valleys began in earnest. At Dolarddyn, near Castell Caereinion, a grateful Henry was presented with a white horse, which he would ride for the remainder of the journey.[35] These were, however, some of the hardest days of the march, comprising a tough climb across Cefn Digoll, the Long Mountain, with its summit above 1,300 feet. With the effort mentally and physically taxing, it is probable that some of the men required regular encouragement to prevent morale dipping too low. It is in these moments that Henry proved himself a leader, galvanising his men and ensuring focus on their goal was maintained. Negativity in the ranks could be infectious if not addressed, particularly when it concerned matters of life and death.

It was during this section of the march, on a high ridge with England in sight below, that Henry gratefully welcomed with open arms the first large-scale defection from Richard III's side, one he had been anxiously awaiting. Beneath his intimidating black raven banner, Rhys ap Thomas appeared on the horizon, riding at the head of as many as 2,000 men, the flower of South-West Wales. This 'great band of soldiers' now stood before Henry, willing to place their lives at his disposal.[36] Despite later attempts by Rhys's descendants to place him at Mill Bay to welcome Henry ashore, the Welshman had remained aloof from his distant relation thus far, with Henry subsequently unsure of his intentions. Instead of heading towards Henry, Rhys had conducted his own steady trek north, starting near his estates in Llandeilo and passing through Brecon, Builth, Rhayader, Llanidloes and Montgomery. This inland route shadowed Henry's own journey, and could be explained if necessary to King Richard as a defensive manoeuvre to prevent the Tudor incursion into England. What is unclear, however, is if the point where Rhys's army finally crossed paths with Henry's marked a predetermined meeting place or if Rhys purposely cut him off to negotiate a deal.

On 16 August, Henry and Rhys met for the first time, exchanged pleasantries and spoke until a pact was struck. In the event of a Tudor victory, Rhys sought complete political dominance in South Wales, which

Henry agreed to honour. It is likely that Jasper Tudor played a leading role in such discussions. Considering his past prominence in the region during the 1450s as earl of Pembroke, it was expected he would be restored to his erstwhile position in the event his nephew became king. Jasper, however, may have been open to the idea of leaving the day-to-day governance of South Wales to Rhys, who, if courted wisely, could prove as useful a servant to the Tudors as his grandfather Gruffydd ap Nicholas had been before him.[37] Though unmentioned by Vergil, Walter Herbert may also have openly embraced his former childhood companion at this moment, or, like Roger Kynaston, reiterated his intention to pursue a policy of non-commitment.

Further raising Henry's spirits at this critical juncture was the arrival of a hardy host from Gwynedd, who journeyed south under the command of Rhys ap Maredudd, an affluent landowner from Golgynwal in the Conwy Valley. Known as Rhys Fawr, or Rhys the Mighty, his pledge of allegiance was the cause of much celebration among Henry's growing Welsh contingent. Rhys Fawr also brought with him fattened oxen and cattle, endearing him to the scores of tired and hungry Scots, English and French in the ranks.[38] Also arriving were Richard ap Hywel of Mostyn, Rhys ap Phillip, Owen Lloyd, David Glyn, Philip ap Rhys, Edward ap Ednyfed, Hywel ap Griffith, Richard Pole, Rheinallt Davy of Pennal, Robert Gethin of Snowdon, Edward Morgan of Aberffraw, William Eynon, William Griffith ap Robin, Rhys ap Llywelyn, and William Griffith of Penrhyn, the latter a descendant of Ednyfed Fychan and therefore another distant kinsman of Henry and Jasper Tudor.[39] At some point during the march, Henry was also joined by someone named David, a scion of the Seisyllt family of Herefordshire. A few generations later, the Seisyllts, under their anglicised name of Cecil, continued to serve the Tudors, albeit in much higher office.

It is not at all accurate to persist in the belief that Henry failed to gain significant Welsh support during his march through his native country. It is patently clear from the record he drew wide backing among his countrymen, and that at Long Mountain a very discernible Welsh touch had been added to his army.[40] George Owen of Henllys, a noted Pembrokeshire antiquarian writing during the reign of Elizabeth I, and admittedly with more than a hint of romanticism in his words, nevertheless has it correct when he observed that Henry 'drew the hearts of the Welshmen to him, as the lead stone does the iron'.[41]

There was, of course, good reason for this. Each Welsh person who observed this growing Tudor force passing through their community would have been drawn towards one of the three swallow-tailed standards that flew high above Henry at each step of his journey. Later described by Edward Hall as 'a red fiery dragon beaten upon white and green sarcenet', this was essentially a red dragon breathing fire on a soft white and green fabric.[42] In the hoist, nearest the flagpole, was the customary red cross of St George, which featured on every English noble's standard. Henry's flag may also have featured red roses, which he claimed signified the House of Lancaster, and a motto, likely *'dieu et mon droit'*, borne by most English kings since Edward III, as a conscious message of continuity.

The green and white had been adopted by Henry as his personal livery colours, in contrast to the blue and reddish-purple, or murrey, of Richard III, the blue and white of his Beaufort kin, or even the red and yellow of the earl of Oxford. From where Henry acquired these colours is unclear, but their connection with the Welsh does seem to date to at least 1346 and the French campaigns on which the sixteen-year-old Edward of Woodstock, Prince of Wales, distinguished himself and won great victories. During that campaign, which culminated in the famous triumph at Crécy, Prince Edward was ably supported by his Welsh levies, distinctively attired in short coats and hats of green and white. One of Henry's kinsmen, his great-granduncle, Goronwy ap Tudur, was noted by the poet Iolo Goch for handing out liveries 'of the finest green obtainable', which suggests by the back end of the fourteenth century these colours had become nationally significant for the Welsh.[43] This could be because of an earlier link with Llywelyn the Last; one poem suggests that the great prince of Gwynedd was able to draw on 200 men attired in green and white, later appropriated by Prince Edward, and subsequently the Tudors, for their own ends.[44]

It was the dragon, however, a fearsome mythical beast, that caught attention, a symbol so recognisable to the Welsh and traditionally associated with Cadwaladr ap Cadwallon, the mid-seventh-century king of Gwynedd whom Henry claimed as an ancestor. Dragons had long been used as heraldic symbols in Britain, having been particularly prominent in Roman military circles, with individual units of cohorts typically brandishing depictions of the beast upon a gilded staff. When the Romans withdrew in the fourth century, the dragon, for so long a symbol of power, was retained by the Romanised British populace, who integrated the beast into their own culture.[45]

Numerous British leaders were associated with the dragon in the following centuries, not least Cadwaladr, whom Henry now sought to emulate as a prophesied deliverer of his people. In his work *Historia Regum Britanniae*, written between 1120 and 1129 and hugely influential in popularising the Arthurian legend for a medieval audience, Geoffrey of Monmouth even linked the dragon with that mythical king, attributing to Arthur a golden dragon banner and noting that his father was Uther Pendragon, or Uther Head Dragon.[46]

Though Geoffrey's work glorifying the British race was unreliable, and its writer even prone to invention, its impact among a Welsh audience was clear. The mid-twelfth-century Welsh prince Owain Gwynedd adopted the dragon as one of his badges, as did later titans of Welsh history like Llywelyn ap Gruffudd and Owain Glyn Dŵr. The latter even raised a banner featuring a golden dragon on a white background when he began his revolt against English rule, and his seal depicted him with a dragon on his helmet. All may have been aware of an early Welsh prophecy which made passing reference to a national deliverer, 'the fated Dragon', who would be 'quick to rise' to liberate his people.[47]

Geoffrey's pseudohistorical account of British history also included the tale of a red dragon battling with a white dragon, which he took from the AD 829 work *Historia Brittonum*, often attributed to Nennius. The two warring dragons symbolised the eternal struggle between the Britons, or Welsh, and the Saxons, or English, and was further embellished in the thirteenth-century prose tale *Lludd and Llefelys*.[48] From the very emergence of the Welsh as a distinct people, the dragon, whether golden or red, was held up as a symbol of national defiance, an emblem of resistance that transcended the various Welsh kingdoms and even the individual.

In fact, this long-standing Welsh reverence for the dragon was noted by at least one English king. During his invasions of Gwynedd in 1245 and 1257, Henry III's army bore the flag of a red dragon breathing fire on both campaigns, appropriating the well-known symbol to broadcast his claim that he and he alone stood as the true successor of the old British kings. As evidenced by continued Welsh resistance to Plantagenet expansion, it didn't have the impact he hoped and was soon dropped.[49]

By the summer of 1485, then, dragons, and in particular the red dragon, were a widely acknowledged part of the Welsh consciousness, embraced as a national symbol and proudly borne by the greatest of Welsh leaders in battle. The dragon had also, in recent times, become associated with Jasper Tudor, regarded by some of the bards during the mid-fifteenth century as the last bastion of Welsh aspirations, at least until his nephew came of age and the focus shifted. In his elegy to Owen Tudor, and harking back to the work of Geoffrey of Monmouth and Nennius, the poet Robin Ddu addressed Owen's son Jasper and urged this red dragon to break the encirclement of their people by a disrespectful white dragon. Another poet, Deio ap Ieuan Du, who flourished during the lean years of Jasper's exile, hoped that '*y draig coch, ddyry cychwyn*' – the red dragon advances. Dafydd Llwyd had even prophesied that Jasper would father a son who was a dragon of the blood of Brutus, though, as time would tell, it was his nephew who would ultimately assume that mantle.[50]

To those who now beheld the fire-breathing dragon in all its defiant splendour, laid against a field of white and green, two separate symbols of Welsh identity had been shrewdly blended into a bold and inspiring spectacle. With the bards having set the groundwork for Henry's arrival, many of these watching Welshmen would have been well versed in his pedigree, and may even have been moved to join the throng of soldiers marching through their communities with intent. Led from the front by the red dragon, these Welshmen were less concerned with partaking in a decidedly English conflict between rival noble factions and more with restoring honour to a people who had long bristled under foreign rule. This was exactly what Henry had intended when he wrote his letters, his standard merely adding to his claim to be the rightful king of these islands, one whose legitimacy stretched back beyond the Norman advent in 1066 to Cadwaladr, Arthur and even Brutus.[51]

Henry's arrival in Wales was not wholly unexpected. For months, indeed years, before he finally resurfaced in his native Pembrokeshire, the Tudors had been implored to return by both their supporters and the zealous poets who championed their cause. These poets were not just the historians of their communities but guardians and preservers of Welsh literary, linguistic and genealogical tradition, sought out by the principal figures of the day to enhance their standing. Though prone to exaggeration, and even invention, in pursuit of their craft, they were nevertheless hugely influential in driving men's ambitions, as evidenced during Owain Glyn Dŵr's revolt when ancient prophecies seamlessly intertwined with contemporary politics to help fuel his crusade.[52]

In the immediate aftermath of Glyn Dŵr's defeat, life had proven tough for the Welsh, handcuffed by a series of punitive laws passed in 1401 which were affirmed by parliaments held in 1431, 1433 and 1447. Absentee lordship had caused a gradual decline in law and order, and a sense of bitterness with little recourse took hold in many Welsh communities. Writing in these lean years after the collapse of the revolt, Siôn Cent captured some of this Welsh disenchantment when he noted that, hour after hour and day after day, he waited to see Wales returned to its former greatness. Each verse was concluded with the quietly optimistic line, 'My hope lies in what is to come.' Guto'r Glyn, meanwhile, cried out more dramatically, 'Woe unto us, born into slavery.'[53]

Some Welsh families, the *uchelwyr*, or landowning class, had been able to carve out a modest existence for themselves in this fifteenth-century power vacuum, even if they were constrained by the Penal Laws and unable to obtain the high offices available only to Englishmen. Some were able to circumvent this by petitioning parliament for English citizenship, but high-flying Welshmen like William Herbert remained a rarity. As the fifteenth century progressed, however, the Welsh economy underwent a revival that enabled the *uchelwyr*, at least, to enjoy the trappings of modest prosperity, one they used to endow a prolific new generation of poets and musicians.

Though their masters may have been content to survive under the English system, the poets' ambitions knew no limit, and merely subsisting was not enough. Many were drawn to the art of *canu darogan*, or prophetic poetry, and desperately sought a new messiah who would reveal himself and free the Welsh from their shackles. Their persuasive works of divination, composed to be committed to memory and easily spread around different communities, helped channel a reawakening of national pride, and fuelled a belief that a descendant of Brutus would soon rise to restore the Welsh to supremacy.[54] Glyn Dŵr, it was reasoned, had clearly not been the foretold liberator.

Though not overly concerned with the dynastic conflict between Lancaster or York, the poets found the Wars of the Roses to be fertile ground in the search for their hero who would advance Welsh interests whatever the outcome. Indeed, around 200 relevant poems, attributed to nearly fifty poets, are known to exist, with the likelihood that many more did not survive.[55] The chief practitioners were Lewis Glyn Cothi of Carmarthenshire, Guto'r Glyn of Powys, Robin Ddu of Anglesey, and the most prolific, Dafydd Llwyd of Mathafarn, though every community had their poet of choice. Two men lauded as potential saviours of the Welsh by these bards of divination were 'the Constantine of Carmarthen' Gruffydd ap Nicholas and 'the guardian of Gwent' William Herbert, and in one case even the distantly Welsh-blooded Edward IV was implored to avenge the wrongs of Wales, being a descendant of Llywelyn the Great through the Mortimer bloodline.[56] It was the Tudors, however, who came to attract considerable interest as the century progressed, and, despite their struggles, this was for good reason.

When Jasper and Edmund Tudor were ennobled in 1452, they were the first Welsh members elevated into the English peerage, and this drew comment. The Gwynedd poet Dafydd Nanmor, for example, noted the brothers' hugely respected patrilineal descent, a lineage that stretched back beyond the Tudurs of Anglesey to Ednyfed Fychan, and further still to revered princes like the Lord Rhys, Hywel Dda and Rhodri Mawr. More recently, of course, they were kinsmen of Glyn Dŵr. In Nanmor's estimations, they were well placed to be the successors of Llywelyn the Last, and would surely defend the honour of their people.[57]

Their maternal connection to the House of Lancaster, as half-brothers of the English king Henry VI, only served to further excite the Welsh poets. When Henry Tudor was born in 1457, his English royal descent from his mother Margaret Beaufort was likewise acknowledged, stirring the most hopeful of vaticinators. When Henry was barely one year old, Nanmor was already suggesting he would be the one to free the Welsh from bondage by obtaining the kingship in old age. Considering the number of candidates in the line of succession at the time, before the bloodletting of the Wars of the Roses had begun in earnest, this seems an almost absurdly premature prediction.[58] After Owen Tudor's execution in 1461, the Glamorgan bard Ieuan ap Gethin even warned, knowingly, that the Welsh should 'look for Jasper and Henry' in future.[59]

Henry himself likely became personally acquainted with the bardic tradition during his decade at Raglan Castle under the guardianship of William Herbert, the greatest benefactor of Welsh culture in the 1460s. Dafydd Llwyd, in fact, addresses Henry during one of his poems to Herbert, counselling his patron to take care of the 'young swallow' under his protection, and to marry the boy to one of his daughters, for he will grow into a 'great eagle'. It is known from Herbert's later will that this is precisely what he intended to do, though it is interesting once more that even as a boy Henry's potential was being discussed.[60]

It was the regime change of 1483, however, that provoked the large-scale outpouring of support for Henry in Welsh bardic circles. When Henry emerged as a prospective candidate for the English crown, the prospect of a Welsh-born, Welsh-raised and Welsh-blooded noble seated upon the throne in London was too irresistible to ignore. Recognised as a descendant of the great Cadwaladr, Henry was implored by one poet to return home at once and claim the land of his grandfather Owen, freeing his people from their severe bondage.[61] To Dafydd Llwyd, Henry's uncle Jasper should be credited for raising a dragon, a leader of the blood of Brutus, that mythical common ancestor of the British nation, who would prove 'the hope of our race'. Henry was, after all, not just a 'high-born Briton' but the 'greatest of sires who will gild all with solid gold' and herald the dawn of a 'long golden summer'.[62]

Another poet, Robin Ddu, a personal acquaintance of Owen and Jasper Tudor, also spoke out in favour of Henry's return. Speaking on behalf of the Welsh, Robin impatiently declared 'we are waiting for him to show', observing that Henry's name was carried down from the mountains like a 'two-edged sword' that would cause the Thames to run red with blood. Gruffydd ap Dafydd Fychan, meanwhile, looked longingly across the sea to the 'youth from Brittany' who would overcome the Saxons and return one of British lineage to the throne.[63]

As the anticipated invasion neared, the relentless Dafydd Llwyd, soon to welcome Henry to his home at Mathafarn during the march, even composed a potent ode to St David, invoking the support of the Welsh patron saint for the campaign ahead. After expressing his desire to see Gwynedd avenged on the field of battle, likely before September, he hoped to see on Henry's side 'all of our race, every district, everybody for David'.[64] The deliverance of the Welsh people from their misery lay, in the bard's estimations at least, in Henry's armoured hand.

One interesting feature of these prognostic poems was that they were often composed in allegory, their subjects typically represented in animal form. Sometimes this simply alluded to their personal badges; for example, Rhys ap Thomas was typically associated with the raven and Richard III with the boar, though often their employment was more abstruse. The Tudors were often represented by black bulls as opposed to the more obvious red dragon or greyhound that Henry later preferred to use. Glyn Cothi, for example, deeply lamented Jasper's time in exile, wailing, 'When wilt thou, Black Bull, come to land; how long shall we wait?', while Robin Ddu referred to Henry as the 'little bull'. To others, he was 'a great bull' and even 'the bull of Gwynedd'. The bull was a symbol of great strength and virility and likely alluded to the family's historic standing in North Wales, the foundations of which were established by the renowned Ednyfed Fychan. Now, this 'bull with the valiant horns' would wage great war on his enemy, not stopping until the 'boar is cold'.[65] Elsewhere, Henry was routinely depicted as a swallow, an eagle and a stag.[66]

Though Henry's ambitions were far more prosaic than the bards', merely seeking to win the English crown for himself and his family rather than conclude an ancient race war, he nevertheless owed a considerable debt to those who prepared his arrival with their rhymes. Wordplay alone may not have been the only reason Henry attracted support on his march through the heart of Wales, with more practical day-to-day concerns naturally taking precedence over the art of divination, but the poets helped make their Tudor subject a more compelling proposition than he had been without their input. Their work was intended to be consumed by the most influential leaders in Welsh society, the *uchelwyr*, those who commanded considerable retinues and could be swayed to the Tudor banner. As shown by those who journeyed to Long Mountain at the head of their households, the bards did their job, and Henry's arrival in Wales was laden with great messianic significance that he exploited well.

A night of celebration likely followed the arrival of the two Rhyses, and no doubt many a song was sung. If any of the poets were present, perhaps they performed their work before the man they had so passionately championed, although careful not to insult the Englishmen present by talking of the Thames running red with Saxon blood. For now, political cooperation to unseat the tyrant was paramount.

On the morning of 17 August 1485, the massive army started descending the ridge towards Shrewsbury, their legs grateful for the steady decline. Aside from perhaps a few minor episodes, Henry left Wales behind having not been challenged, other than by the terrain, and was said by Vergil to be 'in good hope' at this stage of his march.[67] His objective when he landed at Mill Bay, having laid the groundwork through his letters while in France, was to secure the support of influential Welshmen, and with men like Arnold Butler, Rhys Fawr ap Maredudd and Rhys ap Thomas by his side, his journey through the land of his fathers had been an unmitigated success. He had unquestionably recruited, and recruited well.

Now stood on the banks of the Severn, with Shrewsbury's formidable Welsh Gate rising high before them on the northern side of St George's Bridge, the first tangible obstacle to Henry's progress was upon him. From the west, Shrewsbury was, and had long been, the fortified gateway into England, a prosperous market town nestled tightly upon a hill within a meander of the Severn. As Henry approached, foreriders were sent ahead to command the town's senior bailiff, Thomas Mytton, to stand down the men that patrolled the ramparts and raise the portcullis. The stout Mytton, however, was a long-term Yorkist and had already resolved to remain loyal to Richard III, claiming defiantly that he knew the earl of Richmond to be no king. He had, in fact, been closely involved in the arrest of the duke of Buckingham two years previously, handing him over to the king's men to stand trial. Mytton was very much Richard's man.[68]

The bailiff's nervousness was understandable. The army that stood on the other side of the river was vast, boasting perhaps as many as 7,000 men. Of particular concern to the English townsmen was the presence of armed French, Welsh and Scottish soldiers, men they had been raised from childhood to distrust and even detest. The message that came back from Mytton was that if Henry was to enter his town it would need to be over his belly – that is, Mytton would have to be dead.[69]

To bypass Shrewsbury risked wasting time and could be viewed as an embarrassing retreat by someone with pretensions of becoming king of all England. Henry ordered his men to set up camp for the night on Forton Heath, while he spent the night at the house of one Hugh Forton. The following morning, further messages were sent to Mytton assuring him that if he admitted the army it would merely pass straight through the town, harming no one and damaging nothing. Henry had no quarrel with the Salopians, he merely wished to continue onwards in his quest for the crown.[70] It was the arrival of a Stanley retainer, however, that proved decisive in the bailiffs ultimately standing down. Rowland Warburton was sent to Shrewsbury by William Stanley, whose principal estates were just 30 miles north at Holt. After exchanging words, the bailiffs reluctantly raised the portcullis.[71]

Before letting Henry's army into his town, however, Mytton had one request. Having promised his king that nobody would enter Shrewsbury unless it was over his body, Mytton lay on the ground with his belly up. Henry dutifully stepped over the prone bailiff, theatrically absolving him of his oath to Richard III, before pressing on. Henry proved good as his word, and his army passed through the town almost without incident, with the local populace even wishing him well. Another local tradition, first recorded by the noted antiquary Sir William Dugdale in 1663, suggests he briefly stayed in a house on the Wyle Cop, today named Henry Tudor House in his honour, perhaps taking refreshments with the town elders before continuing onwards as promised.[72]

With Shrewsbury at his rear, England now opened before Henry. To this point, his army had marched for eleven days, covering more than 150 miles. The most resistance they had met was at Shrewsbury, and perhaps a minor incident at Aberystwyth, both of which were overcome with little if any bloodshed. Henry had arrived in Wales on the back of passionate support from the bards, who lauded him as the fulfiller of ancient prophecies, raised to wrest the crown back from the English and to restore his race to their former state of prosperity. He was the chosen one: *y Mab Darogan*, the Son of Prophecy. As Henry crossed into England, the hopes of the poets were about to be put to the test.

18

Invincible Giants

On 18 August 1485, Henry Tudor and his army reached the small Shropshire settlement of Newport. Further good news awaited them. As the camp was being set up for the night, scouts alerted Henry to the arrival of Gilbert Talbot, to whom Henry had written earlier in his march. This was not an insignificant development.

Talbot was a younger son of John Talbot, the earl of Shrewsbury who was killed fighting for the Lancastrians at the battle of Northampton in 1460. Though like many families the Talbots had been reconciled to the Yorkist regime of Edward IV, Gilbert clearly had reservations about extending his loyalty to Richard III, and brought with him to the Tudor cause a significant household of 500 men.[1] He was also the first Englishman of note to declare for Henry since the landing at Mill Bay eleven days earlier.

Another hugely welcome defection at this moment was that of Richard Corbet, who arrived at Henry's camp at the head of another 800 men. Corbet had been the man responsible for protecting Henry as a twelve-year-old after William Herbert's execution, and their reunion was tinged with personal significance. Corbet now swore his allegiance to his former charge, and pledged to be Henry's 'true and faithful subject and liegeman' in his 'rightwise quarrel'.[2] Of greater immediate consequence, however, was that Corbet was a stepson of William Stanley, and likely did not act without his stepfather's knowledge. Other men who flocked to Henry's standard at this time, bringing with them scores of fighting men, were Roger Acton of Shropshire, Thomas Croft of Herefordshire, John Hanley of Worcestershire and Robert Pointz of Gloucestershire, all English knights and influential members of the gentry in their respective counties. Some had even been lifelong Yorkists; Hanley, for example, had been in the employ of the duke of Clarence, and Croft was a childhood companion of Edward IV.[3]

After another night's rest, Henry and his bulging army moved on, this time covering the 14 miles to Stafford for his most momentous meeting of the march yet. It was here that he finally met his step-uncle, William Stanley, exchanging pleasantries before settling down to an evening of business. A devoted Yorkist for most of his career, Stanley was likely looked upon with unease by the Lancastrian veterans in Henry's circle, most notably his uncle Jasper and the earl of Oxford, though any disquiet needed to be suppressed in favour of pragmatism. If they were to stand any hope of victory, they needed the Stanleys.[4]

What words passed between Henry and William Stanley are unknown, but based on subsequent events the latter seems to have warned that the king was busily assembling his army at Nottingham and ready to embark on campaign. William surely discussed his brother Thomas's predicament, revealing that the Stanley position was delicate as his nephew Lord Strange remained in the king's custody. If they favoured Henry and showed their hand too soon, Strange would be executed. In fact, Strange had already been caught trying to escape Richard's court, and when interrogated had revealed that his uncle William and cousin John Savage had indeed gone over to Henry's side. Pleading for mercy, Strange implored Richard to give him the opportunity to persuade his father to remain loyal.[5] Lord Stanley's dilemma only deepened, and for the moment he remained openly uncommitted to either side.

Nevertheless, William, now associating with the rebels more freely, was able to advise his step-nephew that Lord Stanley was on the move, having left his seat of Lathom four days earlier with a host numbering several thousand. Though just a baron, Stanley's influence across the north-west of England could be favourably compared to that of the greatest magnates in the realm, and he was able to draw on vast military resources. He also set off with his wife Margaret's pleas to aid her son ringing in his ears, though of course he had his own self-interest to consider. Before William returned to his own sizeable host, he counselled the invaders to turn south as soon as possible and follow the ancient Roman route Watling Street straight to the capital before Richard could cut him off.[6]

The following morning, Henry and his army headed south-east out of Stafford, covering about 17 miles before they reached the city walls of Lichfield, where they bedded down for the night. Very early the next morning, 20 August, a refreshed Henry entered the town, and was 'honourably received' by the people, who were grateful for the absence of disorder and violence. There was no time to waste, however, and onwards they pushed, picking up Watling Street and heading towards Tamworth. Henry had learned upon reaching Lichfield that Lord Stanley had been there just three days earlier, and was now camped somewhere near Atherstone. His cautious stepfather, however, was still unwilling to combine their forces. Despite his unease at this situation, Henry had little choice but to press ahead.[7]

At Tamworth, knights Thomas Bourchier and Walter Hungerford of Farleigh found their way to Henry's side, as did John Savage, Brian Sanford, Simon Digby and others, each rejecting Richard's kingship and pledging their allegiance to the invader. Hungerford was the namesake great-grandson of the Baron Hungerford in whose household Henry's grandfather Owen Tudor once briefly served, a clear indication of the extraordinary revolution of the Tudor family's wheel of fortune.[8] Within two generations, they had emerged from servants to the gentry to contenders for the crown.

Polydore Vergil, who partly composed his account from oral testimony provided by those present on the campaign, records a curious moment on the evening of 20 August when Henry became separated from his main host. Despite his 'noble courage', Henry was overwhelmed by a 'great fear' that the Stanleys would forsake him. Gathering a small band of trusted bodyguards, he sought some space away from his army, a moment of solitude to consider his options. Perhaps at this late stage he even entertained notions of escape. While absentmindedly wandering, however, Henry and his minders lost their bearings, and once night fell upon them they couldn't find their way back to the camp. There was genuine concern they would fall into the hands of Richard's foreriders, who were scouting the area.

When Henry's soldiers woke in the morning to find their leader absent, many started to panic, worrying they had been deserted. Before disorder spread through the ranks, however, Henry made a timely reappearance, loudly proclaiming that the purpose of his brief withdrawal had been to receive 'some good news' from his 'secret friends'. Morale was duly restored, and Henry called to his side his closest advisors to continue laying out their strategy. No more was said about this odd episode in which Henry may have briefly lost his nerve.[9]

Later that morning, the Tudor army left Tamworth and continued down Watling Street until they arrived at Atherstone, where the order was passed down to the captains to halt their men. Here, Henry once more met privately with William Stanley. This time, he was also introduced to Lord Stanley, the stepfather he didn't know. One of the first things Henry likely enquired about was the welfare of his mother, Lady Margaret, with whom he hoped to be reunited in the coming weeks should Lord Stanley's military aid be forthcoming. He had not seen his mother since the autumn of 1470, an absence of some fifteen years. Condolences were also likely expressed regarding Strange's ongoing captivity. Turning towards the matter at hand, Henry attempted to prise solid assurances from the Stanleys that they would stand with him in battle; according to Vergil, writing with the benefit of hindsight, the brothers supposedly assuaged Henry's fears by taking his hand and pledging themselves to him, a moment of 'great joy' to those present.[10]

That evening, Henry retreated a mile or so to the vicinity of Merevale Abbey, in and around the grounds of which his men set up camp for the night, 'greatly replenished' with 'good hope'.[11] The abbey had been founded on 2 October 1148, ironically the birthday of Richard III, and settled with a small community of Cistercian monks. Among its great treasures was the early fourteenth-century Jesse Window, a representation of Jesus's family tree that according to the Book of Isaiah began with Jesse, father of King David and a descendant of Abraham. Previous kings of England to visit Merevale included Henry's lauded ancestors Edward I and Edward III, and during quiet contemplation he hoped to emulate their martial feats.[12] Great kings won great victories in the field, after all.

Later payments suggest that Henry's army caused considerable damage to local agriculture during its brief sojourn in the Merevale area. After three weeks on the move, provisions would have been in short supply, and it seems that at this juncture, knowing that the eve of battle was upon them, the Tudor army sought fresh resources by casting its net wide across the locality. Henry would later reimburse John Fox, a parson of Witherly, and John Atherson £12 2s because their profitable corns and grains were destroyed, while payments were also made to the nearby villages of Fenny Drayton, Atherstone, Mancetter and Atterton. The abbot of Merevale, meanwhile, was also compensated because of the ruin caused to the abbey's pastures.[13] This series of payments clearly places Henry's forces in a range of fields just outside the ancient town of Atherstone, possibly a little north towards Sheepy, with its headquarters at the abbey.[14]

In the camp, thoughts returned to the Stanleys. Together, the brothers commanded an army numbering around 5,000 to 6,000 soldiers – with their backing, the scales would be balanced. It was concerning to Henry they had resisted combining their forces with his, but he could only trust that they could be relied upon when the crucial moment came. As he wandered around the camp, Henry found tired men, but high spirits despite the spectre of war that hung over them all. In just fourteen days, most of the army had marched 220 miles, an extraordinary feat even discounting the week's sea voyage that preceded it. A medieval army could be expected to march up to 15 miles a day, though Edward IV once managed to push his men for 35 miles in one day on the way to Tewkesbury. Carrying their own weapons and equipment, including a tent, a basin, a knife and cup, clothing, plus any other assorted tools they could carry on their person, 15 miles daily for a fortnight was tough going, particularly across challenging terrain without a proper break. For his sake and theirs, Henry hoped their energy reserves were not completely depleted when it mattered.

As Henry made his final preparations, so too did Richard III. Having decamped to Nottingham to await the expected invasion, news of Henry's landing was brought to the king by Richard Williams, his man in Pembroke, on 11 August. According to one observer, Richard 'rejoiced' at the news, for as an experienced military man on home turf he was confident that he would 'triumph with ease' over his contemptible enemies. Richard sprang into action, dictating letters 'of the greatest severity' to his supporters, summoning them to his side so they could stand against the rebels who intended 'our utter destruction'.[15] His mood soon turned into a 'fervent rage', however, when it became known Henry had passed through Shrewsbury without any struggle, the king lamenting the falsehoods of those who had broken their promises.[16] Bernard André later wrote that Richard furiously ranted that he hoped Henry could be brought to him alive, so that 'I may slaughter him, cut his throat, or slay him with my own hands'.[17] While these specific words were the invention of André, such aggrieved sentiments were not beyond an indignant king stung by the betrayal of those like Rhys ap Thomas, William Stanley and Gilbert Talbot.

When the king's scouts reported the rebel position to be somewhere near Atherstone, Richard decided to cut them off before they could continue down Watling Street, forcing a battle. At the head of a royal army considered somewhat hyperbolically by the Crowland chronicler to be 'greater than had ever been seen before in England', Richard and his men followed some ancient tracks until they came to rest in the vicinity of Sutton Cheney.[18] Part of the camp was established upon the nearby Ambion Hill, the end of a ridge which provided commanding and clear views westward across the local landscape. In the distance, Richard and his commanders could not only see the church spire of St Margaret's in Stoke, or perhaps the few houses that comprised the villages of Dadlington, Mancetter and Atherstone, but plumes of smoke that spiralled from dozens of flickering campfires. His enemy was near, only separated from him by wide plains and fenland, part of which was marshland.[19]

Richard's frustration that he would be forced to defend his crown in battle may have been the cause of a disturbed sleep that night. It was reported the king had seen 'dreadful visions' throughout the night, finding himself surrounded by a 'multitude of demons'. In Vergil's judgement, these dreams were sure evidence of Richard's guilty conscience for his recent 'heinous offences'. In the morning, having risen so early and with a countenance more 'livid and ghastly' than usual, his chaplains were unprepared for Mass and there was much scurrying around the camp as the king impatiently waited.[20]

A couple of miles away, Henry Tudor was also stirring, having fallen into a deep sleep if Vergil is to be believed. As he broke his fast that morning, the twenty-second day of August in the year 1485, Henry called together his principal advisors one final time. The battle strategy was finalised, with each commander clear what his role was to be. If the subject wasn't raised, the continued remoteness of the Stanleys no doubt lingered over the group. A messenger was sent to Lord Stanley requesting one more time that he join his forces with Henry's, but the response was negative. Left 'no little vexed' by the Stanley dithering, Henry was 'somewhat appalled' but 'of necessity' had little choice than to order his men to get ready.[21] As his armour was prepared in front of him, he knew there was no going back. Fate had brought him to this moment. Would God now judge in his favour, as the Welsh bards had foretold?

The Battle of Bosworth Field, as it became known to later generations, though known contemporaneously as Redemore or Dadlington Field, changed the face of England and Wales forever. The clash triggered a series of events that would lay the foundations for the eventual formation of a new Britain under the victor's descendants. More than 500 years later, military historians and archaeologists continue to heatedly debate how the battle unfolded and where the action played out. Recent discoveries in the first two decades of the twenty-first century have greatly added to our understanding of one the most pivotal events in the history of these islands, and the expectation is that more will be uncovered by future investigations. The principal facts, however, appear to be broadly accepted.[22]

On that early August afternoon in 1485, two armies gathered under the blue sky on a Leicestershire plain, roughly equidistant between the villages of Fenny Drayton, Dadlington, Stoke Golding, Upton and Shenton.[23] Each man prayed he would live to see one more sunset. All knew that, by the afternoon, hundreds, possibly thousands, would be slaughtered in the most horrific ways imaginable. Some were experienced military men who knew what to expect over the next few hours, battle-hardened soldiers with muscular arms and calloused hands that seemed to be 'made of iron'.[24] Others anxiously awaited their first taste of warfare. As the first battle of the Wars of the Roses in which the two claimants to the throne were present in the field, the day was sure to be momentous whatever the outcome.

As the battle drew near, a cursory glance around the field revealed units of men bearing weapons designed to destroy the human body – swords, arrows, daggers, poleaxes, bills, halberds, swords of varying lengths and styles, and even handguns. Richard also brought a collection of cannon to the field, defensive weapons often positioned at the flanks, and which could hurtle cannonballs horizontally across the terrain so that they bounced through whatever, or whoever, had the misfortune to be in their way.[25]

Most of the soldiers were not adequately attired to withstand the blows soon to be inflicted upon them. When visiting England in 1483, the Italian Dominic Mancini had observed Richard's troops up close and reported upon his finds. Full plate armour fashioned from well-tempered steel was the preserve of the 'better sort', Mancini noted, with only the leading noblemen able to afford the high costs associated with the best protection. Henry had been able to obtain such a suit before leaving France, and was one of those covered from head to toe in steel. Some of the troops had been able to obtain breastplates or brigandines, essentially a front-opening vest made from small armour plates, but most were restricted to the padded jack, a jacket comprising layers of canvas stuffed with wool or straw. The softer the stuffing, the more defence it provided in softening blows, though in close-combat scenarios its wearer was vulnerable. Over this, some wore lengthy tunics or sashes identifying the lord or town to which they belonged; Richard's troops, for example, wore his colours of murrey and blue, and Henry's may even have borne his green and white. All, however, would have had some form of head protection, typically a sallet with a visor, only a thin slit providing vision directly in front of them.[26]

Once fed, watered, and arrayed, Henry's army completed a journey of around 5 miles, heading down Watling Street before turning north-east along a Roman pathway known as Fenn Lane. Scouts had informed Henry exactly where Richard III's force was placed, and that an encounter was now inevitable. Wisely, on their final approach, Henry's men performed a flanking manoeuvre that kept the marsh to their right and placed the high August sun directly behind. Such minor details, exploiting the land and elements to their advantage, could hugely impact the day's outcome, particularly for the militarily weaker force.[27]

Now, as the two sides faced one another across the plain, a range of banners fluttered softly in the breeze. The soldiers hastily 'buckled their helms', the archers nervously 'bent their bows and frushed their feathers', and the billmen 'shook their bills and proved their staves'. All stood ready, waiting on tenterhooks for the call of the trumpet to signal their advance.[28]

During these tense moments, Henry may just have been able to make out the formidable white boar on a background of azure and murrey, or blue and purplish red. Mounted just beneath was the crowned king he refused to recognise. This would have marked the first time Henry had ever cast his blue eyes upon the man whose death he had plotted for the last two years. He may also have noted a separate banner bearing the royal arms of England, quartered with those of France. Having already claimed to be the rightful king of England, Henry himself may even have had a similar banner to hand, although his French benefactors may not have taken too kindly to any claim to their own crown.

Situated on a ridge to one side of the armies, not far from the village of Stoke, and very noticeably detached from either side, were the Stanleys. Their intentions were still not fully known to either side. Richard had tried to appeal to their loyalties through fear, threatening the life of the Stanley heir, Lord Strange, while Henry had sought to exploit his kinship to the family, hoping Lord Stanley would be swayed by the prospect of helping raise his stepson to the throne.

Henry grew agitated that the Stanleys had still not publicly declared for him at this late hour, and his army was noticeably weaker for their absence at his side. Inferior in numbers, possibly by half if any credence is given to Vergil's assessment, the Tudor force was drawn up in a single battle line, with the archers positioned at the front. Tradition in England during this period, following the principles laid out by the Roman writer Vegetius in the fifth century, was to arrange the army in three units, or divisions, and this was precisely what Richard had done across the field. According to Vergil, who would have spoken with veterans of that day, the king positioned his archers 'like a most strong trench and bulwark' before a vanguard full of men-at-arms and horsemen under the command of Norfolk and Robert Brackenbury. Behind followed the main division under Richard's direct command, with Northumberland's ample northern recruits bringing up the rear.[29] The Tudor army, likely because of their lower numbers, did not, or rather could not, follow suit.

Since Henry had no military experience, overall command of his troops was conceded to the 'most valiant soldier' John de Vere, Earl of Oxford, regarded as 'next in rank'. Responsibility for the right flank was given to Gilbert Talbot with the left taken care of by John Savage. Beneath the commanders, knights like John Welles, Edward Woodville, John Cheyne, Robert Willoughby, William Berkeley, James Blount, Thomas Arundel, Richard Edgcumbe, Edward Poynings and Richard Guildford led small units of their own.[30] The French contingent, which comprised much of the heart of the force, was overseen by Philippe de Chandée. Together, Welsh, English, French and Scottish soldiers now sought to overturn the odds against them and raise up the unlikeliest of kings.

Henry remained slightly behind his army, surrounded by a bodyguard that comprised one troop of horsemen and a few footmen.[31] He was accompanied by William Brandon, who had been afforded the honour of bearing the Tudor standard. One person oddly absent from any source at this most crucial point in the Tudor family story is Jasper. When listing those present at the battle that came to define the family's rise, neither the Crowland chronicler nor Polydore Vergil list Jasper among those present. Considering how close he was to the nephew he had for so long guarded, his own heir even, this seems strange.

If Jasper was indeed not at the battle, then age may have been a factor. In his early fifties on this campaign, he may have been feeling the effects of a tough couple of decades on his body, not least the strenuous march in the last fortnight. That said, older men had fought during the various battles of the Wars of Roses, and the earl of Shrewsbury had even been deep into his sixties when he fell fighting the French at Castillon in 1453. Even at Bosworth, the duke of Norfolk on the opposing side was around sixty. Instead, perhaps superstition played a role in his lack of participation. Despite being regarded a 'wise and gifted soldier' by one mid-sixteenth-century observer,[32] Jasper's military record was hardly auspicious, having experienced a devastating loss at Mortimer's Cross in 1461 before being reduced to periodic raids throughout the rest of the decade to make an impact. Perhaps he now opted to take a back seat. Another consideration is that Jasper had been tasked with preparing an escape route for Henry in the event things went awry, which, in light of the Stanleys' continued aloofness, surely remained the most expected outcome of the day.

Of course, Jasper's lack of mention in the sources could even have been a conscious post-battle strategy to not draw attention from Henry by reminding people an older Tudor still lived, although Jasper had no claim to the English throne himself. Soon after the battle, one of Henry's maternal cousins, an illegitimate son of Henry Beaufort, 3rd Duke of Somerset, even had his surname changed from Charles Beaufort to Charles Somerset, possibly for similar reasons. In the interests of elevating his own, dubious, claim to the throne, Henry Tudor could have no potential dynastic rivals, real or imagined, and the decision may have been taken, with or without his command, to minimise Jasper's role in proceedings. It seems deeply unlikely, after everything they had been through together, that Jasper would not be at Henry's side at this moment. They would have risen or fallen together, bonded by blood and hardship.

With his army drawn up, Henry issued final instructions to his men, and likely performed a rousing speech as a last attempt to stir his men's hearts. The chronicler Edward Hall recorded such a stirring performance sixty years later, one almost certainly later adapted for the stage by a certain William Shakespeare.[33] Though Hall's speech derived largely from his own imagination, when considering existing communication from Henry to potential supporters during this period, he probably captured the spirit of this crucial moment.

According to Hall, a fully armoured Henry, minus his helmet, rode along the ranks of his men from flank to flank. Along the way, he spoke 'comfortable words' to these soldiers who were now prepared to die in his pursuit of a crown, his countenance 'cheerful and courageous' despite the occasion. As the moment of battle neared, Henry stood atop a small mound, and 'in a loud voice and bold spirit', spoke about their 'Godly quarrel' against a 'homicide and murderer of his own blood and progeny' that was proving a 'burden intolerable' to his subjects. It was their duty, Henry pressed, to suppress this tyranny, to defeat their 'proud enemies, and arrogant adversaries', to relieve the innocents who chafed under Richard's rule. Having existed in exile for long with 'small livings and little plenty of wealth or welfare', their reward in victory would be an 'abundance of riches'.

As for Richard himself, Henry regarded his foe as someone who 'hath violated and broken both the law of God and man'. Contrary to 'all justice and equity', Henry boldly claimed Richard 'keeps from me the crown', but 'for long we have sought the furious boar, and now we have found him'. As they faced their enemy across the field, he warned that 'backward we cannot fly'. Reaching the end of his speech, Henry, at least as envisaged by Hall, promised his men either 'an honourable death or famous victory', adding, 'Let us therefore fight like invincible giants.' Hall, meanwhile, has Richard criticising the 'Welsh milksop' who dared to challenge him, 'an unknown Welshman whose father I never knew nor him personally saw'.[34] The stage was set for the first military engagement on English soil since Tewkesbury fourteen years earlier.

The battle began with the traditional exchange of arrows which, although causing some degree of disarray on both sides as they fell from the heavens in their thousands, did not prove advantageous to either side. Richard's artillery was employed to try and inflict widespread disorder among the Tudor ranks from a distance, unleashing plumes of disorienting smoke and thunderous explosions across the field of battle.[35] Archaeological investigations have unearthed over thirty cannon shot, ranging from 30 mm to 94 mm in size, suggesting an array of different-sized guns were used during the battle. It is possible the marsh that stood to the right of the Tudor army was able to bear some of the brunt.

At last, the call was made on Henry's side to advance, with Oxford leading the Tudor troops under heavy arrow fire towards Norfolk's vanguard. These two East Anglian titans were long-standing regional rivals who had faced one another at the battle of Barnet fourteen years earlier, and each man probably relished another opportunity to inflict a mortal wound on his adversary. Fearful that his men would be enveloped by the superior numbers of their foe, Oxford wisely commanded his soldiers not to stray more than 10 feet from the banners. This lesson he had learned at Barnet, when indiscipline had caused his defeat at Norfolk's hands. The earl was ably assisted by the French, who pressed on the Yorkist flank.[36]

After a brief pause in the fighting, Oxford regrouped his men and resumed the attack. This time, his force was arranged into tight wedge formations, used to great effect to penetrate Norfolk's bewildered ranks.

The duke's men started to break under such intensely concentrated pressure, until their lines finally splintered.[37] In the melee, Norfolk, a soldier 'very politic and skilful in wars', was killed, possibly by an arrow after Oxford knocked off the bevor that protected his neck, and soon the Yorkist soldiers were starting to abandon their positions to flee. At no point does Northumberland appear to have made a move, though his path appears to have been blocked by the marsh and the hesitancy of some of his men to engage in what was starting to look like a losing effort.[38]

As the battle continued to be fought with the 'greatest severity',[39] a mounted Richard spotted a lapse in concentration on the Tudor side that exposed their leader. Situated to the rear of his main host before the fighting had commenced, Henry gradually became further detached from the bulk of his soldiers until he was surrounded by only a small band of mounted troops and a handful of infantry. According to Vergil, he was easily identifiable to Richard by certain 'signs and tokens', which may be taken to mean his standards, including the red dragon of Wales.[40]

As Richard looked towards the melee, he would have seen that momentum was swinging towards Oxford and the rebels. He may have glanced up towards the ridge where the Stanleys remained perched and drawn the conclusion that the day was lost if they committed against him. In a split second, the man with a crown fixed to his helmet had made his fateful decision. He would hack down Henry himself and bring an early end to the fighting.

Signalling his intention to his household knights and personal retainers, Richard pointed his sword towards where Henry Tudor stood, lowered his visor, struck his horse with his spurs and started his charge. When Richard's prey sighted this fearsome cavalry charge galloping straight for him, a coldly controlled mass of armoured man and beast, it would be no criticism of his character if Henry voiced his alarm aloud. The expectation must have been that in moments he would be dead. There was still enough time, however, for his cries to be heard and his bodyguard to frantically assemble some semblance of defence against the imminent assault.[41]

The very embodiment of a chivalric king defending his crown on horseback, Richard and his household crashed into Henry's bodyguard with a deafening roar, a cacophony of bloodcurdling screams and the snorting of thrashing horses. These final moments of Richard's reign, or conversely the first of the Tudor dynasty, were captured a few days later in a tantalising eyewitness account penned by a French archer, discovered and published in part by Alfred Spont in 1897.[42] This archer, Colinet or Nicholas Leboeuf, reported home that Richard had charged at them with his entire division, a terrifying spectacle that brought a tremble to the most hardened of mercenaries. Rather than fleeing, Henry bravely dismounted from his horse to stand amid the French, in the process making himself a smaller target for the imminent assault. He was quickly surrounded by some of the French troops, whom Leboeuf credited with saving the day.

Richard was frustrated by the desperate defence that had been mounted on Henry's behalf, his initial momentum already lost, but he persevered with his attack. He trusted that soon the day would be his. Fighting with boundless bravery, the king hacked through whatever obstacle was placed in front of him, and was able 'with great force' to even knock down the towering figure of John Cheyne, a man of 'much fortitude' who stood a foot taller than Richard.[43] Henry's standard bearer, William Brandon, was also targeted.

The capture or downing of a standard was a significant act in the ebb and flow of battle, stirring the hearts of men who perceived victory to be within reach and humiliating those who found their flags trampled upon and muddied. Often, the fall of a banner or standard heralded the death or capture of the lord whose heraldry was snatched from the skies. Unlike Cheyne, the newly knighted Brandon was unable to survive the onslaught and was killed. Though Henry's standard bearing the proud Welsh dragon fell from Brandon's lifeless grip, tradition records that Rhys Fawr ap Maredudd reacted bravely to rescue it from the ground and raise it higher than before. A Welshman of ancient lineage, Rhys may have been outraged to see Cadwaladr's dragon degraded in such fashion, but his intervention could have had a more important and prosaic purpose.[44]

To have killed Brandon suggests Richard came within feet of Henry, their eyes perhaps momentarily locking, two strangers whose personal ambitions had brought them to this moment. Aside from their distant kinship – they shared a common ancestor in John of Gaunt – the two combatants weren't all that dissimilar. Richard was older by just four years, and neither man knew his father well. Henry didn't know his father at all, while Richard's had often been absent owing to political obligations and was executed when he was just nine years old. Richard, like Henry, was now the only surviving son of his mother, to whom he had a noticeably close bond to rival that of Henry and Margaret Beaufort, and both were now unmarried and without children. Both had shared time in exile. In different circumstances they might have enjoyed one another's company, but fate had made them adversaries. Only one could prosper, and it seemed as though victory was in Richard's grasp.

From their vantage point, the Stanley contingent watched with wide eyes as Richard gathered his men and charged across the field towards Henry's position. When they saw the Tudor standards fall, there may have been a moment when it was believed that so too had Henry, and that the battle had reached its conclusive moment without their involvement.

Just then, however, the red dragon reappeared, waved frantically above the scrum and indicating that Henry, for the moment at least, remained alive. Having received the initial assault 'with great courage', Vergil later reported that Henry 'abode the brunt' longer than even his own soldiers could have believed, until they were 'almost out of hope of victory'.[45]

It is at this moment the Stanley forces belatedly engaged. Rampaging down from their ridge, William Stanley led his men directly to where Richard was trying to hack his way towards Henry. Just as Henry had hoped, and Richard had feared, the men the Stanleys attacked were wearing boar insignia and the murrey-and-blue livery of the Yorkist king. Many in Stanley's service were Welshmen drawn from his lordships of Bromfield, Yale and Chirk, and very likely some were kinsmen of those fighting for their lives on the Tudor side. These North Welsh Stanleyans, as Vergil called them, knew the prophecies, and may have been conflicted about their master's hesitancy to commit them to the fray.[46]

Once involved in the fighting, the Stanley contingent took no mercy on their exhausted quarry, the menacing whistle of their swords and axes as they cut through the air to find bone or steel accompanied only by the chilling screams of dying men. The air was rank with the smell of blood and bodily fluids, and men stumbled over the corpses of those already felled. If they recognised one of the dead as a friend, perhaps even relation, there was nothing to do except keep fighting.

Richard was surrounded, forced to fend off not just the Welsh and French who desperately sought to rescue Henry, but now the Stanley contingent as well. Despite great bravery, the numbers proved too much, and the reigning king was swept towards the marsh. With his horse stuck in the mire, Richard soon abandoned his saddle, or perhaps was wrenched out by his assailants. Around him his men were slaughtered, including devoted friends like Brackenbury and Ratcliffe. Nearby, a stunned Richard may also have witnessed his standard bearer, Percival Thirwell, have his legs cut from beneath him.[47]

Just minutes previously, it had been Henry's dragon standard fluttering miserably to the ground, bunching up on the bloodstained ground before it was defiantly raised once more. Now, Richard's boar standard followed suit, though this time there would be no proud champion to pick it back up. According to the account of the French archer Leboeuf, the enraged king was heard crying out that 'these French traitors are today the cause of my kingdom's ruin', though in truth it was the Stanley wave which had ultimately made the difference.[48] Richard was encouraged to flee by his men but gallantly refused, declaring how on this day he would 'make end either of war or life'.[49]

Besieged from every side and unable to withstand the onslaught, Richard was gradually overcome, though his death was anything but dishonourable. According to hostile accounts written after his demise and under the reign of a dynasty that stood to prosper by blackening his reputation, Richard had battled 'like a brave and most valiant prince', having fought 'manfully in the thickest press of his enemies'. Such valour, however, was ultimately to no avail. Despite his efforts, in the mire in which he was trapped, Richard was 'pierced with numerous deadly wounds', the last English king to fall in battle.[50]

It's possible there was Welsh involvement in Richard's death. The poet Tudur Aled credits Rhys Fawr ap Maredudd with landing the killing blow on Richard, while Guto'r Glyn paid tribute to Rhys ap Thomas for the act, noting in a poem that his patron had 'killed the boar, he shaved his head'. The Stanley contingent also featured heavy Welsh component, and one of their number may have brought Richard's life to a close. The Burgundian Jean Molinet, meanwhile, reported abroad that it was simply a Welshman armed with a halberd, a lethal two-handed slicing weapon mounted on a pole wielded by the most skilled and competent of soldiers, who slayed the last Plantagenet king.[51] Another name put forward was that of Tamworth native Thomas Woodshawe, though in all likelihood multiple men hold the dubious honour of committing regicide.[52]

When the skeleton of Richard III was exhumed in 2012, perimortem analysis using modern technology revealed the principal wounds inflicted on the king in his final moments. Though the order in which the injuries occurred could not be determined, a total of nine separate wounds were detected on his skull, with two more inflicted on his lower body. Of those that would have proven fatal, one was likely to have been a dagger piercing the right cheek while a narrow rondel dagger was used to penetrate the top of the head. At the base of the skull, meanwhile, a large piece of bone was sliced away, lending credibility to the notion that a bladed weapon such as a halberd was used. These injuries to Richard's skull almost certainly occurred while he was in a prone or kneeling position with his head unprotected. Injuries which only caused soft-tissue trauma are unknown, though the king's body was well protected by his armour at the moment of his death so these may have been minimal.[53] He died in a sustained, frenzied attack carried out by multiple assailants, and therefore it is unclear which man landed the fatal blow. Indeed, apart from the few names mentioned by the poets, which cannot be verified, the names of those involved are now lost to time.

When word spread that the king was dead, the fighting ground to a halt. Those on Richard's side who promptly threw down their weapons were permitted to leave the field unmolested.[54] A few men of note who had survived, like the earls of Surrey and Northumberland, were rounded up and taken prisoner, while those hardy few who refused to yield were slaughtered in the traditional post-battle rout. Richard's bloodied body, covered in mire and filth, was stripped of its armour and clothing before being slung over the back of a horse, ready to be taken to Leicester for public display.[55] In this moment, those present first became aware of some curvature in Richard's spine, a hitherto concealed medical condition soon be exploited to tarnish his reputation in death. Further post-mortem wounds – humiliation injuries – were inflicted on his corpse, 'not exactly in accordance with the laws of humanity', rued one unimpressed chronicler.[56]

The fields which just two hours before had been lush and quiet now lay strewn with bodies and horses. Though the fighting had ceased, the screaming had not, for many men had incurred unspeakable injuries without the mercy of a quick death. Some were tended to as best as the basic first aid of the day allowed, while others were perhaps sombrely dispatched.

The dead were gathered up, and where possible their names recorded. There were around 1,000 on Richard's side, and scarcely 100 on the Tudor side.[57] Some could be identified by their coat of arms, others by distinguishing features known to their friends. The most notable victim on the losing side was the duke of Norfolk, a man who had made his reputation in war. Many more deaths were unrecorded, their participation on this historic day unknown to future generations, their fate perhaps never revealed to their families, just assumed.

Aside from the few members of the nobility who perished, including Norfolk and of course the fallen king, many of the dead were dumped unceremoniously into pits, as had occurred throughout the Wars of the Roses. In some cases, the dead were at least moved by cart to consecrated ground; nearby Dadlington is known to have received its fair share of war dead, and in 1511 the wardens of St James' Chapel in the village petitioned the new king, Henry VIII, for permission to found a chantry to commemorate those who died. In 1868, several skulls were unearthed in the churchyard, commonly believed to belong to soldiers from the battle, with further finds in 1889 and 1950.[58]

Once he had processed what had just occurred, caught his breath and mentally recovered from his close brush his death, Henry was overcome with emotion, 'replenished with joy incredible'.[59] He departed the site of battle, which he would come to regard in coming months as simply the 'victorious field',[60] and headed to a nearby hill. Here, Henry commended his exhausted soldiers and gave thanks to God for their success. During the closing moments of the battle, the golden diadem that had been fixed to Richard's helm had been wrenched loose and lay pitifully 'among the spoil'. According to Vergil, it found its way into the hands of Henry's stepfather, Lord Stanley, who, having maintained a low profile during the battle, now emerged to place it upon his stepson's head.[61]

Another contemporary chronicler, however, pointedly asserts that it was Stanley's younger brother William, the man whose intervention had swung the day, who placed the crown on Henry's head with the impudent words, 'Sir, here I make you king of England.' Given that William would be executed for treason a decade later, it stands to reason that his role at Bosworth was not just minimised but rewritten to grant the honour of approaching Henry with the crown to his elder brother. Whichever Stanley handed Henry the crown that moments earlier had adorned Richard III's helmet, the Tudor supporters nevertheless enthusiastically cheered the historic spectacle, crying out with considerable delight, 'God save king Henry, God save king Henry!'[62] The mount upon which this impromptu crowning is believed to have taken place is still known as Crown Hill.

Henry took this opportunity to issue his first proclamation as king, in which he very noticeably regarded himself as not only king of England and France but also prince of Wales. It was his utmost concern that his victorious men exercise restraint and refrain from pursuing personal vengeance. Henry, after all, had campaigned for the crown on a manifesto of unity, and now had to show himself to be a just king for all:

Henry, by the grace of God, king of England and of France, Prince of Wales, and Lord of Ireland, strictly chargeth and commandeth, upon pain of death, that no manner of man rob or spoil no manner of commons coming from the field; but suffer them to pass home to their countries and dwelling-places, with their horses and harness. And, moreover, that no manner of man take upon him to go to no gentleman's place, neither in the country, nor within cities nor boroughs, nor pick no quarrels for old or for new matters; but keep the king's peace, upon pain of hanging.[63]

It must be wondered whether, amid such overwhelming exhilaration, Henry found a private moment with his uncle Jasper, to share this astounding transformation in their fortunes. It wasn't so long ago that Jasper had been forced to grasp his nephew by the collar and desperately flee their homeland, pursued hard by Yorkists charged with capturing and possibly even killing them. It was a remarkable turnaround, one nobody could have foreseen just a couple of years earlier.

It was for good reason that Philippe Commines, a man Henry had met during his exile, found it extraordinary that Henry, a man 'without power, without money, without right to the crown of England, and without any reputation but what his person and deportment obtained for him', had emerged from these years victorious. It was, however, Commines supposed, simply 'the just judgement of God'. To the Crowland chronicler, the new king of England was even lauded as 'an angel sent down from heaven' to deliver his people 'from the evils which it had hitherto, beyond measure, been afflicted'.[64]

In Wales, however, and possibly in Henry's own mind, there was another reason for his improbable victory, one that had less to do with divine intervention or the efforts of the thousands of men who were willing to lay down their lives for him on that August day in 1485. It was because he was the Son of Prophecy, whose triumph had been foretold for many centuries. When Henry entered the city of Worcester in 1486, he was greeted with a range of pageants extolling his various virtues. In one, somebody cried aloud:

> Cadwaladr's blood lineally descending,
> Long hath be told of such a prince coming.
> Wherefore friends, if that I shall not lie,
> This same is the fulfiller of the prophesy.[65]

The Tudor dynasty had arrived.

EPILOGUE

A Prince of
Our Own Nation

On 30 October 1485 in Westminster Abbey, Henry Tudor, or rather Henry of Richmond as he more properly regarded himself in the manner of the day, was seated upon St Edward's Chair, a high-backed wooden seat covered in cloth of gold. In a resplendent crimson robe lined with the finest ermine, he listened as his claim to the crown received the full assent of the assembled lords and commons, followed by the cry of 'King Henry, King Henry, King Henry'.[1]

A week later, the first parliament of the reign assembled, during which it was confirmed that henceforth the 'inheritance of the crowns of the realms of England and of France' rested in the 'most royal person of our now sovereign lord, King Harry the Seventh' and the heirs of his body.[2] Henry's accession as the seventh king of that name to rule England, just the nineteenth in total since the Norman Conquest in 1066, concluded a remarkable transformation not just in his fortunes but in those of his family.

When Ednyfed Fychan, Tudur ap Goronwy or the Tudurs of Penmynydd, for example, had been waging their wars on the English crown, none could have foreseen a scenario where one of their Welsh-born and Welsh-raised descendants would one day be crowned king of England in London. Even to the grandfather who had briefly known Henry as a child, Owen Tudor, such an outcome of the dynastic wars which cost him his head would have been unfathomable. Apart from a brief visit to the city as a child, Henry had not even stepped foot in London until he was already king. Fortune's wheel may have been fickle, but this was inconceivable.

To the Welsh bards, of course, there was a perfectly rational explanation, and that was that Henry had clearly been the *Mab Darogan*, the fulfiller of ancient prophecy.[3] After many failed dawns, most notably Owain Lawgoch and Owain Glyn Dŵr, the Son of Prophecy had finally revealed himself, the champion of the ancient British nation who would restore their independence and prosperity. Huw Cae Llwyd rejoiced that the 'youth from Gwynedd' sat on the throne in London, while Dafydd Llwyd crowed that there was 'a golden crown on our kinsman'.[4] The great descendant of Brutus and Cadwaladr had restored the island's original ruling house, and the zealous bards now anticipated a new dawn for their people, one in which the English would be cast into the sea.[5]

Of course, Henry could never hope to live up to such an ambitious and, quite frankly, unworkable manifesto, and for this he incurred some soft criticism. Dafydd Llwyd, that close partisan of the Tudors and arguably Henry's greatest champion among his class, grew disillusioned about the presence of English counsellors and nobles around Henry, and Llywelyn ap Hywel even openly admonished the king for his apparent preference for men of the English north over the Welsh. Lewys Glyn Cothi still believed the world to be sad and poor, regardless of the Welshman on the throne. It should be noted that the poets often pitched their expectations unrealistically high, effusively praising their patrons' hospitality, bloodline and character perhaps more than they truly deserved.

Similarly, their expectations for Henry were always unattainable, and there may have been an open acknowledgement they never expected their poetical commentary to form the literal foundations of political policy. Disapproval of Henry's attitude towards the Welsh once king, however, has surfaced in the modern age, with accusations levelled that he merely manipulated the Welsh penchant for myths and legends to advance his own cause, only to betray the land of his fathers once he had achieved his objectives.[6]

This criticism seems unfair. Upon becoming king, Henry had a huge amount of work to do if he was to not only stabilise England after a fresh outbreak of civil war but avoid his own dethronement in the uncertain years after his victory. Through a combination of his natural intelligence, astute administrative prowess and relentless drive, a pragmatic Henry succeeded in this mission, ultimately rehabilitating England's continental reputation, restoring royal authority and reconciling the warring factions behind the crown. In the process however, Henry had to overcome several conspiracies and plots while navigating the perilous minefield of international diplomacy. It is to be expected that Wales, perhaps the most peaceful and obedient part of his dominions, was not a political priority during this difficult period.[7]

Indeed, the political situation in Wales remained complex in 1485, a consequence of the piecemeal conquest of the Welsh by earlier kings of England and their Anglo-Norman barons. In fact, unlike England or even Scotland, Wales as a single polity did not even yet exist in law. After the Edwardian conquest of 1282 brought any Welsh personal rule to a close, the king of England's power personally extended across the Principality, or *Pura Wallia*, which constituted what became known in the English system as Anglesey, Merionethshire, Caernarfonshire, Cardiganshire and Carmarthenshire. The rest of Wales, the *Marchia Wallie*, was a patchwork of lordships, numbering around forty, in the possession of a handful of English barons. These lordships were administered for their own benefit by the dukes of Somerset or York, for example, or earls of Pembroke or Warwick, each with their own set of judicial or legislative processes and customs.[8] Since the Conquest, then, Wales remained an administrative anomaly, part-principality, part-march, some areas under crown control and many others not. As a result, the country was unable to be uniformly governed, an assortment of separate jurisdictions that created a complex structural issue for successive monarchs and governments.[9] Wales was, yet Wales wasn't.

The Wars of the Roses, however, had caused considerable bloodshed among the nobility, resulting in several earldoms and duchies with significant Welsh landed interests reverting to crown possession as proud lineages crashed to sudden halts. Upon becoming king, Henry held sway not only over the Principality shires of Caernarfonshire, Merionethshire, Anglesey, Carmarthenshire and Cardiganshire but also the duchy of Lancaster's Welsh holdings, including the lordships of Monmouth, Grosmont, White Castle and Skenfrith, and the many lordships that were attached to the historic earldom of March like Denbigh, Ludlow, and Ceri and Cedewain. Since the duke of Buckingham was a minor, Henry controlled the lordships of Brecon, Builth and Usk. Upon his uncle Jasper's death in 1495, the earldom of Pembroke and all associated lordships across South Wales passed to Henry. That same year, the execution of the most powerful landowner in North Wales, William Stanley, brought under crown control the lordship of Bromfield and Yale, along with Chirk. One of the few Marcher lords left by the end of Henry's reign was his maternal cousin Charles Somerset, who was lord of Chepstow, Raglan and Gower, with another, the young Edward Grey, holding the barony and lordship of Powys.[10]

The concept of Wales as a single entity to which the king could grant independence, or at least increased autonomy, therefore did not yet exist. Even if Henry was inclined to bestow upon the Welsh some manner of self-governance, this would have represented a significant threat to his own security as a king of England; he had, after all, just invaded England through Wales. As one of the most cautious men to wear the English crown, a king who had exploited his predecessor's dynastic, political and geographic failings to usurp the throne, Henry's policy towards Wales demanded a pragmatic, rather than sentimental, approach. There were to be no extreme measures or novel decisions taken regarding Wales that risked his position in England, whatever the protestations of the bards.

This doesn't mean that Henry didn't seek to address some legislative and judicial anomalies concerning Wales throughout his reign. On

29 November 1489, Henry created his first son, Arthur, Prince of Wales and within a year had re-formed the council of Wales and the Marches under the nominal authority of the prince. This was to govern the Principality and ensure the Marcher lords maintained law and order within their domains, where the king's writ did not run.[11]

Such an administrative body was not an innovation on Henry's part, but rather he closely followed the example set by Edward IV when he first created a council to supervise the region in 1471. Due to his tender age, it wasn't until 1501 that the Tudor prince personally took up residence in Ludlow, where it was expected he would learn the art of governance and kingship. Though Arthur's premature death the following year hampered much of Henry's meticulous plans for his dynasty's future, the council itself never ceased to exist.

If Henry was unable, rather than unwilling, to bestow independence on the Welsh nation, then did he honour his promise to deliver his compatriots from the shackles of their 'miserable servitude'?[12] Since the passing of the debilitating Penal Laws in 1401, Welsh communities had bristled against what they perceived to be unfair punishment. These laws, among other things, prevented Welsh people from owning lands or property in several large towns of note in Wales and the March, from bearing arms or from becoming a chamberlain, justice, chancellor, treasurer sheriff, steward, constable, receiver, escheator, coroner, chief forester or keeper of records in any part of their homelands.[13] Conversely, Englishmen were also forbidden from marrying a Welshwoman and retaining their privileges, which naturally lessened the appeal of cross-community unions. The Penal Laws had been designed to hamper Welsh ambition, and though Henry VII did not have them repealed, towards the end of his reign several charters were granted with the aim of finally enfranchising a handful of communities.

The seven charters, granted between 1504 and 1508 of the king's own volition and on the advice of his council, sought to suspend some of these punitive laws and were naturally welcomed by those who benefited.[14] In October 1504, the first such charter was granted to the people of the Principality counties of Merionethshire and Caernarfonshire. They were henceforth permitted to acquire lands and offices in England or English boroughs and towns in Wales, and to abolish the Welsh custom of partible succession in favour of English common law. A similar charter was granted to the inhabitants of Bromfield and Yale in August 1505 and to Chirk and also Denbigh in July 1506. Anglesey benefited in March 1507, followed by confirmation of an earlier charter granted to the people of Ceri and Cedewain in July that year. Finally, in June 1508, the people of Ruthin were grateful to be made inhabitants of a free borough.[15]

These charters, though limited in their geographic or political scope, were more than any previous fifteenth-century king of England had bothered to entertain. Even so, they cannot be viewed simply as generous grants from a benevolent king. Henry charged hefty prices for the honour of modest liberation, with the Principality alone paying £2,000 for their charter. As these grants came through the royal prerogative rather than the agency of parliament, they may not even have been legally sound; indeed, they were robustly challenged by the English castle boroughs.[16]

Nevertheless, whatever the motivation – and it remains plausible these grants were born out of a genuine desire in Henry to help his Welsh subjects while also sating his acquisitive nature – those who benefitted no doubt viewed them as a liberating gesture after a century of oppressive laws. As far as these Welsh communities were concerned, this was progress, delivered to them by one of their own. For the average Welsh person, it was evolution rather than revolution they craved, an opportunity to simply be treated on par with their English neighbour. This was enough for David Powel, writing at the end of the sixteenth century, to credit Henry, 'who by his grandfather Owen Tuder descended out of Wales' and therefore knew of the injuries done to the Welsh in times past, with having 'granted unto them a charter of liberties, whereby they were released of that oppression'.[17]

Before any further programme could be rolled out throughout the rest of the country, if that indeed was the plan, Henry died, and the legacy of what to do with the riddle of Wales passed to his initially disinterested son. If Henry VIII shared none of his father's favourable disposition towards Wales or the Welsh, then his political and religious tribulations in the 1530s brought Wales's administrative incongruities to the attention of his industrious leading minister, Thomas Cromwell. Together, they would oversee the complete incorporation of Wales into the English system.

Known officially as Laws in Wales Acts, or more commonly if incorrectly as the Acts of Union, this series of legislation owes some of its conception to Henry VIII's tumultuous break with Rome and the English Reformation. When tearing his kingdom away from influence of the papacy, in 1533 Henry declared England to be an empire, appointing himself the final legal authority in his lands. To ensure he exercised complete sovereignty across all his dominions, and to enforce his controversial religious settlement in all parts of his realm, it was considered prudent in subsequent years to remove any political or geographic anomalies still extant, most if not all of which involved the poorly governed Wales and the Marches.[18] Wales, after all, populated by a religiously conservative people, represented a potential security risk with the looming threat of an invasion from Catholic Europe. The Welsh gateway that Henry VII had once used to great effect needed to be closed.

Overseen by Cromwell, the chief architect of the break with Rome, the acts were passed by the sole authority of the English parliament and without any involvement from the people they would affect, the Welsh.

The preamble made it clear that the Principality, ever since the Statute of Rhuddlan in 1284, had been considered 'incorporated, annexed, united, and subject to and under the imperial Crown of this Realm'. Now, these acts sought to bring about a final union between the Principality and the March, formally creating the political entity of Wales that would absorbed into the kingdom of England.[19] There would be one state, and one legal jurisdiction.

As part of this process, new counties were created from the Marcher lordships to join those already in existence, Anglesey, Merionethshire, Caernarfonshire, Cardiganshire and Carmarthenshire. They were Pembrokeshire, Glamorgan, Denbighshire, Montgomeryshire, Radnorshire, Brecknockshire, Flintshire and Monmouthshire. A handful of lordships, like Clun, Oswestry and Archenfield, were transferred to the counties of Shropshire and Herefordshire, and the modern border of England and Wales was, for the first time in law, established.[20]

The acts officially completed what Henry VII's charters had started a quarter-century previously. Though the Penal Laws remained on the English statute books, they were abandoned, with only English law henceforth recognised in Wales. Moving forward, for the first time there would even be Welsh representation in the English parliament, their grievances finally heard in the hallowed corridors of power. English would be the official language of the courts, and anyone using the Welsh language alone would not be able to enter public office. This clause has been interpreted as a conscious decision to eradicate the medium of Welsh, though this is at odds with later attempts to protect and promote the language as one of worship, with the Welsh-language Bible issued in 1588 under Elizabeth I. The principal aim behind this clause was to enforce uniform administration across the king's realm, to have English as the sole language of the judiciary and to eradicate any lingering confusion about different legal systems. Indeed, there doesn't appear to have been any clear decline in the personal usage of Welsh until the Industrial Revolution some 300 years later.[21]

If the express purpose of the acts was to make the governance of Wales more secure and straightforward for the Tudor crown, it had positive implications in Welsh communities, at least for those of means. No longer were Welshmen regarded as legally inferior to their English counterparts, bringing an end to the need to claim letters of denizenship to get ahead, as had been the case for Owen Tudor. The gentry were able to quickly build up vast estates and affluence, and soon Welsh families were becoming nationally prominent in a way never before seen. Though an argument could be made that the Welsh were now, in effect, considered English by law, the opposite can also be said to be true – they no longer had to suppress their Welshness for fear of being at a political or economic disadvantage.

Whatever the consternation in Welsh homes at the political, cultural or religious upheaval imposed on them from distant London, unlike various parts of England, most notably Yorkshire, Lincolnshire and Cornwall, it is telling that the Welsh never militarily resisted these developments as they were occurring. Perhaps George Owen of Henllys, a respected Elizabethan antiquarian who in 1594 was reflecting upon the reign of Henry VII and subsequent events, captured the wider mood of his compatriots when in his commentary he regarded the first Tudor king, 'a prince of our own nation and born in our country', as 'a Moses that delivered us from bondage'.[22]

There are widespread examples in late sixteenth- and early seventeenth-century Welsh scholarship that commend Henry and his accession as a turning point for the Welsh people. Siôn Tudur, also writing during the reign of Henry's granddaughter Elizabeth I, regarded 'Fair Harry' a national deliverer who 'set us free', while Huw Machno believed that 'Jesus gave us Henry VII as our protector' to break the Welsh free of their chains. The foremost Welsh antiquarians of the age, William Salesbury, Humphrey Llwyd and David Powel, as well as the aforementioned George Owen, all heaped significant praise upon Henry's accomplishments in delivering their people from the 'laws of bondage'.[23]

If there was a sliver of disappointment from some of the bards, or later generations of Welsh thinkers who regard the acts and the advent of the Tudors as having a detrimental effect on Wales, that soon there was little to differentiate a Welshman from an Englishman save for perhaps accent, their ambitions exceed the practical confines within which both Henry Tudors were operating. Equality, or mere opportunity, was what the average fifteenth- or sixteenth-century Welsh person was yearning for, and that was precisely what they got. It may be considered that as a consequence of this opportunity the Welsh were drawn away from their traditional culture, language and laws, but our ancestors were not operating with the benefit of hindsight. The question of whether Henry VII and the Tudor dynasty was a force for good for the Welsh people continues to invite heated debate more than 500 years after Bosworth Field, and shows little sign of abating any time soon as Wales's political place within the modern British state is increasingly examined.[24]

If Henry was not able to quench the bards' thirst for Welsh vengeance on the Saxon, then his accession did at least provide ample opportunity for his compatriots to thrive, and for this he would be praised. Soon after his victory at Bosworth Field, Henry turned to rewarding those who had helped him to the throne. This, of course, wasn't restricted just to the Welsh; among those he honoured were his stepfather, Thomas Stanley, who was created earl of Derby and afforded the privilege of bearing the Sword of State during the coronation, and the Frenchman Philibert de Chandée, granted the earldom of Bath. John de Vere, Earl of Oxford, meanwhile, was handed significant responsibility for the security of the realm, filling the offices of chamberlain, constable of the Tower and admiral of England.[25] Others who had experienced exile with Henry were shown favour, with Edward Courtenay created earl of Devon, his maternal uncle John Welles created a viscount, and Giles Daubeney made a baron.

The most significant reward handed out by the new king, however, was reserved for the man who had sought to protect him from birth. In gratitude for this life of service, on 28 October 1485 Jasper Tudor was not only formally restored to his earldom of Pembroke but created the duke of Bedford. A dukedom was the highest rank in the peerage, below only the crown, and in the preamble to Jasper's creation Henry makes clear the affection he has for his uncle. When the king considered 'how great are the services which our most beloved uncle Jasper, Earl of Pembroke, has heaped upon us', and mindful of the great dangers the latter encountered in keeping Henry 'safe from our childhood right up to this time', it was clear he was a man 'worthy to be raised to a higher grade'. Pointed reference was also made to Jasper's pedigree, a 'most ancient nobility', which can only have been a reference to his Welsh lineage.[26]

The dukedom of Bedford had first been created in 1414 for John of Lancaster, the younger brother of Henry V and uncle of Henry VI, and was likely revived at this moment to consciously emphasise the bond between the Tudors and the Lancastrians. Like John, Jasper could also now claim to be a brother – half at least – and uncle of kings. In fact, he did; whenever his presence was announced by heralds, he was introduced as 'the high and mighty prince, Jasper, brother and uncle of kings, duke of Bedford and earl of Pembroke', which was also inscribed on his seal.[27]

A dukedom was no small reward during the kingship of Henry VII – throughout his reign, the only other dukes he created were his three sons, who in descending order by age were created Cornwall, York and Somerset. At the coronation, Jasper was the man entrusted to carry his nephew's crown through Westminster Abbey. To further strengthen the alliance with the Woodvilles, on 7 November Jasper also married Katherine Woodville, the dowager duchess of Buckingham and younger sister of the dowager queen, Elizabeth Woodville. This marriage mirrored the king's own in some ways, the union of a Lancastrian to a prominent Yorkist-aligned bride. There is no suggestion the marriage was anything other than a political alliance, and no children were born to the pair during their decade together.

Jasper's rewards didn't end with titles or marriages. Soon after his nephew became king, Jasper was restored to the lordships of Pembroke, Cilgerran, Llansteffan, St Clears, Ystlwyf and Trane Clinton in South-West Wales, as well as the manors of Westley in Suffolk and Witley in

Surrey. Caldicot, a former possession of his mother's, also eventually found its way back to Jasper's hands, as did the manor of Magor. He also received back a number of manors and lordships he had once held jointly with his brother Edmund, including Solihull, Sheldon, Bolsover and Clipstone in the English Midlands.[28]

On 2 December 1485, he was granted for life the office of steward of the duchy of Lancaster lands in Gloucestershire and Herefordshire, together with the constableships of the castles of Monmouth, Skenfrith, Grosmont and White Castle.[29] On 13 December, he was created justiciar of South Wales, an office to be held for life.[30] The justiciar's role was to represent the king in political and judicial matters, and to maintain royal law and order on behalf of the crown. Its officeholder was, in effect, a vice regent in South Wales, answerable only to the king, and by far the most dominant figure in the region. Though he was content to leave much of the day-to-day matters of governing South Wales to deputies or men like Rhys ap Thomas, Jasper would occasionally attend the Great Sessions in Carmarthen and Cardigan in person, keeping his ear to the ground. One such visit, to Cardigan in September 1492, marked his final appearance in Wales before his death three years later, forty years since he was created earl of Pembroke and began his long association in local politics.[31]

Further rewards would be forthcoming. On 2 March 1486, Jasper was granted the lordships of Glamorgan and Abergavenny, augmenting his authority across South Wales, and on the same day received the confiscated estates of Richard III's close allies, Francis Lovell and William Berkeley, extending his territorial sway into the west of England. The latter grant of nearly thirty manors provided Jasper an extensive landed interest throughout the Severn Valley and even as far north as Shropshire, in the heart of which lay Minster Lovell in Oxfordshire, where he would occasionally host his nephew in coming years. Another hugely significant reward at this time was the palatial castle and lordship of Sudeley, situated roughly halfway between his lands in South-West Wales and London, and which would become his favoured base. Taken together with his existing collection of lordships and manors, and the thirty-five manors he held through his wife, including Thornbury Castle, Jasper was the undeniable master of everything west of the Cotswolds. Finally, on 11 March 1486, he was appointed lieutenant of Ireland, a prestigious office with a good wage, though he would never assume this post personally.[32]

Perhaps Jasper's most integral role, and the one which epitomised Henry's trust in him, was as de facto leader of the council of Wales and the Marches during the minority of Prince Arthur, making him responsible for maintaining stability in the region.[33] It was Henry's intention to avoid any one magnate holding too much power anywhere within his realm, something which had brought previous kings of England to their knees during the fifteenth century. Jasper does seem to have been the exception, granted wide-ranging powers in South Wales and effective control of the council to expand his sway over the Marches. Apart from his mother, Jasper was the one person Henry knew he could completely trust. Others could be swayed by personal interests, lured towards rebellion by the promise of titles or riches, but never Jasper. That there were no major insurrections in Wales during the ten years Jasper survived his nephew becoming king suggests he accomplished his task.

Jasper also played his part in ceremonial aspects of his nephew's reign. After bearing the crown at Henry's coronation, during Elizabeth of York's coronation as queen on 25 November 1487 the duke once more had the honour. He had also accompanied his niece by marriage from the Tower of London to St Paul's Cathedral earlier in the day, his horse's caparison lavishly decorated with red dragons.[34]

Another poignant family scene occurred in Hereford towards the end of April 1493. Having escorted his six-year-old grandnephew Arthur to the Welsh March, where the young Prince of Wales was due to begin his education in Ludlow as a king-in-waiting, both Tudors appeared before the people of the town. The occasion involved pageantry in the market square, and it is easy to imagine that the memory of Owen Tudor was not too far from Jasper's mind; thirty-two years before, Owen had been beheaded in the same square. Perhaps Jasper told the young prince all about his great-grandfather, the daring Welsh squire who had married a queen and helped set the family on their path to political and royal prominence within the English system.[35]

Jasper ended his days alternating between his palatial homes of Thornbury, Sudeley and Minster Lovell in the English West Country, a quiet retirement in plush surroundings after decades in the wilderness. By the time he died in Thornbury on 21 December 1495, aged around sixty-four, he was one of the wealthiest figures in the kingdom.[36] It was perhaps a fitting end to a life in which he had encountered considerable hardship.

Henry made sure he paid his respects to the tireless elder statesman of the family who had guided him through so much, a reassuring presence for so long. When informed of his uncle's death, the king immediately travelled down to Keynsham in Somerset for the interment, taking with him his queen for moral support along with many of the lords. The mayor of Bristol had arranged for 2,000 mounted men to accompany the duke's coffin, for which he received thanks from the king.[37] No trace of Jasper's tomb survived the Dissolution, nor indeed has anything of Keynsham itself, although a chantry was founded in his memory in Thornbury with the assent of the king.[38] In his will, Jasper had been sure to make provision for prayers to be heard for the souls of his father

Owen, mother Katherine of Valois, 'some time queen of England', and brother Edmund. In memory of his father, the Greyfriars in Hereford where Owen was buried was also bequeathed one of Jasper's cloths of gold and a payment of £20.[39]

Despite being the great-uncle of Henry VIII and instrumental in propelling the family to unfathomable heights, Jasper was sadly quickly forgotten after his death. His steadfast loyalty to his kin and redoubtable courage in the face of great danger have only recently been recognised, as has his tenacity, which put lesser mortals to shame. He was, at least, warmly recalled in 1578 by the Welsh antiquarian Rice Merrick as, quite simply, 'the good duke'. Merrick, in fact, records a story, likely apocryphal, that perhaps best underscores Jasper's lasting legacy. According to Merrick, shortly after the landing at Mill Bay in 1485, a very old woman approached the earl of Pembroke and said to him, 'Long mayst thou live! For thou hast better kept thy nephew, than King Richard kept his.' Whether Richard III can truly be blamed for the disappearance and probable murder of his nephews or not, there is no doubt that Jasper did protect his own nephew well.[40] Jasper is, arguably, the mightiest of all the Tudors, a luminary who gave everything he had so that others could strive for greatness.

King Henry's other surviving uncles at the time of his accession, Owen Tudor the younger and David Owen, an illegitimate son of the elder Owen Tudor, were also rewarded, although far more modestly. Both were kept reasonably close to their royal kinsfolk. The younger Owen had not been raised with his brothers Edmund and Jasper, and had instead been handed over to the monks of Westminster Abbey as a child. He evades all known mention in the historical record until 30 July 1498 when, deep into his seventh decade, as 'Owen Tudder' he was rewarded £2 by his nephew and nearest living relative, Henry VII. It may be speculated that Owen's obscurity before the Tudor accession can be explained by a change of name; in his 1603 guidebook on the monuments and epitaphs of Westminster Abbey, the antiquarian William Camden mentioned a monk named Edward as the son of Owen Tudor and Katherine of Valois. Perhaps the younger Owen had changed his name at the height of the Wars of the Roses to conceal his connections to his brother Jasper, a fervent enemy of the ascendant House of York.[41] That he was regarded again as 'Owen Tudder' during the reign of his nephew suggests any adopted moniker was discarded once he was certain he would not be viewed with suspicion by a hostile crown.

Although rewards to a dedicated and elderly churchman were limited for obvious reasons, upon Owen's death in 1501 the king paid the churchwarden of St Margaret's, a smaller church near Westminster Abbey, 6*d* for the 'knell of Owen Tudor with the bell', a touching personal tribute.[42] A monk who had dedicated his life to the abbey, not to mention a close relation to the reigning king, Owen was accorded a burial within Westminster's sacred walls. Later tradition places his interment in the Chapel of St Blaise, at the end of the south transept and later largely appropriated to become Poets' Corner, itself the resting place of literary luminaries like Geoffrey Chaucer, Charles Dickens and Alfred Tennyson.[43] A stone placed in 1873 marks Owen's supposed resting place, alongside the remains of Nicholas Littlington, abbot of Westminster between 1362 and 1386, and William Benson, the last abbot and first dean of Westminster, who died in 1549. Owen is described simply as 'Monk of Westminster, Uncle of King Henry VII'. For overseeing the 'burying of Owen Tudder', on 18 June 1502 a Welshman named Morgan Kidwelly was paid £3 1s 2d from the king's own accounts.[44]

David Owen had been born in Pembroke in 1459, and was two years younger than his half-nephew Henry. They appear to have developed a close bond in exile, and upon becoming king Henry knighted his uncle. It is clear from David's own testimony that he was present at Henry's coronation, his marriage to Elizabeth of York and the baptisms of their sons Arthur and Henry. At Arthur's marriage to Katherine of Aragon, David also served in close attendance on the king – at every significant family occasion, even if only performing some minor political role, it is apparent that David was always close to hand. He would also be one of the leading mourners at Henry's funeral.[45]

David also played his part in public life. On 2 January 1486, as 'the king's knight', David was appointed chief carver for life, with a wage of £50 a year.[46] In November 1487 David was one of twelve knight bachelors who held the canopy at the coronation of Elizabeth of York, and in July 1489 he was granted the office of constable and warden of Winchester Castle along with several manors across England, including in Leicestershire, Norfolk and Northamptonshire. In 1493 he was created a knight banneret, and ten years later he was entrusted by Henry VII to escort Princess Margaret, his great-niece, to Scotland for her marriage to James IV – he was noted for wearing an expensive chain during the festivities. In May 1509, a month after the death of Henry VII, David was even proposed by the earls of Oxford, Surrey and Devon as a candidate for induction into the Order of the Garter, although ultimately the nod went elsewhere. David continued his service into the reign of Henry VIII; at the coronation of the second Tudor to wear the crown, he fulfilled his longstanding role as the king's carver, and in February 1413, mustered a total of 103 men to serve under him for the upcoming military campaign in France.[47]

When peace with the French was secured the following year, one of the terms was that the king's sister Princess Mary would marry the much older Louis XII of France. David was one of the men selected to accompany his eighteen-year-old great-niece to her new home, and was present at the marriage ceremony itself on 9 October 1514 in Abbeville.[48] Upon returning to England, David continued in his role as king's carver, and on 20 February 1515 even helped bear the canopy at the christening of the king's daughter, the other Princess Mary, in Greenwich. On 2 October 1518, David was one of the signatories on the Treaty of Universal Peace, Cardinal Wolsey's great achievement, and two days later he also witnessed the marriage treaty joining together the young princess and the dauphin of France.[49]

In the summer of 1520, meanwhile, he formed part of the royal household that accompanied Henry VIII to Canterbury when the court was preparing to cross the Channel for the momentous Field of the Cloth of Gold summit with the new French king, Francis I.[50] It is known that he also served as Member of Parliament for Sussex in 1491–92 and 1523, and probably on several other occasions in between.[51] By virtue of his blood and competent service to his royal kinsmen for fifty years, David had a front-row seat to some of the most significant political moments of the day, events that would shape much of the turbulent century to come.

Such proximity to the centre of Tudor power was not without its threats, however, and he occasionally came under fire. When Perkin Warbeck was preparing to invade England in 1497, having claimed to be Richard of Shrewsbury, the younger of the Princes in the Tower presumed dead for more than a decade, he issued a scathing proclamation taking aim at the heart of the Tudor court. Among his many accusations of Henry VII's tyranny was one that the king kept around him only 'his kinsmen and friends of simple and low degree', one of which was David Owen. Fortunately for David, Warbeck's campaign for the crown ultimately came to naught and this 'villain of simple birth' was able to continue his career unabated.[52]

David's royal connections had also helped secure a profitable marriage, one likely arranged by his nephew. Around 1489, David was wed to Mary Bohun, an heiress of the Bohun family of Cowdray, Sussex. They had one son, named Henry after the king, who may have stood as godfather. Henry Owen would have sons of his own, one of whom was touchingly called Jasper. David Owen remarried later in life, first to Anne Blount, and later to Anne Devereux. From these unions he fathered further children, including another Jasper and a daughter named Elizabeth, likely for the queen. If the old duke of Bedford was forgotten by the wider population after his death, within the family, his legacy and memory lived on. Likewise, Owen Tudor was also not forgotten by his youngest son. In his will, David made sure he left £10 to the Greyfriars in Hereford for a tomb to be made commemorating his father, though due to the Reformation it is unlikely this was ever honoured. David also left money for prayers to be said for the souls of his half-brothers Edmund and Jasper Tudor, and his royal nephew Henry.[53]

David died before September 1535,[54] having reached the grand age of seventy-six. He had lived not only through the Wars of the Roses, and his nephew Henry VII's astonishing victory at Bosworth Field, but the first quarter-century of Henry VIII's tumultuous reign, observing up close the break with Rome, the fall of Wolsey, the rise of the Boleyns and the early phases of the English Reformation. David maintained a low profile, quietly accruing significant power in his corner of Sussex and retaining the favour of a king increasingly edging towards tyranny. He merely served without hesitation, and avoided letting personal ambition sway his loyalties. In that, he shared much in common with his half-brother – and, considering the age difference, probable father figure – Jasper Tudor.

In Easebourne Church, within walking distance of his home at Cowdray, David is remembered with an alabaster effigy depicting a long-haired knight, in full armour and wearing a Lancastrian livery collar of Esses. The tomb chest beneath once displayed heraldry that associated him with the great Welsh lineage he, like Henry VII, inherited through Owen Tudor. Few today know the story of this somewhat forgotten uncle of the Tudor dynasty.[55]

Outside the family unit, there was wider recognition for other Welshmen who aided Henry in his quest for the crown. One Welshman who benefitted hugely from the Tudor accession was Rhys ap Thomas, rewarded well for throwing in his lot with Henry before Bosworth. Rhys was knighted by Henry moments after the battle, and, staying true to his word on Long Mountain, the new king soon entrusted to Rhys great power in Wales, although cautiously not enough to create another potentially overmighty subject.

Although no man could outrank the king's uncle Jasper, on 3 November 1485 Rhys was appointed constable, lieutenant and steward of the lordship of Brecon, before being appointed chamberlain of South Wales for life and steward of Builth three days later.[56] He was warmly invited to Henry's coronation, later became a knight of the body in the king's household, and was occasionally sought out for his political counsel. In Jasper's physical absence from South Wales, it was Rhys who was assured effective control of the region, and when the great duke died a decade later Rhys stepped officially into the void without missing a beat, adding justiciar of South Wales to his many offices. Rhys would continue to serve the Tudor crown militarily, leading Welsh troops in the battles of Stoke Field and Blackheath, and also on campaign to France in 1492 and 1513.[57]

Through his devotion to Henry, Rhys accumulated considerable riches; by the end of the reign, he could be said to have status matching that of an English magnate. He used his wealth wisely, not least in embarking on a remarkable rebuilding project at Carew Castle to construct a palatial seat on par with anything in England. His greatest honour came in April 1505 when, after a position became vacant, Henry inducted Rhys into the prestigious Order of the Garter, the first Welshman since William Herbert to be afforded the honour and only the fourth in total if Edmund and Jasper Tudor are included. It was a remarkable display of royal favour, and a demonstration of how heavily the king of England had come to depend on his Welsh ally.[58]

That there was mutual respect and trust between the two men is clear from the fact that one of Prince Arthur's closest acquaintances was Rhys's son Gruffydd ap Rhys. For a king as circumspect as Henry, no one who wasn't fully vetted and valued was going to be allowed such close proximity to his treasured heir unless he strongly approved of their character and background. That Gruffydd was also permitted to marry one of the king's maternal cousins, Catherine St John, is further evidence of the close bond between the two families, who did, after all, share common descent from Ednyfed Fychan. Arthur's premature death at the age of fifteen devastated Gruffydd ap Rhys, and following his own death twenty years later, after a storied career, he was buried close to the prince's elaborate chantry in Worcester Cathedral. Rhys himself, meanwhile, continued his distinguished service under Henry VIII, maintaining a firm grip on royal authority in Wales for another two decades until his death aged around seventy-six in 1525.[59] He was buried in the same Greyfriars in Carmarthen as the king's father, Edmund Tudor, a final connection between the two families. Few men, English or Welsh, had done so well out of the Tudor accession.

Another Welsh figure who played his role in the Tudor accession, and was amply rewarded once the dust had settled, was Hugh Conway. It was Conway whom Margaret Beaufort had sent to Brittany with money to help fund her son's conspiracy, and it was he who counselled Henry that Wales was a suitable destination for an invasion.[60] Aged around forty-five when Henry VII became king, Conway's career soon took off with his fellow Welshman on the throne. On 21 September 1485, just a month after the battle, Conway was appointed keeper of the great wardrobe, and knighted just a few months later. Such was his reputation with the king, in 1494 he was created lord treasurer of Ireland, and in 1504 lord treasurer of Calais.[61]

Despite their reluctance to be drawn into the fighting at Bosworth, the Herbert family also quickly came to terms with their childhood companion, quietly abandoning decades of Yorkist sympathies and making peace with the new order. Within the first year of Henry's reign, the earl of Huntingdon, as head of the Herbert family, was pardoned of all fines incurred, and his brother Walter was appointed steward and constable of the lordships of Centrecelly and Talgarth, going on to serve on several commissions across the reign, becoming an important and competent member of the Tudor administration in South-East Wales.[62] In a sign of their friendship, and possibly a commemoration of the great victory at Bosworth, Walter sent the king a hawk every August.[63]

In fact, while grieving for the death of their son Arthur in the summer of 1502, one of the places the king and his queen visited during their western progress was Raglan. Henry perhaps found some solace at his childhood home, however brief, and also relaxed in the company of the Herberts, his erstwhile companions.[64]

Another person of Welsh descent who did well out of the Tudor victory was Henry's cousin Richard Pole, whose mother was a half-sister of the king's mother, Margaret Beaufort. Under Henry's kingship, Pole was knighted, appointed constable of Harlech and Montgomery castles in Wales, created a knight of the Garter, and made chief gentleman of the privy chamber to Prince Arthur. Perhaps the greatest indication of Henry's trust in his cousin was that he oversaw Pole's marriage to Margaret Plantagenet, a Yorkist princess of royal blood. Though Pole lived and died a devoted adherent of the Tudor crown, his offspring would prove troublesome down the line.

Further Welshmen were rewarded. Another distant cousin, William Gruffydd of Penrhyn, was retained as chamberlain of North Wales a month after Bosworth, having first been appointed by Richard III.[65] Hugh Vaughan, one of Henry's companions in exile, climbed the ladder upon his return; starting as a household servant, Vaughan was knighted by 1500 and would become governor of Jersey for nearly thirty years. He married a daughter of the 3rd Earl of Northumberland, a woman of distant royal blood, and was buried in Westminster Abbey. Welshmen also made headway in the church. In 1496, John Morgan was consecrated as bishop of St David's, the first Welshman to fulfil the office since 1248, and though he was succeeded by an Englishman, in 1509 another Welshman, Edward Vaughan, was elected as bishop. Similarly in the north, in 1500 Dafydd ab Ieuan ab Iorwerth was elected bishop of St Asaph followed three years later by Dafydd ab Owain.[66]

There are dozens, if not hundreds, more examples of Welshmen suddenly making headway after a century and more on the sidelines. On 24 September 1485, Lewis ap Rhys was created keeper and bailiff of Hanslope in Buckingham, later becoming bailiff of Blisland in Cornwall and porter of Dover Castle. On the same date, Owen ap Griffith, a yeoman of the guard, was made steward and constable of Laugharne, while a month later Walter ap David ap John was appointed a coroner in Gower. On 17 November, meanwhile, Adam ap Jevan ap Jenkyn was granted the office of king's attorney in Carmarthenshire and Cardiganshire. In January and February 1486, letters of denizenship were granted to William ap Griffith ap Robyn and Richard ap Llewelyn ap Hulkyn, while on 16 February 1486 the doctor Lewis Caerleon was granted 40 marks a year for his role in the conspiracy that made Henry a king, followed by another grant of 20 marks a year six months later.[67]

The gifts of cash and offices continued. On 10 November 1486 William Llewelyn was made receiver of the lordship of Newport, and in March 1487 Hugh ap Howell and John ap Thomas were both granted annuities of 10 marks. On 1 June 1487, Owen Meredith was appointed king's attorney general in all the courts of record in South Wales, and on 26 February 1488 Edward ap Rhys, a yeoman of the chamber, was granted a brewhouse on Fleet Street in London. In perhaps the most visual demonstration of Welsh buoyancy at this time, the pub was called The Welshman.[68]

It wasn't just the Welshmen who were rewarded. On 15 June 1486, Henry granted Joan, wife of Philip ap Hywel and his nurse from his childhood in Pembroke, an annuity of 20 marks. This was followed in 1491 by the grant of a tun of wine to be delivered to Joan yearly. Evidently, she made a good impression on the youthful Henry and he retained a warm affection for her deep into his adulthood.[69]

More generally, scores of Welshmen and women flocked to London in the years after Henry became king. London, for so long associated with the crown which had inflicted hardship upon the Welsh nation, now became a city of untold opportunity where those with ambition could seek to transform their fortunes, not unlike the Tudors themselves. By the early sixteenth century, it was estimated there were at least 660 Welshmen in the English capital and perhaps as many as 1,500, a number that only grew exponentially as the century progressed.[70] Naturally, this exodus did have an effect on Welsh communities forced to endure the loss of some of their brightest minds, but over time the upper ranks of English society were imbued with a Welsh flair. Perhaps the most successful Welsh economic migrant during this period was David Seisyllt, later anglicised to Cecil, who established himself as a landowner near Stamford in Lincolnshire and found employment as a sergeant of the guard.[71] The Cecils would rise to the very highest ranks of Tudor society within just two generations, holding many of the key offices under Elizabeth I and James VI/I and establishing their own formidable political dynasty.[72] Perhaps they all occasionally frequented 'The Welshman' pub on Fleet Street.

While it is true some Welsh had received recognition under previous kings of England, Henry VII's own ancestors among them, under his reign the records clearly show that Welshmen from all walks of life were rewarded in greater numbers than ever before. It is important to note that Henry was not overly sentimental when it came to settling upon those who served him. As shown throughout English history, too many kings had relied on favourites who would prove their downfall. It was those who exhibited characteristics of loyalty and competency that advanced under the first Tudor king. The difference with Henry was that he more than willing for those men and women to be drawn from Wales, no longer looked down upon as an unworthy, even lesser, people.[73]

In gratitude for this opportunity, Welsh attitudes to England underwent a marked change during the reign of the earlier Tudors, content that a man of their race was on the throne and looked favourably upon his compatriots, or at least more favourably than his predecessors. Not without reason did George Owen of Henllys later remark that Henry 'so drew the hearts of the Welshmen to him, as the leadstone does the iron'. So far as the evidence can be followed, the feeling was mutual.[74]

There is much to be said for Henry VII's warmth towards the land of his birth. The very first proclamation he issued as king after the Battle of Bosworth is revealing. Like his predecessors throughout the fifteenth century, Henry regarded himself, 'by the grace of God', king of England and of France as well as Lord of Ireland. He also, however, use the style 'prince of Wales', laying personal claim to a title English kings had traditionally reserved for their heirs. The personal significance to Henry, fully aware of his pedigree and upbringing, consciously associating himself with Wales and the Welsh, is clear.[75]

When it came to settling upon a royal badge or emblem to represent him in public, Henry again looked to his Welsh connection for inspiration. Every king of England bore the royal arms, traditionally accompanied by a pair of heraldic supporters to add an individual element. Henry VI, for example, used two antelopes, while Edward IV employed two lions. Richard III's arms, famously, were supported by two boars. Other supporters used by medieval kings to that point included falcons and harts.

For one of his supporters, Henry VII choose a white greyhound with a red and gold collar, a heraldic device associated with the earldom of Richmond and the House of Lancaster. Among those who had borne the greyhound as a secondary badge were John of Gaunt and John Beaufort, Henry's great-great-grandfather and great-grandfather respectively.[76]

The other supporter he selected was singularly rooted in Welsh history, but it would become synonymous with the first Tudor king of England: the Red Dragon of Cadwaladr. During his march to battle, Henry brandished the dragon wherever he went, consciously positioning himself as the successor of the ancient king of the Britons. Though he would employ multiple badges throughout his reign, ancestral propaganda that included the red rose of Lancaster and the Beaufort portcullis, when it came to his arms, Henry elected to prioritise his Welsh lineage.

The steps Henry took to extol his Welshness were not motivated by political expedience, but rather personal reasons. Once upon the English throne, there was little to be gained in pandering to the interests of the Welsh, a people long treated with suspicion, even disdain, in England.

It was the English nobility and people Henry had to win over, and it was in England rather than Wales that the success of his fledgling and vulnerable dynasty would be judged. He selected the red dragon as his principal badge not because it advanced his position, but because it held great personal significance.

Perhaps because of insecurity about his legitimacy to rule, Henry sought to brand his kingdom with dynastic imagery, and consequently the Welsh dragon featured prominently around the early Tudor court. It was particularly a favourite of royal masons employed to shape the king's pet projects, acting no doubt on detailed instructions from their master. More than 500 years later examples of Henry's dragon can still be viewed, visual reminders of the brief interlude in English history when a consciously Welsh king occupied the throne. In King's College Chapel, Cambridge, Henry's arms liberally adorn the hallowed walls, while on the Great East Window the dragon is situated prominently above the head of Christ. The same arms can still be seen on the Christ Church Gateway that provides access into Canterbury Cathedral, and similarly the dragon is conspicuously placed throughout the majestic Lady Chapel in Westminster Abbey that Henry had erected to serve as a grand royal mausoleum and lasting testament to the dynasty he founded.

The red dragon appeared elsewhere during Henry's reign, his heritage on show for all. On the eve of his coronation, Henry created a new officer of arms known as Rouge Dragon, and during the coronation banquet itself the king's champion, Robert Dymmock, rode into the room astride a horse whose caparison was richly emblazoned with the red dragon.[77] During the stirring water pageant held in November 1487 to celebrate Elizabeth of York's coronation, meanwhile, one striking boat known as the *Bachelers Barge* outshone all others for it featured a 'great red dragon spouting flames of fire' into the Thames.[78] Henry even put the dragon on his coins, so that every subject with money in their pouches, from Cumbria to Cornwall and from Gwynedd to Kent, associated this symbol with their king.[79]

Henry's penchant for mining his Welsh background did not end with emblems, offices or coins. When the much-vaunted Tudor heir, a son of both Yorkist and Lancastrian extraction, was born in the early hours of 20 September 1486, the boy's name and birthplace represented a marked departure from recent English royal history. During his upbringing in Wales, and possibly Brittany, Henry had likely been surrounded by the legendary exploits of King Arthur, a favoured topic of the poets and musicians who enjoyed regaling their audiences with the ancient hero's exploits. That Henry claimed Arthur as an ancestor only served to heighten an interest in Arthurian folklore that he brought to his kingship.

While the subject had been popular as far back as the sixth or seventh centuries among the Welsh, who viewed Arthur as one of their own, the start of Henry's reign coincided with the publication of Thomas Malory's *Le Morte d'Arthur*. Produced by William Caxton's pioneering printing press, Malory's work was one of the first books printed in England and brought the legend to a wider English audience. It also served to establish in the public consciousness Arthur's famed Camelot as 'English Winchester'. Henry, wisely recognising an opportunity to connect his heir with the renowned king of British legend, arranged for his son to be born in England's ancient capital. The newborn was duly christened Arthur, which at once drew comment in Wales – the poet Dafydd Llwyd enthusiastically responded that he would watch on in anticipation for the 'victories that go his name'.[80]

The name was not completely unknown in English royal circles. Just two decades earlier Edward IV had named his illegitimate son Arthur, while a Breton-born nephew of kings Richard I and John also bore the illustrious name. Neither, however, were born heir to the throne. The firstborn legitimate sons of the king of England, from 1485 all the way back to the Norman Conquest in 1066, had been named Edward, Edward, Edward, Henry, Henry, Edward, Edward, John, Edward, Henry, William, Eustace, William and Robert. By naming his son Arthur, Henry VII made a clear departure from a tradition in favour of honouring his personal heritage. Tragically, there would never be a second King Arthur, for the Tudor prince predeceased his father, dying at the age of just fifteen. The cult of the legendary king soon fell by the wayside, and normal service was resumed under Henry VIII, who named his heir Edward.

Moreover, there is no suggestion in the historical record that Henry had any embarrassment about his paternal descent, or his Welsh kin. As already shown, he acknowledged and rewarded three of his closest relations on his father's side, Jasper Tudor, David Owen and the younger Owen Tudor. As for the father he never knew, Henry named his third son Edmund and marked the anniversary of his father's death every year. During the celebrations for his second son's investiture as duke of York in 1494, the king even interrupted the festivities for a week to mark the thirty-eighth anniversary of his father's demise. In September 1491, Henry assigned a £10 annuity to the Greyfriars in Carmarthen for prayers to be said for his father's soul, while in November 1496 the significant sum of £43 10s was handed to Rhys ap Thomas for a new Purbeck tomb to be constructed.[81]

Henry's commitment in embracing his Welshness, to value his ancestry, reward his relations and employ Welsh imagery and myth to construct his own legend, was not without its risk. Indeed, shortly into his reign he was subject to slanderous aspersions that mocked his lowly paternal descent, which some thought unfitting for a king of England. Richard III, after all, had attempted to exploit Henry's Welsh birth in his various proclamations.[82] Henry chose not to shy away from these accusations, personally funding an investigation into his background to establish his British lineage and counteract the insults levelled at him.

The commission was handed to Dafydd ab Ieuan ap Iorwerth, abbot of Valle Crucis, plus a canon of Hereford named Dr Owen Poole and a herald-at-arms named John King, and all three were empowered to travel throughout Wales charged with salvaging the king's paternal reputation. The result of their research was half credible and half fiction, concluding that within 100 degrees the king was descended from Brutus of Troy, the mythical founder of Britain. Nonetheless, this commission provides the only source we have to speculate upon the origins of Ednyfed Fychan and the Welsh background of the Tudor dynasty.

The three principal commissioners recruited several Welsh genealogists, who each assiduously examined all existing manuscripts to glean the information they sought. Pedigrees were a matter of great importance to the Welsh people, and it should not necessarily be treated with caution that such documents existed in the late fifteenth century, with verbal traditions put to parchment. Though writing a few centuries earlier, the cleric Gerald of Wales made much of Welsh preoccupation with ancestry, noting in his work *The Description of Wales* that 'the Welsh value distinguished birth and noble descent more than anything else in this world', adding that 'even the common people know their family-tree by heart'. It was expected they could 'readily recite from memory the list of their grandfathers, great-grandfathers, great-great-grandfathers, back to the sixth or seventh generation'.[83]

The commission found that Henry was, as was commonly known, the son of Edmund Tudor, grandson of Owen Tudor and great-grandson of Maredudd ap Tudur. It traced his ancestry back several further generations to Ednyfed Fychan, revealing that he in turn was the son of Cynwrig, son of Iorwerth. Ednyfed's great-grandfather was Gwrgan, son of Maredudd, and so on until it reached the mythical founder of Britain, Brutus of Troy.[84] Henry was not embarrassed by the results of this investigation, and made no attempt to disown, or downplay, his bloodline.

Henry was an elusive monarch, one who preferred to maintain a personal distance from those he ruled. He was a vigilant man, with a deep-rooted wariness of others often perceived as unwarranted paranoia, and this reputation has persisted through the centuries. The historical record, however, can always provide a glimpse of the real person, particularly when it comes to how they spent their money. Recent examinations into Henry's Chamber Books,[85] which record payments primarily concerned with his most personal needs, have produced a wealth of information that bring to life the first Tudor king, and shed further light on his relationship with the Welsh.

Around St David's Day, for example, bonuses are recorded for the Welshmen in the king's employ so that they can celebrate the saint's feast day.[86] That these payments were maintained in the final years of the reign, a dark period when the king's ruthless avarice had taken a deep hold, suggests the Welsh patron saint was personally significant to the king. As a native of Pembrokeshire, a quality he shared with the saint, Henry was also unique among kings of England to that point in time in recognising St David's importance to the Welshmen in his household.

These same Chamber Books also reveal that Henry never forgot the tastes and sounds of his childhood. Once wealthy and able to afford any fare on the market, he spent significant sums satisfying his urges. Payments are recorded in most years between 1495 and the king's death in 1509 to source significant quantities of metheglin, a type of spiced mead brewed in South Wales, and also for cheese from Llanthony Priory in Monmouthshire. Among those rewarded for this are servants of his Welsh allies, Walter Herbert and Rhys ap Thomas.[87]

Welsh harpists, meanwhile, were known to frequent Henry's court, and in 1501 the king even personally paid for one of their funerals, a touching recognition of an entertainer who had presumably brought him joy and memories of his childhood.[88] It is likely that Henry also enjoyed the work of Welsh poets and minstrels, although it is unknown to what extent he had mastered the Welsh language, the beloved tongue of his ancestors. Henry's intelligence was well noted by his contemporaries, and he was also a known linguist; during his funeral oration, Bishop John Fisher made mention that Henry was 'gracious in diverse languages', reasonably understood to have been English, French and Latin.[89]

Henry had grown up in Wales, surrounded by Welsh-speaking servants including one of his nurses, Joan. If his birthplace of Pembroke, a traditional seat of Anglo-Norman Marcher Lords, was no great centre of Welsh learning, then the same cannot be said of Raglan Castle, where Henry spent his formative childhood years. Under the patronage of William Herbert, Henry's guardian, Raglan became a hub for Welsh culture and arts, both visual and aural, and provided a splendid base for scores of bards, musicians, scribes and others to exhibit their talents in a nurturing environment.

An eager student, it is highly unlikely that Henry, brought up around the Welsh language and with a Welsh nurse in Joan ap Howell, did not pick up at least the basics that would allow him to follow some of the performances, and perhaps key phrases so he could greet visitors or express his gratitude. He was, after all, being groomed by Herbert to be a potential son-in-law, and there would have been an expectation that Henry would be moulded somewhat in his guardian's image. Any potential development in the medium of Welsh was disrupted by Herbert's death in battle and Henry's exile to Brittany, though it must be noted that the languages of Welsh and Breton share a similar root, and some common words. He left Wales at the age of fourteen, and did not depart a place whose culture, language or people he would forget. That he was said to enjoy Welsh poetry as king suggests he retained some basic knowledge into adulthood.[90]

Upon becoming king, Henry also introduced the relatively obscure cult of Armel into England, a saint of Welsh origin he discovered during his lengthy exile in Brittany. Though he publicly venerated English national saints like George and Edward the Confessor, following the example set by previous kings, it was Armel to whom Henry was personally devoted. When finalising plans for his grand new Lady Chapel in Westminster Abbey, the king ordered two carvings of the armoured saint to be produced, and both can still be viewed 500 years later within sight of his tomb, one standing in the third bay of the south triforium and another at the east end of the north aisle.[91]

Henry was also keen to demonstrate his thanks to Armel for winning his great victory in the field. On 6 September 1503, when the king returned to the East Midlands, Henry paid a visit to the Cistercian abbey of Merevale in Warwickshire, where tradition states he camped the night before the battle of Bosworth.[92] He compensated the monks for the damage caused by his army, and before he left commissioned a new stained-glass window. Perhaps intended to imitate some of those he had seen in Brittany, the window depicted Armel in his customary suit of armour, brandishing a Bible in one hand and a bagged dragon in the other.[93] It was a solid testament to this Welsh king of England's enduring personal commitment to a previously obscure Welsh-Breton saint.[94]

Following Henry's example, other public commemorations of Armel occurred under early Tudor rule, some of which still survive. A small chapel dedicated to Armel once stood to the west of Westminster Abbey, while a recently rediscovered reredos in Romsey Abbey in Hampshire depicts a long-haired and bearded Armel taming a dragon, his legs and feet enclosed in armour.[95] He also features on the tomb of one of Henry's closest confidantes, his longtime chancellor Cardinal John Morton, still visible in the crypt of Canterbury Cathedral. An elaborate fifteenth-century alabaster panel, meanwhile, can be viewed in St Mary Brookfield parish church in north London, purportedly found during the late nineteenth century beneath some floorboards in a North Welsh farmhouse, Plas-y-Pentre. The tradition is that the panel had once adorned a wall in Valle Crucis Abbey in Denbighshire but had been quietly rescued during the Dissolution and concealed down the generations in private possession.[96]

Armel has also survived in manuscript form. On a prayer roll presented to the king's son Prince Henry, the saint is featured alongside various representations of Christ, the Virgin Mary, the Archangel Michael and saints Christopher, Anthony and George. The page bearing Armel's likeness explains to the reader that the saint was 'brought out of Britayne

at the ynstans off the kyng oure sovereyne lord Harry the VIIth', and all
who prayed to him would be delivered from their troubles with gout,
aches, agues, fevers and other infirmities.[97]

It may be considered curious that Henry was personally devoted
to a saint celebrated for slaying a dragon, a beast he had adopted as
his principal badge and had even carried into battle. Close inspection
of the various depictions of Armel, however, reveals an interesting
discrepancy. In Brittany and France, Armel is often associated with a
large and fierce dragon, a colossal creature who terrified the people
until he was destroyed. In Welsh or English representations, however,
Armel is often shown with a smaller, submissive dragon, sometimes
docile under the saint's foot. This may have been intended as a none-
too-subtle message to any concerned English parties that just as Armel
had his dragon under control, so too did Henry with the Welsh, for he
was indeed one of them.[98]

All these things taken together, Henry's enthusiastic adopting of Welsh
heraldry and names, his curiosity of his lineage, his penchant for the
tastes and sounds of his youth, and willingness to employ and befriend
Welsh faces strongly suggest a king who embraced his Welsh heritage and
felt a deep affinity for his compatriots. Henry was a subtle man, a natural
pragmatist who may have been one of the most circumspect men to wear
a crown. Everything he did once king, firstly to establish his credibility
and secondly to strengthen his dynasty, was intentional and not without
a great deal of forethought. A king of England had little to gain from
associating himself so strongly with Welsh symbols, legends or people.
Henry nevertheless discarded his cautious nature and went to great pains
to wear his Welshness publicly.[99]

There is good reason that contemporaries, particularly those
from outside England who weren't as hostile to all things Welsh,
acknowledged Henry's Welshness. It was remarked upon in great detail
by his French biographer Bernard André, and drew comment from the
Italian poets Pietro Carmeliano and Giovanni D'Giglis and the Scotsman
Walter Oglivie, who regarded him as Cadwaladr's heir. The theme of
Henry being directly descended from Cadwaladr was also taken up by
the writer of the Worcester pageant that welcomed him to the city in
1486. Perhaps most significantly, however, a noble Venetian ambassador
visiting England around 1496 pointedly noted in his report that the 'most
wise and fortunate' Henry VII was 'a Welshman'.[100]

All were surely broadcasting accurately and without prejudice
the image Henry himself wanted the world to see. His Beaufort and
Lancastrian connections had incurred some criticism, scorn even, but to
Henry this ancient Welsh lineage, stretching back centuries before the
Normans and even the Saxons had arrived on these islands, represented
the very height of dynastic prestige. Considering all the evidence provided,

it must be finally recognised that, though he was a king of England, Henry regarded himself without qualification as a proud Welshman, the heir of a remarkable legacy.

Henry was buried in Westminster Abbey on 11 May 1509, laid to rest in the glorious Lady Chapel he was in the process of rebuilding to serve as his dynasty's personal mausoleum. One in four men of the guard were Welsh, and as many as thirty-five Welshmen were involved in the funeral arrangements, performing one final duty to their compatriot.[101] Above his grave rests an ornate bronze-and-marble tomb in the Italian manner that captured the king's likeness. By placing himself in the pantheon of venerated English kings, and memorialised in greater splendour than any that had ruled before him, Henry was able to make a bold final statement that served to reinforce the legitimacy of the Tudors. Though his reign continues to be overshadowed, Henry's reputation as one of history's great survivors is justly earned.

There is much that we can never know about this enthralling period in Welsh, English and British history. The people who existed several centuries ago remain largely elusive characters, of whom we can only draw tantalising glimpses through often frustratingly vague or compromised historical records. The discussion about whether the Tudors, as we now refer to them, were ultimately a force for good for Wales and the Welsh continues to be heated, a consequence of the political, administrative, judicial, religious and linguistic changes the country experienced during the fifteenth and sixteenth centuries. The reign of Henry VII has traditionally been considered a watershed moment in the historical study of England, covering its emergence from the medieval into the Renaissance. Though this can be problematic for various reasons, Henry's tenure on the English throne most certainly was a pivotal moment in the story of Wales.

Returning to the scope of the present work, chronicling the origins of the family responsible for much of these changes, the bare facts nevertheless have much to commend them. From comparatively humble origins in what is now known as North Wales, there once rose a competent politician named Ednyfed Fychan, a figure of considerable intellect and drive who provided a sound foundation for his descendants to flourish under difficult circumstances, often at odds with their English overlords. He could never have conceived that one of those would have established the greatest dynasty to rule over England, the very kingdom that crushed the Welsh autonomy Ednyfed had spent his life defending. It was a remarkable turnaround, but fortune knows no limits.

And neither, it would seem, do sons of prophecy.

Notes

Abbreviations

Adam of Usk *The Chronicle of Adam of Usk*

AoWR *The Act of Welsh Rulers 1120–1283*

André *The Life of Henry VII*

BL *British Library*

Brut *The Brut or The Chronicles of England*

ByT *Brut y Tywysogion, or The Chronicle of the Princes*

Caradoc *The History of Wales, Written Originally in British, by Caradoc of Lhancarvan*

Chronica Maiora *The Chronica Maiora of Thomas Walsingham*

Commines *The Memoirs of Philip De Commines*

Croyland *Ingulph's Chronicle of the Abbey of Croyland*

CCR *Calendar of the Close Rolls*

CFR *Calendar of the Fine Rolls*

CPR *Calendar of the Patent Rolls*

CSPM *Calendar of State Papers, Milan*

CSPS *Calendar of State Papers, Spain*

ChronLon *Chronicles of London*

DL *Duchy of Lancaster*

EngChron *An English Chronicle of the Reigns of Richard II, Henry IV, Henry V and Henry VI*

Foedera *Rymer's Foedera*

Froissart *Chronicles of England, France, Spain by Sir John Froissart*

Gerald *Gerald of Wales, The Journey Through Wales and The Description of Wales*

Great *Great Chronicle of London*

Gregory *William Gregory's Chronicle of London*

Hall *Hall's Chronicle*

L&P *Letters and Papers Illustrative of the Reigns of Richard III and Henry VII*

Leland *Joannis Lelandi antiquarii De rebus Britannicis collectanea*

Mancini *Dominic Mancini's The Usurpation of Richard the Third*

Materials *Materials for a History of the Reign of Henry VII*

Molinet *Chroniques de Jean Molinet*

NewChron *The New Chronicles*

NLW *National Library of Wales*

OL *Original Letters, Illustrative of English History*

Paris *Mathew Paris's English History*

PL *The Paston Letters*

POPC *Proceedings and Ordinances of the Privy Council of England*

PROB *Public Record Office*

PROME *Parliament Rolls of Medieval England 1275-1504*

Scalacronica *Scalacronica; The Reigns of Edward I, Edward II and Edward III*

SJLM *St John's College Archives, Cambridge*

TNA *The National Archives*

Vergil *Three Books of Polydore Vergil's English History*

WAM *Westminster Abbey Muniments*

Wendover *Roger of Wendover's Flowers of History*

Warkworth *A Chronicle of the Reign of King Edward the Fourth by John Warkworth*

Introduction

1. *A Relation, or Rather a True Account, of the Island of England, About the Year 1500* (tr. C.A. Sneyd, London, 1847) p.19

1 The Terror of England

1. Caradoc of Lhancarvan, *The History of Wales, Written Originally in British, by Caradoc of Lhancarvan, Englished by Dr Powell and Augmented by W. Wynne, to Which is Added, A Description of Wales by Sir John Price* (London, 1774) pp. 331-332
2. *Caradoc* pp.325-334
3. Gerald of Wales, *The Journey Through Wales and The Description of Wales* (tr. L. Thorpe, London 2004) p.251
4. Williams, G., *Renewal and Reformation Wales c.1415-1642* (Oxford, 1987) p.451
5. Lloyd, J.E., *A History of Wales from the Earliest Times to the Edwardian Conquest* (London, 1912) pp.371-392
6. Lloyd, *History of Wales* pp.604-611; Gerald p.182, 233-238, 251-252
7. Alternatively known as Snowdonia
8. Lloyd, *History of Wales* pp.587-613; Gerald pp.193-194; *Brut y Tywysogion, or The Chronicle of the Princes* (ed. J. Williams ab Ithel, London, 1860) p.225, 241, 257
9. *ByT* pp.264-279; Lloyd, *History of Wales* p.621, 634-635; *Caradoc* pp.228-231; *Roger of Wendover's Flowers of History Vol. II* (ed. J.A. Giles, London, 1849) p.225
10. *ByT* p.273; *Wendover Vol. II* pp.256-258
11. *ByT* pp.281-283
12. *Wendover Vol. II* p.308-322; Morris, M., *King John; Treachery, Tyranny and the Road to Magna Carta* (London, 2015) pp.299-311; Jones, D., *Magna Carta; The Making and Legacy of the Great Charter* (London, 2017) pp.130-169
13. *Wendover Vol. II* p.349-364
14. *Ingulph's Chronicle of the Abbey of Croyland with the Continuations by Peter of Blois and Anonymous Writers* (ed. H.T. Riley, London 1854) p.316
15. *Caradoc* p.240; Lloyd, *History of Wales* pp.647-648; *ByT* p.287
16. Stephenson, D., *Medieval Wales c.1050-1332* (Cardiff, 2019) p.22; Lloyd, *History of Wales* p.684; Ellis, T.P., *Welsh Tribal Law and Custom in the Middle Ages Vol. 1* (Oxford, 1926) p.36
17. *ByT* pp.289-291; *Caradoc* pp.240-241; Lloyd, *History of Wales* p.649
18. Lloyd, *History of Wales* pp.652-653; *ByT* pp.299-303
19. *ByT* pp.303-305; Lloyd, *History of Wales* pp.652-654, 684; *Syllabus of the Documents Relating to England and Other Kingdoms Contained in the Collection Known as Rymer's Foedera Vol. I 1066-1377* (ed. T.D. Hardy, London, 1869) pp.23-24; *Rotuli litterarum clausarum in Turri Londinensi asservati 1204-1224 Vol. 1* (ed. T.D. Hardy, London, 1833) pp. 378-379; *The Act of Welsh Rulers 1120-1283* (ed. H. Pryce, Cardiff, 2005) pp.398-400
20. *A Catalogue of the Manuscripts Relating to Wales in The British Museum Vol. 1* (ed. E. Owen, London, 1900) p.357
21. CPR 1215-1255 p.413, 481
22. AoWR pp.419-423
23. *ByT* p.307, 317; Lloyd, *History of Wales* pp.659-669; *Wendover Vol. II* p.444, 509-510; *Caradoc* pp.249-251; CPR 1225-1232 p.436
24. Lloyd, *History of Wales* pp.673-675; *Caradoc* p.252; *ByT* pp.319-321; *Wendover Vol. II* pp.539-540
25. *Wendover Vol. II* pp.540-541; Lloyd, *History of Wales* pp.675-676; *Caradoc* pp.251-252
26. AoWR pp.434-435
27. CPR 1225-1232 p.453; CPR 1232-1247 p.3, 17
28. *Wendover Vol. II* pp.604-606
29. CPR 1232-1247 p.108
30. Hurlock, K., *Britain, Ireland and The Crusades C.1000-1300* (Basingstoke, 2013) pp.72-73; Walker, D., *Medieval Wales* (Cambridge, 1990) p.108; Lloyd, *History of Wales* pp.684-685; CCR 1234-1237 p.101

31. Lloyd, *History of Wales* p.684

32. Yorke, P., *The Royal Tribes of Wales* (ed. R. Williams, Liverpool, 1887) p.36

33. *Caradoc* p.331; *Gerald* p.222; Lloyd, *History of Wales* pp.324-338; *ByT* p.23

34. Watkins, T.G., *The Legal History of Wales* (Cardiff, 2007) pp.44-75; Lloyd, *History of Wales* pp.338-343

35. *ByT* p.55; Davies, J., *A History of Wales* (London, 1994) p.106

36. *ByT* pp.194-195; 199-205; Lloyd, *History of Wales* pp.500-515, 568-572; *AoWR* pp.168-173

37. *ByT* pp.237-241; Lloyd, *History of Wales* p.582

38. *ByT* p.229, 243, 245

39. *Gerald* p.203

40. *ByT* p.245

41. *Gerald* p.251

42. Roberts, G., 'Wyrion Eden'; The Anglesey Descendants of Ednyfed Fychan in the Fourteenth Century' in *Aspects of Welsh History* (Cardiff, 1969) p.183, 273; *Caradoc* p.332

43. *AoWR* pp.443-444; Lloyd, *History of Wales* pp.692-693; *ByT* p.327

44. *Caradoc* p.259

45. *Caradoc* pp.331-332

46. Ellis, *Welsh Tribal Law* p.107, 113-114

47. *Survey of The Honour of Denbigh 1334* (ed. P. Vinogradoff & F. Morgan, London, 1914) p. 228, 261, 265; Roberts, *Wyrion Eden* p.182-184; Ellis, *Welsh Tribal Law* pp.246-247; CPR 1225-1232 p.271; *AoWR* pp.223-224; Yorke, *Royal Tribes* p.193

48. *Caradoc* p.332

49. *AoWR* pp.423-428; Fenton, R., *Tours in Wales (1804-1813)* (London, 1917) p.311

50. Yorke, *Royal Tribes* p.193; *Caradoc* p.332

51. CPR 1232-1247 p.59, 184; *AoWR* pp.457-460; Lloyd, *History of Wales* 695-698; *Mathew Paris's English History Vol. I* (tr. J.A. Giles, London, 1852) p.372

52. *Caradoc* p.268

53. CPR 1232-1247 p.264, 267-268; Lloyd, *History of Wales* 696-698; *AoWR* p.466-467; 477-478

54. *Paris Vol. I* p.488; CPR 1232-1247 p.424

55. *Paris Vol. II* pp.45-46; CPR 1232-1247 p.456; *Annales Cestrienses, Chronicle of the Abbey of St Werburg, at Chester* (ed. R.C. Christie, London, 1887) pp. 63-65

56. Lloyd, *History of Wales* p.705; *Caradoc* pp.265-267; *Paris Vol. II* pp.110-112

57. CPR 1232-1247 p.461; *Annales Cestrienses* p.65

58. *Paris Vol. II* pp.140-141

59. *Annales Cestrienses* p.67; *Caradoc* p.332

60. *The Royal Commission on the Ancient and Historical Monuments and Constructions in Wales and Monmouthshire; IV County of Denbigh* (London, 1914) p. 95

61. Price, T., *The Literary Remains of the Rev. Thomas Price Vol. 1* (Llandovery, 1854) p.333

2 War and Bloodshed

1. *Paris Vol. II* pp.244-245

2. *AoWR* pp.483-485

3. Lloyd, *History of Wales* p.705; *Paris Vol. II* p.111; Roberts, *Wyrion Eden* pp.183-184, 274; *ByT* p.333; *Collections Historical & Archaeological Relating to Montgomeryshire Vol. 1* (London, 1868) p.117; *Fasti Ecclesiae Anglicanae or A Calendar of the Principal Ecclesiastical Dignitaries in England and Wales Vol. I* (ed. T.D. Hardy, Oxford, 1854) p.66

4. Roberts, *Wyrion Eden* pp.183-185; *AoWR* pp.223-224

5. Roberts, *Wyrion Eden* pp.183-184

6. *AoWR* pp.725-726

7. CPR 1232-1247 p.496; CCR 1247-1251 p.72, 518; CPR 1247-1258 p.23; CPR 1258-1266 pp.69-70, 248

8. *Catalogue of Manuscripts Relating to Wales Vol. I* p.357

9. Roberts, *Wyrion Eden* pp.183-184

10. *Caradoc* p.271; *ByT* p.341

11. Lloyd, *History of Wales* p.714

12. *ByT* p.341

13. *Caradoc* p.273; Lloyd, *History of Wales* p.717, 720-721

14. *Paris Vol. III* p.233

15. *Caradoc* p.279
16. *AoWR* pp.499-501
17. *ByT* pp.345-347; *AoWR* pp.505-506
18. Lloyd, *History of Wales* p.731; *Royal and Other Historical Letters Illustrative of the Reign of Henry III Vol. II* (ed. W.W. Shirley, 1862, London) pp. 367-369
19. *AoWR* pp.529-533; *Collections Historical Montgomeryshire Vol. I* p.117
20. *Royal Letters Henry III Vol. II* pp.284-286
21. *ByT* pp. 355-357; *AoWR* pp.536-542
22. *AoWR* pp.543-545
23. *ByT* p.357
24. Owen, M.E., '*Literary Convention and Historical Reality: The Court in the Welsh Poetry of the Twelfth and Thirteenth Centuries*' in Etudes Celtiques 29 (1992) p.81; Lloyd, *History of Wales* p.743; *The Myvyrian Archaeology of Wales Collected out of Ancient Manuscripts* (ed. O. Jones, E. Williams & W.O. Pugh, Denbigh, 1870) p.254
25. CCR 1272-1279 p.506; *AoWR* pp.657-658
26. *AoWR* pp.796-798; Lloyd, *History of Wales* pp.748-750
27. CCR 1272-1279 p.241; *AoWR* pp.568-570; '*Councils and Ecclesiastical Documents Relating to Great Britain and Ireland*' Vol. I (ed. A.W. Haddan & W. Stubbs, Oxford, 1869) pp.506-508
28. *Caradoc* p.283
29. Lloyd, *History of Wales* 759; Morris, J.E., *The Welsh Wars of Edward I; A Contribution to Mediaeval Military History, Based on Original Documents* (Oxford, 1901) pp. 130-135
30. *Caradoc* p.285
31. *Annales Cestrienses* p.105; *AoWR* pp.589-596
32. Lloyd, *History of Wales* p.761; *Caradoc* p.285; *ByT* pp.369-371
33. Roberts, *Wyrion Eden* p.184
34. *AoWR* pp.651-654
35. Morris, *Welsh Wars* pp.153-154; *Annales Cestrienses* p.109
36. *Caradoc* pp.297-298; Morris, *Welsh Wars* p.166, 176-180
37. *Caradoc* pp.287-291
38. *Caradoc* pp.292-293
39. *Caradoc* pp.293-296
40. Roberts, *Wyrion Eden* p.186; Griffiths, R.A. & Thomas, R.S., *The Making of the Tudor Dynasty* (Stroud, 2005) pp.20-21
41. Roberts, *Wyrion Eden* p.185
42. Morris, *Welsh Wars* p.183; *Scalacronica; The Reigns of Edward I, Edward II and Edward III as Recorded by Sir Thomas Gray* (ed. H. Maxwell, Glasgow, 1907) p.3
43. *Annales Cestrienses* pp.109-111; Lloyd, *History of Wales* p.763; *Caradoc* p.299
44. *Annales Cestrienses* p.113
45. Stephenson, *Medieval Wales* p.27

3 Hardship

1. *The Statutes of Wales Collected, Edited, and Arranged by Ivor Bowen* (ed. T. Fisher Unwin, London, 1908) p.2-27.
2. Roberts, *Wyrion Eden* p.186
3. *Scalacronica* p.4
4. Morris, *Welsh Wars.* pp.242-243; Moore, D., *The Welsh Wars of Independence c.410-1415* (Stroud, 2005) p.159; Rex Smith, G., '*The Penmachno Letter Patent and the Welsh Uprising of 1294-95*' in *Cambrian Medieval Celtic Studies, Vol. 58* (Aberystwyth, 2009) p.51
5. Rex Smith, *Penmachno Letter* pp.57-58; *An Inventory of the Ancient Monuments in Wales and Monmouthshire, Vol. VI County of Merioneth* (London, 1921) p.40
6. *Caradoc* pp.307-310; Rex Smith, *Penmachno Letter* pp.52-53
7. CPR 1292-1301 p.223
8. CPR 1343-1345 pp.229-231; *Caradoc* p.310
9. Roberts, *Wyrion Eden* p.187; *Registrum Vulgariter Nuncupatum, 'The Record of Caernarvon'* (ed. H. Ellis, London, 1838) p.215
10. Easterling, R.C., '*The Friars in Wales*' in *Archaeologia Cambrensis Vol. XIV Sixth Series* (London, 1914) pp.333-335; Roberts, G., '*The Dominican Friary of Bangor*' in *Aspects of Welsh History* (Cardiff, 1969) p.218-229
11. Ashton C., *Gweithiau Iolo Goch: Gyda Nodiadau Hanesyddol a Beiriadol* (Croesoswallt, 1898) p.277

12. Ashton, *Iolo Goch* p.276
13. CCR 1313-1318 p.367
14. CFR 1307-1319 p.361; CFR 1319-1327 p.1
15. *Scalacronica* p.45, 74
16. *The Brut or The Chronicles of England* (ed. F.W.D. Brie, London, 1906) pp.239-241.
17. *Croyland* p.331; *Scalacronica* p.85
18. *Caradoc* p.310; Edwards, J.G., 'Sir Gruffydd Llwyd' in *English Historical Review* (ed. R.L. Poole, London, 1915) pp.589-601
19. *Scalacronica* p.87; *Brut* pp.268-272
20. CCR 1330-1333 p.505
21. Roberts, *Wyrion Eden* p.192
22. *Calendar of Ancient Correspondence Concerning Wales* (ed. J.G. Edwards, Cardiff, 1935) pp.230-233
23. *Calendar of Ancient Correspondence* pp.231-235; *Calendar of Ancient Petitions Relating to Wales, Thirteenth to Sixteenth Century* (ed. W. Rees, Cardiff, 1975) p.395
24. CPR 1343-1345 p.492, 500
25. *The Register of Edward the Black Prince Preserved in the Public Record Office Part I* (London, 1930) p.37, 54, 55.
26. *Register of Edward the Black Prince* p.88, 110
27. Gower, J., *The Story of Wales* (St Ives, 2012) p.130; Rees, W., 'The Black Death in Wales' in *Essays in Medieval History* (ed. R.W. Southern, London 1968) pp.181-187
28. *The Record of Caernarvon* pp.12-13, 73, 77
29. Roberts, *Wyrion Eden* p.190; CCR 1330-1333 p.505
30. *Caradoc* pp.314-315
31. Johnston, D., *Iolo Goch Poems* (Llandysul, 1993) pp.12-17
32. Griffiths & Thomas, *Making* p.23
33. CPR 1391-1396 p.4

4 The Great Rebellion

1. Johnston, *Iolo Goch* pp.18-22
2. Williams-Jones, K., 'The Taking Of Conwy Castle, 1401' in *Transactions of the Caernarvonshire Historical Society Vol. 39* p.30
3. Griffiths & Thomas, *Making* p.24
4. CCR 1389-1392 p.49, 52; Roberts, *Wyrion Eden* p.202
5. Roberts, *Wyrion Eden* p.200, Johnston, *Iolo Goch* pp.18-22; CPR 1381-1385 p.100; CPR 1388-1392 p.485; Williams, J., 'Penmynydd and the Tudors' in *Archaeologia Cambrensis Third Series Vol. 15* (1869) p.292; Chapman, A., *Welsh Soldiers in the Late Middle Ages, 1282-1422* (Woodbridge, 2015) pp.88-89
6. CPR 1381-1385 p.104
7. Johnston, *Iolo Goch* pp.22-26; Williams, *Penmynydd* p.292
8. Roberts, *Wyrion Eden* pp.212-213, 274; Williams, *Penmynydd* pp.278-281, 293
9. Griffiths & Thomas, *Making* pp.24-25; Roberts, *Wyrion Eden* pp.199-201
10. Griffiths & Thomas, *Making* p.25; Roberts, *Wyrion Eden* pp.202-203; *Brut* pp.356-357; CPR 1396-1399 p.400; Chapman, *Welsh Soldiers* p.93
11. Jarman, A.O.H., 'The Later Cynfeirdd' in *a Guide to Welsh Literature Vol. 1* (ed. A.O.H. Jarman & G.R. Hughes, Swansea, 1976) p.115
12. Jarman, *Cynfeirdd* p.115
13. Moore, *Welsh Wars* pp.213-215; Davies, R.R., *The Revolt of Owain Glyndwr* (Oxford, 1995) pp.89-90
14. *Chronicles of England, France, Spain, and the Adjoining Countries by Sir John Froissart Vol. 1* (tr. T. Johnes, London, 1857) p.545
15. Moore, *Welsh Wars* pp.164-166
16. *Froissart Vol. 1* pp.545-546; Carr, A.D., *Medieval Wales* (Basingstoke, 1995) pp.103-106
17. Carr, *Medieval Wales* pp.104-105
18. Davies, R.R., *Owain Glyn Dŵr, Prince of Wales* (Talybont, 2009) pp.12-14; Johnston, *Iolo Goch* pp.30-34
19. Johnston, *Iolo Goch* p.30, 38
20. Davies, *Revolt* pp.137-138, 144-145
21. Johnston, *Iolo Goch* p.38; Davies, *Revolt* pp.146-148
22. *Caradoc* p.315
23. Johnston, *Iolo Goch* pp.38-42
24. *Brut* pp.351-356; *The Chronicles of London* (ed. C.L. Kingsford, London, 1905) p.18; *Chronicle of the Grey*

Friars of London (ed. J.G. Nichols, London, 1852) pp.8-9

25. *The Chronicle of Adam of Usk, A.D. 1377-1421* (ed. E.M. Thompson, London, 1904) p.44; *The Chronica Maiora of Thomas Walsingham, 1376-1422* (ed. D. Preest, Woodbridge 2005) p.305
26. *Croyland* p.353
27. *Adam of Usk* p.47, 49
28. *Adam of Usk* p.55; *Brut* p.359; *Chronica Maiora* p.308; *Croyland* p.354; *ChronLon* p.21
29. *Chronica Maiora* p.310; *ChronLon* pp.21-43
30. *Adam of Usk* p.69; *Brut* p.360; *Croyland* p.355
31. Davies, *Revolt* pp.82-83
32. *Royal and Historical Letters During the Reign of Henry the Fourth, King of England and of France, and Lord of Ireland Vol. 1* (ed. F.C. Hingeston, London, 1860) pp.35-38
33. Moore, *Welsh Wars* pp.169-170; *PROME Vol. XIII* p.97
34. Moore, *Welsh Wars* p.170; Davies, *Revolt* p.1, 102
35. Johnston, *Iolo Goch* p.32, 34; Davies, *Owain Glyn Dŵr* pp.30-32
36. Davies, *Revolt* pp.102-103
37. *Brut* p.363; Mortimer, I., *The Fears of Henry IV; The Life of England's Self-Made King* (London, 2008) p.227
38. Griffiths & Thomas, *Making* p.27
39. *CPR 1399-1401* p.386
40. *PROME Vol. XIII* pp.104-105, 136-146
41. *CPR 1399-1401* pp.469-470
42. *CPR 1399-1401* p.451

5 Men of Fame

1. Williams-Jones, *Taking Of Conwy* p.9
2. *Adam of Usk* p.96; Williams-Jones, *Taking Of Conwy* p.10, 22, 25, 34
3. *Adam of Usk* p.96; *PoPC Vol. I* p.147, 150-151
4. *Adam of Usk* p.123
5. *CPR 1399-1401* p.37, 155, 158
6. *CPR 1399-1401* p.470, 475; Williams-Jones, *Taking Of Conwy* p.13
7. *Royal Letters Henry the Fourth Vol. I* p.xxiv, 69-71
8. *Royal Letters Henry the Fourth Vol. I* p.xxiv; *CPR 1399-1401* p.447; Williams-Jones, *Taking Of Conwy* p.15, 42
9. *Adam of Usk* p.96
10. *Adam of Usk* p.100
11. *Adam of Usk* p.107
12. 'Welsh Records: Calendar of Recognizance Rolls of the Palatinate of Chester, to the end of the reign of Henry IV' in *The Thirty-Sixth Annual Report of the Deputy Keeper of the Public Records* (London, 1875) p.207
13. Davies, *Revolt* pp.104-106
14. *Adam of Usk* pp.107-111
15. *Brut* p.393; *Adam of Usk* pp.116-117; Davies, *Revolt* p.107
16. Davies, *Revolt* p.108, 176
17. Davies, *Revolt* p.108, pp.179-180; *Adam of Usk* p.36, 117
18. Mortimer, *Fears of Henry IV* p.241
19. *Adam of Usk* p.122
20. Davies, *Revolt* pp.182-184
21. *Adam of Usk* p.117
22. *Royal Letters Henry the Fourth Vol. I* pp.136-151, 161-162; Davies, *Revolt* pp.112-113
23. *Adam of Usk* pp.122-123; *Brut* pp.363-364
24. Davies, *Revolt* pp.162-163
25. *Adam of Usk* p.127
26. Davies, *History of Wales* p.200
27. Davies, *Revolt* p.192
28. Davies, *Revolt* pp.166-169
29. Mortimer, *Fears of Henry IV* pp.288-289; *Caradoc* pp.317-318
30. *Adam of Usk* p.125, 152; Davies, *Revolt* pp.194-195; *A Collection of the Chronicles and Memorials of Great Britain and Ireland during The Middle Ages Vol. IV* (ed. W. Hardy & E.L.C.P. Hardy, London, 1887) p.92-94
31. Roberts, *Wyrion Eden* pp.204-206
32. Davies, *Revolt* p.295
33. *Adam of Usk* pp.167-168
34. *Adam of Usk* p.168
35. *Adam of Usk* p.166
36. *Adam of Usk* p.166
37. Griffiths & Thomas, *Making* pp.24-27; Roberts, *Wyrion Eden* pp.202-203; *CPR 1396-1399* p.400
38. Griffiths & Thomas, *Making* p.29

39. CPR 1413-1416 p.11
40. Thomas, R.S., *The Political Career, Estates and Connection of Jasper Tudor, Earl of Pembroke and Duke of Bedford* (Swansea, 1971) p.1; Roberts, *Wyrion Eden* p.199; Griffiths & Thomas, *Making* p.30; Williams, *Penmynydd* p.381.
41. Davies, *Revolt* p.308
42. *Adam of Usk* p.183
43. Morgan, P., 'Elis Gruffudd of Gronant – Tudor Chronicler Extraordinary' *in Flintshire Historical Society publications, Vol. 25* (1972) p.10

6 A Gentleman of Wales

1. Davies, *Revolt* p.310-324
2. Roberts, *Wyrion Eden* p.199-201, 204-206; Thomas, *Jasper Tudor* p.4; Williams, *Penmynydd* p.381; Griffiths & Thomas, *Making* pp.24-25, 30
3. Roberts, *Wyrion Eden* pp.205-211
4. 'Deeds: A.13061-A.13672' *in A Descriptive Catalogue of Ancient Deeds Vol. 5* (ed. H.C. Maxwell Lyte, London, 1906) pp. 548-565
5. 'Calendar of French Rolls 1-10 Henry V' *in The Forty-Fourth Annual Report of the Deputy Keeper of the Public Records* (London, 1883) p.622
6. PROME *Vol. XI* p.63; 'Welsh Records: Calendar of Recognizance Rolls of The Palatinate of Chester, from the Beginning of the Reign of Henry V to the End of the Reign of Henry VII' *in the Thirty-Seventh Annual Report Of The Deputy Keeper Of The Public Records* (London, 1876) p.710; *The Ancient Kalendars and Inventories of the Treasury of His Majesty's Exchequer Vol. II* (ed. F. Palgrave, London, 1836) pp.172-175.
7. PoPC *Vol. V* p.47; *Rymer's Foedera Vol. 10* (ed. T. Rymer, London, 1739-1745) pp. 682-695; 710; CCR 1435-1441 p155; CPR 1436-1441 p.344; CCR 1435-1441 p.225
8. CPR 1452-1461 p.494, 532; 'William Gregory's Chronicle of London' *in The Historical Collections of a Citizen of London in the Fifteenth Century* (ed. J. Gairdner, London, 1876) p.211
9. Griffiths, R.A., *The Reign of King Henry VI* (Stroud, 1998) p.33-34, 54-55
10. Strickland, A., *Lives of the Queens of England from the Norman Conquest Vol. III* (Philadelphia, 1841) p.164; Thomas, *Jasper Tudor* p.8
11. *Joannis Lelandi antiquarii De rebus Britannicis collectanea Vol. II* (ed. T. Hearns, London, 1774) p.492; 'Rymer's Foedera Vol. 10 p.710; CCR 1435-1441 p.225; Riley-Adams, A.D., *Elis Gruffydd and Welsh Identity in the Sixteenth Century* (Oklahoma, 2018) pp.121-127; *Brut* p.507
12. Griffiths & Thomas, *Making* pp.31-33
13. Griffiths, *Henry VI* p.56
14. Lewis, K.J., *Katherine of Valois and the Various Vicissitudes of her Reputation* p.4; Wolff, B., *Henry VI* (London, 1983) p.45; CPR 1422-1429 pp.491-492
15. CPR 1422-1429 pp.491-492
16. *Brut* p.451
17. Laynesmith, J., The Last Medieval Queens; English Queenship 1445-1503 (Oxford, 2004) pp.157-159
18. Harris, G.L., *Cardinal Beaufort, A Study of Lancastrian Ascendancy and Decline* (Oxford, 1988) pp. 116-117; PROME *Vol. X* pp.22-26
19. *Gregory* p.159; *Brut* p.432
20. Sayles, G.O., 'The Royal Marriages Act 1428' *in Law Quarterly Review Vol. 94* (ed. P.V. Baker, London, 1978) pp.188-192; Griffiths, R.A., 'Queen Katherine of Valois and a Missing Statute of the Realm' *in King and Country: England and Wales in the Fifteenth Century* (London, 1991) pp.103-113.
21. Riley-Adams, *Elis Gruffydd* pp.121-127
22. Thomas, *Jasper Tudor* pp.8-9
23. PROME *Vol. X* pp.43-44
24. Bennett, M., 'Son of Scotlangle: Sir John Steward' *in Journal of the Sydney Society for Scottish History Vol. 15* (Sydney, 2015) pp.17-19, 26-27, 31
25. Bennett, *Son of Scotlangle* pp.30-33
26. *Incerti Scriptoris Chronicon Angliae de Regnis Trium Regum Lancastrensium: Henrici IV, Henrici V, et Henrici VI, Vol. IV* (ed. J.A. Giles, London, 1848) p.17; Lewis, *Katherine of Valois* p.6

27. *Three Books of Polydore Vergil's English History, Comprising the Reigns of Henry VI, Edward IV, and Richard III* (ed. H. Ellis, London 1844) p.62

28. *Hall's Chronicle, Containing the History of England during the Reign of Henry the Fourth and the Succeeding Monarchs, to the End of the Reign of Henry the Eighth* (ed. H. Ellis, London, 1809) pp.184-185

29. *Holinshed's Chronicles of England, Scotland, And Ireland Vol. III* (London, 1808) p.188

30. *Vergil* p.62; *Hall* p.185

31. Lewis, *Katherine of Valois* pp.5-10

32. *Titi Livii Foro-Juliensis, Vita Henrici Quinti* (ed. T. Hearne, Oxford, 1716), p.75; Lewis, *Katherine of Valois* p.2

33. 'The Borough of Hertford: Castle, Honour, Manors, Church and Charities' in *A History of the County of Hertford Vol. 3* (ed. W. Page, London, 1912) pp.501-511

34. Griffiths, *Henry VI* pp.60-61

35. *Brut* p.507

36. CPR 1452-1461 p.66, 78; *The Victoria History of the County of Hertford Vol. 4* (ed. W. Page, London, 1914) pp.61-63

37. *The Paston Letters, 1422-1509 A.D. Vol. 3, Henry VI 1422-1509* (ed. J. Gairdner, London, 1872) pp.316-320

38. BL Kings 395 f.33r

39. CPR 1452-1461 p.111, 198

40. Griffiths & Thomas, *Making* p.38; *Leland* p.492

41. *PROME Vol. XI* p.63; TNA SC 8/124/6168; CPR 1429-1436 p.212

42. 'Welsh Records', *Palatinate of Chester*, p.710

43. Laynesmith, *Medieval Queens* p.146

44. *Brut* p.470; Strickland, *Queens of England* p.166

45. Bentley, S., *Excerpta Historica; or Illustrations of English History* (London, 1831) p.148

46. Strickland, *Queens of England* pp.166-168; Nichols, J., *A Collection of all the Wills Now Known to be Extant, of the Kings and Queens of England, Princes and Princesses of Wales, and Every Branch of the Blood Royal* (London, 1780) p.244-249

47. Strickland, *Queens of England* pp.168-169; *Brut* p.470

48. Seymour, R., *A Survey of the Cities of London and Westminster, Borough of Southwark and Parts Adjacent Vol. II* (London, 1734) p.546

49. Tomaini, T., *The Corpse as Text; Disinterment and Antiquarian Enquiry 1700-1900* (Woodbridge, 2017) pp.59-61

50. *A Survey of London by John Stow Reprinted from the Text of 1603 Vol. II* (ed. C.L. Kingsford, Oxford, 1908) pp.109

51. *The Diary of Samuel Pepys Vol. VIII* (ed H.B. Wheatley, London, 1905) p.222

52. Ralph, J., *A Critical Review of the Public Buildings, Statues, And Ornaments in and about London and Westminster* (London, 1783) pp.134

53. Gough, R., *Sepulchral Monuments in Great Britain Vol. II Part II* (London, 1796) pp.115

54. Tomaini, *The Corpse as Text* p.57, 76-77, 80-87

55. *PoPC Vol. 5* pp.46-50

56. *Ancient Kalendars and Inventories* pp.172-175

57. Barron, C.M., *London in the Later Middle Ages; Government and People 1200-1500* (Oxford, 2005) pp.164-66; Pugh, R.B., *Imprisonment in Medieval England* (Cambridge, 1968) pp.326-327, 332; 357

58. Chrimes, S.B., Henry VII (London, 1999) pp.9-10

59. *Brut* p.507; *Grey Friars Chronicle* p.17

60. *Rymer's Foedera Vol. 10* pp. 710

61. CCR 1435-1441 p.155

62. *Leland* p.492; *Rymer's Foedera Vol. 10* pp.682-695; Griffiths, *Henry VI* p.67

63. CCR 1435-1441 p.225, 284-285

64. 'The Libell of English Policye' in *Political Poems and Songs Relating to English History Vol. II* (ed. T. Wright, London, 1861) p.190

65. CPR 1436-1441 p.344; CCR 1435-1441 pp.284-285

66. Evans, H.T., *Wales and the Wars of the Roses* (Cambridge, 1915) p.70

7 The King's Uterine Brothers

1. Barnes, T.L., *A Nun's Life: Barking Abbey in the Late-Medieval and Early Modern Periods* (Portland, 2004) pp.13-16; 'Houses of Benedictine nuns: Abbey of Barking', in *A History of the County of Essex: Vol. 2* (ed. W. Page and J. Horace Round, London, 1907) pp.115-122

2. Barnes, *A Nun's Life* pp.54-56

3. *Rymer's Foedera Vol. 10* p.828

4. Barnes, *A Nun's Life* pp.68-69, 112

5. Thomas, *Jasper Tudor* p.26

6. *Rymer's Foedera Vol. 10* p.828

7. *Henry the Sixth; A Reprint of John Blacman's Memoir* (ed. M.R. James, Cambridge, 1919) pp.29-30

8. Thomas, *Jasper Tudor* p.26

9. CCR 1435-1441 p.474; CCR 1441-1447 pp.78-79

10. Thomas, *Jasper Tudor* p.27

11. Thomas, *Jasper Tudor* p.28

12. Wolffe, *Henry VI* pp.180-182; *Gregory* p.186

13. Thomas, *Jasper Tudor* p.28

14. CPR 1452-1461 p.494, 532, 547; CCR 1454-1461 p.405

15. *PROME Vol. XII* pp. 93-106.

16. *The Paston Letters* (ed. N. Davis, Oxford, 1999) pp. 27-28; *An English Chronicle of the Reigns of Richard II, Henry IV, Henry V, and Henry VI* (ed. J.S. Davies, London, 1856) p.69

17. *Three Fifteenth-Century Chronicles with Historical Memoranda by John Stowe, the Antiquary* (ed. J. Gairdner, London, 1880) pp. 94-99

18. *Original Letters Illustrative of English History Vol. I* (ed. H. Ellis, London, 1825) pp. 11-13

19. *ChronLon* p.163; *Brut* p.521

20. *Calendar of the Charter Rolls Preserved in the Public Record Office Vol. VI A.D. 1427-1516* p.122; *Reports from The Lords Committees Touching the Dignity of a Peer of the Realm Vol. V* (1829) pp.293-294

21. *ChronLon* p.164

22. Evans, *Wales and the WotR* p.78

23. Thomas, *Jasper Tudor* p.34

24. Evans, *Wales and the WotR* pp.81-82; *Rotuli Parliamentorum Vol. VI* (London, 1767-77) pp.250-253; Thomas, *Jasper Tudor* p.35

25. Williams, D.H., *Catalogue of Seals in the National Museum of Wales Vol. 1* (Cardiff, 1993); Boutell, C., *Heraldry, Historical and Popular* (London, 1864) p.249

26. Siddons, M.P., *The Development of Welsh Heraldry Vol. 1* (Aberystwyth, 1991) p.117

27. Thomas, *Jasper Tudor* pp.40-44, 94, 105

28. CPR 1452-1461 p.66, 79; 'Welsh Records' in *Palatinate of Chester* p.621

29. *RotParl Vol. VI* p.253, 260-261; Thomas, *Jasper Tudor* p.117

30. Thomas, *Jasper Tudor* p.123-124

31. CPR 1452-1461 p.80, 111-112; Thomas, *Jasper Tudor* p.127

32. CPR 1452-1461 p.104, 110, 116

33. Thomas, *Jasper Tudor* p.116

34. *Third Report of The Royal Commission on Historical Manuscripts* (London, 1872) p.280

35. Bentley, *Excerpta Historica* p.154

36. CPR 1441-1446 p.283

37. *PROME Vol. XII* p.95

38. Jones, M.K. & Underwood, M.G., *The King's Mother: Lady Margaret Beaufort, Countess of Richmond and Derby* (1993) p.38

39. CPR 1452-1461 pp.78-79

40. *PL Vol. I* pp.253-254; Blomefield, F., *An Essay Towards a Topographical History of the County of Norfolk Vol. III* (London, 1806) p.158

41. *Bale's Chronicle, Six Town Chronicles of England* (ed. R. Flenley, Oxford, 1911) p. 140; *PoPC Vol. VI* p.166-7

42. *EngChron* p.70

43. CPR 1452-1461 pp.143-144

44. *PL Vol. I* pp.259-261

45. *PoPC Vol. VI* p.164-165

46. *PL Vol. I* p.265-266

47. CPR 1452-1461 p.153

48. Thomas, *Jasper Tudor* p.153; Lander, J.R., *Henry VI and the Duke of York's Second Protectorate in Bulletin of the John Rylands Library, XLIII* (1960) pp.47-48

49. *PoPC Vol. VI* p.166
50. *PROME Vol. XII* pp.257-259
51. *CPR 1452-1461* p.159
52. *PoPC Vol. VI* pp.220-233
53. *CPR 1452-1461* pp.111-112
54. *PL Vol. I* p.315
55. *Croyland* p.419

8 War in Wales

1. Lander, *York's Second Protectorate* p.49
2. *Rymer's Foedera Vol. 11* pp. 360-370
3. Hicks, M., *Warwick the Kingmaker* (Oxford, 2002) p. 80
4. *PL Vol. I* pp.325-326
5. *PL Vol. I* p.327
6. *The New Chronicles of England and France* (ed. H. Ellis, London, 1811) p. 629
7. *PL Vol. I* p.328
8. *PL Vol. I* p.327-330
9. *EngChron* p.72; *Registra Quorundam Abbatum Monasterii Sancti Albani* (ed. H.T. Riley, London, 1872) p. 168
10. *PL Vol. I* pp.332-333
11. *Gregory* p.198; *PL Vol. I* p.331
12. *PL Vol. I* pp.331-334; *Gregory* p.198; *EngChron* p.72
13. 'Milan: 1455', *CSPM* p.16
14. *PROME Vol. XII* pp.338-345
15. Griffiths, *Henry VI* p.747; *PL Vol. I* pp.344-346
16. *PROME Vol. XII* pp.381-429
17. Thomas, *Jasper Tudor* p.161; *PoPC Vol. VI* p.261; *CPR 1452-1461* p.273
18. Thomas, *Jasper Tudor* pp.162-163
19. Griffiths, R.A., 'Gruffydd ap Nicholas and the Rise of the House of Dinefwr' in *The National Library of Wales Journal, Vol. XIII* (1964) pp.256-65; Griffiths, R.A., 'Gruffydd ap Nicholas and the Fall of the House of Lancaster' in *Welsh History Review II* (1965) pp.213-31; Griffiths, R.A., *Sir Rhys ap Thomas and his Family: A Study in the Wars of the Roses and Early Tudor Politics* (Cardiff, 2014) pp.11-12
20. *PROME Vol. XII* p.446
21. *The Funeral Sermon of Margaret Countess of Richmond and Derby, Mother to King Henry VII, and Foundress of Christ's and St John's College in Cambridge, Preached by Bishop Fisher in 1509* (ed. J. Hymers, Cambridge, 1840) p.111-112
22. Thomas, *Jasper Tudor* p.166
23. Thomas, *Jasper Tudor* pp.166-167; *PL Vol. I* p.392
24. *PL Vol. I* p.378
25. *PROME Vol. XII* pp.431-432
26. *PL Vol. I* p.393
27. Evans, *Wales and the WotR* p.78, 89-90
28. Evans, *Wales and the WotR* p.52, 72, 80-83
29. *CPR 1452-1461* p.627
30. DL 29/651/10534 m.3
31. Evans, *Wales and the WotR* p.45
32. Pugh, T.B., 'The magnate, knights and gentry' in *Fifteenth Century England, 1399-1509* (ed. S.B. Chrimes, C.D. Ross, & R.A. Griffiths (Manchester, 1972) p.72; Thomas, D.H., *The Herberts of Raglan and the Battle of Edgecote 1469* (1967) p.4-12
33. Evans, *Wales and the WotR* p.53, 74
34. Evans, *Wales and the WotR* pp.74-75; Thomas, *The Herberts* p.14
35. Thomas, *The Herberts* p.15; Storey, R., *The End of The House of Lancaster* (Guildford, 1999) p.179
36. Griffiths, *Fall of Lancaster* p.225; Thomas, *Jasper Tudor* pp.168-170
37. Thomas, *Jasper Tudor* p.170
38. Storey, *The End of Lancaster* p.179
39. Griffiths, *Fall of Lancaster* p.226; Thomas, *Jasper Tudor* p.171; *Privy Purse Expenses of Elizabeth of York: Wardrobe Accounts of Edward the Fourth* (ed. N.H. Nicolas, London, 1830) pp.54-55
40. Thomas, *The Herberts* p.16
41. *CCR 1454-1461* p.158
42. Griffiths, *Fall of Lancaster* p.226; *PL Vol. I* pp.416-417; Storey, *The End of Lancaster* pp.181-182; *CPR 1452-1461* p.353, 360, 367
43. SJLM 3/2/1 – St John's College Archives, Cambridge, Wills and Bequests; Tallis, N., *Uncrowned Queen; The Fateful Life of Margaret Beaufort, Tudor Matriarch* (London, 2019) pp.44-45

44. Griffiths, *Rhys ap Thomas* p.49
45. Allen, E., 'The Tomb of The Earl of Richmond in St David's Cathedral' in *Archaeologia Cambrensis Vol. XIII No LII* (1896) pp.315-320
46. Roberts, T. & Williams, I., *The Poetical Works of Dafydd Nanmor* (Cardiff, 1923) pp.41-43; Bayani, D., *Jasper Tudor, Godfather of the Tudor Dynasty* (2015) pp.265-267
47. Bayani, *Jasper Tudor* pp.269-273; *Gwaith Lewys Glyn Cothi* (ed. D. Johnson, Cardiff, 1995) pp.30-33; *The Poetical Works of Lewis Glyn Cothi, A Celebrated Bard, Who Flourished in the Reigns of Henry VI, Edward IV, Richard III, and Henry VII* (ed. G. Mechain, Oxford, 1837) pp.492-496

9 Roots of Rancour

1. CPR 1452-1461 p.306-307
2. *PL Vol. I* p.392
3. Thomas, *Jasper Tudor* pp.51-55
4. CPR 1452-1461 p.359
5. Tallis, *Uncrowned Queen* p.55
6. 'July 1498', in CSPS Vol. 1 p.176
7. *The Itinerary in Wales of John Leland in or about the Years 1536-1539* (ed. L. Toulmin Smith, London, 1906) p.116
8. *Chronicle of the Six Ages*, NLW MS 3054d ff. 324r-324v
9. Bernard André, *The Life of Henry VII* (tr. D. Hobbins, New York, 2011)
10. *OL Vol. I* p.46, 53, 218
11. CPR 1485-1494 p.95
12. *Royal Commission on the Ancient and Historical Monuments and Constructions in Wales and Monmouthshire; An Inventory of the Ancient Monuments in Wales and Monmouthshire Vol. 7 County of Pembroke* (London, 1925) p.286
13. Jones & Underwood, *King's Mother* p.40
14. Jones & Underwood, *King's Mother* p.41; CPR 1452-1461 p.368, 504
15. CPR 1452-1461 p.433; CFR 1452-1461 pp.209-10, 294
16. CPR 1452-1461 p.340, 341
17. CPR 1452-1461 p.326
18. *PL Vol. I* p.408; *NewChron* p.632; *Bale's Chronicle* p.144
19. Laws, E., 'Notes on the Fortifications of Medieval Tenby' in *Archaeologia Cambrensis, Vol. XIII, No LII* (1896) pp.274-289; Walker, R.F., 'Jasper Tudor and the town of Tenby' in *The National Library of Wales Journal Vol. 16, No 1* (1969) pp.1-12
20. *PoPC Vol. VI* pp.292-293; Griffiths, *Henry VI* p.805
21. Griffiths, *Henry VI* pp.805-806; *EngChron* p.77
22. *ChronLon* p.168; *PL Vol. I* p.424; *Brut* p.525
23. *Hall* p.238
24. *EngChron* p.78
25. Thomas, *Jasper Tudor* p.177
26. CPR 1452-1462 p.494
27. Beltz, G.F., *Memorials of the Order of the Garter* (1841) p.clxii
28. *Froissart* p.66
29. CPR 1452-1461 pp.486-487
30. *EngChron* pp.79-80
31. Wolffe, *Henry VI* p.317; *RotParl Vol. V* p.348
32. *Gregory* p.205
33. *Gregory* p.204; *EngChron* p.80
34. *EngChron* pp.81-83
35. *ChronLon* pp.169-170; *Gregory* p.205, 207; *Brut* p.527
36. *Brut* p.527
37. *PL Vol. I* p.499
38. *EngChron* pp.83-84; *PROME Vol. XII* pp.453-462
39. CPR 1452-1461 p.532, 547, CCR 1454-1461 p.405; CFR 1452-1461 p.266
40. Blaauw, W.H., 'On the Effigy of Sir David Owen in Easebourne Church, Near Midhurst' in *Sussex Archaeological Collections Vol. VII* (London, 1854) pp.25-26
41. *PL Vol. I* p.500; CPR 1452-1461 p.541
42. CFR 1452-1461 p.267
43. CPR 1452-1461 p.534, 547
44. Thomas, *Jasper Tudor* pp.180-181
45. Thomas, *Jasper Tudor* p.186; CPR 1451-1462 p.565
46. CPR 1452-1461 p.550, 574
47. CPR 1452-1462 p.485, 562, 564-565
48. Thomas, *Jasper Tudor* pp.186-187
49. *EngChron* pp.94-95
50. *EngChron* pp.94-95
51. *EngChron* pp.96-97

52. *EngChron* p.97; *ChronLon* p.171; *Gregory* p.207; *Brut* pp.529-530
53. Griffiths, *Henry VI* p.884
54. *Gregory* p.208
55. *ChronLon* p.171
56. *EngChron* pp.100-101; *PROME Vol. XII* pp.516-517
57. *EngChron* pp.101-106; *ChronLon* p.172; *Gregory* p.208
58. *PROME Vol. XII* pp.518-528
59. *PoPC Vol. VI* pp.303-305
60. *Gregory* p.209
61. *EngChron* pp.98-99
62. *Gregory* p.209

10 Interminable Treachery

1. *Gregory* p.209
2. *Hall* p.250; *EngChron* pp.106-107
3. Evans, *Wales and the WotR* p.124; Thomas, *Jasper Tudor* pp.188-189; *William Worcestre Itineraries* (ed. J.H. Harvey, Oxford, 1969) p.203
4. *EngChron* p.110
5. *Hall* p.251; *Three Fifteenth-Century Chronicles* p.77
6. *Gregory* p.211; *EngChron* p.110
7. *ChronLon* p.172; *Brut* p.531
8. Some sources, like *Gregory* p.210, say the battle occurred on 2 February
9. *EngChron* p.110; *William Worcestre* p.203; 'Milan: 1461', CSPM pp.37-106; *Gregory* p.211
10. *EngChron* p.110
11. *EngChron* p.110
12. 'Milan: 1461', CSPM pp.37-106
13. *Three Fifteenth-Century Chronicles* p.77; *Gregory* p.211
14. For following, *Gregory* p.211
15. Bayani, *Jasper Tudor* pp.283-285
16. *Gregory* pp.211-212; *ChronLon* p.173; *EngChron* pp.107-108; 'Milan: 1461', CSPM pp.37-106
17. *Gregory* pp.214-215; *ChronLon* p.173; *EngChron* p.107
18. *Gregory* p.215; *Croyland* p.424
19. *Gregory* p.215; *ChronLon* pp.173-174; 'Milan: 1461', CSPM pp.37-106
20. *Croyland* pp.424-425
21. 'Milan: 1461', CSPM pp.37-106
22. *Gregory* pp.216-217; *PL Vol. II* p.5
23. *Gregory* p.217; *ChronLon* p.176
24. *Croyland* p.424
25. *Vergil* p.110
26. Williams, J., *Ancient and Modern Denbigh; A Descriptive History of the Castle, Borough, and Liberties* (1856) pp.86-87
27. 'Milan: 1461', CSPM pp.37-106
28. Evans, *Wales and the WotR* p.132, 134
29. CPR 1461-1467 p.7, 30
30. Evans, *Wales and the WotR* p.136
31. CPR 1461-1467 p.13, 43
32. CPR 1461-1467 p.17, 26, 36, 38, 40, 45, 62
33. CPR 1461-1467 pp.98-99
34. Evans, *Wales and the WotR* p.138; *PL Vol. II* pp.38-41
35. *OL Vol. 1* pp.15-16
36. *PL Vol. II* p.46
37. *PROME Vol. XIII* pp.55-56; Thomas, *The Herberts* pp.25-26
38. Evans, *Wales and the WotR* pp.140-141
39. *PL Vol. II* p.52
40. *PROME Vol. XIII* p.46; *PL Vol. II* p.118
41. *PL Vol. II* p.52
42. *Brut* p.532; *PROME Vol. XIII* pp.11-20, 43-46
43. *PROME Vol. XIII* pp.45-46
44. Beltz, *Order of the Garter* p.lxvii-lxviii
45. CPR 1461-1467 p.114
46. Evans, *Wales and the WotR* p.147
47. CPR 1461-1467 p77, 111
48. CPR 1461-1467 p.114; Thomas, *The Herberts* p.28
49. *Brut* p.532
50. 'Milan: 1461', CSPM pp.37-106
51. Evans, *Wales and the WotR* p.127
52. Bayani, *Jasper Tudor* pp.279-281

11 The Masterlock

1. CPR 1461-1467 p.12
2. CPR 1461-1467 p.114, 197, 212-213
3. *Hall* p.274
4. *André* pp.10-11
5. CPR 1461-1467 p.332
6. *Materials Vol. 1* p.581
7. *The Anglica Historia of Polydore Vergil A.D. 1485-1537* (ed. D. Hay, London, 1950) p.145
8. Nicolas, N.H., *Testamenta Vestusta, Being Illustrations from Wills* (London, 1826) pp.304-305

9. Ross, J., 'The Treatment of Traitors' Children' in *The Fifteenth Century XIV; Essays Presented to Michael Hicks* (ed. L. Clark, Woodbridge, 2015) p.133; Hicks, M.A., *False, Fleeting, Perjur'd Clarence; George, Duke of Clarence 1449-78* (Gloucester, 1980) p.38.
10. Jones & Underwood, *King's Mother* pp.47-48; WAM 6658
11. *OL Vol. 1* pp.42-48
12. Tallis, *Uncrowned Queen* p.91; Hicks, *Clarence* pp.56-57
13. Kenyon, J.R., *Raglan Castle* (Cardiff, 2003) pp.3-4, 10-11, 26-56; Thomas, *The Herberts* p.4-6
14. *Commines Vol. 1* pp.396-397
15. *Vergil* pp.134-135
16. *Materials Vol. 1* p.320
17. *Three Fifteenth-Century Chronicles* p.158
18. 'Milan: 1462', CSPM pp.106-108; Gregory p.218; ChronLon p.177; Scofield, C.L. *The Life and Reign of Edward the Fourth, King of England and of France and Lord of Ireland Vol. 1* (London, 1923) p.231
19. 'Milan: 1462', CSPM pp.106-108
20. Thomas, *Jasper Tudor* pp.200-201; Scofield, *Edward the Fourth Vol. 1* pp.250-251
21. Griffiths, *Henry VI* p.887; Thomas, *Jasper Tudor* pp.201-202; Scofield, *Edward the Fourth Vol. 1* p.252
22. Gregory pp.218-219; ChronLon pp.177-178; Scofield, *Edward the Fourth Vol. 1* p.261
23. Gregory p.219; Thomas, *Jasper Tudor* p.203
24. Gregory p.220
25. *Letters and Papers Illustrative of the Wars of the English in France during the Reign of Henry the Sixth, King of England Vol. 2* (ed. J. Stevenson, London, 1861) p.781
26. Thomas, *Jasper Tudor* pp.205-207
27. Gregory p.223
28. Goodman, A., *Wars of the Roses; Military Activity and English Society, 1452-97* (London, 1981) p.63
29. Griffiths & Thomas, *Making* p.72; Scofield, *Edward the Fourth Vol. 1* pp.318-319
30. *Hall* pp.259-260
31. *Gregory* pp.223-226
32. Ross, C., *Edward IV* (London, 1974) pp.59-63; *Letters and Papers Henry the Sixth Vol. 2 Part II* p.782
33. *Croyland* p.439; *Gregory* pp.232-233; Scofield, *Edward the Fourth Vol. 1* p.334
34. *Gregory* pp.226-227; *Croyland* pp.439-440; 'Milan: 1464', CSPM pp.110-114
35. Ramsay, J.H., *Lancaster and York, A Century of English History (A.D. 1399-1485) Vol. II* (Oxford, 1892) p.305
36. *Croyland* pp.445
37. *PL Vol. II* p.123
38. CPR 1461-1467 p.268, 271, 286, 366
39. CPR 1461-1467 p.425, 526-527, 533; CPR 1467-1477 p.41, 49, 136; Thomas, *The Herberts* p.35
40. CPR 1461-1467 p.100
41. Hicks, *Warwick* p.259, 269-271; Pugh, T.B., 'The Lordship of Gower and Kilvey in the Middle Ages' in *Glamorgan County History III, The Middle Ages* (ed. T.B. Pugh, Cardiff, 1971) pp.260-261
42. *Commines Vol. 1* p.182
43. *PROME Vol. XIII* p.124
44. *Hall* p.261
45. Evans, *Wales and the WotR* p.154
46. CPR 1461-1467 p.355
47. *PROME Vol. XIII* pp.124-126
48. Evans, *Wales and the WotR* pp.165-166; Bayani, *Jasper Tudor* p.114; Scofield, *Edward the Fourth Vol. 1* p.458
49. Evans, *Wales and the WotR* p.166; Gregory p.237
50. 'Milan: 1468', CSPM pp.122-128
51. CPR 1467-1477 p.103
52. Evans, *Wales and the WotR* pp.168-169
53. Evans, *Wales and the WotR* p.169; Gregory p.237; Thomas, *Jasper Tudor* p.213; Thomas, *The Herberts* pp.36-40; CPR 1467-1477 p.152
54. Thomas, *Jasper Tudor* pp.214-217; Gregory p.237
55. Evans, *Wales and the WotR* p.170; Thomas, *The Herberts* p.40
56. CPR 1467-1477 p.113, 154
57. Ross, *Edward IV* p.76
58. Dockray, K.R., 'The Yorkshire Rebellions of 1469' in *The Ricardian*

Vol. 6 No 82 (1983) pp.246-257;
Hicks, *Warwick* pp.271-276; Hicks,
Clarence pp.43-46 *Croyland* p.445

59. Hicks, *Clarence* pp.43; *Warkworth*
pp.46-51; Evans, *Wales and the WotR*
p.173

60. *Croyland* p.445

61. Lewis, B., 'The Battle of Edgecote
or Banbury (1469) Through the of
Contemporary Welsh Poets' in *The
Journal of Medieval Military History
Vol. IX; Soldiers, Weapons and Armies
in the Fifteenth Century* (ed. A. Curry
& A.R. Bell, Woodbridge, 2011) p.105;
Evans, *Wales and the WotR* p.175

62. Evans. G., *The Battle of Edgcote
1469; Re-Evaluating the Evidence*
(Northampton, 2019) pp.9-14, 29-41;
Lewis, W.G., 'The Exact Date of The
Battle of Banbury, 1469' in *Bulletin of
The Institute of Historical Research
Vol. LV* (London, 1982) pp.194-196

63. *Croyland* p.446; *Warkworth* pp.6-7;
Hall pp.273-74; Lewis, *The Battle of
Edgecote* p.107; Evans, *The Battle
of Edgcote* pp.67-73; Thomas, *The
Herberts* pp.60-70

64. *Croyland* p.446; *Hall* p.275

65. Scofield, *Edward the Fourth Vol. 1*
p.497; Nicolas, *Testamenta Vestusta*
p.304; Lewis, *The Battle of Edgecote*
pp.108-109

66. Evans, *The Battle of Edgcote* pp.9-14,
29-41

67. Lewis, *The Battle of Edgecote* pp.105,
107-108; Evans, *The Battle of Edgcote*
pp.107-109

68. *Hall* p.275

69. *Croyland* p.458; Hicks, *Warwick* p.277

70. 'Milan 1469', CSPM pp.128-134; *PL
Vol. II* p.390; Hicks, *Warwick* pp.278-
281

71. *Warkworth* pp.8-9; Scofield, *Edward
the Fourth Vol. 1* pp.509-518

12 The Bloody Sword

1. *Commines Vol. 1* pp.184-186
2. 'Milan 1470', CSPM pp.134-145
3. 'Milan 1470', CSPM pp.134-145;
Vergil pp.131-132; Thomas, *Jasper
Tudor* p.217; Scofield, *Edward the

Fourth Vol. 1* pp.529-531; *Croyland*
p.462; Griffiths, *Henry VI* pp.890-891;
Hicks, *Warwick* pp.293-295

4. 'Milan 1470', CSPM pp.134-145

5. *Hall* p.282; *ChronLon* p.181; *Vergil*
p.132

6. Thomas, *Jasper Tudor* p.218; Scofield,
Edward the Fourth Vol. 1 p.536

7. *Croyland* p.462; Scofield, *Edward the
Fourth Vol. 1* pp.535-536

8. 'Milan 1470', CSPM pp.134-145;
Croyland p.463; *ChronLon* p.182;
Warkworth p.11

9. 'Milan 1470', CSPM pp.134-145;
Hicks, *Warwick* pp.300-301

10. Owen, H, & Blakeway, J.B., *A History
of Shrewsbury Vol. I* (London, 1825)
p.248; Corbet, A.E.B., *The Family
of Corbet; Its Life and Times Vol. II*
(London, 1914) pp.250-256

11. Thomas, *The Herberts* pp.51-53

12. DeLloyd J.G., 'Climbing the Civil-
Service Pole during Civil War:
Sir Reynold Bray (c.1440-1503)', in
*Estrangement, Enterprise & Education
in Fifteenth Century England* (ed.
S.D. Michalove & A. Compton Reeves,
Stroud, 1998) p. 60-61

13. Hicks, *Clarence* pp.56-57; WAM 5472
ff.8V, 38, 41V SQQ

14. *Vergil* p.135

15. Jones & Underwood, *King's Mother*
p.52; WAM 12183 ff.19r-v

16. Jones & Underwood, *King's Mother*
p.52; Lewis, J., *Life of Dr John Fisher,
Bishop of Rochester in the Reign of
King Henry VIII Vol. II* (London,
1855) pp.269 p.269

17. *Vergil* p.134-135

18. Jones & Underwood, *King's Mother*
p.52; Griffiths & Thomas, *Making*
p.80

19. Scofield, *Edward the Fourth Vol. 1*
pp.554-555; *Hall* p.286; *ChronLon*
p.183; *Warkworth* pp.12-13

20. PROB 11/7/2

21. Hicks, *Clarence* pp.97-99; Jones &
Underwood, *King's Mother* p.52; CPR
1467-1477 pp.241-243

22. CFR 1461-1471 pp.283-284; Thomas,
Jasper Tudor p.219, 221-223

23. CPR 1467-1477 p.233, 236, 243, 251-252, CFR 1461-1471 p.293; Thomas, *Jasper Tudor* p.222
24. *Commines Vol. 1* pp.198-199; *Hall* p.289
25. *Warkworth* pp.13-15; *Croyland* pp.454-456; *ChronLon* pp.183-184; *Vergil* pp.136-143; 'Milan: 1471', *CSPM* pp.145-162; *Historie of the Arrivall of Edward IV in England and the Finall Recoverye of his Kingdomes from Henry VI* (ed. J. Bruce, London, 1838) pp.1-17
26. *Warkworth* pp.16-17; *Arrivall* pp.19-21; *Croyland* pp.464-465; *PL Vol. III* p.4
27. *Hall* p.296
28. *Warkworth* p.17; *Arrivall* pp.22-23; *Croyland* p.465
29. *Arrivall* pp.23-24; *Croyland* p.465
30. *Syllabus of the Rymer's Foedera* p.702
31. *Arrivall* pp.26-28
32. *Arrivall* pp.28-30; *Hall* p.300
33. *Warkworth* p.18; *Arrivall* pp.30-31; *Croyland* p.466
34. *Hall* p.302; *Vergil* p.155
35. *The Itinerary of John Leland, the Antiquary Vol. IV* (ed. T. Hearne, Oxford, 1769) p.66
36. *Vergil* p.154
37. *Vergil* p.155; *Hall* pp.302-303
38. Owen, G., *Description of Pembrokeshire* (ed. H. Owen, 1892) p.262
39. Thomas, *Jasper Tudor* p.225; Hore, H.F., 'Mayors and Bailiffs of Tenby' in *Archaeologia Cambrensis Vol. XIV* (London, 1853) pp.115-116
40. *Warkworth* p.21; *Arrivall* p.38; *ChronLon* p.186
41. 'Milan: 1471', *CSPM* pp.145-162
42. 'Milan: 1471', *CSPM* pp.145-162
43. CPR 1467-1477 p.283, 289
44. *André* pp.12-13; Jones & Underwood, *King's Mother* p.58
45. Merrony, M.W., *An Official History of Tenby* (Tenby, 2004) pp.23-26
46. *PL Vol. III* p.17

13 The Only Imp

1. *Commines Vol. 1* p.397; *André* p.14
2. *PL Vol. III* p.17; Allanic, J., *Le Prisonnier de la Tour d'Elven ou La Jeunesse du Roy Henry VII d'Angleterre* (Vannes, 1909) pp.12-13
3. *André* p.14
4. *Vergil* p.155; *Commines Vol. 1* p.397; Allanic, *Prisonnier* p.13
5. Scofield, *Edward the Fourth Vol. 2* p.19; Ross, *Edward IV* p.112
6. Griffiths & Thomas, *Making* pp.88-89; Scofield, *Edward the Fourth Vol. 2* pp.31-35
7. *Commines Vol. 1* p.397, *Vol. II* p.64
8. Jones, M.C.E., '"For My Lord of Richmond, a pourpoint and a palfrey"; Brief Remarks on the Financial Evidence for Henry Tudor's Exile in Brittany 1471-1484' in *The Ricardian*, XIII (2002) p.284
9. *Vergil* p.155
10. *André* p.14
11. Allanic, *Prisonnier* pp.15-16
12. Griffiths & Thomas, *Making* p.89; Pocquet du Haut-Jusse, B.A., *Francois II, Duc de Bretagne et L'Angleterre (1458-1488)* (Paris, 1929) p.180
13. Allanic, *Prisonnier* pp.16-17; Griffiths & Thomas, *Making* p.90; Pocquet du Haut-Jusse, *Francois II* p.176
14. Allanic, *Prisonnier* p.17
15. Henneman, J.B., *Olivier de Clisson and Political Society in France under Charles V and Charles VI* (Philadelphia, 1996) pp.35-71
16. Allanic, *Prisonnier* pp.17-18; Jones, *My Lord of Richmond* pp.286-287
17. Allanic, *Prisonnier* pp.17-18
18. Allanic, *Prisonnier* pp.18-23
19. Le Grand, A., *Les Vies des Saints de la Bretagne Armorique Vol. II* (Paris, 1901) pp.383-387; Asperen, H., 'Saint Armel of Brittany: The Identification of Four Badges from London' in *Peregrinations: Journal of Medieval Art and Architecture Vol. 2, Issue 1* (2005); Gray, M., 'Politics, Power and Piety: The Cult of St Armel in Early Tudor England and Wales' in *Rewriting Holiness: Reconfiguring Vitae, Re-Signifying Cults* (ed. M. Gray, Woodbridge, 2017) p.245
20. Gray, *Politics, Power and Piety* p.246
21. Williams, *Penmynydd* p.402; Pennant, T., *Tours in Wales Vol. III* (ed. J. Rhys, Caernarvon, 1883) p.28
22. *Materials Vol. II* p.394

23. Robinson, W.R., 'Sir Roland De Velville and the Tudor Dynasty: A Reassessment' in *Welsh History Review Vol. 15* (1991) p.354; Gunn, S.J., 'The Courtiers of Henry VII' in *English Historical Review Vol. 108* (Oxford, 1993) p.36, 43

24. CPR 1494-1509 p.47; CCR 1485-1500 p.282

25. Shaw, W.A., *The Knights of England Vol. II* (London, 1906) p.30; *L&P Vol. II* pp.87-89

26. Gunn, *Courtiers of Henry VII* p.36

27. E101/414/6 f.56v, E101/414/6 f.90v, E101/414/16 f.9r, E101/414/16 f.13r, E36/214 f.17r, E36/214 f.138v

28. Gunn, *Courtiers of Henry VII* p.39

29. *L&P Vol. I* pp.395-400

30. Robinson, *Roland de Velville* p.353; E101/415/3 f.51r; Gunn, *Courtiers of Henry VII* p.39

31. CPR 1381-1385 p.100; Williams, *Penmynydd* p292; Chrimes, S.B., 'Sir Roland De Velville' in *Welsh History Review Vol. 3* (1967) p.289; Robinson, *Roland De Velville* p.355

32. Robinson, *Roland De Velville* pp.356-357, 363-364; Williams, *Penmynydd* p.402; *Letters and Papers, Foreign and Domestic, of the Reign of Henry VIII Vol. 1* (ed. J.S. Brewer, London, 1862) p.447

33. Robinson, *Roland De Velville* p.367; Llwyd, A., *History of the Island of Mona or Anglesey* (Ruthin, 1833) pp.166-167; PROB 11/25/364; *Index of Wills Proved in the Prerogative Court of Canterbury 1383-1558 Vol. II* (ed. J. Challenor, London, 1895) p.543

34. Ballinger, J., 'Katheryn of Berain, A Study in North Wales Family History' in *Y Cymmrodor; the Magazine of the Honourable Society of Cymmrodorion Vol. XL* (London, 1929) pp.1-3

35. Christ Church (Oxford) MS 184 f.74t; NLW MS 6495C, 6496C; *Gwaith Siôn Tudur Vol. II* (ed. E. Roberts, Cardiff, 1980) p.42

36. Christ Church (Oxford) MS 184 f220v; *Gwaith Siôn Tudur Vol. II* pp.41-42

37. *Gwaith Siôn Tudur Vol. II* p.42

38. Robinson, *Roland De Velville* p.352-353; Jones, D.C., *The Bulkeleys of Beaumaris. 1440-1547, Anglesey Antiquarian Society and Field Club Transactions* (1961), p.8; Williams, D., 'The Welsh Tudors: The Family of Henry VII' in *History Today Vol. 4 Issue 2* (1954) pp.77-84

39. Siddons, *Welsh Heraldry Vol. 2* pp.577-578; BL Add MS 46354 f.21, 104v

40. Caron, P., *Kerbouric (De) – Réformation De La Noblesse* (Côtes D'armor, 2007) p.2

41. Scofield, *Edward the Fourth Vol. 2* pp.116-120; *Commines Vol. I* pp.251-254, 268-269

42. *Commines Vol. 1* pp.263-264, 272-277

43. *Commines Vol. 1* p.277; Scofield, *Edward the Fourth Vol. 2* p.151

44. Scofield, *Edward the Fourth Vol. 2* p.166; *Vergil* p.164; Pocquet du Haut-Jusse, *Francois II* p.219

45. Pocquet du Haut-Jusse, *Francois II* p.219; *Vergil* p.164; Allanic, *Prisonnier* pp.30-31

46. *Vergil* p.164

47. *Vergil* pp.165-167

48. *Vergil* pp.165-167; Allanic, *Prisonnier* p.32

49. *Vergil* p.166; Allanic, *Prisonnier* pp.34-35

50. *Vergil* p.167; Allanic, *Prisonnier* p.35

51. Pocquet du Haut-Jusse, *Francois II* p.204

52. Thomas, *Jasper Tudor* p.229; Scofield, *Edward the Fourth Vol. 2* p.173; Pocquet du Haut-Jusse, *Francois II* p.204, 248; Allanic, *Prisonnier* p.38; Jones, *My Lord of Richmond* p.287

53. *Molinet Vol. 1* p.405

54. Jones & Underwood, *King's Mother* p.58, 60

55. Jones & Underwood, *King's Mother* p.60; SJLM/4/4/2

56. 'Vatican Regesta 685: 1484-1487' in *Calendar of Papal Registers Relating to Great Britain and Ireland Vol. 14, 1484-1492* (ed. J.A. Twemlow, London, 1960) pp.18-21

57. Jones & Underwood, *King's Mother* p.61; WAM 32378

58. *Croyland* p.483; *ChronLon* p.189

59. *Commines Vol. 2* p.87; *Mancini* p.67

14 Another King

1. Ross, C., *Richard III* (London, 1999) pp.69-70; *Mancini* pp.67-69
2. Ross, *Richard III* p.65
3. *Croyland* p.485
4. *Croyland* p.485; *Vergil* p.173
5. *Croyland* p.486; Lewis, M., *Richard III; Loyalty Binds Me* (Stroud, 2018) pp.252-253
6. *Croyland* pp.486-487; *ChronLon* p.190; *Great* p.230
7. *Mancini* p.77
8. *Croyland* p.487
9. *Mancini* p.79
10. *Croyland* p.482, 487; *Vergil* p.175; *Great* p.230
11. *Croyland* pp.487-488
12. *Croyland* p.488
13. *Mancini* p.91
14. *Croyland* p.488; *Vergil* pp.179-181; *Great* p.231; *ChronLon* p.190
15. Raine, A., 'York Civic Records Vol. 1' in *Yorkshire Archaeological Society, Record Series Vol. XCVIII* (1939) pp.73-74
16. *Croyland* pp.488-489; *Vergil* p.178; Bentley, *Excerpta Historica* pp.14-17
17. *Croyland* p.486
18. *RotParl Vol. VI* pp.124-125
19. *Vergil* p.183; *Great* pp.231-232
20. *Croyland* p.489; *NewChron* p.669; *PROME Vol. XV* pp.13-16; Lewis, *Richard III* pp.289-297
21. *Croyland* p.489; *NewChron* p.668; *ChronLon* pp.190-191; *Vergil* p.182, 187
22. *Great* p.232
23. *Croyland* p.490; *ChronLon* p.191; *Mancini* p.97; *L&P Vol. 1* p.12
24. Jones, M., *Henry VII, Lady Margaret Beaufort and the Orléans Ransom'* in *Kings and Nobles in the Later Middle Ages* (ed. R.A. Griffiths & J. Sherborne, Gloucester, 1986) pp.254-269
25. *Mancini* p.81
26. *L&P Vol. 1* pp.22-23; *Vergil* p.191
27. Thomas, *Jasper Tudor* pp.230-231; *L&P Vol. 1* pp.37-43
28. *Vergil* pp.195-196
29. *Oxford Dictionary of National Biography Vol. 9* (ed. H.C.G. Matthew & B. Harrison, Oxford, 2004) pp.429-430; Kibre, P., 'Lewis of Caerleon, Doctor of Medicine, Astronomer, and Mathematician (D. 1494?)' in *Isis Vol. 43:2, Number 132* (ed. G. Staton, Chicago, 1952) pp.100-108; *Vergil* pp.195-196
30. *Croyland* p.490
31. Stow, J., *The Annales, Or Generall Chronicle of England* (London, 1615) pp.460-461
32. *Great* p.234, 237
33. *Croyland* p.490
34. *The Maire of Bristowe Is Kalendar by Robert Ricart* (ed. L.T. Smith, London, 1872) p.42
35. Wroe, A., *Perkin, A Story of Deception* (London, 2004) p.526
36. Ross, *Richard III* p.100
37. *Mancini* p.93
38. *Vergil* pp.187-188
39. *Vergil* pp.187-188; *ChronLon* p.191
40. *Vergil* p.197
41. *ODNB Vol. 55* pp.959-960
42. *Mancini* p.75
43. Ross, *Richard III* p.77; *CPR 1476-1485* p.349; Evans, *Wales and the WotR* pp.203-204; *Hall* p.382
44. *Mancini* p.91; *Vergil* p.194
45. *CPR 1467-1477* p.261
46. *Gregory* p.218; *Mancini* p.91; Bradley, S., *John Morton; Adversary of Richard III, Power Behind the Tudors* (Stroud, 2019) pp.10-32
47. *Mancini* p.91
48. DeLloyd, *Reynold Bray* pp.54-61
49. *Croyland* p.491; *Vergil* p.196
50. Thomas, *Jasper Tudor* p.236; Roberts, E., 'Seven John Conways' in *Flintshire Historical Society Publications Vol. XVIII* (1960) pp.65-69
51. *Vergil* p.197
52. *Vergil* p.197
53. *L&P Vol. 1* pp.54-55; *Vergil* p.197
54. Pocquet du Haut-Jusse, *Francois II* p.249
55. Pocquet du Haut-Jusse, *Francois II* pp.249-251; Jones, *My Lord of Richmond* p284, 292

56. *PROME Vol. XV* pp.24-25
57. Thomas, *Jasper Tudor* p.234; Griffiths & Thomas, *Making* p.108
58. *Croyland* p.491
59. Griffiths & Thomas, *Making* p.139
60. *Vergil* pp.198-199
61. *PL Vol. III* p.308
62. Kennett, W., Hughes, J, & Strype, J., *A Complete History of England Vol. I, with their Lives of all the Kings and Queens thereof* (London, 1706) p.532; TNA C81/1392/6
63. *ChronLon* pp.191-192
64. *Vergil* pp.199-200; Griffiths, *Rhys ap Thomas* p.205
65. *Croyland* p.492
66. Pugh, T.B., *The Marcher Lordships of South Wales, 1415-1536* (Cardiff, 1963) pp.240-241
67. *Vergil* p.200
68. *NewChron* pp.670-671; *ChronLon* pp.191-192; Blakeway & Owen, *History of Shrewsbury Vol. I* pp.236-239
69. Pocquet du Haut-Jusse, *Francois II* p.251; Chrimes, *Henry VII* p.26
70. *Croyland* p.495
71. *Croyland* p.495; *Vergil* pp.200-202
72. *Vergil* p.202; Pocquet du Haut-Jusse, *Francois II* pp.251-252
73. *NewChron* p.671; *Croyland* p.492
74. *Vergil* p.203
75. *Croyland* p.491
76. Ross, *Richard III* pp.111-112
77. Arthurson, I., & Kingwell, N., 'The Proclamation of Henry Tudor as King of England' in *Historical Research Vol. 63* (1990) pp.100-106
78. *Great* pp.236-237
79. *Commines Vol. 1* pp.396-397

15 Just Quarrel

1. *Vergil* p.203
2. *Lateran Regesta 43: 1396-1397'* in *Calendar of Papal Register Relating to Great Britain and Ireland, Vol. 4, 1362-1404* (ed. W.H. Bliss & J.A. Twemlow, London, 1902) pp.542-546; *Chronica Maiora* p.298; Bentley, *Excerpta Historica* pp.153-4
3. CPR 1405-1408 p.284
4. *PROME Vol. XII* pp.93-106
5. *Vergil* p.203
6. Bradley, *John Morton* pp.47-48; Clarke, P.D., 'English Royal Marriages and the Papal Penitentiary in the Fifteenth Century' in *English Historical Review Vol. CXX No 488* (2005) pp.1024-1026
7. *Vergil* p.203
8. Griffiths & Thomas, *Making* p.115
9. Griffiths & Thomas, *Making* p.117; Allanic, *Prisonnier* p.38; Thomas, *Jasper Tudor* pp.239-241
10. Griffiths, R.A., 'Henry Tudor; The Training of a King' in *Huntingdon Library Quarterly Vol. 49 No 3* (1986)
11. Griffiths & Thomas, *Making* p.118
12. Griffiths & Thomas, *Making* p.117; Skidmore, C., *Bosworth, The Birth of the Tudors* (London, 2013) p.179, 406
13. *Croyland* pp.495-496
14. *PROME Vol. XV* pp.13-16
15. *PROME Vol. XV* p.16
16. Griffiths & Thomas, *Making* p.121; Jones & Underwood, *King's Mother* p.64
17. *Croyland* p.496
18. *OL Vol. I* pp.149-150
19. *Croyland* p.496; *Vergil* p.208
20. *Vergil* p.205
21. *Croyland* pp.496-497
22. *Great* p.236; Gairdner, J, *History of the Life and Reign of Richard the Third* (Cambridge, 1898) pp.185-188, 191; Hillier, K., 'William Colyngbourne' in *The Ricardian; Journal of the Richard III Society, Vol. III. No. 49* (Upminster, 1975) pp.5-9
23. *NewChron* p.672; Gairdner, *Richard III* pp.185-188, 191
24. Griffiths & Thomas, *Making* p.116; *Vergil* pp.203-204
25. *Vergil* p.205; Bridge, J.S.C., *A History of France from the Death of Louis XI, Reign of Charles VIII, Regency of Anne of Beaujeu 1483-1493 Vol. I* (New York, 1978) pp.108-109
26. Chrimes, *Henry VII* p.29; CPR 1476-1485 p.517, 547
27. Griffiths & Thomas, *Making* pp.122-124; Thomas, *Jasper Tudor* p.241
28. *Vergil* p.206

29. *Vergil* p.206
30. Allanic, *Prisonnier* p.38; Thomas, *Jasper Tudor* pp.239-241
31. *Vergil* pp.206-207
32. *Vergil* p.208; Pocquet du Haut-Jusse, *Francois II* p.262
33. Bridge, *History of France* pp.26-30, 126-130
34. Pocquet du Haut-Jusse, *Francois II* p.263; Chrimes, *Henry VII* p.30; Spont, A., *La Marine Française sous le Règne de Charles VIII 1483-1493* (Paris, 1894) p.9; Antonovics, A.V., 'Henry VII, King of England, By the Grace of Charles VIII of France' in *Kings and Nobles in the Later Middle Ages* (ed. R.A. Griffiths & J. Sherborne (Gloucester, 1986) p.173
35. *Vergil* p.208
36. *André* p.21
37. Skidmore, *Bosworth* pp.183-184
38. Spont, *La Marine* p.9; Gairdner, *Richard III* pp.169-170; Antonovics, *Henry VII, King of England* p.173
39. Spont, *La Marine* p.9; Jones, M.K., 'The Myth of 1485; did France really put Henry Tudor on the throne' in *The English Experience in France c.1450-1558; War, diplomacy and cultural exchange* (ed. D. Grummitt, Aldershot, 2002) pp.92-93
40. *Letters of the Kings of England Vol. I* (ed. J.O. Halliwell, London, 1848) pp.161-162
41. Jones, *The Myth of 1485* p.94; BL Add. MS 19398 f.33r

16 The King's Great Rebel

1. Skidmore, *Bosworth* p.194
2. *Molinet Vol. I* pp.405-406
3. *Brut* pp.387-400; *Adam of Usk* p.188, *PoPC Vol. 2* pp.248-249; 'The Siege of Rouen: A Poem' in *The Historical Collections of a Citizen of London in the Fifteenth Century* (ed. J. Gairdner, London, 1876) pp.1-46
4. Castor, H., *Joan of Arc, A History* (London, 2014) pp.189-194; Radford, L.B., *Henry Beaufort: Bishop, Chancellor, Cardinal* (London, 1908)
   p.209; Harris, *Cardinal Beaufort* p.103
5. *The Chronicles of Enguerrand de Monstrelet Vol. 2* (ed. T, Johnes, London 1853) pp.167-170
6. Spont, *La Marine* pp.9-10; Beaurepaire, C.R., 'Entrée de Charles VIII à Rouen en 1485* (Rouen, 1902) p.ix-x, 9
7. Skidmore, *Bosworth* p.186; *Vergil* p.209, 212
8. *BL Harleian Manuscript 433 Vol. II* (ed. R. Horrox & P. Hammond, London, 1980) pp.198-201
9. Griffiths & Thomas, *Making* p.138
10. Scofield, C., 'Early Life of John De Vere' in *The English Historical Review Vol. XXIX* (London, 1914) pp.228-230; Ross, J., *The Foremost Man in The Kingdom* (Woodbridge, 2015) pp.36-42, 48
11. Scofield, *John de Vere* pp.231-245; Ross, *Foremost Man* pp.60-63
12. *Warkworth* pp.26-27; Scofield, *John de Vere* pp.231-240; Ross, *Foremost Man* pp.66-67, 72-75
13. Scofield, *John de Vere* pp.241-245
14. Chrimes, *Henry VII* p.34
15. Ross, *Foremost Man* p.77; CPR 1467-1477 p.297
16. *Vergil* p.208, 212; *Molinet Vol. I* pp.405-406
17. Hutton, W., *The Battle of Bosworth Field, Between Richard the Third and Henry Earl of Richmond, August 22, 1485* (London, 1813) pp.190-191
18. *Harleian Manuscript 433 Vol. III* pp.124-125
19. CPR 1467-1477 p.535
20. Griffiths & Thomas, *Making* pp.135-136
21. Lewis, *Richard III* pp.375-77
22. *Croyland* pp.498-500; *Vergil* pp.211-212
23. Gairdner, *Richard III* p.170; Ross, *Richard III* pp.208-209
24. *OL Vol. I* pp.162-166; *PL Vol. III* pp.316-320
25. Lewis, *Richard III* pp.345-346
26. *Croyland* p.501; *Vergil* p.212
27. *Vergil* p.215

28. *Vergil* p.215; Thomas, *The Herberts* pp.98-99
29. *Vergil* p.215
30. *Vergil* pp.215-216; Griffiths; *Rhys ap Thomas* p.38; Molinet Vol. I p.406
31. *Vergil* pp.215-216
32. *Vergil* p.155; *Hall* pp.302-302
33. CPR 1476-1485 p.410
34. *Vergil* pp.215-216
35. Griffiths; *Rhys ap Thomas* p.183
36. *Vergil* p.214; Ross, *Foremost Man* p.198; Chrimes, *Henry VII* p.38
37. *Vergil* pp.213-214
38. Bridge, *History of France Vol. I* pp.112-132; Jones, *Myth of 1485* pp.89-98
39. Jones, *Myth of 1485* pp.98-101; Spont, *La Marine* p.10
40. Jones, *Myth of 1485* p.98; Beaurepaire, *Entrée* pp.23-24
41. *Materials Vol. 1* p.413
42. Antonovics, *Henry VII, King of England* p.175; Jones, *Myth of 1485* p.99
43. Major, J., *A History of Greater Britain as well England as Scotland* (tr. A. Constable, Edinburgh, 1892) p.393
44. Jones, *Myth of 1485* pp.101-103; *Vergil* p.215
45. *Vergil* p.216; Molinet Vol. I p.407; Pocquet du Haut-Jusse, *Francois II* p.270; Griffiths & Thomas, *Making* pp.142-144
46. Spont, *La Marine* p.10; *Commines Vol. II* p.64
47. Griffiths & Thomas, *Making* p.144
48. *Mancini* p.81; Thorpe, L., 'Philippe de Crèvecoeur, Seigneur d'Esquerdes: two epitaphs by Jean Molinet and Nicaise Ladam' in *Bulletin de la Commission royale d'Histoire Vol. CXIX* (Brussels, 1954) pp.183-184
49. *L&P Vol. I* pp.18-21; Ross, *Richard III* p.201; Thorpe, *Philippe de Crevecoeur* p.201; Antonovics, *Henry VII, King of England* p.178
50. Cunningham, S., *Henry VII* (London, 2007) p.29
51. Griffiths & Thomas, *Making* p.144; *André* p.22, 26
52. Griffiths & Thomas, *Making* p.144; Spont, *La Marine* p.10; Antonovics, *Henry VII, King of England* p.176
53. Antonovics, *Henry VII, King of England* p.393; Major, *History of Greater Britain* p.393; Griffiths & Thomas, *Making* p.145
54. Cunningham, *Henry VII* p.30
55. Spont, *La Marine* p.10
56. *André* p.26; *Vergil* p.216
57. *André* pp.22-23
58. *Vergil* p.216

17 The Fated Dragon

1. *Vergil* p.216; *Great* p.237; Chrimes, S.B., 'The Landing Place of Henry of Richmond, 1485' in *The Welsh History Review Vol. II* (1964-65) pp.173-180; Williams, W.T., 'Henry of Richmond's Itinerary to Bosworth' in *Y Cymmrodor Vol. XXIX* (London, 1919) pp.34-35
2. Harris, O.D., 'The Transmission of the News of the Tudor Landing' in *The Ricardian, Vol. IV, Number 55* (London, 1976) p.8
3. *NewChron* p.672
4. *Croyland* pp.501-502
5. CPR 1476-1485 p.414, 501
6. Evans, *Wales and the WotR* p.214; Griffiths & Thomas, *Making* pp.152-153
7. *Vergil* pp.218-219
8. *Vergil* p.216
9. *André* pp.26-27
10. Chrimes, *Henry VII* p.42; Siddons, *Welsh Heraldry Vol. I* p.59
11. BL Royal MS 2 A XVIII f.31v
12. *NewChron* p.672
13. *Vergil* pp.216-221
14. *Vergil* p.216
15. *Vergil* p.216
16. Griffiths, *Rhys ap Thomas* pp.199-201, 216-217
17. Griffiths & Thomas, *Making* p.160
18. *Vergil* p.216
19. *Vergil* pp.216-217
20. *Vergil* p.217; Skidmore, *Bosworth* p.236
21. Thomas, *Jasper Tudor* p.161

22. Evans, *Wales and the WotR* pp.221-222; Wynne, J., *The History of the Gwydir Family* (Oswestry, 1878) p.48
23. Griffiths & Thomas, *Making* p.162
24. Edwards, O.M., *Wales; A National Magazine for the English Speaking Parts of Wales Vol. III* (Wrexham, 1896) pp.38-39
25. *Vergil* p.218
26. *OL Vol. I* pp.15-16; Evans, *Wales and the WotR* pp.140-141
27. Hicks, *Clarence* pp.56-57
28. Skidmore, *Bosworth* pp.252-253
29. *Croyland* p.501
30. Robinson, W.R.B, 'Henry Tudor's Journey Through Powys and the Lords of Powys in Early Tudor Times' in *Montgomeryshire Collections 90* (2002) p.90
31. Griffiths & Thomas, *Making* p.164; Horrox, R., 'Henry Tudor's Letters to England during Richard III's Reign' in *The Ricardian Vol. 6 No 80* (London, 1983) pp.156-157
32. Robinson, *Henry Tudor's Journey* pp.90-91
33. *Vergil* pp.217-218
34. Evans, *Wales and the WotR* p.223; Blakeway & Owen, *History of Shrewsbury Vol. I* p.244
35. Griffiths & Thomas, *Making* p.165
36. *Vergil* p.217
37. *Vergil* p.217
38. Griffiths & Thomas, *Making* pp.165-166; Roberts, E.P., 'Teulu Plas Iolyn' in *Transactions of the Denbighshire Historical Society Vol. 13* (1964) p.43
39. Evans, *Wales and the WotR* p.223; Chrimes, *Henry VII* p.42
40. Jones, E.W., 'Wales and Bosworth Field – Selective Historiography?' in *NLW Vol. 21 No 1* (1979) pp.58-59, 69-70
41. *The Dialogue of the Government of Wales (1594)* (ed. J.G. Jones, Cardiff, 2010) p.81
42. *Hall* p.423
43. Williams-Jones, *Taking Of Conwy* pp.40-41
44. Lofmark, C, *A History of the Red Dragon* (Llanrwst, 1995) pp.60-61
45. Lofmark, *Red Dragon* pp.40-43; Llywelyn, M.G, *Y Ddraig yn Nychymyg a Llenyddiaeth y Cymry c.600-c.1500* (Aberystwyth, 2017) pp.29-32
46. Lofmark, *Red Dragon* p.43, 49-50; Llywelyn, *Y Ddraig* pp.79-81
47. *Adam of Usk* pp.108-109; John, J.W., *Archaeologia Cambrensis; A Record of the Antiquities of Wales and its Marches, Vol. IV* (London, 1853) pp.193-196; Stephens, T., *The Literature of the Kymry; Being a Critical Essay on the History of The Language and Literature of Wales* (Llandovery, 1849) p.38; Lofmark, *Red Dragon* p.45
48. Barber, R.W., *Myths and legends of the British Isles* (London, 1999) p.40-41; Henken, E.R., *National Redeemer, Owain Glyndwr in Welsh Tradition* (Ithica, 1996) p.55; Llywelyn, *Y Ddraig* pp.77-78, 82-84
49. Lofmark, *Red Dragon* p.54
50. Lofmark, *Red Dragon* p.67; Llywelyn, *Y Ddraig* p.99
51. Owen, I., 'Race and Nationality' in *Y Cymmrodor Vol. VIII Part I* (London, 1887) p.20
52. For general discussion about the role of the Welsh poets, see Roberts, S.E., *Jasper: The Tudor Kingmaker* (Stroud, 2015) pp.124-137
53. Davies, *History of Wales* pp.203-215; Henken, *National Redeemer* p.52
54. Garmon Jones, W., *Welsh Nationalism and Henry Tudor* (London, 1918) pp.15-19
55. Williams, G.A., 'The Bardic Road to Bosworth: A Welsh View of Henry Tudor' in *Transactions of the Honourable Society of Cymmrodorion* (London, 1986) p.14
56. Davies, *History of Wales* p.210; Henken, *National Redeemer* pp.52-53; Garmon Jones, *Welsh Nationalism* pp.21-22
57. *Works of Dafydd Nanmor* pp.34-46
58. *Works of Dafydd Nanmor* pp.43-45
59. Williams, *Bardic Road* p.20
60. Williams, *Bardic Road* pp.20-22
61. Henken, *National Redeemer* pp.53-54

62. Garmon Jones, *Welsh Nationalism* p.17, 32-33, 44-45; Carr, *Medieval Wales* p.125
63. Williams, *Bardic Road* p.43; Garmon Jones, *Welsh Nationalism* p.38; Skidmore, *Bosworth* p.207
64. Williams, *Bardic Road* pp.26-27; Garmon Jones, *Welsh Nationalism* pp.38-41
65. Garmon Jones, *Welsh Nationalism* p.18, 33-37, 47-54; Griffiths & Thomas, *Making* p.158
66. Williams, *Bardic Road* p.23
67. *Vergil* p.218
68. Blakeway & Owen, *History of Shrewsbury Vol. I* p.245
69. Blakeway & Owen, *History of Shrewsbury Vol. I* p.245
70. Blakeway & Owen, *History of Shrewsbury Vol. I* p.245
71. *The Most Pleasant Song of Lady Bessy, the Eldest Daughter of King Edward the Fourth, and how she Married King Henry the Seventh of the House of Lancaster* (ed. T. Heywood, London, 1829) p.39
72. Blakeway & Owen, *History of Shrewsbury Vol. I* p.246-247; *Early Chronicles of Shrewsbury, 1372-1603* (ed. W.A. Leighton, Shrewsbury, 1880) pp.11-12

18 Invincible Giants

1. *Vergil* p.218
2. Blakeway & Owen, *History of Shrewsbury Vol. I* p.247-248
3. Griffiths & Thomas, *Making* p.170
4. *Vergil* p.218
5. *Croyland* p.502
6. Griffiths & Thomas, *Making* p.171; *Song of Lady Bessy* p.42
7. *Vergil* p.218
8. *Vergil* p.220
9. *Vergil* pp.220-221
10. *Vergil* p.221
11. *Vergil* p.221
12. 'Houses of Cistercian monks: Abbey of Merevale', in *A History of the County of Warwick Vol. 2* (ed. W. Page, London, 1908) pp.75-78
13. *Materials Vol. 1* p.188, 201, 233
14. Mackinder, R., *Bosworth; the Archaeology of the Battlefield* (Barnsley, 2021) pp.6-10; Foard, G. & Curry, A., *Bosworth 1485; A Battlefield Rediscovered* (Oxford, 2022) pp.48-49, 181
15. Skidmore, *Bosworth* pp.240-241, 245-246; Harris, *Tudor Landing* pp.10-11; *Croyland* p.501; *PL Vol. III* p.320
16. *Vergil* pp.218-219
17. *André* p.28
18. *Great* p.237; *Croyland* p.502
19. Richmond, C., '1485 and All That, or What Was Going on at the Battle of Bosworth' in *Richard III: Loyalty, Lordship and Law* (ed. P.W. Hammond, London, 1985) p.173; Ingram, M., *Richard III and the Battle of Bosworth* (Warwick, 2019) pp.272-274; Foard & Curry, *Bosworth 1485* pp.38-41
20. *Croyland* p.503; *Vergil* p.221
21. *Vergil* pp.222-223
22. for general battle discussion, see Mackinder., *Bosworth; the Archaeology of the Battlefield*; Skidmore, *Bosworth; The Birth of the Tudors*; Ingram, *Richard III and the Battle of Bosworth*; Foard & Curry, *Bosworth 1485; A Battlefield Rediscovered*.
23. For discussion of battlefield identification, see Skidmore, *Bosworth* pp.377-389; Ingram, *Battle of Bosworth* pp.222-223, 263-266
24. *Mancini* p.99
25. Ingram, *Battle of Bosworth* pp.61-72
26. *Mancini* p.99
27. *Vergil* p.223
28. *Vergil* p.233; *Hall* p.418
29. *Vergil* pp.222-223
30. *Vergil* p.223; *Croyland* pp.502-503
31. *Vergil* p.223
32. *Hall* p.338
33. *Hall* pp.416-418
34. *Hall* p.415
35. *Vergil* p.233
36. *Vergil* p.223
37. *Vergil* pp.223-224
38. *Vergil* p.190; *Molinet Vol. 1* p.408; *Croyland* p.503; Ingram, *Battle of Bosworth* p.245

39. *Croyland* p.503
40. *Vergil* p.224
41. *Vergil* p.224
42. Spont, A., 'La milice de Francs-Archers (1448-1500)' in *Revue des Questions Historiques*, 61 (1897) p.474; Jones, M.K., *Bosworth 1485, Psychology of a Battle* (Stroud, 2002) pp.221-223
43. *Vergil* p.224
44. Jones, *Wales and Bosworth* pp.50-51
45. *Vergil* p.224
46. Jones, *Wales and Bosworth* p.68
47. *Croyland* p.504
48. Spont, *La malice de Francs-Archers* p.474
49. *Vergil* p.225
50. *Vergil* p.224; *Croyland* p.504; *Molinet Vol. 1* p.409
51. Jones, *Wales and Bosworth* pp.51-53; *Molinet Vol. 1* p.409
52. Skinner, R.J., 'Thomas Woodshawe, Grasiour and Regicide' in *The Ricardian Vol. IX No 121* (London, 1993) pp.417-424
53. Appleby, J., Rutty, G.N., Hainsworth, S.V., Woosnam-Savage, R.C., Morgan, B., Brough, A., Earp, R.W., Robinson, C., King, T.E., Morris, M, & Buckley, R., 'Perimortem trauma in King Richard III: A skeletal analysis' in *The Lancet Vol. 385* (2015) pp.253-259
54. *Vergil* p.225
55. *ChronLon* p.193; *Great* p.238
56. *Croyland* p.504
57. *Vergil* p.224
58. Skidmore, *Bosworth* p.382; Harris, O.D, 'The Bosworth Commemoration at Dadlington' in *The Ricardian Vol. VII, No 90* (London, 1985) pp.115-131
59. *Vergil* p.226
60. CPR 1485-1494 p.6, 14, 31, 174
61. *Vergil* p.226
62. *Great* p.238
63. *Letters of the Kings of England Vol. I* pp.169-170
64. *Commines Vol. 1* p.397, *Vol. 2* p.64; *Croyland* p.505
65. Williams, *Renewal and Reformation* p.237

Epilogue

1. Wickham Legg, L., *English Coronation Records* (London, 1901) pp. 219-239
2. PROME *Vol. XV* p.97
3. Skeel, C.A.J., 'Wales under Henry VII' in *Tudor Studies* (ed. R.W. Seton-Watson, London, 1924) p.2
4. *Gwaith Huw Cae Llwyd ac Eraill* (ed. L. Harries, Cardiff, 1953) p.12; Williams, *Bardic Road* pp.27-28; Jones, *Wales and Bosworth Field* pp.63-64
5. Williams, G., *Henry Tudor and Wales* (Cardiff, 1985) p.77, 93-99
6. Williams, *Bardic Road* p.28-29; Williams, *Henry Tudor and Wales* p.77, 83
7. Griffiths, *Training of a King* p.211
8. Williams, *Renewal and Reformation* p.31-54
9. Carr, *Medieval Wales* p.128
10. Skeel, *Wales under Henry VII* pp.3-4
11. *Materials Vol. II* pp.541-542; Williams, *Renewal and Reformation* p.53
12. Wynne, *Gwydir Family* p.48
13. Chrimes, *Henry VII* pp.252-253
14. CPR 1494-1509 p.434, 464-65, 471, 534-35, 586-87
15. Chrimes, *Henry VII* pp.253-255; Smith, J.B., 'Crown and Community in the Principality of North Wales in the Reign of Henry Tudor' in *Welsh History Review Vol. 3 No 2* (Cardiff, 1966) pp.169-171; Skeel, *Wales under Henry VII* pp.11-14
16. Carr, *Medieval Wales* p.129
17. Smith, *Crown and Community* p.145
18. Tanner, J.R., *Tudor Constitutional Documents A.D. 1485-1603* (Cambridge, 1930) pp.40-46; Williams, *Renewal and Reformation* pp.264-278
19. Davies, *History of Wales* p.232; Edwards, G., 'The Principality of Wales, 1267-1967' in *Caernarvonshire Historical Society* (1969) pp.35-39
20. Davies, *History of Wales* pp.232-233; Williams, *Renewal and Reformation* p.35
21. Davies, *History of Wales* pp.233-236

22. *Dialogue of the Government of Wales* pp.80-81
23. Williams, *Henry Tudor and Wales* pp.95-99
24. Owen, *Race and Nationality* pp.21-22; Williams, *Henry Tudor and Wales* pp.101-107
25. CPR 1485-1494 pp.22-23, 63
26. *Materials Vol. 1* p.102; Roberts, *Jasper* p.100
27. Birch, W. G., *Catalogue of Seals in the Department of Manuscripts in the British Museum Vol. II* (London, 1887-1900) pp.360-61
28. Thomas, *Jasper Tudor* pp.253-261
29. *Materials Vol. 1* pp.594-595, 603-604
30. CPR 1485-1494 p.47
31. Griffiths, R.A., *The Principality of Wales in the Later Middle Ages: The Structure and Personnel of Government Vol. I, South Wales, 1277-1536* (Cardiff, 1972) pp.21-33
32. CPR 1485-1494 pp.64-65, 84, 252, 376; *Materials Vol. 1* pp.334-335
33. Williams, *Renewal and Reformation* p.53
34. Roberts, *Jasper* p.108
35. Cunningham, S., *Prince Arthur, the Tudor King Who Never Was* (Stroud, 2016) pp.101-102
36. *Calendar of Inquisitions Post Mortem; Henry VIII Vol. III* (London, 1955) p.396
37. *The Maire of Bristowe* p.48
38. CPR 1485-1509 p.114
39. *Somerset Medieval Wills (1383-1500) Vol. XVI* (ed. F.W. Weaver, London, 1901)
40. Merrick, R., *A Book of Glamorganshire's Antiquities* (ed. T. Phillipps, 1825) pp.34-35
41. Bentley, *Excerpta Historica* p.119; BL Add MS 7099 f.49; Camden, W., *Reges, reginae nobiles et alii in ecclesia collegiata B. Petri Westmonasterii sepulti* (London, 1603); Crull, J., *The Antiquities of St Peter's, or the Abbey Church of Westminster* (London, 1711) p.233
42. Walcott, M.E.C., *The History of the Parish Church of Saint Margaret, in Westminster, from its Foundation, A.D. 1064* (1847) p.57
43. Stanley, A.P., *Historical Memorials of Westminster Abbey* (London, 1868) p.395, 412; Crull, *Antiquities of St Peter's* p.233
44. Bentley, *Excerpta Historica* p.128; BL Add MS 7099 f.75
45. Blaauw, *Effigy of David Owen* p.25-26; *Letters and Papers, Foreign and Domestic, Henry VIII, Vol. 1, 1509-1514* (ed. J.S. Brewer, London, 1920) pp.12, 20-21
46. CPR 1485-1494 p.59
47. Blaauw, *Effigy of David Owen* p.26; *Letters and Papers, Henry VIII, Vol. 1* p.268, 275
48. *Letters and Papers, Henry VIII Vol. 1* pp.1401-1417
49. *Letters and Papers, Foreign and Domestic, Henry VIII, Vol. 2* p.435, 873, 1373-74
50. Blaauw, *Effigy of David Owen* p.26
51. Wedgwood, J.C., *History of Parliament; Biographies of the Members of the Commons House 1439-1509* (London, 1936) pp.654-655
52. Henry, R., *The History of Great Britain, From the Invasion of it by The Romans under Julius Caesar Vol. XII* (London, 1814) pp.387-392
53. Blaauw, *Effigy of David Owen* pp.26-27, 29-43
54. *Letters and Papers, Foreign and Domestic, of the Reign of Henry VIII* (ed. J. Gairdner, London, 1886) pp.146-147
55. Blaauw, *Effigy of David Owen* pp.22-23
56. CPR 1485-1494 p.24, 65
57. Griffiths, *Rhys ap Thomas* pp.45-48; Griffiths, *Principality of Wales Vol. I* pp.162-163
58. Griffiths, *Rhys ap Thomas* p.49
59. Griffiths, *Rhys ap Thomas* pp.49-51, 77
60. *Vergil* p.197
61. CPR 1485-1494 p.22; CPR 1494-1509 p.15, 365
62. Thomas, *The Herberts* p.83, 100-102
63. Condon, M., Harper, S., & Ross, J., *The Chamber Books of Henry VII and*

Henry VIII, 1485-1521: An Analysis of the Books and a Study of Henry VII and his Life at Court p.34

64. Condon et al, *Chamber Books* p.35
65. CPR 1485-1494 p.5; Smith, *Crown and Community* pp.159-160
66. Williams, *Renewal and Reformation* p.130
67. CPR 1485-1495 p.4, 10, 17, 21, 31, 55, 75, 145, 221
68. CPR 1485-1495 p.35, 158, 168, 220
69. CPR 1485-1495 p.95, 365
70. Griffith, W.P., 'Tudor Prelude' in *The Welsh in London 1500-2000* (ed. E. Jones, Cardiff, 2001) pp.9-11
71. Williams, *Renewal and Reformation* p.239, 462-470
72. Henken, *National Redeemer* p.160
73. Skeel, *Wales under Henry VII* pp.10-11, 22-24
74. *Dialogue of the Government* p.81; Owen, *Race and Nationality* pp.20-21
75. *Letters of the Kings of England Vol. 1* pp.169-170
76. Stanford London, H., 'The Greyhound as a Royal Beast' in *Archaeologia or Miscellaneous Tracts Relating to Antiquity Vol. 97* (London, 1959) pp.139-163
77. Griffiths & Thomas, *Making* p.214
78. *Leland Vol. 4* pp.216-222
79. Jones, *Wales and Bosworth Field* p.64
80. *Le Morte D'Arthur, Sir Thomas Malory's Book of King Arthur and of his Noble Knights of the Round Table* (ed. E. Strachey, London, 1897) p. 63; Cunningham, *Prince Arthur* pp. 20-24; Williams, *Renewal and Reformation* p.238
81. Griffiths, *Rhys ap Thomas* p.49; CPR 1485-1494 p.365
82. BL Harleian Manuscript 433 *Vol. III* pp.124-125; *OL Vol. I* pp.162-166; *PL Vol. III* pp.316-320
83. *Gerald* p.251
84. *Caradoc* pp.331-342
85. *The Chamber Books of Henry VII and Henry VIII, 1485-1521* (ed. M.M. Condon, S.P. Harper, L. Liddy, S. Cunningham and J. Ross), accessible online https://www.tudorchamberbooks.org/
86. TNA, E101/415/3, f.86r; E36/214, ff.69r, 120v, 164r; BL Add Ms 59899, ff.14v, 80r, 80v
87. TNA, E101/414/6, f.83r; E101/414/16, f.29r; E101/415/3, f.55v; BL Add MS. 59899, ff.45r, 50v, 79v, 99r; E36/214 ff.109r, 119v, 162r; BL Add MS 7099 ff.30, 41, 47, 69, 96; BL Add MS 21480 f.26v; E36/210 f.47
88. Griffiths & Thomas, *Making* p.220
89. *The English Works of John Fisher, Bishop of Rochester Part I* (ed. J.E.B. Mayor, London, 1876) p.269
90. Williams, *Renewal and Reformation* pp.231-232
91. Gray, *Politics, Power and Piety* p.244; Gray, M., 'Welsh saints in Westminster Abbey' in *Transactions of the Honourable Society of Cymmrodorion* (2007) pp.15-16
92. Bloxham, M.B, 'Merevale Abbey' in *Transactions of the Leicestershire Architectural and Archaeological Society Vol. II* (Leicester, 1870) p.326
93. Jones, *Bosworth 1485* pp.213-214; Skidmore, *Bosworth* pp.370-371
94. Gray, *Politics, Power and Piety* p.253
95. Green, A.R., 'The Romsey Painted Wooden Reredos' in *Archaeological Journal Vol. XC* (1993) pp.306-314; Gray, *Welsh Saints* pp.26-27
96. Gray, *Politics, Power and Piety* pp.247-249
97. BL Add MS 88929 f.4dr
98. Gray, *Politics, Power and Piety* pp.254-255
99. Jones, *Wales and Bosworth* pp.43-64
100. *André* pp.6-7; Williams, *Renewal and Reformation* p.237; *A Relation...of the Island of England* p.19
101. Griffith, *Tudor Prelude* p.22

Bibliography

Manuscript Sources

BL Add MS 46354; BL Add MS 19398; BL Add MS 7099; BL Add MS 59899; BL Add MS 21480; BL Add MS 88929

BL Kings 395 f.33r

BL Royal MS 2 A XVIII

Christ Church (Oxford) MS 184

DL 29/651/10534

NLW MS 3054d; NLW MS 6495C, 6496C

PROB 11/7/2; PROB 11/25/364

SJLM 3/2/1; SJLM/4/4/2

TNA SC 8/124/6168; TNA C81/1392/6; TNA E101/415/3; TNA E36/214; TNA E101/414/6, TNA E101/414/16; TNA E101/415/3; TNA E36/214; TNA E36/210

WAM 12183; WAM 32378; WAM 5472; WAM 6658

Online

The Chamber Books of Henry VII and Henry VIII, 1485-1521 (ed. M.M. Condon, S.P. Harper, L. Liddy, S. Cunningham and J. Ross), accessible online https://www.tudorchamberbooks.org/

Published Primary Sources

A Catalogue of the Manuscripts Relating to Wales in The British Museum (ed. E. Owen, London, 1900)

A Chronicle of the First Thirteen Years of the Reign of King Edward the Fourth by John Warkworth (ed. J.O. Halliwell, London, 1839)

A Collection of the Chronicles and Memorials of Great Britain and Ireland during The Middle Ages (ed. W. Hardy & E.L.C.P. Hardy, London, 1887)

A Descriptive Catalogue of Ancient Deeds (ed. H.C. Maxwell Lyte, London, 1906)

A Relation, or Rather a True Account, of the Island of England, About the Year 1500 (tr. C.A. Sneyd, London, 1847)

A Survey of London by John Stow Reprinted from the Text of 1603 (ed. C.L. Kingsford, Oxford, 1908)

An English Chronicle of the Reigns of Richard II, Henry IV, Henry V, and Henry VI (ed. J.S. Davies, London, 1856)

An Inventory of the Ancient Monuments in Wales and Monmouthshire, Vol. VI County of Merioneth (London, 1921)

Annales Cestrienses, Chronicle of the Abbey of St Werburg, at Chester (ed. R.C. Christie, London, 1887)

Bale's Chronicle, Six Town Chronicles of England (ed. R. Flenley, Oxford, 1911)

Bernard André, *The Life of Henry VII* (tr. D. Hobbins, New York, 2011)

BL Harleian Manuscript 433 (ed. R. Horrox & P. Hammond, London, 1980)

Brut y Tywysogion, or The Chronicle of the Princes (ed. J. Williams ab Ithel, London, 1860)

Calendar of Ancient Correspondence Concerning Wales (ed. J.G. Edwards, Cardiff, 1935)

Calendar of Ancient Petitions Relating to Wales, Thirteenth to Sixteenth Century (ed. W. Rees, Cardiff, 1975)

Calendar of the Charter Rolls Preserved in the Public Record Office Vol. VI A.D. 1427-1516

Calendar of Close Rolls (London, 1911)

Calendar of Fine Rolls (22 vols. HMSO, London, 1911-1962)

'*Calendar of French Rolls 1-10 Henry V*' in *The Forty-Fourth Annual Report of the Deputy Keeper of the Public Records* (London, 1883)

Calendar of Inquisitions Post Mortem; Henry VIII Vol. III (London, 1955)

Calendars of Patent Rolls (54 vols. HMSO, London, 1893-1916)

Calendar of Papal Register Relating to Great Britain and Ireland, Vol. 4, 1362-1404 (ed. W.H. Bliss & J.A. Twemlow, London, 1902)

Calendar of Papal Registers Relating to Great Britain and Ireland Vol. 14, 1484-1492 (ed. J.A. Twemlow, London, 1960)

Calendar of State Papers and Manuscripts in the Archives and Collections of Milan 1385-1618 (ed. A. B Hinds, London, 1912)

Calendar of State Papers, Spain (ed. G.A. Bergenroth, London, 1862)

Caradoc of Lhancarvan, *The History of Wales, Written Originally in British, by Caradoc of Lhancarvan, Englished by Dr Powell and Augmented by W. Wynne, to Which is Added, A Description of Wales by Sir John Price* (London, 1774)

Chronicles of England, France, Spain, and the Adjoining Countries by Sir John Froissart (tr. T. Johnes, London, 1857)

Chronicle of the Grey Friars of London (ed. J.G. Nichols, London, 1852)

Chroniques de Jean Molinet Vol. 1 (ed. J.A. Buchon, Paris, 1827)

Clarke, P.D., '*English Royal Marriages and the Papal Penitentiary in the Fifteenth Century*' in *English Historical Review Vol. CXX No 488* (2005)

Councils and Ecclesiastical Documents Relating to Great Britain and Ireland' (ed. A.W. Haddan & W. Stubbs, Oxford, 1869)

Dominic Mancini's The Usurpation of Richard the Third (tr. C.A.J. Armstrong, Gloucester, 1984)

Early Chronicles of Shrewsbury, 1372-1603 (ed. W.A. Leighton, Shrewsbury, 1880)

Fasti Ecclesiae Anglicanae or A Calendar of the Principal Ecclesiastical Dignitaries in England and Wales (ed. T.D. Hardy, Oxford, 1854)

Gerald of Wales, *The Journey Through Wales and The Description of Wales* (tr. L. Thorpe, London 2004)

The Great Chronicle of London (ed. A.H. Thomas & I.D. Thornley, London, 1938)

Gwaith Huw Cae Llwyd ac Eraill (ed. L. Harries, Cardiff, 1953)

Gwaith Lewys Glyn Cothi (ed. D. Johnson, Cardiff, 1995)

Gwaith Siôn Tudur Vol. II (ed. E. Roberts, Cardiff, 1980)

Hall's Chronicle, Containing the History of England during the Reign of Henry the Fourth and the Succeeding Monarchs, to the End of the Reign of Henry the Eighth (ed. H. Ellis, London, 1809)

Bibliography

Henry the Sixth; A Reprint of John Blacman's Memoir (ed. M.R. James, Cambridge, 1919)

Historie of the Arrivall of Edward IV in England and the Finall Recoverye of his Kingdomes from Henry VI (ed. J. Bruce, London, 1838)

Holinshed's Chronicles of England, Scotland, And Ireland Vol. III (London, 1808)

'Houses of Cistercian monks: Abbey of Merevale', in *A History of the County of Warwick Vol. 2* (ed. W. Page, London, 1908)

Incerti Scriptoris Chronicon Angliae de Regnis Trium Regum Lancastrensium: Henrici IV, Henrici V, et Henrici VI, Vol. IV (ed. J.A. Giles, London, 1848)

Index of Wills Proved in the Prerogative Court of Canterbury 1383-1558 (ed. J. Challenor, London, 1895)

Ingulph's Chronicle of the Abbey of Croyland with the Continuations by Peter of Blois and Anonymous Writers, (ed. H.T. Riley, London 1854)

Joannis Lelandi antiquarii De rebus Britannicis collectanea Vol. II (ed. T. Hearns, London, 1774)

Le Morte D'Arthur, Sir Thomas Malory's Book of King Arthur and of his Noble Knights of the Round Table (ed. E. Strachey, London, 1897)

Letters and Papers, Foreign and Domestic, of the Reign of Henry VIII (ed. J.S. Brewer, London, 1862-1864)

Letters and Papers, Foreign and Domestic, of the Reign of Henry VIII (ed. J. Gairdner, London, 1886)

Letters and Papers Illustrative of the Wars of the English in France during the Reign of Henry the Sixth, King of England Vol. 2 (ed. J. Stevenson, London, 1861)

Letters and Papers Illustrative of the Reign of Richard III and Henry VII (ed. J. Gairdner, London, 1861)

Letters of the Kings of England (ed. J.O. Halliwell, London, 1848)

Major, J., *A History of Greater Britain as well England as Scotland* (tr. A. Constable, Edinburgh, 1892)

Materials for a History of the Reign of Henry VII (ed. W. Campbell, London, 1873)

Mathew Paris's English History (tr. J.A. Giles, London, 1852)

Original Letters Illustrative of English History (ed. H. Ellis, London, 1825)

Parliament Rolls of Medieval England 1275-1504 (ed. C. Given-Wilson London, 2005)

Privy Purse Expenses of Elizabeth of York: Wardrobe Accounts of Edward the Fourth (ed. N.H. Nicolas, London, 1830)

Proceedings and Ordinances of the Privy Council of England (ed. H. Nicolas, 1834)

Registra Quorundam Abbatum Monasterii Sancti Albani (ed. H.T. Riley, London, 1872)

Registrum Vulgariter Nuncupatum, 'The Record of Caernarvon' (ed. H. Ellis, London, 1838)

Reports from The Lords Committees Touching the Dignity of a Peer of the Realm (1829)

Rotuli Parliamentorum (London, 1767-77)

Rymer's Foedera (ed. T. Rymer, London, 1739-1745)

Roger of Wendover's Flowers of History Vol. II (ed. J.A. Giles, London, 1849)

Rotuli litterarum clausarum in Turri Londinensi asservati 1204-1224 (ed. T.D. Hardy, London, 1833)

Royal Commission on the Ancient and Historical Monuments and Constructions in Wales and Monmouthshire; An Inventory of the Ancient Monuments in Wales and Monmouthshire Vol. 7 County of Pembroke (London, 1925)

Royal and Historical Letters During the Reign of Henry the Fourth, King of England and of France, and Lord of Ireland (ed. F.C. Hingeston, London, 1860)

Royal and Other Historical Letters Illustrative of the Reign of Henry III (ed. W.W. Shirley, 1862, London)

Scalacronica; The Reigns of Edward I, Edward II and Edward III as Recorded by Sir Thomas Gray (ed. H. Maxwell, Glasgow, 1907)

Somerset Medieval Wills (1383-1500) Vol. XVI (ed. F.W. Weaver, London, 1901)

Survey of The Honour of Denbigh 1334 (ed. P. Vinogradoff & F. Morgan, London, 1914)

Syllabus of the Documents Relating to England and Other Kingdoms Contained in the Collection Known as Rymer's Foedera Vol. I 1066-1377 (ed. T.D. Hardy, London, 1869)

The Act of Welsh Rulers 1120-1283 (ed. H. Pryce, Cardiff, 2005)

The Ancient Kalendars and Inventories of the Treasury of His Majesty's Exchequer (ed. F. Palgrave, London, 1836)

The Anglica Historia of Polydore Vergil A.D. 1485-1537 (ed. D. Hay, London, 1950)

The Brut or The Chronicles of England (ed. F.W.D. Brie, London, 1906)

The Chronica Maiora of Thomas Walsingham, 1376-1422 (ed. D. Preest, Woodbridge 2005)

The Chronicle of Adam of Usk, A.D. 1377-1421 (ed. E.M. Thompson, London, 1904)

The Chronicles of Enguerrand de Monstrelet (ed. T, Johnes, London 1853)

The Chronicles of London (ed. C.L. Kingsford, London, 1905)

The Dialogue of the Government of Wales (1594) (ed. J.G. Jones, Cardiff, 2010)

The English Works of John Fisher, Bishop of Rochester Part I (ed. J.E.B. Mayor, London, 1876)

The Funeral Sermon of Margaret Countess of Richmond and Derby, Mother to King Henry VII, and Foundress of Christ's and St John's College in Cambridge, Preached by Bishop Fisher in 1509 (ed. J. Hymers, Cambridge, 1840)

The Itinerary of John Leland, the Antiquary (ed. T. Hearne, Oxford, 1769

The Itinerary in Wales of John Leland in or about the Years 1536-1539 (ed. L. Toulmin Smith, London, 1906)

The Libell of English Policye' in *Political Poems and Songs Relating to English History* (ed. T. Wright, London, 1861)

The Maire of Bristowe Is Kalendar by Robert Ricart (ed. L.T. Smith, London, 1872)

The Memoirs of Philip De Commines, Lord of Agenton Vol. 1 (ed. A.R. Scroble, London, 1877)

The Most Pleasant Song of Lady Bessy, the Eldest Daughter of King Edward the Fourth, and how she Married King Henry the Seventh of the House of Lancaster (ed. T. Heywood, London, 1829)

The New Chronicles of England and France (ed. H. Ellis, London, 1811)

The Paston Letters, 1422-1509 A.D. (ed. J. Gairdner, London, 1872)

The Paston Letters (ed. N. Davis, Oxford, 1999)

The Register of Edward the Black Prince Preserved in the Public Record Office Part I (London, 1930)

The Siege of Rouen: A Poem, in The Historical Collections of a Citizen of London in the Fifteenth Century (ed. J. Gairdner, London, 1876)

The Statutes of Wales Collected, Edited, and Arranged by Ivor Bowen (ed. T. Fisher Unwin, London, 1908)

Third Report of The Royal Commission on Historical Manuscripts (London, 1872)

Three Books of Polydore Vergil's English History, Comprising the Reigns of Henry VI, Edward IV, and Richard III (ed. H. Ellis, London 1844)

Three Fifteenth-Century Chronicles with Historical Memoranda by John Stowe, the Antiquary (ed. J. Gairdner, London, 1880)

'*Welsh Records: Calendar of Recognizance Rolls of the Palatinate of Chester, to the end of the reign of Henry IV*' in *The Thirty-Sixth Annual Report of the Deputy Keeper of the Public Records* (London, 1875)

'*Welsh Records: Calendar of Recognizance Rolls of The Palatinate of Chester, from the Beginning of the Reign of Henry V to the End of the Reign of Henry VII*' in *The Thirty-Seventh Annual Report of The Deputy Keeper of The Public Records* (London, 1876)

'*William Gregory's Chronicle of London*' in *The Historical Collections of a Citizen of London in the Fifteenth Century* (ed. J. Gairdner, London, 1876)

William Worcestre Itineraries (ed. J.H. Harvey, Oxford, 1969)

Secondary Sources

Allanic, J., *Le Prisonnier de la Tour d'Elven ou La Jeunesse du Roy Henry VII d'Angleterre* (Vannes, 1909)

Allen, E., '*The Tomb of The Earl of Richmond in St David's Cathedral*' in *Archaeologia Cambrensis Vol. XIII No LII* (1896)

Antonovics, A.V., '*Henry VII, King of England, 'By the Grace of Charles VIII of France*'' in *Kings and Nobles in the Later Middle Ages* (ed. R.A. Griffiths & J. Sherborne (Gloucester, 1986)

Appleby, J., Rutty, G.N., Hainsworth, S.V., Woosnam-Savage, R.C., Morgan, B., Brough, A., Earp, R.W., Robinson, C., King, T.E., Morris, M, & Buckley, R., '*Perimortem trauma in King Richard III: A skeletal analysis*' in *The Lancet Vol. 385* (2015)

Arthurson, I., & Kingwell, N., '*The Proclamation of Henry Tudor as King of England*' in *Historical Research Vol. 63* (1990)

Ashton C., *Gweithiau Iolo Goch: Gyda Nodiadau Hanesyddol a Beiriadol* (Croesowallt, 1898)

Asperen, H., '*Saint Armel of Brittany: The Identification of Four Badges from London*' in *Peregrinations: Journal of Medieval Art and Architecture Vol. 2, Issue 1* (2005)

Ballinger, J., '*Katheryn of Berain, A Study in North Wales Family History*' in *Y Cymmrodor; the Magazine of the Honourable Society of Cymmrodorion Vol. XL* (London, 1929)

Barber, R.W., *Myths and legends of the British Isles* (London, 1999)

Barnes, T.L., *A Nun's Life: Barking Abbey in the Late-Medieval and Early Modern Periods* (Portland, 2004)

Barron, C.M., *London in the Later Middle Ages; Government and People 1200-1500* (Oxford, 2005)

Bayani, D., *Jasper Tudor, Godfather of the Tudor Dynasty* (2015)

Beaurepaire, C.R., '*Entrée de Charles VIII à Rouen en 1485* (Rouen, 1902)

Beltz, G.F., *Memorials of the Order of the Garter* (1841)

Bennett, M., '*Son of Scotlangle: Sir John Steward*' in *Journal of the Sydney Society for Scottish History Vol. 15* (Sydney, 2015)

Bentley, S., *Excerpta Historica; or Illustrations of English History* (London, 1831)

Birch, W. G., *Catalogue of Seals in the Department of Manuscripts in the British Museum* (London, 1887-1900)

Blaauw, W.H., '*On the Effigy of Sir David Owen in Easebourne Church, Near Midhurst*' in *Sussex Archaeological Collections Vol. VII* (London, 1854)

Blomefield, F., *An Essay Towards a Topographical History of the County of Norfolk* (London, 1806)

Bloxham, M.B, '*Merevale Abbey*' in *Transactions of the Leicestershire Architectural and Archaeological Society Vol. II* (Leicester, 1870)

Boutell, C., *Heraldry, Historical and Popular* (London, 1864)

Bradley, S., *John Morton; Adversary of Richard III, Power Behind the Tudors* (Stroud, 2019)

Bridge, J.S.C., *A History of France from the Death of Louis XI, Reign of Charles VIII, Regency of Anne of Beaujeu 1483-1493* (New York, 1978)

Camden, W., *Reges, reginae nobiles et alii in ecclesia collegiata B. Petri Westmonasterii sepulti* (London, 1603)

Caron, P., *Kerbouric (De) – Réformation De La Noblesse* (Côtes D'armor, 2007)

Carr, A.D., *Medieval Wales* (Basingstoke, 1995)

Castor, H., *Joan of Arc, A History* (London, 2014)

Chapman, A., *Welsh Soldiers in the Late Middle Ages, 1282-1422* (Woodbridge, 2015)

Chrimes, S.B., Henry VII (London, 1999)

Chrimes, S.B., '*Sir Roland De Velville*' in *Welsh History Review Vol. 3* (1967)

Chrimes, S.B., '*The Landing Place of Henry of Richmond, 1485*' in *The Welsh History Review Vol. II* (1964-65)

Collections Historical & Archaeological Relating to Montgomeryshire (London, 1868)

Condon, M., Harper, S., & Ross, J., *The Chamber Books of Henry VII and Henry VIII, 1485-1521: An Analysis of the Books and a Study of Henry VII and his Life at Court*

Corbet, A.E.B., *The Family of Corbet; Its Life and Times Vol. II* (London, 1914)

Crull, J., *The Antiquities of St Peter's, or the Abbey Church of Westminster* (London, 1711)

Cunningham, S., *Henry VII* (London, 2007)

Cunningham, S., *Prince Arthur, the Tudor King Who Never Was* (Stroud, 2016)

Davies, J., *A History of Wales* (London, 1994)

Davies, R.R., *Owain Glyn Dŵr, Prince of Wales* (Talybont, 2009)

Davies, R.R., *The Revolt of Owain Glyndwr* (Oxford, 1995)

DeLloyd J.G., '*Climbing the Civil-Service Pole during Civil War: Sir Reynold Bray (c.1440-1503)*', in *Estrangement, Enterprise & Education in Fifteenth Century England* (ed. S.D. Michalove & A. Compton Reeves, Stroud, 1998)

Dockray, K.R., '*The Yorkshire Rebellions of 1469*' in *The Ricardian Vol. 6 No 82* (1983)

Easterling, R.C., '*The Friars in Wales*' in *Archaeologia Cambrensis Vol. XIV Sixth Series* (London, 1914)

Edwards, G., '*The Principality of Wales, 1267-1967*' in *Caernarvonshire Historical Society* (1969)

Edwards, J.G., '*Sir Gruffydd Llwyd*' in *English Historical Review* (ed. R.L. Poole, London, 1915)

Edwards, O.M., *Wales; A National Magazine for the English Speaking Parts of Wales Vol. III* (Wrexham, 1896)

Ellis, T.P., *Welsh Tribal Law and Custom in the Middle Ages* (Oxford, 1926)

Evans. G., *The Battle of Edgcote 1469; Re-Evaluating the Evidence* (Northampton, 2019)

Evans, H.T., Wales and the Wars of the Roses (Cambridge, 1915)

Fenton, R., *Tours in Wales (1804-1813)* (London, 1917)

Foard, G. & Curry, A., *Bosworth 1485; A Battlefield Rediscovered* (Oxford, 2022)

Gairdner, J, *History of the Life and Reign of Richard the Third* (Cambridge, 1898)

Garmon Jones, W., *Welsh Nationalism and Henry Tudor* (London, 1918)

Goodman, A., *Wars of the Roses; Military Activity and English Society, 1452-97* (London, 1981)

Gough, R., *Sepulchral Monuments in Great Britain* (London, 1796)

Gower, J., *The Story of Wales* (St Ives, 2012)

Gray, M., '*Politics, Power and Piety: The Cult of St Armel in Early Tudor England and Wales*' in *Rewriting Holiness: Reconfiguring Vitae, Re-Signifying Cults* (ed. M. Gray, Woodbridge, 2017)

Gray, M., '*Welsh saints in Westminster Abbey*' in *Transactions of the Honourable Society of Cymmrodorion* (2007)

Green, A.R., '*The Romsey Painted Wooden Reredos*' in *the Archaeological Journal Vol. XC* (1993)

Griffith, W.P., '*Tudor Prelude*' in *The Welsh in London 1500-2000* (ed. E. Jones, Cardiff, 2001)

Griffiths, R.A., '*Gruffydd ap Nicholas and the Fall of the House of Lancaster*' in *Welsh History Review II* (1965)

Griffiths, R.A., *'Gruffydd ap Nicholas and the Rise of the House of Dinefwr'* in *The National Library of Wales Journal Vol. XIII* (1964)

Griffiths, R.A., *'Henry Tudor; The Training of a King'* in *Huntingdon Library Quarterly Vol. 49 No 3* (1986)

Griffiths, R.A., *'Queen Katherine of Valois and a Missing Statute of the Realm'* in *King and Country: England and Wales in the Fifteenth Century* (London, 1991)

Griffiths, R.A., *Sir Rhys ap Thomas and his Family: A Study in the Wars of the Roses and Early Tudor Politics* (Cardiff, 2014)

Griffiths, R.A., *The Principality of Wales in the Later Middle Ages: The Structure and Personnel of Government Vol. I, South Wales, 1277-1536* (Cardiff, 1972)

Griffiths, R.A., *The Reign of King Henry VI* (Stroud, 1998)

Griffiths, R.A. & Thomas, R.S., *The Making of the Tudor Dynasty* (Stroud, 2005)

Gunn, S.J., *'The Courtiers of Henry VII'* in *English Historical Review Vol. 108* (Oxford, 1993)

Harris, G.L., *Cardinal Beaufort, A Study of Lancastrian Ascendancy and Decline* (Oxford, 1988)

Harris, O.D, *'The Bosworth Commemoration at Dadlington'* in *The Ricardian Vol. VII, No 90* (London, 1985)

Harris, O.D., *'The Transmission of the News of the Tudor Landing'* in *The Ricardian, Vol. IV, Number 55* (London, 1976)

Henken, E.R., *National Redeemer, Owain Glyndwr in Welsh Tradition* (Ithica, 1996)

Henneman, J.B., *Olivier de Clisson and Political Society in France under Charles V and Charles VI* (Philadelphia, 1996)

Henry, R., *The History of Great Britain, From the Invasion of it by The Romans under Julius Caesar Vol. XII* (London, 1814)

Hicks, M.A., *False, Fleeting, Perjur'd Clarence; George, Duke of Clarence 1449-78* (Gloucester, 1980)

Hicks, M., *Warwick the Kingmaker* (Oxford, 2002)

Hillier, K., *'William Colyngbourne'* in *The Ricardian; Journal of the Richard III Society, Vol. III. No. 49* (Upminster, 1975)

Hore, H.F., *'Mayors and Bailiffs of Tenby'* in *Archaeologia Cambrensis Vol. XIV* (London, 1853)

Horrox, R., *'Henry Tudor's Letters to England during Richard III's Reign'* in *The Ricardian Vol. 6 No 80* (London, 1983)

'Houses of Benedictine nuns: Abbey of Barking', in *A History of the County of Essex: Vol. 2* (ed. W. Page and J. Horace Round, London, 1907)

Hurlock, K., *Britain, Ireland and The Crusades C.1000-1300* (Basingstoke, 2013)

Hutton, W., *The Battle of Bosworth Field, Between Richard the Third and Henry Earl of Richmond, August 22, 1485* (London, 1813)

Ingram, M., *Richard III and the Battle of Bosworth* (Warwick, 2019)

Jarman, A.O.H., *'The Later Cynfeirdd'* in *A Guide to Welsh Literature Vol. 1* (ed. A.O.H. Jarman & G.R. Hughes, Swansea, 1976)

John, J.W., *Archaeologia Cambrensis; A Record of the Antiquities of Wales and its Marches, Vol. IV* (London, 1853)

Johnston, D., *Iolo Goch Poems* (Llandysul, 1993)

Jones, D., *Magna Carta; The Making and Legacy of the Great Charter* (London, 2017)

Jones, D.C., *The Bulkeleys of Beaumaris. 1440-1547, Anglesey Antiquarian Society and Field Club Transactions* (1961)

Jones, E.W., *'Wales and Bosworth Field – Selective Historiography?'* in *NLW Vol. 21 No 1* (1979)

Jones, M., *Henry VII, Lady Margaret Beaufort and the Orléans Ransom'* in *Kings and Nobles in the Later Middle Ages* (ed. R.A. Griffiths & J. Sherborne, Gloucester, 1986)

Jones, M.C.E., 'For My Lord of Richmond, a pourpoint and a palfrey'; Brief Remarks on the Financial Evidence for Henry Tudor's Exile in Brittany 1471-1484' in The Ricardian, XIII (2002)

Jones, M.K., Bosworth 1485, Psychology of a Battle (Stroud, 2002)

Jones, M.K. & Underwood, M.G., The King's Mother: Lady Margaret Beaufort, Countess of Richmond and Derby

Jones, M.K., 'The Myth of 1485; did France really put Henry Tudor on the throne' in The English Experience in France c.1450-1558; War, diplomacy and cultural exchange (ed. D. Grummitt, Aldershot, 2002)

Kennett, W., Hughes, J, & Strype, J., A Complete History of England Vol. I, with their Lives of all the Kings and Queens thereof (London, 1706)

Kenyon, J.R., Raglan Castle (Cardiff, 2003)

Kibre, P., 'Lewis of Caerleon, Doctor of Medicine, Astronomer, and Mathematician (D. 1494?)' in Isis Vol. 43:2, Number 132 (ed. G. Staton, Chicago, 1952)

Lander, J.R., Henry VI and the Duke of York's Second Protectorate in Bulletin of the John Rylands Library, XLIII (1960)

Laws, E., 'Notes on the Fortifications of Medieval Tenby' in Archaeologia Cambrensis, Vol. XIII, No LII (1896)

Laynesmith, J., The Last Medieval Queens; English Queenship 1445-1503 (Oxford, 2004)

Le Grand, A., Les Vies des Saints de la Bretagne Armorique Vol. II (Paris, 1901)

Lewis, B., 'The Battle of Edgecote or Banbury (1469) Through the of Contemporary Welsh Poets' in The Journal of Medieval Military History Vol. IX; Soldiers, Weapons and Armies in the Fifteenth Century (ed. A. Curry & A.R. Bell, Woodbridge, 2011)

Lewis, J., Life of Dr John Fisher, Bishop of Rochester in the Reign of King Henry VIII (London, 1855)

Lewis, K.J., Katherine of Valois and the Various Vicissitudes of her Reputation

Lewis, M., Richard III; Loyalty Binds Me (Stroud, 2018)

Lewis, W.G., 'The Exact Date of The Battle of Banbury, 1469' in Bulletin of The Institute of Historical Research Vol. LV (London, 1982)

Lloyd, J.E., A History of Wales from the Earliest Times to the Edwardian Conquest (London, 1912)

Llwyd, A., History of the Island of Mona or Anglesey (Ruthin, 1833)

Llywelyn, M.G, Y Ddraig yn Nychymyg a Llenyddiaeth y Cymry c.600-c.1500 (Aberystwyth, 2017)

Lofmark, C, A History of the Red Dragon (Llanrwst, 1995)

Mackinder, R., Bosworth; the Archaeology of the Battlefield (Barnsley, 2021)

Merrick, R., A Book of Glamorganshire's Antiquities (ed. T. Phillipps, 1825)

Merrony, M.W., An Official History of Tenby (Tenby, 2004)

Moore, D., The Welsh Wars of Independence c.410-1415 (Stroud, 2005)

Morgan, P., 'Elis Gruffudd of Gronant – Tudor Chronicler Extraordinary' in Flintshire Historical Society publications, Vol. 25 (1972)

Morris, J.E., The Welsh Wars of Edward I; A Contribution to Mediaeval Military History, Based on Original Documents (Oxford, 1901)

Morris, M., King John; Treachery, Tyranny and the Road to Magna Carta (London, 2015)

Mortimer, I., The Fears of Henry IV; The Life of England's Self-Made King (London, 2008)

Nicolas, N.H., Testamenta Vestusta, Being Illustrations from Wills (London, 1826)

Nichols, J., A Collection of all the Wills Now Known to be Extant, of the Kings and Queens of England, Princes and Princesses of Wales, and Every Branch of the Blood Royal (London, 1780)

Owen, G., Description of Pembrokeshire (ed. H. Owen, 1892)

Owen, H, & Blakeway, J.B., A History of Shrewsbury Vol. I (London, 1825)

Bibliography

Owen, I., 'Race and Nationality' in Y Cymmrodor Vol. VIII Part I (London, 1887)

Owen, M.E., 'Literary Convention and Historical Reality: The Court in the Welsh Poetry of the Twelfth and Thirteenth Centuries' in Etudes Celtiques 29 (1992)

Oxford Dictionary of National Biography (ed. H.C.G. Matthew & B. Harrison, Oxford, 2004)

Pennant, T., Tours in Wales Vol. III (ed. J. Rhys, Caernarvon, 1883)

Pocquet du Haut-Jusse, B.A., Francois II, Duc de Bretagne et L'Angleterre (1458-1488) (Paris, 1929)

Price, T., The Literary Remains of the Rev. Thomas Price (Llandovery, 1854)

Pugh, R.B., Imprisonment in Medieval England (Cambridge, 1968)

Pugh, T.B., 'The Lordship of Gower and Kilvey in the Middle Ages' in Glamorgan County History III, The Middle Ages (ed. T.B. Pugh, Cardiff, 1971)

Pugh, T.B., The Marcher Lordships of South Wales, 1415-1536 (Cardiff, 1963)

Pugh, T.B., 'The magnate, knights and gentry' in Fifteenth Century England, 1399-1509' (ed. S.B. Chrimes, C.D. Ross, & R.A. Griffiths (Manchester, 1972)

Radford, L.B., Henry Beaufort: Bishop, Chancellor, Cardinal (London, 1908)

Raine, A., 'York Civic Records Vol. 1' in Yorkshire Archaeological Society, Record Series Vol. XCVIII (1939)

Ralph, J., A Critical Review of the Public Buildings, Statues, And Ornaments in and about London and Westminster (London, 1783)

Ramsay, J.H., Lancaster and York, A Century of English History (A.D. 1399-1485) (Oxford, 1892)

Rees, W., 'The Black Death in Wales' in Essays in Medieval History (ed. R.W. Southern, London 1968)

Rex Smith, G., 'The Penmachno Letter Patent and the Welsh Uprising of 1294-95' in Cambrian Medieval Celtic Studies, Vol.58 (Aberystwyth, 2009)

Richmond, C., '1485 and All That, or What Was Going on at the Battle of Bosworth' in Richard III: Loyalty, Lordship and Law (ed. P.W. Hammond, London, 1985)

Riley-Adams, A.D., Elis Gruffydd and Welsh Identity in the Sixteenth Century (Oklahoma, 2018)

Roberts, E., 'Seven John Conways' in Flintshire Historical Society Publications Vol. XVIII (1960)

Roberts, E.P., 'Teulu Plas Iolyn' in Transactions of the Denbighshire Historical Society Vol. 13 (1964)

Roberts, G., 'The Dominican Friary of Bangor' in Aspects of Welsh History (Cardiff, 1969)

Roberts, G., 'Wyrion Eden'; The Anglesey Descendants of Ednyfed Fychan in the Fourteenth Century' in Aspects of Welsh History (Cardiff, 1969)

Roberts, S.E., Jasper: The Tudor Kingmaker (Stroud, 2015)

Roberts, T. & Williams, I., The Poetical Works of Dafydd Nanmor (Cardiff, 1923)

Robinson, W.R., 'Sir Roland De Velville and the Tudor Dynasty: A Reassessment' in Welsh History Review Vol. 15 (1991)

Robinson, W.R.B, 'Henry Tudor's Journey Through Powys and the Lords of Powys in Early Tudor Times' in Montgomeryshire Collections 90 (2002)

Ross, C., Edward IV (London, 1974)

Ross, C., Richard III (London, 1999

Ross, J., The Foremost Man in The Kingdom (Woodbridge, 2015)

Ross, J., 'The Treatment of Traitors' Children' in The Fifteenth Century XIV; Essays Presented to Michael Hicks (ed. L. Clark, Woodbridge, 2015)

Sayles, G.O., 'The Royal Marriages Act 1428' in the Law Quarterly Review Vol. 94 (ed. P.V. Baker, London, 1978)

Scofield, C., 'Early Life of John De Vere' in *The English Historical Review Vol. XXIX* (London, 1914)

Scofield, C.L. *The Life and Reign of Edward the Fourth, King of England and of France and Lord of Ireland Vol. 1* (London, 1923)

Seymour, R., *A Survey of the Cities of London and Westminster, Borough of Southwark and Parts Adjacent* (London, 1734)

Shaw, W.A., *The Knights of England Vol. II* (London, 1906)

Siddons, M.P., *The Development of Welsh Heraldry* (Aberystwyth, 1991)

Skeel, C.A.J., 'Wales under Henry VII' in *Tudor Studies* (ed. R.W. Seton-Watson, London, 1924)

Skidmore, C., *Bosworth, The Birth of the Tudors* (London, 2013)

Skinner, R.J., 'Thomas Woodshawe, Grasiour and Regicide' in *The Ricardian Vol. IX No 121* (London, 1993)

Smith, J.B., 'Crown and Community in the Principality of North Wales in the Reign of Henry Tudor' in *Welsh History Review Vol. 3 No 2*

Spont, A., *La Marine Française sous le Règne de Charles VIII 1483-1493* (Paris, 1894)

Spont, A., 'La milice de Francs-Archers (1448-1500)' in *Revue des Questions Historiques, 61* (1897)

Stanford London, H., 'The Greyhound as a Royal Beast' in *Archaeologia or Miscellaneous Tracts Relating to Antiquity Vol. 97* (London, 1959)

Stanley, A.P., *Historical Memorials of Westminster Abbey* (London, 1868)

Stephens, T., *The Literature of the Kymry; Being a Critical Essay on the History of The Language and Literature of Wales* (Llandovery, 1849)

Stephenson, D., *Medieval Wales c.1050-1332* (Cardiff, 2019)

Storey, R., *The End of The House of Lancaster* (Guildford, 1999)

Stow, J., *The Annales, Or Generall Chronicle of England* (London, 1615)

Strickland, A., *Lives of the Queens of England from the Norman Conquest* (Philadelphia, 1841)

Tallis, N., *Uncrowned Queen; The Fateful Life of Margaret Beaufort, Tudor Matriarch* (London, 2019)

Tanner, J.R., *Tudor Constitutional Documents A.D. 1485-1603* (Cambridge, 1930)

The Borough of Hertford: Castle, Honour, Manors, Church and Charities' in *a History of the County of Hertford Vol. 3* (ed. W. Page, London, 1912)

The Diary of Samuel Pepys Vol. VIII (ed H.B. Wheatley, London, 1905)

The Myvyrian Archaeology of Wales Collected out of Ancient Manuscripts (ed. O. Jones, E. Williams & W.O. Pugh, Denbigh, 1870)

The Poetical Works of Lewis Glyn Cothi, A Celebrated Bard, Who Flourished in the Reigns of Henry VI, Edward IV, Richard III, and Henry VII (ed. G. Mechain, Oxford, 1837)

The Royal Commission on the Ancient and Historical Monuments and Constructions in Wales and Monmouthshire; IV County of Denbigh (London, 1914)

The Victoria History of the County of Hertford (ed. W. Page, London, 1914)

Thomas, D.H., *The Herberts of Raglan and the Battle of Edgecote 1469* (1967)

Thomas, R.S., *The Political Career, Estates and Connection of Jasper Tudor, Earl of Pembroke and Duke of Bedford* (Swansea, 1971)

Thorpe, L., 'Philippe de Crèvecoeur, Seigneur d'Esquerdes: two epitaphs by Jean Molinet and Nicaise Ladam' in *Bulletin de la Commission royale d'Histoire Vol. CXIX* (Brussels, 1954)

Titi Livii Foro-Juliensis, Vita Henrici Quinti (ed. T. Hearne, Oxford, 1716)

Tomaini, T., *The Corpse as Text; Disinterment and Antiquarian Enquiry 1700-1900* (Woodbridge, 2017)

Bibliography

Walcott, M.E.C., *The History of the Parish Church of Saint Margaret, in Westminster, from its Foundation, A.D. 1064* (1847)

Walker, D., *Medieval Wales* (Cambridge, 1990)

Walker, R.F., *'Jasper Tudor and the town of Tenby'* in *The National Library of Wales Journal Vol. 16, No 1* (1969)

Watkins, T.G., *The Legal History of Wales* (Cardiff, 2007)

Wedgwood, J.C., *History of Parliament; Biographies of the Members of the Commons House 1439-1509* (London, 1936)

Wickham Legg, L., *English Coronation Records* (London, 1901)

Williams, D., *'The Welsh Tudors: The Family of Henry VII'* in *History Today Vol. 4 Issue 2* (1954)

Williams, D.H., *Catalogue of Seals in the National Museum of Wales* (Cardiff, 1993)

Williams, G., *Renewal and Reformation Wales c.1415-1642* (Oxford, 1987)

Williams, G.A., *'The Bardic Road to Bosworth: A Welsh View of Henry Tudor'* in *Transactions of the Honourable Society of Cymmrodorion* (London, 1986)

Williams, J., *Ancient and Modern Denbigh; A Descriptive History of the Castle, Borough, and Liberties* (1856)

Williams, J., *'Penmynydd and the Tudors'* in *Archaeologia Cambrensis Third Series Vol. 15* (1869)

Williams, W.T., *'Henry of Richmond's Itinerary to Bosworth'* in *Y Cymmrodor Vol. XXIX* (London, 1919)

Williams-Jones, K., *'The Taking Of Conwy Castle, 1401'* in *Transactions of the Caernarvonshire Historical Society Vol. 39*

Wolff, B., *Henry VI* (London, 1983)

Wroe, A., *Perkin, A Story of Deception* (London, 2004)

Wynne, J., *The History of the Gwydir Family* (Oswestry, 1878)

Yorke, P., *The Royal Tribes of Wales* (ed. R. Williams, Liverpool, 1887)

Acknowledgements

To pen a non-fiction history book is to stand on the shoulders of generations of esteemed historians who have paved the way for this current work to reach publication. I could not have reached this point without the inspiring drive, insight and encouragement of those who have come before. I can only hope to add something worthwhile to centuries of hard work and illuminating research. In particular, I owe an enormous debt of gratitude to the work of Ralph A. Griffiths, to whom we owe almost all of our understanding of the Welsh background of Henry VII.

I'd also like to express gratitude to my editor, Alex Bennett, publicity officer, Philip Dean, and the team behind the scenes at Amberley for their patience and proficiency in delivering this book.

For assistance, feedback and expertise in their respective fields, I'd like to thank Dave Pilling and David Pilling for assistance and discussion on Welsh history, Samantha Harper for guidance on Henry VII's chamber books and translation help, Katherine Lewis for sharing her thesis and thoughts on Katherine of Valois, Amy Licence for discussing churching rituals, Cyril Jones and Nia Williams for their generous help with Roland de Velville, and Kathryn Hurlock, Christopher Guyver and Lauren Johnson for their help sourcing articles. Huge thanks to Jenny Deadman of Abbey Farm B&B, Merevale, for allowing me time to explore and photograph the ruins, and Eddie Clarkson for his design skills.

I'd also like to particularly thank Adam Chapman, Helen Castor, Heather Darsie, Lacey Bonar Hull, Julian Humphrys, Catherine Ibbotson, Dan Jones, Mike Jones, Matthew Lewis, Andy Saunders and Nicola Tallis for their friendship and encouragement, and also Ian Brandt, Allan Harley, and the Beaufort Companye for their good natured and informative discussions whenever our paths cross. Sadly, during the writing of this book, two supportive historians, Mike Ingram and Deb Hunter, passed away. It is only right to remember them here.

On a private note, thank you to my family for their continued support, my parents Mohammed and Michelle, my sisters Nadia and Yasmin, grandparents Randall and Muriel, and the wider clan. Thank you to Lucy for being a willing travel companion and always providing the fun, and, of course, thanks to Vera, the world's best cat.

Finally, to every reader who has picked up one of my books, listened to me on podcasts or come in person to a talk, thank you deeply. I hope you've enjoyed the journey so far.

Index

Beaufort, Henry, 3rd Duke
of Somerset 145, 146,
148, 151, 157, 159, 160,
166, 167, 179, 181, 182,
183, 185, 300
Beaufort, Margaret, Countess
of Richmond 109,
115-16, 130, 131,
135-37, 140-45, 175,
177, 194-97, 200, 203,
214, 219, 220, 228-30,
232, 233, 235-38,
243-47, 266, 275, 280,
287, 293, 294, 303, 323,
324
Beaufort, Thomas, 1st Duke
of Exeter 257
Beaumaris 46, 57, 68, 71,
92, 157, 179, 212, 213
Beaumont, John, 1st
Viscount Beaumont 102,
154, 155
Beeston 53
Benstead 153
Bere, John de la, bishop of
St David's 130
Berkeley 49
Berkeley, William 237, 299,
317
Bermondsey 97, 100
Berwick upon Tweed 62, 265
Berthelot, Louis 237
Beton, Denis 268
Black Death 53-54, 59
Blackheath, battle of 212,
322
Blacman, John 106
Blakeham 153
Blanche of Castile, Queen of
France 88
Bleddyn Fardd 36
Bleddyn Fychan 45
Bletsoe 130
Blisland 324
Blondeville, Ranulf de, 6th
Earl of Chester 17, 21,
32
Blore Heath, battle of 151,
153, 155
Blount, Anne 321
Blount, James 260, 275, 299
Bodmin Moor 241

Bodrhyddan 236
Bohun, Humphrey de, 3rd
Earl of Hereford 37
Bohun, Mary 321
Boleyn, Geoffrey 148
Bolsover 114, 317
Booth, William, archbishop
of York 118
Bordeaux 117-18
Boston 113
Bosworth, battle of 86, 93,
281, 297-306, 315, 322,
323
Boteler, Ralph, 1st Baron
Sudeley 125
Bourchier, Edward 129, 157
Bourchier, Henry, 1st Earl
of Essex 119, 127, 135,
143, 155, 194
Bourchier, Henry, 2nd Earl
of Essex 212
Bourchier, John, 1st Baron
Berners 125
Bourchier, John, 11th Baron
FitzWarin 268
Bourchier, Thomas,
archbishop of
Canterbury 118, 135,
143, 155, 156, 194, 225
Bourchier, Thomas 294
Bourne 136, 144
Brackenbury, Robert 299,
304
Bradon 114
Bramham Moor, battle of 78
Brampton, Edward 299
Brandon, Thomas 212, 259
Brandon, William 245, 259,
299, 303
Bray, Reginald 195, 236,
240-41, 245
Brecon 15, 20, 25, 33, 35,
45, 65, 76, 132, 134,
161, 169, 189, 234, 238,
265, 282, 311, 322
Brecknockshire 314
Brest 206, 237
Bret, William 259
Bridget of York 219, 248
Bristol 42, 136, 169, 318
Bromfield and Yale 304,
311, 312

Browne, George 237
Bruce, Alexander 270, 273
Brunanburh, battle of 60
Brutus of Troy 285, 286,
310, 329
Brycheiniog 20, 24
Bryn Derwin, battle of 33
Bryn Euryn 27
Brynffanigl 26
Builth 28, 33, 35, 41, 46,
92, 233, 282, 311
Burgh, Hubert de, 1st Earl
of Kent 21
Butler, Arnold 276, 289
Butler, Eleanor 227, 246
Butler, James, 1st Earl of
Wiltshire 118, 120, 125,
134, 149, 150, 151, 161,
163, 164, 167
Byford, Lewis, bishop of
Bangor 76, 80
Cadwaladr ap
Cadwallon 59-60, 284,
286, 288, 303, 310, 326,
332
Caerleon 79, 132
Caerleon, Lewis 229, 230,
266, 324
Caerphilly 133
Caernarfon 43, 45, 46, 52,
67, 68, 71, 74, 79, 170,
233
Caernarfonshire 44, 49, 54,
57, 58, 68, 79, 114, 132,
187, 311, 312, 314
Cade, Jack 110, 117
Caio 265
Calais 148, 151-52, 154,
171, 180, 183, 184, 188,
191, 212, 260, 262, 269,
323
Caldicot 92, 114, 143, 171,
317
Cambridge 68, 326
Camden, William 319
Camulio, Prospero di 164,
167
Canterbury 321, 326, 331
Carbonnel, Henri 240
Cardiff 76, 133
Cardigan 19, 25, 28, 33, 46,
73, 129, 277, 317

Cuff, Georget le 246
Curzon, Robert 212
Cynwal, William 214
Cynwrig ab Ednyfed 26, 31, 33, 34, 37
Cynwrig ab Iorwerth 329
Cwmhir Abbey 22
Cwmliog 32
Cwmllanerch 27
Dadlington 296-97, 306
Dafydd Alaw 214
Dafydd ab Owain 324
Dafydd ap Ieuan ab Iorwerth 324, 329
Dafydd ap Ieuan ap Eynon 186-87, 279
Dafydd ap Llywelyn, Prince of Gwynedd 26, 28-31
Dafydd ap Gruffudd, Prince of Gwynedd 33, 37-41
Dafydd ap Thomas 202, 266
Dafydd Benfras 36
Dafydd Gam 81, 133-34
Dafydd Llwyd 282, 285, 287-88, 310, 328
Dafydd Nanmor 137, 287
Dale 274, 275, 276
Darell, Edward 212
Dartford 110, 111
Dartmouth 192
Daubeney, Giles, 1st Baron Daubeney 236-37, 245-46, 316
Daventry 100
David ap Jerman Rees 53
Dee, river 16, 45
Deganwy 29
Deheubarth 15, 19-20, 25-26, 38, 77
Deio ap Ieuan Du 285
Delapré Abbey 155
Denbigh 45, 49, 52, 68, 79, 133, 153-54, 157-58, 168, 170, 185, 187-88, 311, 312
Denbighshire 314, 331
Despenser, Hugh, 1st Baron Despenser 49
Despenser, Hugh, 1st Earl of Winchester 49
Despenser, Thomas, 1st Earl of Gloucester 77

Devereux, Anne 321
Devereux, Anne, Countess of Pembroke 177, 179, 189, 194-95, 280
Devereux, Walter, 8th Baron Ferrers of Chartley 133-36, 139, 140, 143, 145, 157, 161, 169, 170, 186, 195, 239, 279-80
D'Giglis, Giovanni 332
Digby, Simon 294
Dilby, Robert 53
Dindaethwy 47, 50-51, 57
Dinefwr 25, 40
Dinorwig 27, 32
Dolarddyn 282
Dolforwyn 37
Dover 183, 324
Drayton 92
Dryslwyn 76, 186
Du, Derien le 237
Dublin 155
Dugdale, William 290
Dunstanburgh 181, 183
Dunster 184, 198
Durham 181
Dwnn, John 149, 168-69, 171, 186
Dwnn, Lewys 214
Dyffryn Bryan 129
Dyffryn Clwyd 79
Dyfi, river 16, 280, 282
Dymmock, Robert 326
Dynorban Fychan 26
Eastfield, William 101
Edinburgh 180
Edgcote, battle of 189-90, 193-94
Edgcumbe, Richard 299
Edmund, Earl of Rutland 151-52, 160
Edmund of Langley, 1st Duke of York 156
Ednyfed ap Bleddyn 30
Edward ap Ednyfed 283
Edward ap Rhys 325
Edward, Earl of March *see* Edward IV
Edward, 17th Earl of Warwick 227, 246
Edward of Middleham, Prince of Wales 248-49

Edward of Westminster, Prince of Wales 118, 120, 123, 150, 154, 157-59, 167, 181, 192, 196, 197, 199, 200-01, 202, 217
Edward of Woodstock, Prince of Wales 52-53, 57, 284
Edward I, King of England 33, 37-38, 40-46, 51, 70, 158, 277, 295
Edward II, King of England 46-51, 65, 156, 232
Edward III, King of England 49-54, 58, 59, 61, 65, 87, 89, 109, 110, 114-16, 139, 143, 149, 156, 164, 170, 203, 235, 243, 244, 275, 295
Edward IV, King of England 84, 151, 152, 154, 155, 160, 161, 162, 164-71, 173, 174, 175, 177, 180-88, 190-95, 197, 198, 199, 200, 201, 203, 206, 207, 213, 215-22, 226-28, 231, 233-37, 241, 242, 244, 246-48, 252, 257, 259, 260, 262, 264-66, 287, 292, 295, 312, 326, 328
Edward V, King of England 199 220, 221, 223, 224, 226, 227, 229-32, 233, 235, 238
Edward the Confessor, King of England 331
Edynfed ap Tudur Fychan 55, 56, 57, 58
Ednyfed Fychan, 12, 13, 14, 15-16, 19-28, 30-33, 36, 38, 41, 47, 49, 50, 54, 55, 56, 61, 78, 84, 108, 113, 117, 153, 213, 266, 275, 283, 287, 289, 309, 323, 329, 333
Eifionydd 278
Einion ap Dafydd Llwyd 279
Elen ferch Llywelyn 21
Elen ferch Thomas ap Llywelyn 61-62